Digital Marketing

Vandana Ahuja

Professor of Marketing, Amity Business School
Amity University, Noida
Uttar Pradesh

OXFORD
UNIVERSITY PRESS

Oxford University Press is a department of the University of Oxford.
It furthers the University's objective of excellence in research, scholarship,
and education by publishing worldwide. Oxford is a registered trademark of
Oxford University Press in the UK and in certain other countries.

Published in India by
Oxford University Press
22 Workspace, 2nd Floor, 1/22 Asaf Ali Road, New Delhi 110 002

© Oxford University Press 2015

The moral rights of the author/s have been asserted.

First Edition published in 2006
13th impression 2024

All rights reserved. No part of this publication may be reproduced, stored in
a retrieval system, or transmitted, in any form or by any means, without the
prior permission in writing of Oxford University Press, or as expressly permitted
by law, by licence, or under terms agreed with the appropriate reprographics
rights organization. Enquiries concerning reproduction outside the scope of the
above should be sent to the Rights Department, Oxford University Press, at the
address above.

You must not circulate this book in any other form
and you must impose this same condition on any acquirer.

ISBN-13: 978-0-19-945544-7
ISBN-10: 0-19-945544-9

Typeset in Baskerville
by Tata Consultancy Services, Kolkata - 700156
Printed in India by Rakmo Press, New Delhi 110 020

For product information and current price, please visit www.india.oup.com

Third-Party website addresses mentioned in this book are provided
by Oxford University Press in good faith and for information only.
Oxford University Press disclaims any responsibility for the material contained therein.

Preface

Technological advances and the speed with which new technologies are being embraced by organizations, along with the rising power of the consumers and their ability to get what they want, when they want it, from whomever they want, have opened up new challenges for marketing. With this in mind, the need for understanding the digital world and its application becomes one of the greatest competitive aspects for a business's survival. The buzzword of 'globalization' holds no meaning without the concept of what is being termed as 'digitization'.

Significant to marketing is revenue optimization, by appropriate utilization of resources, and identification of cost-effective means for better marketing asset allocation. The Internet serves as a medium that enhances marketing efficiency in the context of integration of consumer communication, soliciting consumer engagement, building brand value, reducing price sensitivity, escalating consumer brand resonance, and product/brand recall. The transactional ease offered by the medium has increased its popularity manifold.

The ability of the Read-Write Web, or *Web 2.0* as it is termed, to empower the contemporary consumer has gained significantly with the arrival of a generation of *enthusiastic, Internet-savvy consumers* eager to explore, interact, and form social and structural bonds with organizations, and with a keen desire to be heard by organizations and brands. This has resulted in the need to focus on the value perception being created by the brands in the online sphere.

About the Book

The book *Digital Marketing* integrates concepts and developments from the virtual world and analyses how the field of marketing can benefit from these. It has been written for the students and teachers of management courses in digital marketing, Internet marketing, or *e*-marketing, as also for managers interested in the concepts of digital marketing. The content is typically valuable for all those aspiring to pursue a career in Marketing, for, in today's world, the knowledge of marketing is incomplete without the understanding of the digital world.

This book is designed for use either as a stand-alone resource or in conjunction with other modes of marketing education. It explores in detail the various concepts associated with digital marketing and supports them with numerous exhibits, illustrations, and case studies. It is aimed at making an entire package of material available to students and instructors. It not only introduces readers to the intricacies of digital marketing but also enables them to learn from the experiences of a significant volume of organizations that are fast adopting and experimenting with these tools. Examples in the book not only are India-specific but also draw from various Asian, European, and American organizations. The principles and concepts discussed in the book are universally applicable and readers will be able to relate to the book globally.

The book traverses a course, which commences with investigating the rising power of social media and how organizations can benefit from the world of *corporate blogs*, Facebook, *online communities*, *social networks*, and Wikis and proceeds to explore the domain of the Internet, its characteristics and features, the power of individuals online, and subsequently the realm of the online brand. *E*-marketing serves as a significant apparatus to build credibility and trust and enhance the value perception of the consumers for a particular organization, product, or brand. It explores the upcoming domains of Facebook marketing and the digital revolution, gaining momentum through the world of *Apps* and *gamification*.

Highlights

Technology is a ubiquitous tool that empowers; successful application has known to streamline business processes, ease transactions, and reduce marketing expenditure. This book will enable its readers to:

- Become familiar with the usage of Internet as a marketing-planning tool
- Get acquainted with the ability of the virtual world to increase efficiency in established marketing functions
- Understand how organizations can leverage the benefits of social media for maximum benefit
- Embrace cutting-edge business strategies that generate revenue while delivering customer value

Value Addition

- The book provides a lot of practical examples through *Exhibits*, *Case Studies*, and *Practitioner Perspectives*, which help readers to gauge the potential of the virtual medium.
- *Practising Digital Marketing* is a dimension added to the exercises section, which will give students a hands-on experience of real-life developments in the marketplace.
- The book also includes some research illustrations, which draw from the recent research in the field of digital marketing and discuss implications of the same for marketing practitioners. It is this research that paves the way for further analysis, exploration, and usage of the field of digital marketing. This includes my own research in the area and draws short excerpts from the work of my management research students.

Online Resources

The online resource centre provides resources for lecturers. The following resources are available for the faculty using this text:

- PowerPoint slides

- Instructor's manual

Additional case studies are available both for students and faculty. These include digital marketing case studies from various Asian countries such as Malaysia (Air Asia and IKEA Malaysia), Singapore (Maybank and SingTel), Bangladesh (Grameenphone), Sri Lanka (Dilmah Tea), Pakistan (Daraz.pk), etc.

Coverage and Structure

The book has been divided into 4 sections as follows:

The first section, *Marketing in the Digital Era* (Chapters 1 to 4), traces the changing marketing landscape in the context of Internet strategy integration, the behavioural Internet, *individual Internet worth*, the technology catalysis, and the strengths of *e*-marketing. This section starts with the online marketing mix and proceeds to study the characteristics and expectations of a typical online consumer. The section deals with the dynamics and intent of the consumer visit in a digital paradigm and CRM strategies and applications using which organizations can use the online medium to build long-term and profitable consumer relationships. The segment is enriched with:

- Exhibits and illustrations covering recent developments in the field, drawing attention to digital marketing activities at Vodafone, Coca Cola, SBI, Jabong, American Express, Amazon, and eBay.
- Case studies on Louis Vuitton, P&G, and many more, linking academic concepts to corporate practice.
- Practitioner Perspectives from Google, Yahoo, Pinstorm, Adobe, Accenture, Twitter, YouTube, Mahindra & Mahindra, HDFC, Flipkart, Amazon, eBay, comScore, and many more, are significant in this section.

The second section, *Business Drivers in the Virtual World*, addresses the realm of social media, social media analytics and software tools used for analytics in the virtual world, and concepts pertaining to online branding—intricacies of online brand architecture, enriched with strategies directed towards establishing brand resonance, reinforcing brand salience, creating brand identity and meaning, reinforcing brand responses, and forging brand relationships are discussed in detail. The section focuses on how organizations can leverage the Internet for greater marketing profitability and revenue generation. By developing the relevant Web business model, organizations can utilize the Web for generating revenue and visibility and by developing the right keyword management strategies and investing in suitable Web traffic plans, they can maximize returns from their online presence. This section discusses the best practices in the domain of *e*-commerce, online marketplaces, and online distribution and procurement. This section includes:

- Exhibits drawing attention to digital marketing activities at IBM, SAP, Google, Ford, General Motors, Toyota, Pepsico, Groupon, Intuit, Levi Strauss, Aircel, Revlon, Channel V, Standard Chartered, Nokia, Louis Philippe, Aviva, Bacardi, Sony Ericsson, Coke, HDFC, Citibank, Amazon, Snapdeal, and Infosys.

- Case studies such as Starbucks, Jet Airways.
- Practitioner Perspectives from Facebook, Snapdeal, Google, Aviva, TechnoPak, NIIT, Kotak Mahindra, Twitter, eBay, Avendus, and many more.

The third section, *Online Tools for Marketing*, maps the usage of a variety of online tools for disparate marketing activities. Coverage includes consumer engagement, content management, campaign management, sentiment mining, segmentation, targeting and positioning. This section also discusses marketing intelligence and the online domain, as also consumer-generated media and market influence analytics in a digital ecosystem. This section includes:

- Exhibits drawing attention to digital marketing activities at Tata Docomo, Faaso's, HSBC, Coke, AmEx, and eBay.
- Several research-based case studies and cases on Flipkart, Volkswagen, Dell, and Apple.
- Practitioner Perspectives from Cadbury, P&G, HUL, Bajaj Auto, Hyundai, Intel, Vodafone, Wipro, Microsoft, IBM, FoxyMoron, and many more.

The fourth section, *The Contemporary Digital Revolution*, delves into the world of online communities, explores different typologies of online communities suitable to the world of marketing, and shares empirical models built to leverage the virtual space for better marketing resource and revenue optimization. This section further ventures into the world of Facebook marketing, Apps, and gamification in detail. This section includes:

- Exhibits and examples drawing attention to digital marketing activities at Domino's, Heineken, Lego, Starbucks, Dell, Sunsilk, Oreo, ICICI, Brooke Bond, Lufthansa, Horlicks, Philips, Nokia, Godrej, Titan, Marriott, and Nestle.
- Case studies such as MTV, MasterCard, Shopper's Stop, Sahara Star India.
- Practitioner Perspectives from Ogilvy & Mather, General Motors, TVS, Shoppers' Stop, Shemaroo, Mondelez International (Cadbury India Ltd).

Acknowledgements

My special thanks go to all my colleagues from academia and friends from the corporate world who supported me with their inputs during the composition of this title. I also thank the Vice Chancellor of Jaypee Institute of Information Technology, Prof. S.C. Saxena, and the Director, Jaypee Business School, for their unflinching support.

I am grateful to my PhD supervisor, Dr Y. Medury, Director, Bennett Coleman—Higher Education Group, and my mentors, Ms Sunita Joshi, Director, JILIT, and Dr Neerja Pande, IIM Lucknow, for their support and blessings. I thank my management research students, Dr Nidhi Sinha, Dr Shirin Alavi, and Dr Neha Jain, who, over the last several years, co-authored with me several publications in management journals in this sphere.

I feel indebted to my family—my husband, Viman, and my loving daughter, Vanshika, without whose support this endeavour would never have been successful. Above all, I thank my parents for bringing me into this world and teaching me to believe in myself.

Vandana Ahuja

Features of

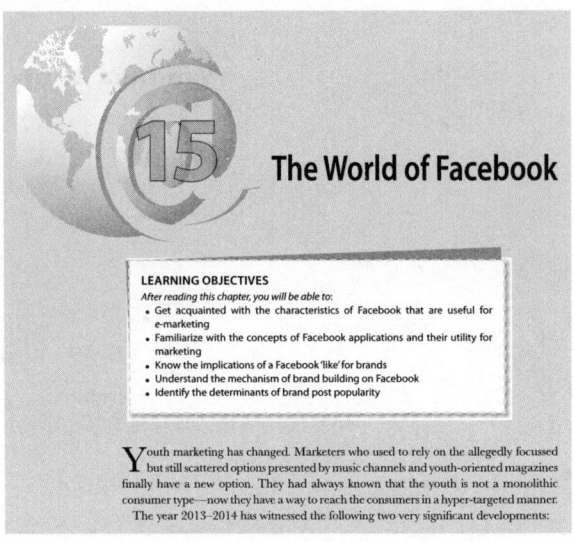

Chapter 15 *The World of Facebook*
A full chapter dedicated to the phenomenon of FB marketing.

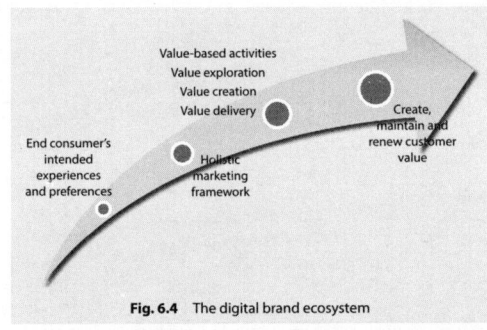

Figures/Tables
Includes numerous figures and tables to support the text.

Exhibits
Several exhibits in all the chapters to bring out the practical aspects of digital marketing.

the Book

CASE STUDY Building Loyalty the Jet Airways Way

Jet Airways, India's premier International airline and JetK
fleet strength of 120 aircrafts and operate over 620 flights c
Economy, Première, and First Class services on its various rou
consolidated low-fare service brand which replaces JetLite a
On 12 October 2011, Jet Airways was conferred three prestig
Travel Honours 2011' in the Most Trusted Airline Brand, the I
Carrier, and the Best International (Economy) Airline categor
  Jet Airways has been able to successfully use its digital pre
brand to an increasingly digitally savvy Indian population. W
Facebook, iGoogle, Orkut, Yahoo, Youtube, Twitter, Foursquare, Pinteres
has been able to carve for itself a special brand image of a sei

Case Studies
Provides case studies for in-depth analysis of digital marketing practiced in various companies such as Jet Airways, Starbucks, Domino's, etc.

Practitioner Perspective
Quotations from the actual practitioners of digital marketing, providing interesting insights into the domain.

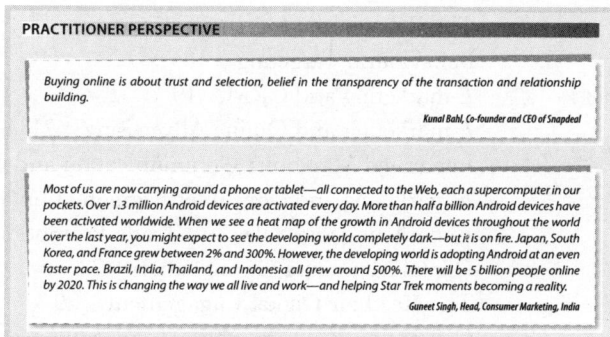

Concept Review Questions
1. How can organizations use digital marketing to build the online value of a brand?
2. Write short n
   (a) Domain r
   (b) Domain r
   (c) Domain r

Critical Thinking Questions
1. Study the brand architecture of one multinational following the house of brand strategy. Discuss with e
2. What strategi
   following pro
   online brandi

Practising Digital Marketing
1. Track the online presence of five product brands. Trace how each brand has used the online world to do the following:
   (a) Create a brand identity in the online sphere
   (b) Generate brand salience and resonance
   (c) Develop a brand personality
   (d) Develop a consumer–brand relationship

3. Differ
   brand

(a) C
(b) V

2. Develc
   above
   presen
3. Sugges
   demor

Chapter-end Exercises
Concept review questions, critical thinking questions, and practicing digital marketing test the understanding of the concepts, both theoretically as well as practically.

Contents

Preface   *iii*
Features of the Book   *viii*

Section 1: Marketing in the Digital Era

Chapter 1   *E*-marketing   3

    The Virtual World   04
    The Changing Marketing Landscape   04
    Web and the New Corporation   08
    The Internet and Business   13
    E-marketing—Strengths and Applications   14
    E-marketing Communication Modes   16
    Online Marketing Domains   16
    The Behavioural Internet   17
    Behavioural Targeting   18
    E-marketing and CRM   19
    E-marketing and Online Advertising   21
    Integrated Marketing Communication and the Internet   21
    E-marketing and Consumer Segmentation   22
    E-marketing and Sales and Trade Promotion   24
    Digital Marketing Optimization   28
    The Need for Digital Engagement   29
    Generation Y—Expectations and Influence   31
    The Implications of Digital Change   33
    Implications for Organizations   34
        Case Study: Blackberry and the Behavioural Internet Theory   36
        Practitioner Perspective   38

Chapter 2   The Online Marketing Mix   42

    E-products—Creating Customer Value in an Online World   46
    Marketing Segmentation   49
    Consumer Segmentation   50
    Consumer Traits   52
    Consumers and Online Shopping Issues   53
    Targeting   54
    Positioning   55
    E-price   55
    The Online Value   55
    E-promotion   56
    Website Characteristics Affecting Online Purchase Decision   57
    Digitization and Implications to Online Marketing Mix Decisions   57

Case Study: Louis Vuitton 61
Practitioner Perspective 64

Chapter 3 The Online Consumer   67

The Digital Ecosystem 67
Online Consumer Behaviour 70
Cultural Implications of Key Web Characteristics 71
Dynamics of Online Consumer Visit 72
Models of Website Visits 73
The Web and Consumer Decision-making Process 76
Behavioural Targeting vs Contextual Targeting 76
Web 2.0 and Marketing 78
Research Illustration 80
Database Marketing 84
Gearing up for New Online Consumers 86
Practitioner Perspective 90

Chapter 4 Customer Relationship Management in a Web 2.0 World   94

What is Customer Relationship Management (CRM)? 94
Why Customer Relationship Management? 95
The Goals of Customer Relationship Management 97
Benefits of Electronic CRM Technology in Online Banking 102
Customer Relation Management Processes 102
Role of Customer Relationship Management Technology 103
Customer Relationship Management and the Customer Lifecycle 104
Bonding for Customer Relationship 105
Electronic Customer Relationship Management 107
Customer Relationship Management—The B2C Dimensions 110
Key Customer Relationship Management Applications 111
Business-to-consumer 2.0 114
SAP Web Channel Experience Management 114
Next-generation CRM—A Mobile App and a Community 116
The New Age *E*-enterprise 116
The Collaborative Web and the Enterprise 118
The Collaborative Web and the *E*-enterprise 122
Case Study: Procter and Gamble 125
Practitioner Perspective 127

Section 2: Business Drivers in the Virtual World

Chapter 5 Social Media   135

Web 2.0 135
Social Media 136

The Social Media Model by McKinsey 137
Marketing with Networks 139
The Social World 142
Social Media Analytics 142
Social Media Tools 150
The Social Web 153
A Broad Look at the B2C and B2B Scenarios 154
Viral Marketing 155
Social Curation and Brands 155
Inbound Marketing and Co-creation 159
Social Media—The Road Ahead 160
 Case Study: Starbucks and Social Media—Striking a Chord with the Indian Consumer 161
 Case Study: Building Loyalty the Jet Airways Way 163
 Practitioner Perspective 165

Chapter 6 Online Branding 169

Cyberbranding 170
Consumers—The New Influential Constituency 170
The Digital Brand Ecosystem 173
Brand Experience 176
Using Consumer Brand Knowledge and Consumer Brand Emotion
 to Develop Consumer Engagement 184
Brand Customer Centricity 186
Brands and Emotions 187
Consumer Brand Emotion 188
 Case Study: Narendra Modi—Developing Brand Modi in the Online World 191
 Practitioner Perspective 193

Chapter 7 Traffic Building 198

The Diamond–Water Paradox 198
Internet Traffic Plan 200
Search Marketing Methods for Traffic Building 200
Internet Cookies and Traffic Building 202
Traffic Volume and Quality 202
Traffic-building Goals 203
Search Engine Marketing 203
Site Optimization 205
Keyword Advertising 205
Keyword Value 205
Keyword Portfolio Evaluation 205
Internet Marketing Metrics 208
Websites and Internet Marketing 208
 Case Study: Domino's India—Building Traffic through Content Propagation 216
 Practitioner Perspective 219

Chapter 8 Web Business Models 223

- The Value of a Customer Contact 224
- Customer-centric Web Business Models 224
- Customer-centric Business Management 226
- Web Chain of Events 227
- Web Chain Analysis 228
- Customer Value Analysis and the Internet 229
- Web Benefits to Firms 231
- Business Models 233
- Revenue Benefits 237
- Financial Services and the Internet 240
- The Indian Web Market 243
- Role of Internet in Impacting Consumer Price Sensitivity 244
- Price Effects in Online Domain 245
- Value Uncertainty 248
- Purchase Importance 248
  - *Practitioner Perspective* 248

Chapter 9 *E*-commerce 253

- Online Distribution and Procurement 253
- Traditional Distribution Management Issues 256
- Fundamental Advantages Offered by the Internet 257
- The Spiral of Prosperity Model 258
- Online Marketplaces 260
- *E*-procurement 261
- *E*-commerce Applications 262
- Measuring *E*-commerce Success 264
- Monitoring *E*-commerce Brands and Social Media in the Indian Market 267
  - *Case Study: Flipkart.com—Shopping Ka Naya Address* 269
  - *Practitioner Perspective* 271

Section 3: Online Tools for Marketing

Chapter 10 Engagement Marketing through Content Management 275

- Building Collaborative Customer Relationships 276
- Consumer Engagement 276
- Engagement Marketing 277
- Social Plugins and their Contribution to Marketing 283
- Online Shopping in the Era of Social Networking 284
- Building Consumer Engagement through Content Management 285
- Need for Greater Organizational Adaptability 290
- Finding Top Loyalty Drivers 291
- Integration and Alignment 292

Case Study: Personal Care Brands and the Indian Consumer   293
Practitioner Perspective   295

Chapter 11   Online Campaign Management   298

What is Campaign Management?   298
Campaign Management using Facebook   302
Campaign Management using Twitter   303
Twitter Marketing   304
Campaign Management using Corporate Blogs   305
Customer Relationship Management   307
Tagging and Folksonomies   307
Campaign Management   308
Sentiment Mining   309
Using Corporate Blog as a CRM 2.0 Tool   309
Customer Liking, Satisfaction, and Involvement   311
Evaluating Consumer Sentiment using Sentiwordnet 1.0   312
Consumer Segmentation based on Consumer Sentiment Score   312
Measuring Campaign Effectiveness I   314
Measuring Campaign Effectiveness II—Quantitative Tag Analysis   314
How Companies can use Blogs for Effective Campaign Management   315
Case Study: The MasterCard—'A World Beyond Cash' Campaign   317
Practitioner Perspective   318

Chapter 12   Consumer Segmentation, Targeting, and Positioning using Online Tools   321

Knowledge Discovery and Data Mining   322
Different Methods for Consumer Segmentation   322
Geographical Segmentation   326
Demographic Segmentation   326
Behavioural Segmentation   326
Psychographic Segmentation   326
Consumer Segmentation in the Virtual Space   326
Popularity of Brand Pages   327
Consumer Psychographic Profiles and Consumer Segmentation   328
Benefit Segmentation   328
Consumer Targeting   328
Online Targeting   329
Deterministic Targeting   329
Non-deterministic Targeting   330
Predictive Targeting   330
Behavioural Targeting   331
Brand Positioning Online   332
Emerging Consumer Segments in India   335

Case Study: Volkswagen India—Effective Positioning in the Virtual World   336
Practitioner Perspective   338

Chapter 13   Market Influence Analytics in a Digital Ecosytem   340

The Digital Ecosystem   341
Knowledge as a Value Proposition   343
Consumer-generated Media and Consumer Behaviour   345
Consumer-generated Media and Opinion Leaders   346
Peer Reviews, Word of Mouth, and the Dissatisfied Customer   346
Correlation between Consumer-generated Media and Sales   347
The Value of the Power of Influence   347
Mining Consumer-generated Media   348
    Case Study: The iPhone   349
    Practitioner Perspective   355

Section 4: The Contemporary Digital Revolution

Chapter 14   Online Communities and Co-creation   361

Co-creation Communities for Brands   362
Co-creation Communities—Some Exhibits   368
Empirical Models to Leverage Product/Brand Online Communities   368
Consumer Trustworthiness Regression Model using Netnography (CTR)   371
A Consumer Co-creation Model using INV Based on Metcalf Law (C-INV)   372
Consumer Price Sensitivity Model using K-means Cluster Analysis   376
Consumer Price Sensitivity   377
    Case Study: MTV India—Co-creation using MTV Music Meter   379
    Practitioner Perspective   381

Chapter 15   The World of Facebook   385

Eight Different Versions of Facebook   386
Facebook—The Origin   387
The Anatomy of Facebook   387
Netiquette—The Facebook Etiquette for Brands   392
The Impact of a Facebook Fan   397
Brand Post Popularity   398
Consumer Visit Schedules and Click-through Rates   403
Top 10 Brands in India and their Facebook Presence   403
    Case Study: Shoppers Stop—Facebook and Apps for Marketing   404
    Practitioner Perspective   406

Chapter 16   The Future of Marketing—Gamification and Apps   409

The Rise of Technology   411
Gamification and Game-based Marketing   412
Consumer Motivation for Playing Online Games   415

Gamification and the Consumer Brand Affinity Spectrum   416
The Anatomy of Gamification   417
Use of Games as Marketing Tools   421
The World of Apps   421
Apps and the Indian Diaspora   424
   Case Study: The 16th Indian Lok Sabha Elections—The Era of Online Apps, Facebook, Google, and Twitter   428
   Practitioner Perspective   432

Index   435
About the Author   439

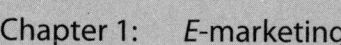

Section 1
Marketing in the Digital Era

Chapter 1:   *E*-marketing

Chapter 2:   The Online Marketing Mix

Chapter 3:   The Online Consumer

Chapter 4:   Customer Relationship Management in a Web 2.0 World

E-marketing

> **LEARNING OBJECTIVES**
> *After reading this chapter, you will be able to:*
> - Understand the concept of *e*-marketing and the changing marketing landscape
> - Explain the technology catalysis along with the strengths and applications of *e*-marketing
> - Get acquainted with the theory behind the behavioural Internet
> - Know the differences between various online marketing domains
> - Get familiar with the idea of digital marketing optimization
> - Know the implications of digital change

The era of digital environment and digital convergence has opened up new opportunities for marketing. The age of individualization, networking, and digitization, along with the evolution of consumers in the virtual domains is posing new challenges for marketers. In this digital age, it is quite imperative to revisit marketing strategies and adapt them significantly to contribute to the marketing value chain. The upcoming discipline of *e*-marketing offers opportunities for innovation, profitability and affordability in the epoch of the empowered customer, who has graduated from standalone media platforms to 'always-on' devices, courtesy digital convergence. This affinity for the Web can be harnessed effectively to leverage its impact on the consumer. *E*-marketing can be put into use to:

- Explore the new tools offered by the world of the Internet
- Access the realm of social media
- Investigate the mindset of online consumers
- Scrutinize the characteristics of the virtual medium which can be of value to the end consumer
- Identify how companies can leverage the online world as a media vehicle, for brand communication and proliferation, building brand and stakeholder relationships and customer relationship management (CRM)
- Understand the consumer online experience
- Examine traffic building activities for marketers.

In summary
- *E*-marketing[1] is the use of information technology in the process of creating, communicating, and delivering value to the customers. It is also used for managing customer relationships in ways that benefit the organization and its stakeholders.
- *E*-marketing is the result of information technology applied to traditional marketing.

THE VIRTUAL WORLD

The Internet, a vast web of computer networks, provides a platform for worldwide users to connect and share data, thereby serving as a huge information repository. The Internet has fundamentally changed the consumers' notion of convenience, speed, price, product information, and service. It has, hence, given marketers a whole new way to create value for customers and build relationships with them.[2] The Internet is allowing greater flexibility in working hours and location, especially with the spread of unmetered high-speed connections and Web applications.

The Internet can now be accessed almost anywhere by numerous means, especially through mobile Internet devices. Mobile phones, data cards, handheld game consoles and cellular routers allow users to connect to the Internet from any point where there is a wireless network technology supporting the device. Within the limitations imposed by small screens and other limited facilities of such pocket-sized devices, services of the Internet, including *e*-mail and the Web, may be available.

Simultaneously, organizations have moved from product based marketing campaign to a customer based relationship approach. Economies have become customer driven. Companies are going global, reaching out to customers located afar as *e*-commerce and online buying facilitate consumer purchase, and thus diminishing geographical restrictions. Increasing competition between organizations is leading to the implementation of relationship strategies and multi-channel relationship programmes, as consumer retention becomes vital for organizational sustenance. As organizations realize the rising importance of communicating with their consumers, the Internet provides an excellent low-cost solution for better connectivity.

THE CHANGING MARKETING LANDSCAPE

The Changing Marketing Landscape (Fig. 1.1) can benefit with the advent of:
- *Internet strategy integration*[3] resulting in combination of market, policy and IT, working in a complimentary or cumulative fashion. The Internet plays a key role in integration of information across suppliers, customers and the organization. Formulation of a clear strategic perspective to this end enables organizations in development of benchmark processes.
- Refined *Internet marketing metrics*[4] for evaluation of marketing performance and identification of key performance indicators, as a result of the campaign's requirement

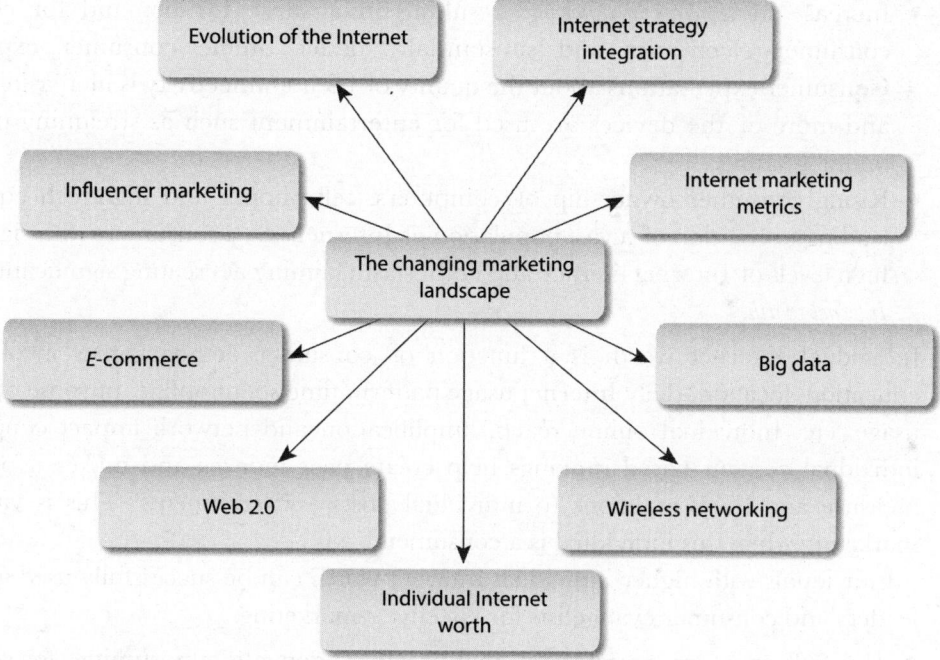

Fig. 1.1 The changing marketing Landscape

to design and send tailored offers and messages to the right consumers. *Length* and *Depth* of *consumer online visits, time spent online, page views, referring sites,* etc. become vital issues to be discussed in the context of *e*-marketing metrics.

- The era of *Big data*,[5] (Fig. 1.2) with the increasing volume and detail of information available online and the need to harness customer intelligence from data extracted by the Web crawlers. Marketing can benefit through better consumer segmentation, forecasting consumer trends and consumer analytics. Consumer profiling can help in extraction of consumer DNA, which can aid decision making in marketing.

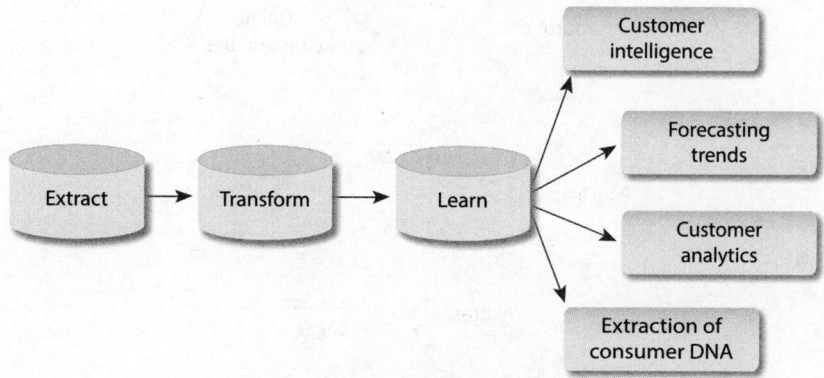

Fig. 1.2 The Era of big data

- Increase in *wireless networking*[6] resulting in a surge for demand for connected consumer electronics and substantially better online consumer experiences. Consumer expectations about the quality of their connectivity is increasing as more and more of the devices are used for entertainment such as streaming movies or online gaming.
- Rising consumer ownership of computers, cell phones and high-tech equipments leading to creation of a vast population of Internet savvy consumers with significantly high levels of Internet literacy and enthusiasm, aiming at creating significant *individual Internet worth*.[7]

Individual Internet worth is a function of consumer demographics involving age, education, location, daily Internet usage pattern, time spent online, purpose of Internet usage, etc. Individual online reach, amplification and network impact coupled with individual content based rankings help create peer indexes and makes it possible to measure and track reactions to individual posts and comments. This is valuable to marketing when this individual is a consumer.

Individuals with higher individual Internet worth can be successfully used as opinion leaders and consumer evangelists for effective *e*-marketing.

- *Web 2.0*[8] or the read-write Web that provides adequate opportunities for companies to practice *e*-marketing by content creation in the virtual world. This enables better campaign management, consumer engagement and consumer interaction (Fig. 1.3).
  - Companies such as Dell are using a series of online Web 2.0 platforms to engage with the consumers. These include blogs (*Direct2Dell*), Dell Online Communities (*Dell Ideastorm*), Facebook pages, and wikis.
  - Organizations such as Apple have created 40 online product communities-each for a separate Apple product, for active engagement with its consumers.

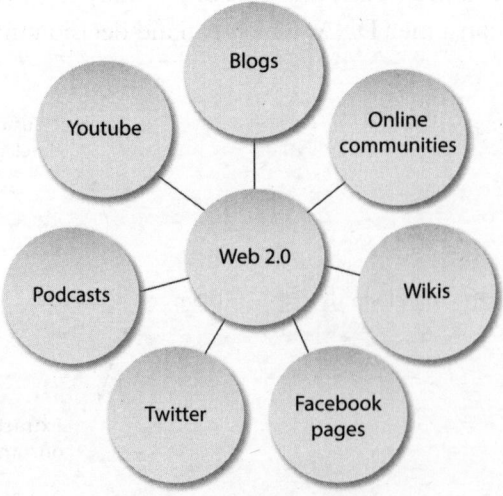

Fig. 1.3 The advent of Web 2.0

- The era of *e-commerce*,⁹ leading to online transactions, in the wake of a population, constrained with time, but willing to spend, for convenience and ease of shopping. Ebay, Flipkart, Jabong and Myntra are some of the *e*-commerce companies operating in India and offering Indians the opportunity to shop online.
- *Influencer marketing*¹⁰ being practiced by top brands. Top brands reach out to influencers for marketing purposes. In the online domain, these are bloggers or social media users with a more-than-average reach among consumers and they are prized by marketers for their ability to spread the word about products or services they believe in. According to a Technorati Media study from December 2012, 65% of top US brands reported participating in influencer marketing. A similar 64% of those were deemed influencers by *Technorati*, which implies that they had more-than-average reach in specific marketplace-made revenue from blogging; either from advertisements on their site or sponsored endorsements from brands.
- *Evolution of the Internet.* The dimensions of Internet usage have changed. This includes the people using the network devices to access the network, the content available using the network and communication happening throughout the network, and technology standards that make the network possible.

Companies that manage learning relationships with customers are able to customize their offerings for them. These customers stay with the company almost forever. The consumer decision process is an intrinsic function of consumer psychology and not achieved objective in terms of product procurement. It is the psychological gain or losses that are the behavioural drivers. This is where the collaborative Web can be utilized. Organizations can focus on reducing the psychological losses and mitigating the impact of any negative consumer thought or negative product information by engaging consumers into meaningful conversations.

EXHIBIT 1.1 Vodafone offers free Twitter access to push data usage

In 2013, Vodafone India tied up with Twitter to offer free access, without any data charges, to the social networking website through their browser (mobile.twitter.com) and 'Twitter for Android' App. The offer was for a period of three months after which regular data charges were applicable. The move was clearly made to increase mobile Internet usage on mobile phones. The aim of the attempt was promoting data usage. Data, unlike voice, did not have a ready market, and the move aimed at netting in some new users, thereby creating a new revenue stream. Apart from these free tie-ups, data operators have entered into multiple agreements to offer Facebook, Twitter, or other specific website access at a fixed price. This is a model that has worked to some extent but is yet to proliferate. Analysts estimate that although there are nearly 100 million Internet users in India, only 1–2% actually use it beyond the basic search or *e*-mail.

WEB AND THE NEW CORPORATION

Web technologies have had a long relationship with the corporation and have had a profound impact on the expression of its identity and the conduct of its stakeholders. That relationship has only strengthened over the years and Web technologies are now manifested in almost every aspect of an organization's operation.

Web 1.0

In 1989, Tim Berners Lee conceived the Web as a way to access inter-linked static documents and navigates the relationships between documents. A language to describe and format such documents was specified and hyper text markup language (HTML) came into being. The application to read such documents was named as the browser and the protocol between the browser and the servers where these documents were stored was called the hyper text transfer protocol (HTTP).

While there were other protocols to access information over the network, the visual rendition of the information and the concept of an 'information mesh' and linkages between documents caused this new paradigm to gain quick traction. The first use-case of this technology was to share data, news, and documentation by academia.

The introduction of the first graphical browser called Mosaic in 1993 at the NCSA was a turning point. The richness of the documents and the ability to organize information in a logical and readable fashion triggered the imagination of many and led to rapid innovation. Between 1993 and 1996, the Web gained commercial recognition and every organization came to realize that presence on the World Wide Web was no longer optional. The companies started to have a 'face' on the Web and used Web to share data, news, and information with its many stakeholders.

Web

The exploding content on the Web (Fig. 1.4) made it increasingly hard to find stuff Web and search engines such as Yahoo and Google were founded to help organize the Web and to search for information. The Web was automatically becoming a medium of communication. As with all other types of media, smart people started imagining and monetizing the 'eyeballs' that the Web was commanding. This was an era of rampant innovation and exploration of new business models. Information directories and portals specialized around specific concepts were abounding. These portals simply served as information aggregators and as navigation assistors. The bond between the organizations and the Web was firmly in place and the organizations had to make sure it was marketing its identity on its Web front. The organizations also had to make sure that it was represented in all the right information portals and directories and that its key stakeholders could find their Web pages. Along with the Internet, though, corporations had also begun to exploit Web technologies to organize internal information and

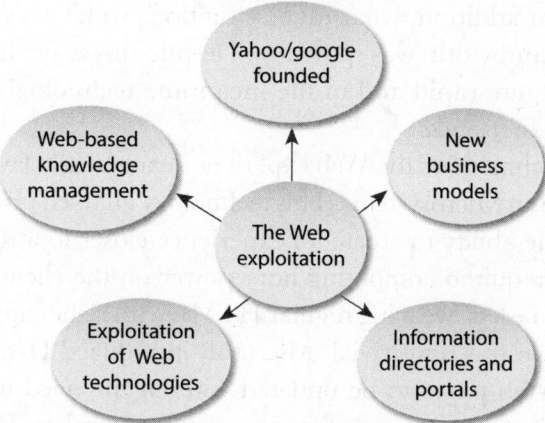

Fig. 1.4 The Web exploitation

knowledge within its employee base. This was the inception of the Web-based knowledge management paradigm. Along with the Internet, the Intranet was gaining popularity among the corporations. The relationship between the corporations and its customers as well as its employees was going through a transformation.

As the Web matured as a platform for broadcasting information, the reliability, security, and privacy of the information became the priority. Corporations in the consumer segment wanted to use the Web as a way to give consumers access to their account information. The authenticity of that information, privacy of the Web transaction, and the authentication and authorization of the consumer to make sure that the right person sees the right information and only see what they are entitled to see were the key business drivers. Information security technologies in the areas of cryptography and PKI (Public Key Infrastructure) came to the rescue. A secure version of the HTTP protocol (HTTPS) evolved and was widely deployed.

The next step in the evolution of the Web was possibility of two-way communication with the server. Technologies like CGI and ASP were introduced and this meant that not only could one pull down information from the server but also one could send information to it and also send commands that the server would execute. The Web was no longer passive and the active Web was born. Customers visiting a Web site could register and enter their information which could be recorded in a database. Now the Web front end for the corporation was not simply akin to an electronic billboard, it now had the potential to be a fully functional electronic storefront. The website could be used to conduct an actual commercial transaction. The *e*-commerce use-case was now very possible. This use-case of course triggered an even greater level of awareness and sensitivity for the security of the Web. The key issue with Web forms/CGI and ASP technology was that all the processing was done on the server side. This prevented the delivery of a rich and interactive user experience. The data had to be sent to the server and processed before a response could be shared with the end user. In addition, what made situations worse was at this stage the speed of connections (bandwidth) was quite low. Despite this issue, the pace of innovation and adoption was quite rapid and in the meantime technologists worked hard to deliver a richer Web experience.

The first enrichment of the Web experience came when Java applet technologies were introduced by Sun Microsystems. This technology enabled processing on the browser side and also had the ability to create an experience closer to a regular desktop application. This however, required computing horsepower on the client end point. Even with this technology, the task of weaving regular HTML with richer applet-based experiences into a seamless whole was non-trivial. Microsoft introduced Dynamic HTML or DHTML which enable Web pages to be updated without the need to make a roundtrip to the server. Through a creative use of images, layouts, applets, DHTML, or even Flex, the Web experience was getting pretty engaging.

Another innovation was the ability to personalize the information being disseminated. Technologies like cookies made it possible for individual visitors to a Web site to be identified enabling the personalization of the information that was being served to these visitors. When a Web user connected to a Web site for the first time, they had to provide personal information. The server stored this information into a token or 'cookie' and sent it back to the browser. The browser stored this and on every subsequent interaction with the server, it sent this cookie back to the server. The server then used the cookie to identify the user and personalize the content. This enabled use-cases around personalization and also interactions that required remembering state. One example of such an interaction is a shopping cart application. The server is able to remember the contents of your cart through the use of cookies.

At this stage, the marketers within corporations were salivating at the prospect of reaching a broad mass of customers with targeted advertising. Web *e*-commerce sites were sprouting up either as adjuncts to brick and mortar storefronts for existing corporations or as stand-alone Web-only storefronts for some new and innovative corporations. The Web was transforming the market capabilities of the corporations yet again. In addition, the Web was playing a crucial role in several other business processes that entailed the customers. This included customer support and service, customer base research, loyalty programmes, and so on.

Meanwhile, for companies, the Web front and Web-based applications were becoming the standard paradigm for front-office and back-office applications. Web-based applications were the standard way for a corporation to interact with its employees not just in terms of updates and news but also the key business processes such as talent acquisition, performance management, product definition, market research, and so on, were all happening at the behest of Web-based technologies (Fig. 1.5). The ubiquity of the browser enabled employee mobility and access to corporate applications even when the employee was not at their designated computer or end-point. The intranet portal was mainstay within the corporations at this stage.

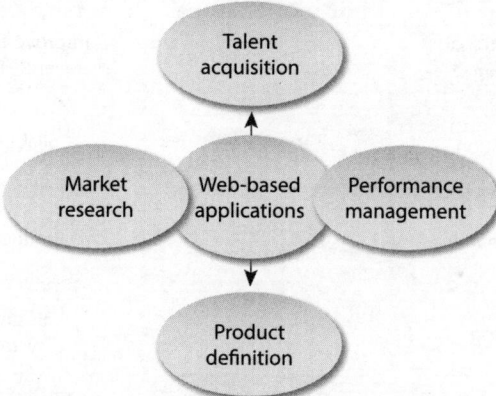

Fig. 1.5 Web-based applications

Web 2.0

The collaborative version of the Internet, termed Web 2.0, as coined by Tim O'Reilly in 2005, has altered the manner in which information was published, consumed, and utilized on the Internet resulting in a concept shift in the way interactions were taking place within the organizational workspace as well as between the organization and the external customers. Web 2.0 is a collection of open-source, interactive, and user-controlled online applications expanding the experiences, knowledge, and market power of the users as participants in business and social processes.[11]

Personal websites were getting replaced by blogs, content management systems by wikis, directories by tagging, encyclopaedias by Wikipedia, and participation was the new keyword connecting organizations, employees, customers, suppliers, partners, and any other intermediaries (Fig. 1.6). Differential patterns of combining data, content, services through collaboration, and increased access to information by consumers was opening up new dimensions for organizations to interact with the various players involved in the business.

Content creation by consumers facilitating the flow of ideas and knowledge has given the corporate sector access to huge volumes of data, which can be leveraged for decision making. Commonly and collectively called *Web 2.0 tools*, these new content-sharing sites, discussion forums and collaborative webspaces, and application design patterns or *mashups* are transforming the consumer Web. They also proffer a significant opportunity

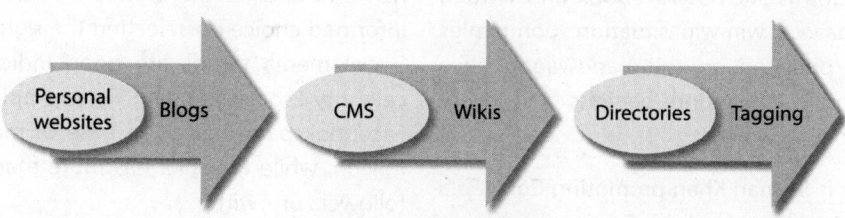

Fig. 1.6 Web 2.0 tools

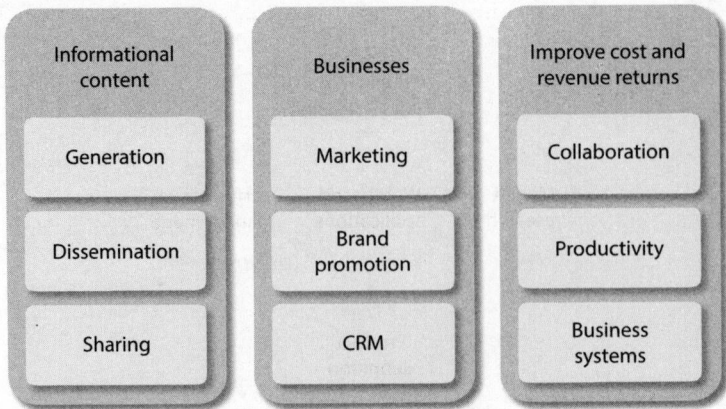

Fig. 1.7 Web 2.0 and the business revolution

for organizations to build new social and Web-based collaboration, productivity, and business systems, and to improve cost and revenue returns (Fig. 1.7).[12]

Web 2.0 is the business revolution in the computer industry caused by the move to the Internet as a platform, and an attempt to understand the rules for success on that new platform.[13] Web 2.0 applications supported the creation of informal user networks facilitating the flow of ideas and knowledge by allowing the efficient generation, dissemination, sharing, and editing/refining of informational content.

Web 2.0 also appears to have a substantial effect on consumer behaviour and on new challenges facing strategists and marketers.[14] Corporate blogs, online communities, social networks, wikis, *micromedia*, and *folksonomies* are some Web 2.0 concepts that were gaining popularity in the field of marketing, brand promotion, and customer relationship management. Web 2.0 also had a substantial effect on consumer behaviour and has contributed to an unprecedented customer empowerment. The consequences were far

---

EXHIBIT 1.2 The Internet changed the way marketing was done

The powerful appeal of a celebrity brand endorsement cannot be over-emphasized. Club that with the seemingly limitless reach of social media platforms such as Facebook and Twitter, and you have a win-win situation. Companies that have pounced on this bandwagon have reaped untold marketing benefits and every rupee spent was worth it.

Whether it is Salman Khan promoting Coca Cola India's Thums Up through his Facebook page, or Priyanka Chopra landing a deal with an Indian health portal to promote their brand through her twitter handle, this winning formula has paid rich dividends to the brands that also made an informed choice on selecting the right celebrity. Social media trends are good indicators of a celebrity's social standing. For example, Salman's Facebook page has a fan base of more than 7 million, while Priyanka has more than 4 million followers on Twitter.

reaching, affecting not only the area of technology development but also the domains of business strategy and marketing owing to changing consumer attitudes, new customer needs, emerging new value perceptions, and the change of consumer search tactics and buying behaviour. Of significance is the emergence of the collaborative Web as a factor influencing consumer buying behaviour and further as a new source of consumer creativity, influence, and empowerment.[15] Consumer behaviour was increasingly influenced by peer opinions and collective intelligence.[16]

Several organizations are using collaborative product-development tools, such as initiating discussions on blogs to test ideas, involving customers in the use of collaborative design tools, or testing how well products sell in virtual worlds. A new type of communities is gaining momentum on the Web and is reshaping online communication and collaboration patterns and the way information is consumed and produced.[17]

Individual desires for self-actualization, belonging to a group and gaining prestige facilitate participation and mutually maximize the collective intelligence of the participants. The value attributed to these applications is not based on the classic customer value approach but rather on some feeling of achievement through personal gratification.

Collective intelligence, which can be defined as the knowledge that is distributed within a group reflects the knowledge of all participants and continuously adapts to changes in environment or opinion leadership.[18]

Web 2.0 is now ushering in the world of Web 3.0, also termed as the *Semantic Web*. The Semantic Web provides a common framework that allows data to be shared and reused across applications, enterprises, and community boundaries.

THE INTERNET AND BUSINESS

The Internet has three technical roles (Fig. 1.8), which are as follows:
- Content providers to create information, entertainment, and so forth that reside on computers with network access

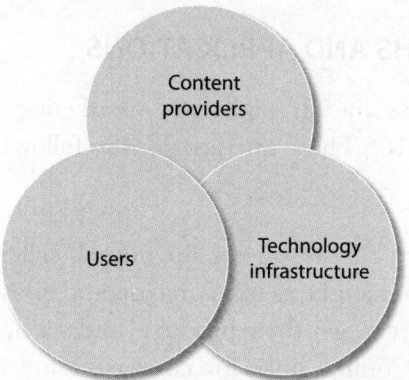

Fig. 1.8 The three technical roles of the Internet

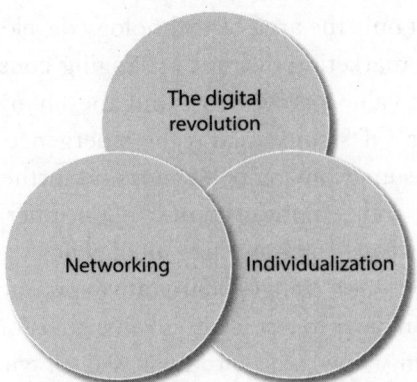

Fig. 1.9 The GPTs of the Internet

- Users who access content and send *e*-mail and other data over the network
- A technology infrastructure to move, create, view, or listen to the content

Individuals can be both users and content providers at various times.

In this context, the three general purpose technologies (GPTs) of the Internet are shown in Fig. 1.9:[19]

There are three important types of networks involved in the formation of the Internet,[20] which are as follows:

- *Intranet* A network that runs internally in a corporation but uses Internet standards such as HTML and browsers. Thus, an intranet is such as a mini Internet but only for internal corporate communication.
- *Extranet* Two or more proprietary networks that are joined for the purpose of sharing information. If two companies link their intranets, they would have an extranet. The access is normally only partial.
- *Web* The portion of the Internet that supports a graphical user interface for hypertext navigation with a browser such as Internet Explorer. The Web is what most people think about when they think of the Internet.

E-MARKETING—STRENGTHS AND APPLICATIONS

This section explores the strengths of *e*-marketing and resultant implications for organizations (Fig. 1.10). Those are described as follows.

E-commerce

E-marketing provides rich resources for buyers, sellers, and learners. Opportunities range from virtual marketplaces like Amazon and eBay to a series of online directories where organizations can get their products and services listed for online transactions and auctions. These online hubs for commerce are useful both in a B2B and B2C context, offering an incredibly wide range of products and services. The USPs of these

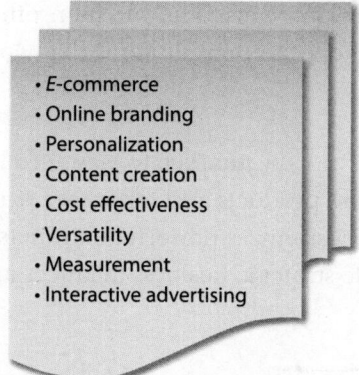

Fig. 1.10 *E*-marketing applications

marketplaces are quite far reaching. They range from their global reach to the increased revenue generation by virtue of enhanced consumer participation and facilities like online auctions, which thrive on healthy ecosystems of sellers and affiliates.

Online Branding

Powerful branding and creation of a successful brand image are very important for any organization. Brands thrive on positioning and the consumer–brand relationship. Online branding offers a myriad of opportunities to enhance *brand identity* and *brand salience*, and increase consumer–brand *resonance*. This subsequently strengthens *brand loyalty*.

Personalization

E-marketing presents unprecedented one-to-one communication and dynamic personalization during an online session by individualizing an impersonal, computer-networked environment; for example, a website may greet a user by his/her name or provide personalized information. Likewise, online advertising allows the customization of advertisements, including content and posted websites. For example, *AdWords*, Yahoo! *search marketing*, and Google *AdSense* enable advertisements to be shown on relevant Web pages or alongside search results.

Content Creation

E-marketing allows the consumers to not only 'consume' the content hosted online by the organization but also generate content. This creates numerous opportunities for marketing and advertising functions to create consumer-specific content for increasing sales and greater revenue generation.

Cost-effectiveness

E-marketing is cost effective, specifically with reference to the ratio of cost to the reach of the target audience. The companies can reach wide audiences for a small fraction of traditional advertising budgets. The medium offers unlimited space on the Web, and, subsequently, marketers can present items that would not be cost effective in print.

Versatility

The Internet opens up the market to new groups of customers and allows them to research and purchase products and services conveniently. The medium is not limited by geography or time, customizes powerful extranets to the company and individuals, and also allows profitable strategic business alliances and affiliations.

Measurement

Internet marketers also have the advantage and ease of measuring statistics, and also inexpensively; and almost all aspects of an Internet marketing campaign can be traced, measured, and tested. This is possible as online marketing initiatives usually require users to click on an advertisement, visit a website, and perform a targeted action.

Interactive Advertising

The immediacy of online content creation and consumption has contributed to the emerging area of interactive advertising and presents fresh challenges for advertisers who have hitherto adopted an interruptive strategy.

The consumer website visit is at the heart of online marketing. These are short visits but organizations face challenges in building higher consumer perceived value for these visits. Organizational objectives are to make these visits believable and persuasive enough to achieve one or more of the above stated objectives of *e*-marketing.

Interaction with the online consumers has been broadly classified in Table 1.1.

E-MARKETING COMMUNICATION MODES

E-marketing involves multiple communication vehicles and platforms. *E*-marketing vehicles include *e-mail, instant messaging,* and *podcasts*. Podcasting derives from Apple's ubiquitous iPod. With podcasting, consumers can download audio files (podcasts) or video files (*vodcasts*) via the Internet to an iPod or another handheld device and then listen to them or view them whenever and wherever they wish. The flexibility offered by the Internet represents its potential as a *mass* medium, (e.g., banner advertisements), as an *addressable* medium (as in case of *e*-mails), and as an *interactive* medium (as in case of live chat). Platforms include PDAs, personal video recorders, and cellphones.

ONLINE MARKETING DOMAINS

The four major online marketing domains[21] include B2C (business to consumer), B2B (business to business), C2C (consumer to consumer), and C2B (consumer to business) (Fig. 1.11 and Table 1.2).

Table 1.1 Interaction with online consumers

Classification of online interaction	Consumer issues raised	Opportunities for marketing
Interaction for information retrieval	Issues of usability Issues of customer support Issues of virtual value	E-marketing can aid the consumer search process, promote information exchange and online transaction, and help organizations enhance value perception by providing more usable and navigable websites.
Information believability	Issues of credibility Issues of trust Issues of completeness	E-marketing can focus on creating online content pertaining to an organization, which can be used for building organizational credibility and enhancing trust, and subsequently building consumer loyalty.
Consumer actions after access to information	Issues of persuasion through marketing material	Internet marketing can be used to persuade consumers, keeping in mind the three principles of *Ethos* (strong credibility of the organization persuading an individual to buy), *Logos* (successful online marketing using logic and reason), and *Pathos* (e-marketing by appealing to human emotion).

	Targeted to consumers	Targeted to businesses
Initiated by business	B2C	B2B
Initiated by consumer	C2C	C2B

Fig. 1.11 Online marketing domains

The low cost of setting up a shop on the Internet has led to many small business start-ups aimed at niches. What these firms have realized is that the best recipe for Internet success is to choose a *hard-to-find* product that customers do not need to see and touch.

THE BEHAVIOURAL INTERNET

The Internet provides a virtual territory where individuals replicate their offline behaviours in the virtual world. This gives rise to the Behavioural Internet theory, which attempts to investigate the various dimensions of the Internet and an individual's behaviour, which can be synchronized together to benefit the domain of marketing. The concept is explained with a case study on Blackberry at the end of the chapter. The case study will demonstrate the attempt of Blackberry to use the behavioural Internet to leverage the *e*-marketing dimensions of the media equation, flow, content accessibility, social and quality cues, and friendly technology.

Table 1.2 Online marketing domains

Domain	Implication	Examples
B2C	Internet consumers differ from traditional consumers in their buying habits and preferences. In the era of a proliferating Internet-savvy consumer population, the Web offers a multitude of experiences to consumers, who initiate and control the contact.	Amazon.com[22] opened its virtual doors in July 1995 with a mission to use the Internet to offer products that educate, inform, and inspire. By early 1999, it became the largest Internet-based seller of books and music and operated one of the most frequently used websites on the Internet, offering over 4.7 million discounted books as well as CDs, DVDs, computer games, audio books, and videotapes. The company had an 85% share of online book sales, with over six million customers in more than 160 countries. Customers used Amazon.com website both to select and purchase products. Specifically, customers were able to use the site to search for titles, browse selections, read and post reviews, register for personalized services, make a credit card purchase, and check order status. Amazon.com continues to communicate with its customers electronically throughout the order process.
B2B	Organizations are fast achieving buying efficiencies and superior marketing productivity by buying and selling online, owing to smoother and faster transactions in the online domain facilitated by greater convenience and price comparisons.	Dell.com has set up customized websites for more than 113,000 business and institutional customers worldwide. These individualized premier/dell.com sites help business customers in all the phases of their Dell computer buying and ownership. Each customer's premier Dell.com website can include a customized online computer store, purchasing and asset management reports and tools, system-specific technical information, links to useful information throughout Dell's extensive website, and more. The site includes all the information that a customer needs in order to do business with Dell, available in one place, 24 hours a day, and 7 days a week.[23]
C2C	When online exchange of goods and information takes place between consumers. In the wake of increased peer-to-peer communications, courtesy the read-write Web, organizations have created online forums where consumer to consumer interaction can take place. Today's consumers not only consume online content, they also create it.	When Nescafe launched its Dolce Gusto coffee maker in France a few years back, it turned to bloggers. It placed an advertisement on French website Blogbang.com, which has a community of more than 2000 bloggers. The site sent a message to its members telling them about the ad campaign, which came in the form of an interactive game. The bloggers were asked to put a link to the game on their sites. In return, Dolce Gusto's home page posted links to blogs that joined up. This created an online buzz and within weeks of its launch, Dolce Gusto's ad was displayed on 500 blogs, and 3,20,000 people had played the online game.[24]
C2B	These include online exchanges where consumers search for sellers, learn about their offers, and initiate purchases, sometimes even driving transaction terms.	Consumers can use websites like Complaints.com to ask questions, offer suggestions, lodge complaints, or deliver compliments to companies.[25]

BEHAVIOURAL TARGETING

Behavioural targeting refers to a range of technologies and techniques used by online website publishers and advertisers, which allows them to increase the effectiveness of their campaigns by capturing data generated by website and landing page visitors. Nearly one-quarter of all interactive marketers use behavioural targeting, and that number is growing faster each year for a good reason. Behavioural targeting[28] cuts through ad clutter and puts the right marketing message before the right people. With market pressures making high performance more important than ever, by concentrating on a few simple elements such as setting objectives, tweaking creative, and leaving time for testing, organizations can get better results through online marketing. When a consumer visits a website, the pages they visit, the amount of time they spend on each page, the links they click on, the searches they make and their interactions are recorded as data. All these factors create a visitor/user/consumer profile that links to that visitor's Web browser. As a result, site publishers can use these data to create defined audience segments based upon visitors that have similar profiles. When visitors return to a specific site or a network of sites using the same Web browser, those profiles can be used to allow advertisers to position their online ads to those visitors who exhibit a greater level of interest and intent for the products and services being offered. On the theory that properly targeted advertisements will fetch more consumer interest, the publisher (or seller) can charge a premium for these ads over random advertising or ads based on the context of a site.

Over 30 Internet companies including Yahoo and Google today have started behavioural targeting. Their methodology is divided into two separate programmes, *AdWords*, which gathers information from user search requests, and *AdSense*, which accumulates information on user activity on Websites.

For the *AdWords* programme, Google serves ads based on the subject matter of consumer search. For example, a consumer search on 'golf' on Google results in golf-related ads. Google also makes ads geographically relevant, which is done with the help of IP addresses. If a consumer is in Delhi searching for cab companies, the consumer wants ads for Delhi-based, not London-based cabs.

Similarly, for the *AdSense* programme, Google serves ads based on the content of the site it views. For example, if a consumer visits a gardening site, ads on that site may be related to gardening. In addition, Google may serve ads based on consumer interests. As individuals browse websites that have partnered with Google sites using the *DoubleClick* cookie, such as YouTube, Google may place the *DoubleClick* cookie in an individual's browser to understand the types of pages visited or content viewed.

E-MARKETING AND CRM

Marketers have practiced *Relationship Marketing* for some time, but the Internet has brought a substantial degree of personalization and subsequently individualization to the world of relationships. Long-term customer retention has become a strategic goal for organizations, rather than several discrete transactions with new customers, courtesy the shift from mass marketing to relationship marketing.

Customer relationship management is used to create and maintain relationships with employees, business customers in the supply chain, lateral partners, and final consumers (Fig. 1.12).

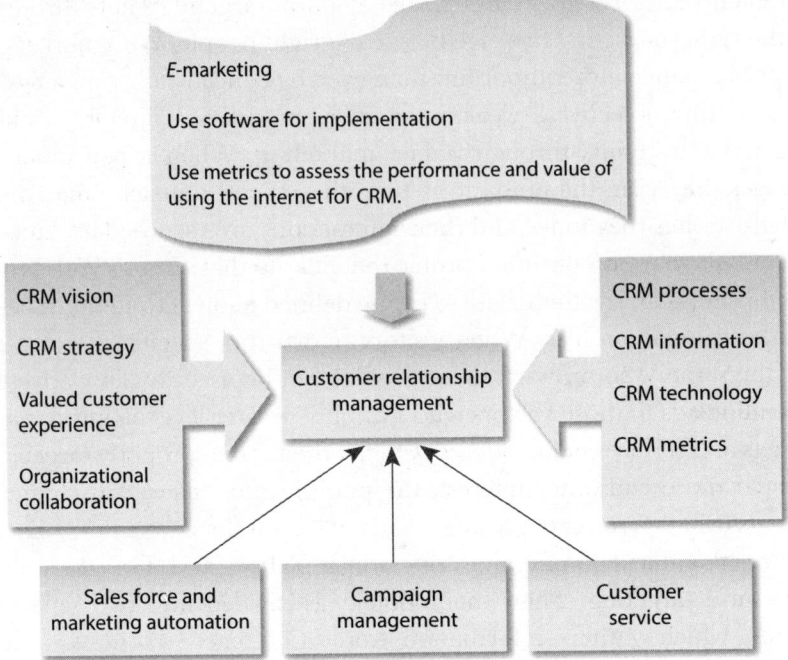

Fig. 1.12 *E*-marketing and CRM

There are various benefits of CRM, as follows:

- Cost-effective acquisition
- Retention
- Growth of current customers
- Word-of-mouth referrals

The three dimensions of CRM are as follows:

- Sales force automation
- Marketing automation
- Customer service

The Gartner Group Model of CRM covers eight building blocks, which are as follows:

- CRM vision
- CRM strategy
- Valued customer experience
- Organizational collaboration
- CRM processes
- CRM information
- CRM technology
- CRM metrics

The CRM vision must include guarding of customer privacy and building user trust. CRM strategy starts by defining what the company wants to accomplish with

CRM technology. Relationship intensity ranges from awareness (the lowest intensity) to advocacy (the highest intensity). Three relationship levels mark the bonds that *e*-marketers build with customers. The highest level of CRM involves creating structural bonds that raise switching costs and build loyalty.[20] *E*-marketers need to think about the experience of their valued customers, how customers prefer to interact with companies and how they can forge ties through community building. CRM depends on information and technology using company-side tools (including cookies, website logs, data mining, real-time profiling, collaborative filtering, outgoing *e*-mail, chat and bulletin boards, and iPOS terminals) and client-side tools (including agents, experiential marketing, individuals' Web portals, wireless data services, Web forms, fax on demand, and incoming *e*-mail). Then *e*-marketers use a variety of softwares for implementation and metrics to assess the performance and value of using the Internet for CRM.

E-MARKETING AND ONLINE ADVERTISING

Online advertising,[29] also known as *online advertisement, Internet marketing, online marketing*, or *e*-marketing, is the marketing and promotion of products or services over the Internet. It is a form of promotion that uses the Internet and World Wide Web to deliver marketing messages to a larger audience. Examples of online advertising include contextual ads on search engine result pages, banner ads, blogs, rich media ads, social network advertising, interstitial ads, online classified advertising, advertising networks, dynamic banner ads, cross-platform ads, and *e*-mail marketing, including *e*-mail spam. Online advertising is a form of promotion that uses the Internet and World Wide Web to deliver marketing messages to attract targeted customers and also includes Web 2.0 content, namely blogs, online community building, and online events.

The use of the Internet by marketers can be understood in the context of the awareness, interest, desire, and action (AIDA) model or the 'think-feel-do', hierarchy of effects model. These models suggest that consumers first become aware of and learn about a new product, develop a positive or negative attitude about it and then decide on purchasing it. The Internet represents a flexible medium that can be used as an addressable medium (*e*-mail messages), as a mass medium (banner advertisements), and as an interactive medium (live chat). The growth of online advertising can be attributed to its agility, interactivity, precision, flexibility, measurability, and responsiveness (Fig. 1.13). The concepts are discussed in detail in Chapter 7 on traffic building.

INTEGRATED MARKETING COMMUNICATION AND THE INTERNET

Sales, marketing, and distribution systems account for a substantial portion of the final cost of a product or service. What makes the potential of the Internet enticing is that companies can save 10 to 20 percent of these costs by using the Web instead of

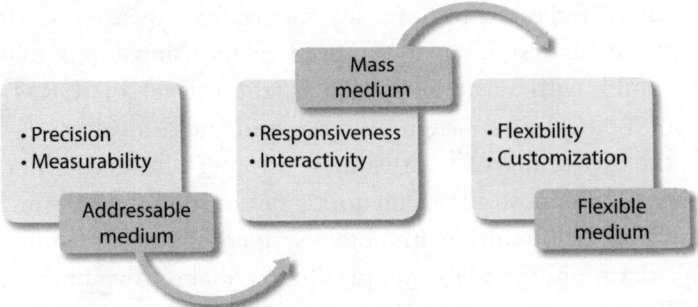

Fig. 1.13 *E*-marketing and online advertising

traditional marketing channels. Marketing should carefully consider the components of advertising, sales support, customer service, public relations, and *e*-commerce when designing and managing an Internet program.[30] A quality integrated marketing communication (IMC) programme can substantially benefit from choosing the functions that the website serves.

In addition to incorporating the Internet into the IMC plan, it is vital for information technology, human resource, production, and shipping departments to be included as the marketing team develops the programme. Placing a significant online promotional campaign on a website and not backing it up with adequate consumer response management strategies can backfire for the organization.

Cyber Branding

Creating an effective website presence is a challenge for IMC. Cyber branding involves integrating online and offline branding tactics that reinforce each other to speak with one voice. The most common method of building an online brand presence is through an offline technique called brand spiralling. These concepts are discussed in detail in Chapter 5.

E-MARKETING AND CONSUMER SEGMENTATION

Time spent by users online can be used as one major variable to segment consumers online along with their online viewing behaviour.

A multiplicity of consumers yields complex segmentation and many opportunities. By applying a cluster analysis, accounting for behaviours and attitudes across the full range of media and technology, McKinsey[31] identified seven distinct consumer segments (Fig. 1.14). McKinsey identified separate groups that vary both in the types of digital experiences they enjoy and the intensity with which they enjoy them.

Two segments showed strong adoption of digital technologies across the media and communication experiences. The *digital media junkies* are extensive users of all digital content (video, music, etc.) available on devices, while the *digital communicators* are more focused on social networking, texting, and *e*-mail. Both have integrated digital media into many areas of their lives.

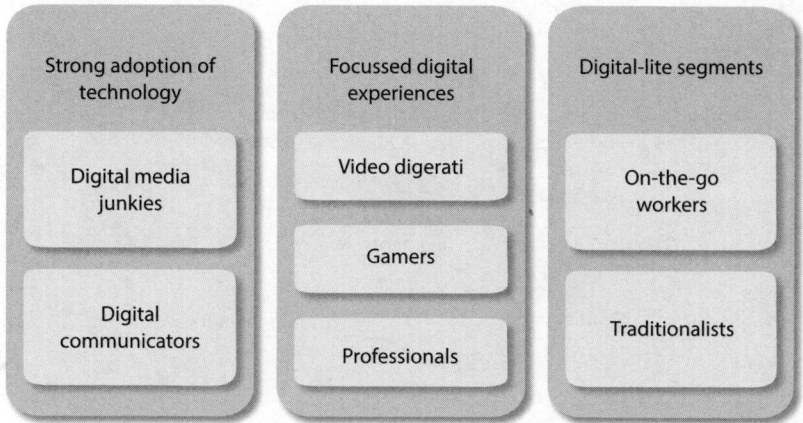

Fig. 1.14 Consumer segments based on digital experiences

Three additional segments have more focused digital experiences. One of the segments is the *video digerati* lead in video usage across all platforms (TV, mobile, PC, and over-the top Web-enabled viewing). *Gamers* focus their digital experiences in single- and multi-player gaming experiences, particularly using gaming console platforms. Finally, *professionals* can buy and avidly use most digital devices but time constraints limit their minutes and type of usage on digital technologies that enhance their ability to communicate and better manage their lives such as *e*-mail or time-shifted videos.

There are also two 'digital-lite' segments. *On-the-go workers* lead the way in use of mobile voice, making them the 'blue-collar' workers of the digital era, but show limited adoption of digital technologies and reflect late-adopter attitudes. Finally, the large but low-digital *traditionalists* have been slow in transitioning to the digital domain and remain focused on traditional modes of behaviour such as reading in print. The average age for *on-the-go workers* and *traditionalists* is 41 and 48, respectively, which is 15–20 years older than the average age of 28 for the social media junkies.

In another such study, McKinsey and Media Matrix identified six user segments based on active user's time spent online, pages/domains accessed, and the amount of time spent per webpage (Fig. 1.15).

Simplifiers want end-to-end convenience. They want to make their lives easier with quick, quality service. These long-time Internet users make half of all online purchases. They spend a total of seven hours online per month.

Surfers want what's new. They view up to four times as many pages as the average user. They move really quickly, always searching for new experiences. Sites capturing surfer loyalty need to be on the cutting edge with design, features, services, continual updates, and assortment of products. Above all, they must have a strong online brand.

Connectors are novelty seekers. They are 'relative novices' who look for reasons to use the Internet. Their main purpose is to build relationships with others through chat rooms and *e*-mail. Sites looking for connector traffic need to have a strong offline presence to attract these beginners.

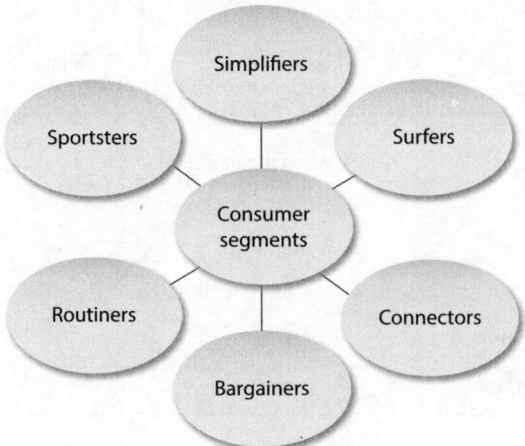

Fig. 1.15 Consumer segments based on active user's time online, pages/domain accessed, and the amount of time spent per webpage

Bargainers look for deals. They spend the least amount of time online. Sites appealing to bargainers satisfy their emotional and rational levels, thus luring them back to search for more deals; for example, eBay.com.

Routiners want something special. They search news and financial sites carefully. They also spend a long time looking at websites, hoping to get something special through superior content.

Sportsters desire highly interactive content. They are a lot like *routiners*, except that they visit colourful, exciting sports and entertainment sites. Sites offering free information will likely lead *sportsters* to eventually pay for information.

Marketers use four coverage strategies to reach consumer segments (Table 1.3),[32] which are as follows:

- Mass marketing
- Multi-segment marketing
- Niche marketing
- Micromarketing

The Internet holds tremendous promise, especially for effective micromarketing.

E-MARKETING AND SALES AND TRADE PROMOTION

The online media can be used by organizations for meeting their trade promotion objectives, namely:

- Increasing distribution using digital channels
- Responding to competitive programmes using social media and organizational websites

Table 1.3 Market coverage strategies

Mass marketing	In addition, known as undifferentiated targeting, occurs when the firm offers one marketing mix for the entire market. For example, A banner ad that appears on portal site home pages (e.g., Yahoo!) tend to appeal to the entire market.
Multi-segment marketing	Occurs when a firm selects two or more segments and designs marketing mix strategies specifically for each. Most of the firms use a multi-segment strategy.
Niche marketing	Occurs when a firm selects one segment and develops one or more marketing mixes to meet the needs of that segment. *Amazon* used this strategy when it targeted Web users exclusively.
Micromarketing	In addition, known as individualized targeting, occurs when a firm tailors all or part of the marketing mix to a small number of people.

- Promotional support to and by channel members including digital networks
- Balancing demand by hosting appropriate online content
- Controlling inventory levels using content marketing
- Promotional support to and by channel members through online partner management

E-marketing can further be used to complement consumer promotions, countering new competitive introductions, and motivating trade support with allowances. By hosting appropriate content relevant to traders, organizations can leverage *e*-marketing for suitable partner relationship management and trade promotion. The digital ecosystem can further be utilized to communicate with consumer's information pertaining to volume discounts, allowances, dealer contests, and point-of-purchase discounts. The virtual medium can also be utilized for conducting online sales training programmes. By showcasing some of their trade promotions online, companies can use their websites for forming strategic B2B alliances as well. While companies can practice B2B *e*-marketing on one side, they can also use dedicated *e*-mail campaigns detailing the latest trade promotions.

Types of Digital Marketing

Digital marketing can be broadly categorized into six types, which are as follows:
- Television advertisements
- Radio advertisements
- *E*-mail marketing (Table 1.4)
- Internet marketing (Table 1.5)
- Mobile marketing (Table 1.6)
- Social media marketing (Table 1.7)

There are several types of television and radio advertising techniques. We shall not delve into them here. We shall, however, briefly discuss the remaining types.

Types of E-mail Marketing

Table 1.4 Types of e-mail marketing

Newsletters and digests	Regularly published monthly or quarterly issues, distributed through e-mail. These can link to content shared through earlier newsletters.
Dedicated e-mails	Specialized e-mails sent to denote only one specific offer.
Lead nurturing e-mails	These are e-mails targeted, with coherent content at those potential consumers who in the past have displayed some specific interest in a product or brand.
Sponsorship e-mails	These are e-mails where one organization pays for the inclusion of its e-mail copy in the content generated by another organization.
Transaction e-mails	Transactional e-mails are the e-mail messages that get triggered by a specific action taken by an e-mail respondent to complete an activity or transaction, such as filling a form or making a purchase.

Types of Internet Marketing

We briefly discuss the different types of Internet marketing in Table 1.5. Most of them have been discussed in detail in subsequent chapters.

Several Indian companies are actively using Internet marketing (Fig. 1.16).

Table 1.5 Types of Internet marketing

Display advertising	The use of Web banners or banner ads placed on a third-party website or *Blog* to drive traffic to a company's own website and increase product awareness.[33]
Search engine marketing	A form of marketing that seeks to promote *websites* by increasing their visibility in *Search Engine Result Pages* (SERPs) through the use of either paid placement, contextual advertising, and paid inclusion, or through the use of free *Search Engine Optimization* techniques also known as organic result.[34]
Search engine optimization	The process of improving the visibility of a website or a Web page in search engines via the 'natural' or un-paid ('organic' or 'algorithmic') search results.
Pay per click	An online advertising model where the advertisers pay the publisher when the advertisement is clicked on, by an Internet visitor.
Social media marketing	The process of gaining traffic or attention through social media websites such as Facebook, Twitter and LinkedIn.[33]
Blog marketing	Refers to using blogs as tools to host content pertaining to a product and brand. Serves like a constantly updated interactive website, where the RSS feed deposits the information into the inbox of users every time new content is posted on a blog.
Viral marketing	A marketing technique where information is passed electronically from one Internet user to the other, through self replicating viral processes.

(Continued)

Referral marketing	A method of promoting products or services to new customers through referrals, usually word of mouth.
Affiliate marketing	A marketing practice in which a business rewards one or more affiliates for each visitor or customer brought about by the affiliate's own marketing efforts.
Content marketing	The process of creating specialized content such as info graphics, blog articles and e-books to attract more customers.
AdSense marketing (Google)	*AdSense* is Google's online advertising platform. Using elements such as the Internet user's geographical location, the current website's content and others, Google is able to deliver ads that target the Web visitor's exact interests.
Inbound marketing	Involves creating and freely sharing informative content as a means of converting prospects into customers and customers into repeat buyers.
Video marketing	This type of marketing specializes in creating videos that engage the viewer into a buying state by presenting information in video form and guiding them to a product or services. Online video is increasingly becoming more popular among Internet users and companies are seeing it as a viable method of attracting customers.[34]
Advergaming	*Advergaming* refers to advertising using games. Advertising can be integrated into online games to promote products and brands online.

Types of Mobile Marketing

Table 1.6 Types of mobile marketing

Mobile Applications	Mobile Apps are computer programs designed to run on smartphones, tablet computers, and other mobile devices. These Apps are profusely used for marketing these days.
Mobile website marketing	Mobile friendly websites are being used for marketing. The content on the website is synchronized for the mobile handset to aid usage for marketing purposes.
SMS marketing	Companies can send text messages using SMS marketing for their mass marketing efforts.
MMS marketing	Companies can send multimedia content regarding their products using the multimedia messaging service on mobile phones.
QR code marketing	QR codes give companies a powerful way to drive traffic to stores and mobile websites. These can be read by any mobile device with a camera and a QR code reader application, allowing organizations to direct customers to relevant online content.
Pay-per-call mobile	The advertiser begins to work with lead generation and affiliate marketing partners that carry the responsibility of creating the campaign and screening the incoming calls for possible customers and the advertiser subsequently pays for valid calls.
Bluetooth wireless proximity based marketing	Proximity marketing is the distribution of promotions or messages to users of devices that have the capability to receive them along with their individual permissions. It can be applied through GPS-enabled devices, cell phones in a particular cell, via a bluetooth or Wi-Fi device.
Mobile banner ads	Banner advertisements are very popular among mobile users.

28 DIGITAL MARKETING

Table 1.7 Types of social media marketing

Social networks	This involves using online social networks like Facebook and twitter for marketing.
Social news	Social news websites feature user-posted stories that are ranked based on popularity. These can be used to share product related information.
Blogs and forums	Corporate as well as individual blogs and online forums are being used for communicating organizational messages and promotional schemes to consumers.
Media sharing	Media sharing allows users to share videos with other publishers in the virtual domain, thereby enabling them to easily manage videos across multiple accounts.
Micro-blogging	Micro-blogs allow users to exchange small elements of content such as short sentences, individual images, or video links. These are more user friendly for usage by marketers.
Bookmarking sites	A social bookmarking service is a centralized online service which enables users to add, annotate, edit, and share bookmarks (*uniform resource identifiers*) of Web documents.

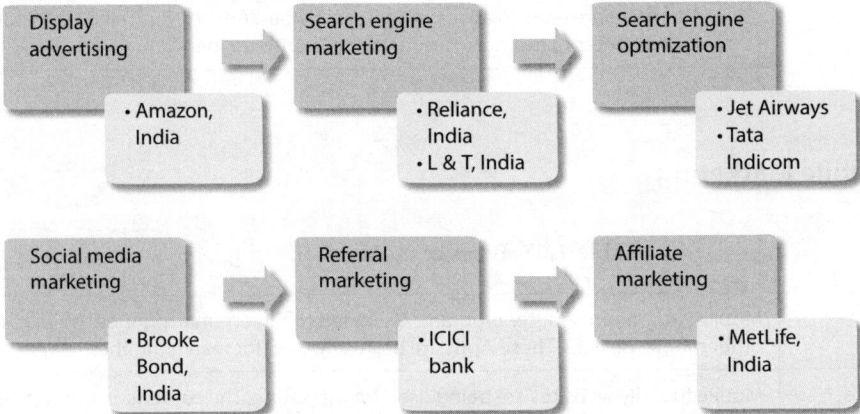

Fig. 1.16 Internet marketing and Indian companies

DIGITAL MARKETING OPTIMIZATION

Digital marketing optimization refers to streamlining of all online marketing activities and analytical techniques, by applying a more focused approach for better marketing resource allocation and achieving higher marketing conversion, for gaining a competitive edge amongst competing organizations.

Why should companies indulge in digital marketing optimization? As the organizational resources are limited, the marketing function needs to plan accordingly to increase the productivity of its actions and an optimal utilization of resources.

An efficient digital marketing programme can be optimized in the following ways (Fig. 1.17):

- Companies need to study how consumers are interacting with the Web.
- Companies can prioritize activities in the context of garnering consumer attention,

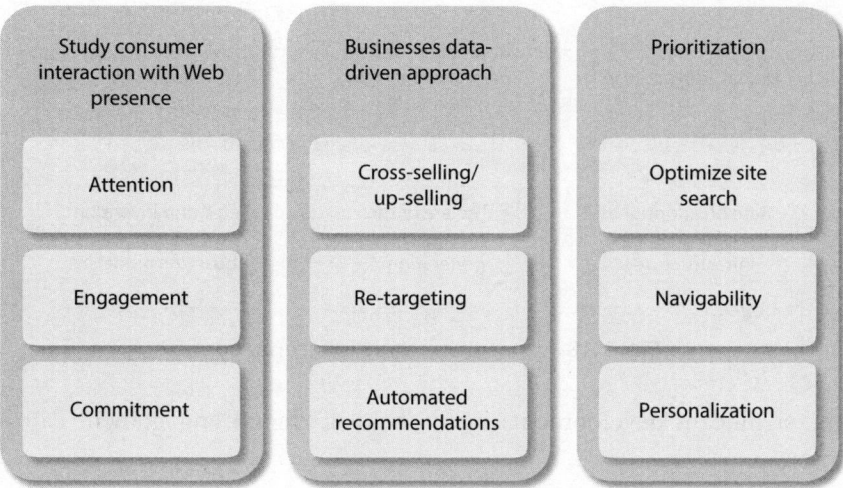

Fig. 1.17 Digital marketing optimization

securing consumer engagement, and finally attaining consumer commitment. A clearer approach can help them to divert resources to the immediate objective at hand—attention, engagement, or commitment.

- A data driven approach to optimization can help companies to maximize customer lifetime value, as they take the necessary steps for cross-selling, up-selling, or re-targeting.
- Companies can optimize site search by pointing visitors in the right direction to the content they are looking for. A better navigability enhances the digital marketing effort.
- Companies can use automated recommendations for consumers as they increase their chances of conversion.
- Companies can indulge in personalization. Personalization enables marketers to enhance the relevance and efficiency of new and repeat visitor experiences, presenting a real opportunity to increase conversion by targeting content based on implicit and explicit data already being collected. The more personalized a consumer experience, the more engaging it becomes.

What do companies gain from digital marketing optimization?

- Greater consumer conversions through digital channels
- Deeper customer loyalties
- Greater competitive advantages
- Higher *customer lifetime value* and long-term customer profitability.

THE NEED FOR DIGITAL ENGAGEMENT

The pace of technology change is increasing exponentially and companies are finding it inevitable to use digital channels to create seamless and consistent engagement (Fig. 1.18).

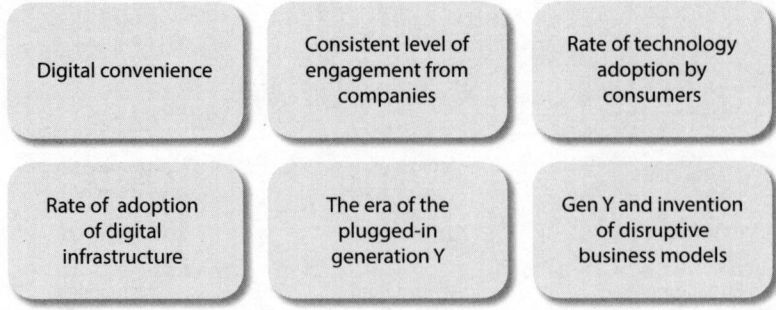

Fig. 1.18 Consumers and digital engagement

Some significant developments in the field of digital engagement can be outlined as follows:

Digital Channels and Convenience

Digital technology has a unique proposition for consumers. The convenience over physical interactions and transactions is quite effective. The convenience of a one-click search and shopping experience saves a lot of time and energy spent on the physical shopping experience. This convenience is allowing companies to gather consumer specific data as the consumer registers himself in the virtual space. This consumer data is subsequently used by companies to garner and harness consumer engagement.

Consumer Engagement

In an era of IMC, companies are sensitive to the need to maintain a substantial degree of uniformity of the marketing message across disparate marketing media vehicles. This consistency of information across the offline and online domains enables companies to develop a relationship with the consumers by moving him up the attention-engagement continuum. Digitally savvy companies have thoroughly integrated their presence across disparate channels to ensure consumer engagement.

Rate of Technology Adoption by Consumers

The rate of technology adoption is very high, specifically for the 'early adopters' and 'early majority' from a marketing perspective. The surprise factor is the acceleration in rate of adoption of this new technology. While it took more than 70 years for telephones to reach 50% household penetration, compared with 28 years for radio and 10 years for Internet access, Google+, the new social media tool from Google, took only 16 days to reach 10 million users, compared with 780 days for Twitter and 852 days for Facebook. It is clear that the acceleration in this rate of technology adoption is huge.

Rate of Adoption of Digital Infrastructure

The pace at which digital infrastructure is growing and being embraced by consumers is equally high. A more technology-enabled governmental development roadmap, backed by a tech-savvy consumer population and with dimensions of technology firmly ingrained in their upbringing, is adopting the new infrastructure at a faster pace.

The Era of the Plugged-in Generation Y

The new generation (Gen Y) seems to be born with a technology background. Youngsters can no longer fathom a world without the Internet, which is so strongly woven into their everyday lives. The 'plugged-in' Gen Y is not intimidated with technology. It regards technology as a friend and a facilitator. With a lifestyle strongly woven around the new digital offerings, this generation has expectations that are different from earlier populations—expectations for good shopping experiences, convenient digital transactions, one-click responses to their search queries, greater and constant connectivity, and faster collaboration. This is a generation that has spawned the dimension of peer-to-peer consumer networking and product advocacy. Online networks of loyal consumers are constantly motivating new consumers to adopt products and services.

Gen Y and Invention of Disruptive Business Models

Gen Y is subsequently responsible for ushering in new business models—models that are innovative, disruptive, and the creation of a population that is not afraid of taking risks. By bringing in new digital products, new communities, new ways of communication, and new Web business models for product proliferation, these youngsters are clearly changing the way business is done today.

GENERATION Y—EXPECTATIONS AND INFLUENCE

This section explores the characteristics and traits of Gen Y, the challenges they pose for organizations, and their evolving expectations.

Organizations[35] that have succeeded in engaging with Gen Y know that, along with accelerating the adoption of new digital technology, this generation also poses additional challenges due to their evolving expectations. This Generation is best perceived not only as a uniform group but also as an evolving mind-set. The demands and expectations of this group are trending upwards to older generations, which makes them all the more important to take note of. Generation Y, today, is the catalyst and the incubators of change, and each day their influence is growing in consumer and corporate environments implying that the organizations must learn to engage effectively now, or risk being eliminated from the game.

To attract this young generation, both as consumers and as employees, a company cannot just *look good*–it has to *be good*. This generation want it all, but above all, it seeks transparency.

It is no longer practical for organizations to state one thing and be another as the digital data trail provides this generation with the methods and tools to spread their opinion about a brand virally and with unimagined consequences. This has significant implications for brand reputation management and customer loyalty. This generation want to ensure that the organizations it engages with are genuine and not a hologram or mirage with a marketing 'front' that belies their reality. Authentic, direct, and personal engagements are

EXHIBIT 1.3 Coca Cola

In March 2013, Coca Cola released a film featuring an experiential campaign which takes forward the brand's 'open happiness' proposition—across borders.

The film, created by Leo Burnett Sydney for Coca Cola, placed two camera-equipped Coke vending machines one each in a mall in Lahore and in Delhi. The film features Indians and Pakistanis interacting with each other via the machine. The machines prompted shoppers in New Delhi to 'make a friend in Pakistan' while mall goers in Lahore were asked to meet someone from India.

Through the simple activities that the participants had to take part in, on both sides of the border, Coca Cola aimed to break down the barriers that have divided both countries with new technology to share common interests in a fun way.

The key to engaging with each other through the machines was simple: people in India and Pakistan could complete a task, such as touching hands, and drawing peace, love, and happiness symbols—together.

The firm used 3D touchscreen technology to project a streaming video feed onto the vending machine screen while simultaneously filming through the unit to capture a live emotional exchange.

Coke successfully managed to build engagement between the two communities, which share a lot of common passions and interests—from food and Bollywood movies, to Coke Studio music, to cricket. This campaign connected the common man in India and Pakistan, giving them hope and building positive consumer sentiment in the process.

Select Success Metrics. The numbers speak for themselves:

- The highest-shared story in the history of Coca Cola.com.
- 10,000 attendees to the live event created 700 connections across the border.
- The effort reached more than 18 million Facebook and Twitter users.
- The video garnered 2 million YouTube views and counting.
- More than 58 million earned media impressions were gained.
- 55% of total reach came from India and Pakistan.

---

even more important than advertising to reach this generation. Above all, Generation Y is no longer content with the old corporate and political model. It demands transformational change, and where they cannot find it, they look to invent it themselves.

According to research conducted by Ernst and Young, other Gen Y expectations include the following:

- *Collaborative, networked learning* The average user spends 55 minutes a day on Facebook
- *Fast, easy, and fun communication* Gen Y adults spend 15+ hours a week on the Internet
- *Visible peer recommendations in decision making* 80% of the consumers believe peer recommendations, but only 14% trust advertisements
- *Immediate feedback* 34% of bloggers post opinions about products and brands

- *Environmentally aware*   96% of Gen Y want an environmentally aware workplace
- *Flexibility*   A total of 56% of Gen Y prefers to work flexibly and chooses when to work, and 79% prefers to be mobile rather than static workers. Gen Y already represents over a quarter of the world's population and the proportion is growing.

Not only will the members of Gen Y be among the most powerful consumers in history; as they enter the workforce, their impact there will be equally impossible to ignore. They display the same lack of patience as employees as they show as consumers, and companies must address their evolving expectations to avoid high recruitment and churn costs. What is more, this generation has significant ideas and is willing to share them company-wide; They represent a useful resource every company should listen to.

THE IMPLICATIONS OF DIGITAL CHANGE

The digital world is changing and smart organizations have realized that. To look at this from an Indian context, India is the third largest country in terms of Internet users in the world, with a highly social and mobile audience. It is estimated that as many as 121 million Indians are logged onto the Internet. The following sections address how the changes in digital scenario are posing challenges for companies and the need for companies to evolve. Subsequently, the chapter quotes a study conducted by Ernst and Young to see how companies can gear up and respond to the changing times.

The Consumer has Changed

The consumer has more choices in terms of making product comparisons at the click of a mouse, can make price comparisons, can discuss product attributes in the virtual world with peers in online communities and can finally take an informed decision after carefully evaluating all alternatives.

The Consumer has a Voice

If a consumer suffers from post purchase cognitive dissonance, as in being doubtful about having made a correct purchase or not, he can openly discuss his feelings across social networks and communities in the virtual spaces. Further, if he is dissatisfied with a company or its product, he can voice his opinions in the online world, for everyone to see. Reputation conscious companies have to keep track of the virtual conversations happening about them, to steer clear of upcoming controversies.

The Consumer Influencer has a Significant Role

The virtual world has given opinion leaders a platform to voice their opinions in front of their audiences (online followers). These opinion leaders if tapped appropriately can serve as consumer advocates for companies, as they can instigate or influence significant volumes of consumers to adopt a company/brand's products.

Consumers Trust other Consumers more than Company Advertising

Research has revealed that consumers trust their peers more than the organizational branding and advertising efforts while making purchase decisions. Hence, companies can benefit by having satisfied consumers on their side, who serve as consumer evangelists in company hosted/independent virtual environments.

Companies are Interacting Digitally with their Suppliers and Marketing Intermediaries

In a fast changing environment, companies can benefit if they engage with their suppliers and other marketing intermediaries in the virtual world, by using these spaces for collaboration and information sharing. A new era of *e*-procurement and *e*-commerce has brought in new tools for supply chain management, which are being increasingly used by progressive companies.

Companies are also using the Web to Interact with their Employees

By using intranets, and other social networks, companies are also interacting with their employees. By giving their employees a platform to voice their thoughts, companies are emerging as futuristic and forward thinking, having dropped their conservative stance and are also using digital platforms like Linkedin for *e*-recruitment.

The Marketplace is Becoming more Competitive

Digital channels are lowering the barriers to entry, for new players, making the marketplace more competitive. Differentiation, personalization, and innovation are the key drivers to organizational success now.

IMPLICATIONS FOR ORGANIZATIONS

The revolutionary changes ushered in by the advent of virtualization have made it mandatory for companies to evolve and re-shape their processes to remain ahead of the game. The following section draws from research conducted by Ernst and Young, to understand how companies can manage and handle change with the arrival of new ways of doing business.

Use Digital Technology to Enhance Traditional Business Models

The following are the ways in which digital technology can be made use of to enhance traditional business models:

- *Using automated digital services to compete with the existing manual services* This will involve making better use of self-service channels including customer service through social media, resulting in reduced cost to serve and reduced time to earn revenue.

- *Shifting the core business model from selling products towards offering services* This brings in a 'pay as you go' model resulting in increased share of value chain and share of wallet.
- *Transforming hardware offerings into service offerings* While integrating products with service engenders combined loyalty, resulting in long-term customer relationships, this also results in increased annuity revenue streams from services and increases customer lifetime value.

Companies can transform Existing Business Models Digitally

They can do this by applying the following drills (Fig. 1.19):

- Offering entirely new services that cannot be provided manually.

This results in adoption of the free service by a larger consumer population, resulting in increased shareholder and reputational value.

- Offering existing services through new digital channels.

The implications are increased customer convenience, which engenders loyalty, increased revenue streams, and reduced cost to serve.

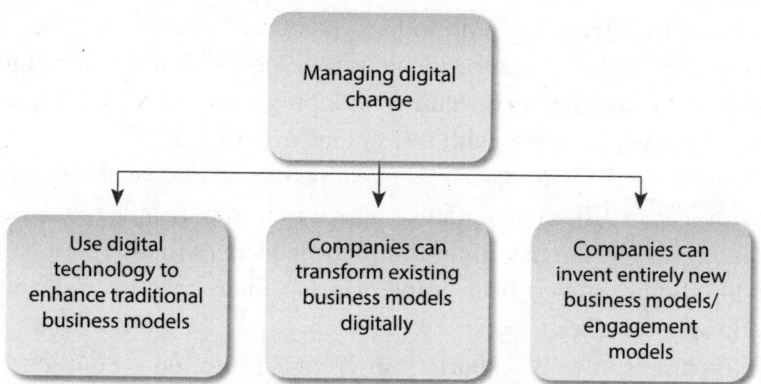

Fig. 1.19 Managing digital change

Companies can Invent Entirely New Business Models or Different Engagement Models

This implies offering entirely new revenue-generating products/services or different engagement models. Examples include virtual currency used in online games and social networks and Google//Yahoo advertising revenue linked to search. Organizations can have the first mover advantage by marketing the products before competition arrives on the scene and can benefit from new revenue streams.

The final verdict is clear—the external marketing environment in which companies are operating has changed, the consumers have evolved into technology-conscious users, and now it is time that companies change the way they function to remain more competitive in a new, globally connected world.

CASE STUDY: Blackberry and the Behavioural Internet Theory

Research In Motion (RIM), a global leader in wireless innovation, revolutionized the mobile industry with the introduction of the BlackBerry® solution in 1999. After several years of staying in business, Blackberry, armed with the tagline *keep moving*, has mounted a make or break campaign to last all through 2013. BlackBerry products and services are used by millions of customers around the world to stay connected to the people and content that matter most throughout their day. The BlackBerry product line includes the BlackBerry® PlayBook™ tablet, the award-winning BlackBerry smartphone, software for businesses, and accessories.

As technology emerges as an enabler for a new generation of strivers, Blackberry has launched an aggressive marketing campaign, to fight competition and to resonate with its consumers. Blackberry continuously launches mammoth campaigns to achieve market transformation and to support and popularize devices based on the BB10 OS. To tap markets with significant potential, markets like India, with a large population and relatively technologically savvy set of youngsters comprising the right target market for its product, Blackberry has added motley of tools to its integrated marketing communication programme, a very interesting one of them being the official Blackberry blog: *Inside Blackberry*.

Indian consumers are characterized by some specific personality traits, which further made this study interesting. The Indian consumer belongs to a close-knit society, which is emotional and takes a lot of pride in its social and cultural fabric. The erstwhile Indian consumer is looking for a convenient shopping experience, loves quality products, and feels very happy if his trysts with technology are friendly.

Blackberry used *Inside Blackberry* to launch an initiative for the Indian population, called *Action Starts Here*. The initiative hoped to inspire people to take action to get things done. Interestingly, the maximum number of pledges made by Indian users centred on friendship. Some ranged from implementing their hobbies and dreams to setting up philanthropic ventures.

In this case study, Blackberry's attempt to use *Inside Blackberry* to leverage the Behavioural Internet across the *e*-marketing dimensions of the Media Equation, Flow, Content accessibility, Social and Quality Cues, and Friendly Technology[27] has been analyzed (Fig. 1.20).

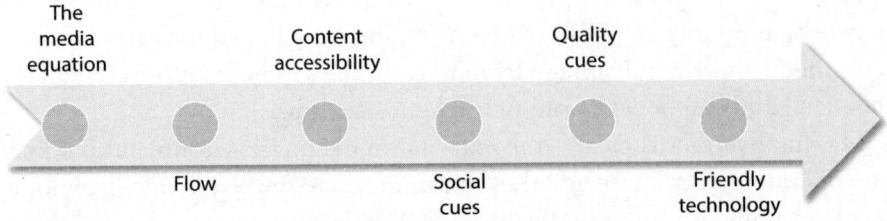

Fig. 1.20 The behavioural Internet

The media equation

The media equation implies that individual behaviour of a consumer in the virtual world is a duplication of their behaviour in their real lives. So, how does *Inside Blackberry* leverage this? The blog attempts to control the media equation by motivating consumers to share their personal experiences with Blackberry products, thereby creating a repository of individual real-life occurrences, soliciting feedback on consumer product and service expectations and reacting to the sophistication and knowledge levels of the users. This way the blog has been able to tap into the sensitivity of the Indian consumer population by giving them a platform to voice their thoughts.

Hoffman and Novak define *Flow* as a state characterized by a seamless sequence of responses, intrinsically enjoyable, accompanied by a loss of self-consciousness and self-reinforcing. Organizations can attempt to achieve *flow* by hosting appealing content, thereby stimulating consumer interest and subsequently involvement. *Inside Blackberry* attempts to achieve flow for its consumers by hosting inspiring user accounts, interesting articles and conversations, supporting videos, and linking with popular social networking sites such as Twitter and Facebook to increase user participation.

Content accessibility

The content on the blog is easily perceivable. It is written in simple language and is highly understandable. The articles have relevant data according to the topics as well as the blog. In addition, navigation through the blog is easy. The content can also be accessed month and category wise.

Social cues

Although the media equation is valid for this blog but in a discussion, group dynamics and personal communication systematically differ online as the tools of communication lack the richness and subtlety of face-to-face messages.

Quality cues

On the blog, the blog manager consistently keeps the members in a loop for feedback and suggestions. He asks for feedback on products, new ideas and modifications, and their expectations. Articles are being posted for complaints and problems and how they are being solved. So, with the help of this blog, the company is able to segment its customers and build quality for them.

Friendly technology

User friendliness of technology acts as a precursor for building social and emotional bonds with the consumers. Needless to say, the Indian consumer can be classified as a sensitive individual, who feels a sense of belongingness to his society. Ventures like these can be excellent endeavours for engaging such consumers by hosting product-specific content, which is a good Internet marketing exercise. Simultaneously, the company can also benefit by moving these consumers up from the state of 'engagement' to the state of 'involvement' with the organization by showcasing the altruistic side of the consumers. The consumers and the brand end up in a simple, friendly relationship with each other—a friendship based on trust, human values, and respect for each other's beliefs and ideologies.

Questions:

1. Blackberry usually launches significant campaigns for the promotion of its product ranges. Perform a Google search and list all recent campaigns where Blackberry has attempted to use the behavioural Internet theory for marketing.
2. Create a brief chart to analyse success–failure points of the campaigns.

PRACTITIONER PERSPECTIVE

Digital media is going to transform the way businesses engage with customers across three key dimensions—customer acquisition, experience management, and insights generation.

Vikas Bali, MD, Accenture

In this age of the empowered and connected consumer, it is essential for brands and marketers to leverage big data analytics for better understanding the consumers, adding context to the content, and creating an integrated and delightful experience throughout the customer lifecycle.

Ashit Panjwani, Executive Director, Sales, Marketing and alliances, SAS India

Twitter is being integrated by brands into their CRM systems, in their marketing campaigns, by HR for prospecting for new talent, and by management to have their voice out and to listen to what their customers are telling them.

Arvinder Gujral, Head, Mobile Business Development, India and South East Asia, Twitter

Relevant and refined content on the Web proves to be of great significance for students and teachers. This can prove to be the next turning point for education.

Benjamin Grubbs, Head of Content and Partnerships, YouTube and Google

SUMMARY

E-marketing is the use of information technology in the processes of creating, communicating, and delivering value to the customers, and for managing customer relationships in ways that benefit the organization and its stakeholders. The changing marketing landscape will benefit with the advent of evolution of the Internet, influencer marketing, *e*-commerce, Web 2.0, individual Internet worth, wireless networking, big data, Internet marketing metrics, and Internet strategy integration. The three general purpose technologies (GPTs) of the Internet are—the digital revolution, networking, and individualization. The behavioural Internet theory addresses the five concepts of the media equation, flow, content accessibility, social cues, quality cues, and friendly technology.

Behavioural targeting refers to a range of technologies and techniques used by online website publishers and advertisers that allows them to increase the effectiveness of their campaigns by capturing data generated by website and landing page visitors. The domains of *e*-marketing, CRM, IMC, advertising, consumer segmentation, sales, and trade promotion significantly tap the domain of the Internet for resource mobilization. Key focus areas can help organizations to embrace digital marketing optimization: content findability, automated recommendations and cross-sells, testing, and personalization. Digital convenience, consistent level of engagement from companies, rate of technology adoption by consumers, rate of adoption of digital infrastructure, the era of the plugged-in generation Y and Gen Y, and invention of disruptive business models are significant dimensions of the need for companies to focus on consumers and digital engagement.

Concept Review Questions

1. What is *e*-marketing? Discuss the salient features of the changing marketing landscape.
2. How has technology catalysis changed the consumer? What are the new ways by which consumers are accessing the Internet? What are the three GPTs of the Internet?
3. Discuss critical strengths and applications of Internet marketing.
4. Discuss the four different online marketing domains. Cite examples other than those given in the text.
5. Discuss the concepts of the behavioural Internet.
6. How can *e*-marketing aid the processes of CRM and consumer segmentation? Demonstrate with examples.
7. Discuss consumer segmentation based on the following:
   (a) Digital experiences
   (b) Active user's time online, pages, domains accessed, and the amount of time spent per Web page
8. Write short notes on the following:
   (a) Digital marketing optimization
   (b) Types of Internet marketing
   (c) Cyber branding

Critical Thinking Questions

1. The behavioural Internet theory allows *e*-marketers to leverage the Internet by understanding various dimensions of consumer behaviour. Examine the following in the context of the theory. Are these online tools structurally sound in the context of behavioural Internet?

(a) Corporate blog of Dell
(b) Corporate blog of General Motors
(c) Corporate blog of Dominos, India
(d) Online communities of Apple
(e) Online Communities of Nestle

Make relevant suggestions on how improvements can be made enabling these online tools to perform better.

2. Make a list of 20 Indian companies using the Internet for marketing and consumer engagement. List the different Internet tools they use. Make a note on how have the companies benefitted from the usage of the Internet. Identify how the online tools are being used for CRM, online advertising, IMC, consumer segmentation, sales, and trade promotion. Does tool popularity vary among specific industry sectors?

Practising Digital Marketing

Assume that you are starting a new fashion portal and intend to promote online sales of garments. The following is what you can start off with:

- Give a name to the portal. Design an Internet marketing strategy for the venture.
- Discuss how you will create the following *e*-marketing tools:
  - Blog
  - Online community
  - Facebook page
- Design a content strategy to facilitate the following marketing activities:
  - Online advertising
  - IMC
  - CRM
- Create a digital marketing optimization strategy for the portal.

References

1. Strauss, J., El-Ansary, A., and Frost, R., *International Business Research*, 2006.
2. Kotler, P., et al., *Direct and Online Marketing—Building Direct Customer Relationships*, Prentice Hall, 2012, p. 426.
3. Hong, P., Tran, O., and Park, K., (2010). 'Electronic commerce applications for supply chain integration and competitive capabilities: An empirical study'. *Benchmarking: An International Journal*, Vol. 17(4), pp. 539–560.
4. Baker, M. and Hart, S., *The Marketing Book*, Routledge, 2008.
5. Manyika, J., et al., '*Big Data: The Next Frontier for Innovation, Competition, and Productivity*', McKinsey Global Institute, 2011, pp. 1–137.
6. Jeffrey, A., Ghosh, A., and Muhamed, R., *Fundamentals of WiMAX: Understanding Broadband Wireless Networking*, Prentice Hall PTR, 2007.
7. Ahuja, V., (2012). 'Market Influence Analytics in a Digital Ecosystem', *International Journal of Online Marketing*, IGI Global Publications, Vol. 2(4), pp. 42–53, ISSN-2156-1753.
8. Kamel Boulos, M.N. and Wheeler, S., (2007). The emerging Web 2.0 social software: An enabling suite of sociable technologies in health and health care education, *Health Information and Libraries Journal*, Vol. 24(1), pp. 2–23.
9. Turban, E., Lee, J.K., King, D., Liang, T.P., and Turban, D., *Electronic Commerce 2010*, Prentice Hall Press, 2009.
10. Hanson, W.A. and Kalyanam, K., *Introduction, Internet Marketing and E-commerce*, First Edition, Thomson South-Western, 2007.
11. Constantinides, E. and Fountain, S.J., (2008). 'Web 2.0: Conceptual foundations and marketing issues', *Journal of Direct, Data and Digital Marketing Practice*, pp. 231–244, 2008, Retrieved January 23, 2009 from

www.palgrave-journals.com/dddmp/journal/v9/n3/.../4350098a.html.
12. Platt, M., (2007). Web 2.0 in the Enterprise, *The Architecture Journal*, Microsoft Developer Network, MSDN Architecture Centre.
13. O'Reilly, T., *Web 2.0 Compact Definition: Trying Again*, O'Reilly.com: The O'Reilly Radar, <http://radar.oreilly.com/archives/2006/12/Web_20_compact.html>, last accessed on 20 January, 2007.
14. Bughin, Chui and Miller, McKinsey, *How Businesses are using Web 2.0: A McKinsey Global Survey*, The McKinsey Quarterly, 2007, Retrieved from <http://www.mckinseyquarterly.com/Marketing/How_businesses_are_using_Web_20_A_McKinsey_Global_Survey_1913_abstract>, last accessed on 5 January, 2008.
15. Gillin, P., *The New Influencers, A Marketer's Guide to the New Social Media*, Quill Driver Books\Word Dancer Press, Inc., CA, USA, 2007.
16. Surowiecki, J., *The Wisdom of Crowds*, Anchor Books, New York, 2005.
17. Kolbitsch, J. and Maurer, H., (2006). 'The Transformation of the Web: How Emerging Communities Shape the Information We Consume', *Journal of Universal Computer Science*, Vol. 12(2), pp. 187–213.
18. Hoegg, R., Martignoni, R., Meckel, M., and Stanoevska-Slabeva, K., *Overview of Business Models for Web 2.0 Communities*, Institute of Media and Communication Management, 2006.
19. Strauss, J., El-Ansary, A., and Frost, R., Convergence, *E-marketing*, Fourth Edition, Pearson Prentice Hall, 2008, p. 28.
20. Kotler, P., et al., *Direct and Online Marketing—Building Direct Customer Relationships*, Prentice Hall, 2012, p. 427.
21. Knight, S., Kobrak, H., and Lewis, P., *Amazon.com*, Case Study Published in Czinkota, Kotabe, Marketing Management, Thomson South-Western, 2007, p. 485.
22. Information for this example accessed at <www.dell.com.html/us/segments/pub/premier/tutorial/users_guide.html/us/segments/pub/premier/tutorial/users_guide.html>; August, 2008.
23. Kotler, P., Keller, L.K., and Jha, K., Identifying market segments and targets, *Marketing Management—A South Asian Perspective*, Thirteenth Edition, Pearson Education, 2009, p. 203.
24. Hanson, W. and Kalyanam, K., Individuals online, *Internet Marketing and E-commerce*, Thomson South-Western, 2007, p. 120.
25. Emily, R., with Rebecca, J., Michael, G., and Emily, B., *Five Ways to Improve the ROI of Your Behavioral Targeting Campaigns*, Forrester Research, 2009.
26. Strauss, J., El-Ansary, A., and Frost, R., Customer relationship management, *E-marketing*, Fourth Edition, Pearson Publications, 2008.
27. Clow, K. and Baack, D., Internet Marketing, *Integrated Advertising, Promotion and Marketing Communications*, Third Edition, Pearson Prentice Hall, 2007.
28. Mohammad, M., Nazerzadeh, H., and Saberi, A., Allocating online advertisement space with unreliable estimates, *Proceedings of the 8th ACM Conference on Electronic Commerce*, ACM, 2007.
29. Bertil, C., Brendan, G., and Parvizi, P., *The World Gone Digital*, Insights from McKinsey's Global iConsumer Research, p. 2, 2011.
30. Strauss, J., El-Ansary, A., and Frost, R., Segmentation and targeting techniques, *E-marketing*, Fourth Edition, Pearson Publications, 2008, p. 236.
31. *Define Online Marketing*. Yourdictionary.com. <http://reference.yourdictionary.com/word-definitions/define-online-marketing.html>, last accessed on 9 January, 2012.
32. *What Is SEM/Search Engine Marketing?*, Search Engine Land, <http://searchengineland.com/guide/what-is-sem>, last accessed on February 1, 2012.
33. *What Is Social Media Marketing, Search Engine Land*, <http://searchengineland.com/guide/what-is-social-media-marketing>, last accessed on 9 January, 2012.
34. Joseph, F., Scam World: 'Get Rich Quick' Schemes Mutate into an Online Monster, The Verge, <http://www.theverge.com/2012/5/10/2984893/scamworld-get-rich-quick-schemes-mutate-into-an-online-monster>, last accessed on May 10, 2012.
35. Ernst & Young, *The Digitization of Everything*, LLP, London, UK, 2011.

The Online Marketing Mix

> **LEARNING OBJECTIVES**
> *After reading this chapter, you will be able to*:
> - Understand the online marketing mix and online promotion techniques
> - Infer the characteristics of the online offer
> - Determine the distribution, segmentation, and targeting in an online world
> - Figure out the pricing strategies for the virtual domain
> - Understand the implication of digitization on online marketing mix decisions

Organizations now need to leverage applications and data to better understand the consumer in order to develop targeted solutions. In the current era, the most important aspect that will help the consumers to choose from the wide array of products available shall be speed and accuracy with which information can be accessed and obtained. In order to reach out to the new customer, organizations need to reinvent the already existing product in the market rather than bring out a new product. As the Internet has pervaded widely into the lives of the new generation, it is vital for organizations to look at the traditional marketing mix in the context of the digital era with greater care. This chapter initially explains the changes in the environment and then proceeds to define the online marketing mix.

Let us now consider the following data gathered from a variety of sources:

- The figures from the Internet and Mobile Association of India (IAMAI) show that the Internet users in India have grown beyond 200 million. Around 25% of the regular shoppers in India fall in the age group of 18–25 years and 46% fall in the 26–35 year range. This has widespread implications for marketing, as it demonstrates a change in the consumer profile that will subsequently result in a change in the way they are addressed by the marketers. The demographics clearly show the growth of a younger, Internet-savvy audience who will be of great interest to online product marketers.
- Presently, the Indian online matrimonial sector is worth $230 million. Previously, the Indian society greatly believed in arranged marriages, and there was a widespread

market for the 'matrimonial' section in the newspapers. This was a service that was being provided by the newspapers wherein the information present helped two interested individuals or families to contact each other and take things further. The online matrimonial sites are not only serving as an excellent source of information for the concerned parties but also providing a great networking environment for them to meet online, interact, and share their concerns. The marketers are particularly interested in the consumer profile, the characteristics of the online environment, and the advantages provided by the Internet in order to provide service to the consumers.

- Worldwide, *e*-commerce is growing at the rate of 28%, and India being a younger market, the growth of *e*-commerce is expected to be 51% in the coming years. India's large population base and the penetration of the Internet in every home has made it imperative for marketers to keep tab on what is happening in the online world. Their desire for convenience, their lack of brand loyalty, willingness to switch, explore other products, and take risks, has given rise to an era of *e*-commerce. This is perceived to be a large and significant terrain that marketers need to explore. Organizations are subsequently advertising their *e*-commerce portals hugely in the traditional media.
- Going with the global trend, India has also started shopping online these days. As per the study by IAMAI, online shopping in India has risen from $11 million between 1999 and 2000 to $522 million in 2007. By the end of March 2010, the rise recorded was above $700 million. All marketers who do not have an online presence are likely to lose the competition. In addition to the online presence, the nature of the products available, the consumer characteristics, as well as the online shopping experience are primary concerns to marketers.
- *Online Shopping: Review and Outlook* in 2013, released by the ASSOCHAM, showed that India's *e*-commerce market (6.5% of the total retail market) rose from about $2.5 billion in 2009, to $6.3 billion in 2011, to $8.5 billion in 2012, and is expected to touch $56 billion by 2013. The upcoming era may see online retail growing immensely. This implies a greater need for product variety and better distribution networks.

The earlier-given statistics point to the need for the evolution of marketing to understand what this spells for the traditional marketer. Double income in families, the era of the busy consumer, willingness to pay a little extra for convenience, and doorstep deliveries are giving consumers greater choice and freedom, and redefining the traditional marketing mix of product, place, price, and promotion.

The various challenges that organizations face include the following:

- Understanding the optimal utilization of the Internet for enhanced marketing efficiency
- Designing the best possible way to position products and services in the online domain for greater marketing productivity
- Creating a value proposition in which the product and the price meet the consumers' expectations

This clearly points to the need for redefining the way marketing is done in the online domain, thereby pointing to the requirement for defining a marketing mix for the virtual world.

The *online marketing mix* can therefore be defined as the set of all those elements that an organization needs to promote its products online. The traditional marketing mix elements comprising *product, place, price,* and *promotion* have to be redefined in the light of the characteristics of the Internet and the opportunities it provides for both marketers and consumers (Fig. 2.1).

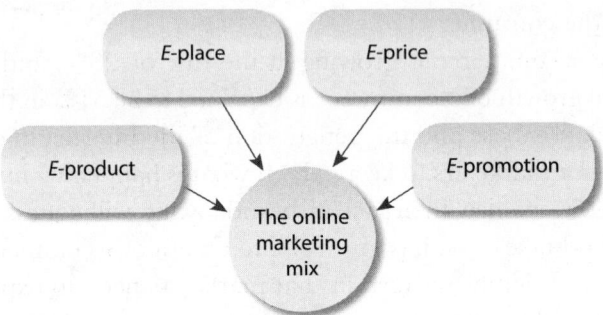

Fig. 2.1 The online marketing mix

The online marketing mix comprises of the following features:

E-products

The *product* element of the marketing mix defines the value proposition offered to the consumer. It is this proposal that signifies a value to the consumer. A consumer feels satisfied when the benefits of the item procured exceed the cost of procuring the item. Value is measured in terms of value creation, value communication, and value delivery. Hence, when defining the product dimension of the marketing mix, a company should be clear about the above-mentioned factors.

The online domain poses some challenges for organizations.

Some products are unique to the Internet (e.g., online Apps—Storiesville, Fundsindia.com, Aapwatch.com, Facetune, Waterlogue, etc.), some use the Internet as a distribution channel (P&G, HUL, etc.), and some others use the Internet as an electronic storefront (Amazon, eBay, Myntra, Flipkart, etc.). The first category of products is sold and can be used only in the virtual world as they are Internet based. The second category of products is those primarily marketed through the traditional means and now the firms have recognized the need to promote them online as well. The third category of products is the *e*-commerce sites that promote all varieties of products online, and these products reach the consumers through an offline distribution channel.

The product dimension of the online marketing mix is subsequently characterized by creating a customer value in the online world by using a set of well-defined strategies for the propagation of products in the online sphere and capitalizing on the benefits offered by the Internet to provide a congenial environment for the consumer.

E-place

The *place* element of the marketing mix refers to the 'where' dimension of marketing. It refers to target markets, places where the product is to be launched or promoted, consumer segmentation, and positioning strategies.

Organizations associated with digital marketing face two major challenges: the first challenge is greater Internet penetration to enhance Internet usage and subsequent benefits from consumers venturing online; the second challenge is greater reach for the products being sold online, in terms of more consumers and visibility, which will come through greater volume of consumer time spent online.

This creates the need for companies to focus on their online distribution strategies and consumer segmentation methodologies. These concepts will be addressed in greater detail in the subsequent chapters.

E-price

The *price* is the amount of money charged for a product or service. It is the sum of all values—money, time, energy, and psychic cost, that buyers exchange for benefits of having or using a good or service. Information technology has changed pricing strategies and transformed the way marketers use this tool, especially in online markets. The online domain provides buyers with many cost savings by virtue of convenience, the fast nature of the Internet, self-service, one-stop shopping, integration, and automation. Convenience allows the shopper to save on costs for travelling to the location of procurement of articles. The fast nature of the Internet and ease of accessibility across various devices allow self-service for consumers and a one-stop shopping location where all comparisons can be made strategically by consumers at a very fast pace. Information from various locations and touch points and across various access devices can be integrated in the virtual domain which fosters cost savings facilitated by automation.

E-promotion

Marketers use the marketing communication tools for advertising, sales promotion, marketing, public relations, direct marketing, and personal selling to achieve their communication objectives. After implementation, they measure the effectiveness, make any adjustments required, and evaluate results. Marketers' use of the Internet can be understood in the light of the Awareness-Internet-Desire-Action (AIDA) model or the 'think-feel-do hierarchy of effects' model. These models suggest that consumers first become aware of and learn about a new product, develop a positive or negative attitude about it, and then move to purchasing it. Each online tool is more or less effective at particular levels of these models.

The four components of the online marketing mix are now addressed in greater detail in this section. The traditional marketing mix has been used as a base and aspects have been incorporated in the same to strengthen marketing by including the needs of the online domain.

E-PRODUCTS—CREATING CUSTOMER VALUE IN AN ONLINE WORLD

A great deal of academic research has gone into identifying the meaning of value of the marketing proposition. To summarize the perspectives, it is clear that value is a sum total of:

- the product experience
- the individual beliefs of the customer
- customer expectations

To define the term *product* in the online marketing mix, we need to look at two types of organizations. First, the virtual organizations that operate only in the online domain; these organizations sell products only through the online media. Second, the other brick-and-mortar companies, which exist in the physical domain and also use the Internet as an additional medium to promote their products.

The online product can encompass an online service or an online offer. In the first case, organizations provide an online service; for example, Amazon, eBay. Here, the online organization is providing the service allowing a consumer to buy a product from the virtual medium. These organizations are *e*-commerce companies allowing consumers to buy and sell online and provide them a virtual marketplace where transactions can take place.

The second case is of companies such as Procter & Gamble, LG, and HUL as examples, which sell their products online through their websites. The online offer provides a consumer the convenience of making a purchase. An online offer is typically characterized by the following features:

- Renders high levels of convenience for the consumer
- Offers good customer service
- Saves consumer time and money
- Provides an enjoyable shopping experience
- Merchandises in the context of product offerings and product information
- Provides site design and transaction security

Consumers are more likely to purchase, via the Internet, products and services that have a low outlay, are frequently purchased, have intangible value propositions, and are relatively high on differentiation.[1] This means that consumers buy products that are popular, are liked by other consumers in the peer group, make consumers happy about the purchase, give them some kind of satisfaction, and appear to be better than those offered by the competitors.

Web users also want effective Web navigation, quick download speed, clear site organization, attractive and useful site design, secure transactions, privacy, free information or services, and user-friendly browsing and *e*-mail viewing. Companies are increasingly promoting and selling their products through social networks.

Three significant product dimensions (Fig. 2.2) where companies can benefit from the use of the Internet are attributes, branding, and co-creation.

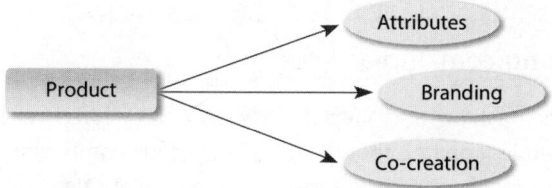

Fig. 2.2 Significant product dimensions

EXHIBIT 2.1   State Bank of India

State Bank of India (SBI) is providing disparate channels and platforms to aid its consumers in using the Internet for greater procurement of SBI products, as also facilitate online trading. Listed below are details on the business vertical SBI Life and online platform SBI FX Trade, which symbolize SBI's efficiency in its tryst with the online world.

- SBI Life has developed a business vertical to tap the potential of online sales of life insurance policies. Through the channel, it distributes products developed exclusively for online business and has gained leadership position in consumer sales.
- SBI provides an online platform called SBI FX Trade to its customers to trade in the exchange traded currency futures. SBI offers its clients the opportunity to trade in four currency pairs, namely, USD/INR, EURO/INR, GBP/INR, and JPY/INR as permitted by regulatory authorities SEBI and RBI. SBI FX Trade is a secure, robust online platform linked to the customer's bank account. The customer can take positions in these currencies from anywhere across the country, after transferring the required margins, through his online trading account. The competitive brokerage rates, the integrated platform of bank account and online trading account, and the provision for lien marking, make this an interesting portal for the consumers. The money continues to remain in the customer's account until the deal is done, thus earning him interest, making it a secure and robust online platform and subsequently allowing SBI to offer this as a product from India's most trusted and transparent bank.

Attributes

The physical components of the product—its shape, size, colour, features, and quality are enhanced by the two most significant benefits offered by the Internet: mass customization and personalization. Companies can reach a wide range of consumers by offering a variety of combinations and tangible and intangible benefits. The ability of the Web to provide the benefit of personalization further allows organizations to engage consumers in a one-to-one dialogue for product proliferation and sale volume. Companies can show-off their product attributes through generating content on a host of online websites, blogs, online communities, and social networks.

> **EXHIBIT 2.2   Jabong.com, India**
>
> Jabong.com is an Indian fashion and lifestyle *e*-commerce portal. It retails apparel, footwear, accessories, beauty products, fragrances, home accessories, furniture, and other fashion and lifestyle products. It sells through its website. The *e*-store at present carries over 1000 brands and over 90,000 products.
>
> Jabong is facing stiff competition from Myntra and Flipkart in India. In a bid to expand its operations and popularity, Jabong employed the following strategies:
>
> - In a bid to position itself as an online fashion destination, the lifestyle portal launched an ethnic women's wear collection designed exclusively for it by well-known designer Rohit Bal.
> - It has launched in-house brands covering apparel, shoes, and accessories to provide a one-stop shopping solution to customers.
> - It has launched an aggressive marketing strategy on Facebook, through a well-structured content marketing strategy.
> - It has created a substantial organic consumer engagement rate using Facebook advertising and sponsored content. This is demonstrated through the number of Facebook fans, likes, shares, number of people talking about it, etc.
> - A well-directed 'relational content marketing' strategy comprising posts related to teacher's day, celebrities such as Deepika Padukone, and women and high heels.
> - In another instance of product differentiation, Jabong intends to score over its peer fashion portals by exclusively retailing high-end brands that are yet to find presence in physical stores in India; the fashion retailer has collaborated with Google to create a shopping hangout to mark the launch of a high-end UK label on its portal. The sale of premium products not only adds a unique dimension to Jabong's brand proposition but will also be instrumental in generating large revenues for the firm.
> - Jabong tied up with 'I am Mumbai', a design lead branding agency which carried out creative duties for Jabong at the Lakme India Fashion Week, 2014. The team created a Jabong Pop-up Shop to enable consumers to get a sneak peek into the world of Jabong. The pop-up shop was titled, 'A Pop of Orange', as research had revealed that Jabong consumers associated the brand strongly with the colour orange due to the orange visual mark within the logo. The experience translated beyond the physical space of the store and went viral via video blogs, makeover pictures, and fashion episodes.

Branding

A *brand* can be formally defined as an individual's perception of an integrated bundle of information and experiences that distinguishes a company or its product offerings from competition.[2] A brand is a promise to customers. Brand equity is the intangible value of a brand measured in monetary terms. Great brands tap into the popular culture and touch customers. The Internet allows brands to form relationships with the customers. A customer first interacts with a brand in the online space, then engages with it, then gets involved with it, and finally starts advocating the brand to others. At the end comes a stage where the consumer and the brand decide to develop a mutually synergistic relationship, as in partnering with each other. The Internet serves as a useful tool in taking the consumer up this ladder from interaction, to engagement, to involvement, and to advocacy. The details are discussed in Chapter 6, *Online Branding*.

Co-creation

With the advent of Web 2.0, customers are active co-creators of the products they buy and use. *Co-creation* is defined as an active, creative, and social process based on collaboration between producers and consumers that is initiated by the firm to generate value for both the firm and the customers.[3] Business online communities are fast becoming excellent tools for operational and collaborative customer relationship management (CRM) with co-creation soon gaining pace as a strategic outcome of collaborative CRM.

E-place

This element of the marketing mix is discussed in the context of distribution, segmentation, targeting, and positioning. We shall discuss each one of them here in detail.

Distribution

The four major elements[4] that combine to form a company's online channel structure and affect Internet marketing strategy are as follows:

- Types of online channel intermediaries
- Length of the online channel
- Functions performed by members of the online channel
- Physical and informational systems that link the channel members and provide for coordination and management of their collective effort to deliver the collective product or service

The associated *e*-business models are addressed in detail in Chapters 8 and 9.

MARKETING SEGMENTATION

Marketing segmentation refers to the grouping or classification of consumers into homogeneous groups based on some similar characteristics, tastes, or preferences. There are several methods of segmenting consumers.

Segmentation is a topic of widespread interest, specifically in the online domain. In the virtual arena, consumers can be segmented on the basis of a wide variety of ways. The following are two different ways of consumer segmentation in the virtual world:

- Consumer segmentation using a combination of the three dimensions of consumer need recognition, website characteristics search, and consumer pre-purchase judgement

- Consumer segmentation using a combination of the two dimensions of consumer traits and online shopping issues faced by consumers

> **EXHIBIT 2.3 Online Portals and the Tourism World**
>
> Most Indian offline travel agencies have reworked their business strategies in the wake of the advent of online travel portals and the huge benefits offered by them. These portals have fundamentally changed the travel buying experience for consumers.
>
> The online travel buying experience is characterized by
>
> - ease of bookings
> - discounts and special offers
> - a host of choices
> - convenience of completing bookings and transactions online
>
> MakeMyTrip.com leads the travel segment in India with a 72% market share. Other players include Yatra.com, Cleartrip.com, TravelGuru.com, Indiatimes.com, and JourneyMart.com among others. These sites offer good networking and connectivity and good content. The user experience generates both loyalty and positive feedback.
>
> A peek at the MakeMyTrip.com site shows how the real-time availability, transparency in prices, and a plethora of choices for hotels, vacations, flights, and cruises make these sites interesting for visitors. This coupled with the company's superior technology and strong relationship with airlines, hotel partners, and other stakeholders allows the company to offer useful solutions to consumers. With the unique facility of customer testimonials available on the website and a generous selection of hotels, business travellers are provided with a wide array of hotel accommodations ranging from 5-star to 3-star hotels, service apartments, and guest houses.

CONSUMER SEGMENTATION

Let us look at the first method of consumer segmentation using the following three parameters:

- Consumer need recognition
- Website characteristics search
- Consumer pre-purchase judgement

These dimensions were constituted using the parameters depicted in Table 2.1.

In a recent study conducted as part of a research project on *e*-marketing and the consumer decision-making process, in Noida, India, data were collected from consumers and the respective dimensions were used for segmentation of consumers. In total, four consumer segments were extracted and the results were tested empirically.

The consumer segments extracted are shown in Fig. 2.3.

The data were analysed and the characteristics of each individual segment (Table 2.2) were profiled.

THE ONLINE MARKETING MIX 51

Table 2.1 Segmentation dimensions

Consumer need recognition	Website characteristic search	Consumer pre-purchase judgement
• Peer influences	• Highest level of interactivity of a website domain	• Price
• Price comparisons	• Ease of navigation	• Brand name
• Product comparisons	• Website readability	• Convenience
• Evaluation of past experiences	• Website reputation and reach	• Special offers
• The role of information Sources	• Specificity of search engine	• Long term benefits
• New schemes and discounts (interaction with recent purchasers)	• User friendliness of interface	• Ease of transaction
• Product purchase without any need	• Keywords used for search	• Consumer reviews
• Comparison through advertisement	• Content diversity of a website	• Affinity for the brand
• Decisions based on standard of living	• Clarity of information on a website	• Secure mode of payment
• Emotional attachments and	• Faster load time/response time	• Awareness of substitute
• Celebrity and brand relationships	• Volume of traffic on the website	• Past purchase experience
	• Presence of adequate searching capabilities	• Trustworthiness of brand
	• Detailed information on a website	• Website customer friendliness
	• Longevity of website existence—domain age	• Product perceived performance
		• Emotional connection with a brand
		• Discussion with family, friends, and peers
		• Attractiveness of transaction offerings

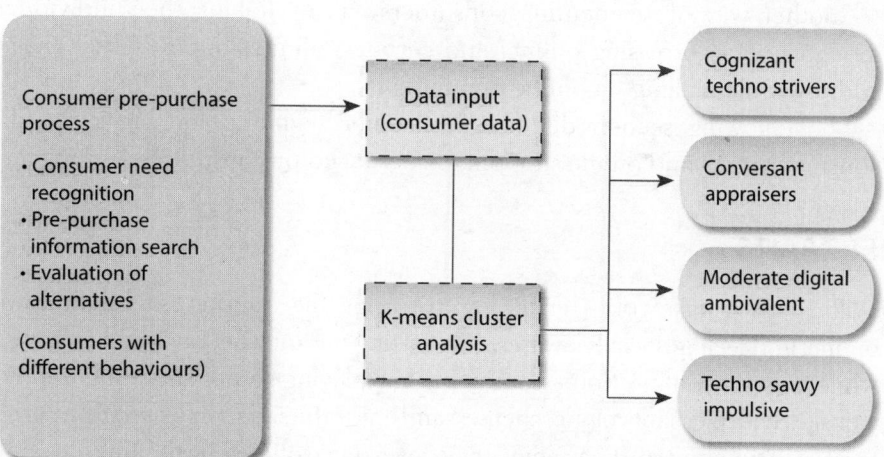

Fig. 2.3 Consumer segmentation based on consumer need recognition, website characteristics search, and consumer pre-purchase judgement

Table 2.2 Consumer segment profiles[5]

Consumer segment	Interpretation of consumer behaviour
Cognizant techno-strivers	Consumers are Internet savvy and use the Internet as a source of information. These consumers take informed decisions and are cognizant towards the website load timings, navigability, readability, domain age, and are influenced positively by efficient Internet presence of product or brand. They are further influenced by affinity of brand, brand name, special offers, quality, and website friendliness. They are slow in recognizing their needs and moderately affected by peer influence
Conversant appraisers	Consumers can easily evaluate alternatives and make informed decisions. They are influenced by brand affinity, brand name, special offers, quality, and website friendliness. But, they are slow in recognizing their needs and somewhat affected by peers, schemes and discounts, prices, and product comparisons. They are not Internet savvy and less influenced by website response time, navigability, and readability
Moderate digital ambivalents	Consumers can easily evaluate and recognize their need and develop a positive stimulus towards product purchase. They are influenced by peers/offers and discounts/surf for more information and consumer testimonials. After identifying their needs, they can easily search all possible alternatives, are Internet savvy, and influenced by website load time, navigability, readability, and existence, but when it comes to purchase they cannot zero in on the best option and fail to choose the best alternative for themselves. So, an enthusiastic beginning ends in a confused response
Techno savvy impulsive	Consumers are influenced positively by the efficient Internet presence of the product or brand. They are further influenced by brand affinity, brand name, special offers, quality, and website friendliness. The consumers cannot identify their needs clearly but are still highly involved in information search through the website after being attracted by the website attributes of better navigability, loading time, and readability, and this information search encourages them to find the best alternative and to shop online

Another way of segmenting consumers will be linking their individual traits, their thoughts while browsing online, and certain online shopping issues that they need to address while making an online purchase.

The following section discusses consumer segmentation using the dimensions of consumer traits and online shopping issues faced by consumers.

CONSUMER TRAITS

Willingness to take risk, seeking joy in surfing the Internet, saving time while shopping online, and feeling socially aware while surfing the Internet are key thoughts of a consumer while browsing online. Some consumers like playing games and using trendy Apps such as websites with pleasant colour schemes, and enjoy the situation when the Internet allows them to voice their opinion. They enjoy the convenience offered by the Internet and participating in online blogs and communities. They enjoy the visual experience offered by the Internet and find the viewpoints of other consumers dependable. They like websites that make their information search easy and enjoy the challenges posed by the online environment.

The Internet helps them to interact with consumer groups and they like websites that provide them up-to-date information. They like visiting virtual sites that offer them better schemes and discounts. Online shopping makes them feel smart in front of their peers. The Internet offers them an emotionally satisfying experience, and online shopping improves their performance and productivity. The Internet allows them to dominate their consumer conversations and they like to shop online because it gives them a sense of excitement. Above all, they find online shopping more adventurous as compared to traditional shopping.

CONSUMERS AND ONLINE SHOPPING ISSUES

Some consumers face several issues while making an online purchase. They do not feel comfortable in sharing their personal details, they cannot touch/feel the product at the time of purchase, may receive products that are different from what they ordered, may feel unhappy about complicated website layouts, are worried that they may not receive the product on time, and may feel that the payment gateway being used is insecure.

Table 2.3 classifies all the issues faced by consumers into four categories:

- Product risk issues
- Interactive risk issues
- Transaction security issues
- Privacy issues

Consumers can be segmented based on a combination of their consumer traits and online shopping issues. The segments extracted are shown in Table 2.4.

Table 2.3 Online shopping issues

Product risk issues	Interactive risk issues	Transaction security issues	Privacy issues
• They cannot see/touch/feel the product at the time of purchase • May receive products which are different from what they ordered • May not receive product in proper shape • Product may not match their requirements • May not return the product • There is a product risk in online shopping • May not receive the product on time • Product does not work properly • May not be able to understand product features	• No offline interaction between company and buyer • Website may not be able to solve all the doubts • May not get an instant reply for query • Have to arrange a specialist visit	• Have to pay extra shipping charges • May feel that the payment gateway being used is insecure • Complicated website layout • Websites will take time to load pages • Difficult navigation system • Complex registration process • Tedious checkout process • Monetary risk • Not willing to pay extra charges	• Do not want to share personal details • Do not want to share credit/debit card details • Worried about privacy

Table 2.4 Consumer segments, based on consumer traits and online shopping issues

Consumer segment	Interpretation of consumer behaviour
Apprehensive conservatives	Consumers who do not feel comfortable in showing their personal details while browsing online feel insecure because they cannot feel and touch the product, they are worried about the product delivery, do not like the complicated layout process of the website, and are not secure about the payment methodologies. Consumers who think that online shopping is not more adventurous as compared to offline shopping, websites do not make their information search easy, they cannot easily get up-to-date information and they enjoy surfing the Internet as they do not lose track of time while browsing
Flamboyant conservative	Consumers in this segment are not hugely impacted by the Internet and are not very fastidious about the online usage as the online medium is not a very significant dimension of their lives
Internet-savvy risk averse	These are individuals who have a penchant for using the Internet and benefit tremendously from the online surfing process. They are adventurous individuals who enjoy the online experience but are limited by their aversion to taking risk. Their conservative behaviour makes them prone to worries with regard to making an online purchase
Internet moderates	These are individuals who possess a moderate degree of Internet saviness. They are not very technical in nature, but are moderately anxious about issues concerning Internet usage for shopping

A careful analysis of the consumer profiles will help companies develop targeting and coverage strategies to engage and convert these consumers separately.

Companies can gain faster conversions by concentrating more on the *Internet-savvy risk averse* individuals and the *Internet moderates*, rather than the *apprehensive conservatives* and the *flamboyant conservatives*. The *Internet-savvy risk averse* candidates will benefit more when given access to a greater volume of Internet tools, but will have to be treated with caution and will need to be demonstrated the importance of safety in their Internet dealings. A greater degree of finesse will be required to handle the *Internet moderates*.

TARGETING

Targeting is a very significant discipline in marketing. A target market is a group of customers towards which a business has decided to aim its marketing efforts and ultimately its merchandise. A well-defined target market is the first element to a marketing strategy. The marketing mix variables of product, place (distribution), promotion, and price are the four elements of a marketing mix strategy that determine the success of a product in the marketplace. This section addresses the need for a more specific online targeting strategy for marketers.

After segmentation of consumers, *e*-marketers can do well with targeting online consumers. The Internet is well suited for the following two targeting strategies:

- *Niche marketing* where a company selects a target segment and develops one or more marketing mixes to meet the needs of the segment.

- *Micro marketing* or individualized targeting, when a company tailors all or part of the marketing mix to a small number of people. Taken to its extreme, it can be a target market of one person.

POSITIONING

Positioning strategies help to create a desired image for a company and its products in the minds of the chosen user segments. Positioning is the process of creating this image, and a position is the resulting view of the firm, or brand from the consumer perspective. To be successful, a company must not only differentiate itself and its products from all others but also position itself among its competitors in the public's mind to carve out its own market niche. Companies can position their brands in the online domain on the basis of product or service attributes, innovative technology image, benefits, user categories, or comparisons with competitors.

E-PRICE

Price is the amount of money charged for a product or service. The Internet focuses on two pricing models—*dynamic pricing*, as the Internet is bringing back the era of varying prices, specifically in cases associated with online bidding, and *price transparency* as both buyers and sellers can view competitive prices for items.

Factors affecting costs in the online domain are:

- Online customer service, which can be expensive.
- High distribution costs for specific customers as products need to be shipped separately.
- Affiliate programmes tend to be expensive as they involve rewarding the referring parties.
- Maintenance and development of websites involve costs.
- The Internet spells low-order processing fee due to self-service
- The Internet world stands for just-in-time inventories and low overheads.
- Costs of distribution of certain digital products like music which is downloadable online are very low.
- Animated shop bots offer online customer service at low cost by replacing service personnel.

THE ONLINE VALUE

In the online domain, companies are adopting one of the following pricing strategies.

Fixed Pricing

The two common fixed pricing strategies used by marketers in the virtual world are price leadership and promotional pricing.

Price leadership

A price leader is the lowest priced product entry in a particular category. Both online and offline, Walmart is a price leader. In the offline domain, economies of scale are the cause of low prices. However, in the online domain, low prices are a function of low costs of small time organizations promoting their products through the Internet.

Promotional pricing

In the virtual world, targeted email messages allow organizations to follow promotional pricing to promote a first time purchase.

Dynamic Pricing

In the online domain, dynamic Web pages allow travel companies to make quick and frequent changes in order to rent cars and fill aeroplane seats or hotel rooms. Dynamic pricing can be initiated both by sellers and buyers. Companies can use *segmented pricing* to sell goods or services at two or more prices, based on segment differentiation, rather than cost alone. Pricing can be devised based on order size and timing, demand and supply levels, and other preset decision factors. With segmented pricing online, companies use decision rules to set pricing levels for segments of customers all the way, to a segment of one person, that is, any customer that is X or does x, gets Y price. For example, any person who books a flight within seven days of departure is quoted the full price.

The Internet allows organizations to customize prices, marketing communication, and products to the individual level. Using cookie files, online sellers recognize individuals and experiment with offers and prices to motivate transactions.

Companies can further opt for *geographic segment pricing* and *value segment pricing*.

E-PROMOTION

Goals of online marketing promotion include the following:

- Driving prospects to the website
- Increasing website registrations
- Increasing online transactions
- Building consumer engagement and involvement.

The online promotional mix is a good conglomeration of online advertising, personalized selling, online promotion through using online coupons, sweepstakes, contests, providing product samples online, rebates, and online exhibitions along with virtual tours. Companies also make use of online public relations activities including *e*-newspaper and magazine articles/reports, and online seminars. Companies also make use of email, interactive consumer websites, online display ads, fliers, online catalogue distribution, and online promotional letters.

EXHIBIT 2.4 Twitter and the Indian Polls, 2014

Twitter emerged as the favourite campaign platform for BJP's Narendra Modi—the Prime Ministerial candidate—AAP's Arvind Kejriwal, and several other political leaders in the Indian Elections, 2014. The microblogging site monetized the Indian Elections and cricket in 2014 by charging political parties and brands for interacting with its user base. Twitter India set up a dedicated vertical whose mandate was to get political parties, politicians, and influencers to engage with their audience on Twitter. The microblogging site foresaw India's 500 million plus mobile users as its potential user base, given that its service could be used even on feature phones via text messaging. The microblogging site subsequently monetized its popularity by

- Enabling real-time marketing
- Encouraging brands to be social
- By ensuring that advertisements were in sync with user experience

Twitter focused on helping brands realize the value and power of real-time marketing. Twitter's CPE and CPF models were used to promote the Indian elections.

The CPE Model

Twitter charges companies based on engagements and followers. So, if a brand advertises on Twitter and a user marks it as favourite, replies to it, or re-tweets, the brand pays Twitter a cost per engagement fee (CPE). In the Indian Elections, political parties paid only when users marked them as favourites or interacted with them online.

The CPF Model

Twitter permits companies to advertise on different levels-for a price Twitter promotes specific accounts, tweets, or trends. Cost per follower strategy is used to rank promoted accounts. Promoted accounts are the first results that emerge in response to an online search query for a particular company or brand. Promoted accounts appear in the 'Who to follow' section for relevant twitter users. Twitter can target potential followers subsequently. In the Indian Elections, political parties had their brands categorized as promoted accounts and paid only for the advantages leveraged subsequently.

WEBSITE CHARACTERISTICS AFFECTING ONLINE PURCHASE DECISION

Online purchases are impacted by certain website characteristics and attributes (Table 2.5). A brief survey helped classify the following website characteristics and attributes as moderately important, very important, neutral, and unimportant. The percentages represent the volume of respondents (consumers) who feel that way.

DIGITIZATION AND IMPLICATIONS TO ONLINE MARKETING MIX DECISIONS

Digitization is a step change even greater than the Internet. Exponential technology advances, greater consumer power and increased competition mean all industries face the threat of commoditization. The winners will act now, and build a strategic advantage that leaves their counterparts wondering what happened.

Table 2.5 Some website characteristics that affect the online purchase decision

Moderately important	Very important	Neutral	Unimportant
• Free trial (20.7%) • Personalized offers (23.4%) • Privacy information (20.3%) • Photo galleries of products (29%) • Consumer reviews and suggestions (27.6%) • Ability to track shopping behaviour (25.7%)	• Customer service (24.3) • Website interface (29.6%) • Security certificates (21.2%) • Perceivable content (29.7%) • Product comparisons (22.6%) • Ease of product search (27.5%) • Large selection of products (27.3%) • Detailed product information (30.7%) • Simplicity of purchase process (28.1%)	• Cost of delivery (20.8%) • Pop up product description (21.4%) • Terms and conditions (243%)	• An online App (19.8%) • Responsiveness to product queries (19.4%)

An imperative for digital innovation and engagement has emerged—businesses have already realized that they must use digital channels to engage with their key stake holders to maintain relevance and drive the conversation. However, few realize how fast the change needs to happen, or how transformational it needs to be. The real imperative in a world where 'everything' is digitized is that businesses need to pursue innovation to disrupt their own business model before the competition does. Without innovative strategies, companies will lose their competitive advantage in an increasingly commoditized world. There is no time to lose, as technology change accelerates exponentially and new digital platforms and devices are emerging. Further more, the expectations of the new 'generation Y' or 'digital natives' mean that companies must keep up with the pace of change or lose relevance. The challenge for businesses is to face the implications of digital change—in particular, the loss of control over the customer relationship, increased competition, and threat of commoditization, and the need to engage digitally with suppliers, partners, and employees in addition to customers.

Companies like Google are engaging in a series of ventures to capitalize on the digital revolution. For instance, Google developed the 'Helping Women Get Online' initiative. The initiative was launched to double the number of women on the Indian Internet. In most markets—US, China, Brazil, and Russia—the number of women and men on the Internet is roughly equal. In India, only 30% users were women. On a percentage basis, India had fewer women than the Middle East. Google launched this initiative to address access, awareness and partner with the ecosystem to double the number of women on the Indian Internet. Google also launched several initiatives to get Indian businesses online. The company also developed a partnership with Nasscom for 10,000 Internet-based start-ups over the next decade.

Product digitization, and the challenges and opportunities stemming from that change, represent a driving force for marketers. The feasibility of digitization of many pre- and post-purchase activities highlights the need for marketers to rethink many marketing mix decisions.

Some key issues pertaining to the online marketing mix, which need to be considered by organizations:

E-product

- Digitization allows firms to create virtual marketplaces. One characteristic of these marketplaces is that, in the context of tangible products, product information can be readily unbundled from the physical product. This allows firms to present an expanded assortment of products and more customized design options.
- Digitization substantially impacts creation, production, and marketing of new products. In the case of digitizable products (e.g., music), offering direct electronic delivery is an important additional benefit for both consumers (i.e., immediate completion of the purchase process) and firms (i.e., no need for costly physical fulfilment activities). Direct and immediate delivery of digitizable products has also created new opportunities related to wireless services (e.g., maps, bill payment, and other information services).
- Digitization impacts the extent to which a product can be evaluated prior to purchase and consumption. Organizations selling products that can be evaluated adequately prior to purchase have a higher success rate.

E-price

Digitization has paved way for three different pricing mechanisms: price set by a firm; price that is negotiated; and price that is established via a competitive bidding process. The implications are as follows:

- Wider and easier availability of price information increases consumer power in the marketplace and creates a tendency of price levels to decrease.
- The biasing impact of seller-provided advertised reference prices is reduced in the online environments because of greater transparency. However, there is also evidence that some psychological biases still persist. For instance, in the case of partitioned prices (e.g., shipping costs showed separately), consumers tend to make price-related judgements that do not adequately adjust for the add-on pricing component in a transaction.
- However, in an online auction setting, consumers may provide higher bids due to two psychological effects: the quasi endowment effect (i.e., consumers develop a sense of product ownership during the bidding process) and the opponent effect (i.e., increase in the subjective value of a product when the behaviour of other bidders is perceived as competitive).

E-promotion

Research suggests that consumers tend to direct attention on a computer screen in a manner that pushes banner ads to the periphery of their visual field. Therefore, as the processing of certain banner ads is likely to be at pre-attention levels, brand awareness and ad recall are more appropriate measures of advertising effectiveness compared to the traditional measures based on click-through rates (CTR). Besides, the contextual factors (e.g., when and where an ad is placed during an online session) can significantly impact advertising effectiveness. In view of such findings, it is evident that firms must devote considerable efforts to develop and implement an online advertising and promotion strategy. Firms can expect a good return on efforts aimed at carefully coordinating online advertising with other channels such as television, radio, and print. Such efforts, collectively, determine a firm's online visibility, an important determinant of traffic levels at the websites of firms.

E-place

Although multi-channel marketing is a topic that preceded the Internet, the emergence of the electronic marketplace has spurred renewed research interest in this area. The consumers' channel choices are explained by making a distinction between two different types of utilities: Product utility (which depends on product characteristics), and process utility (which focuses on how the product is acquired). Process utility can consist of both instrumental components (e.g., getting a lower price in a specific channel) and non-instrumental elements (e.g., enjoyment from the social aspects of a specific channel). Implications to marketing are as follows:

- While having different channel options presents many benefits for consumers, they do have to incur learning costs as they switch from one channel to another.
- From the perspective of firms, the retention rate of a customer can vary significantly depending upon the specific channel in which that customer was initially acquired. Compared to radio, television, and direct mail, initial acquisition via a website is associated with higher retention rates.
- Numerous benefits are visible for firms that implement multi-channel marketing strategies. Customers who shop across multiple channels provide higher revenues, higher share of wallet, and tend to be more active than single-channel customers.
- The likelihood that single-channel customers will become multi-channel customers depends on many factors; the likelihood increases if customers purchase across multiple product categories, engage in more frequent purchases, and/or communicate more frequently with the firm.

Innovative companies are taking the elements of each channel that their customers value most, and combine them to deliver a more valuable experience overall. Some companies have integrated the convenience of Web browsing in their physical stores by adding Internet-enabled kiosks on-site, so customers can browse and check availability on-line, and then try the item on in-store and get the best of both worlds. Others use mobile point of sale terminals to add the convenience of 'click to pay' to their physical shopping experience and provide customers with an email receipt from the POS terminal.

> **EXHIBIT 2.5 Using traditional media to promote online retailing in India**
>
> Indian online retailers, a set of organizations which had to curb it's spending for too long, have now emerged as big spenders on television commercials. This includes Flipkart, Jabong, OLX, Snapdeal, Myntra and Quikr. Top *e*-commerce companies in India which were earlier spending between ₹10 and ₹15 lakh are now spending to the tune of ₹25–75 crore annually. The online retail industry is now estimated at ₹18,000 crore.
>
> Lowe and Partners, Scarecrow Communications and Happy Creative Services are some of the advertising agencies roped in for the television commercials. Brand building, attracting traffic, creating top of mind brand recall value are key objectives of these television commercials. These ads are also directed towards luring talent and investors.
>
> Infact, some portals like Myntra and OLX have used the television to build their online brand. The typical Indian consumer had reservations about online shopping and subsequently many *e*-commerce brands have been using the offline media to convince the erstwhile consumer in doubt.

Brands are facing a loss in the information monopoly and a shift towards two-way communication and conversation. It is vital that brands embrace the shift in consumer power and find ways to make it work for mutual advantage. This is because as customers gain more power to choose where and how they interact, they will begin to choose a smaller number of organizations with which to maintain primary relationships. This is likely to be collaborative organizations that reflect and engage with their values. Other organizations thereby risk becoming mere suppliers. Not all organizations can win the battle to retain the customer relationship—the digital world has thrown organizations into a strictly competitive game.

CASE STUDY Louis Vuitton

Louis Vuitton Malletier, commonly referred to as Louis Vuitton (LV), is a French fashion house founded in 1854 by Louis Vuitton. It is one of the world's leading international fashion houses and sells its products through stand alone boutiques, lease departments in high-end department stores, and through the *e*-commerce section of its website. For six consecutive years (2006–2012), LV has been named the world's most valuable luxury brand.

Louis Vuitton had been promoting its luxury products in the Indian markets for several years, but lately, there was a visible shift in the typical LV customer. The luxury brand earlier had a marketing strategy only to suit the 'royalty' in India. However, the shift in the preferences and profile of the Indian consumer and the upwardly mobile, indulgent section of society, which is smart, savvy, and more aware of the environment around, emerging as the new target segment for LV, has made the company make some significant changes to its strategy. Some of the important changes are visible in the company's online marketing mix.

Louis Vuitton is a trendsetter in the luxury market in India. Their product line—accessories, jewellery, and travel-related goods—start at about ₹25,000 and can go into lakhs of rupees, but it still remains one of the top luxury labels in the country. It sells most of its international line in India with the exception of ready-to-wear clothing, but women's handbags are the clear leader. In a bid to lure the Indian consumer, they opened a LV, India online outlet store with a '100% lowest price plus free shipping' as their unique selling proposition. By offering free membership and savings up to 80% on women's and men's handbags, as well as luggage, and purses, the LV online shopping club provided a convenient way for shoppers to access sales all year round from the comfort of their homes. The club provided 24/7 customer service, streamlined the buying and paying processes, delivered goods at a fast speed and ensured excellence of products.

The challenge in India was to reach out to new clients like the young professionals and entrepreneurs. This was an exciting new challenge and considering the digital proficiency of this target segment, and the inclusion of the online shopping facility, Louis Vuitton was able to spread its wings right across India and appeal to not only the upper class of society, but also the early adopting, risk taking, middle class. Women account for a large part of the company's revenues, although the number of male customers is also going up. Louis Vuitton now sees one-third of India's middle class as potential customers. Growth will be achieved by becoming attractive to the masses.

By becoming price sensitive to a market which promised humongous volumes, considering the large population of India, LV offered products, constantly on sale, with as much as 80% discounts for the Indian market, making it an attractive option for Indians.

Louis Vuitton has been successfully able to leverage the following four tools for its online promotional activities, globally, as well as within India:

- The LV App
- The Quark publishing platform
- The *e*-retail site
- The LV Facebook page

Louis Vuitton developed a new iPad App for internal publications with Quark publishing platform and App studio. The luxury leather goods brand has chosen to use the Quark platform, Quark's enterprise customer communication solution, to produce and deploy an iPad App designed to distribute rich, interactive company communications to iPad equipped employees and stores in France and worldwide. The LV App includes three document types: PDFs, interactive publications (with video, slideshows, websites, specific read models) and videos. It consists of a kiosk, which is used to navigate through the Quark publishing platform tree structure to select and download desired publications before viewing them on the iPad. The App also includes a library for previously downloaded documents (which can be read in offline mode).

When a user visits the kiosk, he can see the 20 most recent documents available with two status options—*update* indicates that a current document previously downloaded by the user has been updated and *new* for publications less than three weeks old.

They have also set up a dynamic search system for keywords, description, and filename as well as a dynamic table of contents to make search more effective. Finally, a public mode is available which, later will enable them to offer their clients access to a certain number of documents at sales sites. The App also includes publications with rich content, such as videos, automatic slideshows and sound-all available in both vertical and horizontal versions.

The Quark publishing platform is a fully customizable publication solution based on HTML 5 which facilitates the creation of targeted, relevant communications that improve client relationships and strengthen their level of satisfaction. The platform allows user and role based distribution of content across mobile and tablet devices. This is the only digital distribution of its kind, which complements mobile device management (MDM) solutions that only manage peripherals and Apps but not the digital content disseminated in the Apps. Louis Vuitton has mastered these capabilities and now draws the full benefits of a high quality, enriched App that adheres to the brand's values.

The *e*-retail endeavours of LV are managed through a separate and independently managed company, known as the Louis Vuitton Moet Hennessey (LVMH), the parent company of LV. LVMH uses eluxury.com as a platform of *e*-retail in the U.S. market for the products of several brands in its portfolio such as LV, Christian Dior, DKNY and Marc Jacobs, among others. This strategy differs from the *e*-retail strategy LVMH executes for some of its brands in the European markets.

Louis Vuitton and Social Media

Social media refers to the means of interactions among people in which they create, share, and exchange information and ideas in virtual communities and networks.[6] Andreas Kaplan and Michael Haenlein define social media as a group of Internet-based applications that build on the ideological and technological foundations of Web 2.0, and that allow the creation[7] and exchange of user-generated content. Furthermore, social media depends on mobile and Web-based technologies to create highly interactive platforms via which individuals and communities share, co-create, discuss, and modify user-generated content. It introduces substantial and pervasive changes to communication between organizations, communities and individuals.[8]

Louis Vuitton has an effective presence on Facebook. Louis Vuitton has been able to understand that social media needs to be fully integrated within the overall brand strategy. It cannot be seen as just a trend anymore, nor as a new way to do marketing. Social media is both a social phenomenon that translates the changes happening in our society and an innovative tool which can be used for marketing, communication, sales, PR and social CRM purposes. But it remains a means to an end, not an end in itself. The company has a well-organized Facebook and Twitter presence and is effectively using several online media for consumer engagement, communication, strengthening brand relationships, increasing consumer brand knowledge and CRM.

New opportunities for LV in the digital space:
- It can adopt a corporate blog for marketing.
- It can use the blog as a CRM tool.

Louis Vuitton is clearly a case of an organization changing its marketing mix to suit the tastes of the local market. From a premium brand, affordable only by the royal class, LV became a trendy brand which could be adopted by the upwardly mobile, aspirational middle class of India—a segment where the number of customers is in millions.

Questions:

1. Who are Louis Vuitton's competitors in a country like India? How does LV leverage its App for its promotional activities?
2. Create a consumer profile for Brand LV in India. How can the company segment its consumers?

PRACTITIONER PERSPECTIVE

Digital marketing involves a very dynamic world. Listed below are the viewpoints of some practitioners from the digital marketing world.

We need to understand that change shall always exist. New lines of businesses are required to come up. During such time, the industry shall also accept failures as well.

Sandeep Menon, Director Marketing, Google

The teams need to be talented in order to be able to leverage the vast database optimally. Talent acquisition and management, both play a critical role in shaping the way modern digital organizations shape up.

Nishant Rao, Country Head, LinkedIn India

Most of the businesses need to understand that the consumer is changing. This enables oganizations to adapt to the rapidly changing markets with ease.

Gurmit Singh, MD, Yahoo, India

One of the most important factors which businesses need to relook at is the way we innovate, in order to be able to offer completely unique and effective solutions to the consumer.

Mahesh Moorthy, Founder Pinstorm, India

> Marketers need to understand how campaigns are performing, which creative to use and how to deliver those campaigns and across which devices. Marketing practitioners also need to take steps to increase their own skill set and skill sets of their teams.
>
> Umang Bedi, Managing Director, Adobe, South Asia

SUMMARY

The online marketing mix comprises-products, *e*-place, *e*-price, and *e*-promotion. Some products are unique to the Internet, some use the Internet as a distribution channel, and some others use the Internet as an electronic storefront. The product dimension of the online marketing mix is characterized by creating customer value in an online world by using a set of well-defined strategies for proliferation of products in the online sphere. Two challenges stare the organizations associated with digital marketing in the face—the first, greater Internet penetration to enhance Internet usage and subsequent benefits from consumers venturing online and second, greater reach for the products being sold online, in terms of more consumers and visibility, which will come through greater volume of time spent online. This creates the need for companies to focus on their distribution strategies and consumer segmentation methodologies. Price is the amount of money charged for a product or service. It is the sum of all values-money, time, energy, and psychic cost, that buyers exchange for benefits of having or using a good or service. Information technology has changed pricing strategies and transformed the way marketers use this tool, especially in online markets. The online domain provides buyers with many cost savings by virtue of convenience, the fast nature of the Internet, self-service, one-stop shopping, integration and automation. Marketers use the marketing communication tools for advertising, sales promotion, marketing public relations, direct marketing, and personal selling to achieve their communication objectives. After implementation, they measure effectiveness, make any adjustments required and evaluate results. Marketer's use of the Internet can be understood in light of the AIDA model or the 'think-feel-do hierarchy of effects model. Each online tool is more or less effective at particular levels of these models. Consumers can be segmented based on a combination of their consumer traits and online shopping issues. Consumers can also be segmented on the basis of consumer need recognition, website characteristics search and consumer pre purchase judgement.

Concept Review Questions

1. Discuss the online promotional mix. How do the characteristics of the online world impact the generic marketing mix? Explain with examples.
2. What are the factors that affect 'cost in the online world? Explain with examples.
3. Discuss one method by which consumers are segmented and targeted in the virtual world.
4. Differentiate between apprehensive conservatives, flamboyant conservatives, Internet-savvy risk averse, and Internet moderate consumers.
5. How can marketers carve the online offer in the virtual world by using fixed pricing and price leadership strategies?

Critical Thinking Questions

1. Study the online marketing mix for one company each in the following industry verticals:
   (a) FMCG
   (b) Automobiles
   (c) IT
   (d) Education
   Prepare a chart to compare between the disparate strategies used by each of the companies in formulating, shaping, and promoting the online offer. How relevant are the decisions of the companies in the light of the competitive position in the respective industry verticals.
2. Visit the Google website. Profile Google's online marketing mix on the basis of secondary data available in the virtual space.
3. Compare the online marketing mix of Myntra.com. How is Myntra.com using the traditional media to complement the online marketing mix?
4. Evaluate the online marketing strategies of Coke. How does Coke make use of a series of online platforms and social networking sites for proliferation of the brand in the virtual domain?

Practising Digital Marketing

Assume that you are launching a fruit-based beverage in India. Give the product a name.
1. Create an online marketing mix for the promotion of the beverage. Define the product constitution, places where it will be launched, pricing strategies, and promotion mix.
2. Collect consumer data for the hypothetical beverage through a survey to create a segmentation strategy using the online medium.
3. Profile the consumers. Use the consumer profiles to create a targeting strategy which the beverage can use for different consumer segments. Discuss the disparity between the targeting strategies used for the different consumer segments and link this difference to the variation in the consumer profiles.

References

1. Phau, I. and Poon, S.M., (2000). 'Factors influencing the types of products and services purchased over the Internet', *Internet Research*, Vol. 10(2), pp. 102–113.
2. Murray, D. and Howat, G., (2002). 'The relationships among service quality, value, satisfaction, and future intentions of customers at an Australian sports and leisure centre', *Sport Management Review*, Vol. 5(1), pp. 25–43.
3. Humphreys, P., Samson, A., Roser, T., and Cruz-Valdivieso, E., *Co creation: New Pathways to Value*, LSE Enterprise, London, 2009.
4. Strauss, J., El-Ansary, A., and Frost, R., (2006). *International Business Research*.
5. Jain, N. and Ahuja, V., (2014). 'Segmenting online consumers using K-means cluster analysis', *Inderscience Publications*.
6. Lee, C., *Social Technographics Report*, Forrester Research, 2008.
7. Cheung, C.M.K., Zhu, L., Kwong, T., Chan, G.W.W., and Limayem, M., (2003). Online consumer behavior: A review and agenda for future research, 16th Bled eCommerce Conference eTransaction, pp. 9–11.
8. Constantinides, E. and Fountain, S., (2008). 'Web 2.0: Conceptual foundations and marketing issues', *Journal of Direct, Data and Digital Marketing Practice*, Vol. 9, pp. 231–244.
9. Hanson, W. and Kalyanam, K., *Internet Marketing and E-commerce*, International Edition 2e, ISBN-13: 9780324422818.

The Online Consumer

> **LEARNING OBJECTIVES**
> *After reading this chapter, you will be able to*:
> - Understand the concepts associated with the digital ecosystem
> - Link between digital paradigms and marketing
> - Understand online consumer behaviour
> - Get acquainted with the dynamics of the online consumer visit
> - Get familiar with metrics and their applications
> - Observe the difference between online behaviour in business-to-business (B2B) and business-to-consumer (B2C) contexts
> - Get an insight into database marketing

Individualization changes the nature and quality of online transactions. It allows the online world to be adaptive, secure, and intelligent. This enables marketing to successfully interact with the customers and react to their sophistication and knowledge. Interaction can build intelligence into the system and by reacting to the specific immediate needs and responding to the access method of the consumers, organizations can interact with the consumers and subsequently host content that is relevant to the consumer.

THE DIGITAL ECOSYSTEM

The digital ecosystem can be defined as the online universe that has a set of unique characteristics opening up a multitude of opportunities for organizations towards a better utilization of the latest offerings from the world of technology and generation of a higher return-on-investment (ROI).

Some of the features of the digital ecosystem (Fig. 3.1a) are as follows:

- The Internet today has been hailed as the most important invention of the twentieth century, and digital marketing is transforming companies' customization and advertising. It is an efficiency enhancer and entertainment provider.
- Online activities can be both time saving and time consuming. Hence, organizations and individuals need to understand how to make *time and money trade-offs* as they

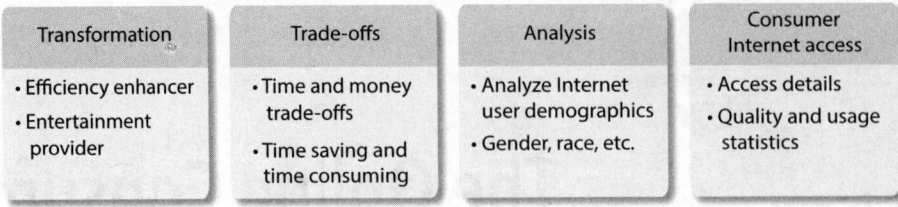

Fig. 3.1a Features of the digital ecosystem

venture forward to utilize the online medium for personal and organizational growth as well as brand proliferation.

- With its increasing popularity, as noticed from more and more number of users coming online, and services being offered online in general, the Internet now occupies a central role in young educated people's lives,[1] all over India. Companies need to analyse Internet user demographics, gender, race, employment status, and education parameters to segment and profile current and prospective consumers effectively.
- In addition, consumer internet access details, quality, and usage statistics are also significant.

The Rise of Digital Marketing

US Corporations were expected to increase their expenditure on digital marketing from 2.5% of revenue to 9% in 2013, overtaking IT spend as a percentage of revenue for the first time. Not surprisingly, social media is where most marketers wanted to increase spending, but mobile and tablet applications were not far behind. Brand building and differentiation are the top reasons for digital marketing, (Fig. 3.1b) followed by customer communication and assessment of customer satisfaction of a product according to a survey by Gartner on 250 firms with over $500 million in annual revenues.

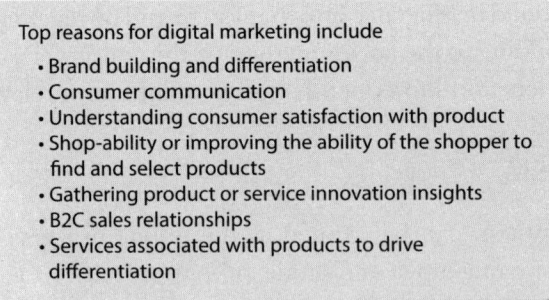

Fig. 3.1b Reasons for digital marketing

Digital Paradigm and Marketing

The digital paradigm (Fig. 3.1c) plays two very significant roles in marketing—influencing consumer behaviour and harnessing consumer intelligence. While it is vital for an organization to evaluate consumer intentions and provide consumers the necessary

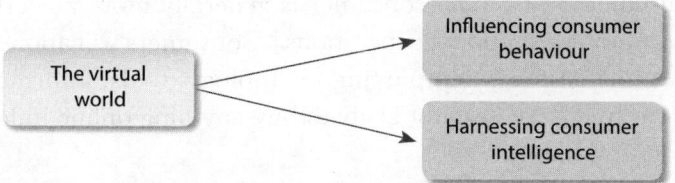

Fig. 3.1c Marketing in a virtual world

information they are looking for, equally important is the need for collecting consumer data by studying the consumer behavioural patterns on the Internet and subsequently nurturing long-term relationships with consumers. The Internet has subsequently commenced playing a very significant role in the marketing value chain (Fig. 3.2) encompassing value identification, creation, and delivery, thereby impacting marketing economics by reducing transaction cost and time. There seems to be rapid adoption of the Internet by consumers for various purposes, including information search and online shopping.[2] Consumer data analysis, content analysis, and predictive modelling are the buzzwords of today and digital marketing coupled with digital media are the twin growth engines for the organizations in contemporary times.

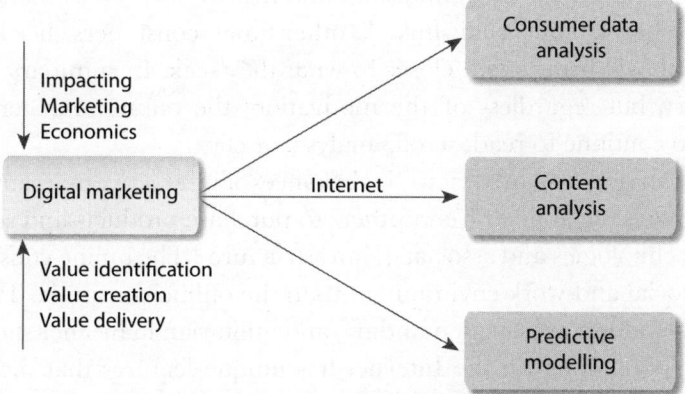

Fig. 3.2 The potential of digital marketing

Consumer behaviour has changed dramatically in the past decade. Nowadays, consumers can order many customized products online, ranging from sneakers to computers. Many have replaced their daily newspapers with customized, online editions of these media and are increasingly receiving information from online sources. This has proliferated because these channels reflect an understanding of consumer needs and consumer behaviour.[3] If experts want to identify the most profound influences on consumer behaviour in recent times, the answer would be the Internet. Consumers also recognize the substantial impact the Internet has had on their shopping behaviour. One of the reasons why the Internet is dramatically changing consumer behaviour is that it helps us search much more easily and efficiently than ever before.[4] The online consumer may also have different social and work environment than the offline consumer. The online consumer is generally more powerful, demanding, and utilitarian in his/her shopping expeditions.[5] Consumers will appreciate business, which value consumer's time by employing technology, tools, information, and customer service. Consumers are also not likely to buy anything online unless complete product information is available.

ONLINE CONSUMER BEHAVIOUR

The Internet has become an important channel for companies to provide product information and offer direct sales to their customers. Firms of all sizes and from all industries have invested in Internet applications and are trying to establish a net presence. People increasingly use the Internet to check out company or product information.[6]

Websites are designed keeping in mind concepts of interactivity, feasibility, convenience, and user requirements. Information regarding products and services must be easily accessible and of high quality in terms of customer satisfaction. A consumer's intention to purchase specific products may vary greatly, and hence predicting general intentions to adopt the Internet for purchasing may be of limited use if customer motives to purchase specific products are likely to differ.[7]

Website visitors may use both distant and nearby cues: consumers may click on a link because they seek that specific link. At other times, consumers click because they believe that the link will bring them closer to what they seek. In summary, the motivations for search vary, but regardless of the motivation, the online searcher continually judges whether to continue to read, scroll, analyse, or click.[8]

Online transactions can be viewed as instances of interactive marketing communications. *E*-commerce is the ability of consumers to purchase products and services online, using Internet technologies and associated infrastructure.[9] The online consumer may also have different social and work environment than the offline consumer. The online consumer is generally more powerful, demanding, and utilitarian in his/her shopping expeditions.[5]

Further, purchasing on the Internet has unique features that make it different from the traditional shopping process.[10] If a website meets a customer's expectations, then the customer is likely to reuse the website in the future, recommend it to his/her peers, and become loyal.

On the other hand, if the website does not meet the customer's expectations, then the customer is likely to switch to another website, and perhaps never go back to the initial one.[11] Therefore, the perceived quality of a website is an important determinant of such expectations, resulting in the development of an attitude towards a particular website and perhaps even garnering visitor loyalty.[12]

Although it has been argued that the capabilities embedded in an *e*-service technology provide many potential benefits for customers, if customers think the technology is too difficult to use, customers may refuse to use the *e*-service technology at all.[13] Significantly, information provided by an online store is an important factor that affects each consumer's site loyalty and purchase behaviour.[14]

EXHIBIT 3.1 Merging Real and Virtual Worlds

You know when you walk into a cosmetics store or an apparel store that you will get to sample or try on the range of products available before you make up your mind on what to buy. Imagine if that was possible from the comfort of your living room where you do not have to visit stores, and everything is delivered to your doorstep.

If the recently launched portal trynbuy.com is anything to go by, your wish might just come true. Still in their infancy in India, trynbuy.com describes themselves as India's first 'discovery' commerce portal. The process is quite simple: as a registered member you get to try samples of the top products of various high-end brands, receive advice and reviews from other consumers, and earn points with every purchase. Every month premium members receive a unique box of requested samples. If you like what you have sampled, you have the option of buying the full product directly from them.

CULTURAL IMPLICATIONS OF KEY WEB CHARACTERISTICS[15]

A major application of the Web can be seen in bridging gaps for organizations by reducing cultural diversity and help in a greater cultural adaptability. Listed in (Table 3.1) are a series of Web characteristics and the cultural implications of those characteristics.

Table 3.1 Culture and the Web

Characteristic	Cultural implication of the characteristic
The Web is a general open network having global accessibility	The Web is viewed by people across culture thus lending itself to vast cultural variability
Interactive nature of the Web	The interactive nature of the Web makes it an ideal medium to create culturally sensitive dialogue
Web is characterized by hyperlinks and self-search option	Hyperlinks and self-search options rely on consumer motivation to browse, therefore if Web content is not customized for global customers on individual bases the interactive efforts might be wasted
Web technologies can help capture customer data that can be used for mass customization	Using customer databases and software, country-specific profiles can be created and used to make the websites culturally adapted
Media convergence and broadband technology make Web an ideal medium to interact with audio, video, graphic, and text	Media convergence on the web can be used to develop country-specific themes, pictures, videos, and sounds to create localized websites
On the Web, the capacity to hold the visitors attention 'the flow state' is an important challenge	The websites that are culturally congruent or closely match the social perceptions of users are more likely to engage the users

DYNAMICS OF ONLINE CONSUMER VISIT

At each visit on an online page, a consumer has the chance to either continue the visit or exit. The average Web visit is less than three page views, as it is totally dependent on the choice of a typical online visitor. The website subsequently has a short time to perform the following drills:

- Communicate with the visitors
- To deliver a message
- To build a brand image
- To engage in commerce
- To persuade visitors

Table 3.2 explains two disparate consumer Web visit models—the random surfer model and the look ahead model.

Table 3.2 Models explaining short visit length

Model	Explanations
The random surfer model	• It explains consumer visits of different length • 50% per page chance of leaving for the first few page views, which then falls to 37% per page chance of exit if the visit continues • Consider web surfing as a flip of the coin • At each page, a visitor has a chance to continue the visit or exit • Exit pages only loosely connected to current page quality • This model appears to be the best match for experiential surfing
The look ahead model	• It explains the same pattern of short visits but with a different model of surfing behaviour • Surfers are not flipping a coin with regard to leaving the pages but carefully balance their time and efforts against the chance of finding the desired information • The connection is higher when the page corresponds to accomplishing a task or clarifying that the website does not match the visitor's goal • This model appears to be the best match for task-directed visits

Source[15a]: Web visit models, Hansom and Kalyanam, 2007.

As the Internet becomes a major and popular source of information, websites offer numerous opportunities for global companies to provide world-wide access to information about a company and its brands. The informational and branding capabilities of websites are now integral parts of integrated marketing communication programmes in organizations. Similarly, creating uniform brand image is one of the key components of global marketing strategy and websites with their global reach are mostly used to serve the purpose of displaying a consistent brand image. Hence, it is becoming vital to understand the cause and relevance of the consumer visit on the website. Well-structured product information that cannot be found easily online is as much of a problem as is having easily accessible information that does not meet consumer's expectations.[16] Visitor choices matter a great deal. Online consumers are time conscious and are often willing to gamble with their money rather than time, as it is impossible to recover lost time, where a moderate financial loss can be compensated.[17] Consumers will appreciate business, which value for customer's time by employing technology, tools, information, and customer service. Consumers are also not likely to buy anything online unless complete product information is available. According to the study on Australian consumers,[18] one of the main emerging characteristics of online users is the growing lack of patience. Many researchers put their attention to online consumer behaviour in order to discover the underlying rules of Internet marketing. It is important to build up a safe and credible market environment for online shopping[19] by understanding the behaviour models of online decision-making behaviours.

The consumer's chance of staying on a website falls as the number of pages viewed increases. This is usually the result of any time constraints the consumer may be facing or an increase in his/her degree of involvement with the product/organization/website which may have prompted him/her to leave at that point of time and subsequently visit again.

How Consumers See and Understand Product Information Online

When buying products and services online, consumers are facing two fundamental differences—removal of physical presence and (as a compensation) abundance and versatility of product information. In other words, a physical product has been replaced by product information.[20] It is important for *e*-retailers to better understand how online consumers interact with the Internet websites, that is, how they evaluate website attributes and that is what makes them remain on the websites.[21] In these days of Web mania, everyone talks about the *e*-commerce and *e*-business revolution and the Internet of the new knowledge-based economy. The Web allows *e*-businesses to provide customers with increasingly accurate, timely, and inexpensive information. As a result, customers can immediately compare prices and choose the supplier with the lowest price.[22]

MODELS OF WEBSITE VISITS

Nowadays consumers spend significant time online and make the purchase decision by making strategic comparisons between alternative and competing products, reading consumer reviews and testimonials, making price and quality comparisons, and so on. What is significant here? Is it the ability of a website to engage the consumer and retain him/her for a significant time period on the site? In this context, it would be vital for organizations to design websites which can cater to consumer need recognition, information search, evaluation of alternatives, purchase decisions, and reduce post-purchase dissonance. It is the ability of a website to respond to the consumer needs that will make the consumer stay on the site or end the Web visit. While the consumer level of interest and degree of seriousness regarding the information search are important determinants in the length of his/her stay on a website, it is the analysis of the type of online consumer behaviour[22]—*task-directed or experiential online consumer behaviour*, that will help an organization to build a consumer Web visit model and then, create ways to increase the longevity of the consumer Web visit (Table 3.3).

Table 3.3 Task-directed vs experiential online behaviour

Type of online consumer behaviour	Models of Web visits
Task-directed behaviour In task-directed website visits, the user attempts to find out information to accomplish a task. A user is actively engaged in judging the appropriateness and credibility of information, and balancing additional information on a page against better alternatives elsewhere.	**Look ahead/surfer option model** The surfers do not have a chance of leaving, but carefully balance their time and effort against the chance of finding the information they desire. The look ahead model appears the best match for a task-directed visit.
Experiential online behaviour Experiential surfing is surfing for one's own benefit as a time using application. A website is a form of programming channel, which either offers quality entertainment or does not.	**The random surfer model** This is a more natural model for an experiential surfer, not actively engaged in the discovery of specific information. The random surfer model appears the best match for experiential behaviour.

Source: N. Jain, V. Ahuja, 2011.

Goal-directed tasks possess an inherent structure that guides consumers when they are engaged in linear, search-directed activities and an experiential task is less structured and supports non-linear, non-search-directed activities.[23] Experiential and goal-directed users would not weigh extrinsic and intrinsic motives in the same way when on the Web.[24] According to the recent research on consumer behaviour on the Internet users, there are distinct consumer groups with different intentions and motivations,[25] they are as follows:

- Exploration
- Shopping
- Quest for information
- Task-directed behaviour other than shopping

The goal for a website designer seeking a highly usable site is to anticipate problems and create a good design from the start. Research indicates that both males and females outline ease-of-use as the most important factor in Web design,[26] though it is generally considered as an important criterion in a user's decision whether to continue using the information system.[27]

The data collected from the online domain has meaning for organizations only if it is quantifiable and measurable. Well-defined *e*-metrics (Table 3.4) help organizations in comprehending the virtual environment.

The types of *e*-metrics gathered will depend on the objectives of the website. Those objectives might include the following:

- Increasing revenue to the organization through direct sales
- Providing after sales service that enhances offline efforts
- Generating sales leads that can be followed up using traditional offline methods
- Brand development complementing offline branding
- Reducing corporate costs by replacing traditional modes of communication with Internet-based technologies

Table 3.4 *E*-metrics used to assess website intent

Website intent	Parameter to be measured

Increase online sales	• Sales generated per visitor
	  – In one individual visit
	  – Through online sale
	  – Through telephonic contact
	  – Through cash-on-delivery option
	• Total number of items per single order placed online
	• Online consumer conversion rates
	• Daily and weekly sales trends and patterns
	• Consumer website entry and exit pages
	• No. of sites linking into the website
	• Source of online visit

Creation of re-purchase intent	• No. of visits to complaints page • Length of the visit • Online registration • Opt-in for company mails • Joining company online forums and blogs • Becoming consumer evangelist (online recommendations)
Identification of potential customers	• No. of organizational online forums joined • Responses to *e*-mails • Responses to company mailers • Responses to organizational campaigns • No. of opt-ins (newsletter downloads, *e*-mail opt-ins, promotional schemes) • Consumer evangelists on online forums • Degree of positivity of online sentiment displayed

The typical traditional consumer decision-making process comprises of the steps as shown in Fig. 3.3.

Fig. 3.3 The consumer decision-making process

THE WEB AND CONSUMER DECISION-MAKING PROCESS

Recognizing the effects of the Web on the consumer's decision-making process, understanding the sources of customer value and the motives of consumers to use the offerings of the Internet are vital for organizations. Web applications are becoming increasingly popular due to the advantages they offer to users (transparency, referrals, contacts with other users, etc.) and their effect on customer power.[28] Interaction with peers triggers new customer needs (often for niche and highly personalized products) and alters buying attitudes. The new buying attitudes are not limited to the online buying behaviour but extend to the traditional one. According to a recent survey of the Sterling Committee, consumers want a seamless buying experience across all channels.[29] As a result, the Internet, and particularly the Web as a new marketplace component, further complicates the time-honoured 'textbook' buying behaviour process. Next to the personal and external uncontrollable factors influencing the buying behaviour, exposure of customers to the company's marketing can affect the decision-making by providing inputs for the consumer's black box where information is processed before the final consumer makes the final decision.[30] Online marketers can influence the decision-making process of the virtual customers by engaging traditional and physical marketing tools but mainly by creating and delivering the proper online experience. The Web experience is a combination of online functionality, information, emotions, cues, stimuli, and products/services. In other words it is a complex mix of elements going beyond the 4Ps of the traditional marketing mix. The prime medium of delivering the Web experience is the corporate website, the interfacing platform between the firm and its online clients.[31] Web experience elements—the marketing tools and actors under the control of the *e*-marketer that can influence or shape the online consumer's behaviour during the virtual interaction, become the basic premise for marketing to explore. The Web experience is in this sense a new and additional input in the traditional buying behaviour frameworks.

BEHAVIOURAL TARGETING VS CONTEXTUAL TARGETING

The target marketing industry is adapting to and shaping the rules of targeting consumers using the Internet. These online marketers use either the user's clickstream data or the IP address and personal information or the frequency of the online activity for the purpose. This encompasses the concept of *behavioural targeting*.

Contextual targeting encompasses placing advertisements where they are in context with the content of the host website or page.

Offline, behavioural segmentation might be based on such elements as benefits sought, purchase occasions, usage frequency, or usage status. The same rules apply to behavioural targeting.

Online Behaviour in a B2C Context[32]

There are two aspects of online behaviour (Fig. 3.4) that can be monitored to help assess the customer's behaviour, they are as follows:

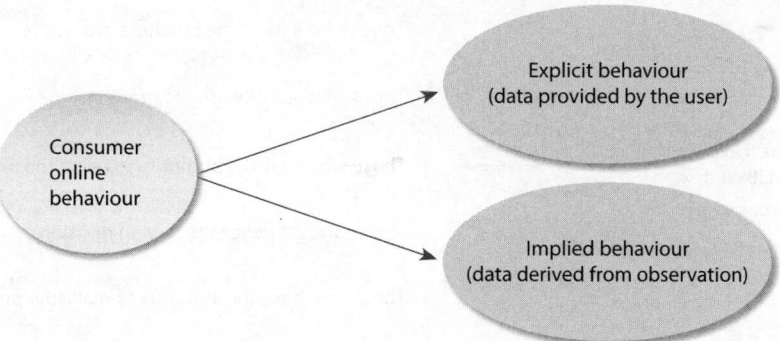

Fig. 3.4 Types of online behaviour

- Explicit behaviour is based on data provided by the user. This could include such things as a user profile if membership or registration details were required to access the site or make a purchase. In addition, any recorded actions on the site, like signing up for an *e*-newsletter or placing an order, would also be included.
- Implied behaviour is based on data derived from the observation of a user's actions as they interact with the site.

Following is an example of online behaviour in a B2C context: Dominos, India interacts extensively with its consumers on the online domain through blogs and online communities. When a consumer logs into the Domino's blog using a well-defined login id and password, his/her explicit behaviour can be monitored by the organization. Dominos further studies consumer response patterns to identify the type of content that drives consumer engagement levels, thus studying the implied behaviour of the participants.

Topographic association

The concept of topographical association takes implied behaviour to a step further, working on the premise that one individual's implied behaviour will be matched by others. Amazon uses the concept well in their book sales. A search on a book title will return a page that not only describes the book in question, but also includes a list of similar or associated books designated as 'customers who bought this item also bought'. To encourage sales, there is also a feature that takes the most relevant of the 'also bought' list and packages it with the sought book as a 'perfect partner', offering the two at a discounted rate if they are purchased together.

Online Behaviour in a B2B Context

The decision-making unit for *e*-marketing (Fig. 3.5), in a B2B context includes the following:
- Those who initiate the purchase procedure
- Those who actually use the product
- Those who have the authority to select the product
- Those who influence the buying decision
- Those who have the authority to make the purchase

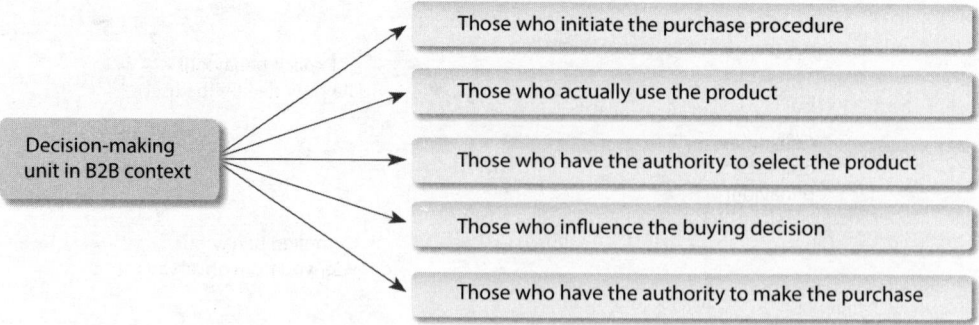

Fig. 3.5 Online decision-making

The above needs to be taken into account while developing an online marketing strategy. For instance, complex technical content might appeal to influencers but put off users. A neutral website that appeals to all might attract none.

Dell's homepage segments the market by providing a gateway to small, medium, and large/global business solutions as well as public sector solutions such as healthcare and education.

WEB 2.0 AND MARKETING

The Read/Write Web or Web 2.0 as it is termed has ushered in a tremendous possibility for *e*-marketers: the opportunity of customer advocacy. Even in the case of product categories previously considered as generic (such as travel and vacation services), vendors discover that they can gain and retain customers by offering something more than only low prices.[33] There is evidence that customer reviews posted on different forums or online communities, Web blogs, and podcasts are much more powerful as marketing tools than expert product reviews,[34] as the influence of blogs and podcasts is increasing significantly. The third way to utilize Web 2.0 media is to engage these as tools of direct, personalized one-to-one marketing. Brick-and-mortar firms such as Nike, Disney, Coca Cola, TIME magazine, The Hearst Media are already experimenting with social media as part of their direct marketing strategy seeking communication, interaction, and customer feedback. They do this by introducing Web 2.0 websites based on user-generated content and encouraging social networking and community forming. These sites offer their customer the possibility to reach their peers, exchange information and experiences.

Another option is to actively participate in the Web 2.0 domain by launching corporate blogs and podcasts. Marketing needs to engage in prospect profiling to address some key issues. A prospect is an individual who might express some interest in becoming a customer. Some of these issues related to finding a new consumer are as follows:

- How does a typical prospect find out about the firm's products?
- Does the message the firm delivers, gain the attention of the intended target audience? Does it address the requirements of the target market, and does it suggest benefits or a means for satisfying them? Is the message appropriately positioned?

- Does the promotion effort effectively inform, persuade, educate, and remind customers about the firm's products?
- Does the firm establish budgets and measure effectiveness of promotional efforts?

Truly good prospects are not only interested in becoming customers, they can afford to become customers, they will be profitable to become customers, they are unlikely to defraud the company and likely to pay their bills, and if treated well they will be loyal customers and recommend others. No matter how simple or sophisticated the definition of a prospect, the first task is to target them. To target the consumers or prospects as they may be called, two issues need to be looked at; they are as follows:

- a marketing communication channel
- what brings the prospect to engage with a particular channel

The collaborative Web offers tools to help a firm address most of these issues by inclusion to the marketing mix. By providing an online medium for interacting to build social and business relationships with consumers, sharing information, collaborating and building consumer engagement, these tools allow marketing to foster brand relationships between consumers and the brand. The shift in customer needs is reflected in the growing demand for online services, particularly in the Web 2.0 domain, where the Web provides a response to the exploratory consumer browsing leading a prospect to online material related to the brand. Customer preferences and experiences about the products and services offered, either in traditional or electronic outlets, is not exclusively based on information made available through traditional mass media or corporate websites any more. In the Web 2.0 era, customer preferences and decisions are increasingly based on inputs provided by parties beyond the control of online marketers which are peer reviews, referrals, blogs, tagging, social networks,

---

EXHIBIT 3.2 Home Shop 18—Billy, Sunny, and the Indian Consumer

HomeShop18 is an online and on-air retail and distribution venture of *Network 18 Group*, India. HomeShop18 was launched in 2008 as India's first 24-hour home shopping TV channel, where anchors performed live demonstration of products on sale. A company, which established itself as a strong name in Indian retail, because of high television penetration, was fast to leverage the growth of the Internet. HomeShop18 launched www.homeshop18.com, which soon became one of the most thriving *e-commerce* portals in India.

HomeShop18s latest 360° media campaign rides on the universally accepted truth of 'if you are sad, go shopping'. The company used cats called Billy and Sunny for the campaign—these represented fluffy, loveable, agile, intelligent, cool creatures.

The company also launched a wacky and engaging micro-site called *Shopping Makes Me Happy*. With Live Contests, FunZones and Saturday Sales, Shopping Zodiacs, Shopping Heavens, and Special Offers, the site provided a cool online hangout for the Indian consumer who wanted an interesting online shopping experience.

online forums, and other forms of user-generated content. When companies began delving into the consumer's cognitive space for value exploration, they used focus groups extensively as one of the several methodologies used to collect feedback on how well customers liked certain products. However, with the increasing complexity and competitiveness in the business world, and with technology offering newer ways to help organizations reach out to consumers in meaningful ways and involve them, the inadequacies of the previously used media made firms try newer options. Companies wanted to get a '360-degree view' of the customers, and the collaborative Web offered a spectrum which helped companies move a step ahead in the direction of market sensing and interacting with their consumers.

RESEARCH ILLUSTRATION

There are some obvious questions for marketers related to websites and online traffic, as follows:

- Why does a consumer venture online?
- If a consumers clicks on a particular feature on a website, what is his/her intention?
- If a consumer is searching for information about a product on the product website, what is the website feature (attribute) he/she is most likely to click on?
- Each website has so many features (attributes such as About us, Contact us). What functions do these features (attributes) perform for the website?

This research illustration attempts to answer these questions.

A research study was conducted to find out the following:

- Calculate a website attribute index which was indicative of website attractiveness
- Classify website attributes according to the online shoppers' intentions they cater to, for visiting product and brand websites
- Examine the relationship between the evaluations of the relative importance of various website attributes, with respect to the function performed by the attribute

Exploratory research was used for this study. Data were collected through hard copy questionnaires and also through online media using the 'snowball sampling technique' for data collection. Snowball sampling is a non-probability sampling technique where existing study subjects recruit future subjects from amongst their acquaintances. Thus the sample group appears to grow like a rolling snowball. As the sample builds up, enough data is gathered to be useful for research. A statistical procedure known as principle components method (PCM) of analysis was used for data reduction.

Pilot Study

Identification of industry verticals and companies.

The list of top 22 industry verticals, Indian Council for Market Research (ICMR) and 4Ps B&M Survey, 2010 was used to identify the following industry verticals—automobile, banking, IT, education, and fast-moving consumer goods (FMCG), and the top 10 companies across all five verticals were subsequently used for the study.

Creation of Research Instruments

Creation of a scoring grid for extraction of website attributes.

Sets of organizational websites, under each industry vertical were evaluated qualitatively to extract an exhaustive list of website attributes, which helped in the formulation of the research instrument—a scoring grid for each industry.

The scoring grid was created to ascertain the presence/absence of the respective website attributes across the company websites (Table 3.5) and was further used to calculate a website attribute index. A value of 1 was assigned when the attribute was present and 0 was assigned when the attribute was not present in the evaluation grid. The *website attribute index* (Table 3.6) was calculated by summing up the attributes for each website and dividing it by the maximum possible number of attributes. *The top three verticals showing a high website attribute index were used for the next phase of the study.*

Vertical-specific evaluation grids were developed to collect primary data from consumers across the automobile, banking, and FMCG sectors, where the consumers were asked to rate each website attribute determining whether they would click on it or not.

The prerequisites for a consumer to fill the questionnaire were as follows:
- An active Internet usage rate of at least 1–2 hours a day
- Active consumption of products pertaining to the respective vertical

Table 3.5 Industry verticals and companies

Industry vertical	Companies
Automobile	Ford, Chevrolet, Audi, Honda, Mercedes, Fiat, Hyundai, Toyota, BMW, Tata
Banking	SBI, ICICI, SCB India, HDFC, OBC, ING VYSYA, Bank of Baroda, Axis, ICICI, IndusInd
IT	Wipro, Dell, Cisco, Accenture, Apple, Reliance, Tata Steel, TCS, Infosys, L&T
Education	DPS:R. K. Puram (Delhi), Ryan International School (Noida), Kothari National School, Mayoor International School (Noida), Amity International School (Noida), Jaypee Institute of Informational Technology (Noida), IIM(Ahmadabad), IIT (Delhi), IMT (Ghaziabad), IIFT (Delhi)
FMCG	HUL, ITC Ltd, Nestle, Dabur, Asian Paints, P&G, Cadbury, Amul, Britannia, Marico

Table 3.6 Website attribute index

S. no	Sector	Attribute index
1	Automobiles	0.72609
2	Banking	0.66207
3	IT	0.36071
4	Education	0.32068
5	FMCG	0.4444

Further research was carried out for the automobile, banking, and IT verticals. The website attributes were linked to the consumer intent behind venturing online.

The attributes empirically loaded onto the ones that follow:

- Consumer intent to explore
- Shopping
- Quest for information
- Task-directed behaviour other than shopping intent

The study aimed at identifying the dimensions of website attributes that represent the intentions of consumers for visiting product and brand websites, and examined the relationship between various website attributes with respect to the functions performed by the attribute.

The following website attributes were empirically identified as contributing to a specific type of consumer intent, across a specific industry vertical (Table 3.7–3.9).

Automobile sector

Table 3.7 Automobile sector

Exploration	Shopping	Quest for information	Task-directed behaviour other than shopping
Price Media centre Customer care Search Dealership enquiry	Request for quote Service booking Buying	About us Online community Contact us E-brochure Test drive Product and model services Accessories Sitemap Privacy Worldwide News events Community	Careers Pre-owned cars

Banking sector

Table 3.8 Banking sector

Exploration	Shopping	Quest for information	Task-directed behaviour other than shopping
Internet banking Complaints and suggestions Whole sale banks Worldwide locations	Phone and mobile banking Ratings Personal banking Agricultural–rural banking NRI services	About us Hindi New and important information Customer care	Career and recruitment Rail tickets

(Continued)

THE ONLINE CONSUMER

| | Corporate banking
SME
Debit andcredit cards
ATM centre
Priority banking
Private banking
Home loans
Deposit schemes
Interest rate | List of holidays
Wealth management
Contact us
Banks open on Sunday | |

FMCG sector

Table 3.9 FMCG sector

Exploration	Shopping	Quest for info	Task-directed behaviour other than shopping
Company structure Reports Society Investors Case studies Awards and recognition Search Press release Cooking Downloads Stock quotes Insider trading Leadership in business Echoupal Shareholder value Collaborate with us	Brands and information	About us History Partner information Employee information social responsibility Calendar Expert help	Careers FAQ

Implications and Conclusions

- The main purpose of the Internet is to make information readily available, and a website should be designed so that finding the required information amongst the website content is as easy as possible. Since it is easy for consumers to move to other sites, website attributes assume substantial significance.
- The purpose of this study was to identify the dimensions of website attributes that represent online shoppers' intentions for visiting product and brand websites and examine the relationship between their evaluations of the relative importance of various website attributes, with respect to the function performed by the attribute. Exploration, shopping, quest for information, and task-directed behaviour other than shopping are the primary consumer intents for venturing online and relevant website

- attributes cater to these consumer intents. The results have been listed separately for the automobile, banking, and FMCG verticals.
- While search engine optimization, online promotions, and viral marketing provide new avenues for generation of Web traffic for organizations, the website remains the most basic organizational entity, that is, the very basic component of any online traffic generation. It is in improving website attributes, navigability, and search ability that increases consumer sensitivity to the websites and while quenching his/her need for information, providing a good sensory experience, can engage the consumer to spend more time on the website.
- This research focuses on linking consumer intents to venture online, with the website attributes of a set of websites across three different industry verticals. The objective is to aid organizations in matching website attributes with relevant consumer intentions and consumer behaviour typology. Satiation, boredom, or the completion of a task results in the culmination of a typical website visit.
- Detailed analysis of consumer behaviour can not only aid manipulation of website attributes to have more and more attributes catering to the relevant consumer intent, but also, aid organizations in choosing the right website visit model, based on specific consumer behaviour.
- These studies will eventually have applications in the domains of connecting the nature of the website visit to the pattern of visit length it generates.

(The above research illustration was extracted from Jain, N., Ahuja, V., Medury, Y., (2012) 'Internet marketing and consumers online: Identification of website attributes catering to specific consumer intents in a digital paradigm'. *International Journal of Online Marketing*, IGI Global Publications, Vol. 2(3), pp. 69–81, ISSN-2156-1753).

DATABASE MARKETING

Database marketing is a form of direct marketing using databases of customers in combination with other databases to generate personalized communications that drive targeted marketing efforts at both strategic and tactical levels. A marketing database is a 'list of customers' and 'prospects' that enables strategic analysis, and individual selections for communication and customer service support. The data is organized around a customer. Compared to other forms of marketing, branding for example, the analysis of the outcome of database marketing efforts is relatively straightforward, for this reason it can be described as 'marketing with measurable results'.

Database marketing involves the gathering, storing, and mining of data that can be used to provide information on customers that might be useful in future marketing efforts (Fig. 3.6). Technology has provided the marketer with the means to collect and store large quantities of data on all their customers. Every company, no matter how decentralized, now has the ability to consolidate customer information and to gain a much better

THE ONLINE CONSUMER

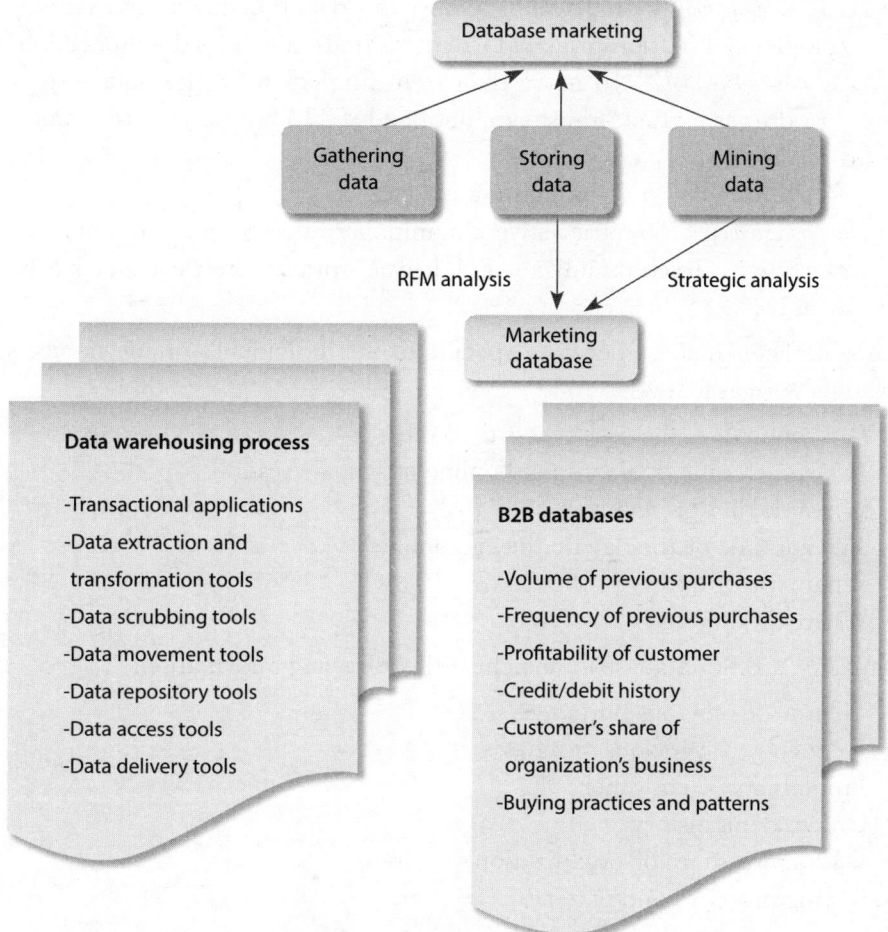

Fig. 3.6 Database marketing

picture of who its customers are, what products and services they buy, and how they like to be served.

As with all aspects of business practice, database marketing must bring an ROI which may be substantial if the practice is to be successful. In mainstream direct marketing, key measures such as recency, frequency, and monetary value (RFM) provide essential data capture elements as part of the electronic customer relationship management (*e*-CRM) and data warehousing functions for marketing purposes. The danger for any database marketer is to design a support system that contains too many fields and holds too much customer data. A balance must be struck between having too much and too little customer data.

Components of a genuine data warehousing process are[35] as follows:

- *Transactional applications*   To ensure data is stored in appropriate format
- *Data extraction and transformation tools*   To read data for business critical applications

- *Data scrubbing tools* To detect or remove raw data that may be inaccurate, out of date, incomplete, or inappropriately formatted. It also includes de-duplication of data
- *Data movement tools* To move data from immediate to the data warehouse mainly referred to as extract, transform, and load (ETL) but now more sector-specific tools are available
- *Data repository tools* To maintain metadata
- *Data access tools* To retrieve, view, manipulate, analyse, and present data
- *Data delivery* To communicate and deliver, store, and retrieve data safely for the end-user access

An *e*-marketer may gather data specific to the individual's online habits, some of the examples are as follows:

- How often does the user access the Web
- How much time do they spend online in a single session
- When do they go online
- At what time of the day do they go online
- What type of access do they have
- Where do they access the Web

Similarly, a B2B database may include the following information:

- Volume of previous purchases
- Frequency of previous purchases
- Profitability of customer
- Credit/debit history
- Customer's share of organization's business
- Buying practices and patterns

GEARING UP FOR NEW ONLINE CONSUMERS

It is clear to organizations that the online world has reshaped consumer behaviour. Companies are gearing up to face the challenges posed by the evolving consumer in three ways, (Fig. 3.7) as follows:

- Companies are focusing on analytics
- Companies have adaptive mind-sets which are open to change
- Companies respond to consumers immediately by scaling offerings rapidly when they see a positive response

Analytical Toolkit

Accenture's research (2011) suggests that organizations should invest in an analytical toolkit. Companies should use advanced analytics to identify and bridge gaps between their businesses and consumers. Many companies are getting much better at understanding customers by using analytics and most importantly, by using data-derived insights to design and improve the customer experience.

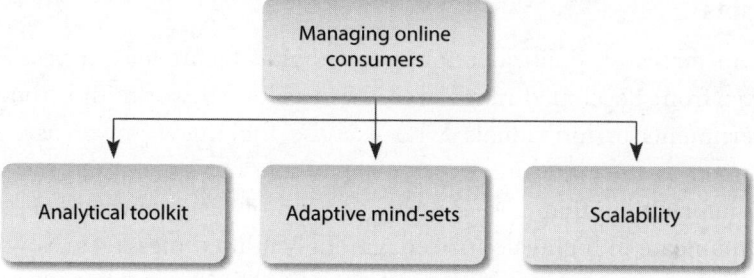

Fig. 3.7 Managing online consumers

Customer analytics is the process by which data from customer behaviour is used to help make key business decisions via market segmentation and predictive analytics. This information is used by businesses for direct marketing, site selection, and customer relationship management. Marketing provides services in order to satisfy customers. With that in mind, the productive system is considered from its beginning at the production level, to the end of the cycle at the consumer. Customer analytics plays a very important role in the prediction of customer behaviour today. Customer analytics helps companies in turning their data into something they can really use—a tool to drive their business forward. It is the intersection of hard science and common sense where data transforms into the ultimate marketing tool for companies. By spending a great deal of time with focus groups and testing ideas on key audiences to extract the nuances of consumer behaviour, business intelligence groups in organizations are able to study what their consumers like and dislike.

In the virtual world, data needs to be collected about the information circulating about a company in the online domain (Fig. 3.8). There are well-defined *social media analytics* tools which aid companies in collecting and analysing this information drawn from the online sphere. This topic is addressed in detail in Chapter 5.

In addition, a key element of an analytical toolkit which is quite significant is the ability to hire, retain, and train in-house analytics talent.

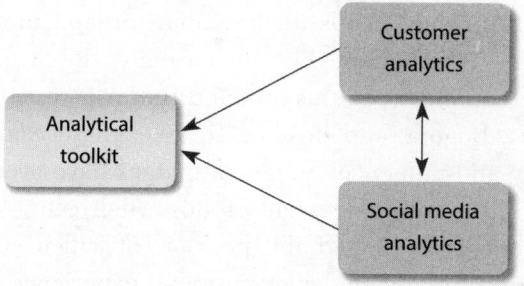

Fig. 3.8 The analytical toolkit for online consumers

Adaptive Mind-sets

The twin forces of political reform and digital technology have shifted the balance of power from developed markets to the developing world and from institutions such as governments to individuals, who exercise their new power as consumers to gain information to their advantage. The digital age has obliterated the scripted, one-way flow of information that existed during the era of just a few channels. Companies used to communicate in highly controlled, carefully crafted messages. Now corporations and consumers are engaged in unplanned, unscripted discussions. Executives now understand that any person has the potential to create a profit-threatening crisis just by hitting 'send'. At the same time, these devices and activities are generating massive amounts of data that can offer insights into consumers' lives.

This change means global markets operate at remarkable speed. Against this backdrop, companies are struggling to adapt to more powerful consumers, the increasingly rapid pace of competition, and the constant threat of disruptive innovation. Manyexecutives are recognizing that the traditional organization—characterized by highly structured processes, functional depth, and the isolation of the consumer perspective in a single function—is too slow, too expensive, and too ineffective for today's consumers and markets. The consumer-focused enterprise reflects an emerging approach that's evident in the organizational discussions, organizational structures, and new approaches to consumer engagement. Companies need to focus on their leadership and strategies to ensure that they develop adaptive mind-sets.

Leadership

The most senior executives have increased their focus on online consumers, who are simply too powerful to be ignored, the chief marketing officer (CMO) leads the cultural transformation, moving the focus on consumer perspective beyond its traditional marketing function and into core processes. This development is similar to how the importance of technology has forced the chief information officer (CIO) to take on a more strategic role. The emergence of new sources of consumer information, such as social media, has made it possible to quantify the impact of marketing efforts in granular detail. Concurrently, consumer behaviour and purchasing habits are generating greater volumes of information, elevating the importance of data analytics to business decision-making. Forward-thinking CMOs are developing organizational capabilities to aggregate and interpret this information. The increasingly global nature of competition adds another layer of complexity to this task and that is companies must cater to consumer tastes in Bombay, Bogota, and Boston. To meet these challenges, CMOs are gaining greater authority and influence. Some companies have even combined the CMO and CIO positions—an acknowledgement of how vital technology has become to serving customers. Others have created the position of chief customer officer (CCO), an executive in charge of marketing, sales, customer experience, communications, and other functions. These moves share a common objective which is to put the consumer at the centre of the conversation and bridge the organizational silos that impede collaboration across departments.

Strategy

The new strategy-development processes are founded on deeper insights about online consumers, not simply how they behave, but what motivates them. Truly understanding consumers in a global context is as challenging, as using these insights to drive disruptive innovations. All these changes are occurring while the process for strategy development moves from a highly scripted, structured process to an adaptive, inventive one.

Agile Organizations Demonstrating Scalability

Accenture's research in the above field further suggests that smart organizations react flexibly to changing consumer behaviour, scaling offerings rapidly after identifying a successful response. In the successful companies two hallmarks identify the agile organization. They respond to change rapidly, through acquisitions and investments. And they learn quickly from the changing environment, immediately sharing what they discover with stakeholders. Online auctioneer eBay's early recognition of what they call resourceful consumers—thrifty types who use online platforms to buy used products or to sell directly to other consumers—backed by an aggressive, rapid-response acquisition strategy, is a perfect example of the first hallmark. In 2000, newly launched *e*-commerce business PayPal, with its popular peer-to-peer electronic payment system, averaged about 50 times more payments per day than eBay's proprietary online payment offering. In 2002, eBay completed the acquisition of PayPal. Following the acquisition, PayPal grew rapidly within the auction site; up until the global economic recession in 2008, eBay's payment business grew more than 30% in revenues each year. By the end of 2011, PayPal accounted for 38% of eBay's total revenues. In 2007, eBay expanded its portfolio of collaborative businesses by acquiring StubHub, the 'fan-to-fan' event-ticket reseller. Like PayPal, StubHub's growth soon began to outpace that of eBay's auction site. Despite its later agreements with larger sports teams and venues, the composition of StubHub's growth was 65% of its tickets in 2011. However, it came from individual and part-time resellers indicating the growing power of the collaborative economy.

Retailers, for example, must meet the expectations of consumers accustomed to buying goods online at competitive prices and having them delivered quickly. And they must do so while creating offerings that are distinct enough to address individual preferences while still meeting expected standards of social and environmental responsibility.

For many, juggling these demands may seem like trying to square the circle, and business leaders might feel daunted by the challenge. The answer lies in responding to change with analytical skill, an adaptive mind-set, and an agile organization. The successful wedding of the scale advantages of the large with the tailored approach of the small, the traditional benefits of the old and the cutting edge of the new should be the target of the organizations. By achieving the right balance between sets of extremes, businesses can convert consumer change to their advantage.

PRACTITIONER PERSPECTIVE

Social media is not a pastime for the CEOs of the twenty-first century but a critical tool for survival in the digital era. CEOs usually spends millions on sophisticated software to set up 'cockpits' that allow them to obtain information throughout their companies, and from their markets. In one fell swoop, social media, particularly Twitter, gives this power to us at no cost! I receive real-time critical feedback, inputs, and market responses from the entire universe of our stakeholders.

Anand Mahindra, Chairman and MD, Mahindra and Mahindra, India

One of the key areas where HDFC is using Twitter is as a channel for customer service as customers expect a quick response to their queries. HDFC is also using the virtual world to promote offers, new launches, news updates, quizzes and polls, cross-linking across platforms.

Kartik Jain, Head, Marketing, HDFC Bank

If companies keep customer needs above their own constraints, it is likely that they will find a way to remove the constraints sooner or later.

Sachin Bansal, Founder and CEO, Flipkart

SUMMARY

The Internet today is transforming companies' customization and advertising. It is an efficiency enhancer and entertainment provider. With its increasing popularity, the Internet now occupies a central role in young educated people's lives, all over the world. Companies need to analyse Internet user demographics, gender, race, employment status, and education parameters to segment and profile current and prospective consumers effectively. The digital paradigm plays two very significant roles in marketing—influencing consumer behaviour and harnessing consumer intelligence. While it is vital for an organization to evaluate consumer intentions and provide consumers the necessary information they are looking for, it is equally important to collecting consumer data by studying the consumer behavioural patterns on the Internet and subsequently nurturing long-term relationships with consumers. The Internet has subsequently commenced playing a very significant role in the marketing value chain encompassing value identification, creation, and delivery thereby impacting marketing economics by reducing transaction cost and time. Consumer data analysis, content analysis, and predictive modelling are the buzzwords of today and digital marketing coupled with digital media are twin growth engines for organizations in contemporary times. The Read/Write Web or Web 2.0 as it is termed has ushered in a tremendous opportunity for e-marketers: the opportunity of customer advocacy. Even in the case of product categories previously considered as generic (such as travel and vacation services), vendors discover that they can gain and retain customers by offering something more than only low prices. Exploration, shopping, quest for information, and task-directed behaviour other than shopping are the primary consumer intents for venturing online and relevant website attributes cater to these consumer intents. Organizations can differentiate between task-directed consumer behaviour and exploratory consumer browsing. Websites have a short time to communicate with the visitors, to deliver a message, to build a brand image, to engage in commerce, and to persuade visitors. There are a host of consumer website visit models including the random surfer model and the look ahead model which can be used by organizations to study and predict consumer behaviour online. Web applications are becoming increasingly popular due to the advantages they offer to users such as transparency, referrals and contacts with other users along with their effect on customer power. Consumer online behaviour in a B2C context can be classified into explicit and implied behaviour. Gaining momentum is database marketing—a form of direct marketing using databases of customers in combination with other databases to generate personalized communications that can drive targeted marketing efforts at both strategic and tactical levels.

Concept Review Questions

1. List the salient features of the digital ecosystem. How is the rise of the importance of the virtual paradigm significant for marketing? Discuss the potential benefits of *e*-marketing for organizations.
2. Discuss the various Web visit models. How can companies empirically analyse the consumer website visit to extract his/her potential behaviour and relevance to the organization?
3. How has the Internet impacted the consumer decision-making process? Discuss.
4. Discuss potential *e*-metrics used for
   (a) Increasing sales
   (b) Generating sales leads
   (c) Maximizing readership
5. Differentiate between
   (a) Task-directed and experiential online behaviour
   (b) Explicit and implied consumer online behaviour
   (c) Behavioural targeting versus contextual targeting
6. How has Web 2.0 provided companies with the opportunity of customer advocacy? Discuss with examples.
7. What is database marketing? How can an *e*-marketer gather data specific to an individual's online habits? What are the typical components of a B2B marketing database?

Critical Thinking Questions

1. Take the example of any FMCG company. Discuss various Web 2.0 tools that the company is using to
   (a) interact with consumers
   (b) build consumer engagement
   (c) share new campaigns
   Develop a case study on the successful usage of one Web 2.0 tool in detail by the company.

2. Visit the Sales and Marketing Department of any Fortune 500 company. Study how the company is using database marketing to increase its sales. What data extraction and transformation tools does the company use?
3. Create a list of 10 websites each from the following sectors:
   (a) Automobile
   (b) Banking
   (c) Consumer durables
   (d) *E*-commerce

   Create a framework to establish which websites across each sector are more user friendly than the others.
4. Conduct an exploratory search on Google for a bank from which you want to secure a housing loan. Which Banking websites feature highest in the search process? How can banks make their websites and products more visible online to cater to exploratory consumer browsing?

Practising Digital Marketing

Assume that you are launching a new bank in an urban setting of India. This bank is a subsidiary of a multinational chain. Create strategies for the following:
(a) Using the Internet to promote offers, new launches, news updates, quizzes and polls, and cross-linking across platforms
(b) Using the Internet for virtual banking
(c) Conduct a survey using a database of 100 consumers for the hypothetical bank, comprising individuals, across different age and qualification parameters. Study their Internet usage volume and statistics. What do you infer for the bank? Do usage patterns vary for different product typologies in the banking domain? Do usage patterns vary on the basis of consumer demographics?

References

1. Majumdar, R., (2010). 'Consumer Behaviour: Insights From Indian Market'. PHI Learning Pvt. Ltd.
2. Ranganathan, C. and Ganapathy, S., (2002). 'Key dimensions of business-to-consumer web sites'. *Information and Management*, Vol. 39(6), pp. 457–465.
3. Long, M.M. and Schiffman, L.G., (2000). 'Consumption values and relationships: Segmenting the market for frequency programs'. *Journal of Consumer Marketing*, Vol. 17(3), pp. 214–232.
4. Rothman, A.J., Bartels, R.D., Wlaschin, J., and Salovey, P., (2006). 'The strategic use of gain-and loss-framed messages to promote healthy behavior: How theory can inform practice'. *Journal of Communication*, Vol. 56(s1), pp. S202–S220.
5. Koufaris, M., (2002). 'Applying the technology acceptance model and flow theory to online consumer behaviour'. *Information Systems Research*, Vol. 13(2), pp. 205–223.
6. Shang, R.A., Chen, Y.C., and Liao, H.J., (2006). 'The value of participation in virtual consumer communities on brand loyalty'. *Internet Research*, Vol. 16(4), pp. 398–418.
7. Coker, B.L.S., Ashill, N.J., and Hope, B., (2011). 'Measuring Internet product purchase risk'. *European Journal of Marketing*, Vol. 45(7/8), pp. 1130–1151.
8. Ventulett, T., Hardy, D.T., Leitess, J.K., Huffaker, M., McNaught, D., and Troxell, B., (2001). U.S. Patent Application 09/760,026.
9. Pavlou, P.A. and Fygenson, M., (2006). 'Understanding and predicting electronic commerce adoption: An extension of the theory of planned behavior'. *MIS Quarterly*, Vol. 30(1), pp. 115–143.
10. Weisberg, J., Te'eni, D., and Arman, L., (2011). 'Past purchase and intention to purchase in *e*-commerce: The mediation of social presence and trust'. *Internet Research*, Vol. 21(1), pp. 82–96.
11. Dadzie, K.Q., Johnston, W.J., and Pels, J., (2008). 'Business-to-business marketing practices in West Africa, Argentina and the United States'. *Journal of Business and Industrial Marketing*, Vol. 23(2), pp. 115–123.

12. Cristobal, E., Flavián, C., and Guinalíu, M., (2007). 'Perceived e-service quality (PeSQ): Measurement validation and effects on consumer satisfaction and web site loyalty'. *Managing Service Quality*, Vol. 17(3), pp. 317–340.
13. Ba, S. and Johansson, W.C., (2008). 'An exploratory study of the impact of e-service process on online customer satisfaction'. *Production and Operations Management*, Vol. 17(1), pp. 107–119.
14. Park, C.H. and Kim, Y.G., (2003). 'A framework of dynamic CRM: Linking marketing with information strategy'. *Business Process Management Journal*, Vol. 9(5), pp. 652–671.
15. Singh, N., Zhao, H., and Hu, X., (2005). 'Analyzing the cultural content of web sites: A cross-national comparison of China, India, Japan, and US'. *International Marketing Review*, Vol. 22(2), pp. 129–146.
15a. Hanson, W. and Kalyanam, K., (2007). Web visit models, *Internet Marketing and E-commerce*, Thomson-South Western.
16. Petrovic, D., (2007). 'Analysis of consumer behaviour online'. *Analogik.com, Tech. Rep.*
17. Koiso-Kanttila, N., (2005). 'Time, attention, authenticity and consumer benefits of the web'. *Business Horizons*, Vol. 48(1), pp. 63–70.
18. Lindstrom, M., (2004). 'Branding is no longer child's play!'. *Journal of Consumer Marketing*, Vol. 21(3), pp. 175–182.
19. Kim, J., Jin, B., and Swinney, J.L., (2009). 'The role of e-tail quality, e-satisfaction and e-trust in online loyalty development process'. *Journal of Retailing and Consumer Services*, Vol. 16(4), pp. 239–247.
20. Kurnia, S. and Schubert, P., (2006). 'Toward achieving customer satisfaction in online grocery shopping'. *Electronic Customer Relationship Management. US: ME Sharpe, Inc*, pp. 177–196.
21. Han, J.K., Chung, S.W., and Sohn, Y.S., (2009). 'Technology convergence: When do consumers prefer converged products to dedicated products?' *Journal of Marketing*, Vol. 73(4), pp. 97–108.
22. Gounaris, S., Dimitriadis, S., and Stathakopoulos, V., (2010). 'An examination of the effects of service quality and satisfaction on customers' behavioural intentions in e-shopping'. *Journal of Services Marketing*, Vol. 24(2), pp. 142–156.
23. Lester, S.W., Tomkovick, C., Wells, T., Flunker, L., and Kickul, J., (2005). 'Does service-learning add value? Examining the perspectives of multiple stakeholders. *Academy of Management Learning and Education*, Vol. 4(3), pp. 278–294.
24. Sánchez-Franco, M.J. and Roldán, J.L., (2005). 'Web acceptance and usage model: A comparison between goal-directed and experiential web users'. *Internet Research*, Vol. 15(1), pp. 21–48.
25. Cotte, J., Chowdhury, T.G., Ratneshwar, S., and Ricci, L.M., (2006). 'Pleasure or utility? Time planning style and Web usage behaviors'. *Journal of Interactive Marketing*, Vol. 20(1), pp. 45–57.
26. Gofman, A., Moskowitz, H. R., and Mets, T., (2009). 'Integrating science into web design: Consumer-driven web site optimization'. *Journal of Consumer Marketing*, Vol. 26(4), pp. 286–298.
27. Morosan, C. and Jeong, M., (2008). 'Users' perceptions of two types of hotel reservation websites'. *International Journal of Hospitality Management*, Vol. 27(2), pp. 284–292.
28. Urban, G.L., (2005). 'Customer advocacy: A new era in marketing?' *Journal of Public Policy and Marketing*, Vol. 24(1), pp. 155–159.
29. BizReport, 30 August, 2007.
30. Andreasen, A.R. and Kotler, P., *Strategic Marketing for Non-profit Organizations*, NJ: Prentice Hall, 2003, pp. 44–53.
31. Constantinides, E., (2004). 'Influencing the online consumer's behavior: the web experience'. *Internet Research*, Vol. 14(2), pp. 111–126.
32. Gay, R., Charlesworth, A., and Esen, R., *Online Marketing: A Customer-Led Approach*. OUP, Oxford, 2007.
33. Gilden, J., (2006). 'Travel websites gain visitors by offering more than low prices', *Los Angeles Times*, 22 January, 2006.
34. Gillin, P., (2007). 'Podcasting, blogs cause major boost'. *B to B.*, Vol. 92(5), pp. 32–33.
35. Kalakota, R. and Robinson, M., *E-business Roadmap for Success*, First Edition, USA: Addison Wesley Longman Inc., New York, 1999, pp. 109–134.

Customer Relationship Management in a Web 2.0 World

> **LEARNING OBJECTIVES**
>
> *After reading this chapter, you will be able to:*
> - Understand the concept of customer relationship management (CRM) and its significance in the era of digital marketing
> - Observe the difference between CRM processes and CRM technology
> - Get acquainted with the concept of ECRM
> - Appreciate key CRM applications
> - Observe the difference among operational, analytical, and collaborative CRM
> - Understand the concepts of Sales Force Automation (SFA), Campaign Management, Customer Service and Support (CSS), Customer Value Management (CVM), and Key Account Management (KAM)

A study of the online marketing mix (Chapter 2) brings some imperative aspects to the forefront. Marketing is now centred on generating consumer engagement in the online world, greater consumer personalization, and subsequently, greater efforts towards building relationships between the brand and consumer in the online domain. The erstwhile concept of CRM has gained more importance in the context of the need for more online consumer traffic on websites and social networks and better online customer experience management. To get a broader perspective, companies have gained access to the online world, which serves as a stupendous medium to interact with the existing customers, retain them, and stimulate re-purchase.

This chapter addresses the various concepts associated with CRM, realigns them to the needs of the online world, and depicts why they are important for organizations.

WHAT IS CUSTOMER RELATIONSHIP MANAGEMENT (CRM)?

CRM is the application of technology that emphasizes on individuals or one-to-one relationships with customers by integrating database knowledge with the long-term prospects of growth and customer loyalty. Managing a successful CRM implementation requires an integrated and balanced approach to technology, process, and people.[1] CRM is an enterprise-wide initiative that belongs to all the areas of an organization.[2] It reflects a comprehensive strategy and the process of acquiring, retaining, and partnering with selective customers to create a superior value for the company and customer. CRM is a term for the methodologies, technologies, and *e*-commerce capabilities used by the firms to manage customer relationships.

WHY CUSTOMER RELATIONSHIP MANAGEMENT?

It is said that it costs five times more to acquire a new customer than to retain an old one. Firms need to invest in building consumer loyalty by trying to cement business relationships and focus on consumer retention. A consistent effort towards enhancing the value proposition offered to customers and transforming customer experiences, while building a rapport with them, is the customer-centric business approach required by organizations today.

Businesses tend to respond to customer attrition on a reactive basis, and by that time it is too late to initiate a reversal in the consumer decision. This is where CRM models and predictive analysis comes into play. By leveraging consumer intelligence appropriately, firms can initiate more proactive marketing strategies directed towards consumer retention. By a frequent examination of a customer's past purchase patterns, spending, past response rates across channels, and other behavioural data, predictive models can identify future patterns in consumer behaviour, and consumer targeting strategies can be developed accordingly. CRM analytics helps identify consumers with a higher likelihood of responding to a particular marketing offer. Additional information about the consumers' demographic, geographic, and other characteristics can be used to make more accurate predictions. Targeting appropriate consumers can lead to a substantial increase in response rates, which can lead to a significant reduction in cost per acquisition.

Analyst firm Forrester Research recommends several CRM 2.0 best practices for organizations to benefit from the *collaborative-web-created* social media technologies. To quote William Band, VP and principal analyst for business process and applications at Forrester Research, the true nature of the 2.0 shift is less about technology and more about the shift in control and power.

'Web 2.0 began as a user-focused revolution, remaking the consumer Web into a landscape that is easy to use, efficient to navigate, populated by self-generated content (versus corporate propaganda), and driven by *adhoc* and established communities of people with similar interests. In a Web 2.0 world, power moves from institutions to consumers, because they can now rapidly connect and digitally converse among themselves about the products and services they buy.'

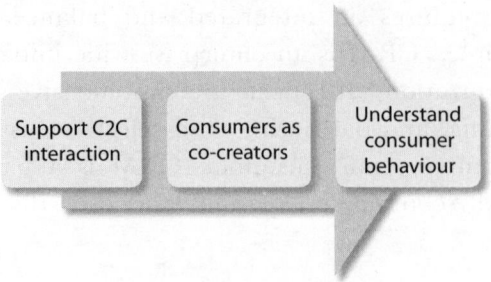

Fig. 4.1 CRM best practices

The following extract is from Forrester's best practices for CRM practitioners' research (Fig. 4.1):

- Support customer-to-customer interaction. Sharing resources via file exchanges (such as VoIP and content networks) allow nodes in the network (individuals) to sustain one another and to rely less on institutional support.
- Embrace customers as co-creators. Soliciting user input is cheaper, better, and faster than more-structured, top-down methods of product development. This means complete strangers can co-develop open-source software and collaborative information banks such as Wikipedia.
- Understand the new consumer-behaviour patterns. Although social computing is having a profound effect on buyers, it affects different types of consumers in different ways. Effective next-generation CRM strategies will be grounded in a deep understanding of social consumer behaviour as well as more traditional demographic and psychographic attributes.

This clearly places the customer at the centre of the CRM function and demonstrates to organizations the value of monitoring and tracking each consumer interaction, as positive peer-to-peer consumer conversations can spell into long-term organizational gains. This shows the companies the need to value the consumer feedback in the context of what they think about current and potential products and the need to study the behavioural patterns of the consumer in detail to ensure that the opportunities generated out of this analysis can be used by companies for greater profits.

CRM assumes manifold significance in the online domain in the following ways:

- CRM software packages aid the interaction between the customer and the company, enabling the company to co-ordinate and integrate all the communication efforts so that the customer is presented with a unified message and image.
- CRM coordinates touch-points around a common view of the customer. As the business gets larger and the number of customer relationships to be managed increases exponentially, it calls for an integration of different business departments to collaborate the customer information to provide a unified view of customer interaction to serve the customers better. In the context of the online world, this integration is required across all the elements of the virtual medium where the company has an online presence, namely websites, blogs, online communities, etc.

- CRM processes shape the interactions between a company and its customers with the goal of maximizing current and lifetime value of customers for the company as well as maximizing satisfaction for customers.[3]

The above characteristics make CRM a vital strategic tool that companies need to embrace for better relationship marketing and greater consumer profitability through enhanced customer satisfaction in the virtual arena.

A detailed analysis of the available definitions in the domain of CRM helped us compile the following definitions:

- CRM is a comprehensive business strategy to empower the internal functioning of an organization with the aim to identify, acquire, deliver, develop, and retain customers (Fig. 4.2). With the use of ever changing technology,[6] this process seeks to integrate various functions of an organization such that it becomes effective and efficient in the long run. This enables the organization to have a high customer share and market share to gain a long-term competitive advantage.
- CRM is important because it costs six to seven times more to acquire a new customer than to retain an existing one. An increase in customer retention rate by 5% can possibly increase the profits by up to 95%. Further, all customers do not contribute equally to the firm's bottom line, and thus are not equally valuable for the company.[7]

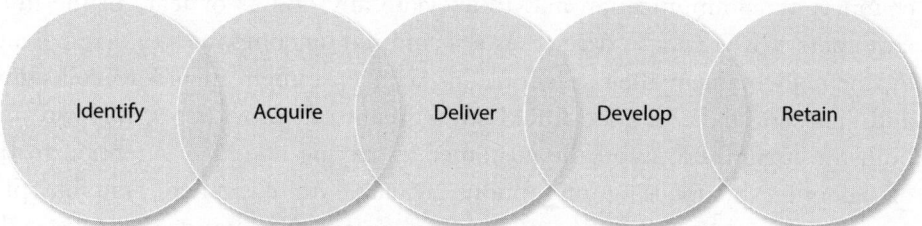

Fig. 4.2 CRM as a business strategy for customers

The value of targeting the right kind of customers using digital marketing has become so important that the entire success and failure of an organization depends on customer acquisition and retention. It is for this reason that online technology has become very important in marketing to provide a wholesome understanding about customers. Effective data generation and data analysis, backed with an appropriate data mining, can help organizations reap significant benefits.

THE GOALS OF CUSTOMER RELATIONSHIP MANAGEMENT

- Build long-term and profitable relationships with chosen customers.
- Get closer to those customers with every point of contact with them.[8]

The primary objective of most organizations (Fig. 4.3) is customer acquisition followed by customer retention. The heart of marketing is relationships, and nurturing long-term relationships should be the goal of marketing practice.[9]

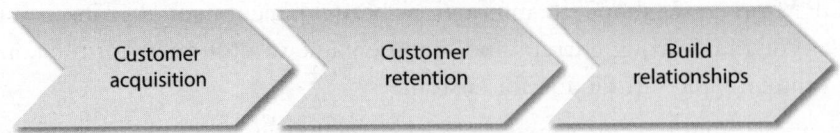

Fig. 4.3 The goals of CRM

Acquisition is a vital stage in building a customer relationship, and a focused and contextual interaction with the customers with respect to their roles (Fig. 4.4) as initiators, influencers, deciders, buyers, and users is required by any organization while moving towards growth or success. Digital marketing needs to act as a facilitator in moving the consumer from the role of an initiator to the role of a user.

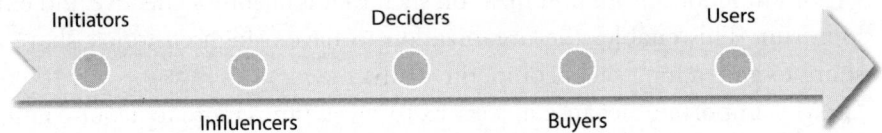

Fig. 4.4 Customer roles

A vital strategy to achieve acquisition is to initiate a forum for open and integrated channels of communication and to alleviate any doubts or fears in the minds of the customers. CRM can be defined as a term used by companies to define concepts used by them to manage their relationships with customers including collecting, storing, and analysing data. A good CRM strategy aims at providing a win-win platform for both the organization and the customer by paying adequate attention to the process of adoption by focusing on options available to customers, suitable promotional campaigns, and concentration on existing customers. The idea is to keep the current and prospective customers abreast with the developments in the organization and also provide clarifications of any information circulating in the environment. An important requisite of a good customer information management (CIM) system is that it should acquire customer database and feedback, serve as an active listening mechanism, and form relationships with customers by focusing on their perspective, thereby achieving customer retention. Customer retention is the process of keeping customers loyal to a company for an unending period by meeting their needs and expectations.

The foundation of CRM (Fig. 4.5) is built on an interactive process of learning and customization. Companies interact with customers and learn about them, and through

Fig. 4.5 The foundation of CRM

the process of incorporating feedback and co-creation, develop a level of intimacy with them. While this serves the objective of better marketing investment prioritization, improving marketing intelligence will definitely aid firms in improving the selling context. Organizational processes need to change in a way that the organization can recognize individual customers and extract information on who they are and what they want. Customers want to be listened to; they do not want to be the passive receptors of a company's sales pitch. CRM is a comprehensive business and marketing strategy that integrates technology, process, and all the business activities around the customer.[10]

CRM is an enterprise-wide approach to understanding and influencing customer behaviour through meaningful communication to improve customer acquisition, customer retention, customer loyalty, and customer profitability. CRM can be viewed as an application of one-to-one and relationship marketing, responding to an individual customer on the basis of what the customer says, and what else is known about that customer.[11] It is a management approach that enables organizations to identify, attract and increase retention of profitable customers by managing relationships with them[5] and further identifying strategically-significant customers.[5]

In the academic community, the terms 'relationship marketing' and CRM are often used interchangeably.[12] The heart of marketing is relationships, and nurturing long-term relationships should be the goal of marketing practise.[13] Five macro environmental factors responsible for the growth of relationship orientation in marketing[14] included the following:

- Rapid technological advancements, especially in the field of information technology
- Adoption of total quality programmes by companies
- Growth of the service economy
- Organizational development processes leading to the empowerment of individuals and teams
- An increase in competitive intensity leading to concern for customer retention

Customers are now more than ever demanding a different relationship with their suppliers, and managing a close relationship has become a central aspect in delivering business goals.[15] A company's product can quickly be compared to another, and many companies are offering very similar products or services to each other. With this in mind, the relationship experience becomes one of the greatest competitive aspects for a company's survival. Increased competition reduces brand loyalty thereby making the job of the marketers more complex. Further, customers also become indifferent to the myriad marketing messages being thrust upon them. As a result, marketing needs to be more well directed and specific, because customers, whether consumers or businesses, do not want more choices. They want exactly what they want, when, where and how they want it, and technology now makes it possible for companies to give it to them.[4]

Customers have hidden or overt preferences, which marketers can reveal by building a learning relationship. Earlier, marketers were attempting to interpret consumer needs on the basis of their buying behaviours. Now, with the arrival of consumer-generated media, which will be discussed in the next section, marketers have another avenue to learn about the consumer. The objective is to keep the consumers satisfied and keep them loyal towards the company or brand. CRM, which has also been described as 'information-enabled relationship marketing',[16] comprises processes used by organizations to manage consumer relationships, which also include collecting, storing, and analysing data and is often termed as data-driven marketing. CRM attempts to provide a strategic bridge between information technology (IT) and marketing strategies aimed at building long-term relationships and profitability. This requires 'information-intensive strategies'.[17] It is vital to maintain appropriate CIM systems by acquiring customer databases and consolidating customer feedback.

Four main CRM strategic capabilities[18] includes the following (Fig. 4.6):

- *Technology* This will ensure the desired functionality for the CRM practise.
- *People*[19] Skills, abilities, and attitudes of the people responsible for the CRM initiative.
- *Process* The processes that the company has identified to ensure that the CRM objectives are fulfilled; these include the transactional interactions with the customers.
- *Knowledge and insight* To ensure stronger and deeper relationships with the right set of customers, companies need to identify the right approaches that will help them gain knowledge to gain insight for enhancing the customer value significantly.

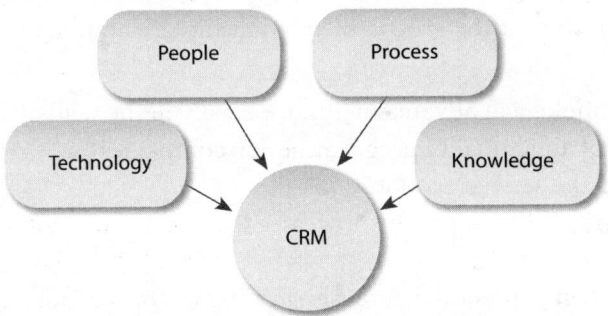

Fig. 4.6 CRM strategic capabilities

Digital marketers can achieve higher levels of success by using the above four main CRM capabilities to their advantage.

The following two definitions of CRM appear practical and meaningful for the domain of digital marketing.

- Customer acquisition and retention are the twin objectives of CRM.
- CRM is a strategic approach that is concerned with creating improved shareholder value through the development of appropriate relationships with key customers and customer segments.

CRM unites the potential of relationship marketing strategies and IT to create profitable, long-term relationships with customers and other key stakeholders. CRM provides enhanced opportunities to use data and information to both understand customers and co-create value with them. This requires a cross-functional integration of processes, people, operations, and marketing capabilities that are enabled through information, technology, and applications. Figure 4.7 shows in detail the building blocks of CRM, which needs to be taken into consideration when an organization incorporates CRM into its strategic plan. Digital marketing companies need to develop a CRM vision, followed

- CRM vision
- CRM strategy
- ✓ Relationship intensity
- ✓ Relationship levels
- Valued customer experience
- Organizational collaboration
- ✓ CRM-SCM integration
- ✓ Extranet
- CRM processes
  - ✓ Identifying customers
  - ✓ Differentiating customers
  - ✓ Customizing the marketing mix
- CRM information
- CRM technology

Fig. 4.7 The building blocks of CRM

EXHIBIT 4.1 ICICI Bank and Online CRM

ICICI Bank is India's second-largest bank with total network of 2,035 branches and about 5,518 ATMs in India and presence in 18 countries. ICICI Bank offers a wide range of banking products and financial services to corporate and retail customers through a variety of delivery channels and through its specialized subsidiaries in the areas of investment banking, life and non-life insurance, venture capital and asset management. The Bank currently has subsidiaries in the United Kingdom, Russia and Canada, branches in United States, Singapore, Bahrain, Hong Kong, Sri Lanka, Qatar and Dubai International Finance Centre and representative offices in United Arab Emirates.

The bank uses Online CRM initiatives for using technology to provide consumers with greater customer convenience, and focuses on automating and improving the business processes associated with managing relationship in the area of sales, marketing and customer service and support.

The CRM software applications are not only intended to facilitate the coordination of multiple business functions but also to support to coordinate multiple channels of communication with the customers as face to face, call centers, ATMs, web, telephones, kiosk, bank branch and sales associates, etc. so as to enable the bank to carryout the cradle to give the customer management more efficiently. ICICI uses SIEBEL software to manage its Customers, for providing an integrated single view of the end customer across product lines and channels.

by a CRM strategy in the context of relationship intensity and relationship levels. The dimensions of the valued customer experience need to be clearly defined. A game plan for organizational collaboration is required at various levels for CRM–SCM (supply chain management) integration and extranets to be established for communication within the organization, both cross functional and across different hierarchical levels. Well-defined CRM processes need to be established for customer identification and differentiation as well as customization of the marketing mix. The utilization of CRM information for deriving actionable intelligence and pillars of CRM technology constitute the other building blocks of CRM in any organization.

BENEFITS OF ELECTRONIC CRM TECHNOLOGY IN ONLINE BANKING

- Complaints and queries management to respond to consumer issues
- Customer retention by tracking consumer behaviour and identifying risky cases
- Cross selling and up selling to already existing consumers
- Customer-contact management
- Mass customization by providing all relevant information to the consumers on the website
- Enabling consumers to manage banking transactions through the Web
- Providing *e*-lobby, a self-service banking centre started by the bank for bill payment, cash withdrawals, video conferencing with customer service executives, online banking, and other such transitions without any assistance

Other benefits of *e*-CRM include the following:

Roaming current account, funds transfer, bill payment, receiving funds, ticket booking, prepaid mobile recharge, online tax calculation, online share trading and online loans, and credit cards.

ICICI is able to further use *e*-CRM by monitoring consumer behaviour and further segmenting and profiling its consumers. The bank is further using consumer feedback to streamline operations to reduce the cost of operation and increase customer loyalty.

CUSTOMER RELATION MANAGEMENT PROCESSES

They can be broadly divided into five categories[20] (Fig. 4.8), which are as follows:

- *The strategy development process* This process requires a dual focus on the organization's business strategy and its customer strategy.
- *The value creation process* The value creation process transforms the outputs of the strategy development process into programmes that both extract and deliver value. The three key elements of the value creation process are: (a) determining what value the company can provide to its customer; (b) determining what value the company can receive from its customers; and (c) by successfully managing this value exchange that involves a process of co-creation or co-production, maximizing the lifetime value of desirable customer segments.

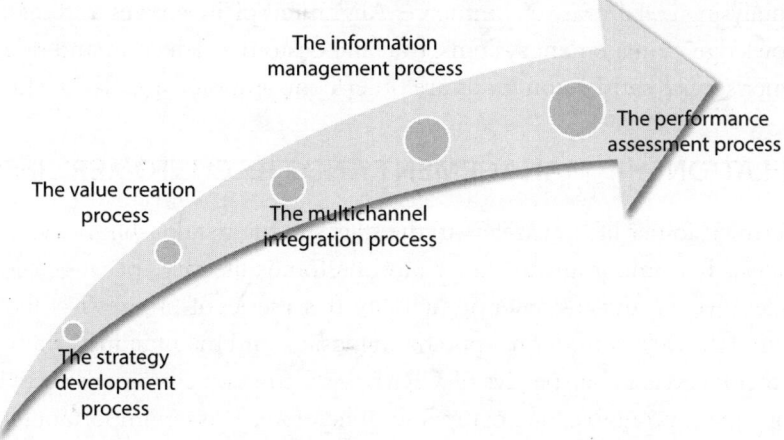

Fig. 4.8 CRM processes

- *The multichannel integration process*   The multichannel integration process is arguably one of the most important processes in CRM, because it takes the outputs of the business strategy and value creation processes and translates them into value-adding activities with customers.
- *The information management process*   The information management process is concerned with the collection, collation, and use of customer data and information from all customer contact points to generate customer insight and appropriate marketing responses. The key material elements of the information management process are the data repository, which provides a corporate memory of customers; IT systems, which include the organization's computer hardware, software, and middleware; analysis tools; and front office and back office applications, which support the many activities involved in interfacing directly with customers and managing internal operations, administration, and supplier relationships.
- *The performance assessment process*   The performance assessment process covers the essential task of ensuring that the organization's strategic aims in terms of CRM are being delivered to an appropriate and acceptable standard and that a basis for future improvement is established. This process can be viewed as having two main components, which are shareholder results, which provide a macro view of the overall relationships that drive performance and performance monitoring, which provides a more detailed, micro view of metrics and key performance indicators.

ROLE OF CUSTOMER RELATIONSHIP MANAGEMENT TECHNOLOGY

CRM technology aims at the analysis of customer revenue and cost data to identify current and future high-value customers to enable organizations to target their direct marketing efforts better. In this context, CRM tools help companies capture relevant product and service behaviour data, create new distribution channels, develop new pricing models, build communities, process transactions faster, and provide better information to the front line. In addition, included are functions for managing logistics and supply chain more efficiently as also catalysing collaborative commerce. Alignment of incentives and metrics, deployment of knowledge management systems, tracking customer defection and retention levels, and customer service satisfaction levels are other contributions of CRM technology.[21]

CUSTOMER RELATIONSHIP MANAGEMENT AND THE CUSTOMER LIFECYCLE

The term customer lifecycle refers to the stages in the relationship between a customer and a business. It is important to understand customer lifecycle, because it relates directly to customer revenue and customer profitability. It is a series of progressive steps that a customer goes through while considering, purchasing, using, and maintaining loyalty to the company. Customer lifecycle in perspective of CRM also focuses on customer selectivity. All customers are not equally profitable for a company.[22] Therefore, it is very important for an organization to customize its one-to-one marketing programmes by carefully targeting and segmenting its customers. The organizations can even go for customer outsourcing such that the company allocates its valuable resources to customers it wants to serve the best. This will not only help an organization filter its customers but, most importantly, it will aid in identifying the methods that are most cost effective, thus creating value for both the organization and the customer. Marketers say there are three ways to increase a customer's value, which are as follows:

- Increase their use (or purchases) of products they already have;
- Sell them more or higher-margin products; and
- Keep the customers for a longer period of time

There are five types of customers in the customer lifecycle (Fig. 4.9). Digital marketers can do well to identify the customers and treat them accordingly.

Fig. 4.9 Types of customers in the customer lifecycle

- *Prospects* People who are not yet customers but are in the target market.
- *Responders* They are prospects who have exhibited some interest, for instance, by filling out an application or registering on a website.
- *New customers* They are responders who have made a commitment, usually an agreement to pay, such as having made a first purchase, having signed a contract, or having registered at a site with some personal information.
- *Established customers* They are those new customers who return, that is, for whom the relationship is hopefully broadening or deepening.

- *Former customers* They are those who have left, either as a result of voluntary attrition (because they have defected to a competitor or no longer see value in the product) or forced attrition (because they are no longer in the target market, for instance, because they have moved).

From the perspective of CRM the customer lifecycle has been divided into five progressive stages, which are as follows:

- *Identification* At this stage, a company identifies the right set of customers to be targeted and offers its products and services in the light of its marketing objectives.
- *Acquisition* A company promotes its products and services to the set of customers identified and acquire the customers by selling its products and services.
- *Delivery* At this stage, the company sells the product or service. This is an important stage as the customers experience the company and its offerings first hand.
- *Development* Here the focus is on maximizing the value of the customers by delivering customized products[23] and cross-selling. Cross-selling increases the existing customer value and also broadens the relationship with the customer.
- *Retention* Customer-retention stage refers to the proactive steps taken by the organization to detect and prevent customer churn. This helps in increasing the customer-base value to the organization.

BONDING FOR CUSTOMER RELATIONSHIP

The CRM industry is presently undergoing a renaissance of sorts. It's moving from the relatively staid function of maintaining customer records and managing trouble tickets to full-on enablement of primary customer engagement itself. The following section discusses different types of customer bonds (Fig. 4.10). Needless to say, companies are increasingly using their virtual presence to build these disparate bonds with their consumers.

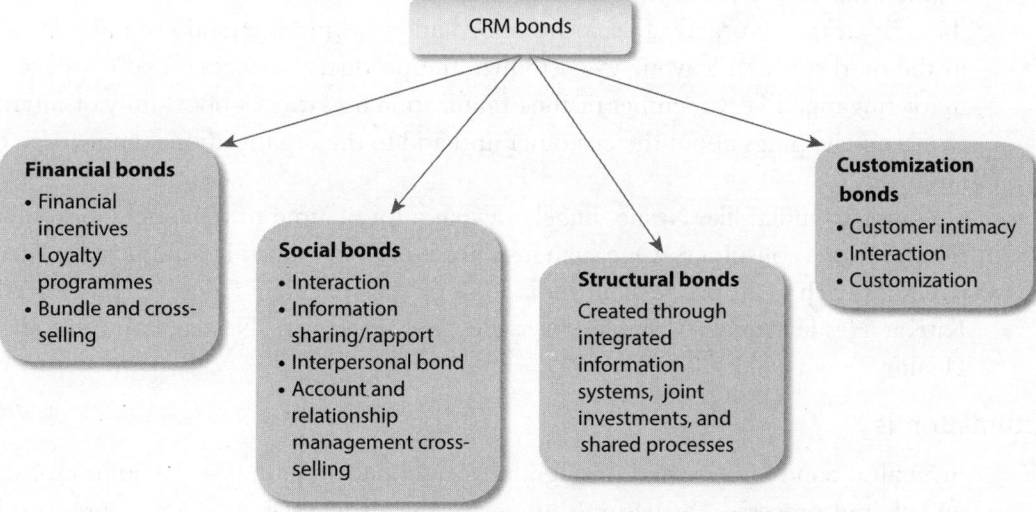

Fig. 4.10 CRM bonds

Financial Bonds

Financial bonds tie in the customer primarily through financial incentives—lower prices for volumes or for customers who have been patronizing the firm over a period of time. Loyalty programmes such as frequent-flyer programmes, reward programmes of hotels, and credit cards are examples of financial bonding through volume and frequency rewards. Bundle and cross-selling is seen in the case of magazine subscriptions, credit cards, telecom, and Internet services in which customers can buy other services provided by the same provider or someone else at a lower cost. For example, the Citibank Suvidha Loyalty Program brings exciting benefits for customers for simply using their Citibank Suvidha account. They earn Suvidha Loyalty points for all banking services they use. They can now redeem their Suvidha Loyalty points online for a wide range of gifts. You can redeem your Citibank Suvidha Loyalty points on Citibank online at www.citibank.com/india.

Social Bonds

Marketers build social bonds with customers by viewing them as clients who are not merely nameless faces. They find ways to keep in touch with them and interact with them to find their changing needs and offer solutions. It is easy to visualize social bonds of the personal kind in the context of professional and personal service providers. During interactions, information sharing and rapport are necessary for providing the service, as they also cement a social, interpersonal bond. Opportunities for social bonding also exist in business markets where the account/relationship managers work very closely with the client's team. This helps them build social bonds that transcend the commercial transactions.

Customization Bonds

Intimate knowledge of customers and their needs developed through a learning relationship is very useful in retaining valuable customers. Customer intimacy connotes that the customer is actively sharing information during interactions and contributing in the marketer's endeavour to customize the products, services, or any aspect of the marketing mix. Every member of the organization uses every opportunity of interaction to learn new things about the customer and add to the organizational knowledge of the customer.

Brands in India, like Nestle, hugely devote a lot of time to building a customization bond with the consumers. One such instance is of Nestle hosting innumerable Facebook pages for each of its products in India—Meri Maggi, Maggi Creative Kitchen, Alpino, KitKat, Nestle Munch, Milkmaid, Nescafe, Nescafe Sunrise, Nestea, Baby and Me, Start Healthy Stay Healthy.

Structural Bonds

Structural bonds are created through integrated information systems, joint investments, and shared processes. Structural bonds are the strongest bonds and subsequently the most difficult to break. Companies like HDFC, India, have developed a structural bond with the customers using Net banking—their Internet banking service. By allowing consumers to perform all transactions without leaving the comforts of their home, HDFC has been able to build a relationship with the customer.

Structural bonds are stronger than customization bonds, and customization bonds are stronger than social and financial bonds. As the bonds become stronger, customer loyalty increases and the opportunities and scope for reaping the benefits of relationship marketing increases.

ELECTRONIC CUSTOMER RELATIONSHIP MANAGEMENT

With the increasing interaction of business applications with the Internet, CRM has enhanced an organization's capabilities by providing access to its customers and suppliers via the Web. This Web experience and communication through the wireless Web is called *e*-CRM.

e-CRM comprises activities to manage customer relationships by using the Internet, Web browsers, or other electronic touch points. A higher degree of interactivity possessed by these channels further allows companies to engage in dialogue, organize consumer redressal, solicit feedback, respond to controversies, and establish and sustain long-term customer relationships. Existing companies are being challenged to rethink the most basic business relationship—the one between the organization and its customers. CRM is a comprehensive business and marketing strategy that integrates technology, process, and all business activities around the customer. Despite media hype about the Internet changing the rules of engagement with customers, it has not changed the underlying fact that addressing customers' needs leads to sustainable profit,[24] which is related to customer satisfaction.[25] In this scenario, where information overload in the Internet age can force people to become passive receptors of information, it is important for an organization to make sure that the right information reaches the right people at the right time. A higher perceived value by the consumer about the organizational information will stimulate consumer interest leading to a desire to interact, thereby achieving '*engagement*' from the organizational perspective.

While CRM can be considered as an approach or business strategy providing seamless integration of every area of business that touches the customer, namely, sales, marketing, customer service, and field support through the integration of people, process, and technology, *e*-CRM, on the other hand, takes advantage of the revolutionary Internet technology to expand the traditional CRM techniques by integrating technologies of new electronic channels and combining them with *e*-business applications into the overall enterprise CRM strategy.

The practice of CRM involves tracking customer transactions and interactions across all contact points and analysing the transactions or interactions to make sense of the customer's behaviour. The terminologies associated with these issues comprise operational and analytical CRM. We now focus on the three components of the *e*-CRM framework, which are as follows: operational CRM, analytical CRM, and collaborative CRM (Fig. 4.11).

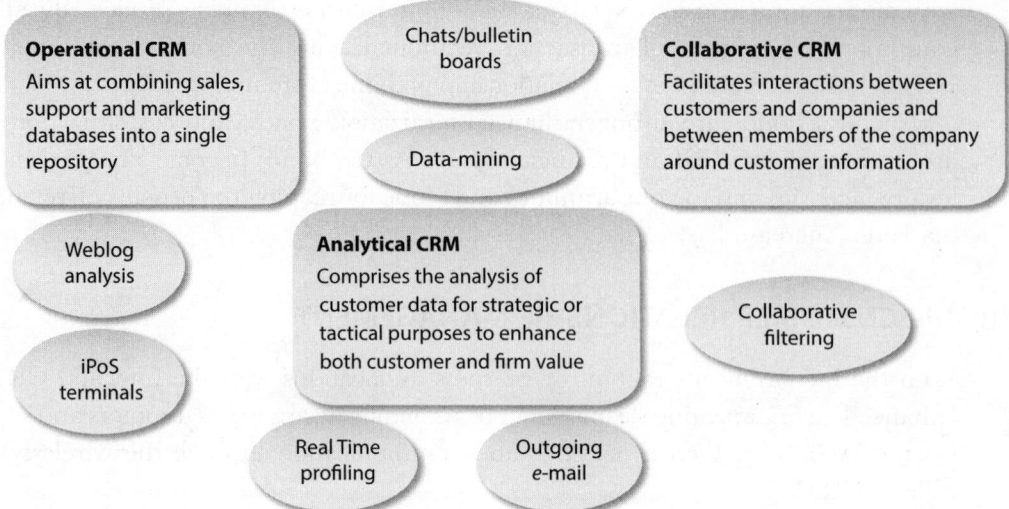

Fig. 4.11 E-CRM meets e-marketing

Operational Customer Relationship Management

Operational CRM aims at combining sales, support, and marketing databases into a single repository that tracks and manages interactions with customers, thereby focusing on improving the efficiency of customer interactions. It is concerned with the customer facing functions and the capturing of data generated as a result of interactions with the consumer, across all contact points. Operational CRM focuses on actual customer interfaces. A company usually in the course of its day-to-day transactions collects large amounts of data about its customers, competitors, and details about its processes and the environment in general. Such data contain hidden implicit knowledge, which could be profitably used by the company. Extraction of this data requires data analysis using statistical and other such techniques. It involves process management technologies across diverse functions of an organization and the automation of horizontally integrated business processes. Thus, channel integration is important for an operational CRM system. Online communities can aid this channel integration by hosting consumer enquiries, order placements, organization–consumer interaction during order fulfilment, and providing a medium for the conversion of consumer-related tacit knowledge to explicit knowledge. Integration of the same through data extraction and dissemination of actionable information across different organizational departments will successfully serve the CRM function.

Analytical Customer Relationship Management

Analytical CRM comprises the analysis of customer data for strategic or tactical purposes to enhance both customer and firm value. It aids decision-making using various tools ranging from simple spreadsheet analysis to sophisticated data mining.[26] The analysis should provide an insight into consumer behaviour and meet the objectives of the CRM initiatives for the purpose of business performance management and improvement. The aspects that could be covered include prediction of consumer behaviour, creating segments of consumers based on their purchase behaviour, understanding consumer-purchase preferences, understanding changing trends, identifying consumers at the risk of churn, analysing responses to campaigns and retention strategies.

Customer analysis applications predict and interpret consumer behaviour, and the integrated customer information is used to build a business campaign strategy and assess results. In addition, predictive models are built to identify the customers most likely to perform a particular activity. Segment selection processes improve response rates and campaign effectiveness and lower campaign costs by reducing the size of the original target segment. Usually, there are three major types of customer analysis applications—online analytical processing, data mining, and statistics. Data mining applications perform the analysis and extract relevant consumer information. Analytical CRM depends on operational CRM for getting the input data on which analysis is to be done.

Collaborative Customer Relationship Management

Collaborative CRM is primarily geared towards increasing the interactions between the customers and the companies. It facilitates interactions between customers and companies and between members of the company around customer information to improve communication and coordination, to raise customer switching costs, and to increase customer intimacy and retention. It involves business collaboration management technologies. Collaborative CRM is an integrated organization-wide system that allows for greater customer responsiveness throughout the supply chain. Organizational collaboration results in productivity enhancement resulting in greater profitability by enhancing cross-functional effectiveness. Some collaborative CRM technologies are voice, conferencing, *e*-mail, web-based and other interactive technologies.

Cookies

CRM applications have focused on extending traditional contact management applications through the collection and maintenance of more robust contextual customer information. An online community can be used in this reference by preserving the context of the consumer interaction.

An important role in CRM is the process of applying lessons learned from customer information to enhance business and customer relationship behaviours. Knowing customer behaviours over time and in the proper context provides companies with the baseline information needed to adapt business decisions and operational behaviours to maximize results. This information also reinforces successful practices and defines the future customer interactions and behaviours likely to generate desired business results.

Detailed below is the list of selected *e*-marketing customization tools that are used by companies to 'push' the products towards the consumer (Table 4.1).

Table 4.1 Selected e-marketing 'push' customization tools[27]

Organizational tools to push products	Description
Cookies	When a user visits a website, small files called cookies are written on the user's hard drive. In the future, when the users revisit the same site, the organization can customize the site for the user's visit based on the information retrieved from the cookie file.
Weblog analysis	Individual user visits are recorded in the Web server's log file. Weblog analysis provides companies with information on user visits, length, depth, and purchase information.
Data-mining	Data-mining involves the extraction of actionable information from large databases through statistical analysis to facilitate decision-making.
Real-time profiling	Companies use special software to track a user's movements through a website. These companies enable the retrieval of compiled information on a moment's notice to facilitate decision-making.
Collaborative filtering	Organizations use collaborative filtering software to gather opinions of homogeneous sets of users. This software is used to return those opinions to the individuals in real time.
E-mail	Marketers use e-mail databases to build relationships with potential customers by providing them relevant information related to the product or brand, from time to time.
Online communities and forums	A firm may create online communities by providing a space for user conversations on the website. These forums can be subsequently used for targeting customers.
iPOS terminals	Interactive point-of-sale terminals located on a retailer's counter can be used to capture consumer-specific data. This data can be subsequently used for consumer targeting.

CUSTOMER RELATIONSHIP MANAGEMENT—THE B2C DIMENSIONS

The marketing enterprise has four main groups of constituents; which are as follows: customers, partners, suppliers, and employees. Web 2.0 tools and technologies and the evolution in the attitudes of the involved constituents present a diverse range of opportunities. The following section discusses the role of customers in the business-to-consumer (B2C) context.

Customers have undergone a substantial transformation. *E*-marketing has evolved and created awareness, using volumes of potential *e*-customers who are themselves aware of the brand, product, or service and are also willingly transmitting the same messages to their peers through word-of-mouth propagation, electronically, and verbally. *E*-commerce challenges the conventional sales channels and offers new opportunities. The changed approach comprises phases of discovery, exploration and evaluation where the consumer purchase, at times, is the culmination of a research operation at the *e*-store.

Consumers are willing to participate in communities, where peer-to-peer interaction in the community also aids in the resolution of consumer issues and sharing of information takes place. To cite an example, companies such as Adobe maintain healthy and active consumer communities, not only to provide resources to the consumers and local user groups, also to enable community participants to help and support each other.

In addition to this, an involved consumer is willing to interact with the organization, participate, even collaborate as his level of engagement increases, and organizations are recognizing the value of these involved consumers. Consumers increasingly rely on their peers as they make online decisions, whether the brands choose to participate or not. In times to come, socially connected consumers will strengthen communities and shift the power away from brands and CRM systems, empowering communities and defining the next generation of products. Technologies are triggering changes in patterns of consumer adoption and brands will soon follow (Fig. 4.12).

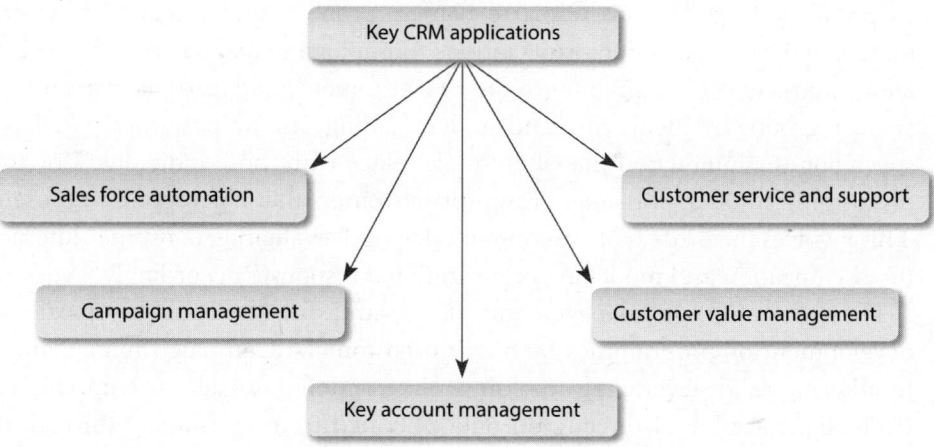

Fig. 4.12 Key CRM applications

KEY CUSTOMER RELATIONSHIP MANAGEMENT APPLICATIONS

Sales Force Automation

Functionalities of sales force automation (SFA) solutions allow interface with campaign management software so that the sales people can receive a comprehensive view of the ongoing and completed marketing campaigns. Some SFA solutions guide the sales representatives through conversations with the customers during first contact. At the higher levels of the sales departments, sales managers must be able to identify their expenses, deploy sales representatives to the proper territories, forecast revenues, and proactively address trends in the markets and shortfalls through proper reassignment. While the contact management functionality stores critical information about each customer contact, account management functionality aids in building a deep understanding of target accounts by documenting the complete account history, key contacts, customer communications, and internal account discussions from lead capture to close. The territory management functionality helps manage and execute sales activities territory wise. Coverage areas usually include order processing, contact management, information sharing, inventory monitoring and control, order tracking customer management, sales forecast analysis, and employee performance evaluation.

Campaign Management

Campaign management solutions help segment customers and develop targeting and positioning strategies for each segment; define products which match customer requirements, price and select appropriate distribution channels for those products; and implement communication strategies to build brand awareness, generate interest, and motivate purchase.[28]

Often, due to lack of data regarding the consumer sentiment for the organization and its products, organizations resort to blanket promotions for their consumers, thereby matching the true consumer expectations. Campaign management software applications allow marketers to segment groups of customers (and prospective customers) into smaller groups by identifying and understanding unique customer patterns and then specifying the interaction that should take place with those individuals, by the creation of customized offers for small groups of customers that correspond to those patterns.[28] This involves the process of response modelling—evaluating consumer interactions with the organization and modelling organizational responses accordingly.

Through campaign management, all the areas of the company participate in the development of programmes targeted to customers. Campaign management involves monitoring and leveraging customer interactions to sell a company's products. Campaigns are based directly on data obtained from consumers through a series of interactions. Hence, marketing managers need to plan, design, coordinate, execute, and assess all campaigns. Simultaneously, metrics are required to calculate the effectiveness of each campaign. Monitoring the success of respective campaigns is importantfor altering unsuccessful campaigns and for response modelling.

Key Account Management

Key accounts or strategic accounts are the most valuable customers for a company. Simply stated, a company cannot afford to lose these customers without experiencing serious difficulties. Key account management (KAM) can be defined as the systematic selection, analysis, and management of the most important current and potential customers of a company. Additionally, it also includes the systematic set up and maintenance of the necessary infrastructure. Without a systematic approach, KAM becomes a process of trial and error, which may miss some necessary elements, create additional costs, and offer no opportunity for corporate learning. KAM is typically associated with the business-to-business context, and most KAM literature deals with industrial relationships.[29]

However, services also include business-to-business situations and KAM clearly has potential in any kind of business relationship. After all, most business relationships include both tangible and service elements.[30] This can also be called systems selling, which involves offering and delivering a comprehensive package or bundle of product/service attributes and benefits to selected customers. KAM plays an important role in this context. Thus, successful KAM often requires an understanding of the logic of both product and service management. Moreover, excellent operational-level capabilities are useless if strategic level management is inferior, and vice versa, the KAM approach combines strategic and operational-level marketing management.

A successful KAM consists of four basic elements,[31] which are as follows:

- Identifying the key accounts
- Analysing the key accounts
- Selecting suitable strategies for the key accounts
- Developing operational-level capabilities to build, grow, and maintain profitable and long-lasting relationships with them

An account manager who works in this role will engage in a variety of tasks including project management, coordination, strategic planning, relationship management, negotiation, leadership, and innovative development of opportunities.

Customer Value Management

Companies can boost profits by increasing annual customer retention as selling a product or service to an existing customer has a higher probability of success than selling to an entirely new prospect. As it costs much more to acquire new customers, the firm should retain customers, once acquired, and realize their customer value management (CVM) to the maximum possible extent. CVM is the present value of the future cash flows, attributed to the customer relationship. Firms should invest in an appropriate consumer-segmentation process once a new consumer is acquired, to target them appropriately. Organizations should manage each customer relationship with the goal of achieving maximum lifetime profit from the entire customer base. Not every individual customer will be profitable but each must be managed to maximize the overall profit, even when the management consists of identifying which customers have little value to the business and focusing development and retention efforts elsewhere.

Customer Service and Support

Customer service and support (CSS) functionalities usually include multiple channel access, solutions knowledge base, managing requests, contract and warranty status, field service and support, and billing.

The following tables provide descriptions of tools offered by Salesforce.com, mySAPCRM, and SiebelCRM. Organizations can choose a tool on the basis of their current organizational objectives, functionality requirements, and business challenges. Identifying relevant customer-focused processes that need to be supported with technology and finally defining the products that support the functionality are crucial aspects that aid organizations in the final CRM product-procurement process.

BUSINESS-TO-CONSUMER 2.0

The offerings of the collaborative Web to the B2C space appear high from the organizational and revenue perspective. By providing added touch-points for aiding customer centricity, the potential of adding to the customer contact, sales, and CRM cycle is enormous. In marketing, the provision of rich, interactive media enables web-based delivery or interaction models, which enable companies to cut the cost of capital and communication with their customers. Creation of online consumer communities solicits consumer participation, thereby enlisting support, resulting in engagement and opening opportunities for consumer evangelism. While providing great volumes of support to the sales staff, especially towards lead generation and contacting prospective customers, this medium also offers support throughout the sales process, particularly with respect to moderating consumer expectations and reducing consumer dissonance.

In the area of customer support, the use of experts in the community as well as customer-to-customer interaction, which at times aids in problem resolution through discussion groups, creates whole new support models. New revenue streams can be built and present revenue streams enhanced through community and social networking. Customers are a business's best sales, marketing, support, and development organization and 'consumer-generated media' or the voice of the consumer can be leveraged by the organization for the promotion of their brands and products as also for co-creation. This is discussed in detail in the subsequent chapters.

SAP WEB CHANNEL EXPERIENCE MANAGEMENT

SAP Web Channel Experience Management (WCEM) is the latest *e*-business suite by SAP. It is a state-of-the-art Web solution that was re-designed from scratch using Web 2.0 and Java standards. It delivers end-to-end processes for *e*-commerce, *e*-marketing, *e*-service, and Web channel analytics on a robust and easily extensible Web channel platform, including third-party solutions.

For some industries, user opinions are given so much weight that evaluation management has become one of marketing's most important tasks. Foremost among these is the hotel industry. The tremendous growth of Trip Advisor, and similar review sites, is evidence of the power of social business. It's fair to say that consumers are storming to Web applications that provide user—in this case—guest reviews. Many websites even bundle guest opinions from other review sites and offer off-course travel booking services. As a result, traditional service providers are struggling to reach the masses. Indeed, they are even experiencing customer churn.

In the wake of customers increasingly informing themselves about the opinions of others, using the online space, they can leverage a wide variety of sources including consumer reviews, blogs, company websites, social networks, price comparison websites, etc. This not only holds true for luxury goods like a new phone or car, but also for commodity goods such as water or paper.

How companies react to social feedback varies from buying fake consumer reviews at one extreme to not caring about what's being said at the other. Most companies attempt to take advantage of modern monitoring capabilities that not only provide us with consumer review data, but also give us data specific to individual brands, products, or services. *SAP Social Media Analytics by Netbase* equips organizations with such advanced monitoring and analysis capabilities. The tool yields these results, thanks to the Natural Language Processing (NLP) and sentiment analysis technology.

The next step is to act based on what's being said. *SAP Social Customer Engagement On Demand* helps companies better manage incoming feedback and service requests from social channels. It achieves this by routing comments from sources such as Facebook or Twitter to the appropriate experts. The solution comes with out-of-the-box integration to social media analytics. This equips organizations with modern CRM ticketing capabilities as well as embedded analytics. Companies can now engage directly with consumers where it makes sense.

CRM 2.0 helps organizations in identifying their value proposition to increase customer loyalty, helps companies understand the degree of customization required for the effective delivery of their services and products and identification of customer tiers.

The virtual world can help organizations build a solid foundation for creating customer loyalty, which includes having the right portfolio of customer segments, attracting the right customers, tiering of services, and delivering high levels of satisfaction. The online domain gives an access into the consumer mind space to the companies, which aids cross-selling, up-selling, and bundling. By further adding value to the customer through loyalty rewards and higher level bonds, firms can identify and eliminate factors that result in a 'churn'—the loss of existing customers and the need to replace them with new ones.

Addressing Key Churn Drivers

Organizations can use the Web to aid *churn diagnostics*. By analysing the contextual content in the realm of the organization–consumer relationship, companies can identify causes that lead to a churn. Proactive analysis of consumer-related content can trigger retention efforts. By the analysis of content created by consumers online, the companies can do the following:

- Identify generic churn drivers
- Minimize inconvenience and other non-monetary costs
- Identify industry-specific churn drivers and create appropriate content to mitigate potential risks for churn

The collaborative Web can further be used for effective complaint handling and service recovery procedures. While the online domain can be used to enable customers to voice their problems with the firm, and then responding with effective service delivery, it can also be used to inform consumers about potential consumer-switching costs.

As per Forrester Research, two significant CRM trends for 2013 included—William Band serves Application Development and Delivery Professionals. The trends are as follows:

- *Trend 1: Enterprises must navigate digital disruption* Thanks to digital platforms, your customers live in a world of heightened expectations and abundant options; they can get more of what they want, in more places, at more times, than ever before.
- *Trend 2: Companies will transform to become experience-driven organizations* More enlightened companies are defining customer-management strategies from the outside in articulating a customer-management strategy defined in customers' terms that can be used to guide organizational improvement efforts.

NEXT-GENERATION CRM—A MOBILE APP AND A COMMUNITY

A 'new' crop of CRM vendors has emerged, either as existing vendors who have reinvented themselves in some way (Salesforce, SugarCRM, RightNow/Oracle) or have reached significant maturity natively in the new CRM space (Lithium, Get Satisfaction, Jive.). However, as evolved as these vendors can be—and technology products often outpace their customer needs by a few years—this time it's different. Customers have gone beyond from just being social and are virtually demanding high function mobile engagement. The best way to provide many customer services, from marketing and sales to customer support and gathering product ideas, is to have a self-self mobile App ready to install in the Apple App store or android market. Thousands of companies are now building their own CRM touch points for mobile devices, typically smart phones and tablets. It's a virtual boomtown perhaps more vibrant than the Web was during the great boom of the 1990s, except that the scale is significantly larger. In this new era, CRM itself is often being reduced to an App (a rich App to be sure), just as it's also being raised up to be a true community experience. It's still unclear where all this will lead, but it's almost certainly going to improve the way we jointly create value with our favourite brands.

THE NEW AGE *E*-ENTERPRISE

Globalization and the resultant transition to virtual work are changing the dynamics of critical business relationships today. The organizational fabric is undergoing a transformation. The new knowledge economy coupled with the modern customer-based relationship approach has transformed the shape of business, catalyzed further by the Internet revolution. Shrinking distance barriers and the emergence of new ways of building and delivering products and services online is enabling the rapid globalization of markets. This chapter traces how the new knowledge economy, along with the modern customer-based relationship approach, impacts the organizational fabric.

The collaborative Web along with the *e*-enterprise has brought into vogue the use of emergent social software platforms within companies or between companies and their partners or customers. This, along with organizational willingness to take risks, has created new opportunities for companies in the domain of innovation, Internet-based collaboration, and co-creation.

This section discusses concepts pertaining to the new knowledge economy, approaches how organizations function, and studies the modern customer-based relationship approaches being followed in organizations. It further details the tools of the collaborative Web, namely corporate blogs, online communities, business and social networks, Wikis, and micromedia Twitter in the context of the *e*-enterprise and proceeds to discuss how Procter and Gamble, a modern day enterprise, uses these new approaches on innovation, harnessing consumers, *e*-commerce, and brand–customer centricity through four case studies.

The New Knowledge Economy

Signifying volatility with extremely fast changes, explosive upsurges, and sudden downturns, the new knowledge economy is characterized by market changes that are fast and unpredictable. The lifecycle of products and technologies is short and innovation and entrepreneurship are the buzzwords. Competition has adopted a global face and differentiation is the name of the marketing game. The pace of business is appreciably faster with ever rising customer expectations.

Change management is the focus area and business development approach has become opportunity driven with dynamic strategies. Knowledge has become the source of strategic planning for the creation of a value proposition for consumers. Market sensing is a core business process and organizations that are able to manage, analyse, and combine knowledge faster for product innovation and improvement in line with customer expectations are succeeding in the competitive scenario (Fig. 4.13). The connected millennium lays tremendous importance on the concepts of market opportunity analysis and global marketing.

Fig. 4.13 The new knowledge economy

Innovation processes are continuous and appropriate human capital is fast becoming a scarce resource. Distinctive capabilities coupled with institutional excellence now spell sources of competitive advantage. Organizations are transforming from hierarchical, bureaucratic, functional, pyramid structures, to interconnected subsystems characterized by flexibility, employee empowerment, and flat or networked structures. People, knowledge, and capabilities are the key organizational assets.

The Organization

Adhoc workgroups and communities are constantly forming and operating in diverse locations over widespread geographic areas, countries, and companies. Geographic proximity is no longer essential for people working together, courtesy the advances made in the field of information and communication technology. People are engaged in project-based work with an ever changing and increasing circle of colleagues, customers, and partners, many of whom they have never met. Employee attrition is frequently ushering in new work partners, leading to an intrinsic need for better documentation that can enable projects to withstand the change in project participants and maintain continuity. Optimum teaming of world-class competencies is the order of the day.

Work is now no longer limited to the office, it can take place in the electronic network. The ability to access vast information resources within a matter of minutes and to communicate across huge distances at ever lower costs, while maintaining quality levels along with dramatic changes in competition; technology; and workforce values, is causing organizations to search for new and more human ways of increasing productivity and competitiveness. Newer systems support collaboration and employee interaction.

Examples of successful projects of this type include worldwide product launches involving training, presentations, and project planning that eliminate the need to bring employees from multiple locations to a single site with substantial savings in travel and associated costs and time.

The Modern Customer-based Relationship Approach

Marketing is shifting from making and maximizing profit from individual transactions to building mutually beneficial relationships with consumers and other parties. Relationship marketing focuses on customer satisfaction and retention as organizations move from product-based campaign marketing to a customer-based relationship approach. Economies have become customer driven. Companies are going global, reaching out to customers located afar as *e*-commerce and online buying facilitate consumer purchase thus diminishing geographical restrictions. Increasing competition between organizations is leading to the implementation of relationship strategies and multichannel relationship programmes, as consumer retention becomes a vital imperative for organizational sustenance. Further, vast opportunities are available to consumers who are well informed and further analyse competing products and make intelligent choices. In view of the increased need for the organization to communicate with its consumers, the Internet provides an excellent low-cost solution for better connectivity between the organization and its partners.

THE COLLABORATIVE WEB AND THE ENTERPRISE

The collaborative version of the Internet, termed Web 2.0, as coined by Tim O'Reilly in 2005, has altered the manner in which information is published, consumed, and utilized on the Internet resulting in a paradigm shift in the way interactions take place within the organizational workspace as well as between the organization and the external customers. Web 2.0 is a collection of open-source, interactive, and user-controlled online applications expanding the experiences, knowledge, and market power of the users as participants in business and social processes (Fig. 4.14).

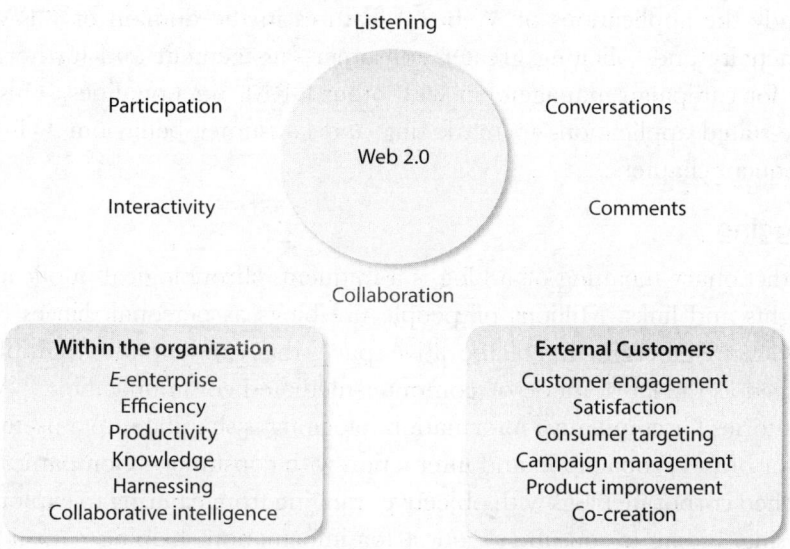

Fig. 4.14 The collaborative Web and the enterprise

Personal websites have been replaced by blogs, content management systems by Wikis, directories by tagging, encyclopaedias by Wikipedia, and participation is the new keyword connecting organizations, employees, customers, suppliers, partners, and any other intermediaries. Differential patterns of combining data content, services through collaboration, and increased access to information by consumers has opened up new dimensions for organizations to interact with the various players involved in the business.

Content creation by consumers facilitating the flow of ideas and knowledge has given companies access to huge volumes of data that can be leveraged for decision-making. Commonly and collectively called *Web 2.0 tools*, these new content-sharing sites, discussion and collaborative web-spaces, and application design patterns or mashups are transforming the consumer Web. They also represent a significant opportunity for organizations to build new social and web-based collaboration, productivity, and business systems and to improve cost and revenue returns.[32]

Corporate blogs, online communities, social networks, wikis, micromedia, and folksonomies are some Web 2.0 concepts being used by businesses in the field of marketing, brand promotion, and CRM. Web 2.0 also appears to have a substantial effect on consumer behaviour and has contributed to an unprecedented customer empowerment. The consequences are far reaching, affecting not only the area of technology development but also the domains of business strategy and marketing owing to changing consumer attitudes, new customer needs, emerging new value perceptions, and the change of consumer-search tactics and buying behaviour. Of significance is the emergence of the collaborative Web as an influencing factor in consumer-buying behaviour. Several organizations are using collaborative product-development tools, such as initiating discussions in blogs to test ideas, involving customers in the use of collaborative design tools, or testing how well products sell in virtual worlds. It is interesting to study the applications of Web 2.0 features in the domain of CRM by improving interactivity and soliciting greater consumer engagement and further integrating the same for campaign management with other CRM functionalities. This along with the above-stated applications to marketing and consumer behaviour will be discussed in subsequent chapters.

Corporate Blogging

The dictionary meaning of a blog is a frequent, chronological publication of personal thoughts and links. Millions of people use blogs as personal diaries on the Internet, and they are emerging as collaborative spaces that can be put to multiple uses and have emerged as the latest mode of computer-mediated communication.[33] As these become repositories for cumulative information, blogging is shaping into a useful organizational tool for brand propagation and interaction with consumers. Companies have effectively launched corporate blogs with objectives ranging from catering to exploratory consumer browsing, aiding a consumer's quest for information, helping consumers gain access to organizational promotional campaigns, to responding to controversies regarding organization or brand or product.

Online Communities

An online community or a virtual community represents a group of people that primarily or initially communicates or interacts via the Internet. The dawn of the information age found groups communicating electronically rather than face to face. A computer-mediated community (CMC) uses social software to regulate the activities of the participants. These are places where people gather to share knowledge, build recognition, and tap opportunities. Initially sensed to be resource pools for value addition, where people ventured to fulfil their need for self-actualization, participation in online communities and forums started as a medium for exchange of ideas and information, and now organizations have started using these communities for marketing through consumer evangelism and support. A web-based communication model utilizes the features of the network for B2C as well as peer-to-peer communication.

Business and Social Networks

Networking on business and social networking groups of individuals and organizations has emerged successful in modern marketing. The high volume of individual presence across these networks makes them viable marketing tools. While increased consumer interaction results in higher levels of trust, these are also being used extensively by salespeople for the generation of leads to drive demand.

Wikis

A *wiki* is a collection of Web pages designed to enable individuals to contribute or modify content using a simplified mark-up language. Wikis are often used to create and power collaborative and community websites. The most prominent wiki application is the 'Wikipedia' on which every Internet user can become the knowledge provider of its contents. In such architecture, both peers and experts are equally welcomed and valued to participate in the knowledge refinement process. Wikis are used in business as effective knowledge management systems.

Wikis enable site visitors to add their own content and build up in an additive fashion on the content created by others. They hence create a common platform for people in the targeted and specified community to not merely participate in the communications but also be the content and knowledge providers of the group. The properties of a wiki platform make it easy to track activities such as the viewing, reading, adding, and editing of content, changes to content over time, the most active contributors, as well as the opportunity to recruit specific users for more focused research projects. When done right, wikis can drive key metrics that online marketers labour to achieve including increased page views, a higher level of consumer engagement, and higher rates of user contributions.

Wikis can also be used for gathering market intelligence by analysing the content added by consumers, which can provide insight into possible future trends or competitor offerings. They can also aid in market research where researchers enter the discussion and conduct focused surveys or discrete experiments. Wikis offer companies the opportunity to encourage user-generated content. User-generated content can serve multiple purposes as a market intelligence tool, a competitive intelligence tool, as a forum for advertising, and as a platform for consumer interaction.

Micromedia—Twitter

A form of text-based 'Micromedia',[34] Twitter is really much like blogging but on a miniature scale. The character limit of 140 calls for simplification of messages. A tool with social network features, Twitter is a next-generation, instant-messaging tool, where users can blast messages to their network, send private messages, or search. When users publish messages, those are often called 'tweets'.

Twitter was founded by Jack Dorsey, Biz Stone, and Evan Williams and began as a research and development project inside San Francisco podcasting company *Odeo* in March, 2006. Twitter helps extend the reach for those individuals or companies that already have a blogging strategy in place and want to further work on strengthening the consumer relationships through increased interaction with the consumer. It can be used by retailers for promotional campaigns and building a buzz and is of special use to companies launching new products or product variants, where it can also be used as part of an organizational branding strategy. Twitter's usability for developing and engaging a community can be leveraged as a tool for market sensing and understanding consumer sentiment.

Folksonomies

With the increased informational and exchange needs, there has been an emergence of new communication models producing incredible amounts of distributed information that knowledge workers need to link, aggregate, and organize in order to extract knowledge. Folksonomies attempt to provide a solution to this issue by introducing an innovative distributed approach that is based on social classification. The huge volume of content available online today has resulted in the evolution of more relevant aggregation and concept matching tools by addressing web-specific classification issues, specifically with reference to the vast volumes of content created by consumers on the Web.

THE COLLABORATIVE WEB AND THE *E*-ENTERPRISE

Enterprise 2.0 is the use of emergent social software platforms within companies or between companies and their partners or customers. This use of Web 2.0 within the enterprise to improve efficiency and productivity finds applications where shared knowledge work becomes the intellectual capital for the company and a smooth flow of communication through the 'connected' enterprise takes place.

Similarly, these tools have widespread application with respect to their application to the organization consumer interface-in improving organization-consumer relationships, increasing brand value, improving the productivity of marketing and enhancing consumer perceived value about the organization.

Harnessing Collaborative Intelligence

Collaborative intelligence as the collaborative ability of an entity or a group.

To succeed, companies need to innovate faster, collaborate better, and operate more efficiently than ever before. To do so, they need to depend on close collaborative relationships with strategic partners, the ability to exchange prudent information rapidly, and to act on that information in real time, across end-to-end business processes. The key to unlocking this performance potential is to tap into the power of communities that drive business success. Relationships matter particularly for the knowledge-intensive activities that make organizations unique (IBM, 2007). Given the increasingly dispersed, project-based work environments that are characteristic of companies today, it is important to help people become better connected with one another and with the information and applications they need. In building on a theme of collaborative intelligence, the following list of features may be considered as the objectives of knowledge content development via *Web 2.0*:

- *Contribution*   Every Internet user has the opportunity to freely provide their knowledge content to the relevant subject domains.
- *Sharing*   Knowledge content is freely available to others. Secured mechanisms may be enforced to enable the knowledge sharing amongst legitimate members within specific communities.

- *Collaboration* Knowledge content is created and maintained collaboratively by knowledge providers. Internet users participating in the creation of content can have conversations as a kind of social interaction.
- *Dynamic* Knowledge content is updated constantly to reflect the changing environment and situation.
- *Reliance* Knowledge contribution should be based on trust between knowledge providers and domain experts.

Enterprises with large employees, partners, and customer bases have long known the value of the knowledge living in employees' heads and in the databases and unstructured documents found across the organization. Attempts to collect this information into knowledge management systems have been made in the past, with varying degrees of success. Web 2.0 technologies such as blogs, wikis, and enterprise search for people and data and are providing a new platform for collaborating on complex and creative tasks in the organizational domains. Technological advances are simplifying online collaboration and communication.

These advances are increasing productivity by helping people to more easily capture, share, and reuse work practices (such as project workflows) and link them to the widest possible range of supporting services (e.g., instant messaging, Web conferencing, and tools for team collaboration). Interactivity interfaced with technology enhances the knowledge base of the community, which includes organizational employees, customers, and partners; hence, the content generated by the community can be harnessed for the collaborative intelligence it offers. Further, the preservation of these intangible assets can form a source of competitive advantage for a firm.

This is slightly complex as they differ from normal assets in a crucial way; most of the firm's intangible assets are locked up in the brains of the employees, who can come and go. Be it the Microsoft Developer Network that hosts a series of employee blogs to share tips on software, programming tips, and solutions to programming issues or the GE research blogs or the Sun Microsystems employee blogs, the volume of company-specific knowledge available on these online web-spaces is huge. Sun Microsystems CEO Jonathan Schwartz uses his blog for product announcements and discussion of new knowledge issues as part of his bid to interact with the community.

The transparency of the channels is breathtaking; for instance, a common Sun consumer can gain access to a Sun whitepaper on *multiplatform virtualization* by merely logging onto the online blog community. Accumulation of company-specific information has also made these online web-spaces virtual repositories to be tapped whenever required. The volume of knowledge that can be retrieved regarding a person's work in an organization post his departure, through his contributions to his blogs, etc., makes these viable organizational endeavours.

Organizations are waking up to the need of extending business processes beyond corporate firewalls. This implies inclusion of people outside the company as readily as they do include people inside the firm. IBM has taken the lead in applying the consumer-based, social networking concept to cross-organizational business networks. With IBM networking services, organizations can securely and easily tap into collective knowledge by enabling formation of fluid communities of interest. Enterprise collaboration platforms offer to employees what social networks offer to consumers–ease of use, speed, and ubiquity combined with a high level of security, availability, quality of service, and reliability that enterprises require. To site an example, *The Greater IBM Connection* is a business social network designed to connect current and former IBMers and to enable them to connect, communicate, and collaborate in a variety of new ways by interacting via a virtual environment. Greater IBM seeks to contribute to advancing societal innovations by creating an *innovation network* that can orchestrate collaborative work, the sharing of insights, and facilitate community-based, productive projects for social and business innovation.

These technologies have the potential to usher in a new era by making practices and outputs of organizational workers visible by knitting together the enterprise and facilitating knowledge work in new ways. Content sharing owing to high degrees of centralization and commonality not only facilitate knowledge capture but also better levels of productivity due to greater accessibility. Mining[35] the inputs of the consumers, with respect to the content they generate on corporate blogs, branded online communities, and other organizational networks, serves as an excellent market sensing tool. The consumer ideas and thoughts can be leveraged by organizations to achieve greater customer centricity through product improvements and co-creation.

EXHIBIT 4.2 Amazon.com

Amazon sells the same products as competitors such as Barnesandnoble.com, and they receive the same product descriptions, cover images, and editorial content from their vendors. However, Amazon has used its user engagement to gain a competitive edge. The high volumes of user reviews and invitations for consumers to participate in varied ways results in enhanced user activity, which can produce better search results.

EXHIBIT 4.3 eBay

eBay's competitive advantage comes almost entirely from the critical mass of buyers and sellers, which make any new entrant offering similar services significantly less attractive. eBay grows organically in response to user activity, and the company's role is as an enabler for the creation of an environment facilitating the collective activity of all involved entities.

CASE STUDY **Procter and Gamble**

P&G and innovation

The world's largest consumer packaged goods giant, Procter & Gamble (P&G), operated one of the most widely admired and successful research and development operations in corporate history. However, their closed innovation model was not up to the task of driving the corporate growth needed to sustain an enterprise of P&G's size. So in 2000, under the leadership of the then newly-appointed CEO, A.G. Lafley, they began looking for a better global innovation model. Lafley's stated objective was the radical idea that half of the company's new products would be acquired from outside the company. In the words of Larry Huston, Vice President, Innovation and Knowledge, P&G, Cincinnati and Nabil Sakkab, Senior Vice President for Corporate R&D at P&G in Cincinnati,

> *We discovered that important innovation was increasingly being done at small and midsize entrepreneurial companies. Even individuals were eager to license and sell their intellectual property. University and government labs had become more interested in forming industry partnerships, and they were hungry for ways to monetize their research. The Internet had opened up access to talent markets throughout the world. And, a few forward-looking companies such as IBM and Eli Lilly were beginning to experiment with the new concept of open innovation, leveraging one another's (even competitors') innovation assets—products, intellectual property, and people.*

What set them off towards an open innovation model was the discovery that there were 200 researchers and scientists just as good or even better outside P&G for each of their own 7500 researchers and scientists. That appeared a humongous volume of talent the company could tap into. It does this through an open innovation program called *Connect and Develop* that reaches out to independent researchers, suppliers, and other industrial companies to solve problems it cannot solve by itself.

The company has also adopted the use of Web 2.0 tools—an example of the resulting model is the *Vocalpoint* program. Engaging users is among the many secrets that underlie successful innovation. The newest innovation in innovation is the use of rich media and online interactivity to involve broad audiences in the process. The technology that underlies Web 2.0 enables full bi-directional conversations online, putting users into the creation seat for the bulk of new Internet content.

From the perspective of firms creating new products and services, this can open innovation to a community of millions of possible innovators, people who may be more likely to adopt the resulting offering as they had a hand in developing it. This suggests that Web 2.0 might offer firms both more leverage on the enormous global corporate expenditure on innovation and increase the likelihood of innovation adoption at the same time. Adaptation of this concept enables consumers to voice their thoughts and then subsequently participate in new product ideas, execution of which represents win-win situations for both organizations and consumers.

P&G—harnessing consumers

P&G has a *Vocalpoint* program for mothers, a *Tremor* program for adolescents and a *Living It* program for lead customers. All three programs use different ways to harness customers as sources of ideas and to test new products before they hit the market. *Vocalpoint* leverages the community for propagation of word of mouth (WOM) and innovation and strikes a careful balance using no-frills packaging that is clearly branded to establish credibility. P&G's role as a trusted broker, protecting the consumer while offering an instant WOM network to clients, has proven successful. These programs give P&G a peep into the everyday lives and thought processes of their customers.

The brief, concise nature of these ventures demonstrates a level of simplicity and honesty. Vocalpoint's FAQ is straightforward in stating that it expects members to participate in the programs, share opinions and feedback, and spread the word about the products to friends. This also gives members a feeling of exclusivity when they get access to items before other consumers and can help improve them before they hit the shelves. This enhances interest in a product and ensures a second wave of buzz once it is fully launched. The right environment where people can contribute, interact, and engage enables creation by the community, by offering a high return on investment when considered at a cost per individual interaction perspective. It is interesting to see that even with the enormous resources of one of the biggest companies in the world at their disposal, P&G recognizes that it cannot do all its innovation in-house. Its further acceptance of the fact that it needs to understand customer needs much better than it did in the past, to drive successful innovation in the future, may well be the key to a successful and brighter future for the business giant.

P&G and e-commerce

Electronic commerce is rapidly changing the way people do business all over the world. In the B2C segment, sales through the Web have been increasing dramatically over the last few years. Customers, not only those from well-developed countries, also those from developing countries, are getting used to the new shopping channel. An organization's key to survival in the new information-age revolution is in its ability to successfully integrate and adapt its management practices with new information technologies offered by the Internet.

P&G has teamed up with PFSweb to launch PGeStore.com representing several popular brands such as Tide, Pampers, and Gillette. Rather than build and operate its own Web store, P&G chose an outsourcing arrangement with an established *e*-commerce service provider so that it can concentrate on how online shoppers interact with its hundreds of brands.

The digital paradigm plays two very significant roles in marketing: influencing consumer behaviour and harnessing consumer intelligence. While it is vital for an organization to evaluate consumer intentions and provide consumers the necessary information they are looking for, equally important is the need for collecting consumer data by studying the consumer behavioural patterns on the Internet and subsequently nurturing long-term relationships with consumers. This is where P&G is attempting to position its new online venture.

Online consumers have noticed that these applications offer new and previously unknown possibilities and empowerment not only in the form of information sourcing, also as forums of dialogue and confrontation of producers and vendors with their social, ethical, and commercial responsibilities. The shift in consumer needs is reflected in the growing demand of online services, particularly in the *e*-commerce domain, where consumers can not only interact with marketers but also access peer communities.

Brand customer centricity of brand P&G

Building customer centricity in a brand is one alternative available to organizations in the wake of the rising vulnerabilities of brands and branding in the face of rising consumer empowerment. It creates new opportunities for brand–customer dialogue, knowledge creation, and, critically, provides a new context in which the interests of a corporation and those of its customers can be more closely aligned. Customer-centric brands represent one effective means for firms to achieve better alignment of their brands with the customers. To become a successful customer-centric brand, however, the brand management function must first acknowledge the effective and efficient determinants of emotional connection and consumer brand knowledge in a brand for the consumers.

Studies have revealed that P&G's product brand *Tide* depicted a 'medium' level of brand customer centricity. A BCCC (brand customer centricity calculator) was used to calculate a brand customer centricity score, which was a weighted sum of the performance of the brand across the functions of *building an emotional connection with the consumer, ability of the brand to cater to a particular consumer lifestyle and image, consumer perception, consumer brand knowledge, trust, responsibility towards the customer.*

Tide was found to have scope of improvement in its ability to build an emotional connection with its consumers and demonstrate higher levels of consumer brand knowledge.

Questions:

1. Create a virtual campaign for P&G. The campaign should have the following objectives:
   - Showcasing P&G as a socially responsible brand
   - Building customer engagement
   - Highlight the ability of P&G to build an emotional relationship with the consumer
2. How does P&G use the virtual world for innovation and co-creation?

PRACTITIONER PERSPECTIVE

Achievement of consistency in the already existent touch points; a 24*7 service delivery does not only mean to meet expectations but also to exceed customer's expectations.

Kedar Gavane, Sr. Director, comScore

> *There's a fine divide between creation and consumption of information. Engaging the customer is possible with the use of a targeted approach customized with the regional consumer.*
>
> — Abhishek Malhotra, VP and Partner, Booz and Company

> *The future of marketing from the perspective of a consumer is destined to be customized. Consumers will be in a position to consume only the content which they like, hence making it convenient for the marketers as well as target audiences.*
>
> — Alok Kejriwal, CEO and Co-Founder, Games2Win

> *Organizations need to look at the way processes are developed. Boards need to start looking at the way organizations are structured, which conveys if we are ready to take on this new age world.*
>
> — Deepali Nair, CMO, Mahindra Holidays

SUMMARY

It is said that it costs five times more to acquire a new customer than to retain an old one. Firms need to invest in building consumer loyalty by trying to cement business relationships and focus on consumer retention. A consistent effort towards enhancing the value proposition offered to customers and transforming customer experiences, while building a rapport with them, is the customer-centric business approach required by organizations today. CRM is a comprehensive business strategy to empower the internal functioning of an organization with the aim to identify, acquire, deliver, develop, and retain customers. The following are the goals of CRM: building long-term and profitable relationships with chosen customers and getting closer to those customers with every point of contact with them. Five macro environmental factors responsible for the growth of relationship orientation in marketing include the following:

- rapid technological advancements, especially in the field of IT
- the adoption of total quality programmes by companies
- the growth of the service economy
- organizational development processes leading to the empowerment of individuals and teams
- an increase in competitive intensity leading to concern for customer retention.

Technology, people, process, knowledge, and insight are strategic CRM capabilities. CRM processes are divided into five categories, namely, the strategy development process, the value creation process, the multichannel integration process, the multichannel integration process, the information management process, and the performance assessment process. From the perspective of CRM, the customer lifecycle has been divided into five progressive stages, which are as follows: identification, acquisition, delivery, development, and retention. Organizations develop financial bonds, social bonds, structural bonds, and customization bonds. The Web experience and communication through the wireless Web is called e-CRM, where in organizations benefit through operational, analytical and collaborative CRM. SFA, campaign management, CSS, CVM, and KAM are key CRM applications for organizations.

Concept Review Questions

1. Define CRM. What are the goals of CRM? What are the building blocks of CRM?
2. Write short notes on the following CRM processes:
   (a) Strategy development process
   (b) Value-creation process
   (c) Multichannel integration process
   (d) The information management process
   (e) The performance assessment process
3. Differentiate between the different types of customers in the customer lifecycle.
4. What are CRM bonds? How can organizations develop bonds with customers and benefit from them?
5. Differentiate between operational, analytical, and collaborative CRM.
6. What is SFA?
7. How can organizations use the concept of KAM to differentiate between strategic accounts and identify organizations where synergistic relationships can be developed?

Critical Thinking Questions

1. Identify a typical CRM software that offers modules for *e*-marketing.
2. Study how Apple is using its online communities for CVM.
3. Discuss how you would develop an online web-space for the purpose of KAM.
4. Develop a comparative analysis of CRM tools used in organizations, across different modules and functionalities. For example, Microsoft CRM and my SAP.com or Siebel and Oracle.

Practising Digital Marketing

The following project can be conducted in groups of 3–4 students.

Student groups can chose from one of the following themes:

- CRM in a *virtual world*
- CRM in the *banking* sector
- CRM and the IT industry
- CRM in hospitality/telecom/airlines
- CRM in logistics
- CRM in international business
- CRM in consulting

Study the CRM processes (internal CRM processes for improving employee productivity and external processes for improving the organization–consumer interface) in the vertical/organization chosen. Based on your study, develop a *conceptual model* to depict the processes. Based on your understanding, develop a questionnaire (12–15 questions). The survey can be administered to either employees or consumers. For an employee-based survey, for the evaluation of internal processes, 50 respondents will be required. For a consumer-based survey, data should be collected across at least 100 respondents. The respondent sample should not be skewed. For data collection, survey can be hosted online (*www.surveymonkey.com*, *www.qualtrics.com* or *google-docs*). Data analysis can be done using statistics tools like SPSS (statistical package for the social sciences) or any open source statistics software. Based on the data collected, CRM strategies have to be formulated for better consumer-segmentation/process improvement/productivity enhancement/identification of customers with greater CLV (customer lifetime value). Strategies can be developed for KAM and campaign management.

References

1. Chen, I.J. and Popvich, K., (2003). 'Understanding customer relationship management (CRM): People, process and technology'. *Business Process Management Journal*, Vol. 9(5), pp. 672–688.
2. Singh, D. and Agrawal, D.P., (2003). 'CRM practices in Indian industries'. *International Journal of Customer Relationship Management*, Vol. 5, pp. 241–258.
3. Rajagopal, Sanchez, R., (2005). 'Analysis of customer portfolio andrelationship management models: Bridging managerial dimensions.'*The Journal of Business and Industrial Marketing*, Vol. 20(6), pp. 307–316.
4. Joseph, P.B., Peppers, D., and Rogers, M., (1995). 'Do you want to keep your customersforever.' *Harvard Business Review*, Vol. 73(2), pp.103–104.
5. Hobby, J., (1999).'Looking after the one who matters'. *Accountancy Age*, pp. 28–30.
6. Buttle, F., The CRM value chain, *Marketing Business*, 2001, pp. 52–55, from <www.wtcbrescia.it/upload/0-FButtlE-CRMvalchain.pdf>, last accessed on 25 January, 2008.
7. Natarajan, R. and Shekhar, B., (2000).'Data mining for CRM: Some relevant issues'. *Proceedings of the First International Conference on Customer Relationship Management*, New Delhi, India, pp. 81–90.
8. Shainesh, G. and Sheth, J., Conceptual foundations of CRM, *Customer Relationship Management: A Strategic Initiative*, Macmillan, 2006.
9. Berry, L. L., Relationship marketing. *American Marketing Association*, 1983.
10. Parasuraman, A. and Grewal, D., (2000). 'The impact of technology on the quality-value-loyalty chain: A research agenda'. *Journal of the Academy of Marketing Science*, Vol. 28(1), pp. 168–174.
11. Peppers, D., Rogers, M., and Dorf, B., (1999). 'Is your company ready for one-to-one marketing'. *Harvard Business Review*, Vol. 77(1), pp. 151–160.
12. Buttle, F., *Customer Relationship Management: Concepts and Technologies*, First Edition, Elsevier Butterworth Heinemann, Oxford, (2009), ISBN: 978-1-85617-522-7.
13. Berry, M. J.A. and Linoff, G.S., *Automatic Cluster Datamining Techniques*, Second Edition, Wiley Publications, (2007), p. 354.
14. Sheth, J.N. and Parvatiyar, A., *Handbook of Relationship Marketing, Response Book*, 2000.
15. Yen, X., et al., *Adopting Customer Relationship Management Technology*, MCBUP Ltd., 2002, pp. 441–452.
16. Ryals, L. and Payne, A.F.T., (2001). 'Customer relationship management in financialservices: Towards information-enabled relationship marketing'. *Journal of Strategic Marketing*, pp. 1–25.
17. Glazer, R., (2002). 'Measuring the value of information: The information-intensive organization'. *IBM Systems Journal*, Vol. 32(1), pp. 99–110.
18. Berry, M. J.A. and Linoff, G.S., Automatic cluster detection, *Datamining Techniques*, Second Edition, Wiley Publications, 2007, p. 354.
19. Payne A. and Frow, P., (2005). 'A strategic framework for customer relationshipmanagement'. *Journal of Marketing*, Vol. 69, pp. 167–176.
20. Reinartz, W., Krafft, M., and Hoyer, W.D., (2004). 'The customerrelationship management process: Its measurement and impact on performance'. *Journal of Marketing Research*, Vol. 41(3), pp. 293–305.
21. Buttle, F., The CRM value chain, *Marketing Business*, 2004, pp. 52–55, from <www.wtcbrescia.it/upload/0-FButtlE-CRMvalchain.pdf>, last accessed on 25 January, 2008.
22. Storbacka, K., Customer profitability: Analysis and design issues. In: Sheth, J.N. and Parvatiyar, A., (eds.), *Handbook of Relationship Marketing*, Sage Publications, Thousand Oaks, CA, 2000, pp. 565–586.
23. Ansari, A. and Mela, C.F., (2003). 'E-customization'. *Journal of Marketing Research*, Vol. 40(2), pp. 131–145.
24. Shan, L.P. and Lee, J.N., *Using E-CRM for a Unified View of the Customer*, ACM Press, New York, NY, 2003, 0002-0782/03/0400.
25. Feinberg, R. and Kadam, R., (2002). 'E-CRM Web service attributes as determinants of customer satisfaction with retail websites'. *International Journal of Service Industry Management*, Vol. 13(5), pp. 432–451.
26. Tanner, J.G., Ahearne, M., Leigh, T., Mason, C.H., and Moncrief, W.C., (2005). 'CRM in sales—intensive organizations: A review and future directions'. *Journal of Personal Selling and Sales Management*, Vol. 25(2), pp. 169–180.

27. Strauss, J., El-Ansary, A.I., and Frost, R., Customer relationship management, *E-marketing*, Fourth Edition, Pearson–Prentice Hall, 2007, p. 403.
28. Boulding, W., Staelin, R., Ehret, M., and Johnston, W.J., (2005). 'A customer relationship management roadmap: What is known, potential pitfalls, and where to go'. *Journal of Marketing*, pp. 155–166.
29. Pardo, C., et al., (1995). 'The key accountization of the firm'. *Industrial Marketing Management*, Vol. 22, pp. 123–43.
30. Grönroos, C., (1984). 'A service quality model and its marketing implications'. *European Journal of Marketing*, Vol. 18(4), pp. 36–44.
31. Ojasalo, J., (2001). 'Key account management at company and individual levels inbusiness-to-business relationships'. *Journal of Business and Industrial Marketing*, Vol. 16(3), pp. 199–218.
32. Platt, Michael, (2007), Web 2.0 in the Enterprise, the *Architechture Journal*, Microsoft Developer Network, MSDN Architecture Centre.
33. Herring, S.C., (1993). 'Gender and democracy in computer-mediated communication'. *Electronic Journal of Communication*.
34. Owyang, J., (2007), *Trendwatch: MicroMedia Provides Bite-sized Voice and Video to Micro Audiences*, Web Strategy, http://www.web-strategist.com/.
35. *Sources for Discussion on Software Platforms—*www.SAP.com.

Section 2
Business Drivers in the Virtual World

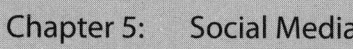

Chapter 5:   Social Media

Chapter 6:   Online Branding

Chapter 7:   Traffic Building

Chapter 8:   Web Business Models

Chapter 9:   *E*-commerce

Social Media

LEARNING OBJECTIVES

After reading this chapter, you will be able to:
- Understand the concept and tools of Web 2.0
- Get familiar with the concepts associated with social media and social media models
- Observe the different tools in the social media analytics space
- Get the concepts related to the new-age *e*-enterprise: Internet-based collaboration, innovation, and co-creation

WEB 2.0

Web 2.0 is not a clearly demarcated period in the history of the Web. Instead, it is a set of capabilities enabling the Web consumer to become the 'prosumer' (a new word coined to describe the ability to produce and consume). As early as 1997, the concept of weblogs (what eventually came to be known as blogs) was gaining mindshare. The Web consumer could now actually participate in authoring the webpage that they were reading. Hence, the term 'prosumer' or participative Web became popular. From multiple prosumers, companies soon found themselves in the territory of collaboration and social networking. It was indeed a simple yet profound change. The foundational capabilities that enabled this were as follows:

- A new way to navigate (tagging, search). Users could comfortably use search engines in their quest for information and also use tags, which are keywords attached to pieces of information, which could describe an item and allow it to be found again by browsing or searching.
- Rich user experience (richness, interactivity, signalling, and syndication). Dynamic content which is responsive to user input, a degree of interactivity by virtue of individuals being able to contribute to the read–write Web, and signals comprising the use of syndication technology, such as rich site syndication (RSS) to notify users of content changes, has enriched the online user experience.

- Federated authorship (wikis, blogs, ratings, comments, uploading audio, and video). A huge volume of content could be created by individual users (who became authors in the new era), using a variety of Web 2.0 tools. This content could subsequently be content syndication, which is an agreement in which an author allows his or her work to be re-posted merged into the plethora of information circulating on the Internet. This ushered in the era of what was termed as social media (Fig. 5.1).

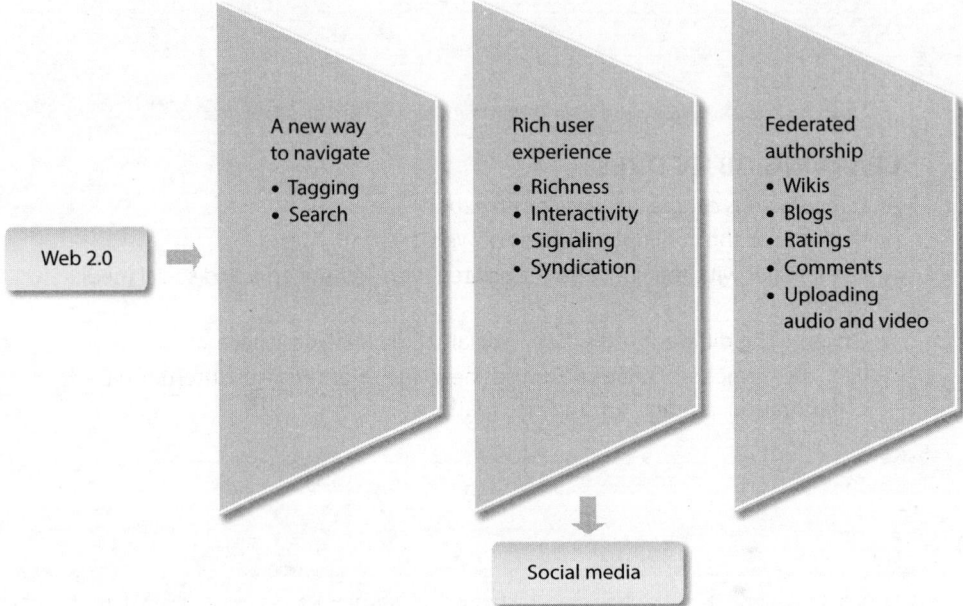

Fig. 5.1 Web 2.0 and social media

SOCIAL MEDIA

Social media refers to the means of interaction among people in which they create, share, and exchange information and ideas in virtual communities and networks.[1] Andreas Kaplan and Michael Haenlein define social media as a *group of Internet-based applications that build on the ideological and technological* foundations of Web 2.0 and that allow the creation and exchange of user-generated content.[2] Furthermore, social media depends on mobile and web-based technologies to create highly interactive platforms via which individuals and communities share, co-create, discuss, and modify user-generated content. It introduces substantial and pervasive changes in communication between organizations, communities, and individuals.[3]

The necessary Internet has ushered in an era of individuals and individualization, wherein while operating at an individual level, person-content-product has become an important dimension of online marketing. At the same time, it spells significant opportunities for social media. This supports secure interaction and is essential for a low-cost personalized information and product customization. The Internet creates more accountability and traceability and is subsequently becoming the base for a wide variety of business practices.

Despite its low cost, social media accounts for about 10% of the advertising budgets worldwide.[4] Consumers care about what other consumers think, and those with the widest reach have the potential to sway lots of friends and followers. According to the survey, blogs were considered more likely to influence an Internet user's purchase decision than any other social channels, including Facebook; only brand and retailer's sites ranked higher. Blogs are the primary place where influencers engage with online fans; 86% of those individuals who Technorati Media deemed influencers blogged regularly and more than half of them operated between two to five blogs.

THE SOCIAL MEDIA MODEL BY McKINSEY

McKinsey's social media model (Fig. 5.2),[5] namely, monitor–respond–amplify–lead enables targeted marketing responses at individual touch-points along the consumer decision journey.

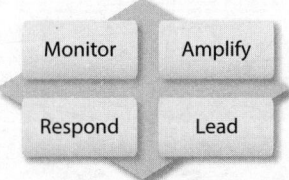

Fig. 5.2 The social media—Monitor, amplify, respond, and lead model

Monitoring involves scrutinizing organizational brands in real time across social media. Companies can track data built, data visualizations, and dashboards and run sentiment analyses around product and campaign launches.

Amplification involves designing an organization's marketing activities to have an inherent social motivator that spurs broader engagement and sharing. It means that the core concepts for campaigns must invite customers into an experience that they can choose to extend by joining a conversation with the brand, product, fellow users, and other enthusiasts.

Responding includes reacting to controversies floating about the organization in the social media space, countering negative comments, and reinforcing positive ones to increase the reputation of the organization.

Leading involves leading customers towards making long-term behavioural changes. This may involve boosting brand awareness by driving Web traffic to content about existing products and services.

What we are witnessing is an unprecedented process of technological democratization. In the context of corporate reporting, the main application of the Web 2.0 technologies and the social media[6] is that of corporate dialogue. This concept means that companies can take advantage of the evolution of the capacities of the Web so that they can provide information in much greater detail and of more use to the users allowing users to participate effectively through the use of these new platforms.

Figure 5.3 shows the multidirectional flows between the stakeholders of any public or private entity (shareholders, owners, managers, employees, customers, users, suppliers, authorities, competitors, local communities, and environment).

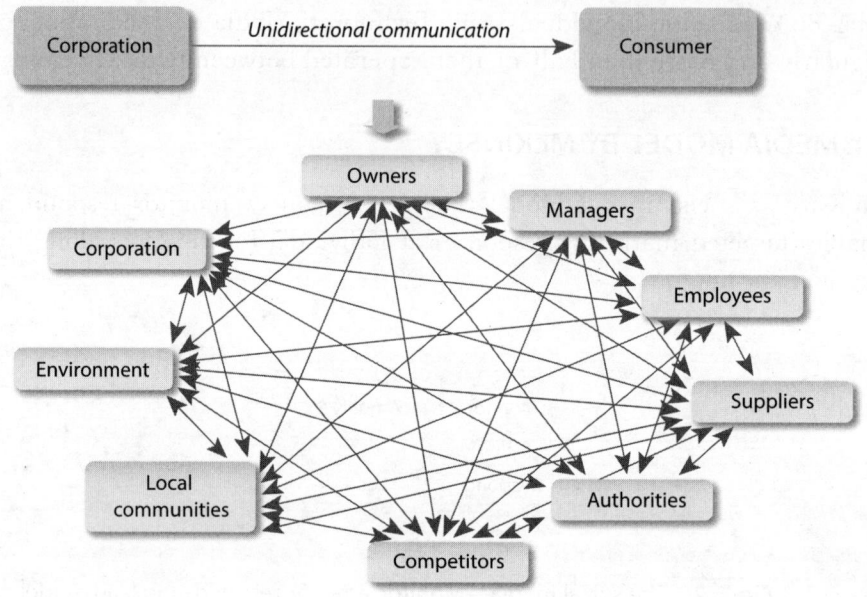

Fig. 5.3 Multi-directional communication flow between corporation and stakeholders (shareholders and customers)

Adopting a corporate dialogue would mean putting aside the current model of unidirectional.

This streamlines communication from the corporation to the user and facilitates.

The following are the examples of relationships between potential corporate dialogue and some underlying Web 2.0 technologies[7]:

Content Syndication Webcasting

Content syndication is an agreement in which an author allows his or her work to be reposted. It allows content to be posted from one website to the other after seeking permission. Companies can make use of RSS, that uses standard Web feed formats to publish frequently updated information, such as blogs and news headlines.

Sharing and Bookmarking Facility

A company may be able to disseminate news and results more efficiently from its corporate website through the various leading social networks such as Facebook and

Twitter, which may result in making it more attractive to specific potential investors or customers.

Mashups

The technology can be optimized to integrate different initiatives in a unique corporate website, avoiding inconveniences of dispersion and providing the opportunity to develop a coherent strategy for Web design and development.

In order to better identify with customers in the social media context, brand managers[8] must learn to think like them. Doing so will also enable them to realize the significance consumers place on the opinions of family, friends, and others within the online communities they frequently visit. A recommendation from these sources will often tip the balance in favour of making a purchase. This fact has not escaped the notice of alert operators who have successfully designed social media programmes that resonate emotionally with customers to an extent that they rush out to inform others about their experiences.

A study by the Lenskold Group found that more than three out of four marketers[9] (77 percent) use social media in their marketing efforts and just over half of those marketers (55 percent) indicate that measurements are a high priority.

The drivers of this high priority for measurements include the need for improved effectiveness, the need for better integration, and pressure from executives. Those companies using marketing return on investment (ROI) metrics to assess and improve their general marketing effectiveness have advantages in outgrowing competitors and have more effective and efficient marketing programmes.

Companies gain significantly if their online consumer engagement programmes yield rich results and their consumers become evangelists. Social media enthusiasts often cite the example of American Airlines where the team received kudos and active defence when the brand was being criticized for claiming that their new logo was an improvement to the customer experience. Defence of organizations by customers is a significant step towards social media success.

MARKETING WITH NETWORKS

Organizations gain significantly by creating value with networks. This can be done because of the ubiquitous nature of online networks, their speed, sharing abilities, specialization, and a host of other virtual value activities. Metcalf's law has significant applications in this field, and this is discussed in detail in Chapter 10, of relevance here is the economic logic of hype.[10]

- Expectations matter when an investment in a network makes sense for the user if the network reaches a critical mass.
- A user will find it valuable to belong to a network if the value of the network exceeds the cost.

EXHIBIT 5.1 IBM

IBM has a site called 'social business at IBM', which is a central resource base for all 'social' engagement. This includes features such as education modules, which explore everything from behaviours to specific tools, which employees can use. There is also something called the 'expertise locator' so that employees who are experts at 'social' can become known within the organization and externally on the IBM sites. In short, this became a way to catalogue expertise (which can be searched). IBM has a long legacy of using collaboration tools, and they have had the good fortune of working in an environment that embraces collaboration. One of the essential events that helped shape this collaboration are their 'jams', which are collaboration sessions that they have been hosting since the 1990s. They helped shape the IBM culture and are a prime reason for IBM being 'social'. The 'Values Jam' was a restatement of the core beliefs of IBM as a company. This was a jam around what it meant to work for IBM, emphasizing what the values are. The IBM CEO and Chairman and the IBM CIO were both there, which showed the company's commitment. IBM has been on a business strategy to integrate the company and break down silos for the better part of the decade.

Some examples of IBM's internal social media footprint today include the following:

- 17,000 individual blogs
- 1 million daily page views of internal wikis, internal information-storing websites
- 4,00,000 employee profiles on IBM connections, IBM's initial social networking initiative that allows employees to share status updates, collaborate on wikis, blogs and activity and share files
- 15,000,000 downloads of employee-generated videos/podcasts and 20 million minutes of LotusLive meetings every month with people both inside and outside the organization
- More than 400k same time instant messaging users, resulting in 40–50 million instant messages per day

Some examples of IBM's external social media footprint today include the following:

- Over 25,000 IBMers actively tweeting on Twitter and counting
- Approximately, 30,000 IBMers on LinkedIn
- This number is growing at 24% per year
- Making IBM the largest employee presence of any firm on the platform
- Approximately, 198,000 IBMers on Facebook

In addition, IBM has a whole group called Blue IQ, which is designed to get sales people to be expert collaborators. The whole social business programme at IBM has courses and training programmes along with policies and governance. The tools and internal environment are always being upgraded as well. Internal communications also continue to reinforce these processes. Executive participation is crucial to make this happen and thus—even the CEO is involved.

(*Source*: Implementing Enterprise 2.0 at IBM, www.ibm.org. Reprinted with permission from IBM)

The Internet explosion ushered in an era of fascination and functionality, an era demonstrating the virtuous cycle of the Web (Fig. 5.4) and an era of network evolution for marketing and business. Digital environments are participatory, procedural, spatial, and encyclopaedic, and this has opened up new vistas for marketing.

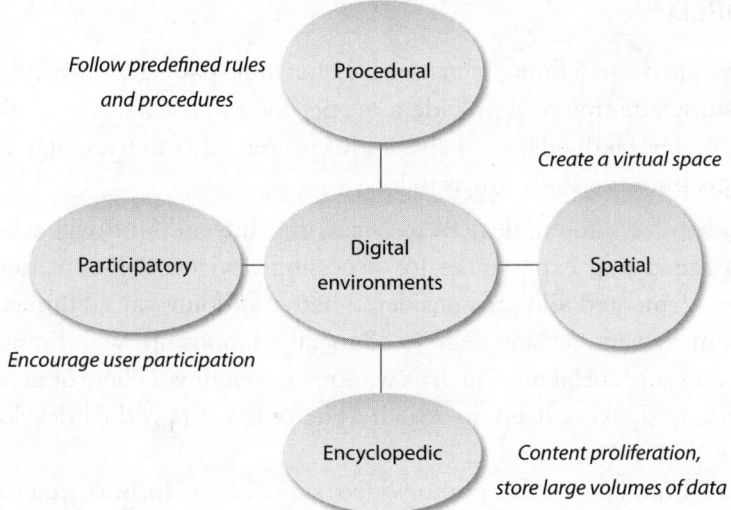

Fig. 5.4 The virtuous cycle of the Web

The US interactive marketing forecast, 2011 to 2016, predicts the need for bigger interactive teams, greater excitement about emerging media, effectiveness of interactive marketing, and greater customer obsession with the Internet. As per the report, we get to know the following:

Social media management is relatively low cost   It is relatively low cost even with widespread adoption. Listening platforms cost only about $5000 to $10,000 per month. Developing owned social assets like a Facebook page could run high costs, but this is a one-time cost, far lesser than a paid search budget.

Social networks tender limited paid inventory   The biggest social media outlets for advertisers such as Facebook and Twitter have only a few pay-per-click advertising options. Twitter offers a few paid media products while Facebook has added some new products such as sponsored stories. It has fewer formats than traditional online portals. So, while social media matters a lot to big advertisers like Hewlett-Packard, they spend more on internal resources to build and oversee social media assets.

Listening will develop into social intelligence   Growth will come as more organizations buy listening platforms like Trackur or Crimson Hexagon to monitor social conversations. However, the bigger investment is expected to come from firms integrating social data into their existing customer database as part of customer relationship management (CRM) upgrades—a spend not typically made by the interactive marketer.[28] Marketing services provider Merkle already positions itself as a specialist at *connected CRM* that tethers the marketing database to digital channels in order to create marketing, sales, and service opportunities.

The *e*-marketer survey for analysing select metrics when evaluating influencers in the social media space, 2012 identifies Facebook *friends* and *likes* and Twitter followers along with a blog's *unique users* and *blog page views* as the most important defining parameters.

THE SOCIAL WORLD

Social media is redefining consumer behaviour patterns. Recently, Lodestar UM's WAVE study attempted to provide a deeper look into what social relations can deliver for brands. The sixth edition of the study covered 62 countries including India.

Excerpts from the study are as follows:

- Marketers have many devices to access the Internet and will subsequently have to customize digital experiences for accessing devices. Different devices have started getting segmented and are considered better at doing varied things.
- Consumers want varying degrees of social relationships with brands. This can range from very superficial ones such as wanting discount vouchers or access to entertaining content, to the very deep ones such as helping with product development or being a part of a brand community.
- Official brand websites, photo/video sites, blogs, forums, microblogs, and social networks are useful social platforms. They are used by active Internet users to meet new people, stay in touch with friends, make contacts for work, promote themselves, learn something new, share knowledge, change opinions, be creative, express themselves, make money, have fun/be entertained, create a sense of belongingness, share new experiences, earn respect, hang out, be up-to-date, explore the world around them, manage lives better and seek other people's opinions.
- Social networks, followed by blogs serve as the most useful platforms for active Internet users by helping them achieve the above objectives.

Hence, social media offers a viable solution for organizations to interact and engage online users in a dialogue. Companies need to keep a consistent flow of information and customize digital experiences across a wide range of access devices ranging from laptops to mobile handsets. Interacting with consumers in their social platforms will help companies use social media as a tool to form significant brand–consumer relationships.

SOCIAL MEDIA ANALYTICS

A significant amount of content is generated via social media in the online domain. Organizations can derive actionable information from this content by performing social media analysis. This is done through a series of analytical tools. For clarity, let us look at some of the following definitions:

- Social media analytics refers to the technology used to monitor, measure and analyse activity by users of the Web 2.0 framework to provide information assisting business decisions. Social media analytics encompasses business intelligence tools such as reporting, dash-boarding, visualization, search, event-driven alerting and text mining. They are applied to information sourced from social media such as Twitter and Facebook.
- Social network analysis is advanced analytics that is specifically focused on identifying and forecasting connections, relationships and influence among individuals and groups.

EXHIBIT 5.2 Digital Conversations

Conversations in the digital age allow organizations and consumers to engage in interactions facilitated by the collaborative Web. Interactivity is one such characteristic that allows two involved entities to exchange information and facilitate learning for each other. This feature of the online media has been found to be favourable with organizations as well as consumers. While participation of consumers aid the domains of co-creation, feeds organizational feedback mechanisms, and contributes to knowledge resources, what is it that leads a consumer to venture into an interactive online organizational domain—In fact, what is the role of interactivity?

Two angles to this thought were that the consumer perspective on the purpose of interactivity and the structural features of an online site that catered to the function of interactivity.

Querying consumers showed that *accepting feedback and allowing a two-way interaction between organization and user* were primary functions of interactivity. *Consumer engagement, the ability to facilitate location of information* and *building brand relationships* surfaced as other key areas where these characteristics played a role. The consumer perceptual system clearly seemed to focus on cooperation and coordination. To evaluate the organizational online domain, for their structural characteristics, corporate blogs of fortune 500 companies were studied. Several parameters catering to the function of interactivity were identified and by further grouping them by virtue of their adherence to the consumer-listed functions, it was observed that a maximum number of structural features appeared to cater to the objective of building a brand relationship.

Using a combination of the two, an interactivity score was calculated and interestingly a positive correlation was observed between the interactivity score and the online reach as well as the Technorati authority of a blog. Increasing the reach and popularity of an online venture is the dream of any organization. Hence, maximizing the interactivity score using linear programming showed that it made more sense for an organization to have a corporate blog with maximum number of interactive features, which aided a consumer's search for information, followed by those that catered to building a brand relationship.

Aiding a consumer's *quest for information* is where a blog can score brownie points. Conversations to build brand relationships are important, but coming to the consumer's aid to help him look for what he set out to locate in the first place could very well help an organization or brand make way into a consumer's heart!

It mines transactions, interactions and other behavioural information that may be sourced from social media and/or just as often from CRM, billing and other internal systems.
- Social media monitoring is real-time analytics that uses complex event processing (CEP) to acquire, filter and display events taking place in social media.
- Social intelligence refers to the trend towards incorporation of social network style interaction models, such as those associated with Facebook and wikis into the BI user experience.

EXHIBIT 5.3 Indian Brands and LinkedIn

Indian marketers, namely, Madura Fashion and Lifestyle, WoodLand, DSP BlackRock Mutual Fund, and IT major Wipro are increasingly using LinkedIn to tap social media to woo professionals. As brands recognize LinkedIn's users as professionals with more purchasing power and disposable income than users of other sites, these organizations are using LinkedIn's platform for carrying out promotional campaigns.

LinkedIn provides specific holistic solutions to brands through its LinkedIn marketing solutions. These are in line with the overall marketing objective of the company that is far more effective.

Brand	Followers (July 2014)
Tata Consultancy Services	665,787
Wipro	463,842
HCL Technologies	320,677
Franklin Templeton India	84,090
Infosys	487,059
Tech Mahindra	116,870
Bajaj Finserv	176,785
Biocon	62,322
Mindtree	–
Bharti Axa General Insurance	–

LinkedIn has more than 26 million users in India, accounting to 9% of its total memberships worldwide, and second only to the U.S.

LinkedIn, the business-oriented social networking service, released its ranking of the top 10 most influential global and Indian brands in 2014. The ranking was based on LinkedIn's content marketing score (CMS) that measures the effectiveness of a company's content marketing efforts on LinkedIn. LinkedIn's CMS can be analysed at any point through a company's campaign. It measures member engagement with sponsored updates, company pages, LinkedIn groups, employee updates and influencer posts. A single score is then calculated and ranked against the company's competitive set.

Top 10 Indian and Global brands released by LinkedIn are as follows:

The list of top 10 global brands released by LinkedIn includes Forbes, World Economic Forum, *Inc. Magazine*, Microsoft, *Financial Times*, *The Wall Street Journal*, Hewlett Packard, Salesforce.com, IBM, and Mashable.

Companies can benefit by using LinkedIn through the following means:

- Send continuous industry news updates to users
- Regularly release new and useful content for users
- Relevant conversations
- Personalized interactions with the audience
- Benchmark content marketing efforts against competitors
- Enhance influence

Interestingly, the most influential brands on LinkedIn in India belong to the IT sector, as against media companies globally. The success of these companies clearly lies in well-crafted content generation strategies.

Social media analytics has applications in managing content creation, scheduling, publishing and moderation. It further strengthens collaboration, workflow and permissions along with data analytics and reporting. Key capabilities may include sentiment analysis, vertical-specific compliance, marketing campaign automation, integration with legacy marketing and analytics platforms and strategic social media consulting services (Fig. 5.5).

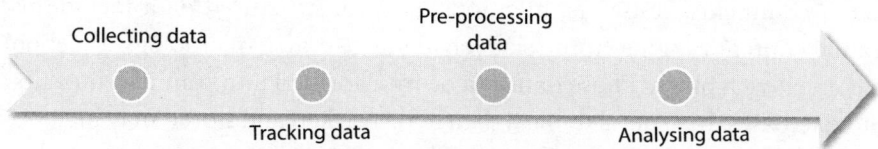

Fig. 5.5 Social media analytics

Information that is available online revolves around the following topics: emotions, opinions and events. This information is available in the form of text, with low to high complexity level, and helps in extracting the emotions and opinions from the written words. Software tools are needed to do the following:

- Collect data
- Extract topics
- Extract sentiments
- Analyse opinions

This section undertakes a generic discussion on the aforementioned topics to generate familiarity with the concept.

Data Collecting

The very first step regarding data collection is to determine the sources of the data. With skyrocketing growth in the user base in recent years, social networking sites and micro-blogging services, with their most prominent examples such as Facebook and Twitter, offer a huge amount of user-generated content in an unprecedented scope. As a longer established social media type, weblogs are not to be neglected either. Regarding Twitter, the data to be tracked and monitored are in the form of public 'tweets'. For Facebook, the most important kind of data represent the content of the 'wall' including 'status updates' and corresponding comments.

Data Tracking

Both Twitter and Facebook offer application programming interfaces (API) for data tracking. The most frequently used API for Twitter are 'search API' and 'streaming API', while Facebook's 'graph API' allows programmers to conveniently track wall postings (i.e., status updates and comments). In contrast, weblogs do not provide such a standardized way to get access to the data. However, most blogs do offer RSS feeds, which can be easily tracked. For those without RSS function, web-crawling techniques such as HTML parsing are necessary.

Data types

Within each data source, there are elements of both structured and unstructured data. While structured data (or more precisely metadata) comprise profile/user demographics, spatial, temporal, and thematic data as well as attention-related data (e.g., number of 'likes', comments, re-tweets, mentions, etc.), unstructured data include user-generated textual content ranging from relatively context-sparse microblogs, Facebook comments, to context-rich blogs. Those data can be transformed into common formats and ingested into databases. In general, typical data to be tracked and stored may include, for instance, ID of the posting, time stamp, username (of the author), content of the posting, and possibly the type of posting (i.e., status update, blog entry, or re-tweet, comment).

Tracking approaches

The several different approaches to data tracking (Fig. 5.6) are as follows:

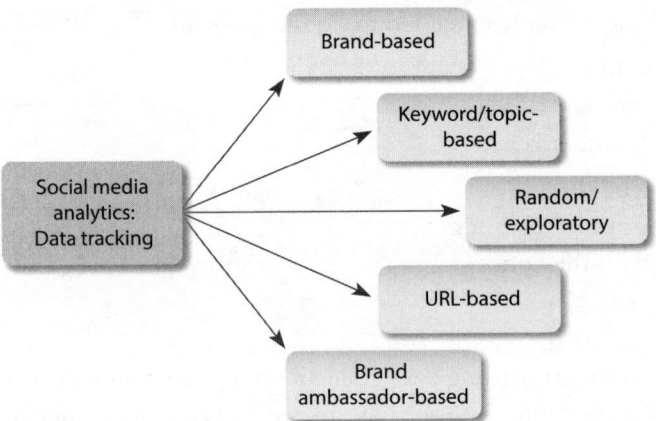

Fig. 5.6 Social media analytics: Approaches for data tracking

Brand-based approach The first approach is applicable when an organizational brand wants to know explicitly how consumers are interacting about them in the social media space. In such cases, the brands can have all tweets collected that contain their name, either as a simple keyword or hashtag. If the brand has its own Facebook presence in terms of a page or group, they should track all posts and corresponding comments published by users or fans/members of their own page or group. Likewise, if the brand also has its own blog, all comments on their blog should be gathered for analysis. Furthermore, it might be useful to collect all Facebook and blog postings that contain the brand name from external pre-defined Facebook groups/pages and blogs, respectively.

Keyword/topic-based approach Brands are interested in the feedback or opinions of social media users for certain brand campaigns and brand-related topics. In this context, the tweets as well as the Facebook and blog postings that involve keywords related to topics of interest can be tracked. To attain a high level of data completeness, relevant keywords representing the topic of interest have to be carefully and systematically chosen in advance. The broader the topic to be analysed, the more keywords should be taken into account.

Random/exploratory approach This approach supports exploratory inductive content mining. The idea behind this tracking approach is to randomly select one or several sets of data (e.g., tweets, Facebook or blog postings) for different time periods for analysis. Based on these random datasets particularly, content analysis might be conducted to identify major brands and detect users' opinions or sentiments associated with those topics.

URL-based approach Given that social media platforms are widely used, among other purposes, to disseminate information, particularly by means of posting URL, organizations may apply a URL-based approach to selectively track content behind hyperlinks shared in tweets, Facebook and blog postings. This might provide additional meaningful insights, especially in case of tweets with a limited length of 140 characters.

Brand ambassador-based approach Brands usually have some celebrities who endorse the brand or function as brand ambassadors. These ambassadors have the power to influence (online) opinion-making processes. Therefore, brands are also interested in monitoring such important users in terms of their generated content. For that, brands track tweets, wall postings, and blog entries as well as corresponding comments specifically contributed by those influential users.

Data Pre-processing

To prepare textual data for further analysis, a pre-processing step needs to be carried out. For example, stop words (i.e., words that only have grammatical significance) are eliminated. In addition, stemming (i.e., reducing inflected or sometimes derived words to their stem, base, or root form) as well as lemmatization (i.e., grouping together the different inflected forms of a word so that they can be analysed as a single item) might also be performed to facilitate further analyses.

Data Analysis

Organizations conduct social media analysis for the following purposes:
- Growing brand equity
- Understanding what customers want by capturing consumer data from social media to understanding attitudes, opinions, trends, and managing online reputation
- Tracking the competition and differentiating the organizational brand by keeping tabs on the most shared content on social media/competitor websites
- Generating consumer engagement by learning what content drives conversions with social audiences and subsequently creating customized campaigns and promotions that resonate with social media participants
- Showing result reports to key stakeholders to articulate the value of social media

- Using the referral source and links directly to company goals and *e*-commerce tracking
- Identifying opinion leaders in the social media space
- Predicting customer behaviour and improving customer satisfaction by recommending next best actions
- Driving more sales, revenue with an integrated approach, to social media analytics

The following section addresses some analysis approaches used commonly in the social media space.

Analysis approaches

There are three major approaches predominantly used for data analysis in the social media space (Fig. 5.7).

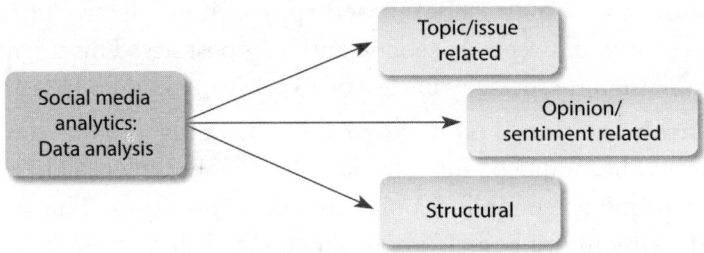

Fig. 5.7 Social media analytics: Approaches for data analysis

Topic/issue/trend-based approach For brands, it is important to identify and monitor discussions regarding specific topics, campaigns, or issues, particularly those that might have a direct or indirect association with sales and brand reputation in the context of potential for creating controversy. In order to identify topics, content analysis or, more specifically, text mining techniques may be applied. Content analysis is a technique for making replicable and valid inferences from texts (or other meaningful matter) to the contexts of their use. Given the massive amounts of social media data, automated quantitative methods of content analysis or text mining are necessary. These methods are suitable for providing answers to a broad variety of questions, among which are the classification of texts and the identification and modelling of recurring topics.

There are different approaches of text classification. Besides descriptive and explorative approaches, such as word-frequency analysis or co-occurrence analysis as well as deductive approaches including dictionary-based coding or rule-based parsing, there are a number of new approaches for automated text analysis, specifically text classification based on unsupervised and supervised learning as well as semantic network analysis. In particular, supervised text classification, which uses statistical algorithms from machine learning, has the potential to become a standard method for automated text mining. In addition, documents might be clustered based on unsupervised learning using techniques such as hierarchical and k-means clustering.

Of substantial significance to this domain are as follows:
- Topic modelling
- Trend-detecting algorithms

Regarding topic modelling, recent advances in natural processing language provide more sophisticated statistical models for discovering abstract topics that occur in documents.

Trends in social networks have recently been a major focus of interest among both research and industry, and there are a variety of algorithms to predict emerging topics pertaining to brands.

Opinion/sentiment-based approach Given the rapid growth of social media, consumers are able to express their views, opinions, or emotions on almost anything in forums, blogs, and on social networking sites more than ever before. This applies particularly to the consumer–brand dialogue that enables organizations to generate a consumer–brand relationship.

Opinions are important because whenever consumers need to make a decision, they want to hear others' opinions. This is not only true for individuals, also for organizations. It is important for companies to keep a track of prevailing consumer sentiment (positive or negative emotions) or opinions expressed by others about themselves as a person or organization. In recent years, sentiment analysis or opinion mining has emerged as a distinct method to study people's opinions in terms of views, attitudes, appraisals, and emotions towards entities, events, and their attributes in a more thorough way. It is vital for companies to find relevant sites, extract related sentences with opinions, read them, summarize them, and organize them into usable forms. Automated opinion discovery and summarization systems are thus needed, which can be accomplished by sentiment analysis.

Sentiment analysis can be performed based on two different approaches. The first one is the traditional dictionary-based classification of sentiment orientation including polarity (positive, negative, neutral) and strength, that is, dictionaries of words annotated with their sentiment orientation are used to extract sentiment from the text. Recently, sentiment analysis makes use of another approach based on machine learning where the classification of sentiment can be formulated as a learning problem with three classes, which are positive, negative, and neutral. Here, sentiment classification can be performed based on supervised or unsupervised learning. This subject has been addressed in greater detail in Chapter 11.

Structural approach Brands might be interested in identifying influential consumers or opinion leaders, in particularly those who are significant to organizations in the context of profit or relationship potential. By monitoring these users, brands might be able to have a certain influence on those users' opinion. Companies use social network analysis for this purpose. One such example is discussed in detail in Chapter 13.

Social network analysis studies the relations linking persons, organizations, interest groups, states, by analysing the structure of these relations. To identify influential users, companies have to measure the influence. There are a number of different measures of influence of a user in a network. Influence is determined by many factors, such as the novelty and resonance of the messages of the opinion leader with those of their audience and the quality and frequency of the content they generate. In particular, resonance in terms of re-tweets (Twitter) and comments (Facebook and blogs) is very important for organizations.

SOCIAL MEDIA TOOLS

There are a series of established tools being used by organizations to perform social media analytics. This section profiles the following social media tools:

- SAP Social Media Analytics by Netbase
- Google Analytics
- Social Crawlytics
- IBM Social Media Analytics

SAP Social Media Analytics by Netbase

The SAP® Social Media Analytics application by Netbase helps organizations track and monitor what customers are saying about a company's products and services on social media sites all over the world. Delivered on demand with data from more than 95 million sources, this solution helps organizations grow their brand equity with insights that they can act on to deliver what the company's customers want.

Objectives

- Grow brand equity
- Understand what customers want
- Track the competition and differentiate an organizational brand

Solution highlights

- On-demand delivery with instant access to volumes of social media data
- Natural language processing to understand what customers really mean
- Analysis tools for more details and deeper insights
- Scorecards to measure brand passion and the status of competitors
- Access via API to integrate with other SAP applications

Benefits

- Better brand management and greater customer loyalty
- Improved competitive analysis and insight
- Low risk and minimal up-front investment with on-demand delivery

Google Analytics

Google Analytics is a service offered by Google that generates detailed statistics about a website's traffic and traffic sources and measures conversions and sales. The product is aimed at marketers as opposed to webmasters and technologists from which the industry of Web analytics originally grew. It's the most widely used website statistics service.

Social media measurement using Google analytics is conducted using social reports, social conversions, and social sources.

Social reports help organizations measure the impact social media has on their business goals and conversions. Integrated Web and social data provides a holistic view of the content and community.

Social conversions report enables social media marketing accountability and clearly shows how social media impacts organizational business.

Objectives

- Shows conversion rates and the monetary value of conversions that occurred due to visits from social networks by linking the visits to consumer goals and *e*-commerce transactions.
- Enables organizations to choose the goals that are important to their business and subsequently review how social media as a source is helping them achieve those goals.

Solution highlights

- Helps companies measure the impact of social media on their goals in simple, ready-to-use reports
- Helps companies learn what content drives conversions with social audiences
- Shows result reports to key stakeholders to articulate the value of social media
- Uses the referral source and links directly to company goals and *e*-commerce tracking
- The reports break out the contribution of social media as being the last referring source of your customer, for example, they come to your site directly from a social site and can also break out the instances where a social site was involved further up in the conversion chain.

Social Sources

Social sources reports help an organization refine its social tactics and move them from 'gut feel' to data driven.

Objectives

- Helps organizations get an overview of key social networks for the organizational brand
- Observes which networks are sending traffic
- Visualizes how visitors flow from social networks through the organizational site
- Uses social sources to discover which social platforms are most relevant to the company

Solution highlights

- The social sources reports automatically segment and group referral traffic from hundreds of *social* networks, allowing organizations to focus on the analysis.
- The originating social networks group referral traffic across platforms, such as YouTube
- It identifies which networks are driving traffic to any specific page
- It identifies which content is popular across all the different social networks
- The comparison charts display all traffic and traffic from social sources

Social Crawlytics

It is a free online tool that analyses how popular or unpopular the content is on a website. It's very useful to assess the performance of a company's competitor's blog.

Objectives

- Analyses the content and produces detailed information on where content is shared and how often it's shared.
- Detailed content analysis can help organizations understand the type of content they can create and share.
- Simultaneously, companies can identify content typologies that do not resonate with their competitors.

Solution highlights

- Identify the most shared content on social media or a competitor website.
- Identify blog authors who get the most shares. This works correctly if the website has implemented Google author tags.

Benefits

- Organizations can *set up scheduled reports*, which automatically provide updated reports on selected websites.
- When social crawlytics traverses through a website, it picks out all the blog posts and displays these posts in order of popularity on social media channels.

The IBM Social Media Analytics Solution

Social media analytics is a powerful tool for uncovering customer sentiment dispersed across countless online sources. As businesses feel the pressure to gain new insights from social media, they require the analytics expertise to transform this flood of information into actionable strategies.

Objectives

- Helps organizations to take control of this data so that they can improve customer satisfaction, identify patterns and trends, and make smarter decisions regarding marketing campaigns.

- Empowers companies with data to help them formulate actionable strategies for strategic issues.

Solution highlights

- Capture consumer data from social media to understand attitudes, opinions, trends, and manage online reputation
- Predict customer behaviour and improve customer satisfaction by recommending next best actions
- Create customized campaigns and promotions that resonate with social media participants
- Identify the primary influencers within specific social network channels
- Drive more sales, revenue with an integrated approach to social media analytics

The IBM Social Media Analytics solution can help an organization gain new insights across marketing, customer service, product development, and supply chain. Built on IBM's leading analytics platform, the solution analyses the social media impact of your products, services, markets, campaigns, employees, and partners. The IBM Social Media Analytics solution can segment the consumer audience across geography, demographics, influencers, recommenders, detractors, users, and prospective users. It enables companies to measure social media activities, behaviours and sentiment, and discover the affinities, associations, and causes that drive them.

Benefits

Companies can transform massive volumes of social media data into highly effective business insights and actions, which are as follows:

- The solution provides customized results in configurable, easy-to-understand charts and dashboards.
- The companies can act quickly to improve customer satisfaction, enhance brand reputation, mitigate problems, and anticipate new opportunities.
- The companies can integrate social media insights with analytics platforms and business processes.

THE SOCIAL WEB

The Forrester report on 'The future of the social Web', April 2009, talks about the five eras of the social Web and traces the role of the changing consumer. The five eras are elaborately explained as the following:

- *The era of social relationships* Beginning in the mid-1990s, people signed up for online profiles and connected with their friends to share information.
- *The era of social functionality* Subsequently, social networking evolved into more than just a platform for 'friending' but one that can support a broader array of 'social interactive applications.' However, identities are essentially disconnected silos within individual sites.

- *The era of social colonization* By late 2009, technologies such as OpenID and Facebook connect began to break down the barriers of social networks and allow individuals to integrate their social connections as part of their online experience, blurring the lines between networks and traditional sites.
- *The era of social context* In 2010, sites began to recognize personal identities and social relationships to deliver customized online experiences. Social networks became the 'base of operation for everyone's online experiences'.
- *The era of social commerce* In approximately two years after that, social networks became more powerful than corporate websites and CRM systems as individual identities and relationships were building on this platform. Brands served community interests and grew on the basis of community advocacy as users continued to drive innovation in this direction.

The following section traces how the social Web impacts the employees, partners, and suppliers in an organization.

Employees Concepts of enterprise 2.0 or the social enterprise lead organizations to embrace the principles of openness, transparency, and collaboration, which are being leveraged internally. The internal culture and values propagate to the customers, partners, and suppliers thereby resulting in an integrated approach leading to increased productivity and cost savings and, further, a readiness to embrace new opportunities and challenges.

Partners and suppliers Organizational partners, especially with reference to the marketing intermediaries offer a channel for market sensing, as they are closer to the consumers. While firms were already following the business practice of making partners an integral part of the R&D, marketing, sales and service organizations, the collaborative Web offers greater opportunities for creating the same culture of openness and transparency with its partners as it does with customers or employees. Creation of partner communities where interaction between the company and partners makes the partners feel valued, while soliciting their opinions, can create synergistic environments for growth, innovation, and development of competitive strategies for better positioning, greater market differentiation, and targeting.

With inevitable cuts in marketing budgets, more and more corporate groups are using the online medium to reach their consumers in a meaningful way. In this context, we explore the usage of a corporate blog as a CRM tool to enable an organization to interact with its customers, employees, and partners later in the chapter. Diverse Web 2.0 initiatives result in better organizational listening via social media monitoring, greater transparency via corporate blogs and Twitter profiles, and higher engagement with customer communities on social networking sites.

A BROAD LOOK AT THE B2C AND B2B SCENARIOS

An analysis of the 100 most valuable brands in the USA (according to *Business Week*, 2007) and how they use 11 different social media channels ranked the following brands as most effective in terms of social Web engagement: Starbucks, Dell and eBay based on their breadth and depth of engagement. Following these came Google, Microsoft, Thomson Reuters, Nike, Amazon, SAP, and Yahoo/Intel that were the top ten brands that were deeply engaged with consumers through the social Web.[10] The study also found out a positive correlation between the use of the social Web and a firm's financial performance. Social Web engagement is seen as a good indicator of an innovative, risk-taking culture and eagerness to engage with the customers. However, it should also be noted that social capital was particularly gained by those organizations that innovated early, often and incrementally.

VIRAL MARKETING

Viral marketing refers to a form of marketing where pre-existing online networks and other technologies are used for marketing purposes by achieving a viral proliferation of a marketing message. Objectives range from trying to produce increases in brand awareness or to achieve other marketing objectives (such as product sales) through self-replicating viral processes analogous to the spread of viruses or computer viruses. These marketing messages can spread from one user to the other virally, either through word-of-mouth or enhanced by the network effects of the Internet and mobile networks.

The most common version of intentional viral marketing occurs when consumers willingly become promoters of a product or service and spread the word to their friends; they are driven to do so either through an explicit incentive (e.g., financial incentives, need to create network externalities) or simply out of a desire to share the product benefits with friends (e.g., fun, intriguing, valuable for others).[11]

Dimensions of the viral marketing strategy include the following:

- Effortless transfer to others
- Scalability
- Exploitation of consumer motivations
- Exploitation of consumer emotions and behaviour
- Utilization of existing communication networks
- Using resources of others for message propagation

Viral marketing may make use of video clips, interactive flash games, advergames, *e*-books, brand-able software, images, text messages, *e*-mail messages, or Web pages for message creation. The most commonly utilized transmission vehicles for viral messages include: pass-along based, incentive based, trendy based, and undercover based. However, the creative nature of viral marketing provides endless possibilities, especially in the era of intensification of the use of mobile devices. Table 5.1 enlists three examples of viral marketing.

SOCIAL CURATION AND BRANDS

Social curation is collaborative sharing of Web content organized around one or more particular themes or topics.

Table 5.1 Viral marketing examples

Ford	General motors	Toyota
The Ford Fiesta movement involved selecting 100 socially-vibrant individuals who were provided with the European version of the Ford Fiesta, 18 months prior to it being manufactured and released in the USA. These socially media aware-fanatics were encouraged to share their experience with the Ford Fiesta over the 6 months on their blogs, Twitter, Facebook, Flickr, and YouTube channels. – 11 million social networking impressions – 5 million engagements on social networks (people sharing and receiving) – 11,000 videos posted – 15,000 tweets (not including re-tweets) – 13,000 photos – 50,000 hand raisers who had seen the product in person or on a video who said that they want to know more about it when it comes out and 97% of those who do not currently drive a Ford vehicle – 38% awareness by Gen Y about the product, without spending a dollar on traditional advertising	Eight teams of social media embark on a combination road trip/scavenger hunt competition from their hometowns to Austin behind the wheel of some of Chevy's newest products. Along the way, they'll need to complete 50 'challenges' in order to determine the winner. The winning team will be the one that not only has completed the most challenges but has done the most interacting with their community on Twitter and their own sites. – Over 60 million social Web impressions – 15,924 online mentions including 13,440 tweets – 1216 blog posts – 1268 other posts (including comments, photos, and videos) – 33,500 page views through Facebook and ChevySXSW.com – More than 300 pieces of positive user-generated content posted to *ChevySXSW.com* (including 250+ videos) – *Chevrolet* added 8764 fans to its Facebook page (upto 12.7% in 3 weeks)	Toyota in the UK put together a social media marketing programme that saw two bloggers attempting a 500-mile road trip in a Toyota iQ, all on a single tank of petrol. The trip would take the two drivers to 18 UK cities and every step of the journey would be shared through social media. – In terms of coverage, the activity resulted in 64 blogs, including *Wired*, the *New York Times* and *Treehugger* reporting the attempt – *Toyota* reaching a potential audience of over 105 million readers worldwide – It reached a possible 3.7 million in the UK alone. – Traffic to the *iQ* blog increased by more than 212%

Social curation involves aggregating, organizing, and sharing content created by others to add context, narrative, and meaning to it. Artists, change-makers, and organizations use social curation to showcase the full range of conversations around a topic, add more nuances to their own original content, and set the stage to crowd source content from their community members.

Among the oldest social curation sites are Digg and Reddit. Both of these sites allow users to suggest links to articles and allow other readers to give approval on Digg, for example, by clicking a 'thumbs up' icon. Higher approval ratings mean that a story will appear more prominently. Delicious, another long-standing social curation site is dedicated to social bookmarking such as users save and share links to websites of interest, arranged according to topics. A newer social curation site, Pinterest, is dedicated to images.

The rise of social curation can be attributed to three broad trends (Fig. 5.8). First, people are creating a constant stream of social media content, including updates,

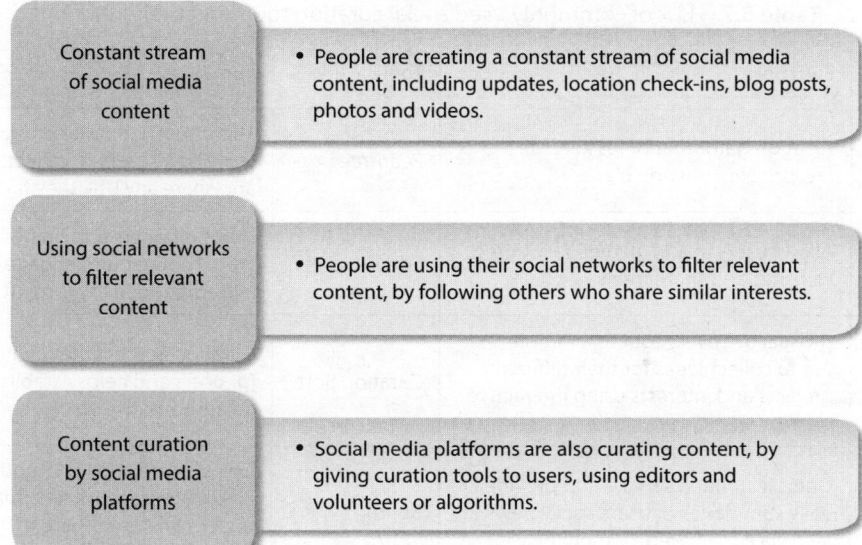

Fig. 5.8 The rise of social curation

location check-ins, blog posts, photos, and videos. Second, people are using their social networks to filter relevant content, by following others who share similar interests. Third, social media platforms are also curating content, by giving curation tools to users (YouTube playlists, Flickr galleries, Amazon lists, Foodspotting guides), using editors and volunteers (YouTube Politics, Tumblr Tags) or using algorithms (YouTube Trends, Auto-generated YouTube channels, LinkedIn Today). As a result, a number of niche social curation platforms have emerged to enable people to curate different types of content—including links, photos, sounds, and videos—into boards (Pinterest), trees [Pearltrees (video)], pages [Scoop.it (video)], and narratives [Storifyvideo, (Cowbird)]. Some social curation platforms are focused on specific niches, for instance, Learni.st(video) helps people curate lessons and Fancy helps people discover cool things to buy. Table 5.2 lists some commonly used social curation tools and their functions.

In addition, media organizations are using social curation to add depth to their programming and media entrepreneurs by creating new media business models around social curation.

- News media organizations are curating conversations around popular topics (The *Guardian #smarttakes*) and important events (Al Jazeera War on Gaza, Facebook and CNN Election Insights, Indian Elections, 2014)
- Entertainment media organizations are using social curation to amplify the participation around sports and entertainment events (Grammy Live, Oscar Buzz, ESPN NCAA Tournaments, Indian Premier League)
- Television shows (X Factor USA, American Idol's Fan Wall, shows on MTV, India)
- Media organizations are also creating hubs to enable fans to connect with anchors and stars (NDTV Social)

Table 5.2 List of commonly used social curation tools and their functions

Tool	Function	Tool	Function
Google reader	An aggregator that helps keep all favourite links in one place	Pearltrees	This visual and collaborative curation tool allows users to collect, organize, and share any URL they find online
Feedly	Allows users to add all their favourite websites and share freely	Listly	Helps bloggers and brands curate, crowd-source, and engage readers via live embedded list content
Pinterest	A visual discovery tool that people use to collect ideas for their different projects and interests using interactive boards	Curation Soft	Curation Soft enables content curation for users and helps establish brands as an authoritative voice
Summify	Offers a curation service that provides daily summaries of users' social news feed via *e*-mail, Web, or mobile	Bundlr	Helps create relevant bundles with any kind of content articles, images, videos, tweets, links and share that content with multiple channels
Alltop	Collects the headlines from the top blogs and presents it to you in an organized manner	Tumble Cloud	Is a place for collaborative digital story telling, where users can easily arrange, display, co-create, share, and manipulate multimedia content
Curata	Enables marketers to create, curate, organize, annotate, and share the most relevant and highest quality content	Delicious	Free online curation tool that acts as a social bookmarks manager

- Media entrepreneurs are building new types of media platforms around posting excerpts from the most relevant stories from around the Web (The Drudge Report, The Huffington Post) or linking to them [Techmeme, mediagazer, Alltop (video)].
- Some brands have started creating short-term social curation hubs to curate the conversations around their own events, like fashion shows (Victoria's Secret and Lakme Fashion Week) and product launches (Ford Fusion).
- Other brands have created social curation hubs around events they are participating in KPMG created the World Economic Forum Live dashboard to showcase the most important conversations and trends emerging at Davos in 2012 and 2013. TaylorMade created a social hub to help fans connect with athletes during the 2012 US Open Golf. During the 2012 London Olympics, GE tied up with NBC to track Twitter conversations around the Olympics.

Another opportunity is to use social curation (as per www.Gauravonomics.com) to create niche communities around a shared profession, passion, or purpose. For instance, in 2009, Microsoft created a unique B2B (business-to-business) community called *ExecTweets*, where people could find and follow top business executives from different sectors and engage with their tweets.

INBOUND MARKETING AND CO-CREATION

Social media nowadays has a great impact on the social behaviour of people and their behaviour as a consumer. Its journey started from digitally empowered desktop computers to super-fast laptops and now mobile phones. This has affected the way brands and consumers communicate, which has given birth to a new technique of marketing, namely, *inbound marketing*. *Inbound marketing* focuses on producing relevant, audience captivating, high-quality content that attracts consumers towards the online presence of a specific organization, brand, or product. It is a way to earn attention organically. The virtual medium presents a good medium for organization–consumer, bi-directional dialogue; companies can use the online arena for soliciting consumer views for their products, promotion mechanisms, thereby enabling consumer participation in the co-creation strategies of organizations with the help of these ideal tools.

Co-creation involves the consumers' participation in the creation of the core offering itself. It can occur through shared inventiveness, co-design or shared production of related goods, and can occur with customers and any other partners in the value network.[12] *Co-creation* occurs when the customer participates through spontaneous, discretionary behaviours that uniquely customize the service experience (beyond the selection of pre-determined options).

The dynamics of business are changing. Earlier, decisions regarding products and services to be launched were taken solely by the organization. These were then expanded to distributors and suppliers who, apart from their pre-determined roles, also started to get involved in new product development strategies in terms of giving ideas for new products to the organization. This was the result of the greater proximity of distributors and suppliers to customers and their eventual ability to comprehend the consumer needs and requirements. This consumer–supplier interaction assumes manifold importance. The suppliers who work collaboratively with the organizations and give consumers a personalized service started to differentiate themselves as experience-based service providers, and the brand value of the organization was endorsed with this differentiating factor. Eventually, organizations realized the benefits of communicating directly with the customers, and with the help of the Internet, this became quite easy. For heterogeneous agents working together to achieve complex goals, teamwork is very significant. So, co-opting the stakeholders' competence in the strategic decisions of the organization becomes the key factor of success of the so called experience-based service providers. This is the basis of co-creation strategy. Co-creation is different from user involvement; co-creation of innovation involves generation of knowledge of latent needs. Some observations—involving users as co-creators to produce ideas that are more creative, highly valued by customers, and more easily implemented—by allowing users to become idea generators and co-creators of new services (or ideas for new services, improvements to already-existing services), it becomes possible to move beyond the customers' expressed needs to a comprehension of their latent or unarticulated needs.

SOCIAL MEDIA—THE ROAD AHEAD

Some examples of companies successfully using social media are as follows:
- The *Mountain Dew* brand of *PepsiCo* has immensely gained with the use of social media. The company has used the virtual domain to gather customer insights via its DEWmocracy promotions, where consumers were invited to vote for the beverage flavour of their choice. For every vote, participants received a free Pizza Hut gift voucher. This led to the creation of new varieties of its Mountain Dew brand.
- Companies can use social media for creating consumer referrals. Online deal sites such as *Groupon* and *Gilt Groupe* provide consumers with credit for each first-time purchaser they refer. Positive word-of-mouth and consumer evangelism serve as great marketing tools for organizations.
- *Levi Strauss* engages in one-to-one personalized interactions with potential and current customers using social media to offer location-specific deals. In one instance, direct interactions with just 400 consumers led 1600 people to turn up at the company's stores, demonstrating the success rate of the company with the medium.
- Telecom service provider, *Aircel India* had launched the 'Joy of Little Extra' campaign on social media for a viral marketing drive to tap the positive sentiment generated in a consumer mind when he/she gets a little extra from a brand. India has had a tremendous relationship with the game of cricket. The campaign features cricketing star, Mahendra Singh Dhoni, who unexpectedly joins a set of youngsters in their game of cricket, thereby not only surprising them, but also delivering a lot of joy to them by playing with them—a simple gesture with huge implications. This not only depicted Aircel's emotional stance with regard to its relationship with its customers but also its seriousness with regard to its consumer-engagement initiatives. In addition, introduced on Facebook was an App that enabled fans to share experiences where they had received something extra unexpectedly and had been filled with joy. Twitter campaigns further promoted trends and contests encouraged the use of the hashtag #AlittleExtra, with gift vouchers as incentives.
- *Mahindra Two Wheelers Limited* (MTWL), a group venture of Mahindra and Mahindra used gamification to launch an exciting campaign on social media for its latest bike, the Mahindra Centuro. The company decided to use the typical youth's obsession with games to resonate with the potential customers. The idea behind the campaign was to gamify each of the bike's cool features for an informative yet entertaining experience for the potential customer. The company gamified several features and hosted six games using Facebook and the company's website, inspiring users to engage with the brand. This resulted in a huge fan base, which wanted to experiment with the games.
- Men's fashion brand, *Louis Philippe,* from the house of Aditya Birla owned Madura Fashion and Lifestyle, had launched an interesting campaign called 'The Louis Philippe Dressing Room' for the promotions of its new Autumn Winter 2013 Collection. The virtual dressing room gave an experience of the new collection to

the company's potential consumers, with an interactive App that enabled a user to mix and match clothes from the collection and create their very own style. Entry through the virtual dressing room led a user to a closet that contained the new Autumn/Winter collection using which the user was supposed to create stylish looks for a mannequin, by clicking on various pieces of clothing from shirts, trousers, blazers, ties, bags, shoes and jeans. Following this, the user could describe the style and the occasion for which the combination had been created. Users could also play stylist to actor Vidyut Jamwal and stand a chance to win a new wardrobe from the collection.

As these social-media activities gain scale, the challenges centre less around justifying funding and more around organizational issues such as developing the right processes and governance structure, identifying clear roles—for all involved in social-media strategy, from marketing to customer service to product development and bolstering the talent base, and improving performance standards. Plentiful new capabilities and social-media best practices are barely starting to emerge. We do know this because social media influences every element of the consumer decision journey; therefore, communication must take place between as well as within functions.

CASE STUDY: Starbucks and Social Media—Striking a Chord with the Indian Consumer

Starbucks expanded its operations to India in 2012. Starbuck's competitors in India were Amalgamated Bean Coffee Trading Company's *Café Coffee Day* (CCD), which has the largest presence among the various coffee chains in the country with around 14,900 outlets. The company focused on digital media and outdoor campaigns for key store launches, for building stronger customer relationships and high-quality consumer engagement.

As part of its social engagement strategy, Starbucks has launched a Facebook App called *My Starbucks Brew* that allows customers to select their favourite Starbucks beverage and a chance to win special Starbucks gifts.

In early 2014, Starbucks had 5363 followers on Twitter and 1,95,000 fans on Facebook. Market leader CCD had 14,896 Twitter followers and 4 million Facebook fans. Other players such as Costa Coffee (669 followers/2,04,000 fans/80 outlets) and Barista Lavaza (1612 followers/2,44,000 fans/200 approximate outlets) are some of the other big coffee chains in the country. This made it clear that Starbucks would have to do something unique to increase its online presence in the Indian space, and it seemed to be a perfect opportunity to replicate and promote the *My Starbucks Idea* in India as well.

Starbucks started in 1971, as a store for coffee, tea, and spice in the touristy pikes place market in Seattle. Starbucks started its online community *My Starbucks Idea* five years ago with the idea of engaging people with affinity for the brand in driving its resurrection. Customers log onto *My Starbucks Idea* to pitch their product/service improvement ideas or new product ideas. They do this by posting on this online community. Once the idea is posted, other customers vote, comment (negative and positive), and give add-ons.

These posts are subsequently rated. This online community has a large number of members, which are increasing day by day.

Starbucks is using the Internet, specifically the social media space, for increasing the degree of involvement of Starbucks with its consumers and the level of consumer participation in the organizational co-creation strategies. Ideas include fresh ideas given by other consumers to Starbucks through posts and the ideas which have been implemented recently in the stores that are updated by Starbucks' employees. The factors that drive consumers to post more ideas on the online community of Starbucks, namely, *My Starbucks Idea* involves the psychological aspects of consumer behaviour and the social connection they have with the company. The *empowerment* felt by the consumers and subsequent *social connection* are the reasons for high consumer participation in the community.

This online community impacts the consumers in two ways. First, Starbucks is able to co-create the change management with consumers, and secondly, it is very much like a social networking website where people post, vote up, vote down, comment, and interact with other members to exchange ideas. So, consumers are also using this space as a social networking website along with giving their feedback to Starbucks and proposing new ideas to them. A primary factor that drives consumers to remain active in terms of posting new ideas or commenting on others' ideas on the community is the psychological factor that makes them assert a sense of control on their coffee brand. The number of positive votes on the consumer's idea is also a major factor in keeping consumers engaged on the community. There is also a leader board to track customers, who are most active on the community in submitting ideas, comments, and voting on other people's ideas. Customers get points on doing the following actions:

- Sharing a new idea
- Receiving positive votes on their ideas
- Commenting on another's idea
- Voting on the other's idea

Customers also get badges like 'Top Commenter', 'Top Voter', and 'Idea Launched'. Another reason for being an active member is that they make new acquaintances.

Consumers feel happy when Starbucks launches their idea or even when people conduct long discussions on it. In addition, for other consumers, it's like a game where being identified as the one whose post got the highest votes or whose idea got implemented becomes a matter of prestige in the community.

Consumers tend to take decisions based more on emotions and lesser on reasons. Hence, to engage and leverage the consumers, appealing to their emotions is essential. Organizations can hence accomplish this by demonstrating an emotional attachment for the consumers and subsequently forming a relationship with them. Emotional branding is a consumer-centric, relational, and story-driven approach for fabricating and abiding relation between consumers and brands.[13]

Earlier, branding strategies were about the market share, mass campaign, acquiring large number of consumers, and the player with a leading share was then considered as a better brand. However, as consumers' standard of living enhanced, marketers segregated mass markets according to the needs and desires of consumers, and the core motive of branding strategies shifted from market share to mind share. This called the need for communication channels for interacting with consumers for targeting narrow consumer segments. Branding is no more only about awareness, it is also about positioning of the product on a higher altitude on the psychological graph of product comparison in the mind of the consumer. The emotional attachment of consumers with the organization gives an organization a competitive advantage. Consumers' involvement and engagement is highly influenced by the emotional connectivity between the consumers and the organization. Consumers' engagement is the centre of gravity in case of 'My Starbucks idea', where Starbucks is using consumers' involvement to co-create strategies for the development of new products and for the improvement of existing products or services through the process of co-creation.

To increase involvement and participation of the consumers on the community page, Starbucks gives psychological rewards in terms of high rank on the page, as it updates top 10 participants every week on the *e*-community page and has demonstrated a growing faith of the consumer in the company through an enhanced participation in the virtual arena. Maybe *My Starbucks Idea* will be the right choice for Starbucks to try and strike a chord with the hugely emotional Indian consumer and gain inroads into the Indian hearts.

Question:

1. Compare the virtual activities of Starbucks, Costa Coffee, and Barista for building consumer engagement and brand propagation.
2. Study the consumer suggestions on *My Starbucks Idea* and analyse the shares, votes, and comments on one specific consumer suggestion (Starbucks Idea).

CASE STUDY Building Loyalty the Jet Airways Way

Jet Airways, India's premier International airline and JetKonnect have a combined fleet strength of 120 aircrafts and operate over 620 flights daily. Jet Airways operates Economy, Première, and First Class services on its various routes. JetKonnect is the new consolidated low-fare service brand which replaces JetLite and Jet Airways Konnect. On 12 October 2011, Jet Airways was conferred three prestigious awards at the 'Times Travel Honours 2011' in the Most Trusted Airline Brand, the Best Domestic Full Service Carrier, and the Best International (Economy) Airline categories.

Jet Airways has been able to successfully use its digital presence for propagating the brand to an increasingly digitally savvy Indian population. With a wide presence across *Facebook, iGoogle, Orkut, Yahoo, Youtube, Twitter, Foursquare, Pinterest,* and *Linkedin,* Jet Airways has been able to carve for itself a special brand image of a sensitive brand.

The Jet Airways Widgets—A Convenient Way for Booking Tickets Online

Jet Airways launched online widgets, where consumers can download and search for the best fares and flight options available. By keying in relevant personalized data and preferences, a consumer can place the Jet Airways widget on their Facebook page and it can be used to check for the lowest fares at any time, thereby giving consumers their personal Jet Airways booking block.

Jet Airways and Social Media

As the airline embraces social media to create new customer touch-points, the emergence of social networking as an interactive marketing communication tool, that works from a relationship marketing perspective, can be witnessed. With a significant presence across Facebook alone, with over 1.2 million *likes*, Jet Airways has proved that the discipline of interaction with the customer has evolved substantially in recent years.

As the online marketing team posts videos and discussion threads on new Jet Airways features, services, and procedures, the group is also being used to foster customer relationships.

A survey of the Jet Airways Facebook group revealed that while more than 60 per cent of group members have joined the group for 'understanding Jet Airways schemes and offerings', about 30 per cent have done so to share experiences. Jet Airways customers and employees have created an interactive environment, with a substantial number of wall posts.

The cost effectiveness of the medium is worth the effort. As Facebook brings new brands to the customers, customers can become 'fans' of a particular brand and showcase them on their home pages. The era of the 'Fansumer' has arrived. Consumers can now even gain access to brand preferences of their friends and peers.

Jet has been on Facebook since 2009 and in the last 5 years, has focussed on the following elements to use Facebook as an online marketing tool:

- Volume (customer focus group size)
- Frequency (of interaction with the customer and between customers)
- Content of brand communication (promotional/relationship building)
- Personalization
- Participation
- Interactivity

These, coupled with low investments, facilitate the ongoing dialogue between enterprise and customer. While increased access to customer information improves marketing performance, enhanced exposure to a brand further increases customer loyalty.

With posts ranging from *Jetfacts* with over 1200 likes and *Fanography* garnering a 1000 likes, Jet has carefully crafted a community which can be gradually used by the company for consumer evangelism. Equally liked are the *Jetescapes holidays* and *Adventure is worthwhile* posts. Jet also uses the forum to provide consumers with useful tips regarding its *Self-check in* services.

Jet also encourages its customers to participate in an online dialogue on the Facebook page. Consumers post in response to the campaigns hosted by Jet or pictures, snippets, thoughts, ideas, and the like, specially crafted by the company to solicit consumer engagement and involvement. The personal relevance of these messages creates an atmosphere of reciprocity, exchange, and participation, and consumers absorb the brand information almost subconsciously. This further accentuates the degree of consumer interest and sends customers on a journey comprising more product-relevant thoughts, thereby influencing customer perception. When these stimuli are processed in the mind of the customer, interest is created and a relationship is developed.

When these cues are reinforced, the impact on customer beliefs and attitudes results in positive buyer responses, thereby rewarding the product with higher customer loyalty.

While Jet has fostered an environment where its customers can interact with the company, at the same time, the forum provides a peer-to-peer, in this case consumer-to-consumer visibility for the ideas and thoughts posted therein. Jet's use of social media to generate positive consumer sentiment is clearly worth exploration.

Question:

1. Analyse Jet Airway's Facebook activity in context of the following parameters:
   - Volume (customer focus group size)
   - Frequency (of interaction with the customer and between customers)
   - Content of brand communication (promotional/relationship building)
   - Ability to generate personalization

PRACTITIONER PERSPECTIVE

Facebook is not about social media, but mass media. Our goal is to solve the biggest business and marketing challenge. It's about reach and engagement, not just fans.

Kirthiga Reddy, Head of Facebook, India

Digital is more in tune with spends. It is more focused as compared to traditional media where there is a lot of wastage. It is better to try using the digital medium as revenues are down and there is pressure on profit margins.

Hemant Dua, CEO, GMR Sports, Owner of Delhi Daredevils, IPL

SUMMARY

Web 2.0 is a set of capabilities enabling the Web consumer to become the 'prosumer' (a new word coined to describe the ability to produce and consume). *Social media* refers to the means of interactions among people in which they create, share, and exchange information and ideas in virtual communities and networks. Social media depends on mobile and web-based technologies to create highly interactive platforms via which individuals and communities share, co-create, discuss and modify user-generated content. It introduces substantial and pervasive changes to communication between organizations, communities, and individuals.[3] McKinsey's social media model,[5] namely, Monitor Respond Amplify Lead enables targeted marketing responses at individual touch-points along the consumer decision journey. Those companies using marketing ROI metrics to assess and improve their general marketing effectiveness, have advantages in outgrowing competitors and having more effective and efficient marketing programmes. Companies gain significantly if their online consumer-engagement programmes yield rich results, and their consumers become evangelists. Organizations gain significantly by creating value with networks. This can be done because of the ubiquitous nature of online networks, their speed, sharing abilities, specialization, and a host of other virtual-value activities. The Internet explosion ushered in an era of fascination and functionality, an era demonstrating the virtuous cycle of the Web and an era of network evolution for marketing and business. Digital environments are participatory, procedural, spatial, and encyclopaedic, and this has opened up new vistas for marketing. Social media is redefining consumer-behaviour patterns. Social media analytics has applications in managing content creation, scheduling, publishing, and moderation. It further strengthens collaboration, workflow, and permissions along with data analytics and reporting. Key capabilities may include sentiment analysis, vertical-specific compliance, marketing campaign automation, integration with legacy marketing and analytics platforms, and strategic social media consulting services. SAP Social Media Analytics by Netbase, Google Analytics, Social Crawlytics and IBM Social Media Analytics are significant social media analytical tools.

Concept Review Questions

1. What is Web 2.0? What are the various Web 2.0 tools of relevance to marketers?
2. What is social media? Discuss McKinsey's social media model for marketers. What do you understand by the '*Economic Logic of Hype*'?
3. Digital environments are participatory, procedural, spatial, and encyclopaedic. Comment.
4. How is social media analytics relevant to marketing? Discuss with examples.
5. List major social media analytics players in the industry today. Contrast their performance in the context of their functionalities.
6. Write short notes on
   (a) Enterprise 2.0
   (b) Business and social networks
   (c) Wikis
   (d) Content syndication
   (e) Viral marketing

Critical Thinking Questions

1. Analyze the social media practices of
   (a) Two *IT* companies
   (b) Two *FMCG* companies
   (c) Two *banking* organizations
   Do the social media practices vary from sector to sector? If yes, identify the causes for variation.
2. McKinsey's social media model, namely, *Monitor–Respond–Amplify–Lead* enables targeted marketing responses at individual touch-points along the consumer-decision journey. Trace the social media practices of *Dell* or *Starbucks* in the context of McKinsey's social media model.
3. Document how *EBay* uses the Internet for
   (a) Internet-based collaboration
   (b) Innovation
   (c) Co-creation
4. *Dove* has been increasingly successful in the viral marketing arena. Document *Dove's* campaigns. Which of them have been most successful and why?

Practising Digital Marketing

1. Identify one brand that is active on social media. Read the information available online about the brand. Browse through the campaigns of the brand in the online domain study their consumer-engagement strategies, and then the consumer-generated comments. Form an opinion paper on the consumer sentiments and opinions, as visible through your reading and qualitative judgements.
2. Use a social media analytical tool to perform analysis on the same brand in the context of consumer sentiments and opinions. What customer intelligence do you derive from the analysis?
3. Do you see any variation in your qualitative judgement and the results obtained after using the analytical tool?
4. How can the brand use the intelligence derived from the analytical tool to its advantage?

References

1. Garton, L., Haythornthwaite, C., and Wellman, B., (2006). 'Studying online social networks'. *Journal of Computer-mediated Communication*, Vol. 3(1).
2. Kaplan, A.M. and Haenlein, M., (2009). "Consumer use and business potential of virtual worlds: The case of 'Second Life'". *The International Journal on Media Management*, Vol. 11(3–4), pp. 93–101.
3. Kietzmann, J.H., Hermkens, K., McCarthy, I.P., and Silvestre, B.S., (2011). 'Social media? Get serious! Understanding the functional building blocks of social media'. *Business Horizons*, Vol. 54(3), pp. 241–251.
4. Hsu, W., Jacobsen, G., Jin, Y., and Skudlark, A., (2011). 'Using social media data to understand mobile customer experience and behaviour'.
5. Divol, R., Edelman, D., and Sarrazin, H., (2012). 'Demystifying social media'. *McKinsey Quarterly*, pp. 1–11.

6. Grajales III, F.J., Social Media: A comprehensive knowledge synthesis, *Doctoral Dissertation*, University of British Columbia, 2012.
7. Gillis, T., *Securing the Borderless Network: Security for the Web 2.0 World*, Cisco Systems, 2010.
8. A more equal footing: How social media have transformed customer relationships, *Strategic Direction*, Emerald Group, Vol. 28(6), 2002, pp. 4–6.
9. Lead Generation Marketing Effectiveness, Lenkold Group, 2012.
10. Hanson, W. and Kalyanam, K., Networks, *Internet Marketing and E-commerce*, Thomson India Edition, 2007.
11. Bruyn, A.D. and Lilien, G.L., (2008). 'A multi stage model of word of mouth influence through viral marketing'. *International Journal of Research in Marketing*.
12. Bolton, R.N., (2011). 'Customer Engagement–Opportunities and Challenges for Organizations'. *Journal of Service Research*, Vol. 14.3, pp. 272–274.
13. Manyika, J.M., Roberts, R.P., and Sprague, K.L., (2008). 'Eight business technology trends to watch'. *McKinsey Quarterly*, Vol. 1, p. 60.

Software Sources

www.Sap.com
http://www.google.co.in/analytics/
https://socialcrawlytics.com/
www.ibm.com

Online Branding

LEARNING OBJECTIVES

After reading this chapter, you will be able to:
- Understand the concept of cyberbranding
- Use the customer-based brand equity pyramid to appreciate the digital brand ecosystem
- Get acquainted with the online implications of brand architecture
- Understand the concepts of online domain names and domain name memorability

The best way to spark a consumer's imagination and then activate their wallet is to combine the physical and the digital experience, meshing data, online connections, and an on-ground experience. Used with imagination and innovation, digital communication allows organizations to work better.

Push strategies in marketing use marketing communication to motivate the consumer to buy. While the traditional media can be used to *push* products towards the consumer, once awareness reaches a certain threshold, it starts to plateau. Marketing then needs to engage and immerse the consumer to give him/her a compelling reason to buy. This is where online brands need to be fashioned.

In recent years, the offline and online spheres of strategic brand management are becoming more and more inter-connected. Firms are increasing their online spend on digital marketing in the realms of social media, mobile applications, customer relationship management (CRM), customer analytics, tablet applications, content management, collaboration tools, predictive analytics, campaign management, search engine optimization, *e*-mail marketing, single view of customer, score cards or dashboards, and reputation management.

This is not just because offline companies sell their products over the Internet as an alternative distribution channel,[1] or even that firms more frequently run integrated brand communication campaigns, both offline and online.[2] The connection goes beyond these links, as companies that commercialize their products offline, now seem to cross over the offline borders and offer new products and services online. The reverse is also possible, and online companies may benefit from launching products that are available on the offline market. Strong brands enter into the consumers' consideration sets, create confidence in purchases, and positively influence product evaluation and choice.[3]

The differential effect of brand knowledge on consumer response to the marketing of the brand[4] helps develop customer-based brand equity. These differential benefits include product evaluation, purchasing rates, market share, quality perceptions, product line extensions, product associations, resistance to negative events, stock market valuation, price sensitivity, advertising recall, and advertising response.[5] The appearance of a brand, both online and offline seems to be a powerful strategy as it allows firms to leverage established brand equity in both contexts. For offline brands, expansion online is all about adding brand value for consumers through additional availability and exposure via the Internet.[6] For online brands on the other hand, expansion offline can create increased brand awareness as the brand is made more tangible by selling offline products, which may foster stronger trust.[7]

CYBERBRANDING

Cyberbranding (Fig. 6.1) involves integrating online and offline branding tactics that reinforce each other to speak with one voice.[8] The most common method of building an online brand presence is through an offline technique called brand spiralling. It is the practice of using traditional media to promote and attract consumers to an online website.[9]

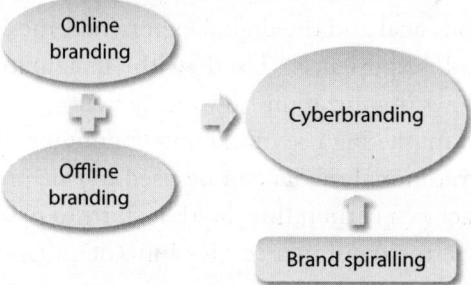

Fig. 6.1 Cyberbranding

CONSUMERS—THE NEW INFLUENTIAL CONSTITUENCY

Global enterprises are struggling today to understand how the use of the Internet makes an impact on their brands. Corporate management is witnessing a new level of activism from an influential constituency rarely heard in the past—ordinary consumers. Many of these new consumer influencers are gaining a large share of voice in the market, thanks to the power of the Internet and the technologies that bring together people who share common interests. Consumers are impacting brand equity as never before.

Strong brands complement online traffic building and online advertising aims at motivating online users to visit a website, where the branding conversation and conversion actually occurs. Branding campaigns require storytelling, technical skills, and sophistication. With the Internet as a tool, marketers and advertising agencies can collaborate for creation of efficient online campaigns.

Organizations need to remember the basics of brandbuilding such as establishing points of parity (convenience, price, and variety) and points of difference (customer service, credibility, and personality).

In research undertaken to understand online service quality, defined as the extent to which a website facilitates efficient and effective shopping, purchasing, and delivery, a study identified 11 dimensions (Fig. 6.2) of perceived *e*-service quality. The dimensions found in the study are access, ease of navigation, efficiency, flexibility, reliability, personalization, security/privacy, responsiveness, assurance, trust, site aesthetics, and price knowledge.[10]

Fig. 6.2 Dimensions of *e*-service quality

Digital marketing agencies provide turnkey solutions to organizations by delivering services that focus on the technical development of Internet-based marketing products. These services can include Web design, *e*-mail marketing, or microsite software development. Additional services may include viral marketing campaigns, banner advertising, search engine optimization, podcasting, or widget development. Digital marketing agencies tend to emphasize web-based tool development as a means to an end, focusing on everything except the most important social media element, which is the quality of the relationship between the firm and the consumer. With this increase, brand ownership is increasingly being shared among consumers and the brands themselves. Through social networks, blogs, and videos, consumers are entrenched in the dissemination of information. Long gone are the days when media would communicate a brand's message to consumers.

Customer-based Brand Equity Pyramid

The customer-based brand equity pyramid (Fig. 6.3) states that the power of a brand lies in what customers have learned, felt, seen, and heard about the brand as a result of their experiences pertaining to the brand. In other words, the power of a brand lies in what resides in the minds of customers.[11]

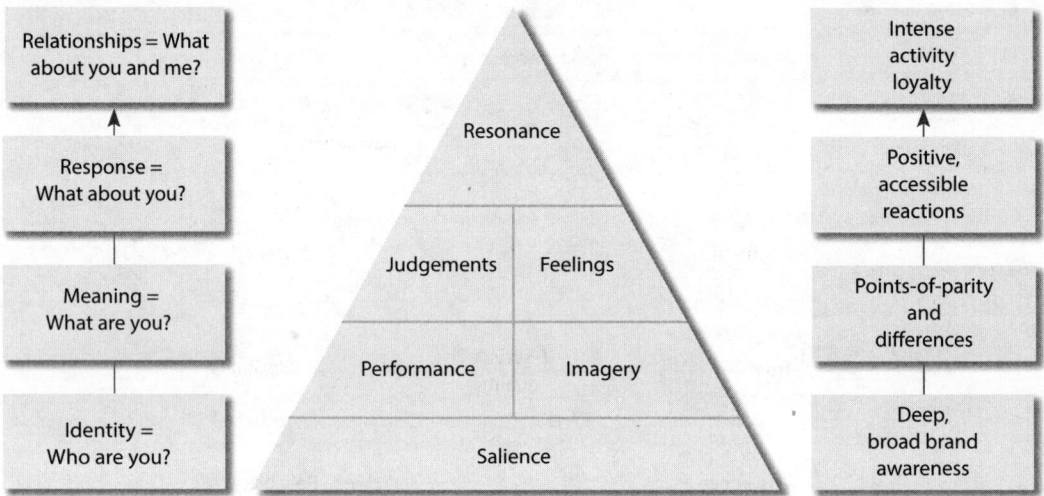

Fig. 6.3 Customer-based brand equity pyramid

The four stages of establishing customer-based brand equity are as follows:
- Establishing the proper brand identity
- Creating the appropriate brand meaning
- Eliciting the right brand responses
- Forging appropriate brand relationships with customers

The challenge for marketers in building a strong brand is ensuring that customers have the right type of experiences with products and services and their accompanying marketing programmes so that the desired thoughts, feelings, images, beliefs, perceptions, opinions, and so on, become linked to the brand.[12] It is through customers learning about and experiencing a brand that they end up thinking and acting in a way that allows the firm to reap the benefits of brand equity.

Although marketers must take responsibility for designing and implementing the most effective and efficient brand-building marketing programmes possible, the success of those marketing efforts ultimately depends on how consumers respond. This response, in turn, depends on the knowledge that has been created in their minds for those brands. The customer-based brand equity pyramid defines the various stages of the brand–consumer relationship, in the context of the stages where the consumer moves up from remembering the brand to having feelings for it. The pyramid defines *brand salience* as the degree to which the brand is thought about or noticed when a customer is in a buying situation. Strong brands have high brand salience and weak brands have little or none. This helps explain to some extent as to why big brands are big and small brands are small. If consumers cannot think about a brand at the moment of buying, the truth is that the brand is going to be relegated to the set of small and unnoticed brands. *Brand performance* is the way the product or service attempts to meet the consumer's functional needs. Brand performance also has a major influence on how consumers experience a brand as well as what the brand owner and others say about the brand. Brand imagery deals with the way in which the brand attempts to meet customers' psychological and social needs. Brand imagery is the intangible aspects of a brand that consumers pick up because it fits their demographic profile (such as age or income) or has psychological appeal in that it matches their outlook on life (conservative, traditional, liberal, creative, etc.). *Judgments* about a brand emerge from a consumer pulling together different performance and imagery associations. These judgments combine into a consumer's opinion of a brand and enable individuals to develop *feelings* for a brand. Brand resonance refers to the extent to which customers feel 'in sync' with the brand. Just as we feel the vibe between us and others, we also experience a vibe that resonates between us and the brands.

The customer-based brand equity pyramid[13] also reflects the impact of the various branding parameters on the consumer. These include the following:

- *Brand awareness* The extent and ease with which the customers recall and recognize the brand and can identify the products and services with which it is associated.
- *Brand associations* The strength, favourability and uniqueness of perceived attributes and benefits for the brand.
- *Brand attitudes* Overall evaluation of the brand in terms of its quality and the satisfaction it generates.
- *Brand attachments* How loyal the customer feels towards the brand. A strong form of attachment, adherence, refers to consumer's resistance to change.
- *Brand activity* The extent to which the customers use the brand, talk to others about the brand, seek out the brand information, promotions, and events.

THE DIGITAL BRAND ECOSYSTEM

A brand is more than just a company's products and services. It is also the ecosystem that surrounds those products and services. The brand also develops a relationship with the members of the ecosystem thereby impacting their role in influencing the spread of a brand message. Ultimately, the strength of a brand is directly related to the connections within that ecosystem. From a strategic perspective, brands can be designed to deliver greater customer value by building a 'brand ecosystem'. This includes the value networks and interactions of these value networks at each stage of brand value building. The value chain[14] framework describes how the activities of a business contribute to its tasks of designing, producing, delivering, communicating, and supporting its products to create value. Similarly, the '3Vs' framework[15] that includes valued customers (who to serve), a value proposition (what to offer), and a value network outlines the principles to deliver the promised product and/or service.

EXHIBIT 6.1   Aviva India—Padding up with Sachin

Aviva's brand strategy, based on the father–child relationship, highlights the importance of a father's role as a protector in his child's life, whether financial, physical, or emotional. With an objective to help young fathers realize the importance of financial planning for their children's secure future, Aviva, India unveiled its social media strategy based on creating and feeding engaging content on the social media channels. The core of the content onion focussed on protection-related content drawing analogies from cricket; the next levels covered content on financial literacy, products, and parenting for young fathers. This was supported by a robust digital advertising campaign to promote content to their target audience—young parents in the age group of 28 to 44 years. Aviva was already among the top players for its online protection plans and with this launch, they expected to further consolidate their position in this category.

Through the new campaign—*Padding up with Sachin* and *Sachin off Guard*, launched in March, 2013, Aviva aimed to further strengthen its association with fatherhood and protection. These were a series of webisodes on cricket tutorials and interviews on importance of protection by Aviva's brand ambassador and the master blaster—Sachin Tendulkar. For the first time ever, netizens had access to innovative, inspirational, and conversational tutorials on cricketing by the little master himself. With 73% of audience on social networking sites consuming video/entertainment on the site, Aviva witnessed an increase of three-fold in its engagement scores on its social media channels such as Facebook, Twitter, and YouTube leading to higher awareness on Aviva's offerings. Aviva shortly released its *Product Center* and a series of engaging product-related videos on Facebook to further enhance the same.

(*Source*: Aviva India, Press Release, 2013)

All activities in a value network are driven by the end-consumer's intended experience and preferences (i.e., desired value proposition). It is well designed and presented as a holistic marketing framework to show how the interaction between relevant actors (customers, company, and collaborators) and value-based activities (value exploration, value creation, and value delivery) helps to create, maintain, and renew customer value (Fig. 6.4).[16] Today, as consumers are demanding more social responsibility from the

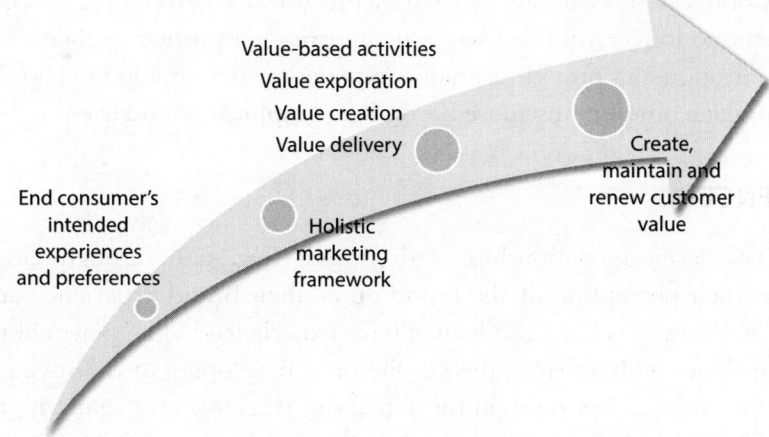

Fig. 6.4 The digital brand ecosystem

brands they use, a brand ecosystem as a whole must reflect the core values associated with the brand. In this respect, the brand's identity provides the DNA for the entire ecosystem,[17] and ultimately brand equity.

The importance of consistent high standards and values throughout the entire brand ecosystem cannot be ignored. Recognizing the holistic nature of a brand ecosystem requires an organization to fully understand and manage its value network(s) and their interactions that are driven by desires and preferences of the chosen target markets. In essence, the brand ecosystem places the brand and related customer experiences as the focal point. The best brands in the world know that it is essential to create a brand ecosystem—a living, breathing organism that is all about stimulating and feeding off conversations that happen within it, then using that to build further brand stories. Millions of micro interactions that happen on the Web (e.g., blogs, Twitter, Facebook, YouTube, Google, etc.) are conversations between people, and many of the conversations happening in social media are about brands.

The brand ecosystem (Fig. 6.5) is an organic model, where the role of the brand is to *listen* to the conversations happening around it and *energizing* those conversations with interesting content and experiences. It is all about giving the *brand community* something to talk about the brand, within their own personal social networks where *influencers* are then able to add velocity to the idea of penetration about a brand.

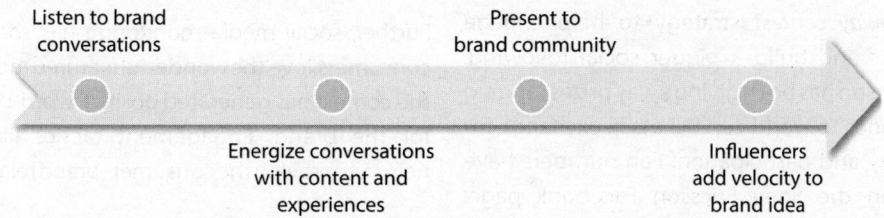

Fig. 6.5 The brand ecosystem: An organic model

In a world where cynicism and scepticism towards advertising are growing rapidly, consumers no longer want messages or information pushed to them. In such a world where activation can provide a unique experience to a limited bunch of people, digital can help reach out to many more beyond geographical boundaries.

BRAND EXPERIENCE

Customers develop relationships with brands (Fig. 6.6) through direct experiences and base their perception of the brand on (a) their brand experience and (b) how that brand compares to other brands they have experienced. The personal experience that a consumer has with a firm is the key factor in developing or destroying trust.[18] A total of 76% of consumers would find it difficult to trust a brand again, if the brand could not meet their needs on the first occasion. Since a firm's brand is a promise of a certain experience, the trust or distrust of a brand depends on the experience of the consumer.[19]

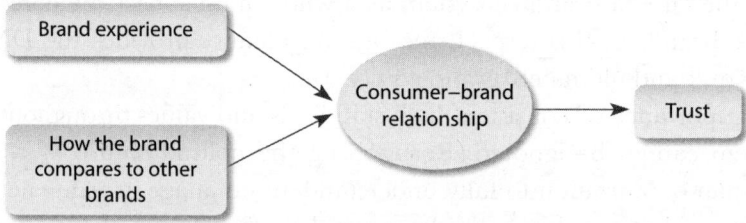

Fig. 6.6 Customers and brand relationships

This is important because it is through this experience that customers will decide whether or not the brand is valuable to them and worth trust.[20] Generally, consumers believe that firms have good intentions and work hard not to repeat mistakes. They believe most firms will do the right thing when faced with a problem with one of their goods. Still, the fact remains true that consumers find it more difficult to trust brands after the first time of having a bad experience with the brand.[21] Customer relationships

---

EXHIBIT 6.2 Sony Ericsson

Sony Ericsson was one of the greatest brands to successfully use social media. The brand used *the giveaway contest* strategy to help engage customers and build a bigger social following. Sony Ericsson has been giving away prizes ranging from phones to world cup tickets in exchange for fan loyalty and participation. Fan numbers have soared on the Sony Ericsson Facebook page, granting absolute success to Sony Ericsson's consumer engagement strategies.

Further, social media monitoring has shown that consumers' love' the wonderful featured models and the contest has generated positive word-of-mouth for the brand. Engagement tactics like these help in improving the consumer–brand relationship.

are longer with a firm, when customers gain high levels of cumulative satisfaction for a brand. Conversely, if a customer has a poor experience with the goods, they will be less satisfied. They will not seek a long relationship with a particular brand. When a consumer is satisfied with a brand, this means they are content with all parts of the goods that are related to their needs. Finally, they also trust this brand.[22]

Organizations need to establish online brand identity. This involves the following functions (Fig. 6.7):

- Establishing brand resonance and reinforcing brand salience
- Creating brand identity and online domain names
- Enhancing brand meaning
- Reinforcing right brand responses
- Forging brand relationships

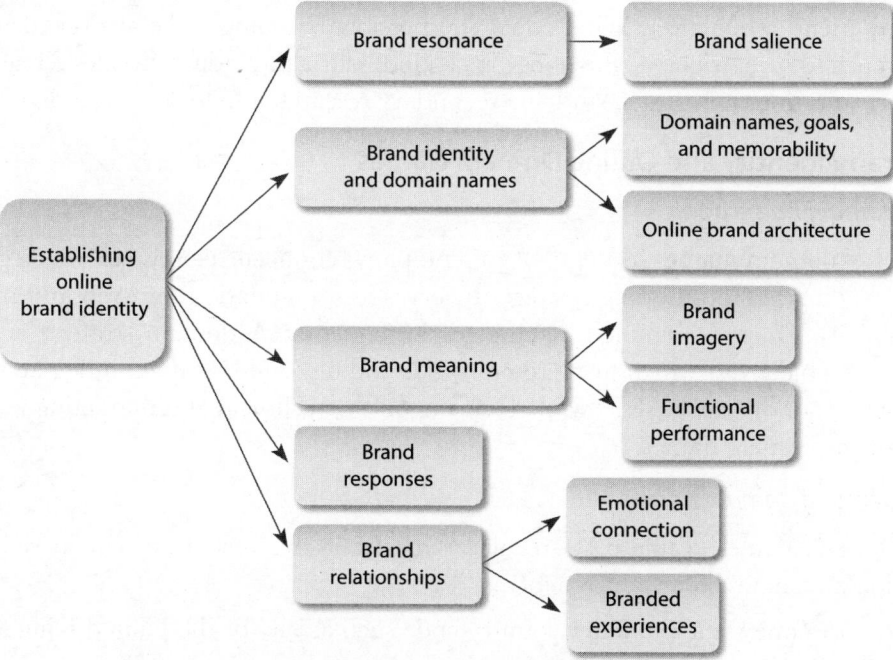

Fig. 6.7 Establishing online brand identity

Establishing Brand Resonance and Reinforcing Brand Salience

The first stage in using the net to enhance a brand is to ensure that the brand has both breadth and depth of brand awareness. The goal is brand salience; when a consumer considers a product category, the brand is automatically included as a possible choice. Reinforcing brand salience occurs through exposure to Web advertising directly or by exposure to the advertiser's website stimulated by brand advertising.[23] Online banner ads resemble print ads and require readers to focus attention away from the main content and to pay attention to the ads. Brand salience is reinforced when the brand's image and advertising are present at content sites specializing in the category.[24]

Brands now also seek to associate with elements of popular culture. The language of social media, 'fans', 'friend request', 'like', 'social network', and yes, 'status update', is increasingly appearing in advertising, irrespective of whether the ads are running on social media, such as Facebook, Twitter, and YouTube or not. Such ads are also increasingly being aimed at mainstream consumers, not just the younger consumers who were the early adopters of social media. The appropriation of the trappings of social media for marketing purposes is an example of a tactic known as borrowed interest, by which brands seek to associate themselves with the elements of popular culture that are pervasive enough to be familiar to everyone. In the words of Bridgett Judd, group director for strategic innovation at Saatchi and Saatchi, describing a campaign for the Toyota Venza crossover, the campaign was centred on 'redefinition of social' and 'socializing' by parents and their adult offspring and how there are two ways to look at 'social life'. A print advertisement in the campaign carried a headline: 'My mom has not accepted my friend request yet. What could she possibly be doing? The answer: driving in her Venza to meet friends—the non-virtual kind—for a day riding bicycles'. The answer for organizations now lies in studying secondary research and looking at individual lives.

Creating Brand Identity and Online Domain Names

Domain name goals

The domain name strategy of a company connects closely to an organization's branding and positioning strategy. It serves as a foundation for Web and promotional activity. Once determined, it changes infrequently. A domain strategy accomplishes three objectives; which are—reinforces branding, builds traffic, anticipates consumer behaviour and mistakes,[25] while focusing on the technical and marketing requirements for the domain names.

Defining domain names

Domain names (Table 6.1) are hierarchical and are read from left to right. Primary domain names come in three forms:

- Form one[26] is a two-letter country code such as .uk for the United Kingdom and .ru for Russia.

Table 6.1 Defining domain names

	The hierarchical structure of domain names			
	Primary domain	Secondary domain	Tertiary	Full address
Examples:	.com	NDTV	Goodtimes TV channel	www.goodtimes.ndtv.com
	.edu	Tata Institute of Social Sciences	Library	www.library.tiss.edu
	.gov	mhrd (Ministry of Human Resource Development)	www	www.mhrd.gov.in

- Form two is based on the type of organization or information involved such as .edu for education, .org for organization, .net for network, and .com for commercial organizations.
- Additional specialized names are also entering the usage. These include .aero, .biz, .int, .museum, etc.

Secondary domain names are the identifying portion of the domain name for most firms. Some firms also use tertiary domain names.

In June 2011, Internet Corporation for Assigned Names and Numbers (ICANN) announced plans to open up the net to make it more local and flexible as organizations often create and keep websites using such new domains for internal use.

Globally, by March 2013, nearly 2000 applications were submitted, but only two dozen were being given clearance. North America topped the list of applications with 911 applications followed by 675 from Europe. The new domain names were costing as much as $1,85,000 to apply and $25,000 for renewal per-year.

The global row over generic names

Globally, there have been concerns over corporations trying to corner generic domain names such as .music or .book, as it may stifle competition and give owners of such domains unique advantage.

Amazon, for instance has applied for .book, .read, and .author, much to the chagrin of other publishers.

Similarly, Google has applied for some hundred generic names. Both Google and Amazon have applied for .search and .cloud, and typically the owner of contested domain names would be decided through an auction. This process will vastly expand the Internet suffixes beyond the widely used .com and .org varieties.

Prominent Indian companies that have applied for new domain names include the following (Table 6.2).

Domain name memorability

The goal of memorability extends beyond substituting words for numbers. Memorability is limited by length, confusing and unusual strings of letters, artefacts of programming languages, homophones, and names that are difficult to express. Some basic guidelines for domain name memorability are listed in Table 6.3.[27]

Online brand architecture

The goal of brand architecture (Table 6.4) is to provide clarity in customer offerings, real synergies in the brands and their communication programmes, and an ability to leverage brand assets.[28] In the online context, the most important challenge faced by the organization is concerning domain naming between *branded house* and a *house of brands*. A branded house, chosen by companies such as Virgin, Healthy Choice, and BMW, treats all its products as an integrated brand. Branding is companywide.[29]

Table 6.2 Companies that have applied for new domain names

Company	Domain name
Bharti Group	.airtel and .bharti
Dabur India Limited	.dabur
HDFC	.hdfc
HDFC Bank	.hdfcbank
Infibeam Incorporation	.ooo
Infosys	.infosys and .infy
Lupin	.lupin
Reliance Industries	.indians and .ril and .reliance
Tata Group	.tata and .tatamotors
Shriram Capital	.sriram
Star India	.star
State Bank of India	.sbi and .statebank
TV Sundaram	.tvs

Table 6.3 Making domain names memorable

Domain memorability	Benefits
Obtain a category domain. For example, www.software.com.	If an upcoming enterprise can secure a category term, it may be able to launch an effective online business.
Avoid complex domain names.	Domain names that are easy to memorize and simple aid recall if they have appropriate visual and sound cues. Companies can benefit if consumers see a simple domain name and are able to retain it in their memory.
Avoid long and complicated domains from third-party hosting arrangements—www.viaweb.com/librarycompany/.	Care should be taken when third-party hosting is being used for domain registration. Complex names again have problems with regard to brand recall.
Register-related items and common types. For instance the Jaypee group in India could have facilitated consumer search if they had registered jp.com and jepee.com as well.	The cost of registering domain names is trivial compared to the cost of acquiring traffic. Registering related names and even common typographical errors, helps build traffic and prevents brand dilution. Hence, if a user misspells the required domain name, it will be interesting, if he still lands on the same website he was trying to locate.

Table 6.4 Online implications of brand architecture

	Branded house	House of brands
Important branding advantages	A good example of a branded house approach is Richard Branson's Virgin empire. The business verticals include credit cards, airlines, music, and so on. Diverse product lines are all wrapped into a single identity, using a single master brand to span a set of offerings operating with only descriptive sub-brands. The company is the brand, and all products draw their energy from the single brand identity. Virgin puts their label to every product. • Provides consistency and centralized value • Efficient use of branding resources • All the products and services can share the same budget, customer, and market position • Inherited attributes can include visual identity, messaging, values, and customer perception • Lower cost of new product introduction and brand extensions • Aids consumer segmentation • Allows traffic-building efforts targeting a single homepage rather than many. Reinforce authority status of site by sharing inbound links • Create multiple reasons for user visits • Allows easier tracking of visitors	The house of brands separates the company into various sub-brands. Each product line is a stand-alone brand that is specifically positioned in a particular market segment independent of other brands in the company. An example is the Dutch giant Unilever with 400 brands. Their brands range from luxurious hair treatments, mouth-watering ice creams, low-cost nutritious foods, antibacterial soaps to germ-killing sprays. • Each set of stand-alone brands focuses on maximizing the impact on the market • Can dominate product category associations with a powerful name • Helps reduce or minimize channel conflict • Allows focused content • Permit short click trails from homepage to main interest areas • Simplifies the imagery and look-and-feel decisions • Allows better measurement of brand-specific campaigns, especially with traditional media
Branding challenges	• This approach limits the degree in which a product or service can be uniquely marketed • Can limit flexibility and reduce the ability of the organization to adapt quickly to changing market conditions and opportunities. In addition, with all the products housed under a single brand, the shortcomings of one can have damaging perception effects that can ripple across the entire portfolio • Complicated content choices can create possible navigation problems for users • Creates difficulties for measuring advertising effectiveness by individual brands	• Each brand needs its own brand-building investment • More expensive and complicated to manage • Hinders cross-selling opportunities • Reduces likelihood of frequent customer visits due to 'content fatigue' • Each brand has to fight its own battles • Relies heavily on customer pull for traffic

At the other extreme is the *house of brands*. Branding is product specific with few, if any, ties to other company brands. The leading example is Procter and Gamble, but it is also a strategy used by many pharmaceutical companies and companies with very separate divisions such as Toyota and Lexus.

Advantages and disadvantages tend to be mirror opposites for a house of brands marketer. Consider the following two home pages of two P&G brands, Crest and Tide. Having separate pages allows the content to be focused. Category-specific material on laundry need not compete with content appropriate on dentistry. Navigation is also much simpler, with a visitor able to focus quickly on a problem or interest.

Enhancing Brand Meaning

Brand imagery and functional performance

Imagery and functional performance[30]-related information create brand meaning. Brand imagery is more abstract and relates to consumers' psychological and social needs. User profiles, purchase and usage situations, personality and values, and the history and heritage of the brand, all contribute to brand imagery. Functional performance aspects of the product include product features, service, and price.

- *Brand personality refers to the set of human characteristics associated with the brand. The personality of the brand allows a consumer to express himself or herself, an ideal self or the specific dimension of the brand. Brand personality differentiates brands in a product category, drives consumer preference, and usage, and is a common denominator for marketing across cultures.*
- *Online media with low-cost archives and flexible formats provides an inexpensive setting to expand brand imagery.*
- *The website of a brand can serve as an authoritative source to share information regarding the brand and serve as a reasonable solution for problems pertaining to the brand.*

EXHIBIT 6.3   The Coke Happiness Machine—Strengthening the brand–consumer relationship

In 2010, Coca Cola started the 'Coke Happiness' campaign where a Coca Cola vending machine started delivering *doses* of happiness on a college campus in New York. This campaign used Coca Cola vending machines to provide Coca Cola consumers who needed some bottles of the beverage, with some flowers, pizzas, and even foot-longs, in an apparently unending doses of happiness. The campaign ended with *Where will happiness strike next*. This campaign represented an idea, which could be experienced by only a few college students. However the Internet provided Coca Cola with an unending amplification of this idea. Social media, YouTube, and digital marketing enabled the viral proliferation of this campaign allowing millions of eyeballs to gain access to the event.

This soon became an example of activation wherein the offline activities when lathered with the layer of digital and technology, yields robust amplification.

The happiness machines are classic Coke vending machines that dish out treats including drinks, pizzas, flowers, and sandwiches. While some give away the freebies to all consumers, others require a specific action to earn a reward.

Some other Coke Happiness machine endeavours which went viral and contributed hugely to strengthening Coke's brand relationship with its customers include the following:

- In South Korea, the Coke vending machine coaxed people to mimic dance moves of a popular band and used Microsoft Kinect technology to register the steps. The machine subsequently dispensed Coke in proportion to the dance moves copied correctly.
- Similarly machines in Singapore dispensed Coke cans after receiving a hug from consumers.

Reinforcing Right Brand Responses

The goal of integrated marketing communications (IMC) is to integrate the organizational message across all IMC tools and media platforms. The integration is required at the following levels:

- Maintaining harmony in the context of marketing objectives
- Maintaining uniformity in the context of creative message content across disparate media vehicles
- Eliciting responses from the consumers
- Maintaining similarity in interacting/responding to the consumers
- Enhancing consumer retention
- Promoting brand switch from competing brands
- Reinforcing messages through testimonials, advertisements, and expert advice

Forging Brand Relationships

Branding is an ongoing process of monitoring brand perception to ensure that a brand is always meeting consumer expectations and evolving with consumers' changing needs. A brand's growth is severely limited if it lacks an emotional connection with consumers. It is up to an organization to create branded experiences that allow people to become emotionally involved with their brand. In branding, the process of creating emotional involvement begins with the emotional triggers created by the brand with their set of audiences.[31] If a brand does not hone in on an emotional trigger, then it will have a much harder time generating word-of-mouth marketing and loyalty. People often do not talk about things they have no feelings for or about,[32] and that applies to brands too. Once the organizations identify the most effective emotional triggers tied to their brand and understand the feelings consumers have for the brand and the competitors' brands, it is time to create branded experiences that allow emotional involvement in their brand to grow deeper.

Branded experiences include the atmosphere in the organization's brick-and-mortar location, the user experience, and content on the corporate website,[33] the conversations on product or brand blogs, the brand behaviour and offerings at events. It is in the interest of the organizations to look for ways to allow consumers to experience their brand first-hand and develop their own emotional connections to it. The brand that makes a connection with the consumer, wins their confidence and their business. Emotionally connecting consumers to a brand is essential. Without it, relationships are not formed, and loyalty can never develop. The consumer has to be touched emotionally more than intellectually today. The key here is to fulfil consumers' desires over their basic needs. That is, to appeal to consumers' emotions over their reasoned, intellectual needs.

A brand relationship is hence the commitment and resonance a customer has towards a brand. It goes beyond simple features, functionality, price, or total cost of ownership. It marks the upper point of the brand equity pyramid and represents a goal only some brands are able to obtain. The role of online content is to deepen this brand loyalty, the attachment of the consumers to a brand, the support and sense of community and to encourage active engagement with the brand.

> ### EXHIBIT 6.4 HDFC
>
> HDFC bank is known to be low on mass media such as TV and print and heavy on digital and activation. The organization targets customers through netbanking and ATM with relevant, customized messages based on data analytics. The company uses these campaigns extensively for driving activation and usage of various banking products and services such as debit card upgrades, bill payment, mobile banking, online deposits, DEMAT.
>
> HDFC bank is successfully leveraging the online domain both in terms of number of channels being used as well as engaging with their customers. Some of HDFC's trysts with the virtual domain are listed as follows:
>
> | Social media channel | Online branding contribution |
> |---|---|
> | HDFC and Facebook | The company's money matters section provides interesting financial news to customers which increase their brand knowledge. The puzzles/jigsaws on the page stimulate consumer engagement. |
> | HDFC and Twitter | Builds consumer engagement, increases brand resonance, stimulate brand responses. |
> | HDFC and YouTube | HDFC has created great advertisements and one such advertisement for HDFC mutual fund garnered over half a million views. |
> | HDFC and LinkedIn | Display of products and getting recommendation from consumers enhances the brand value in a peer-to-peer and consumer-to-consumer context. This builds brand credibility, as the consumer recommendations serve as a live testimonial for other consumers. |

USING CONSUMER BRAND KNOWLEDGE AND CONSUMER BRAND EMOTION TO DEVELOP CONSUMER ENGAGEMENT

In a fiercely competitive environment, organizations that want to retain their consumers and increase consumer–brand loyalty need to focus on increasing the consumer's brand knowledge (CBK) along with the consumer's emotion about the brand. Increasing CBK and emotion contributes to increased consumer perceived value in the brand, which is directly linked to greater consumer–brand loyalty, by building greater brand customer centricity.

It should come as no surprise that humans are emotional creatures. Even a casual glimpse into the nation's brand or product shelves reveals that consumers make buying decisions based on their feelings and emotions about particular brands. And marketers have long recognized the fact that emotions play a key role when consumers are talking about—or purchasing—products in categories as disparate as those represented by brands such as Mercedes, Kodak and Louis Vuitton. Although none of this seems all that newsworthy, marketers appear to be rediscovering the power of human emotions.[34] Suddenly, it seems that the new marketing millennium is all about emotions. And whatever has sparked this resurgence of interest is apparently contagious. In this context, brand positioning gains importance as a strategic marketing function.

It further becomes vital for organizations to recognize the consumer as a significant dimension in evaluating and positioning organizational brands.[35] This can be achieved through adoption of appropriate brand management strategies. Building customer centricity in a brand by leveraging CBK is a significant strategic thought that organizations can explore in the wake of the rising vulnerabilities of brands, in the face of rising consumer empowerment. It creates new opportunities for brand–customer dialogue, knowledge creation, and, critically, provides a new context in which the interests of a corporation and those of its customers can be more closely aligned.[36]

The collaborative version of the Internet has altered the manner in which information is published, consumed, and utilized on the Internet resulting in a paradigm shift in the way interactions take place within the organizational workspace, as well as between the organization and the external customers.

Blogging is shaping into a useful organizational tool for brand propagation and interaction of consumers with several companies having effectively launched corporate blogs, thereby shaping consumer perception, by adding to consumer knowledge about organizations, brands, and products. As blog audiences grow and persist over hundreds of posts, more of the 'back story' is contained in an archive or across conversations throughout the community and more and more is taken for granted as known. In the era of consumer empowerment, the average consumer is faced with numerous product and brand choices. Brands have a simple, common purpose, which is to make it easy for people to express their personal style. Companies constantly evolve their brands to better meet customers' needs—through innovative and inspiring design; through convenient and engaging store experiences; and by communicating with people in a way that connects to how they live, adopt, and use a brand. This is the value that brands deliver to their customers. Brands should strive for the timeliness and classicism and should allow customers to express themselves. Brands should appeal to every customer through the creation of an intimate connection. When customers think of any brand, they should feel comfortable and good about themselves in all kinds of situations.[37] Through changes of social and economical environment (i.e., growth of consumerism), people are pursuing higher-quality living. This in turn leads to the higher demand of product varieties.

The focus earlier was on the traditional 4Ps of marketing where marketers promoted products' tangible benefits, but the focus now is at promoting a product that touches consumers' inner feelings. The consumer–brand relationship evolved from pure monetary transaction to emotional transaction. The value of a product is not only determined by its objective value, also by the way consumers perceive this product.[38] It is argued that cognition leads to conclusion, but emotion leads to action.[39] Marketers therefore promote their products by targeting consumers' emotional impulse and desire. This kind of branding strategy is called emotional branding. This is a customer centric, empathetic, and cultural story-driven strategy that captures customer's deep emotions, and it can therefore be widely applied to different product and service contexts. Through the emotional appeals, consumers tend to give their brands personalities.[40]

Consumers also form communities around their brands. This enables the brands to achieve a unique market position, and the products no longer compete through their basic product attributes.[41] Most of the consumers are driven more by an emotional marketing strategy than a rational marketing strategy.[42]

For companies, the following two aspects are extremely significant:

- Exploring the marketing paradigm for cost-effective consumer communication channels to establish interactive touch-points that can manipulate the consumer mind space and usher greater product adoption by building a consumer–brand connection.
- The dimension of consumer emotion, the ability of a blog to impact consumer emotion, and the connection between CBK and consumer brand emotion (CBE), in an Internet marketing paradigm.

BRAND CUSTOMER CENTRICITY

Increased competition reduces brand loyalty, making the job of the marketers more complex. Further, customers also become indifferent to the myriad marketing messages being thrust upon them. As a result, marketing needs to be more well directed and specific, because customers, whether consumers or businesses, do not want more choices. Customers have hidden or overt preferences which marketers can reveal by building a learning relationship. An increasing number of organizations have specialized in meeting the increased complexity of the individual needs. More and more consumers gain access to powerful new media and information tools to compare brands, products, and services.[43] Organizations in a range of industries are responding by developing advocacy-based strategies and practices.[44] The strategy behind customer advocacy is simple. By assisting consumers to find and execute their optimum solution in a given market, it will be easier for an organization to earn their long-term trust, purchases, and loyalty.[45] In the meantime, in the highly competitive business climate, developing and maintaining unique product features has become hard and costly. Technical progress does not necessarily assure commercial success or sustainable competitive advantages. Products are becoming more and more like commodities.

According to Naomi Klein, author of the much-debated book 'No Logo', leading companies such as Nike, Microsoft, and Tommy Hilfiger put brands before products claiming that they no longer produce things but images of their brands. What consumers know about a brand will influence their reaction when confronted with brand-related stimuli (e.g., a branded product, a brand user, a category). Managing CBK hence becomes a crucial task for brand managers.[46]

Hence it is vital for companies to explore the concept of a brand, from a consumer's perspective. A brand is the perception of value that customers believe he/she receives in purchasing a particular product, service, or experience from a particular organization. Consequently, a great brand effectively retains customers while simultaneously attracting new ones. Branding is the process by which companies distinguish their product offerings from competition.

Hence, it is vital for organizations to establish a healthy and purposeful consumer–brand relationship. This can be achieved by building strong customer centric brands. Companies need to have a thorough understanding of the customer beliefs, behaviours, product or service attributes, and competitors. CBK can be defined in terms of the personal meaning about a brand stored in consumer memory, that is, all descriptive and evaluative brand-related information.[47]

Different sources and levels of knowledge such as awareness, attributes, benefits, images, thoughts, feelings, attitudes, and experiences get linked to a brand and its understanding by the consumer. To be effective, a brand needs to resonate with customers.[48] When a brand faces aggressive competition in the marketplace, brand personality and reputation of the brand help it distinguish from competing offerings. This can result in gaining customer loyalty and achieve growth. A strong brand identity that is well understood and experienced by the customer helps in developing trust, which in turn results in differentiating the brand from competition.

A company needs to establish a clear and consistent brand identity by linking brand attributes with the way they are communicated, which can be easily understood by the customers. The brand can be viewed as a product, a personality, a set of values, and a position it occupies in people's minds. Brand identity is everything the company wants the brand to be seen as. A brand tries to establish a coherent perception of the company for its different stakeholders and reflects a good corporate reputation in the eyes of the general public.[49]

Nevertheless, the single most important public of a brand is its end consumers, who are drowning in the overwhelming abundance of brands and brand communication. Brand identity and image significantly contribute to the degree of customer centricity of a brand.

BRANDS AND EMOTIONS

The concept of brand identity is defined as a unique set of brand associations that a firm can create or maintain. It may involve a value proposition with functional, emotional, or self-expressive benefits. It does not matter whether the associations are tangible or emotional/symbolic or both.[50] The emotional linkage between brand and consumer is equally important in building strong brands. It has also been confirmed in research that consumers look for and buy emotional experiences around what has been bought and no longer buy products and services alone.[51] Emotional attachment to brands has attracted a lot of attention.[52]

It has long been considered that attitudes are insufficient predictors of brand commitment (e.g., loyalty), and suggest that true loyalty requires the customer to form an emotional bond with the brand.[53] Calling for greater research in this area, it is suggested that the boundaries of the attitudes construct need to be recognized so that another construct reflecting emotional attachment can be articulated.[54]

The nature and character of the emotional attachment construct is reflected in discussion of brand relationships, brand love, and brand communities. Brand commitment among others, and various dimensions such as passion, commitment, and intimacy are considered by many researchers to better explain brand loyalty.[55]

CBE is a state of emotional attachment (evoked in response to the brand as a stimulus), which is characterized by strong positive affinity towards the brand and a tendency of the brand to dominate the consumer's cognition. CBE is subject specific. Different consumers may enjoy different levels of emotional attachment with respect to the same brand.

Two experiments were conducted to demonstrate the connection of brand and emotions; the experiments are as follows:

Experiment I

This experiment focused on analysing the improvement in CBK by exposure of the consumer to a corporate blog.[56]

The objective of the experiment was to demonstrate that corporate blogs can be used by organizations for increasing the level of CBK.

Method

A focus group of participants were asked some questions regarding the following brands:

- Facebook
- Volkswagen
- Google
- Cadbury's

Their level of brand knowledge was recorded.

Then, these consumers were asked to surf the Internet blogs of these companies for a fixed duration. Their knowledge pertaining to the brand increased.

Experiment II

The previous experiment was extended to measure the variation in the consumer emotion.

A focus group of respondents was asked to rate their emotion pertaining to a brand, before and after the exposure to the blogs. The variation in the CBE levels, as mapped subsequently, is then, empirically measured (Table 6.5). The key to creating brand loyalty is developing a consistent and salient brand perception through the association of specific emotional experiences with a product or service.

CONSUMER BRAND EMOTION

Before 'emotion' becomes as nebulous a concept as 'satisfaction', it might be helpful to determine the exact response we are trying to elicit. In an effort to get all the cards on the table, let us relate one of the dictionary definitions of 'emotion', which describes 'a psychic and physical reaction—physiologically involving changes that prepare the body for immediate vigorous action'. The 'emotional' revolution that has engulfed the

Table 6.5 Experiment grid to measure CBE levels (pre and post) of participants

	Brand blog		Questionnaire	
Use one word to describe your perception of the given brand on the following attributes				
Active engagement	Superb	Excitable	Constructive	Unnoticeable
Advertising and jingle	Excitable	Full of life	Admired	Disgustful
Appealing	Smart	Magnetic	Excitable	Unnoticeable
Attitudinal attachment	Graceful	Well off	Royal	Disappointing
Behavioural loyalty	Sincere	Genuine	Responsible	Disappointing
Believable	Recognized	Genuine	Responsible	Disappointing
Captivating	Superb	Mesmerizing	Full of life	Unnoticeable
Cheerful	Full of life	Happy	Well off	Disgustful
Empathy	Understanding	Compassion	Responsiveness	Disappointing
Excitement	Terrific	Fascinating	Encouraging	Disappointing
Intense	Associable	Genuine	Intelligent	Disappointing
Likeable	Purposive	Smart	Magnetic	Disgustful
Mesmerizing	Captivating	Purposive	Superb	Unnoticeable
Sensorial experience	Intensely	Spirited	Stunning	Disappointing
Spirited	Splendid	Encouraging	Amazing	Disappointing

marketing world is undeniable. Brands are constantly seeking to win our wallets by way of our hearts. The brand that makes a connection with the consumer, wins their confidence.

Emotionally connecting consumers to a brand is essential. Without it, relationships are not formed, and loyalty can never develop, as the consumer has to be touched emotionally more than intellectually. The key here is to fulfil consumers' desires over their basic needs. That is, to appeal to consumers' emotions over their reasoned, intellectual needs. By paying close attention to the emotions we elicit through design, we can build a positive perception of any brand. For the purpose of this study we have used a CBE score, and subsequently moved ahead to study the correlation between CBK and CBE scores.

Method

The consumers were asked to pick one word for each attribute listed on the screen, before and after exposure to the corporate blog of a product. Each of the words pertaining to a respective attribute under the CBE function had a well-defined sentiment score. These words were lifted from SentiWordNet 1.0, a lexical resource used for sentiment mining.

Each synset of WordNet 2.0 is associated with three numerical scores—*obj, pos,* and *neg*.[57] Both *pos* and *neg* scores were used for our study. For instance, the word 'like' has a positive score of 0.5.

SentiWordNet 1.0

We describe SentiWordNet (version 1.0), a lexical resource[58] in which each synset of WordNet (version 2.0) is associated to three numerical scores *obj(s), pos(s),* and *neg(s)*, describing how objective, positive, and negative the terms contained in the synset are. The assumption that underlies our switch from terms to synsets is that different senses of the same term may have different opinion-related properties.

Each of the three scores ranges from 0.0 to 1.0, and their sum is 1.0 for each synset. This means that a synset may have non-zero scores for all the three categories, which would indicate that the corresponding terms have, in the sense indicated by the synset, each of the three opinion-related properties only to a certain degree. The synset SentiWordNet[59] is freely available for research purposes, and is endowed with a web-based graphical user interface.

The Procedure

- The experiment grid I was administered to the consumers and their responses were tabulated.
- The consumers were exposed to a corporate blog for a period of 10 minutes.
- After the exposure, the respondents were administered with grid I again and their responses were tabulated.
- The variation in their emotion score was calculated.
- Finally, to see the relationship between the CBK and CBE levels, correlation was calculated between variations in CBK and variations in CBE.

It is seen that the content on the blog appears to strike an emotional chord with the consumer, enticing him to engage with the organization. Hence, consumer emotion is a vital parameter, which organizations should attempt to leverage. The experiment shows that the degree of CBE changes with the level of increase in CBK. A corporate blog serves as a touch point between organizations and consumers where a bidirectional-learning process can commence between the two entities. Success of these marketing endeavours of organizations depends on their ability to establish and manage interaction with their customers. The greater the latitude of this interaction, the greater is the organizational ability to generate and manage knowledge about its customers. A corporate blog helps increase the dimension of this interaction by helping the customer ask questions, get responses, look for information, contact customer service, contact senior organizational executives, portray his viewpoint, and at times access other forums related to the same organization/product/service while at the same time helping the organization capture consumer information as also actionable data to aid customization of offerings.

Regardless of the industry, most operators will claim at least a strong working knowledge of the many and varied touch-points at which their company interacts with the customer. What is typically lacking is any real sense of the relative importance of those touch-points in how they forge and reinforce the emotional engagement between the company and customer. Not all touch-points are created equal and focusing on the ones that have the greatest potential to impact the customer's product knowledge and emotional engagement with the company or brand is not just wise—it is required. The most successful companies in the world understand that brand and business growth do not result from the kind of emotion that is manufactured in an advertisement. Instead, these companies channel all of their energy into creating magnificent products that add true, tangible value to people's lives. Emotion—and the financial commitment it inspires—actually emerges as an organic side-effect of satisfied functional needs. To reap the enhanced financial benefits that can result from customer loyalty, marketers have enthusiastically pursued strategies intended to keep customers coming back. In fact, marketers want to move beyond customer 'retention', which is merely a behaviour, to generating customer 'commitment', 'delight', and even 'evangelism'—all of which represent enduring psychological bonds that link a customer to a company.

A higher assimilation of brand-related knowledge results in the improvement of consumer emotion pertaining to the brand. It is in the organizational interest that ways and means are developed to increase the consumer's knowledge with regard to product or brand. Organizations can successfully leverage brand blogs to engage consumers, build a bond with them, and then subsequently increase their knowledge about an organization/product/brand. Subsequent improvements in consumer emotion pertaining to the brands will result in faster product adoption by the consumers. If an emotional connection is truly the key to an enduring customer relationship, companies should not be targeting consumers based on their demography or lifestyle. Rather, they should focus their efforts according to the consumers' evident potential to develop meaningful brand connections. In addition, instead of directing their efforts at stimulating trial through reduced switching costs, marketers should re-focus their attention on establishing and enhancing these powerfully differentiating emotional bonds. *That's the road to a brand relationship, not just to a transaction.*

CASE STUDY   Narendra Modi—Developing Brand Modi in the Online World

Narendra Damodardas Modi is the 15th and the current Prime Minister of India. Modi, a leader of the Bharatiya Janata Party (BJP), also served as the Chief Minister of Gujarat from 2001 to 2014.

Modi was a key strategist for the BJP in the successful 1995 and 1998 Gujarat state election campaigns. He became Chief Minister of Gujarat in October 2001 and served longer by far in that position than anyone else to date. He was a major campaign figure in the 2009 general election, which the BJP led National Democratic Alliance lost to the Congress-led United Progressive Alliance (UPA). He led the BJP in the April–May 2014 general election, which resulted in a majority for the BJP in the Lok Sabha, first time any party has done so since 1984.

Modi is a Hindu Nationalist and a member of the Rashtriya Swayamsevak Sangh (RSS). He is a controversial figure both within India as well as internationally as his administration has been criticized for the incidents surrounding the 2002 Gujarat riots. He has been praised for his economic policies, which are credited with creating an environment for a high rate of economic growth in Gujarat. However, his administration has also been criticised for failing to make a significant positive impact upon the human development of the state.

The virtual world was supposed to have played a very significant role in formulation and propagation of Brand Modi, by garnering huge volumes of visibility and voter engagement through the online world. Brand Modi used the virtual world as a megaphone to connect with the people, conduct rallies, and solicit support. This case study addresses Brand Modi's online presence, after having won the 2014 Lok Sabha elections and being sworn in as Prime Minister.

The following online tools were being used to create an online brand presence for Brand Modi:

- *Blog* http://www.narendramodi.in/blog-detail/
  - The blog was positioned as a platform for people across the world to read his opinion on myriad issues in his own words. Readers could post their feedback on the blog and share the blog on their social networks. On the blog, Narendra Modi was positioned as a soulful writer whose words flowed directly from his heart to touch the hearts of millions. The blog showcased his passion for the country, his vision for development, and his anguish against injustice. In this manner the blog was successfully used as a tool to create a brand identity in the online sphere and then generate brand salience and resonance.
- Brand Modi's Facebook page carries out regular updates on his activities. The Facebook page hosts posts ranging from his swearing in ceremony (20 lakh likes, 68,000 shares) to extracts of his conversation with the Prime Minister of Pakistan, which shared details of the Pakistani PMs personal life, received over 5 lakh likes. The Facebook page is hence being used to enhance Brand meaning. This is being done by strengthening the brand imagery and functional performance by touching the user's emotions and psychology through an emotional brand personality.
- Brand Modi's presence on Twitter provides a very up to date, almost minute by minute performance of Brand Modi by giving users access to his hourly schedule. With 4.52 million followers, the Twitter page has been able to elicit the right responses from users for the brand by maintaining uniformity, harmony, and repeated message reinforcement.
- *Brand Modi's official website* http://www.narendramodi.in/, allows people to interact with the Prime Minister and includes a significant volume of information about him and his ideology. The governance section on his website positioned his government as one which would provide them pro-people good governance, with a minimum government poised to give maximum results. The site clearly reiterates that his government endorsed red carpet for the people and not red tape with the slogan—*Sabka Saath, Sabka Vikas* and has been able to create an emotional connection with the voters.

Objectives of Brand Modi's Online Presence Appear to be as Follows

- Engagement with the masses
- Regularly update people with his activities and performance
- Get user feedback and use the same to his advantage by taking timely corrective actions
- Staying close to public sentiment
- Personify Brand Modi as an emotional individual geared to help the masses and bring in an era of happiness and prosperity for all.
- Use technology to demonstrate 'inclusive governance'
- Crowd source ideas from discerning citizens and civil society who actively follow him on social media. Channel the positive energies into policy decisions and implementation

The online branding strategy for the brand appears to have been successful, considering the volume of people following, liking, and engaging in conversations with the brand in the virtual domain. However, it still needs to be seen how Brand Modi will leverage the benefits of his online promise to facilitate the functioning of his government and impress the people, in the years to come.

Success of this brand will be a function of his ability to monitor brand perception of the voters constantly and to ensure that the brand is always meeting consumer (voter) expectations and evolving with consumers' changing needs. The brand has already been successful in creating an emotional connection with consumers and generated mass appeal. Forming a relationship with his supporters and the general population and winning their confidence will allow Brand Modi to develop a 'relationship' with his consumers. Voter loyalty will be a function of how trustworthy the brand is perceived. It is in capitalizing on this trustworthiness and emotional involvement with the voters in an intellectual way that the future of Brand Modi rests.

Questions:

1. Elucidate the contribution of the following tools in the creation of Brand Modi:
   (a) Narendra Modi's blog
   (b) Twitter campaign
   (c) Facebook page
   (d) Brand Modi's official website
2. What do you think is the most striking feature of Narendra Modi's virtual presence?

PRACTITIONER PERSPECTIVE

Buying online is about trust and selection, belief in the transparency of the transaction and relationship building.

Kunal Bahl, Co-founder and CEO of Snapdeal

Most of us are now carrying around a phone or tablet—all connected to the Web, each a supercomputer in our pockets. Over 1.3 million Android devices are activated every day. More than half a billion Android devices have been activated worldwide. When we see a heat map of the growth in Android devices throughout the world over the last year, you might expect to see the developing world completely dark—but it is on fire. Japan, South Korea, and France grew between 2% and 300%. However, the developing world is adopting Android at an even faster pace. Brazil, India, Thailand, and Indonesia all grew around 500%. There will be 5 billion people online by 2020. This is changing the way we all live and work—and helping Star Trek moments becoming a reality.

Guneet Singh, Head, Consumer Marketing, India

Our vision on social media is to build a community of financially aware young parents and to achieve this, we see a significant role for both entertaining content for parents as well as infotainment around financial planning and Aviva's products as key pillars.

Rishi Piparaiya, Director Marketing and Bancassurance, Aviva India

SUMMARY

Cyberbranding involves integrating online and offline branding tactics that reinforce each other to speak with one voice. The most common method of building an online brand presence is through an offline technique called brand spiralling. It is the practice of using traditional media to promote and attract consumers to an online website. The customer-based brand equity pyramid states that the power of a brand lies in what customers have learned, felt, seen and heard about the brand as a result of their experiences pertaining to the brand. In other words, *the power of a brand lies in what resides in the minds of customers*. The four stages of establishing customer-based brand equity are establishing the proper brand identity, creating the appropriate brand meaning, eliciting the right brand responses, and forging appropriate brand relationships with customers. The best brands in the world know that it is essential to create a brand ecosystem—a living breathing organism that is all about stimulating and feeding off conversations that happen within it, then using that to build further brand stories. Millions of micro interactions that happen on the Web (blogs, Twitter, Facebook, YouTube, Google, etc.) are conversations between people and many of the conversations happening in social media are about brands. So, to break down the brand ecosystem—it is an organic model, where the role of the brand is to listen to the conversations happening around it, energize those conversations with interesting content and experiences. It is all about giving the brand community to talk something about the brand, within their own personal social networks and influencers are then able to add velocity to the idea penetration about a brand. Organizations need to establish online brand identity. This involves—establishing brand resonance and reinforcing brand salience, creating brand identity and online domain names, enhancing brand meaning, reinforcing right brand responses, and forging brand relationships. In the online context, the most important challenge faced by organizations is concerning domain naming between *branded house* and a *house of brands*. A branded house, chosen by companies such as Virgin, Healthy Choice, and BMW, treats all its products as an integrated brand. Branding is companywide.

Concept Review Questions

1. How can organizations use digital marketing to build the online value of a brand?
2. Write short notes on the following:
   (a) Domain names
   (b) Domain name goals
   (c) Domain name memorability
3. Differentiate between house of brands and branded house strategies in the context of the virtual medium offered by the Internet. Use corporate examples to illustrate your viewpoint.
4. How can the brand equity pyramid help organizations in formulating a digital brand ecosystem?

Critical Thinking Questions

1. Study the brand architecture of one multinational following the house of brand strategy. Discuss with examples.
2. What strategies should the sellers of the following products use in the context of online branding:
   (a) Carat Lane solitaire earrings
   (b) Volkswagen Vento
   (c) Harley Davidson motorcycles
   (d) Beverley three seater sofas

Practising Digital Marketing

1. Track the online presence of five product brands. Trace how each brand has used the online world to do the following:
   (a) Create a brand identity in the online sphere
   (b) Generate brand salience and resonance
   (c) Develop a brand personality
   (d) Develop a consumer–brand relationship
2. Develop a chart to rate the brands in the above context and develop a brand online presence (BOP) index.
3. Suggest ways for improvement, for brands demonstrating a low BOP index.

References

1. Levin, A.M., Levin, I.P., and Heath, C.E., (2003). 'Product category dependent consumer preferences for online and offline shopping features and their influence on multi-channel retail alliances'. *Journal of Electronic Commerce Research*, Vol. 4(3), pp. 85–93.
2. Bartel-Sheehan, K. and Doherty, C., (2001). 'Re-weaving the web: Integrating print and online communications'. *Journal of Interactive Marketing*, Vol. 15, pp. 47–51.
3. Keller, K., (1993). 'Conceptualising, measuring and managing customer-based brand equity'. *Journal of Marketing*, Vol. 57, pp. 1–22.
4. Keller, K.L., (2003). 'Brand Synthesis: The Multidimensionality of Brand Knowledge'. *Journal of Consumer Research*, Vol. 29, pp. 595–600.
5. Ibid., Tables 1 through 6.
6. Aaker, D.A., *Building Strong Brands*, The Free Press, New York, NY, 1996.
7. Snyder, 1998; Ries and Ries, 2000; Todaro, 2004; Delgado and Hernández, 2008.
8. Del Franco, M., Mailers say, webwardho!, *Catalog Age* 19, no. 4, pp. 1–3.
9. Clow, K. E. and Baack, D., Integrated advertising, promotion and marketing communications, *Internet Marketing*, Third Edition, p. 444.

10. Parsuraman, A., Zeithmal, V.A., and Berry, L.L., (2003). 'Conceptual model of service quality'. *Journal of Marketing Research.*
11. Keller, K.L., (2003). 'Brand synthesis: The multidimensionality of brand knowledge'. *Journal of Consumer Research*, Vol. 29, pp. 595–600.
12. Aaker, J.L., (1997). 'Dimensions of brand personality'. *Journal of Marketing Research*, Vol. 36(3), pp. 345–55.
13. Lassar, W., Mittal, B., and Sharma, A., (1995). 'Measuring customer-based brand equity'. *Journal of Consumer Marketing*, Vol. 12(4), pp. 11–19.
14. Porter, M., *Competitive Advantage: Creating and Sustaining Superior Performance*, Ch. 1, The Free Press, New York, NY, 1985, p. 1115.
15. Kumar, N., *Marketing as Strategy*, Harvard Business School Press, Boston, MA, 2004.
16. Kotler, P. and Keller, K.L., *Marketing Management*, Twelfth Edition, Prentice Hall, Upper Saddle River, NJ, 2006.
17. Aaker, D.A., *Building Strong Brands*, The Free Press, New York, NY, 1996.
18. Feldwick, P., (1996). 'Do we really need "brand equity"?' *The Journal of Brand Management*, Vol. 4(1), pp. 9–28. Fifth Annual Advertising and Promotion Workshop', 1st February, 1993.
19. Fombrun, C., Gardberg, N., and Server, J., (2000). 'The reputation quotient: A multistakeholder measure of corporate reputation'. *The Journal of Brand Management*, Vol. 7, pp. 241–255.
20. Fournier, S., (1998). 'Consumers and their brands: Developing relationship theory in consumer research'. *Journal of Consumer Research*, Vol. 24, pp. 343–73.
21. Govers, P.C.M. and Schoormans, J.P.L., (2005). 'Product personality and its influence on consumer preference'. *Journal of Consumer Marketing*, Vol. 22(4), pp. 189–97.
22. Keller, K.L., (2001). 'Building customer-based brand equity'. *Journal of Marketing Management*, 11(3).
23. Peter, J.D. and Guy, W.M., (2003). 'Factors affecting online advertsing recall: A study of students'. *Journal of Advertising Research.*
24. Lee, S. and Deighton, J., (2001). 'Banner advertsing: Measuring effectiveness and optimising placement'. *Journal of Interactive Marketing*, Vol. 15(2), pp. 60–64.
25. Hanson, W. and Kalyanam, K., Online branding, *Internet Marketing and Ecommerce*, Thomson, 2007.
26. Hansom, W. and Kalyanam, K., Defining domain names, *Internet Marketing and Ecommerce*, Thomson, 2007, p. 186.
27. Hansom, W. and Kalyanam, K., Domain name memorability, *Internet Marketing and Ecommerce*, Thomson, 2007, p. 188.
28. Aakersnd, D. and Joachimsthaler, E., *Brand Leadership: The Next Level of the Brand Revolution*, The Free Press, New York, NY, 2000, p. 26.
29. Aaker, D.A., *Brand Portfolio Strategy: Creating Relevance, Differentiation, Energy. Leverage and Clarity*, Free Press, New York, NY, 2004.
30. Hansom, W. and Kalyanam, K., Online branding, *Internet Marketing and Ecommerce*, Thomson, 2007, p. 191.
31. Mowen, J. and Minor. C., *Consumer Involvement, Consumer Behavior, a Framework*, Ch. 3, Fifth Edition, Prentice Hall, 2001.
32. Joseph, W.A. and Hutchinson, J.W., (1987). 'Dimensions of consumer expertise'. *Journal of Consumer Research*, Vol. 13(March), pp. 411–38.
33. Ryals, L. and Payne, A.F.T., (2001). 'Customer relationship management in financial services: Towards information-enabled relationship marketing'. *Journal of Strategic Marketing*, Vol. 9, pp. 1–25.
34. McEwen, W. J., *Married to the Brand*, Gallup Press, New York, NY, 2005.
35. Aaker, D.J., *Building Strong Brands*, The Free Press, New York, NY, 1995.
36. Sinha, N., Ahuja, V., and Medury, Y., (2011). 'Corporate blogs: A web 2.0 approach to increase consumer brand knowledge'. *International Journal of Business Economics and Management Research*, Vol. 2(3), pp. 193–205.
37. Bedbury, S., *A New Brand World*, Penguin Group, New York, NY, 2003.
38. Dolan, R.J. and Gourville, J., Principles of pricing, *HBS Note*, 9-506-021, 2005, pp. 149–162.
39. Robertson, T.S., (1976). 'Low-commitment consumers behavior'. *Journal of Advertising Research*, Vol. 16(2), pp. 19–24.
40. Aaker, J.L., (1997). 'Dimensions of brand personality'. *Journal of Marketing Research*, Vol. 34(3), pp. 347–356.

41. Muniz, A.M. Jr. and Schau, H.J., (2005). 'Religiosity, in the abandoned Apple Newton brand community'. *Journal of Consumer Research*, Vol. 31(4), pp. 737–747.
42. Pawle, J. and Cooper, P., (2006). 'Measuring emotion: Lovemarks, the future beyond brands'. *Journal of Advertising Research*, Vol. 46(1), pp. 38–48.
43. Pitt, L.F., Berthon, P.R., Watson, R.T., and Zinkhan, G.M., (2002). 'The Internet and the birth of real consumer power'. *Business Horizons*, Vol. 45(4), pp. 7–14.
44. Achrol, R. and Kotler, P., (1999). 'Marketing in the network economy'. *Journal of Marketing*, Vol. 63 (Special Issue), pp. 146–163.
45. Urban, G., (2004). 'The emerging era of customer advocacy'. *MIT Sloan Management Review*, Vol. 45(2), pp. 77–82.
46. Kapferer, J.N., *The New Strategic Brand Management: Creating and Sustaining Brand Equity Long Term*, Kogan Page, London, 2004.
47. Keller, K.L., (2003). 'Brand synthesis: The multidimensionality of brand knowledge'. *Journal of Consumer Research*, Vol. 29(1), pp. 35–50.
48. Aaker, D.J. and Joachimsthaler, E.A., (2000). 'The brand relationship spectrum: The key to the brand architecture challenge'. *California Management Review*, Vol. 42(4), pp. 8–23.
49. Hatch, M.J. and Schultz, M., (2003). 'Bringing the corporation into corporate branding'. *European Journal of Marketing*, Vol. 37(7/8), pp. 1041–1064.
50. Anselm, K.J. and Kostelijk, E., (2008). 'Identity-based marketing: A new balanced marketing paradigm'. *European Journal of Marketing*, Vol. 42(9/10), pp. 907–914.
51. Brembeck, H. and Ekström, K., *Elusive Consumption*, Berg, Oxford, 2004.
52. Thomson, M., MacInnis, D.J., and Park, C.W., (2005). 'The ties that bind: Measuring the strength of consumers' emotional attachments to brands'. *Journal of Consumer Psychology*, Vol. 15(1), pp. 77–91.
53. Park, C.W., MacInnis, D.J., and Priester, J.R., Research directions on strong brand relationships. In: MacInnis, D.J., Park, C.W., and Priester, J.R., (eds.), *Handbook of Brand Relationships*, Society for Consumer Psychology, M.E. Sharpe, Armonk, NY and London, 2009, pp. 379–393.
54. Oliver, R.L., (1999). 'Whence consumer loyalty?' *Journal of Marketing*, Vol. 63(4), pp. 33–44.
55. Warrington, P. and Shim, S., (2000). 'An empirical investigation of the relationship between product involvement and brand commitment'. *Psychology and Marketing*, Vol. 17(9), pp. 761–782.
56. Sinha, N., Ahuja, V., and Medury, Y., (2010). *Evaluating Brand Attributes for Defining Brand Identity. A Consumer Perspective*. Paper presented at the third National Conference on Contemporary Management Research, Apeejay School of Management, New Delhi, 14 May, 2010.
57. Ahuja, V. and Medury, Y., (2011). 'CRM in a Web 2.0 world'. *Journal of Direct, Data and Digital Marketing Practice*, Vol. 13(1), pp. 11–24.
58. Esuli, A. and Sebastiani, F., (2006). Senti Word Net: A publicly available lexical resource for opinion mining. *Proceedings of Language Resources and Evaluation (LREC)*, http://www.lrec-conf.org/proceedings/lrec2006/, accessed 7 October, 2011.
59. Ahuja, V. and Medury, Y., (2010). 'Corporate blogs as e-CRM tools: Building consumer engagement through content management'. *Journal of Database Marketing and Customer Strategy Management*, Vol. 17, pp. 91–105.

Traffic Building

> **LEARNING OBJECTIVES**
>
> *After reading this chapter, you will be able to*:
> - Distinguish the components of a Web traffic plan
> - Get familiar with the strategic and tactical choices pertaining to Internet marketing
> - Get acquainted with the various search marketing methods
> - Enumerate the traffic-building goals for organizations
> - Understand the concept of search engine marketing

The fragmentation of the media and the rise of the Internet have made media planning and buying much more complicated. Media buyers now have the upper hand in many decisions and by nature prefer more cost-effective and accountable advertising vehicles. Advertisers seek to create and maintain brands, to provide information about new products and services, to advertise sales and price promotions, and to direct consumers to the proper retail outlet for their goods. This is where online branding and advertising have significant roles to play.

THE DIAMOND–WATER PARADOX

Despite the critical role of water and the inessential nature of diamonds, a diamond is vastly more valuable than water. Of course, scarcity is the key! Water literally falls from the sky while diamonds are exceedingly rare. Even extraordinary value can be driven down by abundant supply.[1]

To draw an analogy with the Internet, online content is growing abundantly and so are the number of users; however, what is scarce for organizations is—*user attention*. Novelty no longer drives attention and getting higher traffic on a company website is a major challenge for organizations. With the proliferation of diverse typologies of online content, the four major challenges before companies are as follows:

- Creating the right set of keywords
- Advertising and content

- Driving users to the website
- Making them stay on the website

Significantly, companies need to have well-defined online traffic plans in place and also need to spend on traffic building online. It is in building the right online advertising ecosystem and leveraging the appropriate Web business models that companies will be able to grow in the digital space.

Let us understand the dynamics of an online search.

A visitor goes to a search engine and types a keyword related to his quest and proceeds further. He sees a series of unpaid links which hopefully give him what he wants. Challenges for digital marketing lie in the visibility of a company's website or brand on the search engine in response to the search results. In addition, there is a challenge in the keyword term that is used as well. Presence of that keyword in the content reflected on the company website will throw it (the link) up in the search results.

Search engine marketing (SEM) is the form of Internet marketing that involves the promotion of websites by increasing their visibility in the search engine results page. It may use search engine optimization (SEO) that adjusts or rewrites website content to achieve a higher ranking in search engine result pages or uses pay-per-click listings.

The first, organic SEO is the spending to ensure that search engines rank a site highly on the relevant search criteria and information seekers can organically find the listing and the site. The implication is simple—the earlier (or higher ranked on the search results page), and more frequently a site appears in the search result lists, the more visitors it will receive from the search engine's users. This is addressed in detail as the chapter proceeds.

The second is pay-per-click advertising on major sites such as Google, Yahoo, and MSN and also a number of additional more specialized search engines.

Companies need to have a detailed Web traffic plan in place to use concepts related to digital marketing more effectively.

The three components of an *Internet traffic plan* (Fig. 7.1) are as follows:

- Traffic-building sources (Fig. 7.2)
- Traffic volume and quality
- Traffic-building goals

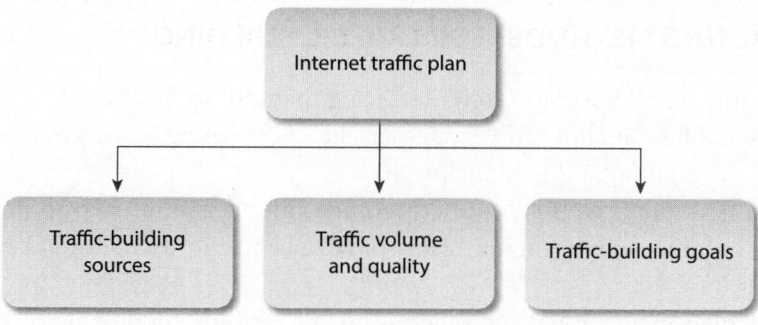

Fig. 7.1 Internet traffic plan

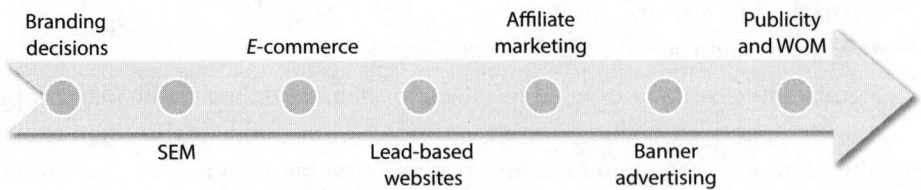

Fig. 7.2 Traffic-building sources

> ### EXHIBIT 7.1 Brands and YouTube
>
> Every month people around the world log in to YouTube to watch more than four billion hours[3] of video. The Indian viewing story is also pretty much along the same growth trajectory.
>
> Every significant brand in India is on YouTube—the reason is the visibility they get. Pepsi India, Hero Motocorp, Lakme, Honda, and Pond's are some significant names garnering the highest views on YouTube. Vodafone, Nokia, OLX, Airtel, and Cadbury Bournville have a very high number of YouTube subscribers.
>
> Brands consistently upload videos to increase views through online circulation. Digital marketing further empowers brands by providing YouTube monitoring tools. Metrics comprise the number of *uploaded video views*, number of *uploaded videos*, number of *subscribers*, or number of *YouTube channel views*. Companies can benefit from understanding their audience, measuring their YouTube marketing success, and optimizing their content. They can further identify key influencers, monitor engagement, and track growth by tracking user interaction on their YouTube channels and comparing performance.

INTERNET TRAFFIC PLAN[2]

An Internet traffic plan is developed using a series of *e*-marketing strategic and tactical choices. It is vital for a company's website presence to generate consumer traffic, as it is the traffic that builds visibility and subsequently consumer engagement. Traffic-building sources (Table 7.1) can fall into seven major categories; which are as follows:

SEARCH MARKETING METHODS[5] FOR TRAFFIC BUILDING

Companies use a host of search marketing methods to increase their online visibility on the Web. These include SEO, pay-per-click advertising, contextual advertising, digital asset optimization, and paid inclusion.

SEO is where a website's structure and content is improved to maximize its listing in the organic search engine result pages according to relevant keywords or search phrases.

Paid placement or pay per click is an advertising model in which advertisers pay their host only when their sponsored ad or link is clicked. Advertisers typically bid on

Table 7.1 Traffic-building sources

Branding decisions[3]	The value of a brand and a well-defined online brand architecture can successfully help an organization develop a substantial amount of Web traffic. This topic has been addressed in detail in the chapter on online branding.
Search engine marketing[4]	Organic search traffic results from a visitor going to a search engine, typing in a keyword phrase, and following one of the unpaid links to a site. It is free traffic, but it is not easy to achieve. The most important success criterion is an appearance high in the list of search returns. This results from strong content, high visibility, and search engine optimization. This has been addressed in detail in the subsequent section.
E-commerce	A model whereby goods and services are sold directly to a consumer or business.
Lead-based websites	A strategy whereby an organization generates value by acquiring sales leads from its website. These prospects are often referred to as organic leads.
Affiliate marketing	A process wherein a product or service developed by one entity is sold by other active sellers for a share of profits. The entity that owns the product may provide some marketing material (e.g., sales letters, affiliate links, tracking facilities, etc.); however, the vast majority of affiliate marketing relationships come from e-commerce businesses that offer affiliate programmes.
Online banner advertising	Companies use online banners to advertise in the virtual world. Decisions involved are regarding the sizes and typologies of those banners.
Publicity and word of mouth	Publicity, promotion, and word-of-mouth are significant traffic sources. Consumers consider word-of-mouth recommendations the most persuasive and credible information source. Building natural links into e-mail communications, online visits, and other electronic material helps spread these recommendations.

keywords or phrases relevant to their target market, with sponsored/paid search engine listings to drive traffic to a website. The search engine ranks ads based on a competitive auction and other related criteria (e.g., popularity, quality). Google AdWords, Yahoo! search marketing, and Microsoft ad centre are the three largest ad network operators, with all three operating under a bid-based model.

Contextual advertising is a form of targeted advertising with advertisements (e.g., banners, popups) appearing on websites, with the advertisements themselves selected and served by automated systems based on the content displayed to the user. A contextual advertising system scans the text of a website for keywords and returns advertisements to the webpage based on what the user is viewing. Google AdSense was the first major contextual advertising programme.

Digital asset optimization or SEO 2.0 is the optimization of all the organization's digital assets (e.g., .doc, .pdf, video, podcasts, music files, images, and other digital media) for search, retrieval, and indexing.

Paid inclusion is where a search engine company charges fees related to inclusion of websites in their search index. Some organizations mix paid inclusion with organic listings, for example, Yahoo! where others do not allow for paid inclusion to be listed with organic lists (e.g., Google and Ask.com).

INTERNET COOKIES AND TRAFFIC BUILDING

Cookies are a unique ID number a site comes up with for each person who visits it. These are called 'name–value pairs'. A name–value pair is simply a named piece of data. It can be considered as a welcoming pass to get an individual back into a website. When an individual visits and then revisits a site, their browser and a site's server use cookies to talk to each other.

Advantages of Cookies

Some of the imperative advantages of cookies are discussed as follows:

- Cookies state information on an individual's (customer's) PC and then share that information with the browser to customize the online experience. Websites use cookies in several beneficial ways for both the user and the site owner.
- Cookies share data about how many people visited the site and which items were clicked on, which helps site managers present the best choices of material to visitors.
- Cookies deliver a personalized experience. To store user preferences and create more personal browsing experiences, for example, by customizing screen and icon appearances.
- Cookies are smart. *E*-commerce sites can create shopping carts and 'quick checkout' options, and make product recommendations based on previous purchases.

It is important to note that all this information is stored on the site, and not the cookie. The cookie can simply be described as an identifying pass. Without it, the Web would not be so easy to navigate or nearly as intuitive.

TRAFFIC VOLUME AND QUALITY

While it is important for digital marketers to generate consumer traffic on the websites through a series of sources, it appears to be more significant for them to constantly assess the volume and quality of this traffic to take corrective action immediately. The following section discusses concepts related to traffic volume and quality (Fig. 7.3). These are Web visibility and competitive analysis and cost per action.

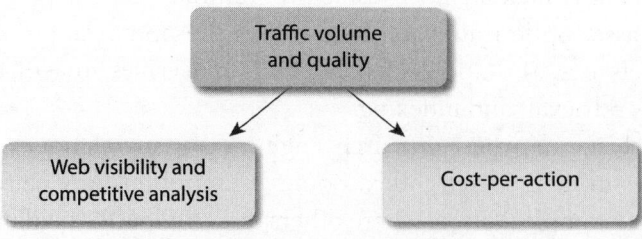

Fig. 7.3 Traffic volume and quality

Web Visibility and Competitive Analysis

Organizations can make use of several online analytical tools to analyse their site's performance, traffic rank, and reputation. The reach of the website can be compared with that of the competitors using a tool such as Alexa.

With the aid of the tools available, one can find the Alexa traffic rank and the site reputation. It further proceeds to list the estimated percentage of global Internet users who visit the site. Figures can be evaluated on a daily, weekly, and monthly basis. Companies can also obtain audience snapshots and profiles that can help organizations to track top search queries pertaining to their company. Tools like Google Analytics provide complete demographic and geographic information to companies regarding their online visitors.

Cost-per-action

Companies indulge in traffic-building analysis by computing the cost-per-action, which is defined as the number of visits that make it to a particular stage (the action) divided by the campaign costs. Companies calculate

- The cost per impression
- The cost per visit
- The cost per eventual purchase

Cost-per-action is a simplification of the full Web chain analysis. A cost-per-action analysis only focuses on the benefits for one specific desired outcome. It has the benefit of simplicity, creating a method of quickly comparing alternative traffic-building campaigns. Other sources of traffic, especially search and banners, are much easier to measure and evaluate.

Visitors decline and cost rises at each stage. For example

- Cost per impression = $15 per 1000 impressions
- Cost per visitor at the rate 2% click through = $0.015/0.02 = $0.75 per visitor
- Cost per purchases at the rate 5% conversion from visitors to buyers = $0.75/0.05
  - Cost = $15.00 per purchaser

TRAFFIC-BUILDING GOALS

The traffic-building goals (Fig. 7.4) of any organization should aim at the following:

- Maximizing short-term/long-term profit
- Minimizing cost-per-action (subject to volume targets)
- Maximize actions subject to spending capacity

SEARCH ENGINE MARKETING

Search engine traffic comes in two basic forms, which are as follows:

- *Organic traffic* Arising from a search return list, automatically generated by the search engine without any commercial arrangements.
- *Pay-per-click* Nature of search marketing establishes a hard number for the cost of generating a visit to a website.

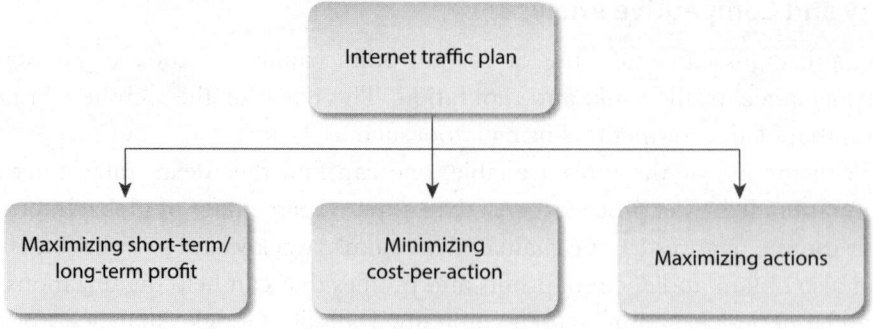

Fig. 7.4 Traffic-building goals

EXHIBIT 7.2   The Indian Premier League and Social Media

One of the TV programmes garnering the highest prime time TRPs is IPL—the Indian Premier League, a Twenty20 cricket tournament where different franchise teams participate for the title. The tournament started in 2008 and from then takes place every year. The event draws a significant amount of interest and attention from cricket fans in India. 2014 saw the formation of an interesting synergistic relationship between IPL and social media.

From title and presenting sponsor PepsiCo to others such as telecom service provider Vodafone, to personal care maker Garnier, and multi-business Muthoot Group, most big advertisers leveraged social media with incremental budgets to connect with their audiences.[6]

Attractions offered in the social media space were as follows:

- Pepsi tied up with Twitter to allow viewers to play cricket on the social media platform. Pepsi created the *Tweet20* dashboard which was a great platform for participants to engage with the brand. Through *Tweet20*, Pepsi allowed cricket crazy consumers to be a part of the game through a platform where technology drives the game play, which in turn results in engagement. By offering users a stadium-like experience, Pepsi was successful in building a strong association with the cricketing extravaganza.
- Google+ initiated special Hangout sessions that generated post-match conversations. YouTube allowed viewers to *live chat* by integrating Google+, thus making the experience more exhilarating for consumers. Top cricket stars participated in the hangouts during some matches, providing an analysis between innings.
- Vodafone used its zoozoos in the online space for an aggressive brand proliferation exercise. Zoozoos, are white creatures with ballooned bodies and egg heads, who are used to promote various value-added services of Vodafone. By having a significant fan following on Facebook, Vodafone could use the event for reigniting its relationship with its consumers. The company launched 25 new advertisements using zoozoos during IPL, 2014, to target first-time users of mobile Internet and popularize them on what all they could do on the Internet. One of the films promoted the service provider's *'Choose your number'* service. It featured a dance reality show starring the zoozoos in a refreshed and engaging creative format to communicate Vodafone's propositions.

SITE OPTIMIZATION

Just as newspaper editors have long put their top-rated stories 'above the fold' to ensure greater readability and visibility to a greater number of eyeballs, similarly, *search engine optimizers* seek to improve search engine placement by the following ways:

- Making the main search engines aware of their site
- Ensuring that content creates the appropriate keywords
- Focusing on details that search engines utilize in their rankings, ensuring that site navigation reinforces search engine algorithm, and cultivating links from other appropriate sites. They provide site guidelines that raise visibility without sacrificing usability and online quality

KEYWORD ADVERTISING

The rise of keyword advertising has been one of the most significant online developments. Small, clickable text-based ads bring organizations significant volumes of revenue. These keyword ads drive traffic to a company's website and in a typical pay-per-click model, organizations pay only when a particular keyword has been clicked. This has emphasized the need for appropriate keyword management.

KEYWORD VALUE

Keyword ads influence billions of website visits. They also establish a benchmark for the value of traffic from all sources. Traffic is relatively cheap if it can be generated for less than the prevailing keyword price in that sector, and should be refocused if the price is higher than this rate. Traffic cost places a burden on website managers and usability experts to ensure their sites are sufficiently productive to justify the visit cost.[7]

A keyword only has value if it leads some viewers to click and visit a site and some fraction of those visitors to convert to a desired action. Keyword value is driven strongly by competition. Although the specifics differ between major search engines, keyword ads are priced by a continuous auction process.

Even if a keyword is extremely valuable to an advertiser, if no other firms bid, its price will be low. However, if there are a number of firms competing for the keyword, the price can be bid up to levels that become unprofitable for some advertisers. Prices can change minute by minute, as new bidders enter and current bidders change their offers.

KEYWORD PORTFOLIO EVALUATION

The competitive bidding process creates situations where seemingly close keywords can have very different prices, at least temporarily. The process of keyword portfolio evaluation comprises the following steps:

Identify main keywords → *Expand the list* → *Test* → *Bid* → *Trim* → *Track*

The most significant step in keyword management is the identification of the appropriate keywords. Organizations can do so by reviewing their own weblogs as a starting point. The weblogs give a company access to terms that current visitors generated on their own and provide a snapshot of keyword-search activity connected to a desire to visit. Subsequently, software systems track these keywords on conversion steps and high performing keywords from this list are considered useful. Of relevance now are *keyword length* and *alternative keyword phrase*. Research has revealed the following information about most consumer searches:

> Most consumer searches
> A total of 39% use one word
> A total of 49% use two words
> A total of 9% use three words
> Less than 5% searches use Four or more words

Search results for Sony Vaio revealed the following keywords being used:

- *Word*   Battery
- *Word*   Laptop battery
- *Word*   Sony laptop battery
- *Word*   Sony Vaio laptop battery
- *Word*   Sony Vaio laptop TR3A battery

Keyword ads[8] vary widely in click-through rates (CTRs), conversion rates, and cost-per-action productivities. It is very useful to test the keyword list and collect some basic conversion rate and cost-per-action data prior to committing to a keyword plan. Search engines allow advertisers to set daily traffic and budget limits. These permit budgeting for easy- and low-risk testing of alternative keyword lists.

Tables 7.2 and 7.3 reflect the competitive bidding processes of Yahoo! versus Google and the key similarities of the two systems.

Table 7.2   Competitive bidding: Yahoo! vs Google

Yahoo	Google
Yahoo! rank ads according to maximum bid.	Google ranks ads by maximum bid times CTRs.
Yahoo! makes public the bid for all keywords allowing an advertiser to understand what the cost would be to acquire any particular position in the bid list.	The Google system is more profitable for the search engine as better CTR ads get promoted higher in the list. As the search engine receives money only for click through, this tends to augment their income by considering low-performing ads in less desirable positions.

Table 7.3 The Reflection of competitive bidding process and the key similarities of the two systems

The bidding process	Key similarities of the two systems
• A keyword bid sets the maximum price an advertiser is willing to pay for a specific keyword • The actual price paid and the position on the list depends on other bids from other advertisers • Assume there are six bidders and a minimum bid of $0.10 • The system first sorts the bids, from highest to lowest (0.95, 0.82, 0.56, 0.35, 0.33, 0.13) • The system works from the bottom • The bottom bidder pays 0.10 and gets the last slot • For an advertiser to show in fifth place instead of sixth, it must bid higher than the sixth place maximum bid • Thus the price of the fifth place is $0.14 • This continues to the top • The bids (0.95, 0.82, 0.56, 0.35, 0.33, 0.13) produce prices paid for the six slots of (0.83, 0.57, 0.36, 0.34, 0.14, 0.10)	• No payment is required until someone clicks through to the website • Higher bids increase the possibility of a higher keyword position • Actual price charged depends on the intensity of the competition • The cost per click in the marketplace establishes a benchmark for traffic-building activities

Companies can invest in a wide variety of online advertisements (Table 7.4) through a series of digital marketing organizations.

Table 7.4 Types of online advertisements

Advertisement	Description
Floating ad	An ad which moves across the user's screen or floats above the content
Expanding ad	An ad which changes size and which may alter the contents of the webpage
Polite ad	A method by which a large ad will be downloaded in smaller pieces to minimize the disruption of the content being viewed
Wallpaper ad	An ad which changes the background of the page being viewed
Trick banner	A banner ad that looks like a dialog box with buttons. It simulates an error message or an alert
Pop-up	A new window which opens in front of the current one, displaying an advertisement or entire webpage
Pop-under	Similar to a pop-up except that the window is loaded or sent behind the current window so that the user does not see it until they close one or more active windows
Interstitial ad	A full-page ad that appears before a user reaches their original destination
Map ad	Text or graphics linked from and appearing in or over a location on an electronic map such as on Google Maps
Frame ad	An ad that appears within an HTML frame, usually at the top with the site logo

Success of the digital marketing endeavours is clearly a function of the organizational ability to measure the impact of the efforts. This can be done through a series of Internet marketing metrics (Table 7.5).

Table 7.5 Internet marketing metrics

Metric	Definition/Formula
Web traffic	Total traffic (visitors) on the website
CPM	Cost-per-thousand impressions (Cost/impressions) × 1000 Impressions = no. of times ad was served to unique visitors
Cost per message	Cost to send an e-mail Cost = no. of e-mails/total cost
Social media sharing	Number of shares across social media channels
Opt-out rate	Percent who opt out of an e-mail list Rate = opt out number/total number
Response time	Time between sending e-mail and click through response
Site stickiness	Length of stay as tracked on website log
Click-through rate (CTR)	Number of clicks as percent of total impressions CTR = clicks/impressions
Inbound links	Number of sites linking into a website
Visitors resulting from click through	A page view on website resulting from a click Visitors = impressions × click through percent
Cost per click (CPC)	Cost for each visitor from ad click CPC = total ad cost/clicks
Cost per lead (CPL)	Pay only for delivered leads from special offer CPL = cost/no. of leads
Conversion rate	Percent of people who purchased from total number of visitors Conversion rate = orders/visitors
Cost-per-order equation	Cost of each order resulting from click-through visits
Customer[9] acquisition cost (CAC)	Total marketing costs to acquire a customer

INTERNET MARKETING METRICS

Web analytics provide organizations with a tool for measuring traffic. These tools, termed as Internet marketing metrics, allow companies to engage in research to understand the volume of traffic and its typology to allow organizations to optimize their online marketing efforts and increase consumer conversions using the digital world.

WEBSITES AND INTERNET MARKETING

Websites play a pivotal role in contributing to the brand identity of an organization and an even greater role in stimulating the brand–consumer relationship. The majority of benchmark and performance criteria for website evaluation follow a

> **EXHIBIT 7.3 Marketing and the Rise of the Information Technology**
>
> The face of marketing is changing rapidly and information technology has risen as a dominant player in the marketing arena. Electronic data-processing equipment is becoming a major tool of scientific marketing not only for reporting data but also for planning and controlling by management.
>
> Marketing is seeing a major computerization of several processes, specifically with regard to data collection, marketing research, MIS reporting, sales force automation, and so on. Digital marketing is witnessing the use of the laptops, desktops, and tablets for building an interaction with the consumer by generating traffic on a website and then monitoring the digital marketing activity through use of relevant metrics. Major considerations for Internet marketing include the following:
>
> - Lower cost of *e*-marketing
> - Timeliness of publication of advertisements at any time with minimal cost
> - Rich format of Internet advertisements which can effectively use the convergence of text, audio, graphics, and animation
> - Personalization of Internet advertisements to specific interest groups
> - Non-intrusive method of reaching the consumer
>
> The Indian automobile sector witnessed tremendous growth in online searches depicting over a 100% growth in 2013–2014, on Google search. The Indian consumers are increasingly relying on the Internet to make auto-purchase decisions. An analysis of search queries also indicates a strong trend in India's growing need for bigger and more luxurious cars. SUVs were the second most searched for cars category.
>
> Indians use Google increasingly to search for car models, auto websites, price comparisons, used-car research, and new-launch research.

generalist quality management approach for website design. This is very useful for website designers but fails to recognize the critical link between brand positioning and website elements. The world of the 'offline' brand has benefitted substantially from the digital medium which websites offer. Nowadays, websites increasingly supplement the value and equity of offline brands. The world of a typical 'online' brand, where products are solely available online, revolves significantly around the Internet. Nevertheless, brand architecture, in today's world is incomplete without the benefits that the digital medium has to offer. Brand websites have become an important tool and provide various functionalities. Consumers can read product or brand information, watch TV commercials, customize virtual products, download music, chat with other visitors, or have a direct dialogue with an organization behind the brand. By supplying a broad range of functionalities, these websites provide the brand with a platform to foster relationship with potential and actual customers, based on a continuous dialogue.

Appropriate consumer experience, good consumer perception, and ability to locate what they are searching for, leads to high consumer satisfaction levels. This further heightens the need for a careful understanding of website dimensions which eventually

> **EXHIBIT 7.4 Google**
>
> The Google reunion advertisement describes the power of Internet search in the digital age.
>
> *Reunion* is a 2013 Google India advertisement for Google search. The advertisement depicts Google's attempt to build a strong resonance with the emotional Indian consumer, who places a lot of emphasis on the value of maintaining relationships.
>
> The advertisement was produced by Ogilvy and Mather, and published on YouTube in 2013. *Reunion* is about the fictional reunion between two elderly men, *Baldev Mehra* from India and *Yusuf* from Pakistan. They were separated as children during the partition of India. Using details of her grandfather's story, *Suman* is able to locate *Yusuf's* sweet shop in Lahore via her laptop and Google. She connects with his grandson, *Ali*, who helps her to plan a surprise visit of *Yusuf* on *Baldev's* birthday.
>
> The campaign has had a strong impact in both India and Pakistan, leading to hope for the easing of travel restrictions between the two countries. The advertisement went viral and was viewed more than 1.6 million times before officially debuting on television on November 15, 2013.
>
> **The Power of Google Search**
>
> Google's ability to tug at the consumer heartstrings with its ads almost parallels its ability to harvest all of our online data to sell to advertisers. The company's latest poignant endeavour which targets Google's ever-growing Indian user base is a tearjerker. That it will be a resounding success in its ability to touch a chord with the masses is a foregone conclusion.

will shape the ability of the websites to contribute to (a) the consumer experience and subsequently, (b) the brand.

The decision makers at *e*-business companies have continued to make vast investments in developing websites for *e*-business without having clear knowledge of what factors contribute to developing a high-quality website and how to measure effects on *e*-business success. The success of an *e*-business company is more likely when its website is developed to provide the highest level of website quality among alternative websites and this study shows that online customers mostly prefer to select the most preferred sites. If more customers select the website, the higher is the likelihood of improved business performance. There exists a relationship between website quality, preference, and business performance.

Online Brand Presence

In recent years, the offline and online spheres of strategic brand management are becoming more and more inter-connected. This is not only because offline companies sell their products over the Internet as an alternative distribution channel, or that firms more frequently run integrated brand communication campaigns both offline and online. The connection goes beyond these links, as companies that commercialize their products offline, now seems to cross over the offline borders and offer new products and services online. Apple is an example with the iPhone and the iTunes shop on the Internet. Another example is Nokia with its Ovi Web portal. The reverse is also possible, and online companies may benefit from launching products that are available in the offline market. For instance, Google has made its Google Docs useable without an Internet connection. Recently, this company has just launched a new mobile phone that uses its own operating system. This new launch created expectations among consumers who waited patiently for the new product.

Websites and Branding

Regular communication between organization and consumer reinforces organizational image and product messages, builds brand awareness, and strengthens brand recall. By creating meaningful brand encounters, the consumer–brand relationship can be strengthened. When consumers are regularly in contact with a brand, they may begin to perceive it as a person, a trusted friend who is part of their everyday life, thereby strengthening their loyalty towards the brand. Customer–brand loyalty in cyberspace demonstrates an evolution from the traditional product driven, marketer-controlled concept towards a distribution-driven, consumer-controlled, and technology-facilitated concept. When consumers engage in a brand relationship, they begin to perceive the value related to the brand. Brand knowledge affects future purchases via a brand relationship path that includes brand satisfaction, brand trust, and attachment to the brand. Finally, consumers who have greater expected benefits and utility from an ongoing relationship are more likely to commit to it. Having a regular touch point to interact with the customer results in learning related to the brand and generates a positive attitude by creating a brand association. When consumers form relationships with brands, they use norms of interpersonal relationships as a guide in their brand assessments. Further, improving the level of interactivity of the online medium being used by the organization increases the 'reach' (percentage of all Internet users who visit a given site) of the medium. By targeting the brand image in the consumer's mind, customer expectations and perceptions can be influenced.

Website dimensions that contribute to the brand in the online space include (Fig. 7.5 and Table 7.6) the following:

Relative importance of the website

We discuss the dimension of *relative importance of the website* in the context of *impact of search engine rank on website traffic*.

Search engine marketing is the fastest growing sector in online marketing (1—IAB, Nov 2003), and more and more people are looking towards the web when making both online and offline purchase decisions (2—iMedia Connection, June 2004). The Web metrics include CTRs (percentage of visitors who clicked on a link or banner) and conversion rates (percentage of visitors who completed a desired action).[10] Relative impressions indicate the number of impressions to expect in relation to the first rank. Relative CTR is the CTR to expect in relation to the first rank.[11]

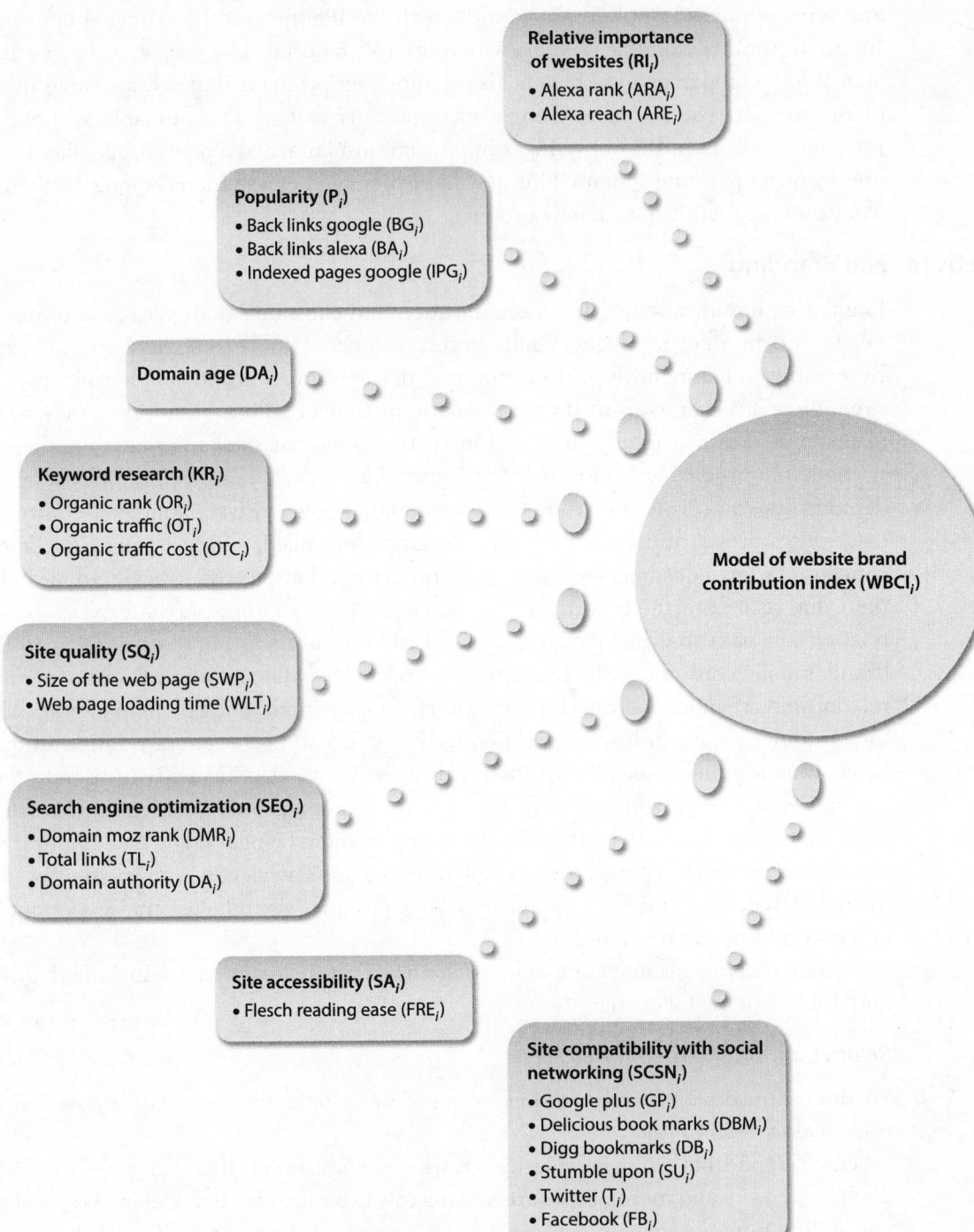

Fig. 7.5 Model of website brand contribution

Table 7.6 Website dimensions and metrics

S. No.	Website dimension	Parameters
1	Relative importance of websites (RI_i)	Alexa rank (ARA_i), Alexa reach (ARE_i)
2	Popularity (P_i)	Backlinks Google (BG_i), backlinks Alexa (BA_i), indexed pages Google (IPG_i)
3	Domain age (DA_i)	Domain age (DA_i)
4	Keyword research (KR_i)	Organic rank (OR_i), organic traffic (OT_i), organic traffic cost (OTC_i)
5	Site quality (SQ_i)	Size of the web page (SWP_i), Web page loading time (WPT_i)
6	Search engine optimization (SEO_i)	Domain mozrank (DMR_i), total links (TL_i), domain authority (DA_i)
7	Site accessibility (SA_i)	Flesch reading ease (FRE_i)
8	Site compatibility with social networking ($SCSN_i$)	Google Plus (GP_i), Delicious Bookmarks (DBM_i), Digg Bookmarks (DB_i), Stumble Upon (SU_i), Twitter (T_i), Facebook (FB_i)

Research has proven that traffic drops significantly by rank. This needs to be taken into account as organizations weigh the profitability of the keywords. While opting for a lower rank may imply a small percentage loss to sales, the losses in customer acquisitions could be huge. Drop in traffic is consistent with drop in rank. This gives rise to the need to discuss the concepts of *Alexa rank* (ARA_i) and *Alexa reach* (ARE_i).

- *Alexa rank* (ARA_i)   This is calculated using a combination of average daily visitors and page views on the site, over the past three months.
- *Alexa reach* (ARE_i)   This comprises the estimated Internet users who visit this site.

Website popularity

The Internet has become main stream in everyday communication and transaction and has been hailed as the single-most important invention of the twentieth century. Purchasing on the Internet has unique features that make it different from the traditional shopping process.[12] Websites are frequently mentioned as the online marketers of a company serving important roles like image creation or image enhancement. The website of a company is such a powerful tool that it conveys huge amounts of information cost-effectively, creates attitudes and action, triggers brand and product awareness, and communicates company and brand image all at the same time, which is a portfolio of benefits that cannot be expected easily from any offline advertising or promotion tool. The visual appeal, creativity, and attractiveness of websites are very important characteristics that influence product choices and purchases for both novice and expert users.[13]

It has been found that a high daily hit rate is strongly influenced by the number of updates made to the website in the preceding three-month period. The number of links to their websites were also found to attract visitor traffic.[14]

Considering backlinks as indicators of website popularity, we discuss *backlinks Google* (BG_i), *backlinks Alexa* (BA_i), and *indexed pages Google* (IPG_i).

- *Backlinks Google* These are incoming links to a website or webpage. In the SEO world, the number of backlinks is one indication of the popularity or importance of that website or page (though other measures, such as page rank, are likely to be more important).
- *Backlinks Alexa* It comprises the number of links to a site from sites visited by users in the Alexa traffic panel. Links that were not seen by users in the Alexa traffic panel are not counted.
- *Indexed pages Google* These enable organizations to learn how many pages of their sites are indexed by Google. Google now claims to be using more than 200 'signals' when determining the rank of a page, with thousands of machines involved in the ranking process for every query.

Search engine optimization

Search engine optimization is a set of techniques used by websites in order to be better indexed by search engines. Search engine optimization allows organizations to capture users who are actively looking for information about a product related to the firm, which converts them into potential clients openly expressing their needs. Search engine optimization is a must for every business to promote their website and they must be successful at implementing it.

Considering SEO as a successful tool for website brand contribution index ($WBCI_i$), the concept of *Domain Mozrank* (DMR_i), *Total Links* (TL_i), and *Domain Authority* (DA_i) are discussed in detail.

- *Domain Mozrank* It is a link popularity score based on how the domain, rather than just pages link to each other. It is an indicator of domain popularity.
- *Total Links* The numbers of links—external or internal to the uniform resource locator (URL). External links are considered better than total internal links because the latter include navigational links within a site that are not indicators of the site impact.
- *Domain Authority* It is a score out of 100 points representing the likelihood for arbitrary content to rank on this domain.

Domain age

It represents the age of a website's domain name. The SEO community currently speculates that older domain names will rank more highly than newer domain names for the same content. Domain Age (i.e., the date at which each domain was registered) has been positioned as an important factor in the ranking of a site, as older domain names are said to be inferred by Google's ranking algorithm as conveying more trust, and therefore should rank higher than newer domains.[15]

Site compatibility with social networking

Socially connected groups use Internet for social interactions, exchanging formal and informal information, and keeping in touch.[16]

In the context of understanding compatibility of a website to diverse social media entities, the following metrics are explored—*Google Plus* (GP_i), *Delicious Bookmark* (DBM_i), *Digg Bookmark* (DB_i), *Stumble Upon* (SU_i), *Twitter* (T_i), *Facebook* (FB_i).

- *Google Plus*   It is an identity service with social networking aspects. The service integrates social services such as Google profile, Google buzz, and introduces new service circles, hangouts, sparks, and huddles.
- *Delicious Bookmark*   Helps to find out how many Delicious Bookmarks are there for this URL.
- *Digg Bookmarks*   Help to find out how many bookmarks the site has on Digg.
- *Stumble Upon*   Helps to find out how many users have stumbled upon this URL.
- *Twitter*   Helps to find out the total Twitter mentions for the page.
- *Facebook*   Helps to see the total Facebook mentions for the page.

Keyword research

A website should be evaluated as to how well it markets its products and services, and also as to how well it keeps the customer in focus. Basically, three objectives are pursued (a) creating awareness, (b) generating traffic, and (c) driving sales. For an effective online presence, and traffic building, creating visibility, and building meaningful traffic is just as important as advertising and promotion activities.

The following three metrics are considered for KR:

- *Organic rank*   Rating of a site by the number of visitors coming from the first 20 Google search results.
- *Organic traffic*   Estimated number of visitors coming from the first 20 Google search results per month.
- *Organic traffic cost*   Estimating cost of purchasing the same number of visitors.

Site quality

Page-loading speed was rated as the most important category by the users.[17] Speed[18] (i.e., slow speed) was the number one complaint of Web users (77%). Most potential *e-*commerce customers do not want to wait for a seemingly endless page to load. Instead, they hit the browser 'stop' button and go elsewhere. Therefore, large, pretty graphic files, and 'cool' animation may come at a price to the Web business owner in terms of lost business. In this context, *size of Web page* (SWP_i) and *webpage load time* (WLT_i) are significant metrics for site quality.[19]

Site accessibility

Web accessibility refers to the degree to which Web information is accessible to all human beings and automatic tools. Accessibility is defined as the art of designing webpages that can be accessible to all Internet users (both disabled and non-disabled), regardless of any Internet browser that they are using.[20] Web accessibility simply means that 'anyone using any kind of web-browsing technology must be able to visit any site and get a full and complete understanding of the information as well as have the full and complete ability to interact with the site if that is necessary'. *Flesch reading ease* (FRE_i),[21] is considered as a popular metric, suited for evaluating more complex texts and is used extensively to evaluate texts as a metric for site accessibility.

Websites are not about individuals, or organizations. They are about visitors. Building strong brands, differentiating them, and maintaining them are critical marketing functions. Strong brands enter into consumers' consideration sets, create confidence in purchases, and positively influence product evaluation and choice. Today, the Web plays a significant role in enhancing this brand equity. Websites contribute to the proliferation of a brand in the online domain and brands will benefit by understanding the various dimensions of the websites which contribute towards this brand proliferation. It is in having the right mix of the parameters contributing to the website dimensions that organizations will benefit. Subsequently, when a brand manager's goals escalate to the higher stage of brand response, the interactive and participatory power of the Web becomes increasingly helpful. In this context, organizations can benefit substantially by making their sites compatible with social networking sites.

CASE STUDY Domino's India—Building Traffic through Content Propagation

Organizations are fast waking up to the methods of generating greater traffic to their company websites by creating content on social media sites. This content can propagate virally by virtue of being significantly important and interesting to the potential consumers. One such organization is Domino's India.

Domino's India has a distinct social media presence across its corporate blog and Facebook and continuously keeps hosting online campaigns on special themes, right across the year. Across 2010–2013, Domino's posted several interesting campaigns on their Facebook page. Domino's has been running campaigns of three types. An analysis of the *likes*, *shares*, and *comments* would be the appropriate indicator of the success of those individual campaigns.

Relational campaigns Which aim at building inter-personal relationships with customers by hosting content concerning topics of their interest. Example: Mothers' day celebrations.

Organizational campaigns Whose objectives are to build a certain identity around the brand. They comprise a pre-determined professional communication intended to share information concerning the achievements of the organization, with the customers.

Promotional campaigns Whose objectives are to promote a new product, or to induce awareness about a certain product or maybe induce sales with various schemes, etc.

Table 7.7a Domino's India—Campaigns

Initiatives	Likes	Comments	Shares	
Teachers' day (30 August–5 September 2013)	11,907	1192	229	
Father's day (7 June 2013)	1214	33	20	
Mother's day (15 May 2012)	5653	82	63	Relationship
Rishta of the day (21 September–5 October 2012)	6790	164	112	
Domino's Rakhi contest (13 August 2011)	917	34		
Domino's Friendship contest (24 July–3 September 2010)	542	156		
Total	**27,023**	**1661**	**424**	
Pizza mania ad contest (5 April–10 April 2013)	2017	85	56	
Biggest partycon contest (29 May–31 May 2011)	293	127		
Biggest Domnicon contest for lazycons (18 May–23 May 2011)	885	102		
Domino's pizza maniacs contest (25 April–28 April 2011)	1202	130		
Domino's pizza yummilicious photo initiative (25 January–1 February 2011)	557	74		
Domino's super fan of the day (22 September–9 October 2010)	2956	826		Promotional
Domino's model of the week	2213	1689		
Domino's happy fan contest (1 September–12 September 2010)	1546	889		
Total	**11,669**	**3922**	**56**	
Domino's pizza coke studio contest (18 June 2011)	1804	171		
Rapid fire quiz (25 November–4 December 2011)	1788	2135		Brand building
Model hunt for TV ads (15 June–19 June 2010)	112	42		
Total	**3704**	**2348**	**0**	

Tables 7.7a and 7.7b show the various campaigns under the aforementioned heads and the number of likes, comments, and shares the campaigns received. *Initiatives* refer to the individual campaigns hosted, for a particular theme.

Table 7.7b Domino's India—Campaigns

Months (2013)	Number of posts	Likes	Comments
November	105	148,392	59,105
October	90	119,377	69,796
September	98	183,112	55,815
August	89	99,890	19,191
July	95	109,082	27,092
June	65	52,654	13,660
May	85	103,145	9,456
April	103	176,114	75,946
March	87	59,824	29,562
February	71	19,590	4,186
January	68	43,853	11,421

An empirical analysis revealed a positive correlation between *likes* and *shares*, a positive correlation between *comments* and *likes* and *comments* and *shares*. This shows that a person liking a Facebook post is most probably, also commenting on the post. In other words *likes* trigger the increase in number of *comments* and increase in number of *shares* is also dependent on number of *comments*.

Further empirical analysis was used to establish the dependency of total comments, posts, and likes on each other.

The progressive incremental relationship between the number of *likes* and *comments* indicates that *comments* are dependent on the number of *likes* a post is able to generate. It goes without saying that liking a post requires less effort than commenting on a post. In a 'click' a post hosted by the organizational page, receives a 'heads-up' or attestation by its customers and as soon as it multiplies in number, customer engagement in terms of comments also increases. This happens because a post with more number of likes draws more eyeballs to it and reflects that the post has been interesting enough to have successfully drawn customer attention.

Further, an incremental progressive relationship between the number of *likes* and *posts* can be observed. The increase in number of likes has been proved dependent on the increasing number of posts which is indicative of better consumer engagement and greater traffic at the organizational page as and when the company indulges in consumer engagement activities in terms of hosting content at their Facebook page. This implies that the more the number of posts, the more the attraction for customers which eventually results in better consumer engagement.

Domino's has been able to generate maximum traffic because of the 'relational' category of campaigns. 'Relational' content touches a chord with the audience.

More than *in the face* or *push marketing*, and *promotional gimmicks*, users at Facebook still look for posts, campaigns, activities that create a sense of involvement for them as customers of a particular brand. The consumers first take a social networking website as a place where they want to create a space of their own and do things they can endorse proudly, than be constantly subjected to brands blowing their own trumpet all the time.

The consumer engagement continuum (Fig. 7.6) hence sees that once a consumer logs into an organizational Facebook page, that is, essentially their brand page or a particular post at the page, and the customer happens to click a *like* which is the primary stage of virtual brand engagement, there is a chance that the first few posts that catch his eye will make him either stay or walk away. The kind of environment built around the brand page, which is determined through the type of content it hosts, will affect the engagement levels of a customer.

Fig. 7.6 Consumer online (Facebook) engagement continuum

The customer engagement continuum reflects that having liked a particular brand page or a particular post, the consumer will comment if the post fits his psychological desires, that is, he feels in *sync* with the brand. The peer-to-peer interaction which then happens due to increased number of comments on that post will increase electronic word of mouth, thus giving way to brand loyalty.

Questions:

1. Who are the competitors of Brand Domino's in India? What are the target consumer segments that Brand Domino's hopes to reach through its virtual presence?
2. What situations influence a consumer to use the online medium to purchase a pizza? How useful would a mobile application be in ordering a pizza?

PRACTITIONER PERSPECTIVE

Subscription models are popular for e-tailers, subscribers tend to buy more, spend more, and therefore margins go up, they are the more profitable customers.

Ankur Bisen, Senior Vice president, Technopak

The NIIT e-solution for tobacco auction will add to the company's credibility as it was a strong player in implementation of procurement, supply chain, sales, and marketing solutions. Under this project, the IT solutions company would provide mobility platforms in the form of handheld devices, and software platform that handles the actual material management and reporting besides back-end technology infrastructure with technical support for a period of six years, Mehrotra said. The company would generate revenues from the project on a transaction-based pricing, which has been arrived at on the basis of average volumes of tobacco auctions of the recent years.

Arvind Mehrotra, President, Asia Pacific, NIIT Technologies

SUMMARY

With the proliferation of diverse typologies of online content, the four major challenges before companies are creating the right set of keywords, advertising and content, driving users to the website, and making them stay on the website. Significantly, companies need to have well-defined online traffic plans in place and also need to spend on traffic building online. It is in building the right online advertising ecosystem and leveraging the appropriate Web business models that companies will be able to grow in the digital space. The components of a Web traffic plan are—traffic building sources, traffic volume and quality, and traffic-building goals. An Internet traffic plan is developed using a series of *e*-marketing strategies and tactical choices. Traffic sources can fall into eight major categories—branding decisions, search engine marketing, *e*-commerce, lead-based websites, affiliate marketing, online banner advertising, publicity and word-of-mouth. Companies make use of several search marketing methods and tactics for Web visibility and competitive analysis. Organizations can make use of several online analytical tools to analyse their site's performance, traffic rank, and reputation. The reach of the website (Fig. 7.1) can be compared with that of the competitors using a tool like Alexa.com. The traffic-building goals of any organization should aim at maximizing short-term/long-term profit, minimizing cost-per-action (subject to volume targets), and maximizing actions, subject to spending capacity.

Concept Review Questions

1. What are the various components of a Web traffic plan? Discuss in detail.
2. Discuss the following:
   (a) Search engine marketing
   (b) Site optimization
   (c) Keyword portfolio evaluation
3. What are different types of online advertisements?
4. The traffic-building goals of any organization should aim at—maximizing short-term/long-term profit, minimizing cost-per-action (subject to volume targets), maximize actions, subject to spending capacity. Comment.

Critical Thinking Questions

1. Use an organizational example to demonstrate how a company can generate online traffic by virtue of its branding decisions, search engine marketing, e-commerce, lead-based websites, affiliate marketing, online banner advertising, publicity and word-of-mouth.
2. Identify five advertisements which demonstrate the usage of the Internet as a tool being used by organizations for leveraging the power of online search. Identify how companies use the following to do so:
   (a) Consumer emotion
   (b) Consumer desire to save money
   (c) Consumer desire to innovate
3. Write a case study demonstrating how corporate houses attempt to build more traffic on their website.

Practising Digital Marketing

1. Use the Alexa tool to draw a competitive analysis of four different organizations which are trying to use the Internet to generate traffic. Make sure all the four organizations belong to the same industry vertical. Create a Web visibility and competitive analysis chart for the same.
2. Repeat the activity by doing comparative analysis for groups of companies from the following:
   (a) The automobile sector
   (b) IT industry
   (c) Education sector
   (d) FMCG vertical
   (e) Healthcare

References

1. Hanson, W. and Kalyanam, K., Traffic building, *Internet Marketing and E-commerce*, Thomson Press, 2007, p. 251.
2. Hanson, W. and Kalyanam, K., Traffic building, *Internet Marketing and E-commerce*, Thomson Press, 2007, p. 253.
3. Tiedt, D., How do brands gain from YouTube, *The Economic Times*, 2013.
4. 'The State of Search Engine Marketing 2006'. Search Engine Land. February 8, 2007.
5. Baines, P., Fill, C., Page, K., and Sinha, P.K., Digital marketing, *Marketing-Asian* Edition, Oxford University Press, 2013.
6. Sharma, R.T., Bhushan, R., and Rathore, V., 'IPL striking gold on social media platforms like Twitter, Google+ and YouTube with corporate advertisers', *Economic Times*, April, 2013.
7. Hanson, W. and Kalyanam, K., Keyword value, *Internet Marketing and E-commerce*, Thomson Press, 2007, p. 271.
8. Hanson, W. and Kalyanam, K., Testing keywords, *Internet Marketing and E-commerce*, Thomson Press, 2007, p. 274.
9. Sources: www.e-marketer.com, www.internetnews.com, www.nielsen-netratings.com, www.doubleclick.com, IAB Internet Advertsing Revenue Report, www.computerworld.com.
10. Weischedel, B. and Huizingh, E.K.R.E., (2006). 'Website optimization with web metrics: A case study'. *ICEC*, pp. 14–16.
11. Nico, Brooks, The Atlas Rank Report: How Search Engine Rank Impacts Traffic, Atlas® Institute, *Digital Marketing Insights*. http://atlassolutions.com/wwdocs/user/atlassolutions/en-us/insights/RankReport.pdf.
12. Weisberg, J., Dov, Te'eni, D., and Limo, A.L., (2011). 'Past purchase and intention to purchase in e-commerce: The mediation of social presence and trust'. *Internet Research*, Vol. 21(1), pp. 82–96. doi: 10.1108/10662241111104893.

13. Mandel, N. and Eeric, J.J., (2002). 'When web pages influence choice: Effects of visual primes on experts and novices'. *Journal of Consumer Research*, Vol. 29(2), p. 235.
14. Dholakia, U.M. and Rego, L.L., (1998). What makes commercial web page popular: An empirical study of online shopping, *Proceedings of 32nd Hawaii International Conference on System Sciences*, January 5–8, 1999, Institute of Electrical and Electronics Engineers (IEEE).
15. Michael P.E., (2007). 'Analyzing Google rankings through search engine optimization data'. *Internet Research*, Vol. 17(1), pp. 21–37.
16. Jordaan, Y. and Ehlers, L., (2009). 'Young adult consumers' media usage and online purchase likelihood'. *Journal of Family Ecology and Consumer Sciences*, Vol. 37, pp. 24–34.
17. Smith, A.G., (2001). 'Applying evaluation criteria to New Zealand government websites'. *International Journal of Information Management*, Vol. 21(2), pp. 137–149. doi: 10.1016/S0268-4012(01)00006-8.
18. Hoffman, D.L. and Thomas, P.N., (1996). 'A new marketing paradigm for electronic commerce'. *The Information Society*, Vol. 13(1), pp. 43–54.
19. Mccune, J.C., (1998). 'Making websites pay'. *Management Review*, Vol. 87(6), p. 36.
20. Eschenfelder, K.R., Beachboard, J.C., McClure, C.R., and Wyman, S.K., (1997). 'Assessing U.S. federal government websites'. *Government Information Quarterly*, Vol. 14(2), pp. 173–189. doi: 10.1016/S0740-624X(97)90018-6.
21. Flesch, M., (1949). *The Art of Readable Writing*. Macmillan Publishing.

Web Business Models

> **LEARNING OBJECTIVES**
>
> *After reading this chapter, you will be able to:*
> - Identify the implications of customer-centric Web business models
> - Understand the concept of a Web chain of events and Web chain analysis
> - Execute customer value analysis
> - Elucidate Web benefits to firms

A well-implemented online system can track an online user from a click on a search engine keyword ad to specific Web pages viewed and onto purchase or exit. Successful online companies such as eBay carefully evaluate their customer acquisition methods, identify the best-performing methods, and re-allocate spending appropriately.[1] Marketing revolves around value creation, value delivery, and above all, increasing the value perception of the end customer. The focus of marketing hence shifts from valuing merely the transaction between the organization and consumer to a more careful analysis of continuous ongoing company and customer contacts, and significantly, their impact on the customer and brand equity as well as enhancement of consumer product adoption. The Internet provides opportunities for improved marketing—valuing electronic contacts to new business opportunities. The power of digitization is empowering companies to connect with their consumers, streamline transactions, and improve the company–consumer contact, eventually spelling greater yields in profitability.

The external and internal capabilities of the Internet can be used to enhance customer value. The big data approach can help create comprehensive customer databases that capture the full range of the online customer interactions. This further enables creation of methods for classifying and categorizing customers so that organization–consumer interactions can be tailored to specific tastes and requirements. Systems can subsequently be developed for consumer segmentation into homogeneous groups, segment profiling for strategic targeting, predicting future customer actions, forecasting customer lifetime value (CLV), and identifying strategically significant customers.

Companies that adopt customer asset management (CAM) procedures and develop systems for allocating effort and resources to maximize the value of the customer base benefit significantly in the long run.

THE VALUE OF A CUSTOMER CONTACT

Internet capabilities create a marketing channel for low-cost individualized interaction. Not all customers spell the same economic benefits to the firm. At the heart of valuing, the individualized interaction between the organization and consumer is the logic behind the actual interaction and its ability to build a long-term relationship between the company and consumer. Online technologies host a plethora of opportunities between the organization and consumer which aid marketing in refining its actions to enhance greater productivity through cross-functional collaboration and, above all, analysis of the data generated through respective consumer interactions. Marketers can hence not only learn from the specific consumer interaction but also respond to the same to generate better return on investment (ROI) for marketing.

CUSTOMER-CENTRIC WEB BUSINESS MODELS

The customer-centric approach to Web management steers organizations towards a more value-oriented, conservative approach. When customers make decisions in current economic scenarios, riddled with increased competition, they seek more value in product or service offerings, are more price sensitive, and are further quiet likely to go with a more trusted source. A more informed consumer who is empowered by the Internet and the resultant pool of information available therein needs greater attention. Ranging from consumer views to peer reviews and other product-related information, the consumer has found a voice in the era of consumer-generated media (CGM) on the Internet. The organizational obligation to respond to the consumer has further resulted in a confident, well-informed individual. A relationship-based approach by the organization may be a deciding factor in the decision process of such prospects. Better strategies towards keeping the consumer satisfied may be the qualifying factor in giving an organization an edge over competition and hence contribute to consumer retention.

The Offerings of the Web 2.0 World

While the 1990s heralded an era of enterprise resource planning (ERP), customer relationship management (CRM), and supply chain management (SCM) adoption, the associated technology investments were complex and high. The users of the systems were assigned by the management and had to comply with the organization-specified diktats. The Web has ushered in an era of collaboration where participation is possible at the level of all of the above players—the *organization*, the *employee*, and the *consumer*. Organizations can use Web 2.0 techniques primarily in two areas: inside the organization to improve efficiency and productivity, and between the organization and customers for customer acquisition, improving revenue, and customer retention. Online communities, corporate blogs, social networks have increased social connectivity to a level beyond imagination. These peer-to-peer tools start to change the flow and balance of information. The ability of marketers to shape perceptions by presenting a unified mass market branding image is faced with a counter flow of opinions which can be positive or negative.

Formation of groups with lightweight technology investments ushers in concepts of employee collaboration, community participation, and broader communication channels. As participatory online environments allow organizations to freely engage and converse with the consumers, the voice of the consumer has gained tremendous importance. An empowered consumer has increased access to organization-specific information, thereby opening up the need for organizations to maintain online reputations and availability of product- and service-specific information. While this represents a significant opportunity for organizations to build new social and Web-based collaboration, productivity, and business systems to improve cost and revenue returns, it has also opened up a low-cost channel for organizations to contact and engage a consumer.

While organizations gear up to handle the change with a series of well-defined strategies in all domains of the business, some consumer-oriented strategies that need to be incorporated in the Web business models in organizations are listed as follows.

EXHIBIT 8.1 Expensive products in an *e*-commerce world

Who would have thought that an Indian consumer would be willing to purchase jewellery online? Thoughts of consumers purchasing a Volkswagen car from an online domain were equally not expected. A change in the social fabric of the upwardly mobile, aspiring middle class, ready to take risks and experiment has made the unthinkable possible.

While convenience is the prime driver of this consumer behaviour, the online world is proving equally attractive to both the professional young female who wants to procure jewellery as well as the housewife, who has the money but not the inclination to travel outside to procure a piece of jewellery. A Google search on 'online jewellery India' reveals a vast range of jewellery being sold in the virtual space by players such as Flipkart, Bluestone, Jabong, Gitanjalishop, Titan, Craftsvilla, and Myntra. Most of these players allow consumers to 'try out' a variety of these items when an online sales representative visits them and pay by the cash-on-delivery option. The 'Tanishq' brand of Titan Jewellery provides consumers the benefit of *enrich online*, where consumers can partake of a variety of schemes such as Golden Harvest, Swarnanidhi, and Goldplus and gain from them. The *Gitanjali shop* sells branded jewellery from the *Asmi, D'damas, Diya, Gili, Sangini, Parineeta, Nakshatra*, and *Lucera* brands—each available online.

The era of websites has provided the consumers with a significant visual appeal, with top-quality product pictures, which are as good as a physical '*look and feel*' experience of the product.

Increased Concentration on Current Customer

Customers respond well to a product when they perceive value in the same. Organizational focus is shifting to providing more value to the customer, greater sensitivity to the consumer need, better customer experience management, and greater interactivity with the customer to gauge consumer sentiment. Managing customer relationships may well be the organizational strategy in troubled times.

CUSTOMER-CENTRIC BUSINESS MANAGEMENT

This would incorporate better lead management and optimization to convert prospects into consumers in view of resource limitations. Progressive consumer profiling and segmentation of consumers for formulation of well-directed targeting programmes would be the important areas. Better campaign management and low-cost campaign optimization strategies, coupled with speedy consumer redressal and customer support programmes and along with co-creation and soliciting consumer participation in new product development, thereby matching consumer expectations and stimulating demand, would be needed.

Improving Communication Flow between Organization and Consumer

As market research budgets dwindle, companies can leverage the vast volumes of online data about the consumers for the above-stated endeavours. This is where Web 2.0 creates enormous opportunities as companies move forward to harness the CGM to gain access to the consumer thought process in a bid to match organizational strategies with consumer expectations. Technology empowers innovation and makes the consumer-specific data on the Internet an important component of the marketing value chain, making consumer-generated media, or CGM as it is popularly called, a valuable organizational resource. These tools may appear inherently disruptive and may initially challenge an organization and its culture; however, they are not technically complex to implement.

Enhancing employee productivity through greater access to information regarding the consumer to aid the process of decision making through analysis of data available. While harnessing the intelligence derived from the CGM is a very significant outcome of the participatory environment offered by the collaborative Web, integration of the same with the organizational functions to aid response management results in more consumer-related gains.

This is the right time to carry out changes at a brisk pace. Employees willing to perform better are keen to embrace new techniques. Organizations are looking for ways to sustain themselves by building relationships with the consumer, and consumers are more than happy to have organizations listen to what they have to say. CRM 2.0 may finally encompass a web-based transformation in ways the organizations interact with their consumers. These innovative techniques may eventually be able to produce positive business outcomes in an age of unprecedented uncertainty.

WEB CHAIN OF EVENTS

A Web chain of events is the sequence of steps taken as the result of an online contact. It can be as short as a single click or a hundred different page views. At various steps, different directions and choices are possible. These are event nodes. Eventually the Web chain leads to one of the possible end points, labelled as result nodes.[1]

Hence, for instance, when a visitor logs on, say, a Facebook page, where company X has placed its advertisement, there are two possibilities: the visitor may see the advertisement or the visitor may *not* see the advertisement. However, if the visitor sees the advertisement, there are again two possibilities: he/she may click on the same to visit company X's website or he/she may *not* click on the advertisement. If the consumer does not click, the situation amounts to a wasted endeavour by company X.

To move further, in case the visitor sees the advertisement, clicks on it, enters the company website, he/she may buy a product, that is, he/she gets converted from a *prospect* to a *consumer* or he/she may *not* buy and not get converted. If he/she does not buy, is this endeavour again a wasteful investment for the company? Not really, as the visitor would have seen the company website, and has moved up the brand awareness continuum. This visibility created for the product brand by virtue of the consumer visit has added to the brand propagation efforts of the company.

The Web chain concept and a flowchart depicting possible sequences of events is depicted in the upcoming excerpts.[1]

Studies pertaining to Web chains of events (Fig. 8.1) can help organizations in the following ways:

- Identification of non-performing advertisements and the sustained impact of an advertisement on a consumer.
- Creation of relevant website brand architecture which increases brand salience, strengthens brand identity, increases brand resonance, and builds a strong consumer–brand relationship.
- Creation of a framework for calculating CLV by tracking his/her online search, click, and transaction activities.

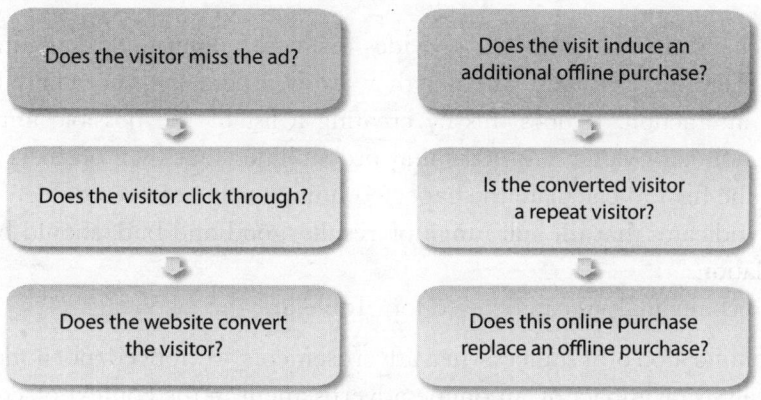

Fig. 8.1 Web chain concept

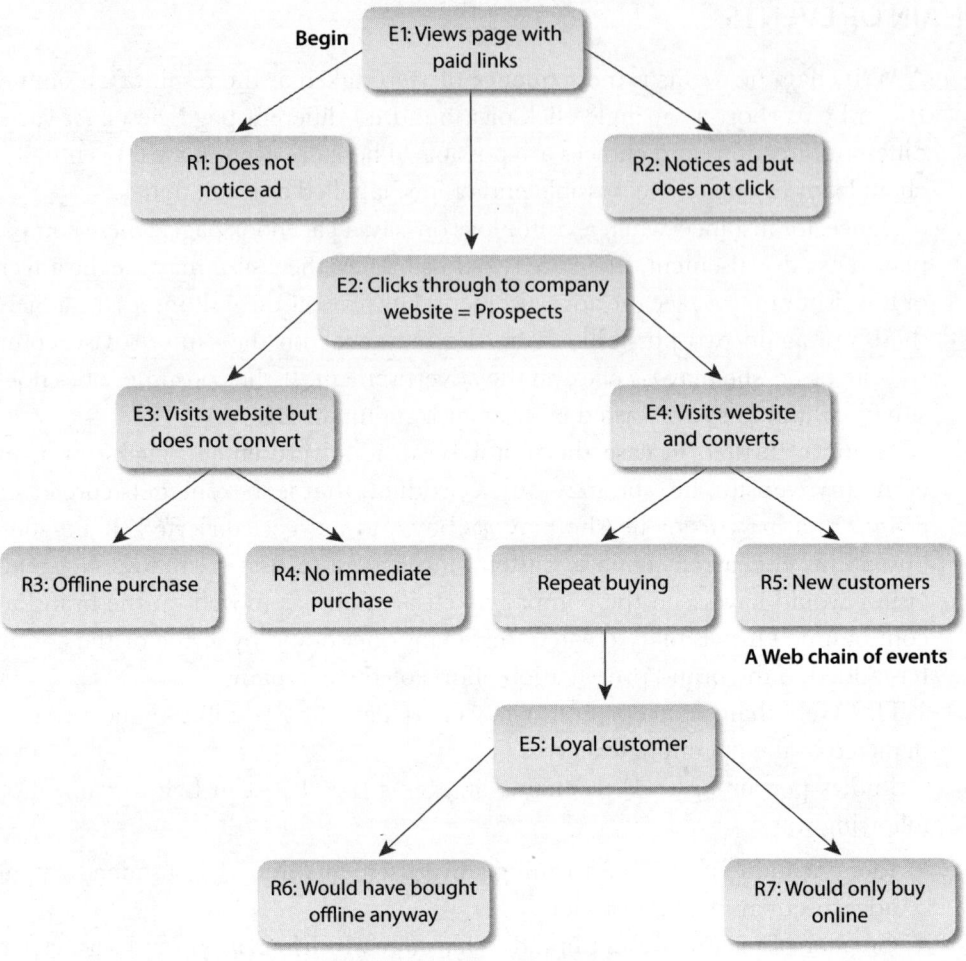

Fig. 8.2 Web chain analysis

WEB CHAIN ANALYSIS

Web chain analysis (Fig. 8.2) provides a starting point for calculating the benefits of these electronic contacts, whether they are visiting a site, receiving an *e*-mail, or some other interaction. It does this by creating a list of the possible impacts, quantifying their monetary value, and assigning probabilities that they occur. These probabilities allow the firm to calculate the expected unified value of the contact. The term unified value indicates that the full range of results, good and bad, should be included in the calculation.[1]

Web chain analysis can be used for (Table 8.1) the following:

- Identification of instances when advertisements are noticed/not noticed by consumers.
- Analysis of impact of an online advertisement in the context of consumers noticing an advertisement, but not clicking on it.

Table 8.1 Web chain analysis

Result	Value
R1: Consumer does not notice the ad	No benefit at all
R2: Notices ad but does not click	Increase in brand visibility—no enhancement in brand relationship
R3: Offline purchase	Has visited the website, hence, increase in product brand visibility and organizational brand visibility + offline profit made from offline purchase by consumer
R4: No immediate purchase	Has visited the website, hence, increase in product brand visibility and organizational brand visibility
R5: New customer	Has visited the website, hence, increase in product brand visibility and organizational brand visibility + online profit because of online transaction during purchase + lifetime value of customer
R6: Would have bought offline anyway	Has visited the website, hence, increase in product brand visibility and organizational brand visibility + offline profit made from offline purchase by the consumer
R7: Would only buy online	Has visited the website, hence, increase in product brand visibility and organizational brand visibility + online profit because of online transaction during purchase

- Contribution of the online dimension of a brand in influencing a consumer purchase decision, in addition to already existing influencers in terms of the generic brand value associated with a product. If a purchase is made offline, the organization benefits from any offline profit accrued.
- Ability of the online presence of a brand in creating a brand impact in the consumer mind-set, even though not stimulating an immediate purchase.
- Identification and analysis of new customers, who after being affected by a product brand, venture online and the brand impact is further strengthened by the online brand presence. These customers, if engaging in an online transaction, become sources of online revenue and need to be tracked as repeat customers and their value needs to be calculated in the framework of CLV, as discussed in the section on CLV.

CUSTOMER VALUE ANALYSIS AND THE INTERNET

The Internet can be used as a tool for customer value analysis (Fig. 8.4). Valuable sources of data are as follows:
- The consumer demographic profile
- The consumer search and browsing history
- The consumer click behaviours
- The consumer online transaction

EXHIBIT 8.2 Femina, India—Monetizing the web

Femina is one of India's most-read women's magazines. Femina has been catering to the urban Indian woman for over 50 years and has always kept a steady process of evolution, thereby sustaining its competitive advantage. Over the years, Femina's readership has grown steadily, with over 60% of its English edition readers being in the age group of 25–45 years and over 76% of its Hindi edition readers being in the age group of 16–45 years.

The magazine communicates information about the latest in fashion and beauty and also covers areas of interest such as stories about women achievers, health, fitness, relationships, career, food, books, and movies.

Femina has up-scaled its digital presence to remain attractive to the youth segment and with a reasonable presence across Facebook, Twitter, Pinterest, Instagram, Mobile and Google+, and other digital channels, has been able to build a brand image online. It launched a series of online initiatives such as Femina Twinterviews, Femina Blogger Bees, Femina Girlfriend Getaways, and Femina PickaPal.

Femina strengthened its digital presence in recent times with the creation of www.Femina.in. The website covered a huge bandwidth of topics including fashion, relationships, beauty, buzz, health, and food.

Femina also launched an online platform called Femina connect, where readers were invited to share their thoughts, ideas, opinions, and be part of Femina's inner circle.

Femina subsequently launched an App which could be used for online magazine subscription.

The Femina Miss India Pageant, 2014 was much hyped across social media and the winner details were live streamed across several platforms simultaneously. As soon as the Indian Budget, 2014 was announced, Femina's social media profiles uploaded posts titled #Moneymatters—what's in the Budget, 2014 for women and simplified details of the budget were uploaded at the given online links.

Similarly, by paying tribute to Zohra Segal on her demise, on their social media platforms, Femina was able to touch the consumer emotion.

By hosting a series of #Trendalerts and getting thousands of shares and likes regarding social posts, Femina is clearly an example of an organization which has been able to leverage the Internet successfully by creating a steady stream of online content which will be *clicked on* by the consumers. The Web chain concept has clearly demonstrated that an organization which is able to get consumers to click on content is definitely able to garner an online brand impact and increase brand visibility and awareness. Monetizing this relationship with the consumer is what the brand manages to achieve at a later stage.

By organizing online contests like #FFF: Can you complete this story and offering users an opportunity to get recognition through publication in Femina, the company has definitely been able to tap the *High Relationship Worth* individuals who have a high relationship potential for organizations by virtue of some opinion leadership qualities, superior networking capabilities, high individual net worth, or high individual network value.

The consumer search and click behaviours have already been discussed in earlier sections. We now discuss the consumer online transaction. Companies should invest in two types of consumers, which are as follows:

- *High relationship worth* Those who have high relationship potential for organizations by virtue of some opinion leadership qualities, superior networking capabilities, high individual net worth, or high individual network value.
- *High profit potential* Those who demonstrate high profit potential, of relevance are those consumers who can indulge in repeat purchases or who are high-value consumers in terms of their revenue prospects.

Online sources of data need to be explored for identification of the *high relationship worth* and *high profit potential* customers.

Customer Lifetime Value

Customer lifetime value (CLV) is the present value of future cash flows attributed to the customer relationship. It depends on the customer's activity level, longevity of his relationship with the organization, the firm's retention spending, and other related costs and benefits attachable to a specific customer or customer segment.

The profitability skew diagram (Fig. 8.3) demonstrates the Pareto effect (Fig. 8.4), which clearly shows that 1% of the organization's top consumers account for the highest revenue, profitability, and ROI. They are, hence, the most significant customers and should be treated with care. Companies will benefit by dividing their customers into *high cost to serve* and *low cost to serve* segments and then serve them appropriately.

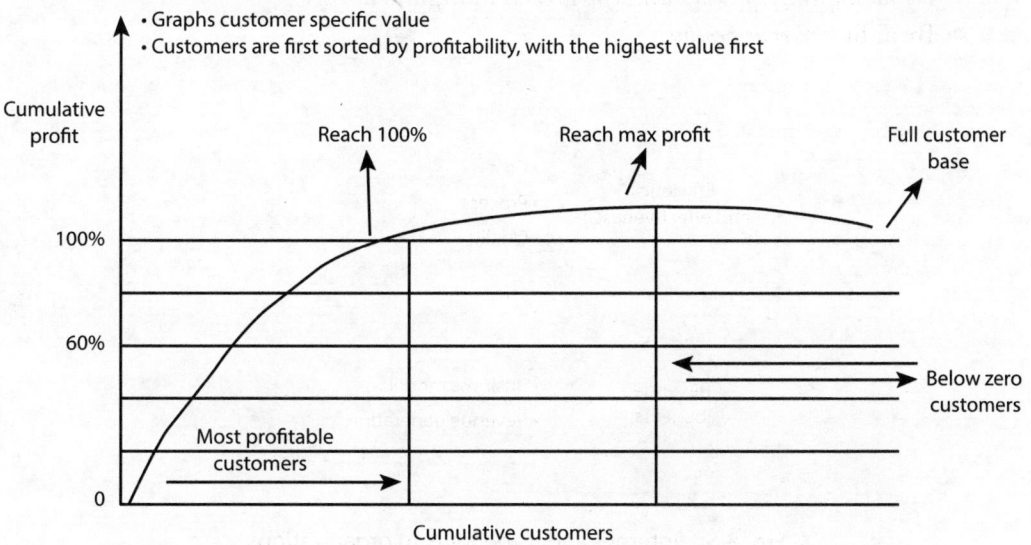

Fig. 8.3 Profitability skew diagram

WEB BENEFITS TO FIRMS

Web metrics are the information that companies use to improve their websites. This information can be based on server logs (clickstream data), customer surveys, and external data collected by web analytics firms. These data fulfil different purposes: clickstream

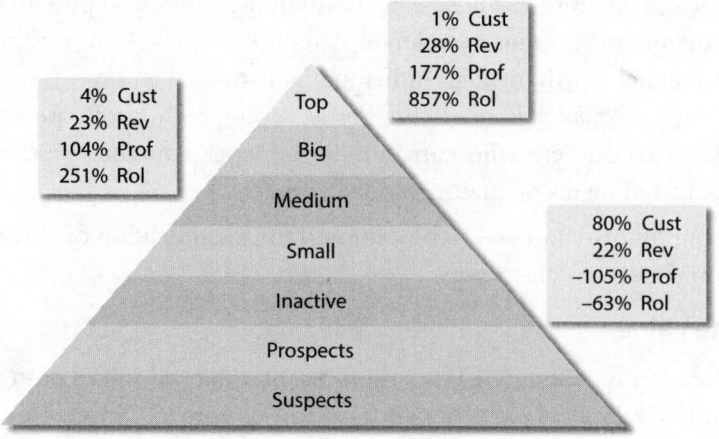

Fig. 8.4 Customer value analysis

data enable managers to answer 'when' and 'what' questions, customer surveys 'why' and 'how' questions while reports from Web analytics firms contain the external yardsticks that enable normative interpretation of the many statistics unavailable until recently.[2]

The Internet can benefit organizations in the following two ways (Fig. 8.5):

- By facilitating *efficiency* and *effectiveness* in organizations
- By aiding *revenue benefits*

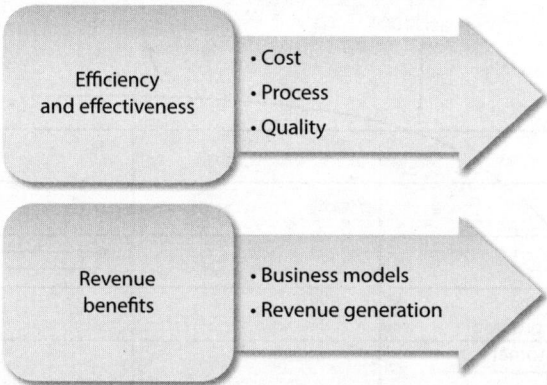

Fig. 8.5 Internet and its benefits to organizations

Internet as a Tool to Aid Efficiency and Effectiveness

The Internet can improve efficiency and effectiveness through the following factors:

- *Cost reduction* In an era of economic downturn, the Internet is a tool which facilitates low-cost advertising and communication budgets, thereby projecting the Internet as a viable media option. With cost effective channels, easy to create, streamlined

Web dynamics, and viral propagation of online content, the Internet is a viable resource for organizations to explore.

- *Improving customer knowledge* Companies are diverting a substantial volume of their resources towards customer knowledge management. Of significance to superior brand proliferation and enhancement of consumer knowledge about products and brands is the online presence of an organization. Appropriate online positioning can improve brand positions with respect to competitors, thereby enhancing consumer perceived value. Greater *consumer* satisfaction with the services offered by a *website* will lead to a greater degree of loyalty towards that *website*.[3]
- *Superior brand architecture* The relevant *house of brands* and *branded house* strategies in the context of online brand architecture can help in enhancement of the brand equity of the product brands and give them a competitive advantage. Brand loyalty is significantly positively related to frequency of *websiteusage*.[4]

The Internet can also be used for *category building* by educating site visitors about an entire category or capability, *quality improvement* through augmentation and enhancement of products with online material and *process improvement* through increased marketing effectiveness and internal savings and changes in consumer attitudes.

BUSINESS MODELS[5]

This section details several business models, being experimented with, in the online world (Fig. 8.6). Principal characteristics of each model are as follows:

(a) E-shop	(b) E-procurement
(c) E-auction	(d) E-mall
(e) Third-party market place	(f) Virtual communities
(g) Value chain service provider	(h) Value chain integrators
(i) Collaboration platforms	(j) Information brokerage, trust, and other services

Fig. 8.6 Business models for the virtual world

(a) E-shop

- Web marketing of a company or a shop
- Done for promotion of the company, its goods and services
- Options to order and to pay, often combined with traditional marketing channels
- Benefits sought for the company are increased demand, a low-cost route to global presence, and cost-reduction of promotion and sales
- Benefits for the customers can be lower prices compared to the traditional offer, wider choice, better information, and convenience of selecting, buying, and delivery, including 24-hour availability

- In situations of repeat visits to the *e*-shop, one-to-one marketing can increase those benefits for both seller and buyer
- Seller revenues are from reduced cost, increased sales, and possibly advertising
- Most commercial websites are business-to-consumer electronic shops, selling, for example, flowers by Fleurop (www.fleurop.com) or air tickets by Travelocity (www.travelocity.com)

(b) *E-procurement*

- Electronic tendering and procurement of goods and services
- Large companies or public authorities implement some form of *e*-procurement on the Web
- Benefits sought are to have a wider choice of suppliers which is expected to lead to lower cost, better quality, improved delivery, reduced cost of procurement (e.g., tendering specifications are downloaded by suppliers rather than mailed by post)
- Electronic negotiation and contracting and possibly collaborative work in specification can further enhance time and cost saving and convenience. For suppliers, the benefits are in more tendering opportunities, possibly on a global scale, lower cost of submitting a tender, and possibly tendering in parts which may be better suited for smaller enterprises, or collaborative tendering (if the *e*-procurement site supports forms of collaboration)
- The main source of income is reduction of cost (automated tender processing, more cost-effective offers)

(c) *E-auction*

- Electronic auctions (on the Internet) offer an electronic implementation of the bidding mechanism
- Can be accompanied by multimedia presentation of the goods
- May also offer integration of the bidding process with contracting, payments, and delivery
- The sources of income for the auction provider lies in selling the technology platform, in transaction fees, and in advertising
- Benefits for suppliers and buyers are increased efficiency and timesaving, no need for physical transport until the deal has been established, and global sourcing. As the cost becomes low, it becomes feasible to offer for sale small quantities of low value, for example, surplus goods
- Sources of income for suppliers lie in reduced surplus stock, better utilization of production capacity, lower sales overheads. The inventory of European electronic commerce related projects (www.ispo.cec.be/ecommerce/ecomproj.htm.) was a particularly useful tool to identify business models and classify projects accordingly, resulting in reduced purchasing overhead cost and reduced cost of goods or services purchased. Examples of electronic auctions are the ESPRIT project Infomar (for ESPRIT and ACTS projects see www.ispo.cec.be/ecommerce/ecomproj.htm) and Fast Parts (www.fastparts.com)

(d) E-mall

- An electronic mall, in its basic form, consists of a collection of *e*-shops, usually enhanced by a common umbrella. It might be enriched by a common, guaranteed, payment method. An example is Electronic Mall Bodensee (www.emb.ch), giving entry to individual *e*-shops.
- Malls specializing on a certain market segment become more of an industry marketplace, such as Industry. Net (www.industry.net/), which can add value by virtual community features (FAQ, discussion forums, closed user groups, etc.).
- The *e*-mall operator may not have an interest in an individual business, that is, being hosted. Instead the operator may seek benefits in enhanced sales of the supporting technologies (e.g., IBM with World Avenue).
- Alternatively, benefits are sought in services (e.g., Barclays with BarclaySquare), or in advertising space and/or brand reinforcement or in collective benefits for the e-shops that are hosted such as increased traffic, with the expectation that visiting one shop on the *e*-mall will lead to visits to 'neighbouring' shops.
- Benefits for the customer are the benefits for each individual *e*-shop with additional convenience of easy access to other *e*-shops and ease of use through a common user interface. When a brand name is used to host the *e*-mall, this should lead to more trust, and therefore increased readiness to buy.
- Benefits for the *e*-mall members (the *e*-shops) are lower cost and complexity to be on the Web, with sophisticated hosting facilities such as electronic payments, and additional traffic generated from other *e*-shops on the mall, or from the attraction of the hosting brand. Revenues are from membership fee (which can include a contribution to software/hardware and setup cost as well as a service fee), advertising, and possibly a fee on transactions (if the mall provider processes payments).
- The commercial viability of the *e*-mall model has been questioned in its current implementation and in the current state-of-the-market. IBM World Avenue, for example, has folded. One of the reasons may be that the 'neighbour' concept does not translate into physical distance in cyberspace, where each location is only one click away. Therefore, not much additional convenience in finding shops is delivered.
- Furthermore, the sophisticated user (i.e., the majority of those on the Web today!) is able to handle a variety of seller–buyer–user interfaces and therefore may be less attached to a uniform user interface. On the other hand, there are also indications that an increasing number of companies wish to outsource their Web-operations, which may increase the opportunity for *e*-malls or third-party marketplaces. Possibly, this reflects the shift from early adopters to mass-market use of the Internet amongst businesses.

(e) Third-party marketplace

- This is an emerging model that is suitable in case companies wish to leave the Web marketing to a third party (possibly as an add-on to their other channels). They all have

in common that they offer at least a user interface to the suppliers' product catalogues. Several additional feature such as branding, payment, logistics, ordering, and ultimately the full scale of secure transactions are added to third-party marketplaces.
- An example for business-to-consumers is to provide a common marketing around a special one-off event profiled by well-known brand names, such as the recent *e*-Christmas experiment. Internet service providers (ISPs) maybe interested in this model for business-to-business, using their Web builder expertise. However, it may equally appeal to banks or other value chain service providers.
- Revenues can be generated on the basis of one-off membership fee, service fees, transaction fee, or percentage on transaction value.

(f) Virtual communities

- The ultimate value of virtual communities is coming from the members (customers or partners), who add their information onto a basic environment provided by the virtual community company. The membership fees as well as advertising generate revenues.
- A virtual community can also be an important add-on to other marketing operations in order to build customer loyalty and receive customer feedback.

(g) Value chain service provider

- These specialize on a specific function for the value chain, such as electronic payments or logistics, with the intention to make that into their distinct competitive advantage. Banks, for example, have been positioning themselves as such since long, but may find new opportunities using networks.
- New approaches are also emerging in production/stock management where the specialized expertise needed to analyse and fine-tune production is offered by new intermediaries. A fee or percentage-based scheme is the basis for revenues. Examples of value chain service providers are the FedEx or UPS (www.ups.com) web-based package shipping support.

(h) Value chain integrators

- These focus on integrating multiple steps of the value chain, with the potential to exploit the information flow between those steps as further added value.
- Revenues are coming from consultancy fees or possibly transaction fees. An example of value chain integrator is the ESPRIT project. TRANS 2000 is in the area of multi-modal transport. Some of the third-party marketplace providers are moving into the direction of value chain integration.

(i) Collaboration platforms

- These provide a set of tools and an information environment for collaboration between enterprises. This can focus on specific functions, such as collaborative design and engineering, or in providing project support with a virtual team of consultants.
- Business opportunities are in managing the platform (membership/usage fees), and in selling the specialist tools (e.g., for design, workflow, document management).

(j) *Information brokerage, trust, and other services*

A whole range of new information services are emerging, to add value to the huge amounts of data available on the open networks or coming from integrated business operations, such as information search, for example, Yahoo! (www.yahoo.com), customer profiling, business opportunities brokerage, investment advice, etc. Usually information and consultancy have to be directly paid for either through subscription or on a pay-per-use basis although advertising schemes are also conceivable. A special category is trust services, as provided by certification authorities and electronic notaries and other trusted third parties. Subscription fees combined with one-off service fees as well as software sales and consultancy are the sources of revenue. An example of a trust service provider is Belsign (www.belsign.be). Many consultancy and market research companies are now offering commercial business information services via the Internet. Search engines are a special category of information services, with the public Internet facility (rather than intranet versions) usually based on advertising as a source of revenue. Advanced information brokerage to support negotiation between businesses is being developed by the ESPRIT CASBA and MEMO projects.

REVENUE BENEFITS

The discussion on revenue benefits associated with the Internet has been divided under three categories, which are as follows:

- Advertising models
- Subscription models
- Transaction models

Advertising Models

For websites relying on an advertising model, it is necessary to attract large and/or highly specialized, differentiated viewership in order to maximize revenues.[6] To be profitable, revenue models based on advertising require high levels of website traffic.[7]

Affiliate model

In affiliate models, websites steer traffic to an 'affiliate' website and, in turn, receive a referral fee or a percentage of the revenues from resulting sales. Facebook, for example, offers organizations or companies the option to create special groups in return for a sponsorship.

In an *e*-commerce context, these models enable firms to generate revenue streams on hundreds (even thousands) of items without carrying inventories, managing orders, processing payments, or handling packaging and shipping. In this arrangement, a website concentrates on a relationship with a very specific group of individuals as its core competence. It develops and continuously upgrades content and services to attract and retain the patronage of this group. Once it has a sizeable number of regular visitors, it can generate revenue by carrying ads or links to merchants with products that its visitors seek or are interested in.

EXHIBIT 8.3 Revenue benefits and mobile App developers

The dominant business models for App developers at present, are user payments or display advertising, however, affiliate marketing could be a new and potentially much more lucrative way of monetizing many Apps. User-payment-driven models can be very lucrative for hit applications, especially games. However, there is an increasing worry that application prices are suffering from downward pressure towards free. New types of payment models such as subscriptions or in-App payments are promising although not all application types are suited to these approaches.

Display advertising can pay the bills on free Apps if there is sufficient scale of usage. Using ad networks like *AdMob* or potentially integrating multiple ad networks using a mobile ad optimizer such as *Smaato* or *Mobclix* can deliver significant revenues for some Apps. However, the growth in mobile inventory, and falling click-through rates mean that it is becoming harder to make this model work.

(*Source*: www.mobyaffiliates.com)

Channel pays

Channel-based revenue models have fees paid to an online service by other companies wanting to reach their users. Examples include content sponsorship, banner advertising, prospect fees, and sales commissions.

- *Permission sponsorship* Sponsored content shows up online, as sites attempt to find the best way to pay for high-quality and popular content.
- *Prospect fees* Click-through ads based on keyword search create a significant connection between user search behaviour and the ads that appear to the right and the top of the page. These keyword ads focus on creating a tight connection between user search behaviour and the ads that appear to the right and the top of the page.
- *Banner advertising* This allows platform operators to charge fees in exchange for the display of advertisements on their website.
- *Sales commissions* Affiliate programmes look much the same to consumers as sponsorship, but differ in their payment structure. Like sponsorship, programmes involve logos on websites that link back to the retail partner. Affiliate programmes base their payment on the actual revenue from sales.

Subscription Models

The second major source of revenue for websites consists of subscription models where a website offers its users content or services and charges a subscription fee for access to some or all of its offerings. Usually, basic features are offered for free, while, for more

> **EXHIBIT 8.4 Affiliate marketing—Amazon in India**
>
> The Indian market and demographics are best suited to an affiliate marketing programme. Right after its foray into the Indian market, Amazon, India introduced this programme, for the Indian consumer.
>
> The Amazon associates programme lets online publishers of all sizes effectively monetize their content by advertising contextually relevant products and referring visitors to Amazon.in. Catering to the ever increasing 'online' Indian population, this programme allows publishers to select from a huge collection of books, DVDs, audio CDs, and consumer electronics, by providing partners an easy to navigate experience while generating revenue for themselves. A satisfying experience for the consumer in the online domain results in greater consumer conversions and subsequently a higher commission figure for the Amazon associates.
>
> *Cost-per-action advertising model*
>
> India has a large number of youngsters, professionals, authors, bloggers, home makers, and other individuals who have a significant online presence on blogs, communities, and social networks. Some of them have significant online network values in the context of having an influential virtual presence as large number of users are linking into these sites. These individuals can be deemed as opinion leaders in these areas and can be used as consumer evangelists. By offering these individuals an opportunity to monetize their online presence, Amazon is actually building a relationship with them.
>
> The features of this advertising model are as follows:
>
> - The Amazon associates cost-per-action advertising model allows the associates to easily create a link to a contextually relevant product from the Amazon.in catalog.
> - Associates earn a percentage-based referral fee when customers click through and make a purchase on Amazon.in.
> - The commission extends to all products the visitor buys and not just the specific product that was advertised.
> - Amazon also has associates central—a dedicated portal for Amazon associates. The Indian associates have also been provided access to this portal, which enables them to build more contacts online.
> - This portal also offers associates an access to a host of convenient and effective widgets, linking tools including text links and rich banners that make this very easy to use for individual and small publishers.

advanced features, the user has to upgrade and pay a fee. Subscription models existed in *e*-commerce already before the advent of Web 2.0, and are becoming more popular with service providers.

Transaction Models

The third possibility for a website or social networking site (SNS) to generate revenues is through a transaction model, where a company receives a fee for enabling or executing a transaction. Two types of transaction models can be distinguished: endogenous and exogenous transactions. Endogenous transactions are carried out when users buy physical or digital goods and services from the platform provider; for example, virtual gifts that can be purchased with so-called micro-payments on the US platform, Facebook. Exogenous transactions take place when the SNS provider sells third-party (or user-generated) content to its users or enables transactions between users, for example, with a yellow pages directory introduced by the US business networking site. In this case, the platform operator can profit from a fee on the volume of transactions conducted over the platform. In order to create sustainable revenues from a transaction model, a critical mass of users is essential.

FINANCIAL SERVICES AND THE INTERNET

The financial services sector can use the virtual world in multiple ways, to improve their client engagement and business processes. A recent report *Impact of Social Media on the financial services Sector*, by Juan A. Virgili and Evgeny Kaganer, studied trends in the financial services sector and analysed the customer perspective in each of the five phases of customer relationship management—discovery, evaluation, purchase, usage, re-engagement, and loyalty. The report highlights two major trends—the convergence of social and mobile, which will boost payment methods via mobile devices and the use of big data to improve customer engagement in the mobile market.

Banks and insurance companies can implement social media primarily in three areas—social marketing, social CRM, and new business models.

EXHIBIT 8.5 Citibank

Citibank posts minimal commercial information on its Facebook pages, but instead focuses on topics of interest to its customers—conversations and polls on their favourite foods or sports teams, which are then linked to its products. For example, it ran a contest to win a trip to the Super bowl which was open to all customers who used their Citibank visa card during a certain period. This kind of social media marketing enables Citibank to gain visibility and communicate with customers. Opportunities for Citibank lie in their ability to integrate their social media marketing with their CRM efforts, since it is primarily social CRM that affects the usage stage. Social CRM is a shade more intimate than social marketing.

Pricing in the Virtual World

The power of pricing

Pricing (Fig. 8.7) has the largest impact on profitability compared with lowering costs or expanding sales. A 1% improvement in price will lead to an 11% improvement in profits, a much larger impact than improvements in other variables.

- The price of a product or service is a number, a formula, or an agreement about how much it will cost.

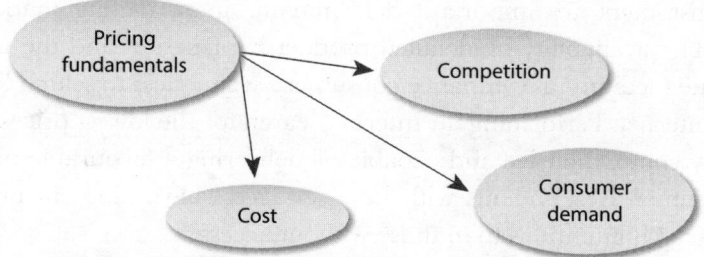

Fig. 8.7 Pricing in the virtual world

- The company's pricing actions are affected by the Internet.
- Consumer awareness of prices is critical to pricing.
- Proper pricing depends on knowledge of different prices from different sources and includes perceptions of fairness.
- It is crucial that a firm can track changes in costs, customer tastes, and actions.

The following three pricing questions are important for *e*-marketers:

- How does the presence of the Internet change the price sensitivity of products and services?
- How can online content be used to influence the price sensitivity of customers?
- What new pricing tools and methods work better on the Internet than through more traditional methods?

McKinsey Marketing Practice in their paper, *Internet Pricing: A Creator of Value-Not a Destroyer*, posit three fundamental ways in which online marketers can benefit from the flexibility of electronic pricing, which are as follows:

- Precision in price levels and price communication whereby companies can identify customer sensitivities to price movements within a range.
- Time adaptability in response to market changes with real time reactions to shifts in demand.
- Segmentation of prices with the overlay of multiple sources of customer data to segment the market with greater precision and then price to the specific segment.

McKinsey argues for the following elements to be present in an online pricing strategy to improve ROI:

- Identify degrees of freedom consistent with strategic objectives and brand values; so while online pricing provides greater flexibility, it supports overall corporate objectives such as entering new markets and market penetration.
- Build appropriate technological capabilities to *e*-pricing, which are relevant and responsive to changes in customer demand, for example, dynamic pricing.
- Build an experimenting and nimble pricing organization based on constant testing and monitoring of demand shifts resulting from price changes and customer reactions to promotions.

Loyal customers are important determinants in predicting market share and profit levels.[9] The availability of detailed product information and the interactive nature of the online medium may enhance consumer's willingness to search for price information on the Internet. Performing an Internet search for the lowest prices will be perceived as relatively comprehensive and capable of delivering a favourable price with less cost to the consumer. Respondents with Internet access have different price perceptions and price—search intentions than those without access.[10]

The price search done by a consumer on the Internet provides low-cost options and demonstrates availability of higher benefits of products which is less likely to be strongly influenced by other promotional cues. The large amount of information about pricing, competitors, and features available on the Internet also helps to create a cost transparent environment. This severely impairs a seller's ability to obtain high margins, because it turns products and services into commodities, and may damage company reputations by creating perceptions of price unfairness.[11]

Many factors affect consumer's price sensitivity. A common perception is that the Internet always raises consumer price sensitivity. This is not always true. On one hand the Internet tends to increase consumer price sensitivity, on the other hand some companies have skilfully used the Internet to lower their specific marketplace price sensitivity and retain premium prices. Having an intuitive understanding of price sensitivity factors helps pricing managers make good decision and for online marketers provides a better understanding of how these factors might be affected by online marketing content. One of the tasks of an online marketer is to understand the implications of the price sensitivity factors for online content.

Different companies will have different objectives. A low-price firm will want to use its online presence to enhance price sensitivity and create a focus on price. A premium service-oriented firm, on the other hand, wants online content that reinforces that position and reduces the focus on price. Each of the price sensitivity factors helps the 'reverse engineering' from price sensitivity factor to online content. One of the major implications can be understood through shared cost effect, it applies when there is a separation between purchase decision maker and purchase payer. The shared cost effect typically lowers market price sensitivity. The main impact of the shared cost effect on Internet strategy is to create separate content aimed at the decision maker or the payer. One or more of the price sensitivity factors can operate at the same time for a particular pricing decision. Thus a thorough understanding of the factors shaping price sensitivity helps pricing managers make good decisions and for online marketers it provides a better understanding of how these effects might be altered by online marketing content.

If proficiency in searching the Internet increases with experience or over time, then reliance on brand names should likewise decrease. Internet search proficiency is likely to increase as users gain more experience with the medium. Increased proficiency decreases the cost of gathering and evaluating information, specifically product information. Alternatively, consumers can rely on well-known brand names as shortcuts in evaluating the merits of different products. Unlike search costs, increased Internet experience is not likely to make consumers more proficient at inferring product quality from brand names.

Therefore, as the price of searching, relative to using brands, falls with increasing Internet experience and if there are substitutes the more experienced consumers should rely less on brands and thus here the various effects of consumer price sensitivity have a significant role to play. On the other hand, the large amount of information about pricing, competitors, and features available on the Internet also helps to create a cost transparent environment. This severely impairs a seller's ability to obtain high margins, because it turns products and services into commodities, and may damage company reputations by creating perceptions of price unfairness. Early work suggested that the Internet could present a threat to branding and erode loyalty. As a result of this cost benefit focus, many *e*-tailers offer low prices and focus on customer acquisition.

EXHIBIT 8.6 Advergaming

Advergaming[8] refers to developing a game to advertise a brand. Companies can merge advertisements and games to create a unique interesting tool which conveys the message pertaining to the brand in a subtle way while the consumer is subconsciously playing a game. Companies like McDonalds are using advergames to interact with their target groups in a bid to capture the ever wavering attention of the consumer. By engaging users in interactive experiences, companies such as Renault are able to build brand awareness in a user-friendly, non-intrusive way, across consumers in Europe, Middle East, Arica, Latin America, and Asia.

The experience of a customer engaged in an advergame is at least four to five minutes as compared to a 30-second exposure to a TVC and 10–15 seconds, as compared to a print and hoardings. In addition, the involvement in advergaming is greater as it requires more concentration and energy on the game. Viral marketing usually supports advergaming, significantly, and the brand benefits consequently. The state of *flow* achieved by a user by virtue of being lost in a game, after being interested in it to a huge extent is what benefits a brand in the long run. In-game advertising has a lot of impact on brand recognition, recall, and revenue. Creativity and enjoyment are normal functions of human beings. Methods esuch as advergaming utilize the dimensions of perceived playfulness and enjoyment from digital resources. If the use of technology allows users to enjoy themselves, it serves as an intrinsic motivator, which brings the consumer closer to the brand.

THE INDIAN WEB MARKET

The Indian online retail sector is growing at the rate of 40% a year and is likely to reach ₹47 trillion (US$792.84 billion) by FY 17, as per a report published by the India Brand Equity Foundation. While a fourth of the total online population is shopping a month, nearly 60% of the buyers are spending ₹500–2000 in a single transaction.

Market Size

- The Indian market is expected to double to ₹7200 crore by 2015. In comparison, China will take the number 1 position, tripling its online sales to more than $360 billion by 2015.
- In India, apparel tops the shopping list in the survey on top categories for penetration of online retail.
- The number of Indian *e*-retailers is estimated at 400.
- The number of estimated Indian Internet users is in the range of 137 million.
- Spending pattern—the preferred price point of purchase was ₹200–500 for 57% people and was ₹2000–50,000 for 26% people.

ROLE OF INTERNET IN IMPACTING CONSUMER PRICE SENSITIVITY

The Internet constitutes a new form and conception of the purchase process carried out by consumers. The more dynamic pricing mechanisms started up in this channel allow prices to adapt quickly to the demand for products.[12] The Internet leads to increased price competition and the standardization of prices. Organizations will have to employ new pricing models when selling over the Internet.[13] The people who use this channel for shopping assign great importance to price when making decisions, which is why they are very sensitive to this aspect. This can further be illustrated through the following:

Role of Online Content in Influencing Consumer Price Sensitivity

A lot of research has been conducted in the past by various eminent researchers to assess this[14] which proposes that when quality-related information becomes a brand differentiating factor for customers, interactive retailing could lead to lower price sensitivity. Online promotions[15] which are indicators of price discounts, lead to higher price sensitivity. When there is high motivation to shop, an increase in information load leads to a high-price level of the product being perceived as more valuable and of superior quality. For the same high motivation situation, the low-price level of the product showed a pattern of results that was opposite to that for the high-price level.[16] Thus, one of the tasks for an online marketer is to understand the implications of price sensitivity factors for online content. Different companies will have different objectives. A low-price firm will want to use its online presence to enhance price sensitivity and create a focus on the price. A premium service-oriented firm wants online content that reinforces that position and reduces the focus on price. Each of the price sensitivity factors helps in the reverse engineering from price sensitivity factor to online content. A major impact of the Internet on price sensitivity throughout the economy is the ability of consumers and firms to rapidly compare alternatives for products and services even when they are not sold online.

> **EXHIBIT 8.7 Flipkart and consumer price sensitivity**
>
> The Indian retail market is characterized as the world's biggest price-sensitive market. Companies offer a value proposition to the consumer where they attempt to combine benefits and price to offer a 'value' that the consumer finds acceptable. A customer may choose a competing product, if it appears to offer the best 'value'.
>
> Flipkart commenced by offering *'Shopping Convenience'* to the Indian consumer. This shopping convenience coupled with an *enriched experience* was the sole value proposition for the customer when Flipkart started its operations. A gradual introduction of the *'Cash on Delivery'* model, providing customers with a convenient payment option, enhanced the value proposition for the customer. Variety and large volumes of *product choices* are other significant characteristics of the customer value proposition being offered by Flipkart.
>
> Other benefits which targeted price-sensitive customers successfully included the following:
>
> - Cost benefits, with additional discounts
> - Free shipping of Products
> - 30-day replacement guarantees
> - Gift packaging options

Ability of the Internet to Increase Consumer Perceived Value

Consumers may use price as an indicator of product quality, which implies that the higher the price, the higher the perceived quality. Such an association between price and perceived quality is essentially a heuristic that enables consumers to use an extrinsic attribute like price to make judgements about a product's quality.[17] Price information plays a dual role in the consumer's judgements. Consumers use price not only to infer a product's quality, but also to determine the monetary sacrifice associated with the purchase of that product.[18] If perceived value represents a trade-off between perceived sacrifice and perceived quality, then the price information is processed systematically,[19] greater weight will be placed on the price sacrifice relationship and the judgements of value will behave in a manner similar to the judgements of perceived sacrifice.

PRICE EFFECTS IN ONLINE DOMAIN

The following are the different price effects in the online domain.

Reference Price Effect

The reference price effect connects price sensitivity with the competitive alternatives that a potential customer uses to judge the product's price.[20] Price sensitivity increases when a product's price is above those of the perceived alternatives. Perception is important and the manner in which the product is compared to alternatives can strongly influence price sensitivity.[21] The reference price effect provides strong motivation for firms to seek the attention of consumers and to provide the information regarding various product and services at their own sites, rather than send consumers to an online site with different comparison sets.[22] The firms competing on low price want that the comparisons revolve around basic features and the low prices of their product and services. Sellers of enhanced features need to ensure that the full range of benefits is required for the comparison set. In reference price effect, price sensitivity rises when price is perceived as out of line with the alternatives.[23]

Difficult Comparison Effect

The difficult comparison effect connects price sensitivity with the presence and awareness of alternatives. *In this effect, awareness of more substitutes and lower search costs work to increase price sensitivity.*[24] The Internet's biggest impact on price sensitivity may be through the comparison effect with increasing information leading to lower willingness to pay.

The Internet has created a cut-throat competition for the retailers as the best prices are available for products at lower shipping costs with the emergence of online services. If the price comparison is easier, it further boosts price sensitivity. The nature of the product or service involved contributes to the challenge of judging new products.

One of the important distinctions is between search and experience goods.[25] A search good is one in which the good's features and characteristics, such as quality and price, are easily observable and comparable. An experience good, on the other hand, is one in which it is difficult to judge the quality and proper price.[26] Experience goods are naturally more sensitive to the difficult comparison effect and consequently less price sensitive.

Switching Cost Effect

For a price-sensitive customer, if switching costs are high, then the customer will not switch over and vice versa. *In this effect, price sensitivity is reduced when the product is part of a system of complementary products.* When a product is part of a system, such as computer plus software product purchases, it is less sensitive to changes in the price of one of the components.

Switching costs are the expenses incurred by changing suppliers.[27] Switching costs have long been associated with customer satisfaction and loyalty. In a low satisfaction relationship, switching costs may act as an exit barrier. Companies attempting to acquire customers often invest money in lowering customer switching costs[28] what is important here is to understand that how important the switching cost effect will be on the price sensitivity. Switching costs are positively associated with loyalty and it is an important mediator between consumer loyalty and its antecedents.

The impact of trust and satisfaction on consumer commitment appears to vary according to contingency conditions of switching cost antecedents.[29] Examples of switching costs include the effort needed to inform friends and relatives about a new telephone number after an operator switch, costs related to learning how to use the interface of a new mobile phone from a different brand, and costs in terms of time lost due to the paperwork necessary when switching to a new electricity provider. Types of switching costs[30] include: exit fees, search costs, learning costs, cognitive effort, emotional costs, equipment costs, installation and start-up costs, financial risk, psychological risk, and social risk. It is important to understand why many consumers do not immediately switch from a product they currently use to the latest innovative improved product, even if the cost difference is minimal.

First, people are sensitive to the relative advantages and disadvantages of any change from the status quo. So, a new, improved product, no matter how great it is on its own merit, must be significantly better than what consumers are currently using before they will switch. Second, different people have different reference points. For example, a hi-tech travelling salesman would evaluate the advantages of a cellular over a landline phone from a much different perspective than a home-bound, fixed-income retiree. Third, people exhibit loss aversion. The pain of giving up a benefit is much more significant than the pleasure of gaining that benefit.

Online shoppers may have additional technology-related efficiency needs[31] compared to traditional shoppers. A Web user may go through a learning curve before skilfully browsing a commercial site and identifying targeted information. This may build a high technology-related switching cost.[32] Perceived switching cost[33] is a component of perceived relationship value. When consumers think that switching to another retailer is costly, they are more likely to stay with the current retailer and exhibit brand preference,[34] and relational market behaviour.

Price Quality Effect

For certain specific goods which provide consumers with a unique experience or value, the price of the product influences consumer evaluation of a product.[35] *In this effect when price is a signal of quality, price sensitivity is lower.* A product's price may act as a trigger to consumers of some underlying characteristics of the product that is hard to observe directly. In particular, consumers may believe that a high price signals high quality. If this is true then price becomes a less responsive tool. The reason is simple; when a firm cuts its price, it makes its product more affordable to a wider customer base.

The positive benefit of cutting price is partially offset by the negative perception that quality maybe lower. Price premium research demonstrates that consumers are willing to pay a higher price for higher-quality brands.[36] A price increase makes items more expensive, but for those consumers using price as an informational cue[37] about quality, there is a positive perceived quality impact. Inexperienced consumers tend to rely on the natural correlation between higher price and higher quality.

Websites targeting these consumers should address this price quality effect directly through product education, hence, increasing acquisition value perceptions.[38] The price quality effect works to the advantage of well-established brands in the face of aggressive price competition by start-ups and discounters. Each company is trying to use its online content, at least partially, to reinforce the view of the price quality effect most advantageous to its own pricing strategy.

Pricing in organizations is a function of the following:
- Market research
- Pricing intuition
- Experience

Price sensitivity factors can be divided under value uncertainty and purchase importance.

VALUE UNCERTAINTY

- Value uncertainty rises when customers cannot determine the precise quality or applicability of different products to their needs.
- Consumers may not be able to easily understand the product and make relevant trade-offs and comparisons.

Some value uncertainty effects include reference price effect, difficult comparison effect, switching cost effect, and price quality effect.

PURCHASE IMPORTANCE

- The monetary and social importance of a purchase increases its price sensitivity.
- While this may seem obvious, it has interesting implications when pricing is combined with online offerings.

Some purchase importance effects include total expenditures effect, end-benefit effect, shared cost effect. The list of effects is included in Table 8.2.

Table 8.2 Price sensitivity effects help connect online strategies and pricing

Price sensitivity factor	Description
Value uncertainty	
Reference price effect	Price sensitivity rises when price is perceived as out of line with alternatives
Difficult comparison effect	Awareness of more substitutes and lower search costs work to increase price sensitivity
Switching cost effect	Price sensitivity is reduced when the product is part of a system of complementary products
Price quality effect	When price is a signal of quality, price sensitivity is lower
Purchase importance	
Total expenditures effect	Expensive products, either in absolute or percentage terms, will have higher price sensitivity due to increased search
End benefit effect	Important inputs to a production process have higher price sensitivity than less critical items
Shared cost effect	Separating the decision-maker and the payer for a product or service lowers price sensitivity

PRACTITIONER PERSPECTIVE

We are seeing keen interest by brands in categories such as telecom, OEMs, DTH providers, banks, each of whom have their own interpretation of what they can do with Twitter.

Arvinder Gujral, Head—Mobile Business Development, India and South East Asia, Twitter

> *Our overall business objectives include being a relevant banking services provider to the new India, which includes digital natives. Jifi enables us to provide relevant and meaningful services to the young and digital-savvy banking customer of today and tomorrow.*
>
> *Karthi Marshan, Executive Vice President and Head—Group Marketing, Kotak Mahindra*

SUMMARY

A well-implemented online system can track an online user from a click on a search engine keyword ad, to specific web pages viewed, and onto purchase or exit. Successful online companies such as eBay carefully evaluate their customer acquisition methods, identify the best-performing methods, and reallocate spending appropriately. Marketing revolves around value creation, value delivery, and above all, increasing the value perception of the end customer. The focus of marketing hence shifts from valuing merely the transaction between the organization and the consumer to a more careful analysis of continuous ongoing company and customer contacts, and significantly, their impact on customer and brand equity as well as enhancement of consumer product adoption. *The customer-centric approach to Web management steers organizations towards a more value-oriented, conservative approach.* When customers make decisions in current economic scenarios, riddled with increased competition, they seek more value in product or service offerings, are more price sensitive, and are further quiet likely to go with a more trusted source. A more informed consumer who is empowered by the Internet and the resultant pool of information available there in needs greater attention. Technology empowers innovation and makes the consumer-specific data on the Internet an important component of the marketing value chain, making consumer-generated media, or CGM as it is increasingly called, a valuable organizational resource. A Web chain of events is the sequence of steps taken as the result of an online contact. It can be as short as a single click or a hundred different page views. At various steps, different directions and choices are possible. Web chain analysis can be used for identification of instances when advertisements are noticed/not noticed by consumers, analysis of impact of an online advertisement in the context of consumers noticing an advertisement, but not clicking on it, and several other purposes. Organizations can use this for identification and analysis of new customers, who after being affected by a product brand, venture online and the brand impact is further strengthened by the online brand presence. These customers, if engaging in an online transaction, become sources of online revenue and need to be tracked as repeat customers and their value needs to be calculated in the framework of CLV, as discussed in the section on CLV. The Internet constitutes a new form and conception of the purchase process carried out by consumers. The more dynamic pricing mechanisms started up in this channel allow prices to adapt quickly to the demand for products. The Internet leads to increased price competition and the standardization of prices. Organizations will have to employ new pricing models when selling over the Internet. The people who use this channel for shopping assign great importance to price when making decisions, which is why they are very sensitive to this aspect. Price sensitivity factors can be divided under value uncertainty and purchase importance.

Concept Review Questions

1. What is a Web chain of events? Explain the Web chain concept.
2. What is Web chain analysis? What do companies use Web chain analysis for? Give examples.
3. Explain how an organization can use data available on the Internet to identify consumers that are strategically significant?
4. For websites relying on an advertising model, it is necessary to attract large and/or highly specialized, differentiated viewership in order to maximize revenues. Explain the *affiliate model* under the category of *advertising models* in the online space in the above context.
5. The Internet can benefit organizations in two ways: by facilitating *efficiency and effectiveness* in organizations and by aiding *revenue benefits*. Explain the various benefits of the Internet to organizations, using examples.
6. How does the presence of the Internet change the price sensitivity of products and services? How can online content be used to influence the price sensitivity of customers?
7. Differentiate between value uncertainty factors and purchase importance factors for pricing in the online world.
8. Write short notes on the following:
    (a) *E*-shop
    (b) *E*-procurement
    (c) *E*-mall
    (d) *E*-auction

Critical Thinking Questions

1. Your friend intends to set up an online business for selling fashion garments online. Develop an *e*-business model for the virtual world, for your friend.
2. Study the *e*-business models of eBay, Amazon, and Myntra.com. Profile the business models. Study the benefits offered by the organizations in the context of revenue and efficiency benefits.

Practising Digital Marketing

1. Create a Web chain of events for a set of prospective customers for the following:
    (a) A shoe brand
    (b) A jewellery brand
    (c) A watch brand
2. Create a list of 20 digital marketing companies in India. Study their operations and identify the most common digital marketing practices being used by them.

References

1. Hanson, W.A. and Kalyanam, K., *Internet Marketing and E-commerce*. Thomson South-Western, 2007.
2. Weischedel, B. and Huizingh, E.K.R.E., (2006). 'Website optimization with web metrics: A case study.' *Proceedings of the 8th International Conference on Electronic Commerce: The New E-commerce: Innovations for Conquering Current Barriers, Obstacles and Limitations to Conducting Successful Business on the Internet*, ACM.
3. Flavián, C., Guinalíu, M., and Gurrea, R., (2006). 'The role played by perceived usability, satisfaction and consumer trust on website loyalty.' *Information and Management*, Vol. 43(1), pp. 1–14.
4. Thorbjornsen, H. and Supphellen, M., (2004). 'The impact of brand loyalty on website usage.' *The Journal of Brand Management*, Vol. 11(3), pp. 199–208.
5. Timmers, P., (1998). 'Business models for electronic markets.' *Electronic Markets*, Vol. 8(2), pp. 3–8.
6. Laudon, K.C. and Traver, C.G., *E-commerce*, Pearson Prentice Hall, 2007.
7. Weinreich, N.K., (2006). What is social marketing? *Weinreich Communications*, 10.

8. Baines, P., Fill, C., Page, K., and Sinha, P., *Digital Marketing*, Oxford University Press, 2013.
9. Ferguson, R. and Hlavinka, K., (2007). 'The COLLOQUY loyalty marketing census: sizing up the US loyalty marketing industry.' *Journal of Consumer Marketing*, Vol. 24(5), pp. 313–321.
10. Jensen, T., Kees, J., Burton, S., and Turnipseed, F.L., (2003). 'Advertised reference prices in an Internet environment: Effects on consumer price perceptions and channel search intentions.' *Journal of Interactive Marketing*, Vol. 17(2), pp. 20–33.
11. Campbell, M.C., (1999). 'Perceptions of price unfairness: Antecedents and consequences.' *Journal of Marketing Research*, pp. 187–199.
12. Martinez, M.E.A., Borja, M.A.G., and Jimenez, J.A.M., (2011). 'Yield management as apricing mechanism.' *Review of Business Information Systems (RBIS)*, Vol. 15(5), pp. 51–60.
13. Allen, E. and Fjermestad, J., (2001). 'E-commerce marketing strategies: An integrated framework and case analysis.' *Logistics Information Management*, Vol. 14(1/2), pp. 14–23.
14. Peterson, R.A., Balasubramanian, S., and Bronnenberg, B.J., (1997). 'Exploring the implications of the Internet for consumer marketing.' *Journal of the Academy of Marketing Science*, Vol. 25(4), pp. 329–346.
15. Kacen, J.J., Hess, J.D., and Chiang, W.K., (2013). 'Bricks or clicks? Consumer attitudes toward traditional stores and online stores.' *Global Economics and Management Review* Vol. 18(1), pp. 12–21.
16. Kulkarni, A.A., Consumers' use of an expected future price as a reference: An investigation of the psychological and contextual antecedents, Dissertation. University of Illinois at Urbana-Champaign, 2011.
17. Pechmann, C. and Ratneshwar, S., (1991). 'The use of comparative advertising for brand positioning: Association versus differentiation.' *Journal of Consumer Research*, Vol. 18(2), pp. 145–60.
18. Suri, R., Long, M., and Monroe, K.B., (2003). 'The impact of the Internet and consumer motivation on evaluation of prices.' *Journal of Business Research*, Vol. 56(5), pp. 379–390.
19. Grewal, D., et al., (1998). 'The effect of store name, brand name and price discounts on consumers' evaluations and purchase intentions.' *Journal of Retailing*, Vol. 74(3), pp. 331–352.
20. Lilien, G.L., Rangaswamy, A., and Van den Bulte, C., Diffusion models: Managerial applications and software. *New-product Diffusion Models*, 2000.
21. Lichtenstein, D.R., Burton, S., and Karson, E.J., (1991). 'The effect of semantic cues on consumer perceptions of reference price ads.' *Journal of Consumer Research*, Vol. 18(3), p. 380.
22. Urbany, J.E., Bearden, W.O., and Weilbaker, D.C., (1998). 'Advised comparative price effects on buyer perceptions and behavior: A model and empirical test.' *Advances in Consumer Research*, Vol. 15(1).
23. Briesch, R.A., et al., (1997). 'A comparative analysis of reference price models.' *Journal of Consumer Research*, Vol. 24(2), pp. 202–214.
24. Moon, S. and Russell, G.J., (2004). 'A spatial choice model for product recommendations.' *Marketing Science Institute Report*, pp. 4–120.
25. Klein, L.R., (1998). 'Evaluating the potential of interactive media through a new lens: Search versus experience goods.' *Journal of Business Rresearch*, Vol. 41(3), pp. 195–203.
26. Huang, P., Lurie, N.H., and Mitra, S., (2009). 'Searching for experience on the web: An empirical examination of consumer behavior for search and experience goods.' *Journal of Marketing*, Vol. 73(2), pp. 55–69.
27. Lanen, W.N. and Thompson, R., (1988). 'Stock price reactions as surrogates for the net cash flow effects of corporate policy decisions.' *Journal of Accounting and Economics*, Vol. 10(4), pp. 311–334.
28. Park, C. and Lee, T.M., (2009). 'Information direction, website reputation and *e*WOM effect: A moderating role of product type.' *Journal of Business Research*, Vol. 62(1), pp. 61–67.
29. Sharma, N. and Patterson, P.G., (2000). 'Switching costs, alternative attractiveness and experience as moderators of relationship commitment in professional, consumer services.' *International Journal of Service Industry Management*, Vol. 11(5), pp. 470–490.
30. Burnham, G., et al., (2006). 'Mortality after the 2003 invasion of Iraq: A cross-sectional cluster sample survey.' *The Lancet*, Vol. 368, pp. 1421–1428.
31. Ha, S. and Stoel, L., (2009). 'Consumer *e*-shopping acceptance: Antecedents in a technology acceptance model.' *Journal of Business Research*, Vol. 62(5), pp. 565–571.

32. Wu, J.-H. and Wang, S.-C., (2005). 'What drives mobile commerce?: An empirical evaluation of the revised technology acceptance model.' *Information and Management*, Vol. 42(5), pp. 719–729.
33. Balabanis, G., Reynolds, N., and Simintiras, A., (2006). 'Bases of *e*-store loyalty: Perceived switching barriers and satisfaction.' *Journal of Business Research*, Vol. 59(2), pp. 214–224.
34. Armstrong, M., Vickers, J., and Zhou, J., (2009). 'Prominence and consumer search.' *The RAND Journal of Economics*, Vol. 40(2), pp. 209–233.
35. Dodds, W.B., Monroe, K.B., and Grewal, D., (1991). 'Effects of price, brand, and store information on buyers' product evaluations.' *Journal of Marketing Research (JMR)*, Vol. 28(3).
36. Chintagunta, P., et al., (2006). 'Structural modeling in marketing: Review and assessment.' *Marketing Science*, Vol. 25(6), pp. 604–616.
37. Brucks, M., Zeithaml, V.A., and Naylor, G., (2000). 'Price and brand name as indicators of quality dimensions for consumer durables.' *Journal of the Academy of Marketing Science*, Vol. 28(3), pp. 359–374.
38. Grewal, D., Monroe, K.B., and Krishnan, R., (1998). 'The effects of price-comparison advertising on buyers' perceptions of acquisition value, transaction value, and behavioral intentions.' *Journal of Marketing*, Vol. 62(2).

E-commerce

> **LEARNING OBJECTIVES**
>
> *After reading this chapter, you will be able to:*
> - Understand the concepts related to online distribution and procurement
> - Get familiar with the fundamental advantages offered by the Internet in online distribution
> - Understand the spiral of prosperity mode
> - Get acquainted with shopping carts and online payment gateways

The *e*-commerce industry in India is growing at a fast pace. The current adoption of *e*-commerce may be lesser than most countries across the globe, but the growth rate of this industry is much higher in India. As a result, this becomes a sector with significant potential for greater exploration.

As per a recent report on *E-Com Opportunity: India versus BRIC Nations*, published in the *Economic Times* in April, 2013:

- The online population in India is 11%, and 9% netizens shop online.
- The size of the *e*-commerce market in India was $0.8 billion in 2012.
- Traditional retailers do not have any significant online presence. New *e*-commerce players are experimenting with niche offline models.
- India demonstrated 3.46 orders per online shopper per year, which was greater than China.
- Most popular categories of *e*-shopping in India include apparel, accessories, electronics, personal care, books, home appliances, cosmetics, shoes, and bags (Table 9.1).

ONLINE DISTRIBUTION AND PROCUREMENT

Distribution, logistics, and purchasing activity have been at the cutting edge of information technology and inter-organizational relationships, especially within the business-to-business (B2B) sector with the exchange and auction models.

Table 9.1 Future of India's *e*-commerce market

	December 2012	December 2016
Internet users	140 million	390 million
Conversion to shoppers	9%	12%
Online shoppers	13 million	47 million
Orders/shopper	3.46	2.94
Order value	$18	$26
Online shopping market	$809 million	$3.62 billion

The Internet is an effective distribution channel for the delivery of digital products by electronic means with minimal cost through a virtual network (Fig. 9.1). However, attention has focussed on the changing channel interactions between manufacturers, service providers, suppliers, distributors, and consumers of physical products.

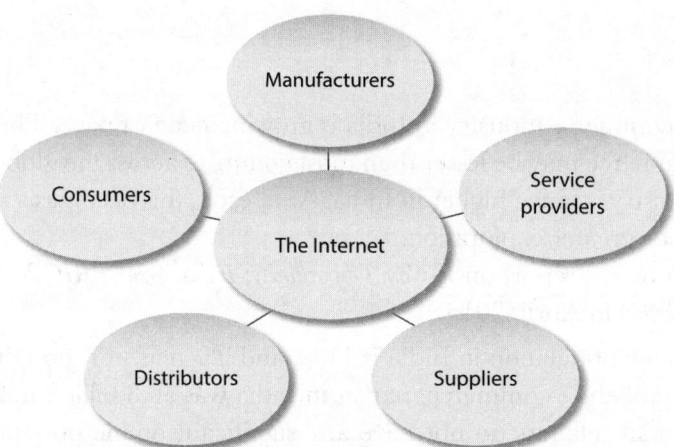

Fig. 9.1 The Internet as a distribution channel

Many Web visionaries predicted a far-reaching reformation of the supply chain with the elimination of layers of intermediaries (disintermediation). This, in turn, reduced transaction costs as customers went direct.

However, other layers have emerged (re-intermediation) with *cybermediaries* or *infomediaries* performing distribution activities, especially information exchange, brokering, and selling information products.[1]

Glazer[2] discusses marketing in an information-intensive environment and the value of what a firm knows to help the exchange process. He cites three sources requiring integration, which are as follows:

- *Downstream* Between firms and customers, including channel intermediaries (distributors)
- *Upstream* Between the firm and its suppliers
- *Internal* Information held internally within the organization and ideally shared and accessible across functions

Glazer argues that as information value increases, the traditional support role played by intermediaries becomes more important. Re-sellers have closer relationships with

---

EXHIBIT 9.1 Amazon.com—The India launch

One of the world's largest online retailers, Amazon.com ventured into India in June 2013. Amazon set foot into India with what it termed as a 'Marketplace model' that it hoped would help it overcome the regulatory binds on foreign *e*-commerce providers. India is a good marketplace for any online retailer, which is able to make a good online proposition. India has over 130 million Internet users and is regarded as a virtually untapped market for online retail. However, *e*-commerce has not picked up as a very successful trend in the Indian market. The problem lies in the failure of *e*-commerce players to successfully leverage the consumers they added in a rush.

The online retail market at the end of fiscal year 2013 was around $41.5 billion (₹8400 crore) and is expected to grow nearly by 100% every year.

Amazon.in, the Indian edition of the online retailer, does not own the merchandise promoted by Amazon but stores it and sells it on behalf of those who showcase their products on the website. The seller owns the inventory and pays for the storage, charged per cubic feet of storage per month. Shipment charges are subsequently added. Amazon is able to maintain the model as they have built it over the years and can maintain a multi-seller logistics operation at a very high scale. Amazon subsequently does the invoicing for all products sold through the Amazon space. Once the customer places the order, he/she is charged. Amazon takes a fee out and deposits the rest in the seller's account.

Regulations do not allow foreign online retailers to have a fully owned Indian arm selling directly in India. By literally interpreting the definition of online retailing, Amazon has created a very clever model, where they claim not to be buying or selling anything themselves. Amazon is hence serving as an aggregator to all the retailers exhibiting their products on its site.

To begin with, Amazon plans to sell some 7 million book titles and nearly 13,000 movie titles. It plans to expand into other categories such as cameras and phones in the near future. Amazon has a fulfilment centre on the outskirts of Mumbai to handle the twin operations of warehousing and delivery, for which they use their own delivery network and third-party carriers. Amazon has a two-fold objective in the endeavour. One is to provide fast and reliable service to customers, and the second is to ensure that they are a relevant service for every one of the 14 million retailers in India.

Amazon is also supported by an online price comparison portal called Junglee.com, which serves as a complementary website for Amazon. Consumers can compare selections from Flipkart and eBay, and other smaller sellers and then subsequently make the buying decision. Amazon.in aspires to gain customer trust to be the place where customers can buy.

customers through transactions and interactions such as communications and customer service.

The future of these relationships depends upon the organization's ability and desire to eliminate channel layers.

TRADITIONAL DISTRIBUTION MANAGEMENT ISSUES

Some of the imperative distribution management issues using traditional channels are as follows:

- Typical intermediary functions include collecting, distributing, and analysing marketing information; facilitating the exchange process; linking suppliers; setting promotional objectives and activities; pricing; managing risk; and physical distribution management (Fig. 9.2).

Fig. 9.2 Typical intermediary functions

- The number of intermediaries involved in channel length varies from business-to-consumer (B2C) and B2B markets as well as by product or service.
- In order to reduce channel competition and conflict, a channel member may seek greater control through merger, acquisition, or alliance through different channel levels. This is termed as a *vertical marketing system*.
- Channel co-operation and co-marketing and managing channel conflict are key issues.
- In both B2B and B2C markets, traditional channels are characterized by linearity as goods and services are pushed through the system. The linear relationship model changes in a variety of ways where intermediaries disappear or emerge, or demand for customized products increases.
- Transactional value, where the intermediary considers issues with respect to how effectively they position and promote themselves in the target market, marketplace

effectiveness of the producer/other intermediaries, effectiveness in connecting buyers and sellers and matching needs.
- Nature of channels and the support required vary in the context of complexity of products on offer, their monetary value, the competitive advantage offered by the model, and known customer service expectations.

FUNDAMENTAL ADVANTAGES OFFERED BY THE INTERNET

The advantages offered by the Internet are as follows (Fig. 9.3):
- *Connectivity* The Internet facilitates communications between buyers and sellers, service/information providers to information seekers.
- *Promotion* The Internet can be used as a site for product or brand promotion.
- *Communication* Automated technologies bring communication benefits in terms of cost and speed for all parties in the exchange process.
- *Efficiency* Calculation of cost–benefit ratios can highlight efficiency of the Internet vis-à-vis other channels.
- Facilitating price negotiations where dynamic pricing and online auctions take place.
- Matching products, both in range and quantity, to the buyer's needs.
- *Aids logistical value* The virtual medium facilitates distribution of services through new channels or by new intermediaries (re-intermediation).
- The distribution of digital content such as subscription newspapers, software, or music downloads, formerly delivered physically.
- Cost-effective and flexible delivery with *e*-learning.

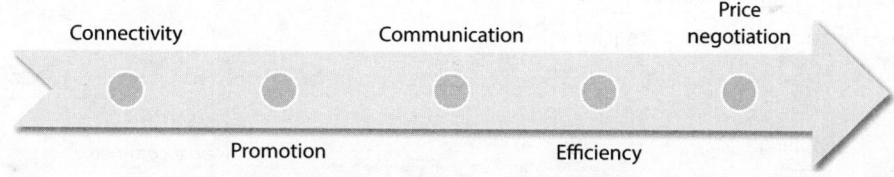

Fig. 9.3 Advantages of the Internet

Clearly, there are several channel design issues to be considered if a value is to be added at each stage of the value chain. The nature of the channels and the support required will vary for the following reasons[3]:
- The complexity of the products on offer
- The monetary value of the products
- The competitive advantage offered by the channel
- The known customer service expectations

In this light, a comparison can be drawn between the distribution paradigm and the buying process support paradigm (Table 9.2).

Table 9.2 Online value paradigms[4]

Distribution paradigm	Buying process support paradigm
• Spatial convenience • Lot size to match the consumption process. Requires effective forecasting • Waiting and delivery times to meet customer's expectations • Product variety	• Local inventory provided by channel members • Sales process supports through all the phases of the buying process including pre-sales, sales, and after-sales support • Order handling; pick, pack, and ship; inventory updates and billing, especially real-time expectations

THE SPIRAL OF PROSPERITY MODEL[5]

The spiral of prosperity is an important model in the *e*-commerce domain. The model presumes that the more we know about a customer, the more we can offer tailored and relevant solutions.

Relevant customization should help achieve the aims of the spiral of prosperity, because the more we know about the client, the more we can tailor to their needs. If we add classic 'direct' profiling techniques, and believe in the premise that 'birds of a feather flock together', the application of collaborative filtering software has considerable potential for communicating appropriate product suggestions.

People with similar profiles using basis for segmentation such as age, sex, income, and lifestyle should have similar likes and dislikes. It will depend on the knowledge and understanding of the segment and sub-segments.

New intermediaries are also playing vital roles in the following two key areas of the purchasing process (Fig. 9.4):

- Shopping cart services[6]
- Payment service providers (PSP)

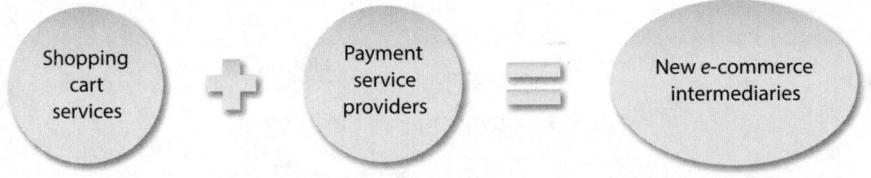

Fig. 9.4 New intermediaries

Shopping Cart Services

Early online shopping experiences were characterized by droves of prospects exiting sites at various points upto and including entering of their credit card details. Complexity in site design, poor usability, and unwieldy order forms led to site dropout rates of upto 70%.

Companies need to pinpoint those areas where prospects choose to leave a site before completing a research transaction. This is where *shopping carts* perform a significant role.

Shopping carts perform two fundamental functions as shown in Fig. 9.5.

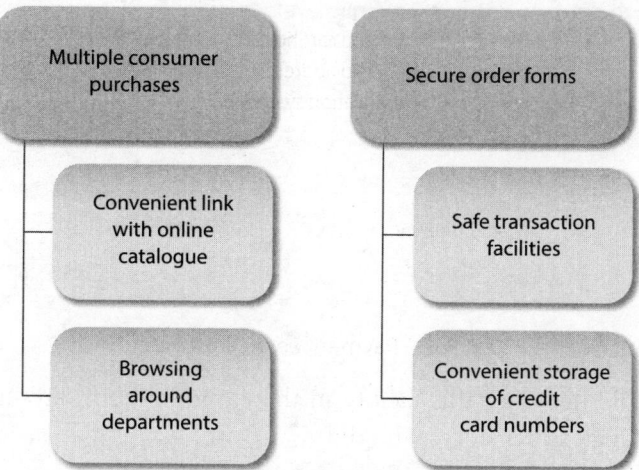

Fig. 9.5 Functions of shopping carts

First, they enable consumers to purchase more than one item at a time offering a convenient link with their online catalogue. The number of single-purchase transactions between a buyer and seller may be significant as online shoppers may wish to browse around different online departments.

Second, most shopping cart services incorporate secure order forms and transaction facilities with safe, convenient storage of credit card numbers.

Payment by credit card remains the most popular method for Internet-based transactions. Internet-based transactions require firms to set up a merchant account separate to the firm's bank account to provide a unique identification number to the PSP who collects the card details and forwards it to the acquiring bank for authorization.

Many *e*-commerce software companies, particularly those with experience in shop design, incorporate shopping cart software coupled with integrated functionality payment processing systems. An example of such a processing system is Electronic Retail Online (www.erolonline.co.uk) that offers a range of flexible shopping cart systems for SMEs with linked facilities to leading payment gateways such as *Netbank*, *Paypal*, and *WorldPay*, which provide ease of use to customers.

Payment Service Providers

Numerous payment solutions are now available from separate arms of established financial institutions or new online intermediaries. *Worldpay*, the Internet payment operation set up by the Royal Bank of Scotland, is an example of a market-leading intermediary with global merchant accounts and more than 12,000 strategic banking and *e*-commerce partners. Consumers take the products and services offered for granted, but they provide fundamental functions that influence the continuous expansion of *e*-commerce (Fig. 9.6).

WorldPay provides facilities to handle payment by instalments, which can be very important in a purchase decision online. Not surprisingly, many decision-making units like to spread payments and budget with higher value purchases. Majority of online

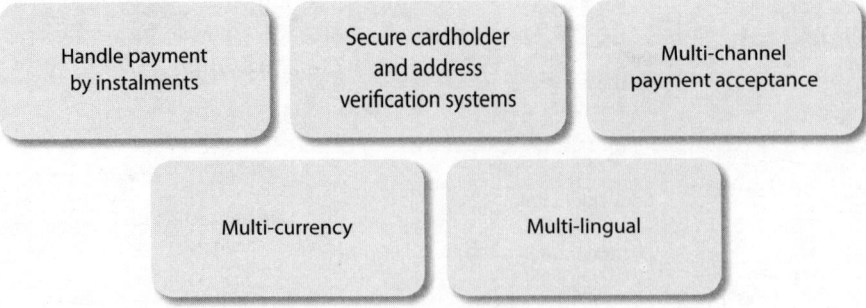

Fig. 9.6 Payment service providers

businesses did not offer this facility in the early dot-com days and lost business to the established high street stores who did.

Other PSP services include the following:

- Secure cardholder and address verification systems
- Multi-channel payment acceptance
- Multi-currency and multi-lingual systems designed to support global transactions

---

EXHIBIT 9.2   Payment solutions making online buying easier

Many technology startups are offering newer payment solutions aimed at weaning people away from paying cash for buying online. Their improved technology helps to make the process faster and safer for shoppers. Online payment gateways are being employed. These are *e*-commerce application service providers that authorize credit card payments for *e*-businesses, online retailers, bricks and clicks, or traditional brick and mortar. These are the equivalent of a physical point-of-sale terminal located in most retail outlets. Payment gateways protect credit card details by encrypting sensitive information, such as credit card numbers, to ensure that information is passed securely between the customer and the merchant and also between the merchant and payment processor.

Benefits of an online payment solution include the following:

- Cost-effective solutions
- Secured payment gateways
- Diverse payment acceptance modes
- Robust technology platforms for faster integration with *e*-commerce websites

Some significant Indian players in this space are as follows:

- Citrus Pay
- PayZippy
- EBS
- PayUIndia
- DirecPay

ONLINE MARKETPLACES

The emergence of online marketplaces, exchanges, hubs, or intranets, especially B2B has resulted in the coming together of buyers and sellers, often beyond normal trading areas and networks and has resulted in significant benefits to participating organizations.

Companies are starting to realize that the potential goes way beyond the price and extends to the entire supplier relationship affecting the end product.

This includes dimensions such as customer service levels, delivery, and product quality which add value in the chain. There are two types[7] of exchanges or hubs that have emerged in the B2B online marketplace. *Vertical* and *horizontal* hubs meet different marketing needs.

Vertical hubs are where commercial arrangements exist with organizations operating within a specific sector. The hub can involve a single dominant company wielding power, or more likely where a number of players form a trading consortium.

Horizontal hubs are where non-industry-specific products and services are sold across a range of industries. Typically, office supplies and maintenance, repair, and operations (MROs) are traded in such marketplaces where homogeneous items are needed by every organization.

E-PROCUREMENT[8]

E-procurement (*electronic procurement*), sometimes also known as supplier exchange, is the B2B, B2C, or business-to-government (B2G) purchase and sale of supplies, work, and services through the Internet as well as other information and networking systems, such as electronic data interchange and enterprise resource planning (Fig. 9.7).[9]

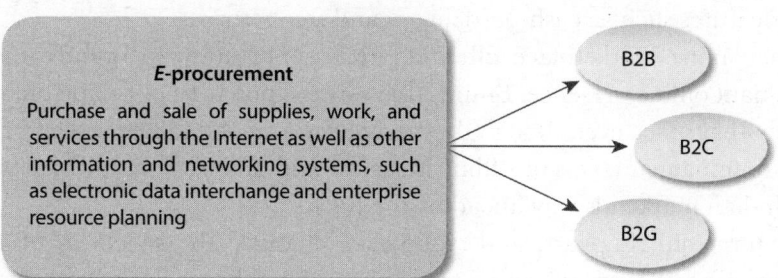

Fig. 9.7 *E*-procurement

The *e*-procurement value chain consists of indent management, *e*-tendering, *e*-auctioning, vendor management, catalogue management, purchase order integration, order status, shipping notice, *e*-invoicing, *e*-payment, and contract management (Fig. 9.8). Indent management is the workflow involved in the preparation of tenders. This part of the value chain is optional, with individual procuring departments defining their indenting process. In works procurement, administrative approval and technical sanction are obtained in an electronic format. In goods procurement, indent generation activity is done online. The end result of the stage is taken as inputs for issuing the NIT.

Elements of *e*-procurement include request for information, request for proposal, request for quotation, RFx (the previous three together), and *e*-RFx (software for managing RFx projects).

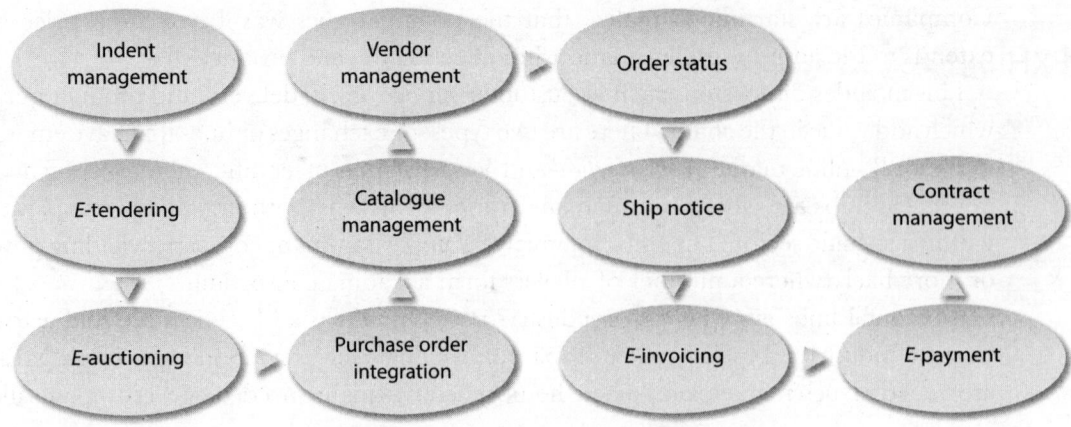

Fig. 9.8 *E*-procurement value chain

Some Major *E*-commerce Players in India Today

India is seeing the evolution of modern trade and online retail almost simultaneously. The organizational requirements to succeed in both formats are very different, as is the profile of the customer. Retailers are realizing this as most of their offline customers prefer shopping at bigger fashion websites, which offer a wider range of products coupled with features such as cash-on-delivery and free returns.

The online marketplace offers a great opportunity to brands that do not have a dominant offline presence. Brands that saw the potential of selling online early are doing well in that space even though they may have a small offline presence. For instance, Nike may dominate in terms of offline business, and online, Puma, which was a latecomer to the Indian market, is way ahead of the pack.

Myntra.com, Flipkart, and AOL have changed the spectrum of the entire Indian market. Today, over 20% of all trade volumes on the stock exchanges and about 35% on the commodity exchanges are done online. One reason for this has been the customer becoming more tech-savvy and comfortable about doing transactions online.

E-COMMERCE APPLICATIONS

Consumers who are shopping online need help on a wide variety of issues. They might need help to navigate an online site better and make better product choices. Consumers may need aid from a customer service representative in the online domain to respond to any queries or doubts they may have with regard to the online experience. They may want to compare prices between different product brands or even different product services. The message for *e*-commerce players is clear: They need to be:

- More visible for the consumer
- More accessible
- More navigable

> **EXHIBIT 9.3   Globus India and online fashion retail**
>
> www.Globusstores.com is the online shopping portal being offered by the Raheja Group-owned Globus chain in India. Globus is one of the first few companies in the fashion arena allowing consumers to make purchases from the online domain. The online apparel Industry is growing rapidly. According to a report released by a consulting firm Technopak, the $130-million apparel 'e-retailing space' in India has attracted investments worth $70 million, after 2010.
>
> Globusstores.com is powered by Mumbai-based digital commerce startup SociaLinked, which is working towards streaming retailers online and selling to increase consumer confidence in online buying.
>
> Globusstores offers apparel including formals, T-shirts, jackets, coats, jeans, skirts, jumpers and cardigans, ethnic wear, and accessories for men and women. The website is offering free shipping on all orders over ₹1,000.
>
> Gift vouchers for amounts starting from ₹101 to ₹1001 are also being offered on the site, which can be redeemed in the physical outlets but not online. Globusstores.com ships to over 5000 pin codes in India, and the company has tied up with courier company Aramex to deliver across India.

There are online applications which help consumers in their online shopping experiences. These Apps are social commerce platforms which can easily be integrated by a brand on its page. These Apps offer complete suites of social discovery and commerce tools. Some of these Apps give page owners the ability to add a shopping tab on their Facebook pages and allow brands to showcase products from their existing online stores. Others allow brands to create a Facebook fan page store. Certain Apps offer social relationship platforms which help brands leverage social channels to drive highly engaged customer relationships that result in a measurable business impact. These Apps provide customer affinity databases that utilize proprietary relationship intelligence technology to provide actionable insights to optimize marketing in all channels—not just social. These Apps enable companies to increase brand awareness, improve customer care, and drive customer conversations. Companies can use these Apps to plan and execute social content, reach and engage target customers, grow their social databases, understand their markets, scale social across the enterprise, and measure social impact. Five of such applications are depicted in Fig. 9.9:

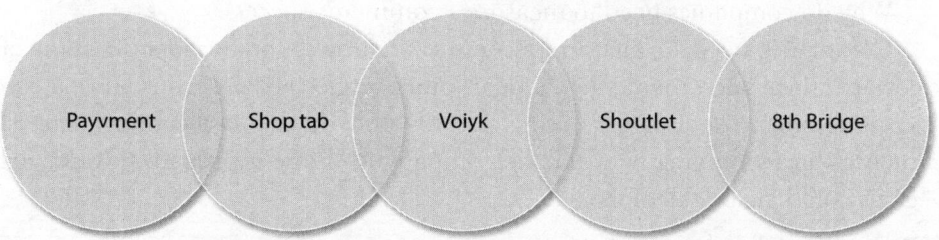

Fig. 9.9   Facebook and *e*-commerce applications

These Apps stimulate product-driven conversation among fans, allowing them to add a social element to their online shopping experience by instantly sharing their purchasing decisions with friends on Facebook and other social sites. Some of them also provide social discovery platforms to brands that want to empower people to discover new product ideas from each other, inspire the creation of crowd-sourced content, and gain a far deeper understanding of their customers.

EXHIBIT 9.4 *E-commerce players and the need to make effective use of colours and image psychology on consumers*

Sight is the strongest-developed sense in most human beings. It is only natural that 90% of an assessment for trying out a product is made by its colour alone. There are many factors that influence how and what consumers buy on the Internet. However, a great deal is decided by visual cues, the strongest and most persuasive being colour. While marketing for the new products on Internet, it is crucial to consider that consumers place visual appearance and colour above other factors such as sound and texture.

Colours and images have a significant impact in stimulating recall of products seen on the Internet, which implies that it is vital for e-commerce players to understand which colour or combination of colours has an enduring impact on a customer's memory in recalling the particular product or brand which they have seen on different sites during their online exploratory experiences.

Research has proven that the mentioned colours attract the following types of online shoppers:

- Orange, black, and blue—impulse shoppers
- Navy blue and teal—shoppers on a budget
- Pink, sky blue and rose—traditional buyers

As *e*-commerce players attempt to attract more consumers, it is advisable for the organizations to select the correct combination of colours and images for their advertisements so that the right types of customers can be pushed towards making the right types of purchases.

MEASURING *E*-COMMERCE SUCCESS

Companies are making large investments in *e*-commerce applications but are hard-pressed to evaluate the success of their *e*-commerce systems.

Why do companies need to measure *e*-commerce success?

Companies need to measure *e*-commerce success for the identification of progress towards their sales, marketing, and customer service goals. For instance, a company has an *e*-commerce goal of increasing sales by 30% in the forthcoming year. Measurable metrics for identifying whether the company is on the right path towards achieving its goals could include the following:

- Number of unique visitors
- Type of traffic sources

- Short-term revenue generation
- Conversion rate
- Customer service calls
- Average order size
- New customer orders
- Product affinity (what products are purchased together)
- Affiliate performance
- Volume of social media followers

The DeLone and McLean information systems success model can be adapted to the measurement challenges of the new *e*-commerce world (Fig. 9.10).

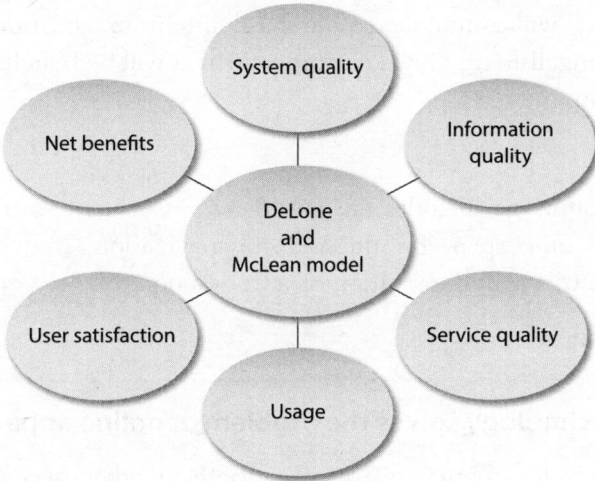

Fig. 9.10 Measuring *e*-commerce success—the DeLone and McLean model

The updated model consists of six interrelated dimensions of information systems success:

- System quality
- Information quality
- Service quality
- Usage
- User satisfaction
- Net benefits

System Quality

It is vital to have a framework in place to measure system quality in the Internet environment. Navigability, usability, accessibility, reliability, adaptability, and response time are examples of qualities that are valued by users of an *e*-commerce system.

Information Quality

Along with the quality of the system, it is equally important to monitor the quality of the content available on the Internet. Good-quality content will attract more visitors and subsequent buyers to the site. Good quality implies content that is authentic, accurate, personalized, updated, relevant, easy to understand, and secure if prospective buyers or suppliers are to initiate transactions via the Internet and return to a site on a regular basis.

Service Quality

Consumers are concerned about the quality of the service they receive. This applies regardless of whether the support is delivered by the information systems department or a new organizational unit or is outsourced to an Internet service provider. Good service quality will stimulate re-purchase intent in consumers, and will result in consumer evangelism and loyal customers which will be beneficial for the organization in the long run.

Usage

The quality of usage includes all parameters associated with a consumer Web visit, including the time spent on the website, navigation, frequency of usage, etc., to information retrieval and execution of a transaction.

EXHIBIT 9.5 Technology solves the problem of online apparel sellers

The biggest deterrents for consumers while making an online apparel purchase are as follows:

- The worry that the product would not fit them well
- The possible need to return a product and ask for replacement or reimbursement
- The possibility of post purchase dissonance if the consumer peer group does not approve of the purchase
- The need to alter a product that has been purchased online

Technology has solved these problems, making life easier for the *e*-commerce players.

- Technology has introduced what is being termed as a virtual try-on system which enables the *e*-commerce website to project clothing onto users as though they were looking into a mirror. Users stand about two feet away and hold out their hands as if they were pulling clothes off a rack. Consumers can 'virtually try on' these clothes as they would in a showroom before making an offline apparel purchase.
- A new feature allows consumers to share pictures of their choices on social media to gain the approval of their peers.
- A Bangalore-based fashion and lifestyle *e*-store has introduced the *Alterations* service. This service provides product alterations without the customers having to step out of their comfort spaces, thereby increasing their personalization quotient and convenience level.

User Satisfaction

This represents customers' opinions with regard to their satisfaction with usage and transactions in an *e*-commerce system. This covers the entire customer experience cycle from information retrieval through purchase, payment, receipt, and service.

Net Benefits

Success of an *e*-commerce system can be measured in a holistic way when the complete positive and negative impacts of *e*-commerce have been measured on customers, suppliers, employees, organizations, markets, industries, economies, and even society as a whole.

MONITORING *E*-COMMERCE BRANDS AND SOCIAL MEDIA IN THE INDIAN MARKET

Indian brands are leveraging their social media presence by targeting young consumers, who are Internet savvy, to influence purchase. The social networks most preferred by brands for this purpose are Facebook and Twitter.

It is important for companies to continuously monitor their presence on the Web (Fig. 9.11). What is it that companies need to measure and why?

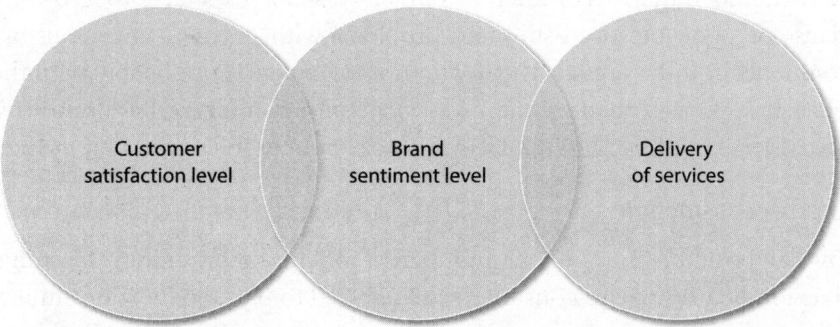

Fig. 9.11 Monitoring social media presence of *e*-commerce brands

Customer Satisfaction Level

It is important for *e*-commerce companies to monitor customer satisfaction with the *e*-commerce site in the context of the following:

- Navigability of the site
- Ease of transaction
- Choice of products available
- Visibility of site
- Security

Higher customer satisfaction levels will result in consumers revisiting and repurchasing and strengthening loyalty bonds between the company and consumers.

Brand Sentiment Level

It is vital for companies to monitor positive and negative sentiments pertaining to the brand to take corrective action as and when required. These can be tracked everytime the company launches an online campaign. Companies can identify types of campaigns which stimulate more positivity in consumer conversations and accordingly manipulate their campaigns and seed online communities with brand-specific conversations.

Delivery of Services

It is important for *e*-commerce companies to focus on the delivery of their services. In some cases the companies are dependent on their marketing intermediaries to carry the products to the end consumers. Similarly, logistical support and payment gateways actually represent the quality of service provided to the *e*-commerce buyer and subsequent satisfaction of the buyer with the same.

E-commerce endeavours of eBay in India and its customer satisfaction, brand sentiment, and service delivery-related endeavours are described in this section.

India is a critical market for eBay. This is further proven by eBay's latest round of funding in *Snapdeal* worth ₹830 crore. Flipkart is one of the most significant players in India today. eBay is facing tough competition from both Flipkart and Amazon.

Earlier, the Indian *e*-commerce market was not expected to grow the way it has because of poor logistics issues and problems with payment mechanisms; eBay's latest investments in India are clearly an attempt to engage more deeply with the country.

eBay has globally made some investments in *e*-commerce in countries such as South Korea, Germany, UK, and the USA with different models than that in India.

Customer satisfaction

eBay has hosted a humongous number of online communities, learning centres, and discussion boards, where consumers are allowed to participate. Consumers continuously participate and upload community stories and images. The head office further maintains a section called *Feedback to India team* where all the stakeholders of the company can login and post their concerns to be addressed in time. Research says that a large volume of consumers become dissatisfied as a result of the perceived indifference of the company. Endeavours like these move the consumers up the *customer satisfaction* and *brand–consumer relationship ladders*.

Brand sentiment

eBay's efforts at modernizing the trading community have generated positive brand sentiments by consumers because of the following factors:

- Global reach to an average of 31 international markets.
- Convenience offered by Internet-enabled trade which overcomes distances and makes the world 'flatter' with fewer barriers to business.
- Creating a level-playing field for small and large entrepreneurs.

- Internet-based trade boosts national trade as *e*-commerce platforms support the domestic economy and bring remote sellers and buyers closer together.
- Growth in interstate flows. The five largest interstate trade flows in India are from Maharashtra to Karnataka as well as to Tamil Nadu, followed by flows from Delhi to Karnataka, Maharashtra, and Tamil Nadu.
- Improvements in national welfare as Internet-enabled trade enhances competition and reduce prices because it offers businesses very low market-entry barriers.
- Better Internet connectivity.

Service delivery

eBay will be further able to enhance service delivery as the business environment in India starts supporting a 'less-cash' economy, a simplification of custom procedures, a liberalization of overly strict trademark regimes and competitive shipping rates for sellers.

EXHIBIT 9.6 Snapdeal opens *E*-window for startups

Termed as India's largest online marketplace, Snapdeal ships products to over 4,000 Indian towns and cities, features more than 6,000 brands in over 500 categories. Products range from apparels, fashion accessories, footwear, jewellery, books and movies, toys, perfumes, health- and nutrition-related products, computers, peripherals, automotives, mobiles, tablets, music instruments, TV, and audio and gaming products.

Online marketplace Snapdeal recently launched a platform that will allow innovators to showcase consumer products designed by them on the portal. The platform is termed as *Launchpad*. Snapdeal Launchpad aims to encourage innovators and inventors across the country and provide them a national reach for their product(s). It provides a platform for individuals/companies to share their latest innovation, and the best ones get to leverage Snapdeal's brand and reach for making their innovation a commercial success. The *e*-commerce company hopes to provide entrepreneurs building products access to its more than 2.5 crore users and provide access to its payment gateway, distribution, and reverse logistics services.

Snapdeal is partnering with IIM Ahmedabad's Technology Incubator Centre for Innovation, Incubation and Entrepreneurship and IIT Bombay's Entrepreneurship Cell, which will not only act as feeders but also screen products on parameters such as innovation and marketability.

CASE STUDY Flipkart.com—Shopping *Ka Naya* Address

Flipkart had a big challenge on its hands when the company was launched in India. It had to appeal to the heart of the conservative Indian shopper who was looking for value for money, convenience, and security. The company found its place in the Indian consumers' choice set for online shopping through a series of heart-warming and funny advertisements. They launched advertising campaigns showing three generations of families benefitting from Flipkart. The flipkart *Nokidding, Noworries* advertisement leveraged acting skills of kids and served their awesome expressions to family audiences, garnering mass appeal in return.

Flipkart has been successful by crafting a careful consumer segmentation, targeting, and positioning strategy, as it has been successful in understanding the Indian consumer's mentality and has taken appropriate steps to establish itself. Flipkart needed to cater to the Indian consumer both in the context of services provided to gratify his/her subconscious needs such as comfort and safety as well as the right products on offer to satisfy his/her needs.

Moreover, Flipkart offered considerable discounts as compared to physical stores attracting the customers. The company quickly achieved a variety-based positioning in the Indian market and became the trusted name in *e*-commerce, selling electronic articles, mobiles, laptops, and their accessories, along with books, apparel, household items, etc. This brought out the need to penetrate the markets further.

Flipkart's primary consumer segment comprised Internet-savvy consumers, who were looking for the convenience of making a purchase from home. These were people who preferred a hassle-free approach to shopping and comprised an equal proportion of males and females, specifically in the context of the urban population. Flipkart's consumer research told them that people were comfortable spending about ₹5000 on shopping online, wanted a comfortable, hassle-free environment for shopping, and were not very particular about discounts on electronic gadgets being sold online. They were impressed with the diversity in choices available, while shopping through an online portal.

Flipkart defined its target consumers as those who were not emotional about the shopping process and who considered shopping as a task. They were rational, calculative, and focused individuals. They were looking for a brand which was reliable, trustworthy, honest, and credible. Flipkart supported this targeting and positioning strategy with an aggressive round of visibility on television, in the digital media, and the offline media, including advertising heavily on bus stops. The Indian consumer was still apprehensive about online transactions and use of credit cards. To overcome this issue, Flipkart launched cash-on-delivery (CoD) system and also a 30-day no-questions-asked return policy. Although this considerably increased sales, it led to other problems. The cash returns became slow and Flipkart was at the mercy of the courier companies. Subsequently, Flipkart Logistics was born to take care of the entire logistics for Flipkart and also with a vision to expand further into a logistics provider. Providing so many features, they appealed to the young and old consumers alike who were willing to shop quickly and easily, and were guaranteed excellent delivery times and service by the most trustworthy name in *e*-commerce in India. Flipkart has now achieved a strategic position in the market, which is not possible for other firms to imitate.

Questions:

1. How is an *e*-commerce portal like Flipkart promoting online shopping? What are the latest business associations Flipkart has ventured into?
2. Profile Flipkart's first festive campaign, for example, Campaign for Diwali, 2014, in India.
3. Snapdeal, Flipkart, and Amazon are the top *e*-commerce players in India that are striving towards changing the face of *e*-retail.

PRACTITIONER PERSPECTIVE

After having been at the point of inflection for a while now, e-commerce in India has finally taken off. Consumers understand that shopping online offers them far more variety as compared to offline. Besides, the larger stores have not penetrated the smaller towns yet.

Muralikrishnan B., Country Manager, eBay India

Markets like the USA have seen a natural progression where today there are purely online retailers and old businesses that have found a way of leveraging their existing strengths to make the transition online. By offering incentives, like free in-store pick up, the retailers are trying every trick in the book to hold on to their customers. In India, the existing retailers are looking at online selling as an additional channel other then from having their own stores and presence in multi-brand outlets (MBOs). This will get you traction, but it is not enough to make you a leader.

Aashish Bhinde, ED and Head—Digital Media and Technology, Avendus Capital

SUMMARY

Distribution, logistics, and purchasing activity have been at the cutting edge of information technology and inter-organizational relationships, especially within the B2B sector with the exchange and auction models. The Internet is an effective distribution channel for the delivery of digital products by electronic means with minimal cost through a virtual network. However, attention has focussed on the changing channel interactions between manufacturers, service providers, suppliers, distributors, and consumers of physical products. Typical intermediary functions include collecting, distributing, and analysing marketing information; facilitating the exchange process, linking suppliers, setting promotional objectives and activities, pricing; managing risk and physical distribution management. The Internet offers ease in terms of connectivity, communications, facilitates price interactions, etc., thereby offsetting several problems faced in traditional distribution channels. Shopping carts perform two fundamental functions. First, they enable consumers to purchase more than one item at a time offering a convenient link with their online catalogue. The number of single-purchase transactions between a buyer and seller may be significant as online shoppers may wish to browse around different online departments. Second, most shopping cart services incorporate secure order forms and transaction facilities with safe, convenient storage of credit card numbers. The emergence of online marketplaces, exchanges, hubs, or intranets, especially B2B, has resulted in the coming together of buyers and sellers, often beyond normal trading areas and networks and has resulted in significant benefits to participating organizations. Companies are starting to realize that the potential goes way beyond the price and extends to the entire supplier relationship affecting the end product.

Concept Review Questions

1. List the typical issues being faced by organizations when they use the traditional distribution channels.
2. What are the advantages offered by the Internet that make it a viable distribution platform?
3. Differentiate between the online value paradigms in the context of the *distribution paradigm* and *buying process support paradigm*.
4. Explain the spiral of prosperity.
5. Write short notes on the following:
   (a) Shopping cart services
   (b) Payment service providers

Critical Thinking Questions

1. Study Amazon's marketplace model in detail. Compare and contrast the same with the model used by eBay. What are the opportunities for eBay in India?
2. What are the *e*-commerce models that are being followed by Indian players such as Myntra.com and OLX? Study the business model being used by Indian player Flipkart and create a table to compare the models of the three Indian players.

Practising Digital Marketing

1. Your friend wants to set up an *e*-commerce portal selling a variety of products online.
   (a) Create a questionnaire which can be administered to potential customers to analyse the following:
      (i) Types of products that can be sold
      (ii) Consumer expectations and preferences for the success of the *e*-commerce venture
   (b) Create an *e*-commerce model in the context of logistics and payment methods to demonstrate how your friend will put operations in place.

References

1. Gay, R., Charlesworth, A., and Esen, R., Online distribution and procurement, *Online Marketing*, Oxford Publications, 2012, p. 448.
2. Glazer, R., (1991). 'Marketing in an information-intensive environment: Strategic implications of knowledge as an asset'. *The Journal of Marketing*, pp. 1–19.
3. Hanson, W.A. and Kalyanam, K., *Internet Marketing and E-commerce*, Thomson South-Western, 2007.
4. Simmons, G., (2008). 'Marketing to postmodern consumers: Introducing the Internet chameleon'. *European Journal of Marketing*, Vol. 42(3/4), pp. 299–310.
5. Daniel, MAREŞ Marius, M. A. R. E. Ş. Valerica, and ILINCUŢĂ Lucian Dorel. "BUSINESS STRATEGY THROUGH IT&C." REVISTA ECONOMICĂ: 109.
6. Eggebraaten, T.J. and Prentice, J.A., (2001). 'Reorder and default order mechanisms for a shopping cart of an *E*-commerce website'. U.S. Patent Application 09/910, 534.
7. Kaplan, S.N., Valuation and new economy firms, *Asset Price Bubbles: The Implications for Monetary, Regulatory, and International Policies*, 2003, pp. 391–401.
8. Baily, P.J.H., (2008). *Procurement Principles and Management*, Prentice Hall Financial Times, Harlow, England, 2008, p. 394.
9. Delone, W.H. and McLean, E.R., (2004). 'Measuring *E*-commerce success: Applying the DeLone and McLean information systems success model'. *International Journal of Electronic Commerce*, Vol. 9(1), pp. 31–47.

Section 3
Online Tools for Marketing

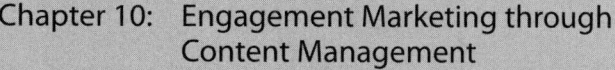

Chapter 10: Engagement Marketing through Content Management

Chapter 11: Online Campaign Management

Chapter 12: Consumer Segmentation, Targeting, and Positioning using Online Tools

Chapter 13: Market Influence Analytics in a Digital Ecosystem

Engagement Marketing through Content Management

> **LEARNING OBJECTIVES**
>
> *After reading this chapter, you will be able to:*
> - Understand the importance of consumer engagement
> - Understand consumer engagement in the virtual world
> - Get familiar with the types of content that can be used to drive consumer engagement
> - Get acquainted with the measurement of online consumer engagement

Information overload in the Internet age can force people to become passive receptors of information. It is hence important for an organization to make sure that the right information reaches the right people at the right time. A higher perceived value by the consumer in the organizational information will stimulate consumer interest leading to a desire to interact, achieving 'engagement' from the organizational perspective.

Each customer touch-point has a significant role to play in the consumer life cycle by influencing the customer experience. The customer experience does not begin and end at a transaction, website visit, or conversation with an agent. The customer experience process encompasses the moment the customer becomes aware of the organization, products, or services comprising multiple independent interactions, transactions, and contacts along the way. Consumer engagement can be defined as 'repeated interactions that strengthen the emotional, psychological, or physical investment a customer has in a brand'.[1] Hence, these consumer touch-points can exist long before a customer actually makes a purchase and long after they have made their first transaction. The goal of every company interested in leveraging customer experience as a competitive advantage is to create a positive and consistent experience at *all* of the touch-points. The collaborative Web offers a series of these consumer touch-points which can subsequently lead to consumer engagement.

BUILDING COLLABORATIVE CUSTOMER RELATIONSHIPS

Creating more social or collaborative relationships is the third major wave of thinking in customer-centric business management (CBM) over the past two decades (Fig. 10.1). In the 1990s, the so-called customer relationship management (CRM) was mostly about managing customer information, a company-centric view of the relationship.

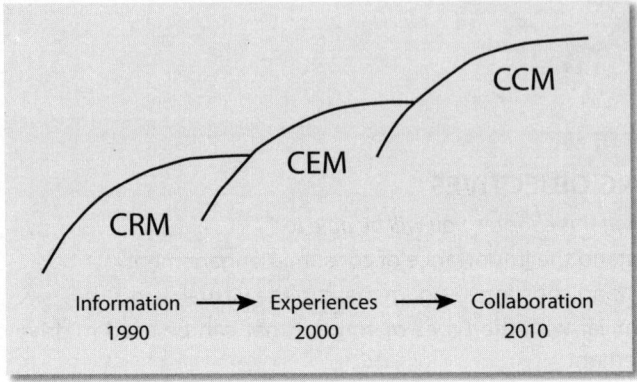

Fig. 10.1 Evolution of customer-centric business management

There was more to a customer relationship than data management and process automation. The limitations of CRM's internal orientation and technology obsession led to the rise of customer experience management (CEM), which was focused on designing and delivering loyalty-building experiences—CEM was not just about using technology. Then emerged the third wave driven by social media or the media generated by organizations and consumers as part of customer collaboration management (CCM), which is about engaging with customers in a real dialogue.[2]

CONSUMER ENGAGEMENT

The ability of marketing to cause consumer engagement is significant as this is the first step to enable consumers to perceive value in a product. The engagement theory comprises the dimensions of involvement, interaction, intimacy, and influence.[2] Online engagement involves a series of interactions as visitors return to a site prompted by different offline and traditional media. Marketers need to go beyond the status quo of traditional communication models if they intend inducing user behaviour and create opportunities in a domain where organizations understand consumer intent and needs, causes of consumer interaction with a brand, and above all the means for consumer conversion. Continued interactions can be stimulated after the initial contact, brand exposure, or transactions, namely lead, sale, or registration result in consumer involvement. *Influencing, measuring,* and *analysing softer emotional measures* as well as the number and type of interactions comprises the study of consumer engagement as this enables organizations to understand how engaged the online audience is with an organizational brand. Web 2.0 applications offer opportunities beyond the static website, as interactivity offered by these tools acts as a catalyst in engaging the consumer, and consumer engagement is visible through the means of publishing, posting comments, subscribing, favouriting, bookmarking, *e*-mailing, distributing, networking, etc. Engagement is a vital factor with respect to Web traffic, CRM, sales, and brand loyalty. Time spent with a brand and subsequent actions with a product's message, related media, and Web 2.0 applications through which they are communicated are significant parameters contributing to the process of consumer engagement. Engagement is hence a function of a series of involved user actions and there is a need to understand what content resonates with the consumer, consumer visits, and pages visited and inbound links to be able to optimize campaigns.

While the return on investment (ROI) may not be immediate, an investment in engagement is better than an investment in retention. The key to future profitability is not in simply keeping customers, it is from deepening their relationships. And engagement is a necessary pre-condition for that to happen.

ENGAGEMENT MARKETING

Engagement marketing, sometimes called 'experiential marketing', 'event marketing', 'live marketing', or 'participation marketing', is a marketing strategy that directly engages consumers and invites and encourages consumers to participate in the evolution of a brand. Rather than looking at consumers as passive receivers of messages, engagement marketers believe that consumers should be actively involved in the production and co-creation of marketing programmes, developing a relationship with the brand. Consumer engagement is the ultimate point in which a brand and a consumer connect in order to offer a true experience related to the brand's core values. It is a long-term connection that must be enhanced over time.

The ability of marketing to engage and endear consumers will ultimately determine whether a user eventually enters into a greater relationship with a brand or organization. It is important to measure the engagement of customers, prospective customers, and detractors with an organizational brand in every area of engagement. Engagement needs to be understood by type, the factors leading to engagement, and the value associated with each in terms of ultimate adoption, sales, and brand loyalty. The engagement theory comprises the dimensions of involvement, interaction, intimacy, and influence. The level of user engagement achieved by interaction between an organization and consumer is an important factor contributing to product adoption, thereby driving sales and brand loyalty.

In the Web 2.0 context, consumer engagement is visible through the means of publishing, posting comments, subscribing, bookmarking, *e*-mailing, distributing, and networking. When measuring engagement, the level of user interaction is an obvious and important component, and each of the aforementioned user actions indicate a different level of engagement.

Some significant observations are as follows:
- The customers can be positively or negatively engaged with a company/product.
- A more in-depth examination of this kind would reveal its content, usually a mixture of emotional states and rational beliefs, such as in the case of positive engagement, sympathy, trust, pride.
- The degree of positive or negative engagement lies on a continuum that ranges from low involvement, namely, the psychological state of apathy, to high.
- An engaged person is someone with an above average involvement with his/her object of relatedness.

EXHIBIT 10.1   Facebook in India

The presence of Indians on Facebook, Twitter, Linkedin, and other social networking sites is increasing continuously. The volumes are tough to ignore. The writing on the wall is very clear for each marketer—jump in or face invisibility.

Increase in broadband connectivity, an adventurous, experimental young Indian consumer, driven by the empowerment offered by these networks and the psychological boost offered by increased visibility has ensured the entry of social media in every household. The gratification faced by the consumers on being recognized and considered significant enough to have an opinion has made this a popular medium.

Companies are now investing in digital campaigns to reach the masses.

Millions of consumers are logging onto the social network through myriad computers, tablets, and mobile phones, and brands and companies have morphed to aggressively targeting social networkers with bespoke plans and initiatives as they seek new avenues for growth today.

High volumes of usage, increased volume of time spent online, good online navigational skills, and increased participation and reciprocity in the virtual medium are making companies contemplate innovative and thought-provoking online campaigns.

Consumer Engagement and Web Analytics

As it is very clear that the virtual world is being increasingly used by companies to build consumer engagement, it becomes important to understand the factors contributing to consumer engagement. While it is difficult for organizations to qualify the time that a consumer spends in the virtual world; however, attempts are being made to study and analyse the consumer visit in terms of how engaged they are.

Subsequently, companies can identify consumers who are highly engaged and treat them as consumer advocates, while at the same time provide additional support to consumers who are less engaged. Table 10.1 details some metrics for analysing the consumer visit to study his/her level of engagement.

Similarly, most online metrics are only able to capture the *degree* not *kind* of engagement. These include the following activities, a study of which enables companies to understand how engaged their consumers are with the product or brand:

- Subscribing (feed, *e*-mail, newsletter)
- Registering
- Feedback (comments, complaints, inquiries, etc.)
- Rating/tagging/filtering/bookmarking its content
- User submissions (UGC)
- Printing or downloading a piece of content

Table 10.1 Factors contributing to consumer engagement in the virtual world

No. of unique visits	Refers to the number of times a consumer logs in afresh on a website.
Frequency of visit	How often a consumer visits a website indicates his/her intertest in the company or product, or depicts level of interest in the organization.
Recency of visit	The more *recently* the visitor came to a website, *the higher the potential value* of the visitor, since they are more likely to come back and generate revenue for the website in the future, relative to other visitors.
Depth of visit	Describes the length of a visitor's journey in terms of number of pages visited. A deep journey signifies a high degree of engagement. Does not distinguish between type of engagement.
Time spent on the site	Time spent correlates with degree of engagement but it does not discriminate between quality of time, it may simply be negatively spent merely in search of some content.

Degree of Engagement

No Web metric, or combination of metrics, can discriminate between the kinds of engagement, that is, positive engagement. This requires primary research. All that the Web metrics can do is discriminate between relative degrees of engagement. Basic metrics can only discriminate between low degrees of engagement. A customer with a high score in his/her visit metrics may nevertheless feel apathetic towards the brand. Response rate of consumers falls as number of days since last contact increases.

The level of user engagement achieved by interaction between an organization and consumer is an important factor contributing to product adoption, driving sales, and brand loyalty as demonstrated in the case of a corporate blog which allows consumers to interact with products, brands, and organizations. When measuring engagement, the level of user interaction is an obvious and important component, and each of the aforementioned user actions indicate a different level of engagement.[3] A user who comments on an organizational post on a corporate blog is at a 'higher level of engagement' than one who simply reads the post. Similarly, a user who creates content about organizational initiative, namely shares content about the organization on his/her personal blog is more engaged than both the above-stated ones. The degree of consumer involvement is expected to influence both the amount and quality of a consumer's cognitive response. Involved consumers engage in more laboured research and acquisition strategies.[4] Number of comments a blog entry attracts and the number of individuals that write the comments are indicators of participation that significantly load onto involvement.[5]

EXHIBIT 10.2 Indian hotels—Using Pinterest for consumer engagement

Pinterest is a photo-sharing website that allows users to 'pin' images to online bulletin boards and hence form theme-based image collections. These include events, interests, and hobbies; and users are allowed to browse other pinboards for images, re-pin images to their own pin boards, like images, and subsequently share them. Several organizations are actually using Pinterest as a catalogue to drive online sales.

In India, several Indian hotel chains have established a presence on *Pinterest*. These include Oberoi Hotels and Resorts, Trident Hotels, ITC Hotels, Neemrana Hotels, and Sun N Sand. Pinterest is being actively used by these organizations to engage and subsequently leverage their customers by allowing consumers to share photos on the online space.

Content hosted by hotels includes information on the following:

Festivals, spa sojourns, fine dining experiences, exotic resorts, timeless weddings, performance arts, comparisons with other hotels, national presence, latest offers, global cuisine offerings, luxury experiences, and signature restaurants.

ITC Hotels hosts chef's special recipes and pictures of their delicious delicacies, wine and drinks, and celebrations on Pinterest along with other information.

Oberoi Hotels additionally hosts information about deals for summer holidays, cruises, luxury beach resorts, photo galleries, etc.

With over 11 million users and growing, Pinterest has proved itself as a powerhouse in the *e-*engagement space. With so many users engaging on the new platform, it is obvious to see the potential. For hotels that have already mastered the other top social channels, have a good following, and beautiful photos to show off, Pinterest is definitely worth trying out.

While user actions in the direction of *adoption*, such as adding to a group, may be indicative of low engagement, rating, commenting, voting, endorsing, and favouriting signal medium engagement. Further content creation activities such as blogging or participation in a fan community are indicators of a high degree of engagement. Similarly, adding friends, networking, and creating a fan community are factors contributing to the highest degree of engagement.

Ghuneim's Typology of Engagement

Each user action can provide different levels of attention as well as influence further interactions. While the viewing of a video online is considered an impression, there are different and unique tiers of attention and engagement in each play such as the length of active viewing as well as subsequent sharing, rating, favouriting, forwarding, and adding, which are all secondary interactions that form the engagement. Figure 10.2 depicts different types of consumer engagement.

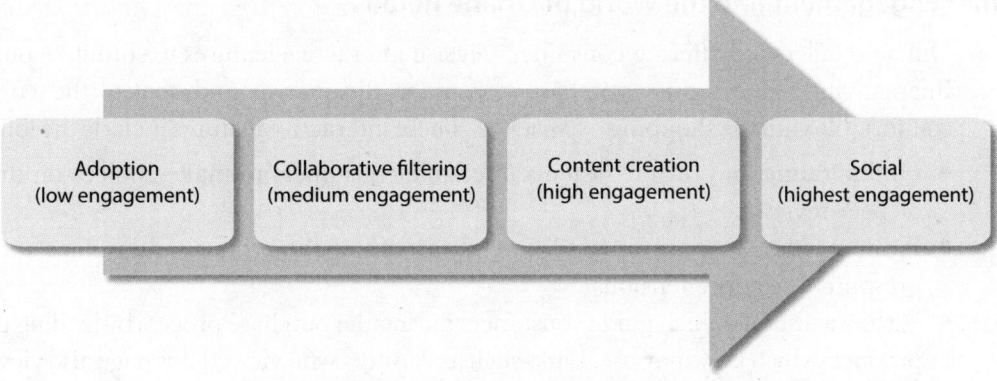

Fig. 10.2 Different types of engagement

Forrester's customer engagement framework (Fig. 10.3) defines four dimensions of the consumer brand relationship and proceeds to identify ways to measure the same. As per this framework, the four dimensions can be outlined as follows:

- *Involvement*   Refers to the presence of a person at various touch-points and can be measured through the frequency of web visits.
- *Interaction*   Refers to the actions that people take while present at key touch-points and can be measured through the online forms they fill, the average page views, the website login details, online transactions, site searches, and average time spent per website.
- *Intimacy*   Refers to the affection or aversion a person holds for a brand. This can be measured through brand affinity surveys, sentiment mining, customer satisfaction surveys, and analysis of customer complaint data.
- *Influence*   Depicts the likelihood that a person will advocate on behalf of the brand and can be measured by the frequency of his/her written reviews, comments, blog posts, etc.

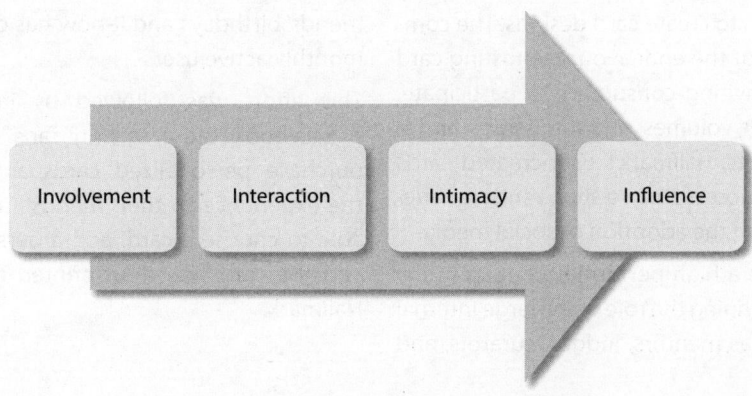

Fig. 10.3 Customer engagement framework

Consumer Engagement and the World of Online Retail

Online retailers are offering consumers several interactive features to stimulate purchase. Interactivity reduces post purchase consumer dissonance and makes the consumer comfortable with the shopping experience. These interactive features include the following:

- Online rating and review systems to enable consumers to make choices on the basis of peer reviews.
- Product videos to get a visual virtual experience of the product and reduce consumer pre-purchase apprehensions.
- Virtual assistants which guide consumers during the purchase process by leading them to products which they may use. Links such as 'Visitors who viewed this page also viewed ...' are common and help a user navigate through the site to possible areas of interest.
- 3D modelling finds its uses in online retail by virtue of the dimension of vividness. Vividness is the way in which an environment presents information to the senses. 3D product visualization techniques makes the product more appealing to the consumer. A 3D presentation enables consumers to interact with products, enriches their learning processes, and creates a sense of being in a simulated real world.
- Bar code scanners for smart phones aid onsite social commerce by making the transaction sites more secure for the consumers.
- Documentation of consumer experiences in social networks. These networks promote peer-to-peer consumer interaction and let consumers interact.

Further addition of functionalities echoing the reputation and feedback mechanisms of major transaction sites has enabled social networks to develop into full-scale recommendation centres.

EXHIBIT 10.3 Hallmark cards and social commerce

Hallmark cards were an early adopter of social commerce. Hallmark used the digital world to involve consumers in co-creation. The company used consumers to create card designs. The company went about the endeavour by hosting card contests and inviting consumers to participate. After significant volumes of submissions and a series of contests, Hallmark's user-created cards represented a success story, a story rendered successfully through the adoption of social media.

The outcome is a high-performing line of funny cards, thus redefining the role of the large internal creative teams as mentors, judges, curators, and idea generators.

Hallmark subsequently introduced a *Facebook application* termed as the *Social Calendar*. This App reminds users of key dates such as their friends' birthdays and it now has over 1.3 million monthly active users.

This effort was followed by introduction of a Facebook Store, giving fans the ability to purchase personalized cards and recommend the experience to their friends. Customers were able to choose a card, add a personal message, and the card was then printed and posted by Hallmark.

Forward-thinking businesses are moving away from reliance on the centrally controlled mass broadcast, and towards the development of personal and localized relationships with well-informed and demanding customers. This group of consumers increasingly expects consistent engagement with their preferred brands across a range of online and offline channels.

Issues that are significant for *e*-retailers include the following:

- The need to have relevant advertisements for consumers and build subsequent engagement between the context of an advertisement and a prospective consumer. This engagement increases the effectiveness of the endeavour.
- The need to recognize the growth of applications facilitating online collaboration through social networks, video/photo sharing sites and blogs, because of the enhancements to broadband Internet access.
- The need to recognize the volume of consumer activity on social networks.
- The need to respect the consumer networks and the number and quality of individual connections on these social networks, which can be valuable for an online retailer.
- The need to recognize the ability of consumer engagement to generate consumer recommendations and subsequent evangelism.
- The need to recognize the ability of consumer engagement to increase feedback for the company with regard to consumer preferences and expectations. This can subsequently be used to forecast the consumer demand and reactions to products.
- The need to appreciate the changing climate of trust and influence by peers on consumer behaviour.
- The growth of networks, such as Facebook, with regard to their ability to direct traffic to retailer websites. Every time a user interacts with a brand on Facebook, that activity is displayed in the newsfeed of their Facebook friends. This is viral distribution and generates referral traffic that has the potential to create a significant network effect.
- The need to recognize the ability of the online networks as tools for brand positioning.

SOCIAL PLUG-INS AND THEIR CONTRIBUTION TO MARKETING

Social plug-in is the new contribution of the world of technology to the world of marketing.

A social plug-in is a widget that can be added to a website to extend the benefits of online marketing beyond a social networking space. Companies like Facebook are offering social plug-ins to marketers to extend their Facebook marketing efforts beyond Facebook. This is a method of getting more marketing ROI out of the Facebook marketing initiative on a company's own website. Facebook currently offers 11 plug-ins. These are the *Like* button, the *Send* button, the *Comments* box, the *Activity* feed, the *Recommendations* plug-in, the *Like* box, the *Subscribe* button, the *Registration* plug-in, the *Login* button, *Facepile* plug-in and *Livestream*. Several product brands are now using these plug-ins, for instance, the Like button on their organizational webpage or corporate

> **EXHIBIT 10.4 Volkswagen–Das Auto—Positioning VW as the *People's car***
>
> Volkswagen is using Pinterest, the social bookmarking site, in order to expand its customer base. The main strategy of using Pinterest is to enhance customer engagement through its 25 boards, each aimed at different customer segments. Volkswagen has created various boards such as *VW Stories, VW Inspired, VW Road to happiness*, and *VW was there* in order to create a virtual community of Volkswagen customers and enthusiasts who can share their experiences, desires, expectations, and perceptions with regard to the VW brand. This instills a sense of belongingness to the group and reinforces brand loyalty.
>
> The company also hosts boards such as *VW enthusiasts*, VW concept cars, and VW owners targeted at consumers of the product brand, car buffs, and industry experts. These boards are meant to share the latest brand models and their concept cars. This forum brings together VW owners and instills a sense of pride in them. Efforts like these spread an indirect message that VW customers are special and the brand cares for them in a special way. The company has aligned all its boards to sync with its tagline *Das Auto*—promoting the brand as a *People's car*.

blog or news site. Hence, if a consumer likes a brand's content, they can *Like* it or *Share* it using a Facebook or Twitter plug-in.

Functions of social plug-ins are as follows:

- They drive deeper engagement with customers.
- The plug-ins can be used by other websites to provide people with personalized and social experiences. When one interacts with social plug-ins, they share their experiences with their friends and others on the sites.
- Users of a product or brand website can comment on the posts hosted there using comment plug-ins or even embed a public post from a post on, say Facebook, to any blog or website. The user can also share the comment on Facebook to post to their own wall and in their friends' streams.
- Users can give personalized suggestions for pages on product sites, based on what people are sharing.
- They give prominence to socially relevant articles tailored for each visitor with the activity feed plug-in. Activity feed displays the most interesting recent activity taking place on a site so that people can see what their friends are reading, sharing, and liking.

ONLINE SHOPPING IN THE ERA OF SOCIAL NETWORKING

Online shopping has evolved. It is true that the consumer has changed. At the same time, it is important to understand and integrate the following:

- The intricacies of the online medium
- The dynamics of the consumer experience
- The opportunities for online retailers in the era of technological developments

Consumers on social networks such as Facebook value the importance of social interactions on the networks more than shopping. They venture on these networks for enjoyable, social, and interactive experiences and one of them is shopping. They come to locate information and the people they 'socialize' with on these networks are rarely those who they do not know in real life. Consumers often post information on these online networks that directly or indirectly recommend products. Reasons for this range from excitement to gaining peer approval to merely showing off. Consumers who spend times on these sites often 'ask' their friends and families for advice on shopping and product issues. Most of the consumers find this advice useful.

E-retailers have a tough challenge in engaging these consumers in terms of enticing them and satisfying them through personal exchanges. The interesting development in the contemporary times is this: Consumers welcome combining social networking with online shopping.

Consumers value the online shopping experience. If they enjoy their forays and attempts at shopping, they engage in that behaviour again. Research studies pertaining to the technology acceptance model (TAM) in consumer behaviour clearly show that *perceived enjoyment, perceived ease of use*, and *perceived usefulness* are key factors that impact consumers' behaviour intention to adopt new technological innovations such as *e*-shopping in a social context. The challenge for retailers now lies in making these experiences interesting, enjoyable, useful, and easy.

Social networking sites such as Facebook allow online retailers to offer a more 'social' purchase experience, either by integrating Facebook features into their own sites or by operating within Facebook itself. As a result, retailers can commence linking fan membership with behavioural data such as consumer visit frequency and purchase details. Customers can already log onto a site using their Facebook credentials, and once they are able to pay and checkout without any other form of registration required, a dramatic enhancement in the purchase experience is significantly acquired.

It is important to understand that triggers in the form of recommendations from friends and trial of appropriate systems result in significant changes in consumer behaviour towards online shopping. This clearly suggests that marketing is really all about leveraging a consumer's social graph to sell more products. Success for online marketers will be a function of how well they are able to get consumers to engage with their products in the online domain. Searching for product information via Google is, understandably, the main means of searching for information, yet, since information from friends is trusted more, consumers often buy on the basis of friends' recommendations without realizing that they are participating in social *e*-shopping.

BUILDING CONSUMER ENGAGEMENT THROUGH CONTENT MANAGEMENT

Organizations can build relationships with their prospective and current consumers through posts on a corporate blog and encourage consumers to participate by commenting on the blog, thereby stimulating consumer involvement. By categorizing the content

> **EXHIBIT 10.5   Cinthol—Making its online presence count**
>
> *Cinthol*, a Godrej consumer product brand, has proved to be a classic example of a brand which crafted itself as an adventuresome brand in the online space. The company used its *Alive is awesome* campaign to create commercials which resonated with the consumers and generated ample excitement for the brand in the consumer mind space. Shot at different scenic locations with young people singing and bathing, the campaign generated enough interest. Cinthol subsequently made the best use of its social media accounts to promote the campaign, especially their Facebook page using a well-designed content marketing strategy. The company posted *Awesome Getaways* which featured amazing and adventurous destinations around the world. The campaign was simultaneously hosted on Twitter and generated huge consumer comments, courtesy the *#MakesMeAlive* hashtag contest where the company ran campaigns to giveaway a poster of Virat Kohli—the star of Indian cricket.
>
> A teaser film hosting Virat, the inspiring superstar, was hosted on the microsite www.cinthol.com/deo showed a tense Virat Kohli sitting in the dressing room before a match. The film ended with a simple question posed by Virat to Cinthol Deo: 'Do you know what's going on in my head?' Capitalizing on social media, the teaser phase was led by the microsite where Kohli personally responded to tons of interesting, surprising, and entertaining comments via a video in a candid tone. Within five hours of its official launch on Twitter, #InVirats Head was trending worldwide. The total reach and impressions generated by the campaign are humongous enough for the campaign to be classified as a thundering success!

posted on the blog, by classifying the same on the basis of organizational objective, the importance of the content type in building a relationship with the customer was studied. The dependency of consumer engagement on the volume of content posted by the organization was then analysed. It is important for companies to analyse the impact of content and volume of brand communication hosted in the virtual medium on the degree of consumer engagement it is able to generate.

Organizations use corporate blogs to post content for consumer consumption. Objectives range from catering to exploratory consumer browsing, aiding a consumer's quest for information, helping consumers gain access to organizational promotional campaigns to responding to controversies regarding organization/product. This creates consumer involvement with this organizational endeavour and eventually achieves consumer engagement for the organization as the consumer commences participation. Content categorization is achieved to enable organizations to post consumer-relevant content to induce greater consumer participation. Dependency analysis and regression are used to study the relationship between the volume of content posted by the organization and its ability to stimulate greater consumer engagement. This section addresses the need for hosting the appropriate content on an organizational initiative which, by matching consumer requirements, develops a relationship between the organization and consumer.

Brand Communication

Regular communication between organization and consumer reinforces organizational image and product messages, builds brand awareness and strengthens brand recall. By creating meaningful brand encounters, the consumer-brand relationship can be strengthened. When consumers are regularly in contact with a brand, they may begin to perceive it as a person, a trusted friend who is part of their everyday life. When consumers engage in a brand relationship, they begin to perceive the value related to the brand. Finally consumers who have greater expected benefits and utility from an ongoing relationship are more likely to commit to it. Having a regular touch-point to interact with the customer results in learning related to the brand and generates a positive attitude by creating a brand association. By targeting the brand image in the consumer's mind, the customer expectations and perceptions can be influenced. It is the volume and content of brand communication that are vital parameters in this context.

Need for Content Categorization

A corporate blog—*a good answer to exploratory consumer browsing*—is being heralded as a paradigm shift in the way companies interact with their consumers. While the key idea is to cater to a long-term brand impact, attracting consumers and motivating regular visits through appropriate content are the simple methodologies.

An additional tool in the company's self-presentation efforts, these blogs attempt to change the flow and balance of information and are emerging as tools for marketers that allow them to shape perceptions by presenting a unified mass market branding image, which can be confronted by a counter flow of dissenting opinions, alternative sources of information, and messages.

In this dynamic blog landscape, the typology of content which attracts greater consumer interest and generates subsequent engagement by soliciting participation and involvement through comments needs to be identified to enable organizations to post in accordance with consumer receptivity. While a corporate blog serves as an excellent value delivery vehicle, it is imperative to understand the organizational thought behind the content-creation process. Customers will devour the content only when they perceive value in the same. This can happen only when the organizational objectives for content creation match the consumer expectations at the time of contact.

Content Typologies

The content posted by an organization on a blog can be categorized into four categories (Table 10.2), which are as follows:

- *Organizational content* Organizational posts can be directed specifically towards sharing news on organizational growth, new projects and endeavours, organizational activities directed towards corporate social responsibility, employee experiences, to those talking about cultural events, awards, and other organizational achievements. The aim is to use the blog as an outreach mechanism to enhance organizational brand image and build greater respect and value for the organization.

Table 10.2 Content categorization

Organizational	Promotional	Relational	General
Posts on	Posts on	Posts on	Paste
Organizational growth	Product features	Soliciting feedback	Economic issues
Organizational culture	Product prices	Bloggers meet	New book/movie/music/jokes
CSR activities	New product	Dealer issues	Environmental issues
Organizational event	Promotional campaigns	Response to rumours/criticism	Political issues
Projects and research	Product comparisons	Controversy/media report	
Employee experiences	Product grievances	Consumer worries	
Awards	Persuasive to try product	Consumer help	
	Technological issue	Celebrations	

- *Promotional content* They include posts sharing factual data with respect to product features, prices, new products, product comparisons, promotional campaigns, and response to any product-related grievances. In addition to these, there are posts passively persuading consumers to embrace the product and those addressing technological issues.
- *Relational content* This category includes posts soliciting feedback, those addressing controversies or rumours about the organization, brand, product, or service. In addition to these, there are posts addressing dealer issues, bloggers meets, consumer worries, and those directed towards consumer redressal.

All other posts are classified under the *general category*.

Research[6] has shown some very interesting results pertaining to blogs. When the company increases posting online, the rate of consumer participation (commenting and liking) also increases. Significantly, companies such as Dell and General Motors have used blogs to interact with their consumers and build engagement. The best results are obtained with relational posts—those that develop some kind of consumer brand relationship.

The volume of the organizational efforts can stimulate consumer engagement as represented by the volume of comments on the blogs. An increased organizational effort in terms of repeated contacts with the consumer through increased number of posts in a virtual environment can create an *e*-relationship between the organization and consumer by stimulating consumer interest and achieving his/her participation by commenting on the posts hosted by the organization. Relational posts appear to induce a higher degree of consumer engagement as measured by the volume of comments on the posts, thereby indicating that organizations should host greater volume of relational posts. The content attractiveness of the relational posts (Table 10.3) appears to strike an emotional chord

Table 10.3 Analysis of posts, comments, and per post comment rate

Item	Dell	GM	Southwest	Marriott
Percentage of organizational posts to total posts	30.04	28.99	30.23	27.77
Percentage of organizational comments to total comments	6.19	15.78	19.67	20.48
Per post comment rate for organizational posts	7.34	20.06	15.89	12.43
Percentage of promotional posts to total posts	32.77	36.68	14.18	20.37
Percentage of promotional comments to total comments	34.31	44.63	26.21	15.37
Per post comment rate for promotional posts	37.3	44.83	45.13	12.72
Percentage of relational posts to total posts	32.14	20.11	37.2	30.55
Percentage of relational comments to total comments	58.58	31.06	45.73	46.51
Per post comment rate for relational posts	64.94	56.9	30.01	25.66
Percentage of general posts to total posts	5.04	14.2	18.37	21.29
Percentage of general comments to total comments	0.91	8.51	8.37	17.62
Per post comment rate for general posts	6.45	22.08	11.12	13.95

with the consumer enticing him/her to engage with the organization, thereby showing that companies can achieve success in these *e*-CRM endeavours.

The emotional appeal and immediacy generated by a relational post, especially with those responding to controversies or soliciting feedback from consumers, strike an instant chord with a consumer, enough to make him/her establish contact with a corporate blog, thus achieving engagement and exposing him/her to a wide range of brand content. Organizations aiming at soliciting consumer engagement through the virtual world should follow a consumers' cognitive thought process, his pre- and post purchase confusion and dissonance by posting content which will reassure the consumer. A regularity in posting, leading to increased consumer contacts, aids in strengthening brand recall and develops a brand relationship, thereby inducing participation and leading to consumer involvement, and an increased perception of value in the organization/product. Engagement leads to purchase intent, and brand loyalty thereby enabling the organization to achieve the twin CRM goals of customer acquisition and customer retention.

EXHIBIT 10.6 Tata Docomo on Twitter

One of the first brands that started using Twitter in a big way was telecom brand Tata Docomo with Twittcom that allowed its users to purchase packs and VAS services by sending tweets to the brand with pre-defined hashtags. Twitter is a great platform, not just for conversations, also for transactions, since a large number of youth are moving away from SMS and browsing.

Twitter can do many things for a brand as part of its business process which includes operations from creating an instantaneous feedback and sales loop to providing a real-time customization or real-time service.

Owing to the real-time nature of the medium, its ability to create positive or negative buzz cannot be undermined. However, there is immense potential as a business enabler for seeking high-quality referrals and rewarding customer loyalty.

The company also went ahead in making social networking more accessible on mobile by offering daily packs at ₹1. It launched a customer value proposition in the data domain by launching data packs that enabled Tata Docomo GSM customers to enjoy popular social networking sites with specially customized value for money plans. The Social Combo pack offered 150 MB of free Facebook, Facebook Messenger, and Twitter with a validity of 15 days. The Monthly Social Combo Pack for ₹30 offered 300 MB usage of Facebook, Twitter, and Facebook messenger.

These packs were especially useful for youngsters as well as professionals who needed to stay 'connected' constantly.

EXHIBIT 10.7 Twitter and the Indian brand Faaso's

Faaso's, the fast food chain operating in Mumbai, Pune, and Bengaluru, started taking orders through Twitter in 2011 and has over 5000 registered customers who use it regularly. It is one of the best mediums where referral really works for the brand. In an age where engagement is dropping, most chief marketing officers (CMOs) have a tough task of building and inculcating such loyal behaviour among fickle consumers.

NEED FOR GREATER ORGANIZATIONAL ADAPTABILITY

Voice of the customer (VOC) programme is being implemented across the world to drive greater consumer loyalty.[7] Net promoter score or NPS is one significant tool being used by companies to study the VOC. However, it is more than just identifying who loves an organization and who hates the organization and ranking them accordingly. It is about finding out why customers feel and react the way they do. This intelligence allows companies to improve the customer experience, create more relevant and successful products, and build loyalty.

Companies are now developing ways to track or analyse the customer experience through better analysis and integration of customer data.

FINDING TOP LOYALTY DRIVERS

The key to better analytics is the ability to unearth the loyalty drivers that will have the greatest impact on business performance. This not only means gaining 'quick wins' with one customer at a time but also with structural improvements that have significant, long-term influence on customer loyalty. There are several approaches to identify these areas for improvement, which are as follows:

Today's technology makes collecting, analysing, and disseminating customer comments easier and faster. These systems are able to aggregate and categorize customers in terms of their open-ended ideas, issues, and comments by frequency. However, comment analysis by frequency alone is not the strongest indication of customer loyalty drivers.

Another technique that captures customer top-of-mind ideas is idea ranking. Several companies are using this in their online communities with features that allow visitors to post a suggestion and click to vote on what others have submitted. However, there are potential traps with popularity ranking. For one, there is an inherent bias to go along with the crowd. And, like categorization by frequency, what's popular does not necessarily equate to what's most important to the customer and his/her loyalty.

An innovative approach designed to discover the root cause of loyalty and prioritize opportunities is called as *adaptive conversation*, a Darwinian process that works in sequence to identify and/or validate not just the most frequent and popular ideas, also the ones that are most important to loyalty behaviours namely, purchases and referrals (Fig. 10.4).

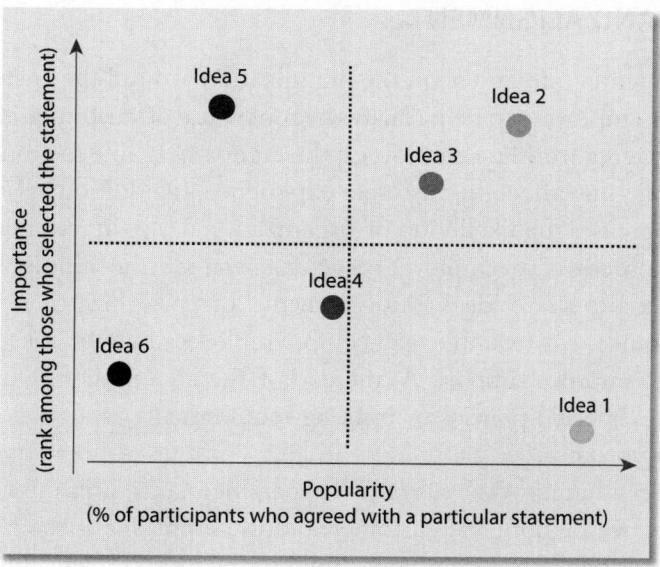

Fig. 10.4 Adaptive conversation® chart

Take, for example, a cookware manufacturer looking to launch a new line of pots and pans. Customers may select offering them in new colours as the most frequent as well as top-ranked popular idea. However, does that mean it is an important factor in the customer's purchasing decision?

Adaptive conversation begins with profiling questions to facilitate customer segmentation and a 'focal question' that allows participants to select ideas 'seeded' by the brand and contribute their own ideas. Once this is completed, respondents are then asked to vote on the most frequently mentioned ideas, which are rotated for each visitor to reduce bias. The most popular ones rise to the top of the list and the unpopular ones go into extinction.

Using the cookware example, the focal question would ask customers to select which new features they would like. The majority of them selected new colours, clear tops, and lighter weight from among the seeded ideas, but many of them also added ergonomic handles. When they ranked the three ideas by popularity, colour ranked first; followed closely by ergonomic handles with lighter weight a distant third.

Customers are then asked to rank order their favourite ideas in terms of how likely they are to purchase the products with given features. Ideas are netted together and prioritized. The results of this process enable brands to assess ideas based on both popularity and importance. From the profile data, you can dig deeper by prioritizing the ideas based on customer segmentation (e.g., lifetime value, geography, promoters, detractors, etc.).

In the cookware example, the company discovers that ergonomic handles is both a popular and important idea among the masses and thus becomes a top priority of the company. Colours, a popular idea but not as important as others, becomes a lower priority. By virtue of the adaptive conversation, the cookware manufacturer makes the decision to launch its new line of products with ergonomic handles versus new colours.

INTEGRATION AND ALIGNMENT

To fully integrate and align the organization around the customer, organizations often involve employees to help clarify the root cause of customer issues and design solutions. By engaging frontline employees, the company is able to gain relevant insight from the very folks that affect the customer experience. In addition, it brings a sense of ownership that increases the likelihood of organizational buy-in and adoption of changes.

The process of an employee *adaptive conversation* is the same as with customers. Employees are asked to share ideas and comments and prioritize them based on popularity and importance. For example, call centre employees may be asked to share their insight on ways to improve support. At the end of the idea process, employees may help identify issues in specific policies or training requirements as a result of analysis of popularity and importance.

Understanding the customer experience and areas for improvement from the perspective of both the customer and the employee is the key to increasing customer loyalty. While many companies understand this concept, finding a way to easily and effectively identify the root cause of dissatisfaction and prioritize action is a challenge.

As companies look for ways to improve the customer experience and respond to the voice of the customer, they will benefit from a comprehensive analysis of the root cause of customer loyalty that includes *adaptive conversation* to prioritize actions. By identifying inherent causes and closing the loop with customers, companies can greatly improve the customer experience, resulting in improved retention, repurchase, and referrals. (*Source*: www.customerthink.com.)

EXHIBIT 10.8   HSBC and the virtual world

Instead of relying on existing social media platforms, HSBC, Hong Kong launched its own platform hkYFi.com.hk in June 2010 to target the Gen Y market. The portal builds on the habits of Gen Y and serves as an innovative knowledge-based platform to enable learning, sharing, and interacting with peers and financial experts through the use of social media and content geared towards Gen Y interests.

The platform offers blogs by celebrities and financial gurus, a talk show, question and answer, and financial news and games to engage the target segment. The idea was to get influencers, such as celebrities, bloggers, and financial gurus to share their views and experiences on financial management to raise awareness among the target segment. The platform was built in an interactive way, allowing members to chat with those influencers and incentivizing them to create user-generated content through interactive activities, such as Y backpacker, Y manifesto, Y debate, and offering prizes for sharing travel budget plans, concert tickets, or cash coupons. The platform was intended to promote free and open discussion, and the bank monitored the content 24/7 for abusive content, which could be removed if necessary.

The bank also involved representatives of the target segment to support the development of the social media strategy, banking services, the hkYFi.com.hk portal, campus activities, and Gen Y banking products and services in the form of a summer internship programme called the 'Gen Y ambassadors programme'. The new hkYFi.com.hk portal was viewed over 1.16 million times and attracted over 5,13,000 visits, building on a basis of over 28,000 registered users. The adaptation of Gen Y to this new way of financial education is reflected in over 200 questions received at the expert corner. The target segment also responded positively to the new strategy resulting in customer growth and double-digit growth in Gen Y cards and accounts.

CASE STUDY   Personal Care Brands and the Indian Consumer

India is characterized by an unusually large population. This represents a wide range of consumers in the personal care products section. These consumers are very sensitive to their personal needs, and the Internet is further sensitizing them to the need for greater self-care, the world of glamour and self-indulgence. An unusually high degree of Internet savviness, a desire to stay in line with current trends, and their inherent propensity to compare products, makes these consumers attractive for brands. Subsequently, the concerned organizations are aggressively targeting the consumers in the online space.

Online Brand Presence

The personal care brand sector (Fig. 10.5) makes great use of Facebook and Twitter for social media, in India.

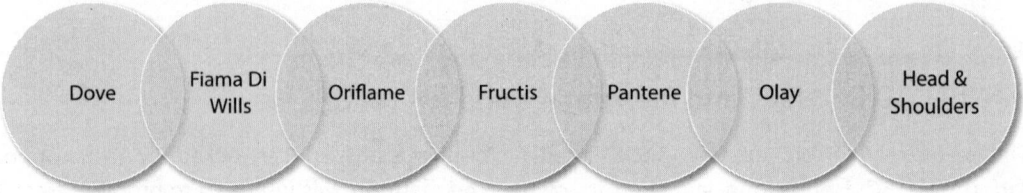

Fig. 10.5 Personal care brands

All the brands are significantly active on Facebook and post regularly to create a community of enthusiasts who can bond over personal care and beauty tips. Maintaining strong images of women, and pictures of people happily pampering themselves have made Facebook pages witness a high consumer engagement growth rate.

Olay has a very successful presence on Facebook with each of its posts garnering over 10,000 likes. With Olay Beauty projects and contests, the page is characterized by a large number of videos which are extremely popular and bear testimony to consumer satisfaction with Olay.

Pantene promotes a fun-filled environment with communities like *Let us Unfrustrate* allowing groups of females to bond together. With live chats and hair care contests, the page hosts information about latest trends for youngsters, which keeps them coming back for more.

Dove is committed to help all women realize their personal beauty potential by creating products that deliver real care. The company has the largest online community of consumers with over 22 million users considering its frequent trysts with the viral world, consumer co-creation endeavours, and consumer involvement. With an overwhelmingly female audience, most brands post female-centric content ranging from make-up tips, hair styles, and fashion along with several contests to engage with the audience. Product description and details comprise the primary content strategy in the content posted by all the brands.

Content Strategy for Consumer Engagement

- The content strategy for Facebook clearly aims at building consumer knowledge about the brands, followed by a relationship building endeavour by appearing to be emotionally sensitive brands, providing service to the consumer.
- The virtual world clearly aims at enriching the brand experience by helping to integrate real world brands into the lifestyles of the users.
- As people turn to social media, for product recommendations, and listening to the opinions of others, they are also forming networks based on shared interests and tastes. These networks gradually form homogeneous groups.

Benefits to Companies

Word-of-mouth (WOM) conversations stimulate online influence. They also provide companies with valuable feedback. Channelizing this feedback aids better decision making.

Most of the consumers, in their subconscious minds, feel that they will be rewarded (in some form or the other), for being a friend of the brand. This actually works for most of the companies who use their Facebook pages to identify customers for Reward and Sampling programmes.

Companies understand the need for integrating their marketing efforts and bring in the rest of the brand's marketing channels into the mix to maximize total reach and to bridge online and offline brand experiences.

The focus is clearly on *Engagement* and *Community*, not on *Sales*.

Questions:

1. Conduct a qualitative study using a focus group of participants to understand how consumers make decisions with regard to personal care brands.
2. What role can the virtual world play in influencing these decisions?

PRACTITIONER PERSPECTIVE

Digital allows very effective and tighter targeting of a message to a consumer. If you think simplistically about men and women, in TV advertising that is going to everybody, you can much more carefully target content to a recipient in a digital environment.

Jon Moeller, Chief Finance Officer, P&G

Digital is high priority for us given that our products are targeted at younger people.

Chandramouli Venkatesan, Director, Snacking & Strategy, Cadbury India

Consumers engaged in the digital medium are far bigger consumers of our brand than those exposed to TV.

Sapan Sharma, Category Head, Ice creams, Hindustan Unilever

In the absence of product news, the digital medium helps in keeping the buzz alive.

Shyam Narayan, DGM, Marketing, Two-wheelers, Bajaj Auto

We understand the importance of online research and we leverage that through digital marketing.

Arvind Saxena, Director, Sales & Marketing, Hyundai

SUMMARY

Information overload in the Internet age can force people to become passive receptors of information. It is hence important for an organization to make sure that the right information reaches the right people at the right time. A higher perceived value by the consumer in the organizational information will stimulate consumer interest leading to a desire to interact, achieving 'engagement' from the organizational perspective. Each customer touch-point has a significant role to play in the consumer life cycle by influencing the customer experience. The customer experience does not begin and end at a transaction, website visit, or conversation with an agent. The customer experience process encompasses the moment the customer becomes aware of the organization, products or services comprising multiple independent interactions, transactions, and contacts along the way. Consumer engagement can be defined as the repeated interactions that strengthen the emotional, psychological, or physical investment a customer has made in a brand. Engagement marketing, sometimes called 'experiential marketing', 'event marketing', 'live marketing', or 'participation marketing', is a marketing strategy that directly engages consumers and invites and encourages consumers to participate in the evolution of a brand. As it is very clear that the virtual world is being increasingly used by companies to build consumer engagement, it becomes important to understand the factors contributing to consumer engagement. While it is difficult for organizations to qualify the time that a consumer spends in the virtual world; nevertheless, attempts are being made to study and analyse the consumer visit in terms of how engaged they are. The purchase of goods from online stores is now a mainstream activity globally. Increasingly, online retailers are offering interactive features to engage customers and encourage them to buy. These include rating and review systems, product video, virtual assistants, 3D modelling, or barcode scanners for smart phones (onsite social commerce). Hence, *e*-retailers should focus on engaging consumers through the virtual medium. Three issues are now significant for *e*-retailers, which are as follows:

- The extent to which consumers are incorporating recommendations and purchase activity into their social networking behaviour,
- The changing climate of trust and influence upon consumer behaviour,
- Efforts by online retailers to become more social. Consumers on social networks, like Facebook, value the importance of social interactions on the networks more than shopping, and *e*-retailers have a tough challenge in engaging these consumers in terms of enticing them and satisfying them through personal exchanges.

Consumers welcome combining social networking with online shopping. These consumers value the online shopping experience.

Concept Review Questions

1. What is engagement marketing? How can companies use the tools offered by the virtual world for engagement marketing?
2. Explain Ghuneim's typology of engagement. Use examples.
3. What parameters help companies in measuring the level of consumer engagement in the virtual world?
4. Write a short note on *adaptive conversation*.

Critical Thinking Questions

1. Compare and contrast the type of content being hosted on the blogs of two Indian organizations. Do a qualitative analysis to identify the type of content that is able to garner the maximum number of comments and views.
2. Identify an organization which is using a corporate blog, Facebook, and Twitter, for building engagement with its consumers in the virtual space. Compare the type of content hosted by the company in the three disparate virtual media.
3. Study the blog of Dominos, India. How is Dominos using different types of content to practise engagement marketing?
4. Study the use of social media and disparate virtual tools in the Indian Elections, 2014. Identify one political party or candidate who used this medium to build a brand for them by using specific content to drive voter engagement.

Practising Digital Marketing

1. Go to www.facebook.com/pages/create/
2. Create a page on Facebook, as a
   (a) Local business,
   (b) Company/organization/institution,
   (c) Product or brand,
   (d) Artist, band, or public figure,
   (e) Entertainment, OR
   (f) Cause or community.
3. As a college student, you can create a page for any college event. Maintain the page for at least six months. Illustrate the following:
   (a) What type of content increases traffic on the page? and
   (b) What type of content helps you 'engage' with your audience?

References

1. Ron Shevlin, author of *Everything They've Told You About Marketing Is Wrong* and an analyst at Aite Group, LLC.
2. The Forrester Customer Engagement Framework, Forrester, 2007.
3. Ghuneims, M., Typology of Engagement, Wiredset, 2007.
4. Cummings, M.N., Consumer engagement perspectives: A tool for ensuring advertising's impact? *Dissertation*, Rochester Institute of Technology, 2007.
5. Dwyer, P., (2007). 'Building Trust with Corporate Blogs', International Conference on Weblogs and Social Media, <http://www.icwsm.org/papers/2–Dwyer.pdf>, last accessed on 24 October, 2007.
6. Ahuja, V. and Medury, Y., (2010). 'Corporate blogs as *e*-CRM tools–Building consumer engagement through content management'. *Journal of Database Marketing and Customer Strategy Management*, Vol. 17(2), pp. 91–105.
7. Eastman, D., Satmetrix, Customer Think, 2009.

11 Online Campaign Management

> **LEARNING OBJECTIVES**
> *After reading this chapter, you will be able to:*
> - Understand the concept of campaign management
> - Appreciate the characteristics of a good campaign management solution
> - Study how companies are using Facebook, Twitter, and corporate blogs for campaign management

A lot has been said about the usage of varied tools in the online space to build brand presence, increase visibility, and build consumer engagement. Of significance for an organization, is the ability to build a virtual presence and then leverage it to enhance the productivity and efficiency of its marketing efforts.

This chapter profiles the world of online campaign management using Facebook, Twitter, and corporate blogs. Virtual campaign management for Facebook and Twitter has been addressed using two tools for campaign automation. Subsequently, a case study demonstrates how a blog can be used for online campaign management.

WHAT IS CAMPAIGN MANAGEMENT?

Marketing automation is the backbone of creating customized organizational campaigns, which are automated, traceable, and easy-to-repeat processes, thereby providing to the marketing function a campaign which is more targeted to the right consumer base. More important to marketing is the measurement of performance after a campaign is over. Analytical abilities in campaign management tools help organizations turn insights into competitive advantage. Meaningful customer dialogue can be subsequently converted into long-term loyalty by organizations. Companies can assess customer profitability; create highly accurate retention, cross-sell/up-sell, and response models(Fig. 11.1).

The process of campaign management helps organizations to streamline product mixes and next-best offers, and communicate more effectively with customers. This subsequently results in better consumer response rates and improved ROI.

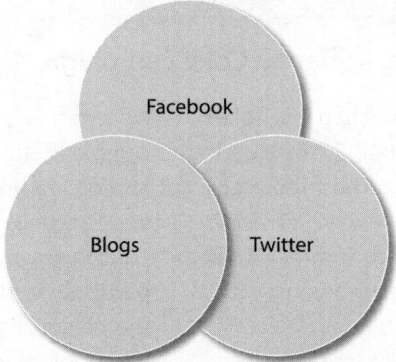

Fig. 11.1 Campaign management in the virtual world

The online social data are channelized through superior data quality processes, de-duplication, standardization, cleansing, and appending, resulting in a complete customer profile that powers more efficient marketing programmes.

A good campaign management solution offers the following:

- *Usability*   Straightforward navigation, intuitive search capabilities, effortless information sharing, and easy reuse of treatments, campaign components, etc.
- *Embedded data management*   Addresses every aspect of managing customer data—from extract, transform, load (ETL) to data quality.
- *Unmatched analytics*   Includes multiple methods for campaign and component testing, as well as analytically based clustering, segmentation, modelling, and priority optimization.
- *Painless integration and customization*   Includes a common, open data model, and custom node functionality for creating custom processes and selecting data attributes.
- *Targeted segmentation and cross-channel execution*
- *Real-time interaction management*
- *Superior operational reporting*

In the online domain, companies will benefit by performing a careful analysis of customer habits and preferences. Customer experiences need to be integrated across channels with graphically rich interfaces. As customers move across online, mobile, and social channels, organizations can build individual profiles that capture their interests, activities, and interactions. This subsequently helps marketing in creating more relevant marketing experiences.

It is in better-targeted segmentation and cross-channel execution that companies will be able to leverage the benefits offered by the virtual medium and subsequently enhance marketing productivity.

In the following sections we will see how organizations are using Facebook, Twitter, and corporate blogs for campaign management, by analysing specific tools and tracing case studies.

EXHIBIT 11.1 The Coke—Share a Coke campaign

The *Share a Coke* campaign launched by Coke was created by Ogilvy and Mather, Sydney, and was launched in Australia in 2012. The integrated campaign was launched in Britain on 29 April 2013 and ran until the end of the summer. The soft drink giant replaced its usual branding with 150 of the UK's most popular names. It was a multimedia effort, with TV adverts, billboards, and experiential marketing in the form of Coca Cola 'tours' where participants could have their own custom bottle made. Each bottle also carried the hashtag #shareacoke to encourage users to share bottles with their names, as well as those of friends and family, using social media.

The summer of 2013 saw a flurry of activity down the supermarket drink aisles, across the USA. Adults and children alike scrambled through stacks of Coca Cola, all eager to grab a bottle bearing their name. It seemed like almost everyone was sucked in by the *Share a Coke campaign* which exploded across Facebook, Twitter, and TV advertising.

The campaign had three unique selling propositions (USPs), which are as follows:

- A unique approach to *personalization*. People loved that this campaign spoke to them directly by using their names, or those of their friends and family.

Fig. 11.2 Share a Coke

- A *dynamic* nature which enabled the campaign to cut across multiple mutually-reinforcing mediums, including TV, Twitter, and Facebook.
- The *participative* element of the campaign, particularly because of sharing images of the personalized Coke bottles on Twitter and Facebook, made them feel more connected to the brand and to one another.

YouGov used actual exposure which came from panellists who completed daily media consumption surveys, allowing YouGov to access their social media feeds and let it track their Web behaviour. Brand perception came from its daily BrandIndex survey—monitoring views on over 900 brands across 15 metrics each day.

Combining the two meant YouGov could accurately assess the impact of the campaign and understand the impact of each element. In this case, it looked at the impact of TV, Twitter, and Facebook by taking those exposed on each platform and assessing how their perceptions of Coca Cola compared to matched samples that were not exposed.

YouGov focused on the following four measures that were most relevant to the aims of the Share a Coke campaign:

- *Buzz* Over the *past two weeks*, which of the following brands have you heard something *positive/negative* about (whether in the news, through advertising, or talking to friends and family)?
- *Impression* Which of the following brands do you have a generally *positive/negative* feeling about?
- *Recommendation* Which of the following brands would you *recommend*/tell a friend to *avoid*?
- *Consideration* When you are in the market next to make a purchase, which brands would you consider?

(*Continued*)

Results

TV

Consumer perception of Coca Cola, Diet Coke, and Coke Zero improved substantially on virtually every measure for those who were exposed to Share a Coke TV adverts. The uplift in perception for Diet Coke and Coke Zero was slightly more modest than for Coca Cola, but still impressive. The data show that 18–24-year-olds who were exposed to the campaign view the brand much more positively than those who were not exposed to the adverts.

Social media

As with those who had seen the TV advertisements, respondents who were exposed to the campaign on social media had a substantially better view of Coca Cola than the nationally representative sample. Consumers who had seen the TV adverts and those exposed to #shareacoke on Twitter experienced a similar uplift in consumer perception. However, the consumers who were exposed to the campaign on Facebook showed the most dramatic improvement in how they perceive Coca Cola, Diet Coke, and Coke Zero (up to 18%).

What can other brands learn?

Share a Coke has emerged as one of the most compelling campaigns in the recent history. The overarching theme that gave *Share a Coke* its edge is the way a brand reached out to consumers and spoke to people as individuals.

- The campaign showed that when personalization works it can be highly engaging and effective.
- Another element for marketers to consider is that in the world of social media, personalization only works if it is something that can be shared with the wider community. This campaign provides people with a reason to share, but one that users can choose to do in their own way—there is a choice, it is customized and left up to individuals to be creative in how and when they use it.

The analysis process

The market research agency combined data sets covering media consumption, brand perception surveys, and social media exposure, to understand whether some consumers were being influenced by the campaign even if they did not necessarily remember seeing one of the TV adverts or posts on Twitter and Facebook. The agency could also analyse which elements of the campaign were working the hardest.

While Share a Coke was extremely effective across all mediums, the greatest benefit emerged on Facebook, where several Coke fans were already hooked onto the medium.

(Reproduced with permission from www.thedrum.com)

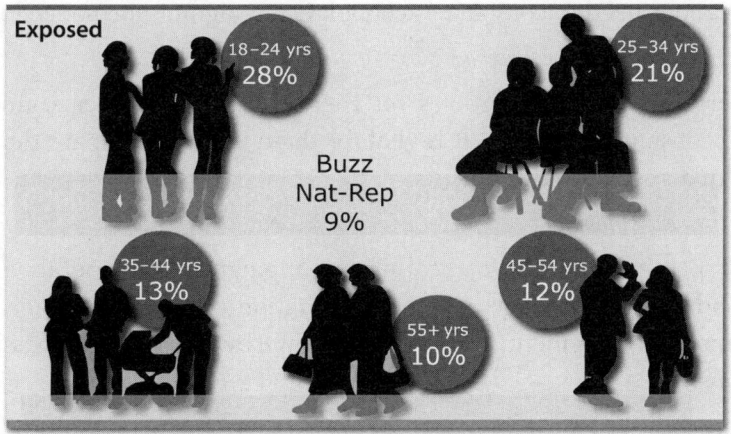

Fig. 11.3 The consumer profile

CAMPAIGN MANAGEMENT USING FACEBOOK

When a company runs a new campaign, it runs it across a diverse set of media. What is required now is to ensure the following:

- Measure the success of the campaign
- Identify the media that was most successful

The following section profiles a tool, Qwaya.com, which is being used by companies to optimize their campaigns and enhance productivity in the online space, using Facebook as a means.

Companies need to optimize campaigns by scheduling the campaign running times, automating campaigns with rules and synchronizing with Google analytics. Companies need to boost their productivity by creating new Facebook Ad variations, saving ad campaigns in templates and organizing ad campaigns.

Tools such as Qwaya allow organizations to connect their campaigns completely from Facebook.

Integrating the campaign management efforts of an organization using Facebook includes the following actions:

- *Collection of Facebook assets*

Companies can collect all their Facebook assets by connecting multiple Facebook user accounts, thereby maintaining all their ad accounts, pages, Apps, and events in one place.

- *Using Google analytics*

Companies can subsequently use Google analytics to track campaign and ad performance on any key performance indicators (KPI) such as goals, conversions, transactions, or revenue.

- *Comparison of Facebook campaign performance*

Organizations need to compare Facebook Campaign performance to other channels.

- *Use consumer profiles on Facebook*

Marketers use consumer profiles on Facebook for consumer segmentation and well directed consumer targeting. It is vital for them later, to compare the performance of a campaign across various segments.

- *Advertisement planning*

A lot of planning goes into creating a campaign. It is imperative for organizations to find out, at a later stage, which combination of text and image make up the best performing advertisement, and save lots of time by generating all possible advertisement variations.

- *Adplacements*

In addition to understand all sorts of ad types and placements, including news feed ads for an organizational website and mobile App install ads are of significance.

Companies which use *Facebook marketing* and *Facebook advertising* to drive business, through direct response or branding can improve ROI and productivity in the following ways:

- Optimizing Facebook advertising workflow by using templates. Companies can use software tools to save ads and target audiences in templates to streamline their workflow. This way they do not have to do the same thing again and again.
- Companies can structure their work in dedicated folders—this saves a lot of time when they need to keep campaigns separated for different markets or product categories or just want to keep the clutter away to focus on *e*-Facebook ad campaign at a time.
- Graphical reporting can give companies quick overviews of their campaign performance and help in spotting trends early to optimize return. Easy drill down from campaign to ad level graphs to identify winning and losing marketing message and target audience combinations, is greatly helpful to organizations.
- Companies can run their advertisements at specific times with day parting. Hence, they can improve ROI by scheduling campaigns to run on certain days of week or time of day. They can run their ads when their campaigns are most likely to generate the response they are looking for.
- Companies can automatically pause ad spends with rules which make a campaign stop if certain criteria are met. For example, *pause the campaign if CPC exceeds* $1.
- Organizations can keep their campaigns alive by rotating the advertisements. They can make sure that the best performing ads are played by rotating the variations specified.
- Software tools can be used to streamline the campaign management function through intuitive collaboration. Effective sharing of ads, campaign, and targeting details allow all team members to contribute and reuse work done by others.

CAMPAIGN MANAGEMENT USING TWITTER

EXHIBIT 11.2 AmEx—Building payments on Facebook and consumer engagement on Twitter

AmEx is venturing into daily deals business, striking a deal with Facebook that allows AmEx cardholders to link their cards to their Facebook accounts. Once they do so they will get a dashboard of deals from brands such as Whole Foods, Dunkin' Donuts, Virgin America, and Sports Authority. Unlike Groupon or Living Social, these AmExdeals do not require anyone to pre-purchase the deal or present coupons at the merchants. The Facebook twist is that the deals are influenced by what customers and their friends 'like' using the Facebook like button.

The AmEx platform illustrates a big difference in business model. Groupon and other daily deal providers make their money on one-time deals with merchants. Whereas a considerable amount of those one-time deals is bad for businesses, AmEx is building a long-term relationship with the merchant that pays off over time. This allows AmEx to drive traffic onto its network for existing merchants over VISA and MasterCard, providing a clear differentiator to encourage new merchant accounts and encouraging new cardholders. The merchant benefits as AmEx only earns on the payments transaction fees, but not the deal itself such as Groupon.

Merchants also benefit from analytics that AmEx can provide, because it processes all the transactions through its network and therefore tracks metrics such as total spend. Tracking beyond initial sales of offers is another significant area where Groupon and Google offers fall short. Analytics also has high potential for the future for services using transaction history, for targeted marketing, or rewards programmes. With transaction history, merchants could better target card members, only targeting those who are really interested in an offer sorted by criteria such as preference, location, or overall spending. Membership rewards integration allows consumers to redeem points at any merchant on the AmEx network, similar to the way in which consumers can redeem points for Amazon purchases.

Generally, AmEx is worth looking at for its use of social media. Besides the most popular Twitter account in the financial services industry with over 1,50,000 followers to resolve anything from queries and complaints, AmEx hosts a business community called Open Forum on its website enabling businesses to connect and collaborates well as source for new ideas. The community offers tools such as the 'ConnectodexSM', which can help generate new leads by intelligently matching businesses with similar needs and interests or 'Idea Hub', a digital trading post of ideas and insights from industry experts and owners. The community is fully integrated with Twitter through an embedded live feed.

(*Reproduced with permission from the* www.theasianbanker.com)

TWITTER MARKETING

Twitter marketing is a great way to advertise and promote a consistent brand image for an organization. Twitter is fast emerging as a medium where organizations can get new customers engaged with a company, by running exciting contests, special promotions and advertising events. Companies are also using Twitter to share tips or links to interesting stories to keep a consumer's Twitter feed personal and interesting.

Companies can use tools such as *Simply Cast* to aid their Twitter marketing efforts. Tools such as these help in the following ways:

- Organizations can *randomize* the time of day that their tweets are posted, so that they appear more organic. Tweets can be designed to automatically target specific audiences based on age, gender, and location, by making the Twitter feed more engaging to an organization's followers by making it more personalized and relevant.
- Companies can create *interesting* posts which are up to date with trending topics, current Twitter trends, and industry news, and bring in consumers to share their experiences and personal testimonials, thereby creating a climate of trust and subsequently building consumer engagement by responding and appreciating the participating consumers.
- Companies can use software tools for *tweet scheduling*—schedule multiple or single tweets, repeat the same tweet at specific intervals and even make their tweets seem less automated with organic tweet timing, thereby keeping their Twitter feed updated and fresh.

- Companies can manage multiple Twitter accounts and tweet from a single account for better campaign management, switch between accounts, and view recent activity across all other accounts. This serves as a useful mechanism for large corporations with several departments, where multiple accounts can be used for different functions or products.
- Companies can follow other organizations and study their own reports to identify the most performing tweets which garnered the maximum number of followers or re-tweets.

EXHIBIT 11.3 Automobile companies in India—Driving online campaign management

Audi

A twitter campaign by Audi, India was hosted to engage with Audi fans asking them to give reasons on why they loved Audi. Fans were asked to give reasons and win attractive prizes such as iPhones, iPads, iPods, and exclusive Audi merchandise.

This subsequently evolved into a tremendous campaign as willing users participated eagerly and expressed their love for the brand. This resulted in voluminous tweets, customized videos, poetic blog posts, and a fully-fledged micro site which made #LoveAudi trend nationally (for two consecutive days) on Twitter. Audi was successfully able to use the digital medium to engage with its consumers.

Maruti

Maruti hosted several online campaigns for its car brand Ritz

Ritz *Moment of the Day*—the brand philosophy of *Live the Moment* was taken forward on the virtual space by creation of an online site called Ritz *Moment of the Day*. Consumers were asked to participate and share interesting stories and pictures regarding the most significant moment of their day. The most engaging story of the day was adjudged the *Moment of the Day* by means of polling by the fans themselves. This ongoing initiative gained huge popularity amongst Ritz's consumers. The success of the online campaign flowed into the next level by creation of the Ritz 'Moment of the Year'.

Ritz also hosted another online campaign called the 'Live the moment' contest—Ritz users were invited to share their driving experiences on an interactive website. The best entry was awarded a brand new Ritz. It was the first time that a car was given away as a prize in India through Facebook. The contest saw participation of around 49,000 stories being shared by Ritz owners and the consumer generated content was further used to build a national brand campaign on magazine media.

CAMPAIGN MANAGEMENT USING CORPORATE BLOGS

Organizations use blogs for campaign management, by using the organizational posts for delivery of promotional campaigns to consumers, and further by extracting consumer related information from the comments posted by consumers in response to these posts.

The consumer comments can be mined to gauge consumer sentiment and to serve as a decision support system for better segmentation and response management. This case study traces the usage of a corporate blog as a customer relationship management (CRM) tool, to be utilized for contributing to the CRM functionalities of campaign management, customer service and support, and support to marketing communication, and product development for aiding the organization in developing consumer targeting strategies appropriately.

Corporate blogs are frequently utilized by organizations for increasing the perceived value of the consumers by showcasing organizational, product and brand related achievements, thereby enhancing the brand image, aiding consumer learning, and also serving as a useful touch-point to enhance the consumer–brand relationship. Usage of posts on corporate blogs to apprise consumers of new promotional campaigns and product launches is fast becoming a useful marketing and CRM strategy. Consumers can use the comments feature to voice product or service related complaints thereby increasing consumer involvement. These can be subsequently practiced by the organization.

Consumer related information can be extracted from the comments posted by consumers in response to an organizational post on a corporate blog. The consumer responses, namely consumer comments can be aggregated using tags and folksonomies and further mined to gauge consumer sentiment and to serve as a decision support system for better segmentation and response management. Consumer responses can be subsequently categorized and redirected to the CRM functionalities of campaign management, customer service and support, and support to marketing communication and product development.

The dictionary meaning of a blog is a frequent, chronological publication of personal thoughts and links. As millions of people use blogs as personal diaries on the Internet, they are emerging as collaborative spaces that can be put to multiple uses and have emerged as the latest mode of computer mediated communication. This concept has found widespread acceptance in the corporate world with the emergence of 'corporate' or 'organizational' blogs. These are people who blog in an official or semi-official capacity at a company, or are so affiliated with the company where they work that even though they are not officially spokespeople for the company, they are clearly affiliated and endorsed explicitly or implicitly by the company. In addition to being termed as a hybrid of the personal blog, they are increasingly being explored by public relations practitioners and feature the insights, assessments, commentary, and other discourse devoted to a single company. Organizational blogs have evolved from both online and offline modes of communication and have characteristics of both personal and professional communication. An effective blog fosters community and conversation, drives traffic to the product website, and serves as a medium for interaction with consumers thereby shaping consumer perception, eliciting responses, and through a two way thought exchange process, aids in fostering a connection with the consumers *External* corporate blogs are primarily tools used by organizations to interact with consumers, partners, marketing intermediaries, associates, and components of the external environment, namely media, government agencies, and other general bodies. They offer a more up-to-date view of the organization as compared to other traditional communication channels. Tapping into this new channel to listen to and interact with their customers requires new initiatives from corporations. They further provide a tremendous opportunity for forward-thinking companies and management to have a significant positive impact on their public perception. Launching a corporate brand blog is representative of an organizational desire to share information and engage in a conversation. This is especially true when the blog allows visitors to post their own comments. The informality of communication helps companies build trust, converse with people and even manage public perception by posting suitable responses. The ability of a blog to induce consumer participation by making consumers comment on the posts hosted by the organization creates a dialogue and helps the organization achieve consumer engagement. By further varying the content typologies, organizations can engage in maintaining good consumer relationships by better content management.

While the ability of a blog to achieve higher volumes of engagement in terms of volume of comments is significant, of greater importance is the knowledge capital created through exchange with consumers which can be mined to extract explicit information which can be leveraged by the organization as a decision support system for consumer segmentation and strategy formulation. For the purpose of this study we focus on external blogs being used by organizations to build brand relationships with consumers and induce participation and engagement.

CUSTOMER RELATIONSHIP MANAGEMENT

(CRM), which has also been described as *information-enabled relationship marketing*, is an enterprise-wide initiative that belongs to all areas of an organization. It comprises processes used by organizations to manage consumer relationships which also include collecting, storing, and analysing data and attempts to provide a strategic bridge between IT tools and marketing strategies aimed at building long-term relationships and profitability. A blog can be used by an organization to acquire customer information and consolidating customer feedback.

Companies can use a blog to interact with customers, learn about them and through the process of incorporating feedback and co-creation, develop a level of intimacy with them. This can help improve marketing intelligence and support decision making. Consumer specific data can help in targeting the appropriate set of consumers with the appropriate marketing campaigns. This consumer data can be obtained by analysis of consumer generated content on a blog, in the form of comments.

TAGGING AND FOLKSONOMIES

The emergence of new communication models resulting in increased informational and exchange needs, and the availability of incredible amounts of distributed information that can be linked, aggregated, and organized in order to extract knowledge, has created the need to structure this information to derive meaning. Folksonomies attempt to provide a solution to this issue by introducing an innovative distributed approach based on social classification,[1] hence, addressing these web-specific classification issues. Folksonomy (also known as collaborative tagging, social classification, social indexing, and social tagging) is the practice and method of collaboratively creating and managing tags to categorize content. *Folksonomy* describes the bottom-up classification systems that emerge from social tagging.[2] Tags are created with the intent of signifying or suggesting concepts that are potentially or accompanying or associated with possible content ontology. If consumers can be allowed to tag their comments, a better aggregation of user generated information can be achieved to serve as an aid in response modelling. This requires consumers to associate keywords with content. The best judge of classification of one's comment under a blog post would be the consumer himself, who can tag his comment with the closest possible option of consumer segmentation available from an organization specified list. Tags are inexpensive, scalable, and very near the language and mental mode of the users. If consumers tag the comments themselves, relevance and consistency of the relation of the content in the comment to the tag will be greater. Problems pertaining to lack of terminological control in the tags can be omitted by allowing consumers to choose from a predefined list only. Grouping tags under folksonomies related to consumer liking, satisfaction, and involvement, aids data redirection to respective CRM functionalities. Further, a quantitative tag analysis can help explain the dominant consumer viewpoint.

CAMPAIGN MANAGEMENT

Some functions performed by a campaign management solution include the following:
- Segmentation of customers
- Developing, targeting, and positioning strategies for each segment
- Defining customer requirements
- Implementing communication strategies to build brand awareness generate interest and motivate purchase[3]

Often, due to lack of data regarding the consumer sentiment for the organization and its products, organizations resort to blanket promotions for their consumers, thereby not matching the true consumer expectations. CRM entails constant integration of marketing, sales, and service activities, and applying customer knowledge to continuously improve performance.[4] A corporate blog can be used to increase the knowledge and understanding of customers,[5] and can be utilized for campaign management[6] by segmenting groups of customers (and prospective customers) into smaller groups by identifying and understanding unique customer patterns and then specifying the interaction that should take place with those individuals, by creation of customized offers.

SENTIMENT MINING

Sentiment mining is a computational approach used to identify expressions made about topics within a span of text.[7] With the growing availability and popularity of opinion-rich resources such as online review sites and personal blogs, new opportunities and challenges arise as people now can, and do, actively use information technologies to seek out and understand the opinions of others. The sudden eruption of activity in the area of opinion mining and sentiment analysis, which deals with the computational treatment of opinion, sentiment, and subjectivity in text, has thus occurred at least in part as a direct response to the surge of interest in new systems that deal directly with opinions as a first-class object.[8] Given an opinionated piece of text wherein it is assumed that the overall opinion in it is about one single issue or item, it is possible to classify the opinion as falling under one of the two opposing sentiment polarities or locate its position on the continuum between these two polarities.[9] This concept of sentiment mining is adapted for mining sentiment of consumers, as represented by their comments under an organizational blog post to determine positive or negative sentiment polarity.

USING CORPORATE BLOG AS A CRM 2.0 TOOL

Leveraging the Power of Folksonomies

Let us consider a system where consumers are allowed to tag their comments, from a set of organization-defined options which would enable aggregation of user-generated information to serve as an aid in better response management. The objective is to derive a model to assign each comment to a class as accurately as possible. Allowing a consumer to tag his comment will enable classification under the theme which most closely reflects the consumer intent, thereby enabling a better aggregation of content reflected in the comments section located under each blog post. A total of 24 comment typologies have been observed. A tag representing each comment typology can be created by the consumer for his comment whenever he interacts with the organization. By allowing the consumers to tag the comments, under respective categories using tags, namely liking, feedback, appreciation, praise, happiness, approval, anger, disappointment, etc., better content aggregation is possible (Table 11.1).

Further, it is possible to identify sentiment-bearing words depicting respective sentiments, from consumer comments posted under the blog posts hosted by the organization.

Clustering of these tags, using empirical methods, under folksonomies of liking, satisfaction, dissatisfaction, or involvement with the organization/product, can aid in routing comments under the tags to the respective CRM functionalities. Therefore a folksonomy can be a low-cost community option for response modelling.

The diverse comment typologies are classified into six different categories (Table 11.2)—liking, satisfaction, involvement I, involvement II, involvement III, involvement IV.

Involvements I–IV together represent various levels of consumer involvement. It is further possible to segment consumers on the basis of their sentiment score as lying

Table 11.1 Comment typologies and sentiment-bearing words

Comment	Comment typology for tag creation	Sentiment-bearing words
A comment expressing liking	Liking	Like, love, good, fair, nice, favourite
A comment where consumer is thanking the organization	Thanking	Thanks, thank you, grateful
A comment where consumer is congratulating the organization	Congratulating	Congrats, congratulations, applaud, well done
A comment where consumer is providing feedback in response to organization query	Feedback_prod, feedback_org, feedback_comp	
A comment where consumer is giving a suggestion	Suggestion_prod, suggestion_org, suggestion_comp	
A comment where consumer is giving his approval	Approval	Commend, respect
Expressing happiness with organization/product	Happiness	Pleased, impressed, proud
A comment where consumer is praising/appreciating the organization	Praise	Surprised
A comment where consumer is praising/appreciating the organization	Appreciate	Appreciate, wow, great, terrific, smartest, awesome
A comment where consumer is agreeing with the organization	Agreement	Agree
A comment listing a complaint	Complaint	Complain
A comment expressing disappointment	Disappointment	Unfortunately
A comment expressing anger	Anger	Worst, rude, most miserable
A comment expressing dislike	Dislike	Bitter, never
A comment expressing unhappiness	Unhappiness	Distressing
A comment expressing doubt	Doubt	Intrigued, confusing, doubtful, mixed, restricted
Recommendation the product to someone	Recommend	Recommend

on the continuum between liking, satisfaction, and involvement. Hence, tags can be created for aggregation of consumer comments and folksonomies can be used to extract information from tags and the same can be diverted to the respective functions in an organization for response modelling.

Table 11.2 Classification of consumer comments

Liking	Satisfaction	Involvement I	Involvement II	Involvement III	Involvement IV
Like Dislike	Thanking, Approval, Congratulating, Happiness, Appreciation, Recommend, Praise, Agreement, Disappointment, Anger, Unhappiness	Complaint Query	Complaint Query	Feedback, suggestion, and complaints regarding organization	Feedback, suggestion, and complaints regarding products

CUSTOMER LIKING, SATISFACTION, AND INVOLVEMENT

A consumer passes through several stages, namely liking, satisfaction, and involvement in his relationship with the organization. Liking can be defined as a state of fondness, affection, or preference for product, brand, or organization. This is a preliminary stage of consumer developing a tertiary interest in a product. A consumer moves to the next stage when he starts perceiving greater value in an organizational offering. The perceived value is now equated with perceived quality by customers and due to this customer satisfaction is enhanced.[10] This improves as firms customize offerings for customers and further when firms improve the reliability of consumption experiences by ensuring timely processing of various customer requests. Consumers also tend to express their happiness and appreciation in the relationship with the organization and brand. This expression can be treated as representative of consumer satisfaction. IT tools can help in this regard. Consumer involvement is the perceived personal importance and/or interest attached to the acquisition, consumption, and disposition of a good service or idea.[11] As involvement increases, the consumer has greater motivation to comprehend and elaborate on information. Several factors influence the level of the consumer's involvement—type of product being considered, characteristics of the communication received by the consumer, characteristics of the situation within which the consumer is operating, personality of the consumer, exposure to information or product usage. At times consumers depict a consistent high-level interest in a product and frequently spend time thinking about the product. As the consumer involvement levels increase, consumers tend to process more products and brand related information, and are likely to give more diligent consideration to information relevant to a particular decision. By identifying the level of consumer involvement organizations can formulate strategies accordingly. While high involvement segments may be early adopters, others may have more extended decision-making processes. For the purpose of response management, four levels of consumer involvement are identified from the consumer comment typologies. Consumers who express doubt or worry regarding product, brand, features, etc. are considered to be on the low end of the involvement scale. The next level represents consumers who have a complaint and seek grievance redressal, followed by those who have suggestions for marketing and corporate communications. The consumers who provide feedback in response to an organizational request or suggestions by a personal initiative with regard to product features and scope for improvement are considered to be highly involved with the organization.

EVALUATING CONSUMER SENTIMENT USING SENTIWORDNET 1.0

For evaluating consumer sentiment companies use SentiWordNet 1.0,[12] a lexical resource in which each WordNetsynset is associated with numerical scores Obj(s), Pos(s), and Neg(s), describing how objective, positive, and negative the terms contained in the synset are. Considering comments as sets of opinionated text, with the assumption that the text (each set of comments on a single post) is related to a single issue or item, it may be interesting to see that the opinion would be either positive or negative or feature somewhere on the continuum between these two polarities. This can be done by converting each comment into a feature vector by using a text-processing tool and then identifying the sentiment bearing features. By using a sentiment-mining tool, where each opinionated word has been allocated a sentiment score on the basis of its WordNetsynset, a sentiment score can be calculated for each individual comment. In this context, term occurrence has to be used as an indicator and not term frequency because in traditional sentiment classification, increased term occurrence, does not emphasize/change the sentiment polarity. Further, considering the algebraic sum of the term orientations as representative of the sentiment behind the comment, the score can be calculated. It is important here to correlate each term to the correct WordNetsynset it belongs to, as that holds the key to the score. Volumes of consumers depicting positive and negative sentiment polarity are calculated.

CONSUMER SEGMENTATION BASED ON CONSUMER SENTIMENT SCORE

By using corporate blogs for segmentation, marketing managers can segment customers (and prospective customers) into smaller groups and then specify the interaction that should take place with those individuals. Segmentation is the process of identifying groups of customers around whom to conduct marketing efforts by analysing the existing customer base. It is a very important functionality of any tool as this allows the marketing manager to fine tune the deliverables of the campaign. While this helps identifying most appropriate targets for specific campaigns by understanding a consumer's relationship with the organization, it also aids the process of consumer retention by identifying consumer groups which need special attention or redressal.

Traditionally, only a few broad segments could be defined based on overall demographic information. With changing times, as volumes of data being collected internally have grown, it is possible to define many more segments at a finer and finer level of granularity. In addition, it is now possible to define the segments based on their actual interaction with the company (rather than general demographic information) and to automate different responses to each segment. These consumer comments on the organizational blog posts conceal a wealth of information. While consumers with positive sentiment polarity can be subjected to consumer acquisition strategies, consumers with negative polarity represent a state of consumer dissatisfaction and can be subjected to strategies for consumer retention. All consumers falling under the 0–0.5 bracket are assumed to represent a state of liking. All consumers, more than a score of 0.5 can be assumed to represent a state of satisfaction. Consumers with comments classified under involvement are segmented separately and assigned a score of 1 for ease of tabulation Fig. 11.4.

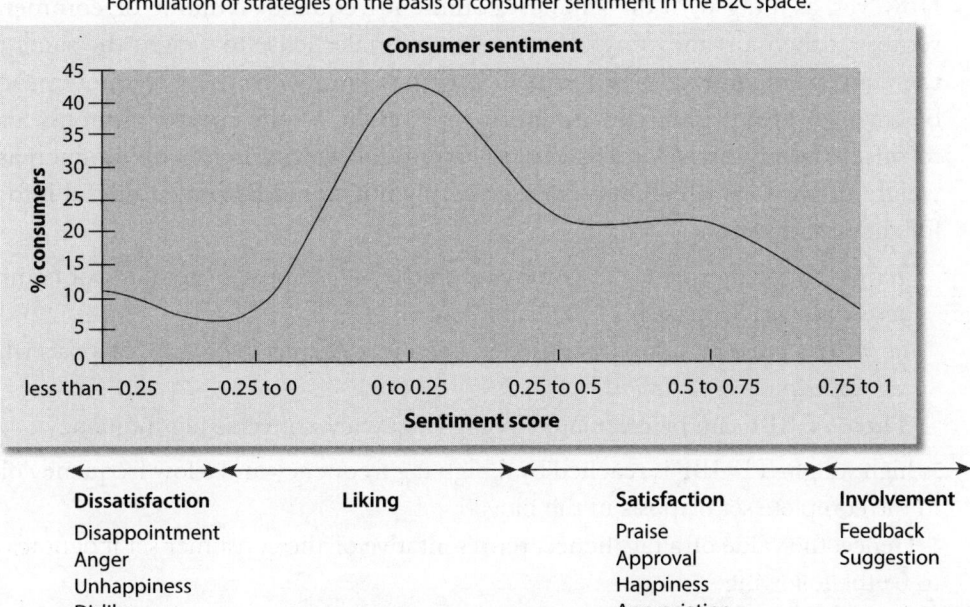

Fig. 11.4 Consumer segmentation

MEASURING CAMPAIGN EFFECTIVENESS I

Campaign effectiveness can be calculated on the basis of the following:
- Mean sentiment score for individual campaign—effectiveness of individual campaign can be calculated by calculating the mean sentiment score of each campaign. As per the central limit theorem in statistics, the distribution of these means sentiment scores across various campaigns reflects the average of the entire population.
- Volume of consumers demonstrating positive and negative sentiment polarity.

MEASURING CAMPAIGN EFFECTIVENESS II—QUANTITATIVE TAG ANALYSIS

A quantitative tag analysis for tags representing comments under each post can help generate a tag cloud which can further help understand the dominant consumer viewpoint.

Tag Frequency–Inverse Blog Frequency

A variation of the term frequency–inverse document frequency (TF–IDF) criteria, often used in information retrieval and data mining, can be used. This can be used as a statistical measure to evaluate the results of a particular campaign represented by a post. The number of comments under a particular tag representing the comments for a blog post can be represented by a numerical figure (equivalent to term frequency). This will be indicative of the number of consumers adhering to a particular comment typology, thereby representing the thought process of the population. However, as a tag with the smallest comment frequency (volume of comments) may represent the most meaningful input, it may make sense to weight the same through the concept of inverse blog frequency. Hence, an inverse blog frequency factor can be incorporated which can diminish the weight of the most commonly used tags to offset the importance of the most commonly occurring terms by increasing the weight of the tags which may be used rarely but would hold meaningful information for the organization.

Tag frequency = (frequency of comments under tag i in post j)/(total no. of comments across all tags for post j)

Inverse blog frequency = log [total no. of posts in a corpus (blog)/no. of posts where a tag appears]

Then TF–IBF can be calculated by tag frequency × inverse tag frequency

A high weight TF–IBF is reached by a high tag frequency and a low frequency of the tag in the complete set of posts in the blog.

Hence, the value of a tag, hence, representative of the consumer set it denotes appears to be the following:

- To increase proportionally to the no. of times a consumer posts a comment in that typology.

- However, offset by the frequency of that tag usage in the entire blog (percentage of blog posts the tag appears in)
- This can be used to create a tag cloud for each campaign (blog post). Tag clouds are visualizations of tag frequencies. In this case a tag cloud for the consumer comments on a blog post (campaign) will reflect the predominant consumer thought, represented by the tag with the maximum frequency of consumer comments in response to the post (campaign).

Determination of Inter-campaign Similarity

The TF–IBF measure can be used to determine similarity of results (consumer thought process as represented by the comments under the respective tags) between two blog posts (campaigns). For this purpose, cosine similarity can be used. Cosine similarity is the measure of similarity between two vectors of n dimensions by finding the cosine of the angles between them. By using the tag frequency vectors of two campaigns, cosine similarity method can be used to normalize the number of comments in a post. With values of these similarity measures ranging between -1 and $+1$, determining similarity between the responses to two campaigns can help organizations improve targeting of future campaigns.

The cosine similarity of two vectors (C_1 and C_2) can be defined as follows:

$$\cos(C_1, C_2) = (C_1 \times C_2)/||C_1||\,||C_2||,$$

where, $C_1 \times C_2 = C_{11} \times C_{21} + C_{12} \times C_{22}\ldots$

$$||C_1|| = \text{sqrt}(C_{11}^2 + C_{12}^2\ldots)$$

Tag dominance representing the tag dominating the view of the maximum number of consumers can be analysed by studying a TF–IBF measure for each campaign. Tag clouds can be used to view the dominant consumer viewpoint.

HOW COMPANIES CAN USE BLOGS FOR EFFECTIVE CAMPAIGN MANAGEMENT

Folksonomies related to consumer liking, satisfaction, and involvement is established. All comments tagged under the tag cluster visible under the folksonomies of liking and satisfaction can be diverted for *sentiment mining* to aid consumer segmentation. All comments under the tag cluster representing the folksonomy of involvement I and II are routed to the '*customer service and support*' functionality. All comments under the tag representing the folksonomy of involvement III are directed to the '*marketing communication*' function and all comments under the tags clustered under involvement IV are sent to the '*product development*' function.

It is important for organizations to understand what their consumers are saying when they are interacting with them. The aforementioned case study demonstrates the usage of a corporate blog to extract and classify the consumer responses to posts hosted by an organization on the blog. By treating each post put up by the organization as a campaign and then using the comments to understand the dominant consumer viewpoint, companies can use this online tool to gauge the effectiveness of their campaigns. Companies can also segment the consumers on the basis of their sentiment scores and implement targeting strategies appropriately. Organizations can make use of the information available about their prospective and current customers by structuring and mining the vast volumes of data available on the Web and formulate strategies for consumers by segregating them on the basis of some factors such as the sentiment score represented in the earlier discussion.

While consumers depicting a positive sentiment polarity can be grouped on the basis of their sentiment featuring on the continuum between liking and involvement, consumers with negative sentiment polarity, who are most likely to defect from the company, can be subjected to a well-directed retention campaign. Usage of a blog as a CRM tool can be achieved by routing the outcomes of the campaigns (Fig. 11.5), represented by individual blog posts to the other organizational functions. By routing the aggregated consumer responses to functions of customer support, marketing, etc., organizations can frame responses to the consumers or develop appropriate targeting strategies. Corporate blogs can definitely be used as Web 2.0 tools to become parts of successful CRM initiatives in organizations.

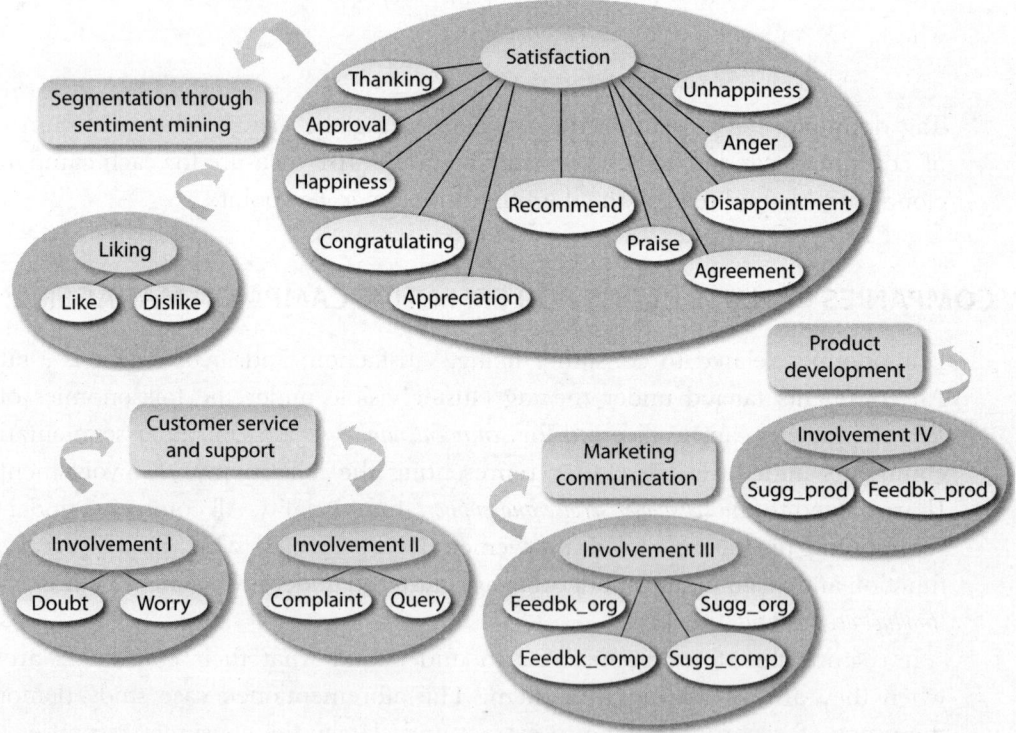

Fig. 11.5 CRM 2.0—Using a corporate blog for campaign management

CASE STUDY: The MasterCard—'A World Beyond Cash' Campaign

It is a cashless world. Paying digitally is the mantra of the day. That is what an individual does if he is trendy and in sync with the times. Using cash for transactions is simply old fashioned. Thanks to the advent of the Internet and *e*-commerce, more and more consumers are opting to pay digitally.

New age tools comprise credit cards, debit cards, prepaid cards, and mobile wallets.

Cash-less society is taking advantage of the offerings of the digital world and companies such as MasterCard are leading the way where electronic payment solutions are more efficient and secure and lead to greater opportunity for people and businesses everywhere.

MasterCard, India and Hindustan Times teamed up to bring to users the MasterCard—a world beyond cash campaign. Categorized as the technological pillar of the global payments industry, MasterCard's campaign comprised a pan-India digital contest, that aimed to target the youth to generate ideas on what the future of payments might hold—ideas that were innovative, cool and witty; and could hold the key to the way individuals make payments worldwide.

This was clearly an initiative to shift social consciousness towards a cashless society. For the past several years, MasterCard has dedicated itself to a strategy that will set a standard and become influential to the future of payments. By pushing urbanized centres to adopt the trendiness of going cashless, MasterCard hopes to influence the behaviour of consumers at large and generate positive perceptions towards a cashless society. MasterCard's seriousness with the campaign has already been seen in its endeavours across some African countries where the company strived to promote schemes such as digital discounts for tech savvy customers and giving consumers incentives to go cashless. Cashless is easier and convenient. This seemed to be MasterCard's ideology, as it launched the contest in India.

Salient features of the campaign included the following:

- Invitation to technology savvy youth across Indian colleges and institutes to submit their ideas for a world beyond cash. The youth represents a demography that is clearly an early adopter of technology and hence, shall clearly define the future in times to come.
- Use of a Facebook App for generating traffic. Facebook is the most popular network in India, and the campaign platform will help spread the word amongst the target community.
- Use of a crowd-sourcing platform—talent-house for leveraging creative talent. This will definitely aid in brand building for the company as MasterCard will be able to generate for itself an image of a trustworthy organization, an organization sensitive to the thoughts of the consumer base, an organization with credibility and desire to contribute to society at large.
- Ideas could be submitted by an individual or as a group, in the form of text, photo, or video.

The 'A World beyond Cash' campaign helped to not only catalyse the brand's vision towards a world without cash but also build engagement with the growing youth of the nation—a significant demographic considering that India is all set to be the youngest country by 2020. The growth of smartphone sales in the country coupled with young minds will also impact the way payments are made in the future.

Question:

1. Electronic payment solutions are more efficient and secure and lead to greater opportunity for people and businesses everywhere. Comment in the Indian context.

PRACTITIONER PERSPECTIVE

As part of our National Digital Literacy Mission, Intel has been working with the government to enhance technology adoption and digital literacy for boosting productivity and impacting livelihoods in a phased manner across the country. We are extremely encouraged by the findings of the first phase of the program where we saw over 52 per cent women participants and it was heartening to see them use the newly acquired knowledge and skills to better support their families. Given the size and diversity of our country, we as an industry, need to do a lot more and hence we feel Google's helping women get online (HWGO) program will help them use technology for a better life.

Debjani Ghosh, Managing Director—Sales and Marketing Group, Intel South Asia

Digital is a dynamic medium and brands need to experiment with the kind of content they create.

Anuradha Aggarwal, Senior Vice President, Brand Communication and Insights, Vodafone India

Designing a great customer-engagement strategy and experience in digital times require businesses to have complete understanding of exactly how people interact with a company throughout their decision journey. The goal is to reach the customer at moments that most influence their decisions.

Sachin Mulay, GM, Head of Corporate Brand and Applications Marketing, Wipro

India is at the forefront of mobile advertising innovation. Despite low digital penetration, India is learning to innovate in the digital space. And since traditional media is thriving, India is at the forefront of bringing old and new media together to unlock alchemies with innovations such as augmented reality. It really is a very exciting time to be a marketer in India.

Shafalika Saxena, CMO, Microsoft, India

SUMMARY

Marketing automation is the backbone of creating customized organizational campaigns, which are automated, traceable, and easy-to-repeat processes, thereby providing to the marketing function a campaign which is more targeted to the right consumer base. More important to marketing is the measurement of performance after a campaign is over. Analytical abilities in campaign management tools help organizations turn insights into competitive advantage. Meaningful customer dialogue can be subsequently converted into long-term loyalty by organizations. Companies can assess customer profitability, create highly accurate retention, cross sell/up-sell, and response models. In the online domain, companies will benefit by performing a careful analysis of customer habits and preferences. Customer experiences need to be integrated across channels with graphically rich interfaces. As customers move across online, mobile, and social channels, organizations can build individual profiles that capture their interests, activities, and interactions. This subsequently helps marketing in creating more relevant marketing experiences. Companies can use Facebook, Twitter, and blogs as tools for campaign management in the virtual world.

Concept Review Questions

1. What is campaign management? What defines a good campaign management solution?
2. How can a software tool help in integrating the campaign management efforts of an organization using Facebook?
3. What is Twitter marketing? List the names of five Indian brands which are indulging in Twitter marketing.
4. Explain how an organization can use the performance of customers across the liking, satisfaction, and involvement continuum for consumer segmentation in the virtual medium.

Critical Thinking Questions

1. Study the last Twitter and Facebook campaigns of BJP during the Lok Sabha polls, 2014. Compare and contrast the success and failure of the campaigns.
2. Study 20 different posts on the Facebook page of Cadbury's India. Treat each post as a campaign. Define a mechanism to measure the success or failure of each campaign.
3. Design an online campaign for promoting an automobile. Create well-defined consumer segmentation and targeting strategy. Define the objectives of the campaign. Profile parameters indicative of analysis of campaign performance.

Practising Digital Marketing

1. Identify and list tools being used by companies for online campaign management.
2. Visit the website of Adobe. Profile the online campaign management solutions being

offered by the company. Study the different attributes of the following:
(a) Adobe analytics from SAP
(b) Adobe social from SAP
(c) Adobe media optimizer from SAP
(d) Adobe target from SAP
(e) Adobe experience manager from SAP

References

1. Quintarelli, E., (2005). *Folksonomies: Power to the People*, ISKO Italy UniMIB meeting, Milan.
2. Smith, G., (2008). *Tagging People-powered Metadata for the Social Web*, New Riders, Berkeley, CA, ISBN: 0321529170.
3. Sheth, S., Components of ECRM solutions, *Customer Relationship Management—A Strategic Perspective*, 2006, p. 115.
4. Gebert, H., Geib, M., Kolbe, L., and Brenner, W., (2003). 'Knowledge enabled customer relationship management: Integrating customer relationship management and knowledge management concepts.' *Journal of Knowledge Management*, Vol. 7(5), pp. 107–123, ISSN: 1367-3270.
5. Chablo, E., (1999). The importance of marketing data intelligence in delivering successful CRM, CRM Forum.
6. Goodhue, D., (2002). 'Realizing business benefits through CRM: Hitting the right target in the right way,' *MIS Quarterly Executive*, Vol. 1(2).
7. Heng M., Hongcheng M., and Quiaot, J., *Sentiment Mining and Indexing in Opinmind*, ICWSM, Boulder, Colorado, USA, 2007.
8. Pang, L., Foundations and trends in information retrieval, *Opinion Mining and Sentiment Analysis*, Now Publishers Inc., http://portal.acm.org/citation.cfm?id=1454712anddl=andcoll=.
9. Pang, B. and Lee, L., (2008). Opinion mining and sentiment analysis, foundations and trends in information retrieval, *Sentiment Polarity and Degrees of Positivity*, Vol. 2(1–2), pp. 1–135, Now Publishers Inc.
10. Mithas, S., Krishnan, M.S., and Fornell, C., (2005). 'Why do customer relationship management applications affect customer satisfaction.' *Journal of Marketing*, Vol. 69(4), pp. 201–209.
11. Mowen, J. and Minor. C., Consumer behavior, a framework, *Consumer Involvement*, Fifth Edition, Ch. 3.
12. Esuli, A. and Sebastiani, F., (2006). 'Sentiwordnet: A publically available lexical resource for opinion mining', downloaded from http://swn.isti.cnr.it/download_1.0/.

Consumer Segmentation, Targeting, and Positioning using Online Tools

LEARNING OBJECTIVES

After reading this chapter, you will be able to:
- Appreciate the concepts of knowledge discovery and data mining (KDD) used for segmentation of consumers in the virtual paradigm.
- Study the concepts of sentiment mining used for evaluating consumer sentiment online and those related to consumer segmentation and profiling.
- Understand how Apps can be used by companies for consumer segmentation in the virtual space (Fig. 12.1).

Companies spend a lot of time in engaging the consumer in the virtual domain and building participatory environments. Now, the companies need to be able to harness this consumer engagement and participation. This is done by understanding what the consumer is stating online and segmenting the consumer on the basis of his demographic profile, psychographic preferences, thoughts, and comments.

Following the process of segmentation, the companies can build consumer profiles. These profiles help companies in the following ways:

- Targeting consumers separately to achieve greater conversions; and
- Building brand positioning.

This chapter traces the concept of KDD which is used to extract meaningful information from the online dialogue. Along with the process of discovery, it also addresses how

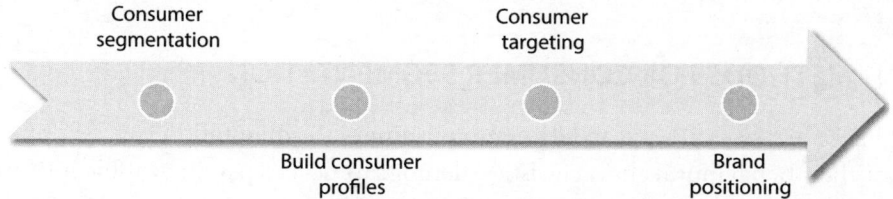

Fig. 12.1 Consumer segmentation in the virtual world

companies are analysing consumer sentiment and using that as a new basis for segmentation in the online space.

The consumers have shown their willingness to purchase online. Companies that are able to modify their processes and invest their marketing resources and align their messages to suit the online consumer, who are more interested in a targeted campaign, will benefit the most.

KNOWLEDGE DISCOVERY AND DATA MINING

Knowledge discovery is the non-trivial process of identifying valid, novel, potentially useful and ultimately understandable patterns form large collections of data. Data mining is concerned with the actual extraction of knowledge from data. The Web captures several aspects of human endeavours and provides a fertile ground for data mining, which is playing an important role in meeting the challenges of the intelligent Web. Gaining insight into the consumer thought process, enables prediction of consumer behaviour, creating segments of consumers, identifying consumers at the risk of churn, analysing responses to campaigns, and retention strategies.

Data-mining applications perform the analysis and extract relevant consumer information. Knowledge discovery and data mining is an interdisciplinary area focusing on methodologies for extracting useful knowledge from data for business intelligence. The ongoing rapid growth of online data due to the Internet and the widespread use of databases have created an immense need for KDD methodologies. The challenge of extracting knowledge from data draws on research in a wide variety of fields to draw on tools that can synthesize and organize knowledge on any given topic of interest from a corpus of documents/content. There is an increasing realization that effective digital marketing can be done only based on a true understanding of the needs and preferences of the customers. In this context, data-mining tools can help to uncover hidden knowledge in online content, thereby enabling better understanding of the consumer and a systematic knowledge management effort can channel the knowledge into effective marketing strategies. Customer profiling is one of the major areas of the application of data mining for knowledge-based marketing. This is of relevance because consumer behavioural data are a more valuable source of information than consumer demographic data. Sentiment mining is one such data-mining technique (covered in Chapter 11).

DIFFERENT METHODS FOR CONSUMER SEGMENTATION

There are several ways to segment consumers. Segmentation can be done on the basis of their behavioural characteristics, demographic and psychographic information, social status, or even benefit segmentation. The following sections explore various ways of segmenting and targeting online consumers (Fig. 12.2).

CONSUMER SEGMENTATION, TARGETING, AND POSITIONING USING ONLINE TOOLS 323

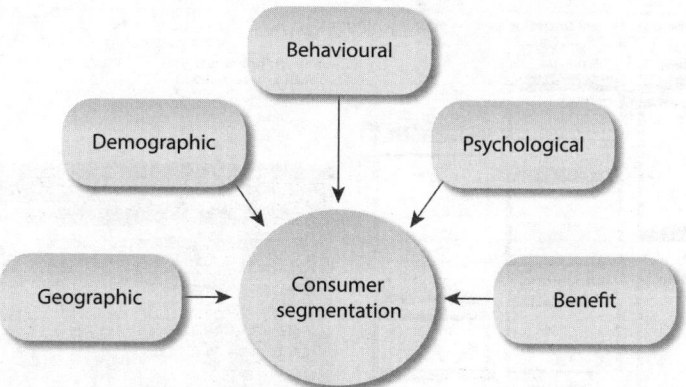

Fig. 12.2 Different methods for consumer segmentation

Efficiency and significance of marketing activities change according to the market segmentation. The traditional marketing segmentation methods have to be adapted to the online domain as the market structure changes. We briefly address segmentation on the basis of geographic and demographic characteristics, followed by segmentation on the basis of behavioural attributes and psychological characteristics of consumers (Fig. 12.3). In addition, benefit segmentation is of significance in the virtual domain. Chapter 2 has already addressed some new methods of consumer segmentation in the online space (Fig. 12.4).

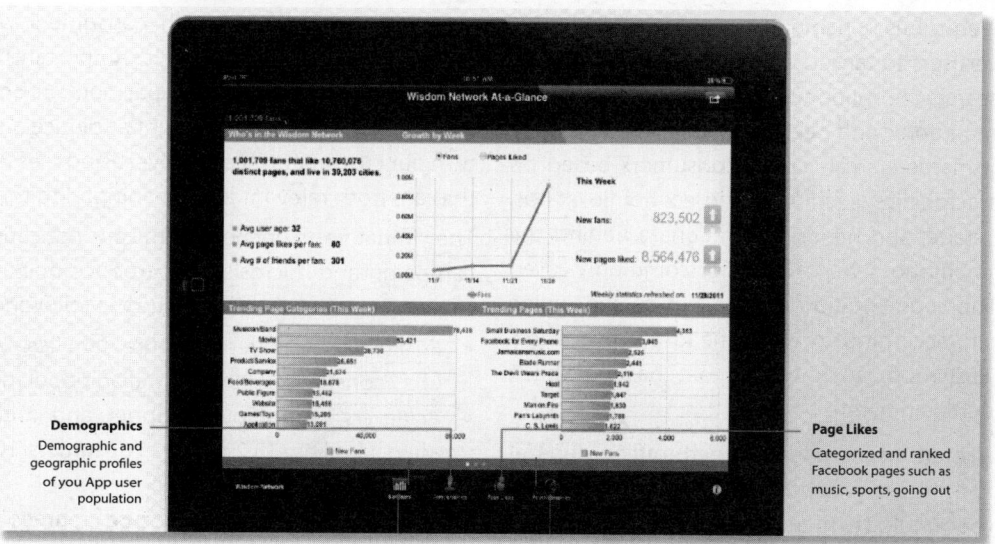

Fig. 12.3 Using page likes and demographic information for consumer segmentation

(Reproduced with permission from Microstrategy, Wisdom)

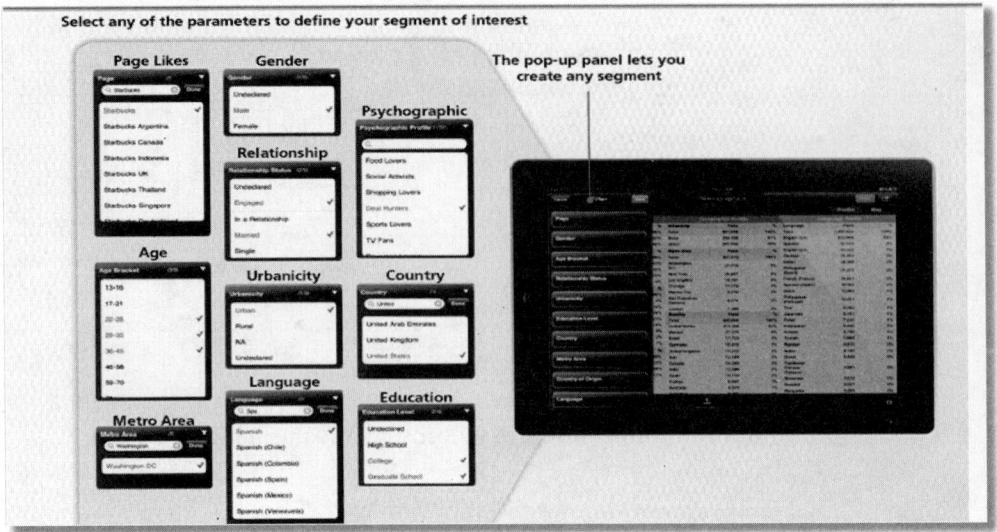

Fig. 12.4 Consumer segmentation online

(*Reproduced with permission from Microstrategy, Wisdom*)

EXHIBIT 12.1 eBay—Consumer segmentation and behavioural targeting

eBay has employed a segmentation of its users to promote its behavioural targeting abilities using 15 'geo-tribes' or named consumer archetypes for advertisers to target. With the assistance of RDA Research, the online auction site conducted a geo-demographic and needs-based segmentation so that marketers can target consumers based on characteristics such as socio-economic status, life stage, and needs. The rationale behind the segmentation was to bring commonly used offline segmentation approaches to the online world, according to eBay's head of advertising, JJ Eastwood, an initiative that has not been undertaken before.

'Marketers who are familiar with offline geo-demographical and needs-based segmentation, but have struggled to map them to digital campaigns, now have a tool that brings offline audience segmentation to online advertising', Eastwood says.

'E-commerce is now a $30 billion industry here in Australia and marketers are looking for opportunities to connect with consumers while they shop online. Therefore it's important that as we bring new advertising partners on-board, we connect them with the right audience and in turn our customers receive advertising messages that are both relevant and meaningful to them.'

The initiative launched with an educational campaign and microsite to introduce marketers to the geo-tribes, which include the following:

- *Rockafellas* Affluent mature families, 7.0% eBay consumers/7.0% Australian population.
- *Achievers* Ambitious younger and middle-aged families, 13.2% eBay consumers/10.1% Australian population.
- *Fortunates* Financially secure retirees and pre-retirees, 3.5% eBay consumers/6.5% Australian population.

(*Continued*)

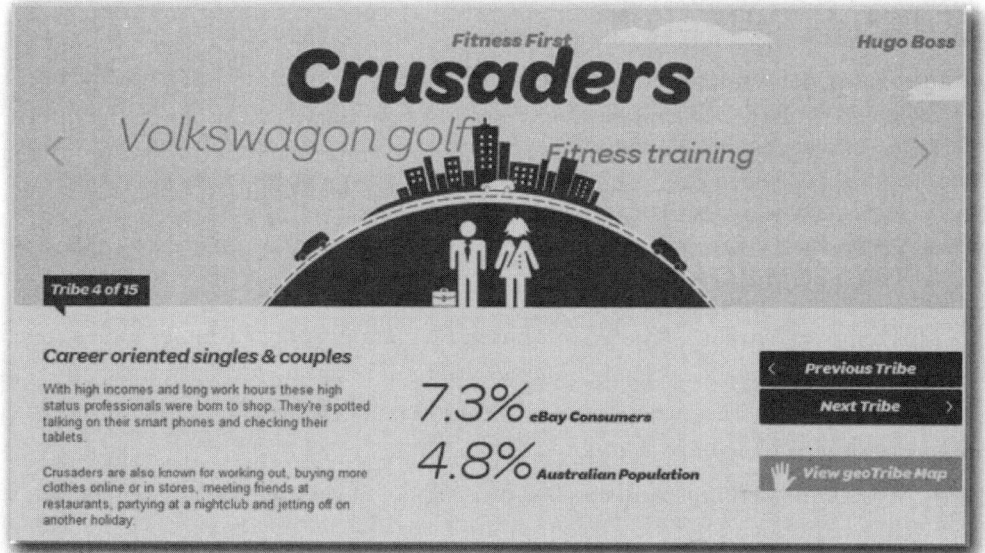

- *Crusaders* Career-oriented singles and couples, 7.3% eBay consumers/4.8% Australian population.
- *Preppies* Mature children of affluent parents, 6.4% eBay consumers/3.7% Australian population.
- *Independents* Young singles and couples, 6.6% eBay consumers/5.0% Australian population.
- *Suburban splendour* Middle-class mature families, 7.5% eBay consumers/8.3% Australian population.
- *Twixters* Mature children living at home, 6.9% eBay consumers/4.2% Australian population.
- *DebtStars* Financially extended younger families, 14.6% eBay consumers/10.6% Australian population.
- *Boomers* White collar post-family pre-retirees, 4.8% eBay consumers/7.0% Australian population.
- *True Blues* Blue collar mature families and pre-retiree singles, 4.4% eBay consumers/6.4% Australian population.
- *Struggleville* Struggling young and middle-aged families, 10.5% eBay consumers/7.3% Australian population.
- *Grey Power* Better-off retirees, 1.4% eBay consumers/5.1% Australian population.
- *Survivors* Retirees living on minimal incomes, 1.4% eBay consumers/8.9% Australian population.
- *Slender Meanz* People living in underprivileged circumstances, 4.5% eBay consumers/5.1% Australian population.

The microsite incorporates an interactive tool for marketers to generate a free report based on age, gender, and geographic location that can be linked to the offline world by allowing marketers to look up where the archetypes are most likely to live.

During an introduction phase, eBay claims to have achieved a four-fold increase in click-through rates and reports from clients of a two-fold increase in return on investment as a result of the geo-tribes targeting.

(Reproduced with permission from The Marketing Magazine www.marketingmag.com.au)

GEOGRAPHICAL SEGMENTATION

Internet-penetration and Internet-usage rates of the consumers in a specific geographical location will become the basis of geographic segmentation. In addition, the Internet-usage trends, purchasing patterns and preferences of consumers, and response to changes in technology across a geographical location in a specific product category will be significant.

DEMOGRAPHIC SEGMENTATION

This refers to market segmentation based on demographic variables such as age, gender, family size, family life cycle, income, occupation, religion, ethnicity, race, and nationality. Demographic factors are the most common criteria for dividing the market into groups of customers, which are as follows:

- Most of the demands and needs show a significant change in the effect of demographic change.
- These variables are much easier to measure than other variables.
- Demographic data of online consumers is easily available from their online profiles.

BEHAVIOURAL SEGMENTATION

Customer behavioural segmentation based on usage time, usage situation, usage, and loyalty helps to divide the consumer population into different groups. Associated factors are occasion, expected benefits, user characteristics, etc.

PSYCHOGRAPHIC SEGMENTATION

In psychographic segmentation, customers would be divided into different groups based on their lifestyle, personality, interests, expected benefits, and consumer personality traits. These consequently influence needs, desires, and shopping behaviour, including choice of media usage, activities and interests, and eventually consumer buying patterns.

CONSUMER SEGMENTATION IN THE VIRTUAL SPACE

There are several automated tools available to organizations for consumer segmentation in the virtual space. For Facebook, a tool such as *MicroStrategy*—social intelligence, stresses on the need to build Facebook applications, to aid an organization's consumer segmentation efforts.

Facebook is fast mushrooming into the world's most inclusive and contemporary database of information regarding users worldwide—their interests, their demography, their product purchase patterns. It is time marketers realize the value of this information and leverage it for the benefit of marketing. Two important observations are as follows:

- Facebook pages provide news and dialog with consumers but cannot be targeted.
- Facebook advertising allows targeted messages but offers very limited dialogue.

Both Facebook pages as well as advertising offer rich interactivity. This is where Facebook applications come into play. Facebook applications strive towards bringing targeted, personalized content and rich interactivity directly to consumers. These Apps have the ability to access and use the personal data contained within Facebook. Apps can use a person's Facebook data to enhance the overall App experience.

Facebook and Database Management

Facebook collects a wide range of data. This information pertains to understanding the following:

- Consumer demographics
- Page likes
- User (consumer) activity
- Users reach and influence through network information

Companies can make use of analytical applications such as *Microstrategy Wisdom* which can be used to deliver valuable insights about an organization's Facebook App users.

Salient Features

- Ready-to-use dashboards which provide information with regard to user demography, interests, and psychographic analysis.
- This information can be used by companies to segment and understand their users.
- Campaigns can be personalized and users can be appropriately targeted.

Hence, an organization can use a tool like this to extract all consumers within a specific age group, with a specific qualification, and who are located in a specific geographical location. The right content can then be directed to these individuals and subsequent consumer conversion achieved.

Benefits

- The tool allows organizations to choose from hundreds of segmentation criteria. Once a company has decided on the segmentation criteria and psychographic profiles, the company can divide the potential consumer base into homogeneous groups.
- Analysis of these segments by investigating and understanding the details can enable companies to personalize the App experience or marketing campaigns for individually defined segments.

POPULARITY OF BRAND PAGES

The heat map visualization helps organizations to identify pages 'liked' by a population segment. Each page is organized into its Facebook category, with size and colour code according to the number of fans and an affinity index score. Hence, companies can find what pages are most popular with their Facebook fans. More importantly, they can use the 'affinity index' to find how much more popular some pages are with a segment compared to the entire fan population.

CONSUMER PSYCHOGRAPHIC PROFILES AND CONSUMER SEGMENTATION

Segmentation tools provide complete libraries of psychographic profiles. These libraries can be used by companies to profile consumers. Companies can assign psychographic profiles to their App users based on demographics, activities, and page-like interests.

Some examples of psychographic profiling are as follows:

Basic communicators	Consumers that use the Internet mainly to communicate via e-mail
Lurking shoppers	Consumers that employ the Internet to navigate and to shop heavily
Social thrivers	Consumers that exploit the Internet interactive features to interact socially, by means of chatting, blogging, video streaming, and downloading

BENEFIT SEGMENTATION

Benefit segmentation provides a valuable window into the mind of the consumer by addressing the question: What does the Web offer consumers and what do consumers seek from the Web? Convenience in shopping is one of the most obvious advantages. Similarly, the ease with which information can be accessed can also become a strong point of the online environment. Security of information (e.g., related to credit card transactions) is a primary worry for potential *e*-commerce consumers. Good customer service, vendor reliability, financial security, convenience/ease of use of the Web-based system of merchandising and competitive pricing, generally lower than those in the offline market, are some of the most significant benefits of the Web. Companies can also make use of benefit segmentation as a method of segmenting consumers into homogeneous groups to identify ways to target them on the basis of their expectations from the online experience.

CONSUMER TARGETING

Past research studies have explored the usage of the Usenet on the Internet as a marketing tool. The Usenet was a collection of online groups which were typically theme based. The accuracy in the identification of possible target segments made Usenet a very attractive proposition for marketers. It was observed that readers of specific news groups tended to be highly involved with the topics of the news group. Significantly, researchers also found that people who were absorbed in one news group demonstrated a low involvement in the activities of another news group. This subsequently enabled marketers to believe in the potential of online product and brand groups, which could be used for consumer segmentation and targeting.

Involvement implies momentarily diverting all our resources to the achievement of a specific activity. When an individual is involved in a particular online activity, he/she wants to see the completion of the activity and is affected by all the information floating in that environment, which impacts the activity in question.

Garnering high involvement of consumers for specific online product groups could result in the development of superior online targeting practices (Fig. 12.5).

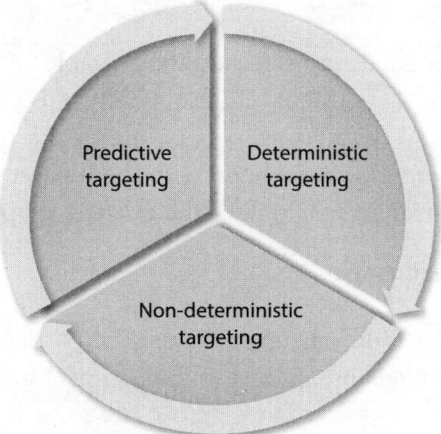

Fig. 12.5 Online targeting

ONLINE TARGETING

Mass marketing was proven ineffective since a majority of targeted consumers may not be interested in an advertised product. Mass marketing is very expensive and since only a small percentage of targeted consumers may be interested in the product, this mode of marketing and advertising is very cost ineffective. This creates the base for effective consumer targeting.

The likelihood of the consumer response forms the basis for the marketer's targeting efforts. As per Suresh Vittal's research on applying customer value to online targeting strategy, Forrester, 2009, consumer targeting in the online world can be classified into three types:

DETERMINISTIC TARGETING

It is also known as rules-based targeting, this is the most commonly used approach and takes the form of 'If visitor performs the following actions, then offer $x, y,$ or z'. Or, even simpler, 'If visitor belongs to segment A, then offer product x'.

Marketing Implication

In an offline scenario, this would employ offering specific products to consumers at the point of sale (PoS). For instance, offer cheese and ketchup to a consumer who has purchased burger buns. In an online scenario, this would imply throwing up information such as 'People who viewed this page also viewed....'

Typically, *deterministic targeting* implies that not only do consumers receive promotional information at the time of a purchase, based on their purchase behaviour, but also the marketers and advertisers can push the promotions to the consumers in an effectively real-time manner, specifically in the context of retailers for FMCG products.

Hence, organizations can make changes and optimize their promotional campaigns accordingly.

In the online space, deterministic targeting enables marketers to create a hierarchy for the promotions that are offered. Subsequently, it is possible to make the promotion choice deterministic. Websites can, depending on the priority or weight given to the promotions, display only the promotion with the highest priority/weight; for which it is expected that the consumer would have the greatest propensity to purchase.

NON-DETERMINISTIC TARGETING

In addition, known as 'self learning', this is when a decision system applies advanced analytics to train a model and apply it to making decisions based on visitor behaviour.

PREDICTIVE TARGETING

This takes the second approach further and applies business rules, constraints, pre-existing segmentation, and analytical techniques such as decision trees and neural networks to drive the targeting process. Not surprisingly this approach also requires the most complete profile of the customer. What is not often discussed is the cost associated with each approach.

Marketing Implications

What marketers must recognize is that the act of targeting is not 'free' and has a cost associated with it. This cost is made up of system costs, data costs, analytical costs, and experience costs. Of these costs, the hardest to assess is the experience costs, that is, the cost of presenting an offer to a customer and the subsequent reaction and impact on future value.

Companies also invest in *response modelling*, where consumer responses are used to drive organizational actions. For instance, if a consumer positively interacts with an organization or likes the company-generated content, his future actions can be predicted based on the degree of his affinity to the organization.

This is exactly where customer value should fit into the equation. Before marketers decide to target a visitor in the online domain, they must understand the overall value of the visitor to current and future business and use that value to help in guiding the targeting approach. For instance, let us discuss the case of an organization hosting a financial services website that sees hundreds of prospects each day, the organization should be able to assign a 'value' to each visitor based on what it knows about them and people like them. This does not have to be a detailed metric such as customer lifetime value but can be a simpler proxy. Once this value can be assigned, the company can use either rules-based targeting or a complex (and expensive) approach with a higher likelihood of success such as predictive targeting. Or, better still, the value or a value proxy should help the company understand that some customers are not worth targeting at all.

> **EXHIBIT 12.2 Dell.com—Targeting consumers using Cookies**
>
> Dell was investing substantially in promoting its products to its customers. However, the mass marketing approach did not seem to work very well as several consumers were visiting the website, but not making a purchase. Dell's strategy of generating large volumes of online traffic was clearly wrong. The company had to bring in traffic of 'interested' people potential customers on the website and not just any visitor. The company decided to leverage stored data from cookies—which could clearly indicate which products or type of products each shopper was interested in or maybe even intending to purchase—to increase engagement and keep their Dell.com experience interesting to consumers.
>
> Dell subsequently developed a focused targeting strategy for its online consumers. The salient features of the strategy were as follows:
>
> - Increasing the relevance of the advertising message seen by individual users, while minimizing wastage and increasing engagement.
> - The company developed a model that merged behavioural targeting with capturing the visit history of potential customers with dynamic creative tools that built customized messaging. Based on each visitor's history, the right advertisements were served to the consuming population.
> - When a consumer visits a website, he searches for information, views specific pages, or places products on his shopping cart—all this consumer information was stored to customize the user's visit when he visited the site again. Cookies were used for the purpose. This clearly targeted consumers who 'considered' a purchase, but did not execute it. On the repeat consumer visit, when he was provided information regarding certain 'schemes' being offered on the product he had 'considered' earlier, an immediate sale was made.
> - This clearly improved Dell's online prospects greatly with its customers.

BEHAVIOURAL TARGETING

Another technique that is proving to be an effective targeting methodology for consumers visiting online stores is behavioural targeting. For instance, during a visit to an organization's online store, a consumer may have viewed items from a particular brand and the behavioural targeting tool may then use that information to show those consumers corresponding banner advertisements depicting information on the same brand he had viewed earlier.

Some of the tools may also focus on the amount of time that a person spent on the website, or certain links that they clicked on or items they searched for, but ultimately all behavioural targeting tools aim to show consumers personalized advertisements based on their actual, expressed interests. There is a wide range of behavioural targeting tools (e.g., BTBuckets, Personyz, audience science) available for small businesses advertisers depending on the approach they are looking for.

Significant features of these tools include the following:

- Profile visitors to a company website in real time in order to provide them with customized offerings.
- Most of the tools can work in synchronization with Google analytics.

- Primary information of value includes data pertaining to cookies, consumer IP addresses, links clicked by the consumer, keywords used for search, products clicked on, etc.
- Some tools try to assess consumer intent on the website and time spent on the site to judge the degree of consumer interest in buying. Interested consumers are targeted with special discount offers or related content which will serve to increase the interest of the potential buyer.

Behavioural targeting, hence, aims at increasing conversion rates, traffic to a website, sales, and even profit if used effectively. The strategy is simple—instead of wasting time, effort, and resources in interacting with disinterested consumers, a well-directed campaign towards interested consumers can speed up their decision and make them buy.

> **EXHIBIT 12.3 Timed or targeted advertisements on social media**
>
> Most impulse buyers respond to 'triggers' that push them to make a purchase. For instance, the buyer of a fast food chain may log online around lunch time and encountering the right advertisement may elicit the right organizational objective that of stimulating a purchase. As mapped browsing provides specific information to companies about consumer behaviour, companies are using analytics to study the patterns with regard to optimal usage of resources.
>
> These studies are enabling retailers to choose the day and time of hosting specific online advertisements to achieve high reach and visibility, based on consumer Internet usage statistics. The digital footprints of consumers are shaping the entire targeting strategies of companies today.

BRAND POSITIONING ONLINE

Brand positioning is about differentiating a brand to stand out before a target audience by demonstrating it as more significant than the competing brands. Traditional positioning strategies are based on one of the several variables such as the following:

- Category
- Image
- Unique product feature
- Benefit

However, companies need to follow a structured approach to gain a competitive edge with regard to their positioning strategies in the online world. Figure 12.6 details the steps for effective brand positioning in the virtual world.

Establishing Differentiation in the Online World

It is important for a brand to demonstrate its 'differentiation' with regard to competing brands in the online space. However, organizations need to clearly remember that

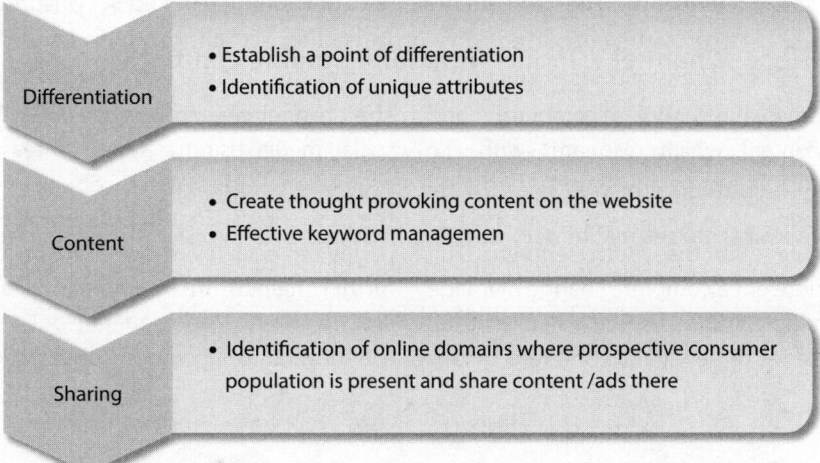

Fig. 12.6 Effective brand positioning in the virtual world

consumers do not go online to buy what is different. They go online to buy what they remember. Brands need to be attractive enough to generate recall. That is where the dimension of differentiation should focus on.

Identification of Unique Attributes

Companies need to identify what their brand has that is unique and share that in the digital world. Unique attributes, riding on unique brand stories is the need of the online world. Skilfully crafting a high valued positioning is the need of the brand.

EXHIBIT 12.4 Nokia Lumia

Nokia Lumia is characterized by a 41 megapixel camera, high-resolution zoom features, xenon flash, and touchscreen technology. Brand differentiation will clearly be a function of the consumers' ability to recall and link these attributes with the brand. The brand created an online community and launched a campaign to highlight its product attributes and increase consumer recall. On the community, 'Nokia Zoom Agents' were supposed to investigate and solve murder mysteries. The participants were allowed to use the smartphone's high resolution features for the purpose. A microsite was created. The site had social logins of Facebook and Twitter and participants had to zoom into the photos taken at the crime scene to extract the clues to solve the mystery. The fastest solvers of the mysteries won Nokia Lumia smartphones.

Create Thought-provoking Content on the Website

Content marketing is fast catching on as an effective branding strategy. As consumers start consuming text, audio, and video content online, organizations are under pressure to create a regular stream of engaging and creative online content.

> **EXHIBIT 12.5 Channel V, India—Appealing online content**
>
> Thought provoking, soul searching, and emotional content which resonates with the target audience is key to any brand's targeting strategy. Channel V, in India, was positioned as a channel meant for the youth segment. The Channel underwent a complete change of image to appeal to the youth by ushering in a youthful logo and a series of new youth oriented shows. The channel created positive WOM for itself on social media using a series of teaser updates, promotional videos and Facebook updates about the new shows. Creation of dedicated Facebook pages for each TV show aired on the channel further helped the company weave a story around the show and generate online support for the shows through viewer conversations.

Text is the most significant form of content and is the foremost tool in *search engine optimization*, which helps product websites acquire higher ranks, and reach, engage, and convert targeted audiences. As a result, companies constantly feed Web content, blogs, white papers, how-to guides, *e*-books, press releases, etc. The right choice of words steers the targeted consumers in the appropriate direction. Images, graphics, photos, pictures, designs, textures, infographics, cartoons, etc., are also very popular amongst the Indian audiences because of their impressive visual appeal. Images trigger imagination and build trust. Video content is increasingly used by brands in India as video marketing takes up a more innovative and creative avatar. Companies are using video marketing to build their brand identity. *Viral video marketing* and *Brand storytelling* are the buzzwords in the era of an exponential growth of mobile applications, mobile advertising, mobile video marketing, and marketing using popular mobile networking Apps such as *WeChat, Line, Whatsapp, Vine, Snapchat, Instagram,* and others.

Effective Keyword Management

In the world of digital marketing, user experience and Web design are ever evolving, where interactivity, rich content and speed are essential components. Brands can position themselves better by employing the right keyword management strategies, as discussed in earlier chapters.

Identification of the Online Consumer Audience

This relates to what is termed as the *humanization* of digital marketing, as brands humanize further, by understanding the importance of online conversations and online consumer engagements. Google is kind to content which has been liked and shared by the online consumer audience. Brands have to break the barriers and identify these online consumer audiences, which are happy to generate positive word-of-mouth (WOM) for companies. For effective personalization, businesses have to deeply understand their customer behaviour and click-stream, and analytics helps them a lot to understand this. Techniques such as *conversion rate optimization* help brands in identifying and understanding their online audiences. Multichannel integrated marketing further enables brands to engage with potential consumers across a variety of platforms.

EMERGING CONSUMER SEGMENTS IN INDIA

KPMG Advisory Services Pvt. Ltd, an Indian limited-liability company and a member firm of the KPMG network of independent member firms affiliated with KPMG International, conducted a survey to differentiate Indian consumers into seven segments (Fig. 12.7). The following section studies those segments and discusses the marketing implications of the same in a significantly digital environment. The segments are shown in Table 12.1.

Table 12.1 Indian consumer segments and the marketing implications

Indian segment	Segment details	Targeting strategies in an online world
First-time users	High aspiration value and significant input from influencers drive first-time consumers' purchasing decisions. Successful players have used influencers and reduced purchase related risks effectively to engage first-time shoppers. Consumers are increasingly trying out modern trade driven by aspirations or pull factors and inputs from influencers.	These are consumers which have aspirations to rise in society and are socially active. In an increasingly Internet-savvy world, they are definitely part of some online social group. Companies should influence their purchase decisions through online opinion leaders, by seeding the relevant online forums with positive WOM. The Internet can be used for leveraging consumer evangelists and opinion leaders to influence the consumers which will generate a 'pull' factor for specific products.
Bottom of pyramid (BoP) users	Increasing media penetration and brand exposure have led to a noticeable change in the BoP segment's buying behaviour. Local influencers determine the purchasing habits of the BoP segment in small cities. Successful business models for BoP consumers are typically built around low-cost delivery systems coupled with high degree of product customization and scalability.	The Internet can be used to connect with the BoP users by providing these individuals with an opportunity to make price comparisons, providing them information with the most economical product options, latest schemes for low-cost products and coupons which benefit them. Well directed e-mail and mobile marketing campaigns can be used for such consumers.
Time-starved consumers	Hectic urban lifestyles, coupled with growing incomes has led to the growth of the segment that values convenience.	These consumers are fast to adopt the convenience offered by the online domain, considering that they are less sensitive to price comparisons and value the online experience and its simplicity.
Value-conscious users	The constantly deal seeking value conscious consumer segment, impacted by economic factors such as high inflation, limited disposal income.	The digital world can be used to improve and create value for the brands using benefit-positioning strategies. Impacting consumer price sensitivity by hosting meaningful online discussions further strengthens the brand value and builds relationships with value-conscious consumers.
Urban consumers	Consists of a large number of heterogeneous sub groups that remain largely underserved. Characterized by increased brand consciousness.	The urban consumers are very brand conscious. Specific Internet marketing strategies can be used to target the urban consumers.
Emerging affluents	Growing urbanization and incomes has led to emergence of a segment seeking better service and tailored solution to set them apart from the masses.	Interactivity, personalization, and customization are the strengths of the Internet which can be used to target the emerging affluent. Leveraging technology is soon expected to become the key factor to enhance consumer reach and convenience.

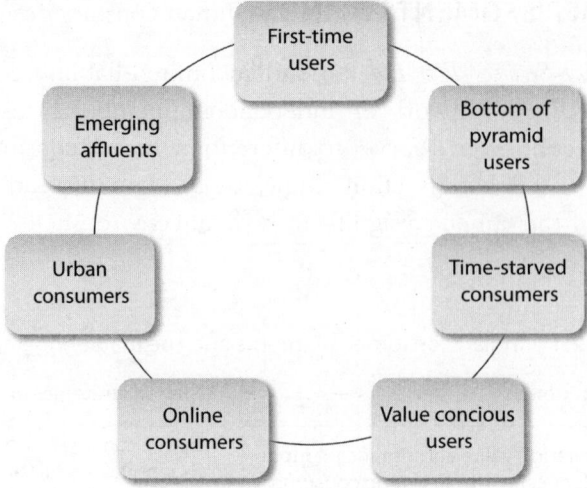

Fig. 12.7 Emerging consumer segments in India

Companies can hence effectively make changes to their supply chain models and their marketing communication techniques, make online transactions popular and target each of the consumer segments appropriately. Well-defined models will enable progressive organizations to leverage the services of the Web world, along with the offline presence of product brands to target consumers across disparate diaspora and economic strata.

CASE STUDY Volkswagen India—Effective Positioning in the Virtual World

Consumer brand association with Volkswagen classifies the brand as trendy, adventurous, stylish, fashionable, luxurious, upmarket, magnificent, and urban. The company represents brands from the low-consumption, small cars to luxury-class vehicles and has developed a positive relationship with the consumer base.

Surveys by the company for targeting the Indian consumers revealed a population comprising a large consumer base—a population that was aspirational and demonstrative.

The Volkswagen group, India is a part of Volkswagen AG, which is globally represented by 12 brands from seven European countries. Eleven automotive brands, namely, Volkswagen passenger cars, Audi, Bentley, Bugatti, Lamborghini, Porsche, Scania, SEAT, Skoda, Volkswagen commercial vehicles, (Volkswagen Nutzfahrzeuge), and MAN; and one motorcycle brand, namely, Ducati.

Superior benchmarking and classification make VW an advanced brand which adds to its popularity in the consumer mindset.

The highest-volume brand of the group is Volkswagen, which has strategically made acceptable inroads into the Indian market.

The company has been sensitive to the Indian consumer segments which value their convenience and have incomes to match their expectations. The company decided to target this segment using carefully crafted online campaigns on LinkedIn. LinkedIn was chosen as the platform for marketing because of its professional image as compared to other channels and networks. The company was hoping to reason with a proficient set of individuals, who would be quick in decision making and reflect significant goal clarity. Through the strategic use of LinkedIn, Volkswagen India was able to garner nearly 3000 car recommendations in under a month.

SEGMENTATION

Surveys had told VW that consumer professional identity affects their car choice. As a result, the company decided to use LinkedIn as an effective component of its social media strategy to target young urban professionals. The idea was clear—this set of dedicated individuals would also be influenced by the testimony of others which would drive positive WOM.

Volkswagen India launched a company page on LinkedIn and subsequently consumers started posting reviews and comments about the car.

TARGETING

LinkedIn allows companies to create personalized campaigns for specific target groups. In this case, VW created a series of recommendation advertisements, which showcased some of the brand's recommendations from their page to other LinkedIn users that fit their targeted demographic. The objectives were driving traffic to the company website and increasing engagement with potential consumers and marketing intermediaries.

POSITIONING

Volkswagen India was attempting to increase its exposure in a relatively new market among working professionals. However, instead of simply running a conventional advertising campaign, they wanted a viral component that emphasized the positive sentiment of the current customers and influenced decision making.

An effective viral campaign, a clear understanding of the segmentation demographic and well-defined targeting and positioning strategies were behind the success of VW's endeavour. The company was able to successfully garner huge volumes of recommendation from happy consumers and was able to create thousands of new fans interested in information regarding VW.

Question:

1. Design a new viral marketing strategy for VW, India. Create a detailed campaign and illustrate how the same can be leveraged.

PRACTITIONER PERSPECTIVE

Lack of easy access to Internet, lack of knowledge on how to use the Internet and its relevance in their daily lives are the biggest barriers for women to get online. 'Helping women get online' is an initiative that aims to overcome these barriers and empower women to improve their lives.

With this initiative we are aiming to help 50 million additional women to get online by end of 2014 by undertaking a variety of initiatives across India. We have already seen many cases of women benefiting greatly by using the Internet and we are really delighted to partner with leading brands in the country to join us in this ambitious project.

Rajan Anandan, MD and VP Sales & Operations for Google India

Social commerce is becoming an integrated element of digital marketing. The opportunity for marketing will be to build foot print on social media, increase their social media diversity, explore social ads on a pay-per-click model, build original content across channels and manage and engage your community to build brand advocates.

Sachin Mulay, GM, Head of Corporate Brand and Applications Marketing, Wipro India

SUMMARY

Companies spend a lot of time in engaging the consumer in the virtual domain and building participatory environments. Now, the companies need to be able to harness this consumer engagement and participation. This is done by understanding what the consumer is saying online and segmenting the consumer on the basis of his demographic profile, psychographic preferences, thoughts, and comments. Following the process of segmentation, the companies can build consumer profiles. These profiles help companies in (a) targeting consumers separately to achieve greater conversions and (b) building brand positioning. Knowledge discovery is the non-trivial process of identifying valid, novel, potentially useful, and ultimately understandable patterns form large collections of data. Data mining is concerned with the actual extraction of knowledge from data. The Web captures several aspects of human endeavours and provides a fertile ground for data mining, which is playing an important role in meeting the challenges of the intelligent Web. Gaining insight into the consumer thought process enables prediction of consumer behaviour, creating segments of consumers, identifying consumers at the risk of churn, analysing responses to campaigns, and retention strategies. There are several ways to segment consumers. Segmentation can be done on the basis of their behavioural characteristics, demographics, psychographic information, social status, or even benefit segmentation. The likelihood of the consumer response forms the basis for the marketer's targeting efforts. Consumer targeting in the online world can be classified into the following three types: deterministic, non-deterministic, and predictive targeting.

Concept Review Questions

1. Explain the concept of knowledge discovery and data mining. How do companies use this concept for consumer segmentation?
2. How can companies use the virtual space to gauge the consumer sentiment for their product or organization?
3. What are the different methods used for consumer segmentation?
4. Write short notes on
   (a) Behavioural segmentation
   (b) Benefit segmentation
5. Differentiate between deterministic, non-deterministic, and predictive targeting.
6. How can companies use the virtual world to position their brands?

Critical Thinking Questions

1. Conduct a consumer survey for the brand *Cadbury*. Use a segmentation strategy to divide the consumers into disparate segments. Suggest a *targeting* and *positioning* strategy where *Cadbury* can use the virtual world to build *brand positioning*.
2. Identify the security concerns of consumers who make purchases online from *Amazon, Flipkart,* or *eBay*. Create consumer profiles by studying their personality traits with regard to their willingness to take risks. Link the same with their Internet-savvy nature and create consumer segments accordingly.

Practising Digital Marketing

1. Study the site www.yahoo.com/info/advertising. What does this tell you about advertising options on the Internet?
2. Create a list of five online tools available for segmentation of consumers. Profile them.
3. Visit the site www.comscore.com. Collect information available on the site pertaining to segmentation and targeting strategies that companies can use for online consumers.
4. Visit the website www.foresterresearch.com. Study the company's latest research articles pertaining to online segmentation.
5. Create a PowerPoint presentation about consumer psychographic profiles. How are these used for consumer profiling and segmentation?

Market Influence Analytics in a Digital Ecosystem

LEARNING OBJECTIVES

After reading this chapter, you will be able to:
- Understand the concept of consumer-generated media (CGM)
- Determine the need to harvest CGM
- Get familiar with the concept of individual Internet worth
- Understand the ability of CGM to influence the consumers

The Internet, used for digital-network-individualization general purpose technologies, provides opportunities for marketing which extend from the micro level of electronic contacts to the macro level of new business opportunities. As the democratization of consumer expression leads to a viral proliferation of information online, the new age communication ecosystem has prompted the need for a careful evaluation of the potential of what is being called consumer-generated Internet content, creating new challenges for *marketing intelligence*. With the ability to impact business environments, these offerings of the information age have garnered adequate potential to engineer business transformations. Consumer-generated media, comprises the content generated by consumers within online venues such as Internet forums, Blogs, Wikis, discussion lists. This has ushered in discussions about the empowerment of consumers, thereby besieging the studies of consumer behaviour with the ability of this medium to influence purchase decisions, hence, creating an intrinsic need to mine this data.

Leveraging CGM and channelizing it appropriately has become critical for organizations for understanding and managing market performance, product positioning, and driving brand reputations. The biggest challenge in front of organizations now is to *harvest* CGM to help marketers gain insight into the online market conversations taking place. This chapter will focus on tools being used to do the same. Efforts are on by marketing in organizations to track the volume, origin, flow, and trajectory of the conversations in real time as they evolve, study the domain of *individual Internet worth* and map the scope, reach and influence of the same on topics that might have a positive or negative impact on a company's products, promotions, and reputation.

This chapter focuses on the need for organizations to analyse the volume of CGM and discusses how it can be used as an organizational resource which can be tapped during the formulation of marketing strategy, tracing the outcomes of marketing strategies, and identifying influencers who can be recruited as customer evangelists.

THE DIGITAL ECOSYSTEM

Online technologies provide the ability to refine marketing actions.[1] The Internet today has been hailed as the single most important invention of the twentieth century and digital marketing is transforming companies, customization, and advertising. With its increasing popularity, as noticed from more and more number of users coming online, and services being offered online in general, the Internet now occupies a central role in young educated people's lives, all over India.[2] The digital paradigm plays two very significant roles in marketing-influencing consumer behaviour and harnessing consumer intelligence. While it is vital for an organization to evaluate consumer intentions and provide consumers the necessary information they are looking for, it is equally important for them to collect consumer data by studying the consumer behavioural patterns on the Internet and subsequently nurturing long-term relationships with consumers.

EXHIBIT 13.1   Dove—Engineering influence in an online world

Dove launched its new hair fall treatment product in India through an online viral campaign. Dove invited a series of women who had used this product to share their thoughts through a series of digital tools such as blog posts and videos. Dove started what it called the *Dove hair fall rescue diary*.

The Product

The 'Dove hair fall rescue treatment' was launched in India, with claims of abilities to strengthen and nourish hair from the roots, giving users the freedom from hair fall in just two weeks.

On YouTube, the brand designed a home page to look like a diary. This leads to a series of women sharing product-related experiences using blogs.

The women are socially savvy bloggers who have a distinct presence in their own spheres—can be called opinion leaders in their specific domains ranging from make-up experts to fashion and travel bloggers and authors.

Dove has always campaigned around real women and their stories. Dove has been consciously reaching out to women who are active on social media, especially women bloggers. By giving product hampers at blogger meet-ups to hosting a blogging contest around 'My beautiful hair story' on one of the largest platform of Indian bloggers, Dove has been on a continuous journey of building a community of women interested in hair care.

The Internet has subsequently commenced playing a very significant role in the marketing value chain encompassing value identification, creation, and delivery thereby impacting marketing economics by reducing transaction cost and time. There seems to be a rapid adoption of the Internet by consumers for various purposes, including information search and online shopping.³ Consumer data analysis, content analysis,⁴ and predictive modelling are now the buzzwords and digital marketing coupled with digital media are twin growth engines for organizations today.

A new dimension of *individual Internet worth* is fast gaining momentum. Individual online reach, amplification, and network impact coupled with individual content-based rankings help create peer indexes and make it possible to measure and track reactions to individual posts and comments. This is valuable to marketing when this individual is a consumer.

Consumer behaviour has changed dramatically in the past decade. Today, consumers can order many customized products online, ranging from sneakers to computers. Many have replaced their daily newspapers with customized, online editions of these media and are increasingly receiving information from online sources. This has proliferated because these channels reflect an understanding of consumer needs and consumer behaviour.⁵ If nowadays, experts want to identify the most profound influences on consumer behaviour, the answer would be the Internet and their peers who use the Internet. One reason the Internet is dramatically changing consumer behaviour is that it helps consumers search much more easily and efficiently than ever before.⁶ At the same time, the Internet can be used to influence the consumers by hosting the right content about products in the online space.

EXHIBIT 13.2   Nestlé India—Seeding the digital media

Nestlé KitKat is one of the most loved brands across the world. In 2013, Nestlé launched a video campaign in India, featuring dancing babies. The objective of the campaign was to appeal to the emotional Indians, by demonstrating how taking a KitKat break helps people notice something good, which would have otherwise been missed. The video emphasizes the need to look beyond the obvious and seeding the campaign on YouTube, prior to its launch on television proved to be a smart move. The video went viral on YouTube garnering over 1.5 million views within a week. The advertisement was subsequently released on television, with digital and Facebook forming key dimensions of the campaign.

The Web-based participatory media is growing at a fast rate and altering the way consumers consume and create content. Hence, companies need to monitor and maintain online reputations in today's world. Reputational challenges emerge as consumers commence posting their thoughts and views online. If these thoughts are positive the company benefits; however, if these thoughts are negative, the company can lose if the controversy in question is not addressed immediately.

Effective 'listening' by companies helps in the following ways:

- Understand emerging issues
- Maintain relationships with key stakeholders
- Create a network of consumer evangelists

Some companies not only use cutting-edge attitudinal-segmentation techniques to better understand the concerns of stakeholders but also mobilize cross-functional teams to gather intelligence and respond quickly to far-flung reputational threats.

These activities, strengthened with consumer research can enable companies to take pre-emptive action to manage challenges that arise.

KNOWLEDGE AS A VALUE PROPOSITION

Knowledge has become the source of strategic planning for the creation of a value proposition for consumers. Market sensing[7] is a core business process and organizations which are able to manage, analyse, and combine knowledge faster for product innovation and improvement in line with customer expectations are succeeding in the competitive scenario. The connected millennium lays tremendous importance on shifting the concept of marketing from making and maximizing profit from individual transactions to building mutually beneficial relationships with consumers and other parties. Relationship marketing focuses on customer satisfaction and retention as organizations move from product-based campaign marketing to a customer-based relationship approach. Economies have become customer driven. Companies are going global, reaching out to customers located afar as *e*-commerce and online buying facilitate consumer purchase thus diminishing geographical restrictions. Increasing competition between organizations is leading to the implementation of relationship strategies and multichannel relationship programmes, as consumer retention becomes a vital imperative for organizational sustenance. In view of the increased need for organizations to communicate with their consumers, the Internet provides an excellent low cost solution for better connectivity between the organization and its partners.

In this context, the collaborative Web opens myriad opportunities by providing a channel for organizations to interact with the consumer, formulate brand–consumer relationships, promote products, and also leverage the consumer generated content as a source of business intelligence to formulate consumer acquisition and retention strategies as well as product improvements and service enhancements.

The Web has ushered in an era of collaboration where participation is possible at all levels between the organization, the employees and the consumers. Organizations can use Web 2.0 techniques primarily in following two areas:

- Inside the organization to improve efficiency and productivity and
- Between the organization and the customers for customer acquisition, improving revenue, and customer retention.

Consumer-generated Media

'Consumer-generated media' encompasses the millions of consumer-generated comments, opinions, and personal experiences posted in publicly available online sources on a wide range of issues, topics, products, and brands. It is also referred to as online consumer word-of-mouth or online consumer buzz, Nielsen.[8] Consumers place far more trust in their fellow consumers than they do in traditional marketers and advertisers.[9] For any marketer, advertiser, or business professional trying to be heard or break through the clutter, understanding and managing this high-impact CGM is critical for marketplace understanding and success. A large number of online users trust consumer reviews posted online over other forms of advertising, before making a purchase.[10] The dictionary meaning of a blog is a frequent, chronological publication of personal thoughts and links. Blogs, which are essentially Web spaces maintaining data in a chronological order, represent a substantial amount of text containing factual information and information about the author's communicative intentions.

EXHIBIT 13.3 Cadbury

Creation of a social campaign launched against a lifestyle situation is another way where organizations are touching a chord with the consumer. The changing pace of life is making several people in society very serious—as in solemn and sombre.

Cadbury's 5 star, a product with an adventurous, spirited and light-hearted image, launched an *Anti-seriousness* campaign called 'Inki Condition serious hai'. In the campaign, *seriousness* was considered as a social disease that needs to be eradicated with a chocolate bar.

The company organized a five day blogging campaign to build audience support for the concept. The contest invited bloggers to blog about their encounter with someone or something whose condition was serious. This was accompanied by Facebook and Twitter contests inviting the community to share information about 'serious' people.

The remedy was obvious—*eating a five star bar*, which could extract a person from the social disease.

While not every such conversation is product related, it stands to reason that in a consumerist society products and product related experiences have substantial mention. Blogs have a comparative advantage of speedy publication—they have a first mover advantage in socially constructing interpretive frames for current events.[11]

Corporate blogging pundits, such as Scoble and Israel, recommend the following two courses of action in responding to this phenomenon:

- Monitoring (the most important action) and
- Participation

As millions of people use blogs as personal diaries on the Internet, they are fast emerging as collaborative spaces that can be put to multiple uses and have emerged as the latest mode of computer-mediated communication today.[12] Consumer behaviour is witnessing the impact of Internet content, which is also affecting product positioning and driving brand reputations in such a big way, that the power of the ordinary content creator can no longer be ignored, raising needs for detailed consumer sentiment mining.[13]

These new Internet tools, by giving birth to CGM have changed company relationships with their consumers from a unidirectional 'attract customer' strategy to a culture of participation and co-creation. As consumer voices start echoing, the need is to establish a meaningful interaction with them and use them as advocates for the company.

A case in point has been the recently launched Apple iPhone—the new handheld media device—which combined functionality from the iPod, mobile telephony, and the Internet via touch screen. The product launch resulted in CGM levels higher than any other product announcement.

CONSUMER-GENERATED MEDIA AND CONSUMER BEHAVIOUR

Consumer-generated media is impacting consumer behaviour deeply. The following section traces the way CGM has empowered the consumer, impacted the role of opinion leaders, and become a vital tool for influence in the marketing game.

Consumer-generated media enables a feeling of empowerment[14] in the consumer. It gives a consumer an immense sense of satisfaction to know that they have a tool to provide feedback to the organization they have sourced a product from. However, the thought that content generated by him may later be read and analysed by the concerned company gives a consumer a feeling that he has the ability to contribute to the customer management and feedback analysis systems of the company and becomes a primary motivator to make him create content. Therefore, CGM has a cathartic effect since it provides a medium to the common man to unload his thoughts and sentiments. It also has the ability to create a conversation tool and build a community of people using similar products and airing their views.

EXHIBIT 13.4 **Standard Chartered Bank, India and the Mumbai Marathon**

As part of its corporate social responsibility endeavours, Standard Chartered Bank, hosted one of the biggest charity events in India—the Mumbai Marathon. The event garnered a lot of support from media and traditional publicity channels, primarily because of its association with a social cause. The official charity partner was *United Way of Mumbai*, a non-profit organization that endeavoured to leverage corporate, employee and leadership talent for community development.

The idea to embark on this unique journey, called the good deed Marathon, was associated with starting a movement of *smiles* in the country. The campaign was successfully able to engage the citizens, with the promotion of the value of running—the need for better health, and achievement of ideal body weight. Activities on Facebook, YouTube, and Instagram carried the campaign forward with applications on Facebook and mobile that helped people to be part of the movement. The campaign, #GoodDeed Marathon ensured a common conversation topic across the networks.

CONSUMER-GENERATED MEDIA AND OPINION LEADERS

Opinion leaders[15] have an informal influence over consumer behaviour and impact consumer acceptance of new products and services. Consumer-generated media has provided a new source of communication for these opinion leaders who adopt CGM for the following reasons:

Self-projection and self-confirmation

The consumer gathers a feeling of superiority or status by demonstrating expertise by generating content and on being considered an authority on a subject. Research shows that individuals categorized as opinion leaders are four times more likely to be asked for advice/voice their opinion on any subject under discussion. This acts as a channel to reduce own post-purchase dissonance or self-doubt regarding a purchase, by discussing the product features in a medium which will garner some comments, which if positive, will reassure the concerned individual regarding the appropriateness of his/her purchase.

Social involvement

Some people love sharing product related experiences and use these conversations as the means of being a part of the community. As the keen desire for knowledge and information drives an opinion leader to be an innovative consumer and share his experiences, his gregarious nature and access to the community coupled with the fertile opportunities provided by the collaborative Web, can be utilized by organizations by creating customer evangelists and generating favourable conversations about their products and services.

EXHIBIT 13.5   Titan—The joy of gifting

Titan industries, India's leading watches, jewellery, and eyewear manufacturer and retailer unveiled a new corporate identity to express and celebrate its transformation over the last 25 years. Under its new identity, the Titan Company Limited, with a new logo—*Titan Star* was unveiled, conveying the company's commitment to drive innovation, nurture talent, create value, and delight consumers by maintaining highest global standards.

When Titan decided to extend its brand concept—the joy of gifting, Titan decided to use an emotional quotient to make inroads into the consumer heart, through social media platforms. Social media was leveraged to enable the community to be part of the Titan signature tune, with interesting contests. A website was built where the community could share their very own version of the Titan tune, by either whistling or playing it on piano. The site was powered by Facebook and Twitter logins. Involving consumers in activities like these built trust and loyalty towards the brand.

PEER REVIEWS, WORD OF MOUTH, AND THE DISSATISFIED CUSTOMER

More and more online buyers are turning to peer reviews for product-related advice, before adopting a product.[16] 'When asked to note their most trusted information source, sixty per cent of online buyers said consumer reviews compared to 31 per cent who said newspapers or magazines.' Further, a large number of online buyers indulge in comparison shopping and are early adopters of social networking such as writing or reading blogs, customer reviews, and community websites and are more likely to share their opinions and give reviews online than people who shop the old-fashioned way. An unsatisfied customer reaches out to a larger audience, as compared to the word-of-mouth generated by a satisfied customer, thereby damaging consumer perception about a company and its products. As it is now clear that a consumer's pre-purchase research finds more value and credibility in an informal source of information, rather than a company's advertising campaign or its sales people, CGM, and opinion leaders are fast becoming forces to reckon with. It is hence vital for companies to identify these 'influencers' or opinion leaders and analyse the content generated by them. A case in point has been Dell which embraced corporate blogging to become part of the conversations in the blogosphere which its customers were having without it, as seen from the blog hosted by an irate Dell consumer Jeff Jarvis.

CORRELATION BETWEEN CONSUMER-GENERATED MEDIA AND SALES

The high impact of the ability of CGM to generate incremental publicity for certain products, enough to affect their commercial prospects, has prompted marketers to formulate a role for CGM in the marketing mix. This has prompted the need to mine this CGM as there appears a strong correlation between buzz and sales and buzz also helped in generating accurate forecasts.

THE VALUE OF THE POWER OF INFLUENCE

With the role of opinion leaders and influential personnel in influencing consumer behaviour, being defined, it is clear that influence,[17] defined as 'the ability to indirectly control or affect the actions of other people or things' is a key psychological driver affecting the behavioural outcomes of individuals. It is, hence, important for organizations to analyse this media generated by the consumers to identify the influencers, the key drivers affecting consumer behaviour, monitoring consumer perceptions, and measuring the magnitude of this influence and outline strategies to harness the influencers for organizational gain.

Influence Analytics

Vital to marketing is the need to measure online influence. This can be done in several ways as follows:

- Identify the key influencers driving online conversations
- Measure the impact of an online campaign on influencing consumers
- Identifying consumer behaviour types that impact online influence
- Identifying important consumers who publish online content
- Identifying important consumers who consume online content

Tools such as *Klout* help companies in *influence analytics*.

> **EXHIBIT 13.6 Influence analytics**
>
> Klout represents an analytical tool that enables the determination of how influential a person is in comparison to other persons, and as a secondary data point how influential that person is about particular topics. The tool assigns a number (1–100) that serves as a literal and figurative measure of the influence of an individual.
>
> The key to effective use of influencers is their ability to cause behaviour, and that ability varies not just by topic, but even more so by platform.
>
> Any analytical tool will have to take into account: action (clicks and other engagement) and activity (online posts).
>
> Channel influence analytics:
>
> - *Twitter influence analytics* 'Plexus Engine' instantly gives companies a list of topical influencers and allows them to create a list, custom search engine, and blog feed in a single click.
> - *Brandfluencers* It ties Twitter data to your Google analytics account to determine who in the Twitterverse is driving the most visits and page views to your website. From the perspective of focusing on ACTION not just audience, it's a simple yet terrific tool.
> - *Pinterest influencer analytics* 'Pinfluencer', which provides shockingly valuable data to its *e*-commerce and retail customers (such as Zappos) about which pinners are driving the most re-pins, clicks, and even hard revenue.
> - *Blog influencer analytics* It helps companies to identify influential bloggers, for example, GroupHigh.

MINING CONSUMER-GENERATED MEDIA

The online information clutter needs to be processed to convert the myriad of online voices, references, and opinions into crystal clear insight and to extract valuable knowledge and actionable intelligence. The following are reasons why CGM is an important tool:

- Market sensing to gain an insight into the consumer's mind, and secure inputs on consumer perceptions on organizational products and brands.
- Build stronger bonds with influencers and channelize them for good word-of-mouth.
- Measure the impact of marketing strategies and understand emerging trends.
- Uncover the ideas for new products and identify opportunities for improving current products.
- Disseminate this market intelligence data across the organization and formulate strategies to create customer value.

Measuring where a message appears and how many people see it is no longer enough. Companies need to track the volume of CGM and the richness of the dialogue among people to understand how a message evolves. The following section illustrates how an organization can track the buzz generated online to extract meaning out of it. Tools used for the purpose are Blogpulse and Buzzlogic.

CASE STUDY: The iPhone

The Apple iPhone was announced in January 2007 giving rise to an unprecedented pre-launch buzz, which concentrated on parameters on which consumers search information, namely product features, sales, and viability and drove anticipation tremendously.

This case study attempts at studying the evolution and flow of conversations regarding a sample product 'iPhone' in the blogosphere.

The case explores:

(i) The volume of user-generated content
(ii) Key influencers
(iii) Volume of CGM as a function of *sales*, *price*, and *features*

The Nielsen Buzz metrics tool, Blogpulse, for trend analysis, was used to track the volume of the content generated across the introduction stage of the product life cycle, that is, across product announcement, introduction, launch, and controversy (Figs 13.1–13.4—iPhone and Blogpulse graphs).

Tracking all posts about iPhone

The insights are as follows:

- The volume of the consumer-generated data was highest around the time of announcement—January 2007, dipped during the interim period and peaked again around the June 29 launch (Fig. 13.1).

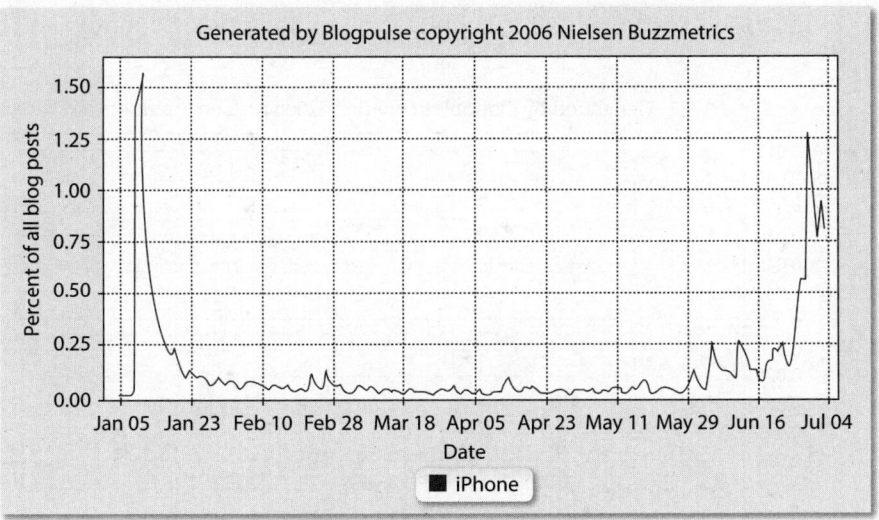

Fig. 13.1 CGM related to 'iPhone', January–July 2007

- A visible jump in the Blogpulse CGM graph in September 2007 coincided with the increased volume of CGM owing to an angry backlash by dissatisfied consumers when Apple slashed the prices of the iPhone by $200 leaving a series of early adopters of the product feeling cheated and angry (Fig. 13.2).

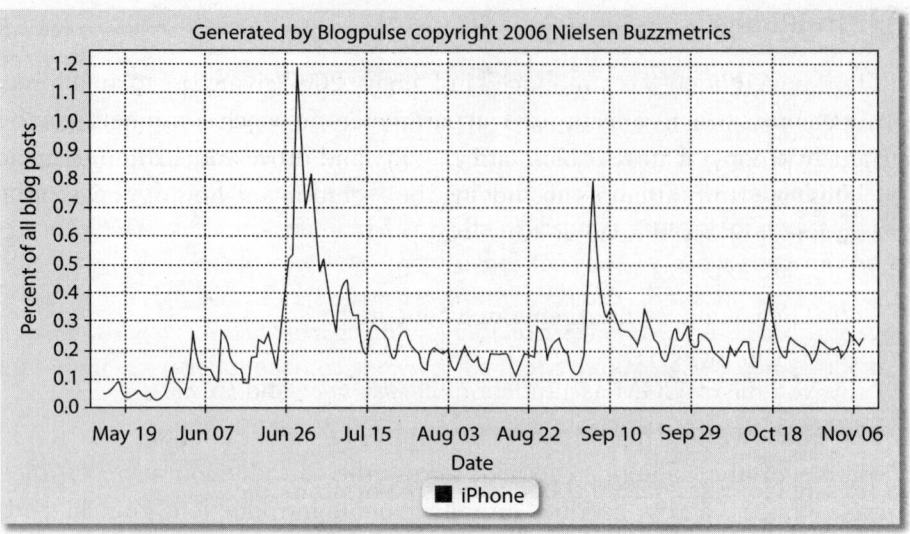

Fig. 13.2 CGM related to 'iPhone', May–November 2007

- Using a combination of 'sales', 'price', and 'features' terms with the iPhone yields graphs which indicate the highest level of CGM related to the 'features' of the iPhone prior to its June 2007 release. The post release phase witnessed an equivalent increment in the levels of CGM related to all 3 parameters (Fig. 13.3). However, by July, there was an increase in the volume of CGM corresponding to the 'sales' parameter. This was followed by a huge increment in the CGM level corresponding to the 'price' parameter which coincided with the pricing controversy (Fig. 13.4).

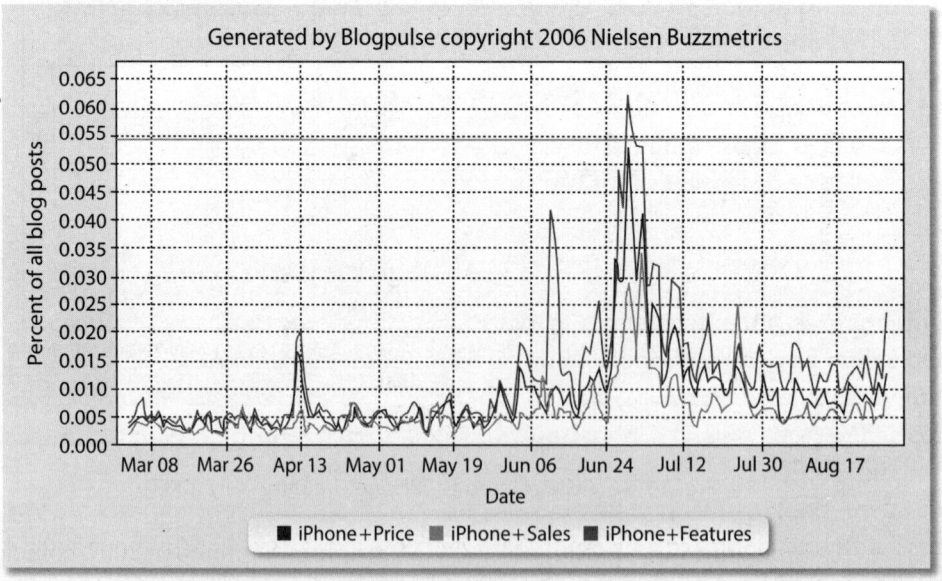

Fig. 13.3 CGM related to 'iPhone' with the combination of 'price', 'sales', and 'features' terms, March–August 2007

MARKET INFLUENCE ANALYTICS IN A DIGITAL ECOSYSTEM

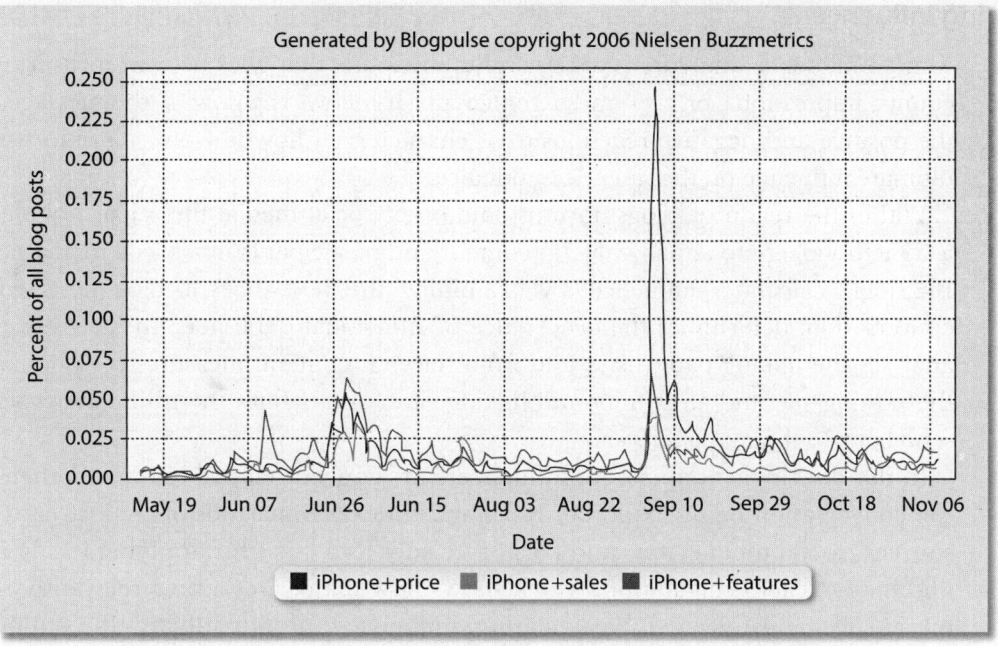

Fig. 13.4 CGM related to 'iPhone' with the combination of 'price', 'sales', and 'features' terms, May–November 2007

IDENTIFYING INFLUENCERS IN CONVERSATIONS

The Buzzlogic tool for identification of key influencers across the blogosphere was used (Fig. 13.5 Buzzlogic + iPhone conversation).

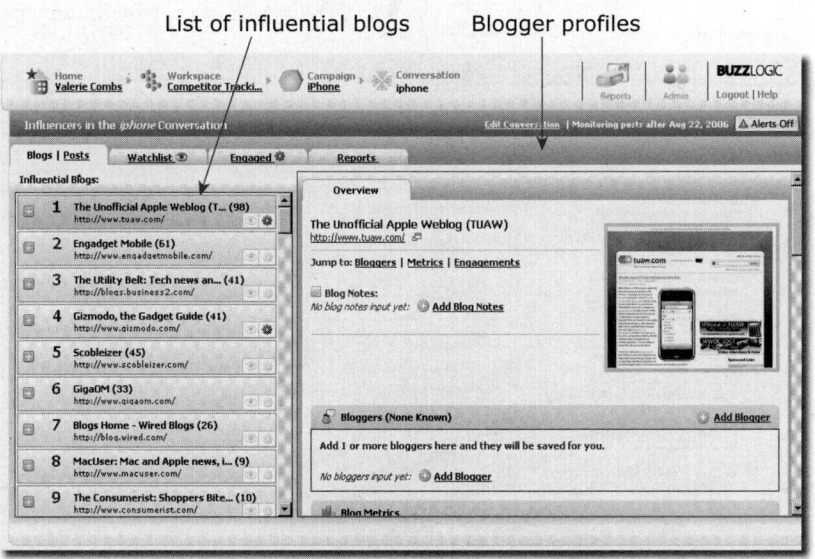

Fig. 13.5 'Buzzlogic' tool for identification of key influencers across the blogosphere in 'iPhone' conversation

Measuring Influence

Market influence analytics is an emerging discipline that goes beyond measuring story counts, impressions, or even message pick up. It follows the flow of the message, tracks the positive and negative reactions to it, characterizes how it evolves, and measures its ultimate influence on the intended audience.

Within the realm of blogs, forums, and other social media, the science of influence is a methodology to attach value to content and participants in a social media network. Buzzlogic calculates influence, by examining the relevance of blog posts within a conversation; determines the occurrence of individual publishers' messages over time; analyses the linking patterns to and from relevant content; measures the popularity of the posting site and all its inbound linking sites, and defines the traffic these blog sites send back to the marketer's site.

In the Buzzlogic application, influencers are ranked relative to one another within the conversation being explored. Buzzlogic indexes thousands of mainstream media sources, social media sites, and corporate sites as a basis for applying its algorithms and has a 'reach' calculation, which shows how many sites a blog relevantly reaches on a specific subject. By calculating influence and identifying the influencers, organizations can formulate strategies to engage the influencers for organizational benefit. After monitoring the *relevance* between user queries and publisher content, the *occurrence* of relevant posts by a publisher during a given time frame, *popularity*, and *recency* of inbound links to an item of a conversation, Buzzlogic calculates influence (Figs 13.5–13.7).

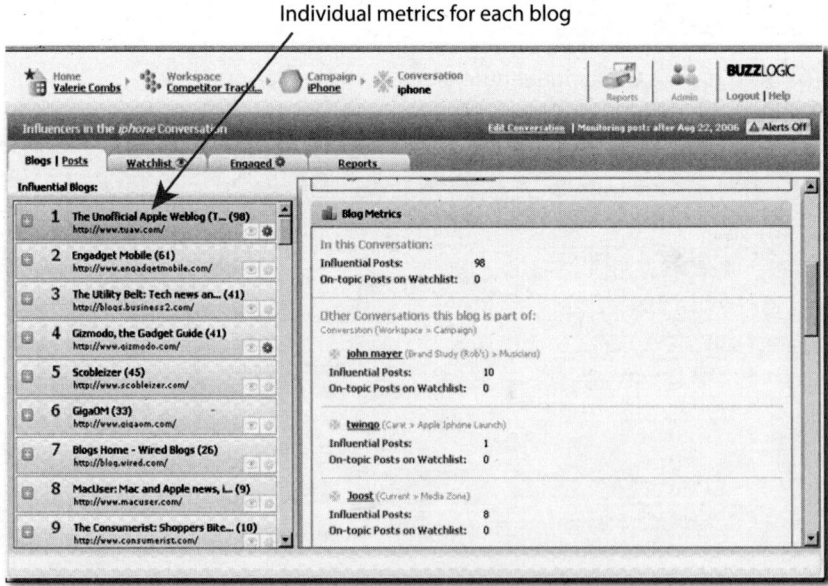

Fig. 13.6 'Buzzlogic' tool in 'iPhone' conversation calculates influence across the blogosphere for individual metrics

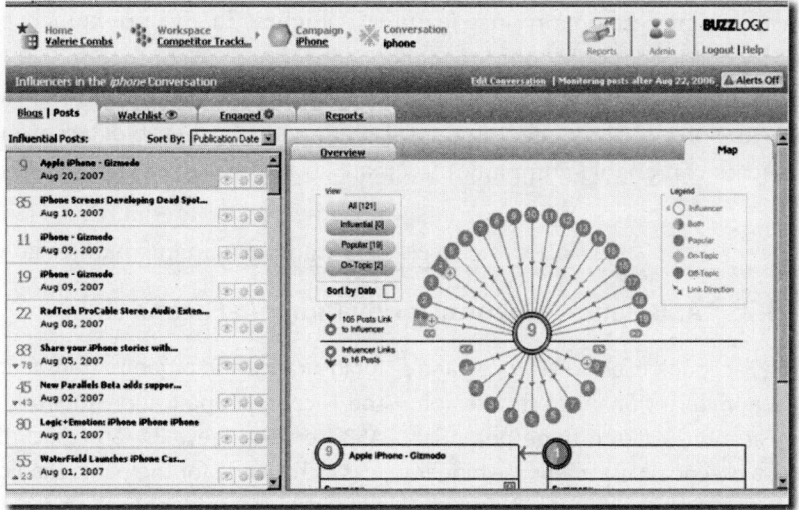

Fig. 13.7 Social maps display track backs and linking behaviour

The insights are as follows:

- The *unofficial Apple weblog*, followed by *engadget mobile* were the most influential blogs with respect to conversations for the Apple iPhone (Fig. 13.1).
- A study of detailed blog metrics shows the number of influential posts (August 2006–August 2007) and also provides data on other conversations the original blog is a part of (Fig. 13.2). While the unofficial Apple weblog (http://www.tuaw.com/) had 98 influential posts about the iPhone, engadget mobile (http://www.engadgetmobile.com) had 61.

Figure 13.3 for the iPhone a social map is the visual representation of relationships between posts and other participants within a conversation. It can hence understand the neighbourhood of CGM for the iPhone. Neighbourhood can be defined as asset of all those relationships by linking around a social media post. In a given neighbourhood, links may be made by relevant, popular, and influential neighbours.

CONSUMERS AND THE ONLINE SPACE

Consumer interest in a product is highest at the time of announcement, followed by launch and peaks whenever there is a controversy. Consumer dissatisfaction spills out in the form of content generated by them and they tend to form communities of like-minded people with similar levels of discontent. In the Apple iPhone case, the volume of content generated by unsatisfied consumers was so high that it, along with other factors, prompted Apple CEO, Steve Jobs to carry an apology letter, addressing the issue on the Apple website. The letter was referenced/linked in over 80 blog postings in the first two days. Apple's acknowledgement of the empowered consumer was complete.

Consumer interest on product features is highest in the pre-launch phase, following which discussions on sales and price take centre-stage. A controversy on any issue results in high volumes of explicit and descriptive commentary on the subject under discussion. In the realm of CGM, detailed study of key influencers, their blogger profiles and detailed blog metrics can enable companies to create strategies for 'creating customer evangelists'

EXHIBIT 13.7   ASB Bank—Channel innovation *ala* Facebook

With 1.7 million Facebook users in New Zealand and basically a number of financial services on this platform, Facebook offered huge potential for tapping into a potential customer base bigger than any city in the sparsely populated country. The bank sought to position itself as an innovative bank and build an engaged community.

ASB's new Facebook application 'Virtual Branch' is a world's first using Facebook as an additional, full-fledged channel allowing customers to bank as if in a branch, but from the convenience of their home with extended opening hours. The application enables a live, secure and real-time conversation between the Facebook user and a choice of ASB specialists.

The new application focuses on 101 conversation, listening, and feedback not viral marketing and broadcasting of promotions and advertisements. This is supported by the fact that ASB specialists on Facebook do not have any sales targets yet, unlike the regular branch staff. The virtual branch allows vital tasks such as security checking and identity verification protocols which are based on the system operating parameters mirroring those of its contact centre and branches.

This allows customers to discuss specific accounts, chat on banking products, open accounts, apply for insurance and organize transactions. Aligning the Facebook application to work through the ASB servers, firewalls, and security protocols was a challenge for the bank. Data generated by the virtual branch application are not stored by Facebook or any third party. Only ASB has access to the information and protects it by the same level of security monitoring and software that is used for the bank's Internet banking. A backend monitoring and reporting system ensures the quality and compliance with internal and regulatory guidelines.

An interesting feature in the virtual bank is the avatar greeting customers landing on the main page. This avatar can be customized to draw attention to new promotions, events or services. Another feature making the application more personal is that customers are able to select an ASB specialist of their choice from a list of photos.

The virtual branch was a major success for ASB Bank. Within 2 months after launch the application was downloaded 13,000 times and was liked by 13,600 Facebook users. This number grew to 18,000 likes by July 2011. In November 2010 the virtual bank attracted almost 10,000 customers per month. A survey showed that the initiative raised the bank's awareness by more than 10%.

(*Source*: www.theasianbanker.com)

through suitable 'blogger relations programmes'. The best bet for Apple, in reference to its product, iPhone is to foster partnerships with the two blogs (the unofficial Apple weblog and engadget mobile) as a medium to reach out to its consumers and shape the online conversations.

Questions:

1. Why is it important for companies to monitor influence in the virtual world?
2. How can companies like Apple make use of influential individuals after identifying them? Discuss. Can the company benefit from a blogger outreach programme or a community programme or use *Whatsapp* for leveraging influential customers?

PRACTITIONER PERSPECTIVE

Marketing in the new India is that we will continue to be in a hybrid media environment. While a large number of our consumers will be digital, a significant chunk of our consumers will still live in media dark geographies beyond TV's reach. To that extent, the role of a brand manager would become interesting where he will leverage content across different media. Great campaigns will continue to be based on singular, sharply differentiated propositions, but the advertising idea would be communicated through content that would work in vastly different media ranging from YouTube and Facebook to a direct contact programme in a village market. From campaign management to content management will be an exciting journey.

Hemant Bakshi, Executive Director, Home and Personal Care, Hindustan Unilever

Twitter can do many things for the brand as part of the business process: from creating an instantaneous feedback and sales loop, to provide a real time customization or real-time service.

Harshil Kalra, Co-founder, Foxy Moron

Indian marketers were more focused on promotions and events that create the buzz around the brands; but they do not go into understanding consumers. Chief marketing officers have to lead by example and should learn to blog, tweet and interact with the Facebook community.

Virginia Sharma, Vice President—Marketing and Communication, IBM India/South Asia

SUMMARY

As the democratization of consumer expression leads to a viral proliferation of information online, the new age communication ecosystem has prompted the need for a careful evaluation of the potential of what is being called consumer-generated Internet content, creating new challenges for *marketing intelligence*. With the ability to impact business environments, these offerings of the information age have garnered adequate potential to engineer business transformations. Consumer-generated media, or CGM as it is being termed, comprises the content generated by consumers within online venues such as Internet forums. The digital paradigm plays two very significant roles in marketing—influencing consumer behaviour and harnessing consumer intelligence. While it is vital for an organization to evaluate consumer intentions and provide consumers the necessary information they are looking for, equally important is the need for collecting consumer data by studying the consumer behavioural patterns on the Internet and subsequently nurturing long-term relationships with consumers. Knowledge has become the source of strategic planning for the creation of a value proposition for consumers. Market sensing is a core business process and organizations which are able to manage, analyse, and combine knowledge faster for product innovation and improvement in line with customer expectations are succeeding in the competitive scenario. Consumer interest in a product is highest at the time of announcement, followed by launch and peaks whenever there is a controversy. Consumer dissatisfaction spills out in the form of content generated by them and they tend to form communities of like-minded people with similar levels of discontent. In the realm of consumer generated media, detailed study of key influencers, their blogger profiles and detailed blog metrics can enable companies to create strategies for 'creating customer evangelists' through suitable 'blogger relations programmes'.

Concept Review Questions

1. What is CGM? How can companies use CGM as an organizational resource to generate positive word-of-mouth for its consumers?
2. What is individual Internet worth? How is it important for organizations?
3. How can CGM be used for consumer empowerment? Illustrate with examples.
4. Write short notes on
   (a) Engineering influence in the virtual world
   (b) Mining CGM
5. Companies can use the virtual medium inside the organization to improve efficiency and productivity, and between the organization and the customers for customer acquisition, improving revenue and customer retention. Comment.

Critical Thinking Questions

1. Use the Facebook page community for a product of your choice. Conduct a survey on the page and try to identify the key influencers amongst the consumers on the page.
2. Form an online research group on LinkedIn or Facebook. Make sure all the participants have something in common in terms of product usage or expertise in a field. Post a

query there. Trace how an online forum can be used for functioning as
   (a) A focus group for ideation
   (b) A group for co-creation
   (c) Collecting marketing intelligence
   (d) Generating influence on peers
3. Identify an FMCG brand whose consumers are active on the Internet. Trace the presence of the consumers across myriad sites on the Web.
   (a) Study what is written in terms of CGM, for the organization. Form an opinion about the organization or its products on the basis of what you see online. Formulate a strategy to
      (i) Enable the organization to channelize positive CGM for benefit
      (ii) Control and respond to negative CGM
   (b) Contact a few of the active consumers who have created content in the online domain. Ask them to detail how the Internet has served to empower them, as consumers.

References

1. Hanson, W. and Kalyanam, K., (2007). Web business models, *Internet Marketing and Ecommerce*, Thomson Press, p. 146.
2. Blackshaw, P. and Nazzaro, M., (2007). '*Consumer Generated Media 101: Word-of-Mouth in the Age of the Web-fortified Consumer*', Nielsen Buzzmetrics.
3. Ranganathan, C. and Ganapathy, S., (2002). 'Key Dimensions of business-to-consumer websites', *Information and Management*, Vol. 39, pp. 457–465.
4. Ahuja, V. and Medury, Y., (2010). 'Corporate blogs as ECRM tools-building consumer engagement through content management', *Journal of Database Marketing and Customer Strategy Management*, Palgrave-Macmillan Journals, Vol. 17(2), pp. 91–105, ISSN: 1741-2439.
5. Schiffman, G. and Leslie, K., Introduction-diversity in the marketplace, *Consumer Behavior*, Seventh Edition, Prentice-Hall, India, 2002, p. 4.
6. Schmidt, J., (2007). 'Blogging practices: An analytical framework.' *Journal of Computer-mediated Communication*, Vol. 12(4), pp. 1409–1427.
7. Ahuja, V., (2012). 'Market influence analytics in a digital ecosystem'. *International Journal of Online Marketing* (IJOM), Vol. 2(4), pp. 42–53.
8. Nielsen Buzzmetrics and BASES, (2007). 'The Origin and impact of CPG New Buzz: Emerging Trends and Implications', http://nielsenbuzzmetrics.com/files/uploaded/whitepapers/Nielsen_Report_Buy_Blog_Buzz_07_17_07.pdf.
9. Blackshaw, P. and Nazzaro, M., Word-of-mouth in the age of the web-fortified consumer, *Consumer-Generated Media* (CGM), 101, 2006.
10. Nelson, P., (1970). 'Information and consumer behavior', *The Journal of Political Economy*, Vol. 78(2), pp. 311–32.
11. Drezner, W. and Farrell, H., (2004). 'The power and politics of blogs', pp. 14–18.
12. Schiffman, G. and Leslie, K., Consumer Influence and Diffusion of Innovations, *Consumer Behavior*, Seventh Edition, Prentice-Hall, India, 2002, p. 398.
13. Ahuja, M., (2011). 'Corporate blogs as tools for consumer segmentation-using cluster analysis for consumer profiling', *Journal of Targeting, Measurement and Analysis for Marketing*, Vol. 19, pp. 173–182, doi: 10.1057/jt.2011.
14. Wathieu, L. and Zoglio, M., Empowering Consumers, '*HBS Working Paper Series*', 2001.
15. Burt, S., (2000). 'The network structure of social capital', *Research in Organizational Behaviour*, Vol. 22, pp. 345–423.
16. Grant, T., (2007). '*Online Buyers Scouring for Deals*', Report on business.com.
17. Gill, K., How we can measure the influence of the blogosphere, University of Washington.

Section 4
The Contemporary Digital Revolution

Chapter 14: Online Communities and Co-creation

Chapter 15: The World of Facebook

Chapter 16: The Future of Marketing—Gamification and Apps

14 Online Communities and Co-creation

LEARNING OBJECTIVES

After reading this chapter, you will be able to:
- Understand the concept of an online community
- Classify the different models of branded co-creation communities
- Understand how organizations are using online communities for co-creation and collaboration
- Distinguish between the use of online communities for identifying trustworthy consumers
- Gain familiarity with the use of online communities for impacting consumer price sensitivity
- Gain clarity on creating consumer profiles on the basis of their online participation

An online community is a group of people with some shared interest who connect and interact with each other over time. Relationship of some sort is implied. The dawn of the information age found groups communicating electronically rather than face-to-face. A computer mediated community uses social software to regulate the activities of the participants. These are places where people gather to share knowledge, build recognition, and tap opportunities.[1]

Initially sensed to be resource pools for value addition, where people ventured to fulfil their need for self-actualization, participation in online communities and forums started as a medium for exchange of ideas and information, and now organizations have started using these communities for marketing through consumer evangelism and support. A Web based communication model utilizes the features of the network for B2C as well as peer-to-peer communication. On the Internet, electronic tribes structured around consumer interests have been growing rapidly.

To be effective in this new environment, managers must consider the strategic implications of the existence of different types of both virtual community and community participation.[2] Consumers join these forums because of the multifaceted opportunities they provide to members. Not only do they provide information on products and services and latest promotional schemes, they are also triggers for innovation. As like-minded people converge together, these are new cliques where organizations can use opinion leaders for evangelism, while harnessing consumer-generated content for product improvement and co-creation.

Collaborative co-creation can be considered as a case of marketing nirvana where customers help an organization to create products, promotions, and advertisements. The levels of co-creation include ideas, product concepts, product screening, product components, product upgrades and updates, and even complete products, as well as creating advertisements, brand names, and ultimately the products themselves.

This chapter aims at linking concepts of collaboration, co-creation, and marketing with one of the most significantly emerging tools from the virtual world today—online communities. The chapter discusses the use of co-creation communities for brands, and various models associated with them and further proceeds to focus on relevant illustrations in the field. The discussion is completed with coverage of suitable empirical models to leverage product/brand online communities.

CO-CREATION COMMUNITIES FOR BRANDS

Brand online communities are virtual spaces where companies interact with customers, treat them as organizational assets, learn about them, and through the process of incorporating feedback and co-creation, develop a level of intimacy with them. Firms aim towards better marketing investment prioritization which yields greater sales from consumers. These online communities help in improving marketing intelligence through interaction between firm and consumer, which aids collection of consumer-related data which definitely help firms in improving the selling context. Finally, consumers drive the actions of the companies who are trying to lure them. In the words of A. G. Lafley, former CEO and Chairman of P&G,

'Consumers are beginning in a very real sense to own our brands and participate in their creation…we need to begin to learn to let go.'

This section discusses a set of models proposed by industry practitioners and academicians in understanding how online communities can be leveraged by organizations towards achieving their branding endeavours, building consumer engagement, and involving consumers in co-creation processes.

Branded co-creation communities can be classified into the following three models[3] (Fig. 14.1):

- Branded challenges on niche crowd-sourcing platforms
- Branded co-creation challenge platforms
- Ongoing co-creation communities

Model 1

In the *first* model, brands run short-term public or private challenges on niche crowd-sourcing platforms to tap into their specialized communities such as designers, developers, animators, filmmakers, engineers, or scientists. There are two types of challenges (Fig. 14.2)—creativity-driven challenges and solution-driven challenges (Table 14.1).

ONLINE COMMUNITIES AND CO-CREATION

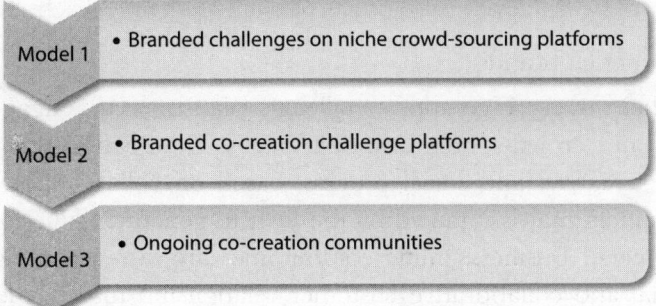

Fig. 14.1 Models of branded co-creation communities

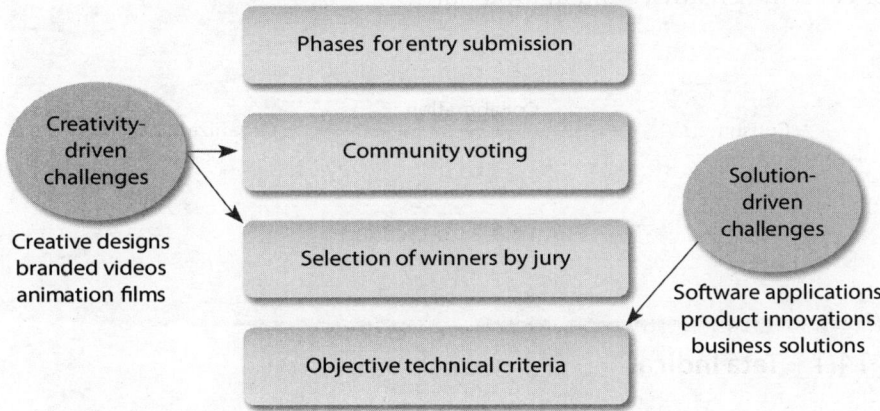

Fig. 14.2 Types of branded challenges

The process

Challenges typically have phases for entry submission, community voting, and selection of winners by jury members or objective technical criteria.

Table 14.1 Creativity-driven challenges vs. solution-driven challenges

Creativity-driven challenges	Solution-driven challenges
Creativity-driven challenges related to creative designs, branded videos, and animation films are typically public, and winners are often selected based on a combination of community voting and jury judgment.	Solution-driven challenges related to software applications, product innovations, and business solutions are sometimes private and winners are sometimes selected based on objective technical criteria.
For example, www.Zooppa.com is an online community which under the theme of 'People powered brand energy', invites entries to brand sponsored video contests and graphic design contest for cash awards. Brands provide a creative brief for each competition, and award prizes for the best ads. Participants can make money, meet other creative minds, grow their portfolios, and achieve visibility for their work.	For example, www.Kaggle.com is a consulting platform that connects companies to the most significant data scientists from its community of over a lakh members. This is a platform for data prediction competitions. Companies, organizations, and researchers post their data and have it scrutinized by the world's best analysts in the field.

Model 2

In the *second* model, brands

- Create their own co-creation challenge platforms to engage their community members and crowd-source branded videos. Co-creation (Fig. 14.3) is defined as an active, creative, and social process, based on collaboration between producers and consumers that is initiated by the firm to generate value for both the firm and the customers.[4] Business online communities are fast becoming excellent tools for operational and collaborative customer relationship management (CRM) with co-creation, soon gaining pace as a strategic outcome of collaborative CRM. Much of the research on online communities suggests that the nature of these communities with permeable boundaries and self-organization makes them a new powerful locus of collective creativity and innovation.[5]

Fig. 14.3 Co-creation

EXHIBIT 14.1   Tata Indica

In 2007, Tata Indica, scheduled to launch the car model, the Indica V2 Xeta, launched the *Xeta Shout out* contest. The customers were asked to submit their own versions of the Indica Xeta advertisement, centred around the theme, *You Gotta be dumb if you miss the Xeta*. Participants had the choice of either shooting a video or presenting a storyboard with pictures clicked by them. The winner of the contest was scheduled to win an Indica V2 Xeta.

The contest was an extension of the long-running 'You Gotta Be Dumb' TV commercial created by FCB-Ulka. The humorous commercial showed four girls trying to flirt with a handsome young man, who just cannot 'get it'. Tata Indica had been using various versions of the commercial for different car variants. Through the above endeavour Tata decided to leverage the impact of consumer-generated media for viral propagation of the theme and utilizing word of mouth for lead generation and sales enhancement. Studies had indicated that the young population revelled in uploading videos on YouTube and having them rated by the Internet populace. By using the same concept, Tata used co-creation to engage the consumer in the development of the brand campaign through some significant creative thinking.

- Create product innovation platforms

  An online community can be built and managed with the aim of product innovation and engaging customers in co-creation. These product innovation platforms (Fig. 14.4) can cater to four distinct dimensions which are providing limited edition designs, discussing, and creating new food and beverage flavours, communities aiming at soliciting new product designs and communities aimed at deriving new business solutions.

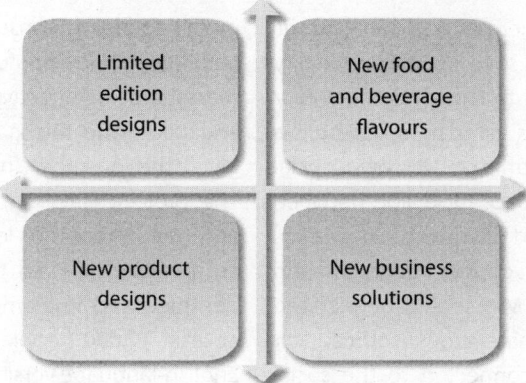

Fig. 14.4 Product innovation platforms

- *Limited Edition Designs*

EXHIBIT 14.2 Nestlé

To involve consumers worldwide in a product innovation venture, Nestlé invited its consumers to participate in a contest to design the new coffee machine Melody 3, by soliciting participation in a euro design contest. The participants could vote for their favourite designs as well. From the 10 designs with the most votes, a UK jury subsequently selected a finalist to represent the UK and Ireland in the European final and win *a trip to the awards in Milan*, Italy—Europe's design capital. Two European winning designs, highest voted and jury selected, were produced as the new Limited Edition *Melody®* machine for *Spring 2014*.

- *New Food and Beverage Flavours*

EXHIBIT 14.3 The Domino's Social Pizza campaign

The Domino's Social Pizza campaign comprised a crusade on the Domino's Facebook page where fans were asked to vote on the favourite parts of the pizza they wanted to savour. New sets of options on a daily basis, namely choices of crust, sauces, and toppings added to create their first 'social pizza'. Domino's India has a significant online presence with a host of blogs, website, Facebook, and twitter, along with encouraging people to order online. The Domino's India blog constantly engages consumers in conversations regarding topics such as *WollaWicky* and *Pehli Kamai Initiatives*.

- *New Product Designs*

> **EXHIBIT 14.4   Fiat Mio**
>
> A campaign created by AgenciaClick, Isobar, Brazil, for the Fiat Mio combined social media and reality in an unprecedented way to launch the first-ever crowd-sourced car. In this campaign, Fiat built a forum at http://www.fiatmio.cc—its own social network, and created a space for dialog between the designers of the car and Fiat drivers. Consumers answered questions about gadget integration and what kind of driving the Mio should be planned for, as well as the ultimate crowd-sourced car question—should it be connected to the social Web? The car was launched at the 26th annual automobile show in Sao Paulo. By telling Fiat exactly what they wanted in a car and using social media to do it, consumers believed they were helping to shape the future of the industry. Brand message gains effectiveness when customers are engaged—and this is the ultimate engagement, giving the consumer a hand in creating the product. The project, Fiat said, drew 10,000 suggestions and was a process of 'learning again how to make an automobile'. Even though the campaign was designed and implemented in Brazil, it reached at least 17,000 people in 160 countries, with an English-language version as well as one in Brazilian Portuguese. The campaign lived across the Web, including *YouTube*, where a series of videos that documented the project can be viewed.

- *New Business Solutions*

Product innovation platforms aimed at creating new business solutions function in the following two ways:

- Some brands host the challenge on niche crowd-sourcing platforms to tap into the community. They also promote them on their own branded destinations, for example, Domino's.
- Other brands need to create their own branded destinations to provide sophisticated dashboards to community members to pick and choose product options to customize their product (Nike ID, McDonald's Mein Burger, Fiat Mio).

Some challenges offer separate community prizes based on community voting, and jury prizes based on jury selection, and some reward community members who offer constructive comments and feedback with prizes.

Domino's India launched a campaign with a series of six questions they posed to their consumers. Participants were asked to respond in a single comment on the Domino's India blog and the winner would receive a free Domino's Pizza and a Butterscotch Mousse Cake within 24 hours!

Model 3

In the *third* model, brands build and nurture their own co-creation communities and encourage contributions through a series of challenges, for example, The Heineken Ideas Brewery launched a series of successful challenges. The third of its challenges was directed towards the 60+ population, with the objective of creating innovative products specifically for this age segment. By asking people across the globe to share their thoughts regarding the ideas and expectations of the aging population, Heineken went a step ahead and requested the acclaimed Director of 'Grumpy Old Men', Donald Petrie, to solicit the ideas from the people online, as well as be a part of the jury to judge the entire challenge. People from 20 countries across the globe were invited to start filming, photographing or writing the experiences, expectations, and thoughts of the golden population.

EXHIBIT 14.5 Brand Program—LEGO CUUSOO

In 2011, LEGO (Fig. 14.5) opened up its Japanese crowd-sourcing platform CUUSOO to global audiences, inviting adults to submit and vote for new LEGO product designs. LeventOzler, editor-in-chief of Dexigner, summarized the process:

Ideas that are supported by 10,000 votes have a chance of being selected to become part of the LEGO Group's product portfolio and sold in LEGO Brand retail stores and the LEGO online shop. Consumers who have their ideas chosen will earn 1% of the total net sales of the product.

CUUSOO's 10,000 vote requirement helps streamline the crowd-sourcing process. The Idea Connection team noted:

Lego receives original ideas but is not weighed down by too many which can be costly and time consuming to examine. And fan support can provide some kind of indication of the potential popularity of a concept.

The fan-facing effort has challenged LEGO to increase the speed of its product release cycle. Matthew Kronsberg, a writer at Fast Company, said:

Such an outpouring of [fan] interest would be squandered though, if that consumer desire was left to wither through a traditional product development cycle. And this is where the second and possibly more significant piece of the Cuusoo endeavor comes into play: Lego Minecraft will go from concept to release in roughly six months, rather than Lego's typical two- or three-year process.

There are currently 3,787 live projects at LEGOCUUSOO. Three co-created products have been launched to date, and a fourth one is in production. LEGO has launched several efforts to nurture and enable a spirit of creation amongst adults and children alike, with digital tools *LEGO Digital Designer* and *LDraw*, and social networks *LEGO Club* and *ReBrick*.

Fig. 14.5 Lego Cuusooonline

(*Reproduced with permission from Lego Cuusoo*)

In Heineken's contest, people were allowed to access the idea, (Fig. 14.6) as well as vote for their favourite ideas. Participants were also encouraged to promote their ideas via social networks, as number of votes was factored in to the winning decision.

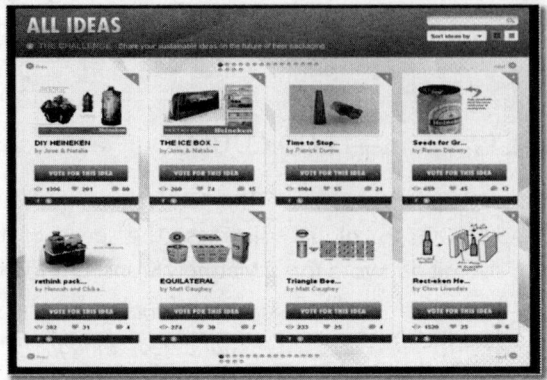

Fig. 14.6 The Heineken ideas

(*Reproduced with permission from Heineken*)

CO-CREATION COMMUNITIES—SOME EXHIBITS

Proceeding further, research helped develop some empirical models to study the effective usage of business online communities.

EMPIRICAL MODELS TO LEVERAGE PRODUCT/BRAND ONLINE COMMUNITIES

(This section contains excerpts from research published by S. Alavi, V. Ahuja, 2011).

Research[6] in the domain of online communities helped us build three empirical models (Fig. 14.7) in the context of product and brand online communities. These models were

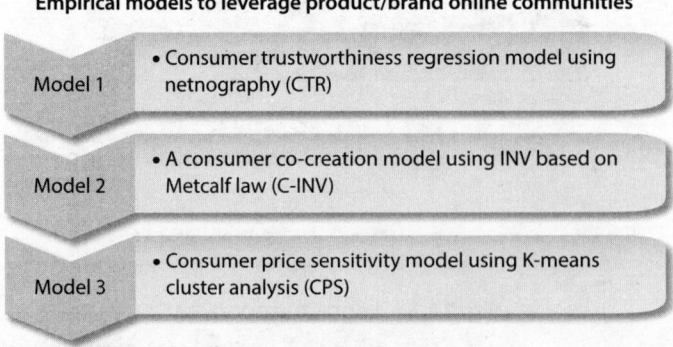

Fig. 14.7 Online communities—empirical models

EXHIBIT 14.6   MyStarbucksIdea.com

The MyStarbucksIdea website, where Starbucks does its business crowd sourcing, has been actively engaging customers for over 3 years now. It encourages customers to submit ideas for better products, improving the customer experience, and defining new community involvement, among other categories. Clearly, Starbucks has seen and believes what Peter Drucker has to say about business adaptability— *within 5 years, if you're in the same business you are in now, you're going to be out of business.*

Customers can submit, view, and discuss submitted ideas along with employees from various Starbucks departments—'Idea Partners'.

The company regularly polls its customers for their favourite products and has a leader board to track which customers are the most active in submitting ideas, comments, and poll participation.

The site is at once a crowd sourcing tool, a market research method that brings customer priorities to light, an on-line community, and an effective Internet marketing tool. By combining the concepts of change, experimentation, social media, customer engagement and market research, Starbucks has emerged as a dominant brand.

In April 2014, Starbucks had the following volume of ideas (Table 14.2).

Table 14.2   My Starbucks Ideas

Product ideas	Experience ideas	Involvement ideas
33,549 coffee & espresso drinks	8,035 ordering, payment, & pick-up	4,961 Building community
3,534 Frappuccino® beverages	14,572 atmosphere & locations	9,091 Social responsibility
9,807 tea & other drinks	11,097 other experience ideas	5,559 Other involvement ideas
15,410 food		1,529 Outside USA
8,107 merchandise & music		
16,475 Starbucks card		
2,994 new technology		
10,818 other product ideas		

EXHIBIT 14.7   Dell Ideastorm

Dell IdeaStorm positioned Dell as a forward-thinker that recognized that the people they served might have some good thoughts on how to serve them. Ideastorm was an online space where people can logon and post ideas related to products and services. In its five-year-tenure, IdeaStorm has received nearly 15,000 suggestions and has made about 500 refinements based on them. Most were nice little tweaks such as backlit keyboards. The most famous was a Linux-based operating system.

EXHIBIT 14.8 Sunsilk Gang of Girls.com

Co-creation challenges around crowdsourcing designs, videos and stories have already become the norm for adding a social media component to brand campaigns, and many creators are becoming fatigued with them, forcing brands to support them with bigger paid media budgets, more attractive prizes, and celebrity endorsements. Branded online communities, set up by companies for Building brand equity, are now tying up with the electronic media for greater visibility. As the interest of the youth increases in social networking, with humongous volumes of youngsters not only hanging around networking sites, but also eagerly participating in consumer communities, these branded online communities have found themselves most wanted on television.

In recent developments in India, Hindustan Unilever's SUNSILK GANG OF GIRLS, an online community, and Zoom television had come together to present a singing reality show called *Sunsilk Gang of Girls - Spotlight Mein*.

In response to online applications at the Sunsilk GOG site, this new television series presented four talented girls in the country who were groomed and mentored by maestros from the music and entertainment fraternity, in preparation for a live finalé performance in front of a big audience. Reality TV, it's success, the impact generated and the huge volume of viewership it draws has opened a new dimension for synergy between the Internet and media. As branded online communities embrace television, the euphoria created by such shows will further increase traffic on the site-increased membership is a foregone conclusion.

Kelly Mooney's thoughts in an ADAGE article on For Relevance, Think Three-Way threw light on how companies can leverage such situations. By looking at the brand, the consumer and online communities as three components of a love triangle, she reiterates the need for brands to intersect with online communities, to be able to connect with their consumers.

'There are no diminishing returns when brands think three-way, when they 'triangulate' to communicate in a b-to-we world. Online communities are an infinite resource bringing not only preexisting participants within the brand's range, but new i-citizens formerly uninvolved until their passions are sparked by a marketing campaign or message that inspires them to spread the love.'

In Sunsilk's case, the three sides of the triangle are aptly covered—the brand connects to each girl and the fan community; the girls connect to the brand and each other—all tied to the community or the event as the centre. While acting as excellent repositories for information, such communities help the brand marketers by providing information to validate their understanding of the market, while further bifurcating consumers with respect to preferences, expectations, and level of brand loyalty.

EXHIBIT 14.9 Oreo, India's Dunkathon

Oreo represents a cookie brand in India. Oreo India's Daily Dunks that were created by the cookie brand to capture the day's most happening event, had launched Dunkathon to create special dunks from their fans' memorable moments. A Facebook App enabled fans to create their own customized Oreo dunks, while Twitter was leveraged to create buzz on #Dunkathon. Apart from positive branding, Dunkathon also helped Oreo India, bond better through co-creation with its online community.

developed for peer-to-peer consumer communities for products and brands where organizations can benefit from the interaction taking place amongst the consumers. Community evangelists and opinion leaders were taking up problem solving roles in communities, impacting consumer price sensitivity and creating credibility for the communities.

I. CONSUMER TRUSTWORTHINESS REGRESSION MODEL USING NETNOGRAPHY (CTR)

What is Netnography?

Netnography is an online marketing research technique. With the help of netnography, online community research can be done by either actively integrating the members of the community or passively monitoring the community and integrating the gathered information, knowledge and ideas into the new product development process.[7] Netnography involves a researcher becoming a part of a community, understanding its working and culture and soliciting reciprocity for himself by engaging into a dialogue in the community. This way a researcher can function at the grass-root level and understand the problems of the community, as well as the differences between the online and offline environments.

Steps in the netnography process are explained in Fig. 14.8.

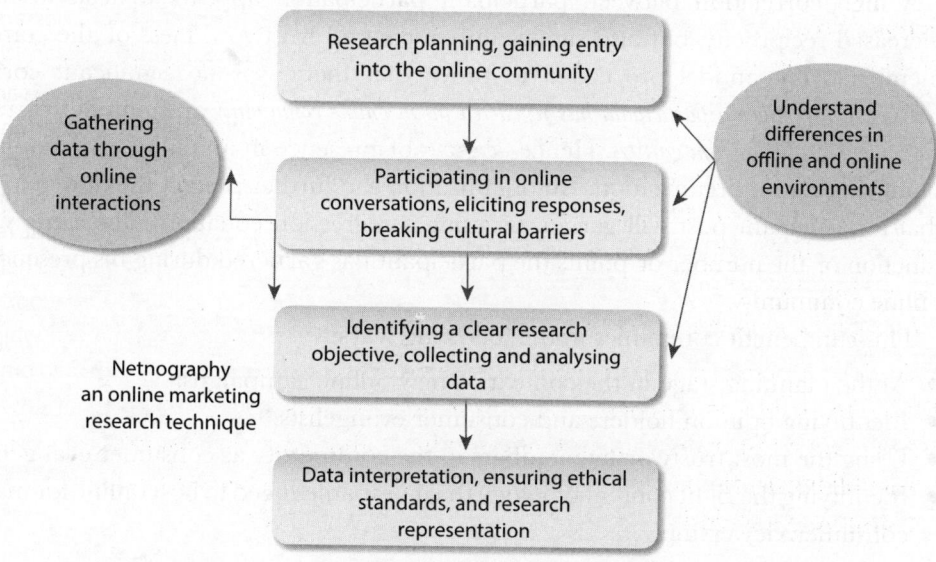

Fig. 14.8 Netnography

A netnography of 40 online product communities of Apple was conducted. Research objectives were to identify the following:
- What drives participants to participate in the community?
- What type of posts garners the maximum consumer views?
- Whose posts are the most viewed? These would be the most trustworthy members in the online community.

Most of the communities had a point system where embers accumulated a specific number of points based on frequency and degree of participation, on the basis of a well-defined formula.

The results indicated a high correlation between the *number of views* a product-related post gets in an online community and the *number of points* a community participant accumulates by participating in the online community[8] (Fig. 14.9).

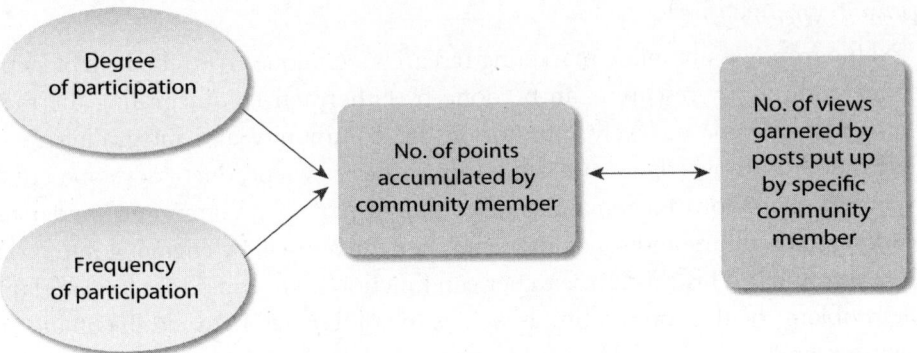

Fig. 14.9 Community member points

A high correlation between participant participation appears to lead to not only increased reciprocity, but also significantly increased trustworthiness of the community members. The model proceeded to prove that there was no significant correlation between *days since a participant has registered in an online community* and number of *views that the content created by him garners*. Hence, *longevity* of presence in an online community is not significant for an organization. An organization can further predict the number of views that a participant post will garner, by using a regression equation. The same will be a function of the number of points the participant has garnered during his presence in the online community.

This can benefit companies in the following ways:

- At the planning stage in the context of new online campaigns.
- Identifying opinion holders and consumer evangelists.
- Using the most trustworthy members in the community as consumer evangelist.
- Identifying the right content typology that companies need to host online for maximum consumer viewership.

II. A CONSUMER CO-CREATION MODEL USING INV BASED ON METCALF LAW (C-INV)[10]

What is Metcalf's law?

Metcalf's law is often cited as an explanation for the rapid growth of the Internet today and can be used to explain the rising wave of information technology that we are riding in the twenty-first century. It relates to the power of an interconnected network to enable collaboration and extend the reach of an organization. We often forget that

Internet is short for 'Interconnected network'. Marketers should continually review how to make the best use of this network as this law is widely believed to apply equally to electronic marketplaces. A network's value grows quickly/exponentially as participants join. Named after a networking company founder who popularized it, Metcalf's law captures the idea that the number of possible connections between members of a network expands much faster than the count of the members.

- Metcalf's law relates the value of a digital network to the number of connections (or users or members) it has.
- This law helps explore the use of the virtual paradigms in the context of enabling collaboration and extending the reach of an organization.[9] This finds applications in the domain of online marketing with respect to *e*-commerce with the Web adequately proliferating as an electronic marketplace.
- Of significance is the global reach of the Internet[10] in creating a larger marketplace which is also a function of the number of eyeballs that view a website,[11] considering that reach is the most visible difference between *e*-commerce and the physical world.
- The power of the network grows in relation to the number of players in the network. This is true in innovation as well as any other business process.[12]
- Metcalf's law illustrates the important difference between an individual's value of a network and the value of the network as a whole.
- As per Metcalf's law, the full value of the network, the community value, is the summation of the individual values of the members in the community.[13]

Community network value = $\sum$ *(Individual values in a network)*
CNV (C1) = INV (M1) + INV (M2) + INV (M3) + INV (M4) + INV (M5) + INV (M6)

- The law is also very much related to economics and business management, especially with competing business communities of a company looking to merge with one another. If there are n number of members in a network, they can connect to $n - 1$ members (Fig. 14.10). The community value of the network grows at a rate of $n \times (n - 1)$.

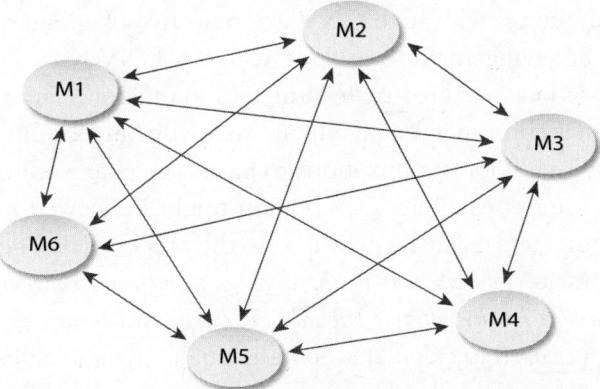

Fig. 14.10 Community C1—Each community member can have an individual connection with ($n - 1$) other community members

The bigger the network, the more valuable it is and the more valuable a new member is. According to Metcalf's law, with everyone connected, each valuing connections at R 1 is R 1 = R 2 × n × (n − 1)/2 = R n × (n − 1).

- For other situations, it is useful to define network value based on individual values. Each member of the network above contributes an individual value to the network. This is the benefit that the individual gets from joining the network. In the situation above, everyone benefits the same from a connection.

More simply, 'The value of a network increases with the square of the number of participants'.[14] This value accrues to those who are collaborating within the network or those who are providing their services across the network. The value of the network to the individual actually increases linearly—with three people, there are two people to communicate with and with six people, there are five people to communicate with (the value is proportional to $n − 1$, where n is the number of members in the network). This law gives an idea of how consumer-generated media (CGM) has become so popular in comparison with conventional marketing practices.

Where communities are created as part of a business proposition, the law shows the importance of supporting the growth of the networks through the difficult initial phase until a 'critical mass' of participants is achieved. Many communities never make it through this phase.[15]

Individual network value serves as an important metric in identification of valuable customers. Participation appears to be the most important determinant of individual network value. Valuable customers demonstrate high participation, high emotional attachment, high loyalty and commitment, and low attitude towards switching. Organizations can use comparisons of community network values of different product communities to gauge the effectiveness of new products launched and effectiveness of new campaigns launched. Based on Metcalf's law, online communities will signify more value to the parent organization when they have more users.

The comparison of community network value (CNV) of different product communities (say, of Apple) is also reflective of product performance from a consumer perspective. Product communities with high CNV are reflective of greater consumer appreciation, association, and engagement than those with low CNV.

The organizations need to create strategies to build a relationship with the consumer through greater consumer engagement, reducing uncertainty and greater consumer motivation. It is vital for organizations to have a mechanism in place, which is useful to identify significant consumers. Co-creation might be viewed as an aspect of customer knowledge competence which encompasses the processes that generate knowledge about specific customers. *Participation in the community network, emotional attachment, online trust, commitment, member loyalty, attitude towards switching,* and *period of association with the network* were parameters used to calculate the individual network value.

The empirical model helped generate five consumer profiles[16] (Fig. 14.11) which can help organizations understand their consumers as co-creators on the basis of their individual characteristics.

ONLINE COMMUNITIES AND CO-CREATION

Classification of consumers participating in product online communities

- Impending co-creators
- Vacillating Indecisives
- Unauthentic non-chalants
- Passionate unfaithfuls
- Potential protagonists

Consumer co-creation model using INV based on Metcalf law

Fig. 14.11 Consumer profiling

The detailed consumer profiles are depicted in Table 14.3.

Table 14.3 Consumer cluster profiles

Cluster number	Cluster profile	Consumer segment	Implications
Cluster 1	Consumers score medium to high on participation, medium to high on emotional attachment, medium to high on online trust, high on commitment, high on member loyalty, medium to high on attitude towards switching and medium to high on period of association with the network.	Impending co-creators	Consumers with *high potential* to become *loyal to* the organization. High end loyalty programmes, incentives, and value added benefits will work towards cementing the consumer–organization relationship.
Cluster 2	Consumers score medium on participation, low on emotional attachment, medium on online trust, medium on commitment, low on member loyalty, and medium on attitude towards switching and high on period of association with the network.	Unauthentic non-chalants	Consumers with high longevity with the company and low emotional connection, depicting *spurious loyalty* and placid nature, will need significant marketing intervention for revitalization of their relationship with the company.

(Continued)

Cluster 3	Consumers score high on participation, high on emotional attachment, high on online trust, very high on commitment, high on member loyalty, medium on attitude towards switching and high on period of association with the network.	Potential protagonists	*Sustainable loyal* customers with greatest potential for becoming *consumer evangelists*, if barriers to switching are high. Loyalty schemes and reward mechanisms will work best with these consumers. Have the highest potential for being used for *Co-creation*.
Cluster 4	Consumers score high on participation, very low on emotional attachment, low on online trust, very low on commitment and medium on member loyalty, high on attitude towards switching and low on period of association with the network.	Passionate unfaithfuls	Enthusiastic people willing to interact with the organization online, but *not loyal* to the organization.
Cluster 5	Consumers score medium on participation, low on emotional attachment, medium on online trust, medium on commitment, medium on member loyalty, medium on attitude towards switching and medium on period of association with the network.	Vacillating indecisives	Ambivalent consumers demonstrating low loyalty

III. CONSUMER PRICE SENSITIVITY MODEL USING K-MEANS CLUSTER ANALYSIS

This model studied the usage of online communities to study consumer price sensitivity in the context of the type of product purchased, that is, expensive, medium, or low-cost products. The consumer profiling was done on the data collected using *K-means clustering* and cluster memberships were extracted and the most significant consumers across all three product categories were identified.

The objective of the study was to enable organizations to identify consumers demonstrating future *profit* or *relationship* potential and devise strategies to impact price sensitivity by the following ways: (Fig. 14.12)

- Responding to price search intentions
- Improving product perceptions
- Improving consumer experiences
- Informing consumers about new schemes
- Improving product perceived value

Online business communities maintained for effective customer relationship management can help to reduce price sensitivity, enable price premiums, and create opportunities for up and cross selling. The communities create barriers for customers to exit and for competitors to enter and facilitate database development.[17] Loyal customers are important

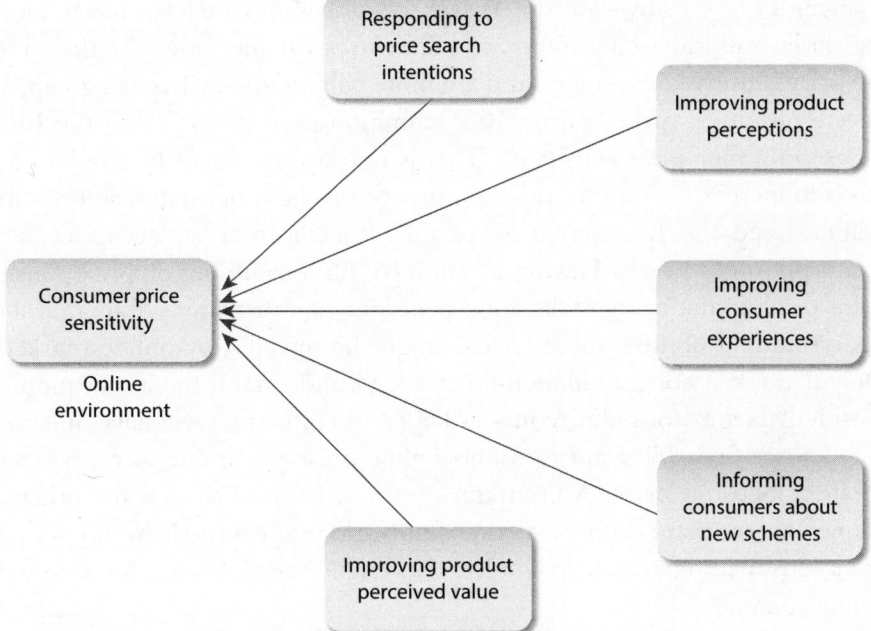

Fig. 14.12 Using the virtual world for impacting consumer price sensitivity

determinants in predicting market share and profit levels.[18] The availability of detailed product information and the interactive nature of the online medium may enhance consumer's willingness to search for price information on the Internet. Performing an Internet search for the lowest prices will be perceived as relatively comprehensive and capable of delivering a favourable price with less cost to the consumer. Respondents with Internet access have different price perceptions and price-search intentions than those without access.[19] The price search done by a consumer on the Internet provides low-cost options and demonstrates availability of higher benefits of products which is less likely to be strongly influenced by other promotional cues. The large amount of information about pricing, competitors, and features available on the Internet also helps to create a cost transparent environment. This severely impairs a seller's ability to obtain high margins, because it turns products and services into commodities, and may damage company reputations by creating perceptions of price unfairness.[20] Transaction marketing is focused on profitable customers and relationship marketing focused on building consumer relationships. Smart marketers will benefit by identifying strategically significant consumers who show noteworthy profit or relationship potential for the company, rather than investing resources in blanket promotions and mass marketing to all consumers.

CONSUMER PRICE SENSITIVITY

Price sensitivity depends on the ability of the consumer to compare alternatives, evaluate deals, and addresses whether the total costs justify the time and effort to find better prices. Price sensitivity encompasses how consumers react to price levels and price changes. Price sensitive consumers seek low prices and are less likely to buy when prices rise. Price insensitive consumers are willing to pay higher prices for the same goods than are price sensitive consumers, and are more willing to buy if prices go up. Many factors affect consumer's price sensitivity. A common perception is that the Internet always raises consumer price sensitivity. This is not always true. On one hand the Internet tends to increase consumer price sensitivity, on the other hand, some companies have skilfully used the Internet to lower their specific marketplace price sensitivity and retain premium prices. Having an intuitive understanding of price sensitivity factors helps pricing managers make good decisions and provides online marketers a better understanding of how these factors might be affected by online marketing content. One of the tasks of an online marketer is to understand the implications of the price sensitivity factors for online content. Different companies will have different objectives. A low price firm will want to use its online presence to enhance price sensitivity and create a focus on price. A premium service oriented firm, on the other hand, wants online content that reinforces that position and reduces the focus on price. Each of the price sensitivity factors help the 'reverse engineering' from price sensitivity factor to online content.

One of the major implications can be understood through shared cost effect, it applies when there is a separation between purchase decision maker and purchase payer. The shared cost effect typically lowers market price sensitivity. The main impact of the shared cost effect on Internet strategy is to create separate content aimed at the decision maker or the payer. One or more of the price sensitivity factors can operate at the same time for a particular pricing decision. Thus, a thorough understanding of the factors shaping price sensitivity helps pricing managers make good decisions and for online marketers it provides a better understanding of how these effects might be altered by online marketing content.

If proficiency in searching the Internet increases with experience or over time, then reliance on brand names should likewise decrease. Internet search proficiency is likely to increase as users gain more experience with the medium. Increased proficiency decreases the cost of gathering and evaluating information, specifically product information.

Alternatively, consumers can rely on well-known brand names as shortcuts in evaluating the merits of different products. Unlike search costs, increased Internet experience is not likely to make consumers more proficient at inferring product quality from brand names. Therefore, as the price of searching, relative to using brands, falls with increasing Internet experience and if there are substitutes the more experienced consumers should rely less on brands. Thus the various effects of consumer price sensitivity have a significant role to play.

On the other hand, the large amount of information about pricing, competitors, and features available on the Internet also helps to create a cost transparent environment. This severely impairs a seller's ability to obtain high margins, because it turns products and services into commodities, and may damage company reputations by creating perceptions of price unfairness. Early work suggested that the Internet could present a threat to branding and erode loyalty. As a result of this cost benefit focus, many *e*-tailers offer low prices and focused on customer acquisition.

Figure 14.13 depicts a classification of Consumers into three categories, namely high profitability consumers, high potential consumers, and underperforming consumers. Firms can use the virtual space to classify consumers (Fig. 14.13) on the basis of how well they can be impacted, using the virtual medium, specifically if the consumers are highly profitable, repeat purchasers, capable of long-term relationship with the organization. Strategically significant consumers deserve more time and cost investment from the firm than those which do not have a long-term profit or relationship potential. Hence, the firm can depute its resources towards leveraging these consumers by interacting with them through online spaces.

Consumer price sensitivity for low, medium cost, and expensive products

Underperforming	High potential	High profitability
• Cannot resist a purchase if price is lesser than alternatives • Not impacted by price quality effect, moderate respect for product quality and convenient buying experiences	• High relationship or revenue potential • Stable customers-desist to purchase competing brands and Internet can be used to enhance consumer perceived value • Give importance to reference price effect	• Strategic customers • Reliable customers • Impacted by reference price effect and price quality effect • Customer retention through good customer experience management

Fig. 14.13 Classification of consumers

CASE STUDY MTV India—Co-creation using MTV Music Meter

MTV India is the Indian version of MTV, a channel specializing in music, reality, and youth culture programming.

'MTV India' is one of the oldest music television networks in Asia. The Indian population has always had a distinct taste in music, thus MTV India has been very successful in India. In fact, MTV India enjoys the maximum popularity among music channels across the Indian subcontinent, having viewership shares in India and also countries such as Bangladesh and Sri Lanka.

MTV India primarily caters to the youth population. The channel creates shows across several themes which includes the following:
- Genres of music (Coke Studio, MTV Unplugged)
- Reality Television (MTV Roadies, Splitsvilla), and
- Youth-based sitcoms (MTV Reality Stars).

Co-creation

The rise of co-creation can be attributed to three broad trends.

First, with CGM gaining respect and visibility, millions of people all over the world are expressing themselves not only by posting blogs, photos, and videos, but also by hacking software and hardware, and making art and craft.

Second, growth in visibility has instilled more confidence in people, who are increasingly thinking of themselves as creators, showcasing their creations in online portfolios selling their creations in peer-to-peer online marketplaces.

Third, people are teaching each other how to create things and learning by making things together, in online and offline communities, often building upon easy-to-use open-source.

As a result, we are seeing a number of platforms focusing on different aspects of co-creation.

In essence, all co-creation communities are designed around four dynamics (Fig 14.14): connect, catalyse, crystallize, and celebrate.

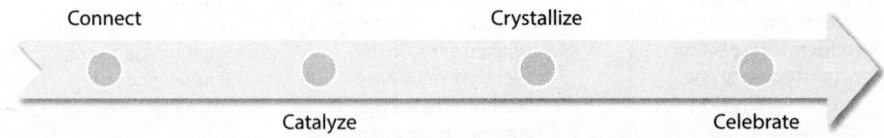

Fig. 14.14 Design dynamics of co-creation communities

Most co-creation platforms enable community members to submit contributions, activate their social networks, and rate, vote, and comment on contributions. Some also provide gamification features such as points and levels to encourage community members to participate. A few platforms also enable community members to collaborate with others and form teams. Some platforms are more restrictive, and only allow community members to vote on options. Most co-creation platforms rely on challenges to attract contributors and encourage participation, so community members often end up competing with each other. However, many co-creation platforms incentivize community members to support others' contributions by rewarding them with social influence or cash for creating a culture of quid-pro-quo collaboration.

MTV India makes more money by co-creating products with brands than by selling on-air, thereby strengthening the case for content co-creation.

MTV Music Meter

MTV Music Meter is an application that gives visibility to upcoming stars. Channels such as MTV are clearly under pressure to retain their popularity in an ever competitive world. By giving upcoming stars more visibility, the company is able to leverage good quality talent available in the environment.

The App allows users to find new artists that other people are discovering and talking about. The platform provides a channel for new talent to shine and come to the forefront of mainstream music. New bands and singers have been empowered to showcase their music and let fans know more about them and the inspiration behind their music. For those who are interested in learning about new types of music, browsing through the different categories and lists provides them with new music experiences and introduces users to artists they may not already know. The lists are continually changing which provides a dynamic perspective to those who want to remain knowledgeable about the type of music and artists that are currently trending. However, only the top 100 artists are ranked across various categories. With over one million artists available on the MTV Music Meter App, it is possible for the artists to make their way towards the top of the list and receive more exposure.

The MTV Music Meter gained popularity by the real-time buzz created on the Internet about fresh, interesting or new music. As people sent tweets, wrote news articles, mentioned artists in various formats or bought the music of these artists, MTV Music Meter acknowledged these activities and pushed such artists to the front of the meter. In addition, MTV joined forces with Samsung to provide the MTV Music Meter across all Samsung platforms including smart TVs.

The proliferation of digital channels and devices gives consumers greater means for communication and collaboration. The physical world is being replicated in the digital world through digital communities, businesses, and assets, fundamentally changing the way consumers engage with businesses and each other. MTV is gaining significantly by embracing the changing customer mindset and leveraging the opportunities provided by the digital world.

Questions:

1. Explain the process of co-creation. How can a company like MTV use the concept of co-creation to leverage good quality talent to enrich its offerings to the consumers?
2. What other ways can MTV use to make MTV Music Meter more popular amongst its consumers?

(*Source*: lego.cuusoo.com)

PRACTITIONER PERSPECTIVE

At present, all products offer features that are almost the same as others. To gain strong brand loyalties, companies are looking at the online space to develop value that is different from other brands.

Kaizad Pardiwala, Vice-President, Ogilvy One, Ogilvy & Mather's Online Marketing arm

> *The innovative use of the Internet is an example of how companies can meet brand expectations by keeping the content relevant and enhancing brand features so that the audience can learn more about the product and relate to it at the same time.*
>
> Prasad Narasimhan, Vice President, Marketing, TVS Motors

> *The Web is fast moving from a publishing mode to a participation mode. It is a medium where community participants are opinion leaders who help in adopting brand values by sharing personal experience, views, and suggestions with other members.*
>
> Anisha Motwani, Marketing Director, General Motors India

SUMMARY

An online community is a group of people with some shared interest who connect and interact with each other over time. A computer-mediated community uses social software to regulate the activities of the participants. Brand online communities are virtual spaces where companies interact with customers, treat them as organizational assets, learn about them, and through the process of incorporating feedback and co-creation, develop a level of intimacy with them. Brand online communities are virtual spaces where companies interact with customers, treat them as organizational assets, learn about them, and through the process of incorporating feedback and co-creation, develop a level of intimacy with them. In the *first* model, brands run short-term public or private challenges on niche crowd-sourcing platforms to tap into their specialized communities: designers, developers, animators, filmmakers, engineers, or scientists. In the *second* model, brands create their own co-creation challenge platforms to engage their community members and crowd-source branded videos. In the *third* model, brands build and nurture their own co-creation communities and encourage contributions through a series of challenges. The chapter covers three empirical models used to leverage product and brand online communities. These models were developed for peer-to-peer consumer communities for products and brands where organizations can benefit from the interaction taking place amongst the consumers. These include (a) the consumer trustworthiness regression model using netnography. Netnography is an online marketing research technique. With the help of netnography, online community research can be done by either actively integrating the members of the community or passively monitoring the community and integrating the gathered information, knowledge, and ideas into the new product development process. (b) A consumer co-creation model using INV based on Metcalf law (C-INV) which classifies typical community members in a branded online community into five different segments, namely, impending co-creators, impending nonchalants, potential protagonists, passionate unfaithfuls, and vacillating indecisive. (c) The consumer price sensitivity model using K-Means cluster analysis studied the usage of online communities to study consumer price sensitivity in the context of the type of product purchased, that is, expensive, medium, or low-cost products. The model helps in consumer profiling and extraction of cluster memberships to identify the most significant consumers across all three product categories.

Concept Review Questions

1. What are online communities? How can organizations successfully leverage online communities for marketing?
2. What are the different types of branded online communities?
3. Differentiate between *creativity-driven challenges* and *solution-driven challenges* in the context of branded challenges on niche crowd-sourcing online platforms. Cite examples other than those given in the text.
4. Identify two companies which are using online communities to engage consumers for co-creation to develop new food and beverage options.
5. Write short notes on
   (a) *Netnography*
   (b) *Metcalf's law*
   (c) *INV*
   (d) *CNV*
6. Differentiate between *impending co-creators* and *vacillating decisives*.
7. How can organizations use online communities to impact consumer price sensitivity?

Critical Thinking Questions

1. Choose an industry vertical—FMCG/automobile sector/banking. Select an online community which is being used by an organization for marketing.
   (a) Conduct a netnography of the online community. Identify a research problem, collect and analyse data. Draw appropriate interpretations.
   (b) Draw a framework to calculate the value of an individual in the online community.
   (c) Draw a framework to calculate the total value of the community.
   (d) On the basis of data collected, classify consumers into different segments based on any variable.
   (e) Name the consumer segments.

Practising Digital Marketing

1. Develop an online community called digital marketing enthusiasts on Facebook, LinkedIn, or any other platform of your choice. Operate it for a year and use it to promote digital marketing concepts and build a group of like-minded people who are keen to share their ideas or details of successful digital marketing campaigns they have executed.
2. Develop an online contest for Hindustan Unilever Limited. What online vehicle can be used to launch the contest? How can the success of the contest be measured?

References

1. Alavi, S., Ahuja V., and Medury Y., (2011) 'ECRM using Online Communities.' *The IUP Journal of Marketing Management*, Vol. X(1), pp. 35–44, ISSN: 0972-6845. (Indexed in SSRN, Proquest, Ebsco). *Abstract further published in Economics of Networks e Journal Sponsored by Networks, Electronic Commerce and Telecommunications ('NET') Institute,* New York University, Vol. 3, No. 75: May, 2011.
2. Kozinets, R. V., (2002). 'The field behind the screen: Using netnography for marketing research in online communities.' *Journal of Marketing and Research*, Vol. 39(4), pp. 61–72.
3. Misra, G., www.Gauravonomics.com, 2012.
4. Humphreys, P., Samson, A., Roser, T., and Cruz Valdivieso, E., Co creation: New Pathways to Value, LSE Enterprise, London, 2009.

5. Lee, G.K. and Cole, R.E., (2003). 'From a firm-based to a community-based model of knowledge creation: The case of the Linux kernel development.' *Organization Science,* Vol. 14(6), Nov–Dec, pp. 633–649.
6. Alavi, S., Ahuja, V., and Medury, Y., (2011). 'An empirical approach to ECRM—Increasing consumer trustworthiness using online product communities.' *Journal of Database Marketing and Customer Strategy Management,* Palgrave Macmillan Journals, Vol. 18(2) pp. 83–96, ISSN-1741-2439.
7. Kozinets, R.V., (2002), 'The field behind the screen: Using netnography for marketing research in online communities.' *Journal of Marketing and Research,* Vol. 39(4).
8. Alavi, S., Ahuja, V., and Medury, Y., Building participation, reciprocity and trust—anetnography of an online community of Apple—using regression analysis for prediction, *International Conference on Management Practices and Research,* Apeejay School of Management, Proceedings, ISBN: 978-81-906991-1-2, 2010, p. 19.
9. Hendrickson, D., (1999). 'Metcalf's law may be the true definition of net firm values.' *Mass High Tech,* p. 9.
10. Klein, L. and Quelch, J., (1996). 'The Internet and international marketing.' *Sloan Management Review,* Vol. 37(3), pp. 60–75.
11. Evans, P. and Wurster T.S., (1999). 'Getting real about virtual commerce.' *Harvard Business Review,* Vol. 77(6), pp. 84–94, Nov–Dec.
12. Grady, E.M. and Matthew, F., (2000). 'Strategic innovation in the new economy.' *Journal of Business Strategy,* Emerald group publishing limited, Vol. 21(3), pp. 25–29.
13. Hanson, W. and Kalyanam, K., Internet Marketing and *E*-commerce, International Edition 2e ISBN-14: 9780324422818, 2007.
14. Muhammad, T. and Wahid, F., (2011). 'Assessing effectiveness of social media and traditional marketing approaches in terms of cost and target segment coverage.' *Interdisciplinary Journal of Contemporary Research in Business,* Vol. 3(1), pp. 1049–1074.
15. Alavi, S., Ahuja, V., and Medury, Y., Internet Marketing-applying Metcalf Law for identifying consumers with high Individual Network Value through business online communities, *International Conference on Facets of Business Excellence,* Institute of Management Technology, Ghaziabad, October, 2011.
16. Chaffey, Fiona Ellis-Chadwick, F., Johnston, K., and Mayer, R., Internet Marketing: Strategy, Implementation and Practice, Fourth Edition, Financial Times, Prentice Hall, 2008.
17. O'Malley, L. and Tynan, C., (2000). 'Relationship marketing in consumer markets: Rhetoricor reality.' *European Journal of Marketing,* Vol. 34(1), pp. 717–815.
18. Ferguson, R. and Hlavinka, K., (2006). 'Loyalty trends 2006: Three evolutionary trends to transform your loyalty strategy.' *Journal of Consumer Marketing,* Vol. 23(5), pp. 292–299.
19. Jensen, Thomas, Kees, Jeremy, and Burton, Scot, (2003). 'Advertised reference prices in an Internet environment: effects on consumer price perceptions and channel search intentions.' *Journal of Interactive Marketing,* Vol. 17(2), pp. 20–33.

15 The World of Facebook

LEARNING OBJECTIVES

After reading this chapter, you will be able to:
- Get acquainted with the characteristics of Facebook that are useful for *e*-marketing
- Get familiar with the concepts of Facebook applications and their utility for marketing
- Know the implications of a Facebook 'like' for brands
- Understand the mechanism of brand building on Facebook
- Identify the determinants of brand post popularity

Youth marketing has changed. Marketers who used to rely on the allegedly focussed but still scattered options presented by music channels and youth-oriented magazines finally have a new option. They had always known that the youth is not a monolithic consumer type—now they have a way to reach the consumers in a hyper-targeted manner.

The year 2013–2014 has witnessed the following two very significant developments:

- The rise of Facebook as a tool for marketing and
- The rise in stature of *e*-commerce

When Facebook announced its results for the second quarter in 2013, increasing user traffic and advertising on the mobile was the talking point. Revenues from mobile spiked 75% in the quarter and accounted for 41% of the company's revenues, against 14% a year ago. Central to Facebook's strategy for 2013–2014 was India—which is on pace to become Facebook's biggest user base within two years—and the mobile.

Mobile advertising revenue, which Facebook faces mounting pressure to grow as more users migrate away from the desktop, constituted 41% of total advertising revenue for the quarter. Facebook has been reporting steady gains in mobile advertising revenue since the company first launched mobile ads in 2012.

Facebook has hence been successful in its three objectives—growing the Facebook community, building consumer engagement, and driving revenues (Fig. 15.1). The company has demonstrated strong growth in adoption by local businesses and user growth. Facebook's greatest attraction lies in its versatility.

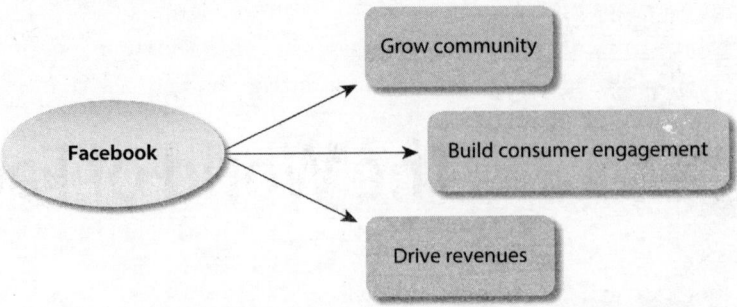

Fig. 15.1 The world of Facebook

EIGHT DIFFERENT VERSIONS OF FACEBOOK

Success of any online platform is a function of its versatility and adaptability. Above all, a medium is useful for consumers if it can be easily used. Contemporary times are witnessing the advent of the mobile into our daily lives—so much so that the handset is replacing the desktop as the 'more useful' gadget. If the rate of increase in mobile usage remains as high as it currently is, companies will have to gear up to make their digital offerings mobile friendly.

Increasingly, a large number of mobile users are coming from emerging markets such as India. Not all of these consumers use smartphones. Facebook subsequently has eight different versions for desktops, smartphones, feature phones, Android, iPhone App, Windows App, Blackberry, and 2G phones (Fig. 15.2). When a user logs onto Facebook, its backend recognizes the operating system, device specifications, and network and chooses one of its eight versions. This foresight will help the company in benefitting from the wave of adoption of new tools, gadgets, and mobiles—all of which happen to be Facebook friendly.

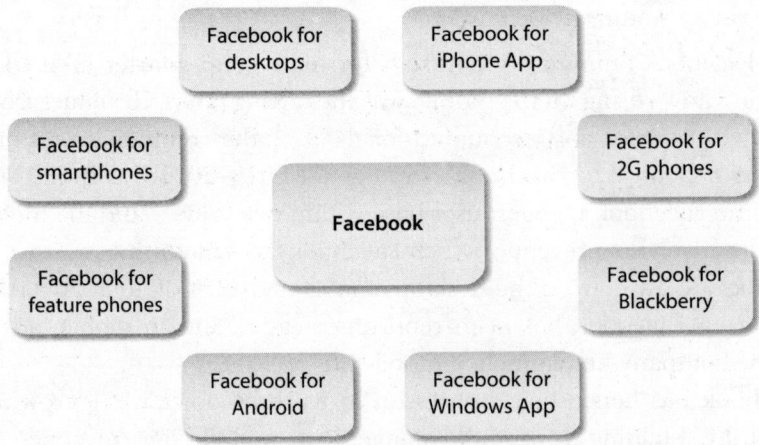

Fig. 15.2 Eight different versions of Facebook

When a user logs onto Facebook, its backend recognizes the operating system, device specifications, and network and chooses one of its eight versions. The company is aware of the humongous increase in mobile adoption and is focussed on building new mobile products at a fast pace.

FACEBOOK—THE ORIGIN

Facebook is an online social networking service, which has become increasingly popular between users across the globe by virtue of its ability to allow participants to share information, photographs, like products and brands, and interact with each other in a friendly, virtual environment.

Facebook was founded in February 2004 by Mark Zuckerberg with his college roommates and fellow Harvard University students Eduardo Saverin, Andrew McCollum, Dustin Moskovitz, and Chris Hughes.

What initially started as an online meeting ground for Harvard students got expanded to other colleges in the Boston area, the Ivy League, and Stanford University. The network gradually expanded across the USA, and over the years, it has become popular across the globe.

Facebook offers profound opportunities to the world of *e*-marketing.

THE ANATOMY OF FACEBOOK

Facebook is not only limited to marketing but can be enhanced to analysis and research as it gives insights about products and services and is able to generate immediate responses from customers. Some of Facebook's general characteristics (Fig. 15.3) that have applications in the field of marketing are as follows:

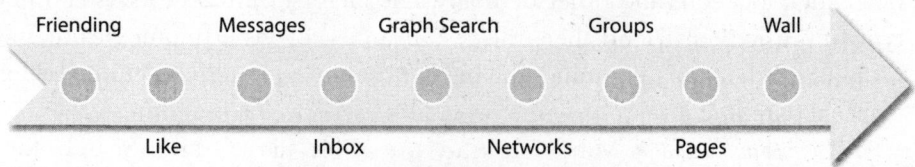

Fig. 15.3 Facebook and *e*-marketing

General Features

Friending

Friending is a term commonly used in the world of Facebook when one user links to the other, by sending him/her a friend request on Facebook. Acceptance of the Facebook request by the receiving party links (adds) the two users together in a virtual network. Every user has the right to accept/decline another user's friend request.

Marketing implication   Companies can identify groups of homogeneous customers having the same preferences, likes, and dislikes by studying the networks on Facebook. Friends on a network also represent the *peers* of consumers who will be influential in a network.

Facebook like

The word *like* represents a positive sentiment. An individual displaying a positive sentiment about a picture, product, or another individual *likes* the same on Facebook. *Liking* implies giving positive feedback and connecting with things people care about. Users *like* updates, comments, pictures, and links posted by their friends and other people on the network. This makes the content appear in their friends' news feeds.

Marketing implication   Companies need to formulate strategies to promote their products and brands on Facebook by getting individuals to *like* the content hosted by them on their company pages. This will stimulate a positive word-of-mouth about a company.

Messages and inbox

Facebook allows users to interact with their friends separately using messages and inboxes. The system is available to all the website users, combining text messaging, instant messaging, *e*-mails, and regular messages, and includes privacy settings similar to those of other Facebook services.

Marketing implication   Marketers can personalize their marketing message and send customized communication to potential customers in a one-to-one interaction, where they do not want others to see the content of the interaction openly.

Facebook Graph Search

Facebook Graph Search allows individual Facebook users to understand the people in their network. For instance, a user can post a query differentiating between his friends by gender, location, and other demographic factors. Similarly, users can find out what type of music their friends like, the restaurants they visit, the movies they watch. The Graph Search feature combines the big data acquired from its over one billion users and external data into a search engine providing user-specific search results.

Marketing implication   Marketers can use tools like Graph Search for consumer segmentation, profiling, and targeting to identify the type of marketing message that will yield better results for specific target groups.

Networks, groups, and pages

Facebook allows organizations to set up different networks and groups. These can be joined by different users and are used for activities such as discussions and events. These groups enable homogeneous groups of people to come together to share information and discuss specific subjects. These groups are increasingly used by clubs, companies, and public sector organizations to engage with stakeholders, be they members of the public, employees, members, service users, shareholders, or customers.

Marketing implication Product brands can use these groups to share product-related news, photos, promotional messages, videos, etc., and invite consumers to participate in discussions pertaining to these issues.

Timeline

The timeline represents the entire journey of an individual on Facebook, ranging from the day he/she joined to his/her current set of activities represented through the posting of messages, often short or temporal notes, for the user to see while displaying the time and date the message was written.

Marketing implication As users share information on their profiles, their timelines are visible to their friends. If marketing makes an effort to get more and more information about their product brand shared on the walls of other users, the results will be a greater visibility for the product brand.

News Feed

Users can get a continuous feed of the Facebook activity of their friends on an alternative homepage created by Facebook. This includes information such as profile changes, upcoming events, and birthdays, among other updates.

Marketing implication When a user likes the page of a product or brand on Facebook, the corresponding information is visible to all his/her friends in their News Feed. This is what marketing wants: A continuous stream of product evangelists or people who unwittingly, by showing their affinity towards a particular brand, recommend the same to their friends.

Facebook Applications

Events

If a user is organizing an event, they can inform their friends about the same and invite them to attend the event using Facebook events. By posting information regarding the event name, network, host name, event type, start time, location, and a guest list of friends invited, invitations can be sent.

Marketing implication Companies can host brand-related events and invite all the people who like their Facebook pages or are friends of their brands.

Marketplace

Facebook Marketplace allows users to post free classified ads.

Notes

Facebook Notes is used as a blogging feature that allows tags and embeddable images; and users are able to import blogs from Xanga, LiveJournal, Blogger, and other blogging services.

Marketing implication Companies can promote the import and sharing of their posts on their corporate blogs on Facebook. This will aid propagation of marketing messages.

Deals

Facebook Deals allows users to check in from restaurants, supermarkets, bars, and coffee shops using an App on a mobile device. The users can be subsequently rewarded through discounts, coupons, and free merchandise.

Marketing implication   Companies can use Facebook Deals as the digital version of a loyalty card or coupon where a customer gets rewarded for loyal buying behaviour.

Developers

The Facebook Developers platform provides a set of APIs and tools which enable third-party developers to integrate with the 'open graph', whether through applications on Facebook.com or external websites and devices. The Facebook platform has evolved from enabling development just on Facebook.com to one also supporting integration across the Web and devices.

Marketing implication   Facebook is being embedded in the social fabric of people's lives and marketing will benefit as more and more Apps and tools are developed to aid marketers in enabling online product proliferation.

Insights

Facebook Insights is a new tool which helps organizations manage and track their campaigns, helps provide meaningful quantitative information regarding a Facebook page with attributes such as likes, shares, followers, comments, and their activity regarding trends (increase/decrease), the sources of followers, the number of fans, virality of a post as well as information on which posts and which customers are interacting the most. It helps in monitoring the dynamic response from an audience. One can determine the reaction of their audience and act accordingly to boost or promote the page increasing its significance.

Marketing implication   Facebook Insights can be leveraged by marketers to promote their business and can be a significantly beneficial tool to manage online promotion.

Questions

Facebook Questions facilitates short, poll-like answers in addition to long-form responses, allows people to get recommendations, and also links directly to relevant items in Facebook's directory of fan pages.

Marketing implication   Companies can use Facebook Questions to run polls regarding products and brands, collect consumer feedback and recommendations for products.

Photos

Facebook allows users to upload their photographs and lately, uploading pictures of their abroad trips, their achievements, and time spent with the family are becoming very popular. Users can upload albums of photos, tag friends helped by face recognition technology, and comment on photos. The photo feature is being used by more and more users to build a personal identity—Facebook profiles are gradually

> **EXHIBIT 15.1 Brands in the era of Facebook's Graph Search**
>
> Ever since Facebook introduced Graph Search, brands are under pressure to invest in genuine relationships and generate love for them. Facebook Graph Search clearly leverages the consumer evangelists, opinion leaders, and people who genuinely recommend a brand. The ideology is clear. When an individual in Delhi, in India wants to visit a restaurant, rather than going in for a Google search for famous restaurants, the individual now logs onto Facebook to identify the restaurants visited by his/her friends. In one such search query on Facebook, all the people who have posted details about a restaurant visit on their timelines, inadvertently serve as consumer evangelists. They are acting as influencers for the friend who made the Facebook Graph Search.
>
> Graph Search allows users to search for information relevant to their lives—on people, places, products, and services—using data of their friends on the social networking site. Marketing of movies, books, and music can greatly benefit from this feature, considering that users really love to show off their experiences to their friends and acquaintants.

becoming reflections of the persona of individuals by showcasing what they do, their value systems, beliefs, and what they like.

Marketing implication A picture speaks much more than words. People are using their Facebook profiles to intimate their friends about what they do, places they visit, restaurants they eat at, products they use, social occasions they celebrate, movies they watch, vehicles they drive, clothes they wear, the latest gadgets they have acquired, and the foreign locations they have visited. All this is of massive interest to marketing. Brands have to create campaigns and photo-tagging contests to encourage consumers to indulge in the above practices. This generation of positive word-of-mouth, results in a lot of publicity for brands. Monitoring, managing and seeding *peer-to-peer influence* will benefit marketers significantly.

Videos

Facebook allows users to share videos—these can be their own creations, recorded using the webcam recording feature, as well as those that belong to others. This can be done by uploading the content online through user laptops, desktops, tablets, and mobiles. Additionally, users can 'tag' their friends in the videos they add.

Marketing implication Companies can create contests and campaigns where consumers can be encouraged to shoot product- and brand-related videos and upload them online. Encouraging consumers to upload videos demonstrating their product usage, such as driving a particular car and tagging their friends, will garner substantial visibility for the products.

All the above features and applications of Facebook make it an ideal platform to be used by organizations for user engagement and customer relationship management.

Companies can use Facebook as an effective marketing tool for product propagation and sharing new campaigns with customers.

The growth of social media and the rise of the era of Facebook are making marketing focus on increasing the engaging and collaborative aspects of advertising. Creating advertising that does not appear to be advertising is the latest challenge confronting marketing people, and online social networks represent an important resource for experimenting with this new type of endeavour (Fig. 15.4).

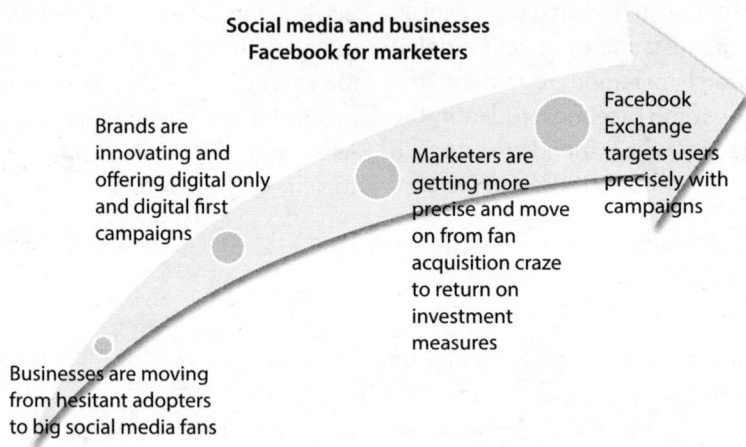

Fig. 15.4 Facebook and the world of Apps

NETIQUETTE—THE FACEBOOK ETIQUETTE FOR BRANDS

The world of Facebook provides a different environment where brands can proliferate by following a distinctive set of rules. The objective for brands is clearly propagation in a virtual environment. The idea is to understand the dynamics of this environment, and to identify best practices which when adopted in the right contextual environment will yield the best possible results. This section discusses netiquette (Fig. 15.5)—the Facebook etiquette for brands and marketers which will enable them to obtain a higher return on investment (ROI) for their virtual endeavours.

- *Conversation is the new advertising*

The role of one-way media was to clearly create brand awareness, enable brand positioning, and keep the brand in the top-of-mind of the consumers.

Interactive media offered a new dimension to this by serving to generate repeat purchases, communicate with prospects that have expressed interest, enable companies and customers to trust each other. It is in this context that companies can make use of Facebook. They can present users with the opportunity of creating a group of friends, of remaining in contact with them, and exchanging information. Users (potential brand consumers) can engage in dialogue, which will eventually benefit the companies, who in a

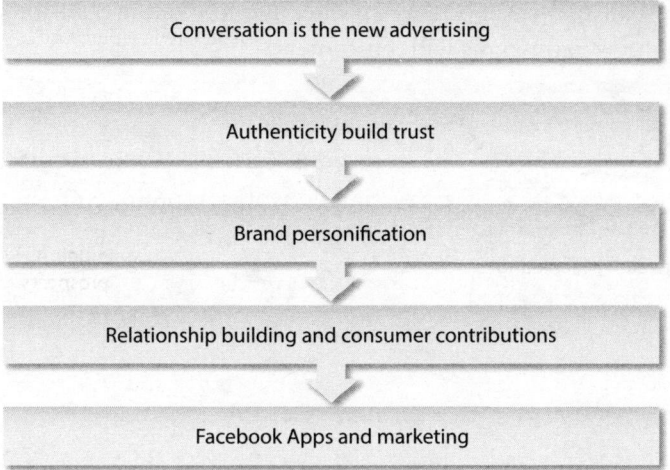

Fig. 15.5 Netiquette

EXHIBIT 15.2   MTV India—Communicating with the youth segment

MTV, a popular brand in India for music, reality shows, live concert broadcasts, and a youth orientation, is on Facebook. The positioning of the brand, clearly targeted towards the youth, was that of a channel resonating with the youth, in their language through programmes and issues they identified with. However, considering that the content hosted on the channel was more for the youth and not exactly in line with the culturally sensitive, moral expectations of the socially responsible Indian society, at large, MTV was careful in crafting its online positioning strategy.

The official Facebook page of MTV India hosted the tagline *Peace, not Pieces*. This was intended at positioning MTV as a socially responsible brand in India. By providing opportunities for users to engage in Snapchat—the livechat, to engage in discussion with MTV stars and celebrities, the hottest gossip, dating tips, and opinion polls on social issues such as user views on Mahatma Gandhi, MTV continuously kept users engaged in an interaction. Hottest Bollywood stories, celebrity love triangles, philosophical quotes, foodart, and information regarding upcoming programmes keep the viewers coming back for more. This fosters an environment for trust and promotes viewer loyalty for the channel.

---

subtle fashion are exploiting these social outings of the consumers for stimulating brand-related conversations. These conversations will eventually generate repeat purchases, initiate first-time purchases, and foster an environment of trust (Fig. 15.6).

- *Authenticity builds trust*

Hosting authentic information and maintaining transparency in discourse and action enables brands to build sustainable consumer relationships. A brand's unpretentious, relevant, and natural way of interacting with its customers is undoubtedly appreciated far more than demonstrative, melodramatic advertising.

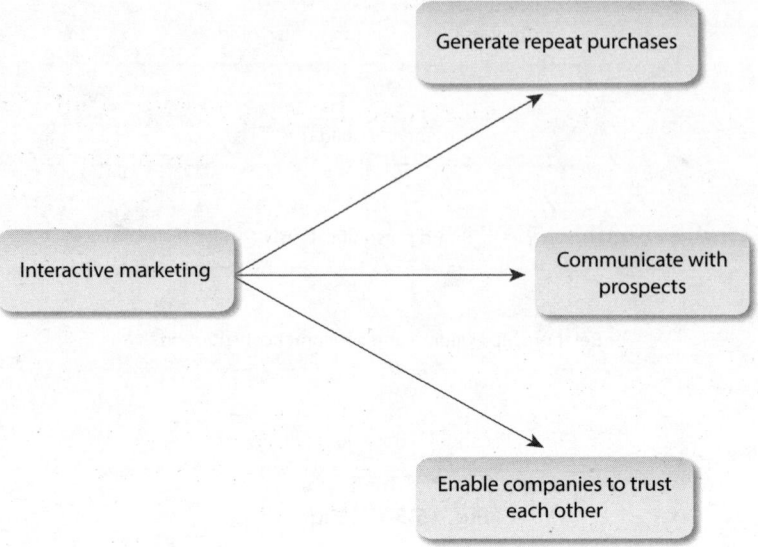

Fig. 15.6 Conversation is the new advertising in Facebook marketing

---

EXHIBIT 15.3 Hyundai i10—Building trust online

The Facebook page of Hyundai i10 commences with a message saying 'Thank you India, for choosing the real family sedan'. This is followed by a photograph of a family standing beside a Hyundai car, with a tagline, *Xcent—The real family Sedan, Multiplies your life*. The page hosts numerous campaigns (posts) such as *The waistline moulding design of the Hyundai Xcent not only makes the car look irresistible, also protects it from scratches*, followed by a picture of the car and interactive queries to customers such as *Zoom through the city roads in comfort and style with the Hyundai Verna. Which is your favourite feature of the car?* The company also uses the page to announce its pre-monsoon car check-up camps. The total volume of likes and the degree of participation received by the Facebook page is clearly indicative of the success of the page in building a relationship with the customers.

- *Brand personification*

Companies can use Facebook to develop and manage brand personalities by providing information about themselves in the *About Us* section on Facebook and subsequently, constantly hosting content which depicts their missions, visions, and values. Maintaining a continuous stream of posts about their social endeavours, new campaigns, and relationship-building tactics can show the consumers what the brand is about and what it stands for.

EXHIBIT 15.4 Nestle India—Creating a brand persona using Facebook

Nestle India has been able to create a distinct brand personification for itself on Facebook. With a tagline, *Bringing Good Food, Good Life*, to Indians for over 100 years, Nestle has been able to position itself on Facebook as a brand that is trustworthy enough to be adopted for use, for those we care the most about. The company has built for itself an image of an organization that enhances lives by offering tastier and healthier food and beverage choices for all stages of life and at anytime of the day. The family fabric is the most important social group for traditional Indians, and by giving consumers a product which helps them care for these families, Nestle has been able to strike a chord with the consumer. Further image building has been done by demonstrating Nestle's commitment to environmental sustainability by showcasing their endeavours towards product development, packaging, and product labelling using materials from sustainably managed renewable resources.

The company's profile on Facebook clearly states its objective of becoming the world's leading nutrition, health, and wellness company. The company has attempted to engage customers in meaningful conversations by hosting a set of what it terms as 'House rules'—rules for participating in the Nestle Facebook online community. People are encouraged to share information and comments for a constructive debate, which does not hurt any sensibilities. By bringing in surveys to collect consumer feedback and posting consumer-sensitive content such as *When do you give sweets to your children, Low-calorie recipe tips for shopping healthy*, Nestle is demonstrating its concern for society and coming across as a socially responsible brand.

- *Relationship building and consumer contributions*

Brands need to focus on creating relationships and engaging consumers in conversations on Facebook, rather than on selling products. This is more important than ever as social networks create relationships between persons, above all. It is important for brands to be proactive and create interaction opportunities, as people who already feel connected to the brand will most probably be open for further dialogue. Nurturing the community requires constant effort, stimulating topics, engaging content, and listening to individuals—not applying mass marketing techniques. This can help companies to encourage fans to return to their page in search of exclusive content. Offering help and sharing content from other members are also useful in establishing an image of credibility and involvement.

- *Facebook Apps and marketing*

Facebook applications are useful for marketers as they can extend their brand profiles and also have the potential of spreading virally throughout the network.

Digital channels have clearly brought about a change in brand communication models: the *one-to-many* classic model is currently on the verge of extinction, as it is rapidly replaced by a new paradigm—*many-to-many*. Social networks can obviously play the part of a mediator between brands and consumers, but the terms of communication have drastically changed in the era of *Web 2.0*, when consumers are able to respond and even alter advertising

> **EXHIBIT 15.5 Facebook's acquisition of WhatsApp**
>
> Facebook recently acquired *WhatsApp*—the instant messaging network which boasted 450 million monthly users. *WhatsApp* had demonstrated very high consumer engagement usage rates. The instant messaging service was becoming so popular that Facebook had started struggling to maintain content levels to keep the interest of the youngsters alive.
>
> *WhatsApp* was very popular because it enabled one-to-one or group messaging along with the ability to send images, video, audio, contact info, and current location data. This created two opportunities for marketers: (a) enabled brands to build a relationship with consumers and (b) individual consumer profiles can be used by brands to send push messages directly to fans' phones, where they are notified.
>
> If *WhatsApp* stays away from meaningless gimmicks and advertisements, there are greater data-led opportunities to monetize the service.

> **EXHIBIT 15.6 Facebook Global Pages for brands—The success of BlackBerry**
>
> BlackBerry has been able to successfully leverage Facebook to generate visibility, build positive word-of-mouth for itself, and get a huge product endorsement from consumers by virtue of a significant number of Facebook likes. BlackBerry has further tweaked its Facebook page in different countries to reflect its endorsements or 'likes' from all over the world.
>
> *Global Pages*
>
> Facebook has launched a new structure for global brands, using a new feature called Facebook Global Pages. This new feature allows for one global Facebook page to track insights and metrics across all of its pages, thereby allowing companies to understand consumer behaviour across specific locations and pages.
>
> Using this feature, Facebook offers users a better localized experience while letting the brand maintain its global presence. This feature allows users across geographic regions to be automatically redirected to the most relevant brand page, based on their location, and also permits brands to link to the main global page with a single vanity URL.
>
> BlackBerry used the *Global Pages* tool to get a spike in the consumer response for the BlackBerry page. The tool allowed the brand to create individual localized versions of its pages while maintaining the same page name and global metrics across all pages. Each local page had its own timeline, cover photo, profile picture, insights, and Apps. Subsequently, Facebook used the feature to migrate all fans to the best local pages for them.
>
> Hence, users always end up hearing from the best markets for them. By allowing a brand to maintain a cohesive global image, while having country-specific versions for product/communication differences that vary by market, Facebook has offered brands an interesting way to communicate with their consumers.
>
> Unilever's *Dove*, Nestle's *Kit Kat*, and Disney's *Frankenweenie* have already adopted Global Pages.

messages. By following the discussed netiquette, brands can definitely succeed in building a brand identity using Facebook, an identity that is well received and propagated extensively.

THE IMPACT OF A FACEBOOK FAN

A lot has been said about the need to build large social networks online. While studies have been directed towards identifying the individual network value or the contribution of one individual to the value of the entire network, equally important is to attempt to quantify the impact of one individual in the network.

Forrester research attempted to calculate what they termed as the Facebook factor—by developing a Facebook impact model that quantified the impact of one Facebook fan.

Marketers have always felt the need to understand the impact of Facebook on their brands. It makes sense to study the likelihood of Facebook fans to purchase, consider, and recommend brands and the greater probability of their positive behaviour, as compared to non-fans.

Forrester studied four major brands as case studies to assess the Facebook factor for Coca Cola, Walmart, Best Buy, and BlackBerry [Research In Motion (RIM)]. The research company studied the increased likelihood of product adoption by the fans, as also the positive impact of Facebook vis-à-vis other brand engagement-driving factors such as convenience of shopping.

The outcomes of the study were as follows:

- Facebook fans are much more likely to purchase, consider, and recommend the brands that they engage with, on Facebook than non-fans.
- Forrester did not examine the impact of Facebook fans in a silo. The company compared the impact of engaging with these brands on Facebook with the impact of other driving factors of brand engagement on these metrics. For example, being a Facebook fan has almost double the impact on purchasing from Walmart as having a Walmart near a consumer's home.

EXHIBIT 15.7 Pockets by ICICI Bank

ICICI Bank, India's second largest bank, launched a Facebook App called *Pockets by ICICI Bank* to promote a safe, simple, and social way of banking through Facebook. The features of the App included *Pay a Friend* (for sending money to friends anonymously), *Split and Share* (for splitting up group expenses and sharing them amongst friends), *Recharge Mobile* (for chatting with family and friends), *Book Movie Tickets, Transact and Track*.

Positioning of the service has been done in the following way:
- Showcasing *Banking with ICICI* as a new experience
- Using Facebook as a one-stop shop for performing all the activities
- Offering convenience and user-friendliness to consumers
- Safety equivalent to the ICICI net banking platform

Implications for Organizations The fact that Facebook fans are more likely to buy (and spend more on), consider, and recommend the brands they engage with, on Facebook shows that the purchase process is not a dead-end road. Brand engagement is a driver of loyalty and purchase for companies, and Facebook is a great channel for advocates to share brand experiences with others.

BRAND POST POPULARITY

Little is known about the factors that influence brand post popularity, that is, the number of likes and comments on brand posts at brand fan pages.

Members of social networking sites can become friends with other members, but they can also become fans of brands on dedicated brand fan pages. Brand fans can share their enthusiasm about the brand on these dedicated pages and be united by their common interest in the brand. Brand fan pages reflecting part of the customers' relationship with the brand broaden the brand–customer relationship and provide a source of information and social benefits to the members. On these brand fan pages, companies can create brand posts containing anecdotes, photos, videos, or other material; brand fans can then interact with these brand posts by liking or commenting on them.

The Determinants of Brand Post Popularity, that is, the Number of Likes and Comments

By liking or commenting on a brand post, brand fans state their opinion publicly. The determinants of brand post popularity (Fig. 15.7) are[1] as follows:

- Vividness
- Interactivity
- The content of the brand post (information, entertainment)
- The position of a brand post
- The valence of comments on a brand post are related to brand post popularity (i.e., the number of likes and the number of comments)

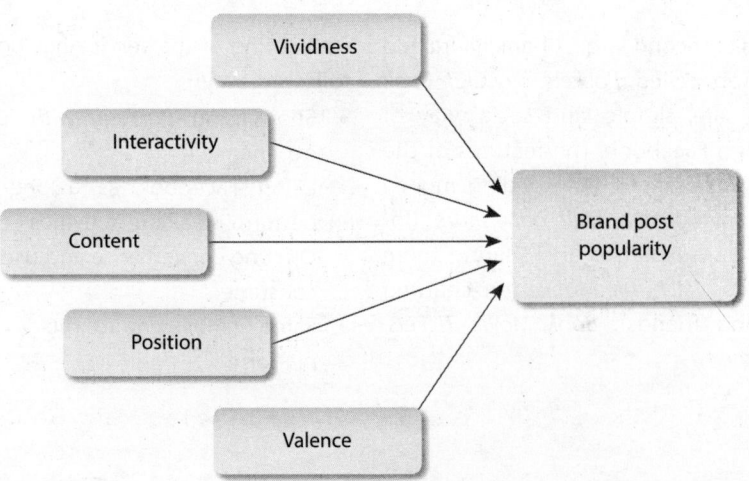

Fig. 15.7 The determinants of brand post popularity

In addition, the day of the week the brand post is placed, message length of the brand post, and the product category are also significant.

> **EXHIBIT 15.8 Brooke Bond Red Label—An emotionally attractive virtual presence**
>
> Hindustan Unilever's largest tea brand, Brooke Bond Red Label, had a distinctly visible and consumer-friendly presence on Facebook. Creating emotional posts to generate mass appeal, the brand had successfully used its Facebook presence to build a relationship with the emotionally sensitive tea-loving population in India. A simplistic image, coupled with the beauty of human relationships, made Brooke Bond popular on Facebook. When the brand garnered a little over 96,000 fans on the Facebook page, it decided to celebrate the journey towards one lakh fans in an innovative and engaging way.
>
> The brand page began a countdown with a dynamic Facebook cover photo—every time a fan liked a page, it was reflected dynamically on the cover page countdown and a tea cup kept filling up little by little. Symbolizing the role of tea in bringing families together, the dynamic cover photo campaign sought to celebrate the accumulation of one lakh tea fans.
>
> Regular contest, questions, and emotionally attractive statements make this page very attractive. Simple messages such as people with differences coming together over a steaming cup of tea, depicted with visually attractive photographs, garnered as much as 2,51,154 likes, 3452 comments, and 4141 shares. The success clearly lies in the volume of consumers being engaged through the medium.

Vividness

One way of enhancing the salience of brand posts is to include vivid brand post characteristics.

Vividness reflects the richness of a brand post's formal features; in other words, it is the extent to which a brand post stimulates the different senses.[2] Vividness can be achieved by the inclusion of dynamic animations, (contrasting) colours, or pictures. The degree of vividness can differ in the way that it stimulates multiple senses.[3] For example, a video is more vivid than a picture because the former stimulates not only sight, but also hearing. Research shows that highly vivid banners are more effective with respect to intention to click and click-through rates. Moreover, higher degrees of vividness appear (Fig. 15.8) to be most effective at enhancing attitudes towards a website.

Interactivity

Another way of enhancing the salience of a brand post is interactivity. Interactivity is defined as the degree to which two or more communication parties can act on each other, on the communication medium, and on the messages and the degree to which such influences are synchronized.[4]

Interactivity is characterized by a two-way communication between companies and customers as well as between customers themselves. It is vital to understand that all posts on social networks such as Facebook, posted by organizations with regard to their

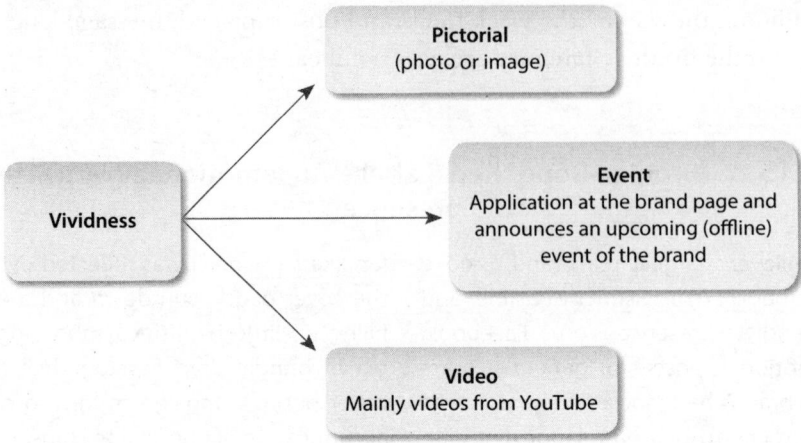

Fig. 15.8 Operationalization of vividness

EXHIBIT 15.9   Lufthansa India—Increasing brand salience through online interactivity

If a brand interacts with its consumers, through Facebook, its salience increases. An excellent example of this is Lufthansa, India, one of the leading European airlines in India, which had unveiled a fun Facebook game called Reveal the Plane for its fans.

The profile picture on the Facebook page of the brand depicts a plane with a caption—*Fanhansa*. The page depicts constant interaction with consumers through questions such as—*You all know the crane on our aircraft. However do you know what is hidden under the 'red dot' below the crane?*

The Reveal the Plane App

Fans were supposed to use the Facebook App to answer questions about each of the Lufthansa aircrafts. Every correct answer revealed a part of the plane. The month-long campaign involved daily sweepstakes that gave away 30 miniature A380 aircraft models to the most knowledgeable fans of its aircraft.

Interactive activities like these clearly improve consumer attitudes towards the brand.

---

brands, differ in the degree of interactivity. For instance, a brand post with only text is not at all interactive while a link to a website is more interactive since brand fans can click on that link. Moreover, a question acts as a highly interactive brand post, as a response is expected from the customers of the brand. Since the objective of brand posts is to motivate brand fans to react (i.e., liking and/or commenting), a higher degree of interactivity will generate more likes and comments. Hence, it makes sense for organizations to implement interactivity at the organizational level.

Hence, operationalization of interactivity (Fig. 15.9) will imply the following:

- Link to a website (mainly to news sites or blogs, but never to the company website)
- Voting [brand fans are able to vote for alternatives (e.g., which taste or design they think is best)]

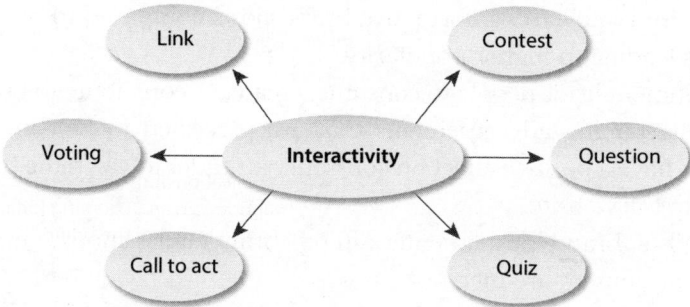

Fig. 15.9 Operationalization of interactivity

- Call to act [urges brand fans to do something (e.g., go to certain website, liking, or commenting)]
- Contest [brand fans are requested to do something (e.g., Tweet or like a website) for which they can win prizes]
- Question
- Quiz (similar to question, but now brand fans can win prizes)

EXHIBIT 15.10   Horlicks—Using contests to drive interactivity online

Horlicks Nutribic, a digestive biscuit from the house of Glaxo SmithKline Consumer Healthcare, has been positioned as a tasty nourishment food product for the working person. The company used an innovative, interactive method to introduce the product on Facebook. Fans had to guess the storyline of the new television commercial before it was officially revealed on Facebook or television.

The teaser updates were used to make the Facebook fans guess the visual clues on the wall. Each guess resulted in the cover photo being revealed in parts and the fan, with all the correct guesses, won a Samsung smartphone.

Content

People use social networking sites for the following reasons:

- Seek information
- Participate in virtual communities
- Contribute to Facebook groups
- Entertainment

This is why people consume brand-related content. Hence, if a brand post contains information about the brand or product, then the brand fans' motivations to participate or consume the content are met.

Additionally, research shows that people tend to have positive attitudes towards informative advertisements on social networks. Therefore, brand fans might have more positive attitudes towards informative brand posts compared to non-informative brand posts, thus leading to higher popularity.

Entertainment leads people to consume, create, or contribute to brand-related content online. Entertaining advertisements that are perceived to be fun, exciting, cool, and flashy—do have a positive effect on consumer attitudes towards the brand, and the desire to return to the website.

Hence, if a brand post is entertaining, brand fans' motivations to participate or consume the content are met.

EXHIBIT 15.11 Philips

When a brand creates a positive and exciting experience for consumers, they tend to develop a positive attitude towards the brand. LED lighting solutions brand, Philips Lighting teamed up with *Maharashtra Tourism Development Corporation* (MTDC) to illuminate the Gateway of India with its advanced LED lighting systems having a 16 million colour palette. Philips experimented with both offline and online media to involve as many people possible across the city. The message—*'See what light can do'* was also propagated amongst the Philips customers through live streaming the illumination using a microsite as well as an App which enabled Philips fans to experience the illumination.

Position of brand posts

The more important information is printed in the first half of the newspaper front page, and is clearly more visible than the information that is printed on the bottom half of the page. Similarly, advertising research shows that the position of a banner advertisement on a website has a positive effect on attention paid to the advertisement.[5] Moreover, recent research on search advertising shows that position plays an important role for click-through rates; namely, advertisements on top of the page generate more clicks.[6]

To look at this in the context of Facebook, brand posts are located in the middle of the brand fan page. The most recently placed brand posts appear on the top of the brand fan page, shifting older brand posts further down on the brand fan page.

If frequency of organizational posting is high, the older posts shift down quickly, which means these are less noticeable and will receive less attention than brand posts that are located at the top of the brand fan page.

Valence of comments

Brand fans can comment either positively, neutrally, or negatively on brand posts. Research shows that consumer' online discussions about positive products or brand experiences can generate empathy and positive feelings among readers.[7] This exchange of information and experiences between consumers leads to a peer-to-peer, consumer-to-consumer (C2C) dialogue. This inadvertently has a positive effect on the perceptions of the value of a product and the likelihood of consumer evangelism. The positive comments on a brand post might have a complementary value on the company's brand post and thus increase the attractiveness of the brand post.

However, brand fans can also comment negatively on a brand post. Much negative information appears to produce a negative effect on attitude towards the ad and the brand. Negative consumer reviews have a negative effect on purchase intentions or sales.

CONSUMER VISIT SCHEDULES AND CLICK-THROUGH RATES

Research suggests that users perform less Internet searching during the weekends than on weekdays. Advertising research further suggests that message length may affect outcome measures such as click-through rates either positively or negatively.

Companies should take the following measures to enhance the number of likes:

- Companies can place a highly vivid or interactive brand post such as a video or a contest on their Facebook page.
- Sometimes posting a question (highly interactive) may have a negative effect on the number of likes. A question demands an answer, which cannot be given by liking the brand post. Questions increase the number of comments, not likes.
- Longevity of the presence of a brand post at the top of the brand fan page increases the probability that brand fans are exposed to it, which indeed has a positive effect on the number of likes.
- Positive consumer comments on a post are positively related to the number of likes for the brand post in question.

Companies should take the following measures to enhance the number of comments:

- Posting a highly interactive brand post, such as a question on their Facebook page.
- Placing a low-level interactive brand post with say, a website link, even has a negative effect on the number of comments.
- Longevity of the presence of a brand post at the top of the brand fan page increases the probability that brand fans are exposed to it, which indeed has a positive effect on the number of comments.
- Presence of a controversial issue or discussion enhances the general interest in the brand post, which leads to more commenting. Previous research shows that people differentiate their opinions and the variance in posted comments seems to generate subsequent comments.[8] For managers this is an important finding because it indicates that negative comments are not necessarily bad.

TOP 10 BRANDS IN INDIA AND THEIR FACEBOOK PRESENCE

Table 15.1 details the Facebook performance of the top 10 brands, in India, extracted from the most trusted brands survey conducted by the Economic Times in 2013.

Table 15.1 Indian brands and their Facebook presence

Brand		Likes
Nokia	Nokia India	10 million
Samsung	Samsung Mobile India	10 million
Sony	Sony	5.2 million
BMW	BMW	17 million
Tata	Tata Safari	1.3 million
	Tata Nano	3.8 million
	Tata Docomo	13 million
	TCS	2.1 lakhs
Godrej	Godrej Appliances	1.7 million
Reliance	Reliance Mobile	1.4 million
	Reliance Entertainment	2.7 lakhs
Bajaj	Bajaj Pulsar	1.1 million
	Bajaj Finserv	1.1 million
Airtel	Airtel India	5.3 million
LG	LG India	1.8 million

Success for Facebook marketing now lies in the quality of content the organizations create online and identify the kind of content that engages people. Then companies need to start tracking the behaviour of these individuals to learn over time about the things they do, to contribute to the sales.

CASE STUDY Shoppers Stop—Facebook and Apps for Marketing

Retailing is a thriving business in India and Shoppers Stop is among the first retailers in India to acknowledge and use the potential of digital and social media to connect and engage with its customers. The brand has increasingly focussed on social media and the digital space to market its products. Shoppers Stop has a well-entrenched presence on major social media platforms such as Facebook, Twitter, and YouTube.

Shoppers Stop is using a 'Perfect for Me App' on Facebook to build consumer engagement and drive sales, and approached this objective by celebrating the acquisition of a million fans on Facebook by giving a ₹200 discount to all their Facebook fans. Loyalty analytics has enabled the retail giant to get repeat business from Facebook, as this activity earned the brand ₹2 crore business from 10,000 customers. The retail player has been successfully able to leverage its online presence to expand its consumer base.

By using business intelligence technology, the company is able to garner consumer-specific intelligence and is now moving towards integrating social media data with customer buying behaviour to understand consumer trends and behaviour, and to churn out more well-directed, targeted consumer-specific campaigns. The *Perfect for Me* (Fig. 15.10) App is a step further in this direction.

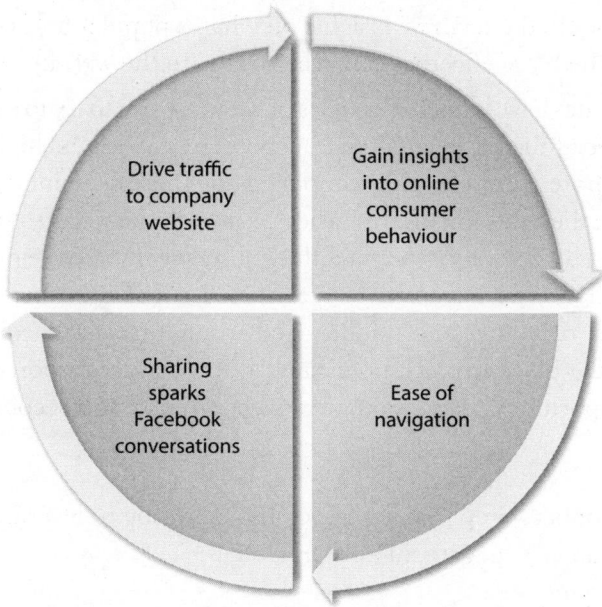

Fig. 15.10   The Perfect for Me App—The benefits

The *Perfect for Me* App

The *Perfect for Me* App is a dedicated Facebook App which is hosted on the Shoppers Stop Facebook page. The idea behind the App is to help a consumer discern what he/she and his/her friends like the most from a catalogue of clothes made just for them. The consumers have to like the page to use the App. While they wait for the App to launch, they can watch a video that pops up on the screen. As a consumer enters the App, he/she is given access to a variety of videos showcasing Shoppers Stop offerings. The consumer can traverse through a collection of apparel and accessories that pop up on the screen. The App allows consumers to choose their favourites and also see what their friends like. Once a consumer likes a particular product, a pop up screen stimulates the consumer to share the product on his/her wall, also telling others why he/she likes it.

The advantages of using the Facebook App are as follows:

- The App allows organizations to gain insights into consumer behaviour online.
- Ease of navigation allows consumers to identify products on offer, make choices, and share their choices with their friends. While enhancing consumer self-belief and

garnering peer appreciation for the consumer, Apps like these serve as excellent tools to influence the consumer thought process.
- The process of sharing on Facebook sparks conversations related to products in the virtual space and may intrigue consumer's friends enough to stimulate trial and purchase.
- Consumers can like certain things from the App, following which the App shortlists the same, making it easier for consumers to take buying decisions. The benefit to Shoppers Stop accrues in the form of insights on what is popular and what consumers like.
- Apps like these are effective in driving traffic to the website.

Social media sites have launched a series of new features to try to cater to businesses looking to ride the social media revolution. Facebook recently launched Facebook Exchange to target users more precisely with campaigns for those searching for home loans with ad campaigns on their news feeds. Elsewhere, LinkedIn launched a targeting tool used by the likes of American Express to target affluent users with bespoke programmes. Even newer sites such as Pinterest have seen a heightened corporate interest to observe the social media interest of young and middle-aged women's social media habits. While Twitter has become the place to track politicians, celebrities, and sportsmen, businesses too are sensing an opportunity to use promoted tweets, trends, and accounts to build their brands.

Questions:

1. How is Shoppers Stop making use of the following to leverage the virtual medium to build consumer engagement and drive sales?
    (a) Loyalty analytics
    (b) Business intelligence technology
2. How does the *Perfect for Me* App facilitate the consumer experience on the Shoppers Stop Facebook page?

PRACTITIONER PERSPECTIVE

Any brand with a large fan base will see a lot of conversation on its pages. Graph Search now provides an opportunity for an actual endorsement from others, which has much more meaning and convincing power than our advertisements.

Vinay Bhatia, Vice-President, Marketing, Shoppers Stop

Our endeavour is to build strong connections with our fans day-in and day-out, hence we strive to look at this space not as social media but more like social relationship marketing.

Chandramouli Venkatesan, Director, India (snacking) and Asia Pacific Developing Markets (chocolates), Mondelez International (Cadbury India Ltd.)

> *Digital marketing will bring together people with common interests; so say if there are R. D. Burman fans, a marketer will be able to filter that out and use that information in his/her strategies. Entertainment marketing will get a big boost.*
>
> Hiren Gada, Director of Shemaroo Entertainment

SUMMARY

Year 2013–2014 has witnessed two very significant developments: the rise of Facebook as a tool for marketing and the rise in stature of *e*-commerce. When Facebook announced its results for the second quarter in 2013, increasing user traffic and advertising on the mobile was the talking point. Revenues from mobile spiked 75% in the quarter and accounted for 41% of the company's revenues, against 14% a year ago. Central to Facebook's strategy for 2013–2014 was India—which is on pace to become Facebook's biggest user base within two years—and the mobile. Facebook has hence been successful in its three objectives—growing the Facebook community, building consumer engagement and driving revenues. The company has demonstrated strong growth in adoption by local businesses and user growth. Facebook's greatest attraction lies in its versatility. Companies can use Facebook as an effective marketing tool for product propagation and sharing new campaigns with customers. Marketers should follow a step-by-step approach to build a brand on Facebook to explore and experience the possibilities of brand–consumer engagement on the social network. They should display authenticity in discourse, create a brand persona personifying the brand on Facebook, focus on building relationships, generating contributions, and creating Facebook applications that subtly integrate brands, while at the same time offering users added value.

Companies should focus on creating specific Facebook content, not importing advertisements from offline media, inviting fans to contribute in creating new products, developing new features, and improving existing ones. They should be brave enough to accept criticism and the possibility of failure.

Concept Review Questions

1. Discuss the following features of Facebook in the context of their application to marketing:
   (a) Facebook like
   (b) Facebook News Feed
   (c) Facebook Graph Search
2. Differentiate between the following Facebook applications. Give examples to illustrate: Facebook Events, Facebook Platform, and Facebook Marketplace.
3. How can companies use Graph Search as a brand positioning and consumer segmentation tool?
4. *With Facebook, brands have been offered the chance to actually understand what their consumers want, without deducing or listening to intermediaries. However the first thing they need to do in order for that information to be available is to listen.* Comment on this using Indian brands as examples.
5. Create a research-based equation to demonstrate how companies can quantify the 'likes' on a brand page on Facebook and link the same to the degree of consumer engagement.
6. How can companies calculate the value of a 'Facebook fan'?

Critical Thinking Questions

1. Create a chart to differentiate between the features offered by Facebook, Twitter, and Google+ in the context of accessibility, ease of use, volume of traffic, and user-friendliness in the context of the suitability of these platforms as online marketing venues for
   (a) An FMCG brand
   (b) An automobile brand
   (c) A laptop brand
   (d) A television brand
2. Experiment with the Graph Search option on Facebook. Identify ways it can help you group your Facebook friends into different segments. In what ways can Graph Search help you in understanding preferences of your Facebook friends?

Practising Digital Marketing

1. Compare the Facebook campaigns of two cosmetic brands which are popular in India. See the volume of activity on the pages. Identify the drivers of consumer engagement and increase in traffic volume on the Facebook page.
2. Visit the Facebook page of two automobile brands that are popular in India. Study the consumer participation level. Identify the frequency of consumer participation. Contact 10 Facebook consumers on each of the brand pages. Collect their views on the Facebook activity of the brand. Prepare a feedback document for the brands on the basis of the consumer interactions.
3. Develop a prototype Facebook page for the following:
   (a) A chocolate brand
   (b) An automobile brand
   (c) A cosmetic brand
4. What does a company need to keep in mind while designing a Facebook page for its product brands? How does the target segment define the contents, colours, and characteristics of the Facebook page?

References

1. De Vries, L., Gensler, S., and Leeflang, P.G.H., (2012). 'Popularity of brand posts on brand fan pages: An investigation of the effects of social media marketing', *Journal of Interactive Marketing*, Vol. 26(2), pp. 83–91.
2. Steuer, J., (1992). 'Defining virtual reality: Dimensions determining telepresence', *Journal of Communication*, Vol. 42(4), pp. 73–93.
3. Coyle, J.R. and Thorson, E., (2001). 'The effects of progressive levels of interactivity and vividness in web marketing sites', *Journal of Advertising*, Vol. 30(3), pp. 65–77.
4. Goldfarb, A. and Tucker, C., (2011). 'Online display advertising: Targeting and obtrusiveness', *Marketing Science*, Vol. 30(3), pp. 389–404.
5. Xavier, D. and Hussherr, F., (2003). 'Internet advertising: Is anybody watching?' *Journal of Interactive Marketing*, Vol. 17(4), pp. 8–23.
6. Rutz, O. and Bucklin, R., (2011). 'From generic to branded: A model of spillover in paid search advertising', *Journal of Marketing Research*, Vol. 48(1), pp. 87–102.
7. Bickart, B. and Schindler, R., (2001). 'Internet forums as influential sources of consumer information', *Journal of Interactive Marketing*, Vol. 15(3), pp. 31–40.
8. Moe, W. and Trusov, M., (2011). 'The value of social dynamics in online product ratings forums', *Journal of Marketing Research*, Vol. 48(3), pp. 444–456.

The Future of Marketing— Gamification and Apps

> **LEARNING OBJECTIVES**
> *After reading this chapter, you will be able to:*
> - Learn about the changes in the marketing landscape
> - Observe the advent of the era of Apps and gamification
> - Get familiar with some common Apps that are being used by Indian marketers and consumers
> - Understand how companies are using games for marketing
> - Get acquainted with the elements, structure, mechanisms, and dynamics of games to understand and identify future opportunities for marketing

The fabric of society is changing and what interests the younger generation is changing even faster.

Digital marketing is about to enter a more challenging territory. Building on the vast increase in consumer power brought on by the digital age, marketing is headed towards being on-demand—not just always 'on', but also always relevant, responsive to the consumer's desire for marketing that cuts through the noise with pin-point delivery.

What is fuelling on-demand marketing is the continued, symbiotic evolution of technology and consumer expectations.[1]

Search technologies have changed the face of marketing in the following ways:

- Product information has become omnipresent
- Social media encourages consumers to share, compare, and rate experiences
- Mobile devices put pressure on everyday product environments to become digital

Consumer expectations have evolved. For instance, travellers expect a few taps on a smartphone App to deliver a full complement of airline services; similarly, net banking applications allow consumers to complete their banking transactions using mobile devices.

When a consumer decides to make a purchase, he/she will venture online to search for information. Marketers have learnt to pre-empt consumer expectations and his/her search behaviour. By optimizing search positioning for their products, companies can make sure their products end up in the consumer choice set. Search marketing is becoming one of the biggest media outlays. Companies have well-directed digital marketing campaigns in place, making perfect use of websites and social medial channels, by trying to promote consumer advocacy and evangelism through the proliferation of positive consumer-generated content.

Companies are creating new and improved ways for engaging and involving their consumers. Playing games, both online and using the mobile, and the use of Apps, both online and using the mobile, is becoming rampant—in fact, it is the new lifestyle trend today. Internet-savvy smartphones are the ubiquitous gadgets that adorn the hands of most urban consumers.

Voluminous downloads are common from the Google Play store and India secured third position globally, in this regard, according to App Annie Index for 2013. Games and image-based Apps are witnessing a global rise in adoption, by consumers across the world.

Marketers have been smart to capitalize on the consumer's desire for more urgency and ubiquity, a desire for greater convenience and value for money. Smartphone Apps are making the need for physical contact between brands and consumers redundant. For instance, several young consumers use a range of mobile services to manage their accounts and rarely interact with the brand physically.

EXHIBIT 16.1 Marriott and gamification

Farmville caught on as a very popular game across social media. The game allowed players to cultivate their farms by ploughing, planting, and harvesting crops and trees. While playing, players also care for their farm animals, and get completely engrossed in the activity.

In a bid to acquaint users with the hotel industry, Marriott has developed a game, similar to Farmville, where the players have to juggle all the responsibilities of a hotel kitchen manager.

Users commence playing the game, all the while earning virtual rewards that will enhance the image of the industry in their eyes.

Users can start playing this game at the *My Marriott Hotel* page on Facebook by selecting a language from English, Spanish, French, Arabic, and Mandarin, and then begin managing a virtual hotel restaurant kitchen.

Hospitality is a fast-rising sector and as Marriott expands in growth markets outside the USA, the company seeks to attract more millenials, those between the ages of 18 and 27 years. Getting people interested towards a particular subject becomes easier when they are engrossed in an activity they enjoy. Games make absorption of information easier because they are enjoyable for everyone.

Subsequently, it is the monetization of these games and Apps, that is, the next logical step marketers can take in this direction. Consumers, who are using Apps for the first time, tend to use the free Apps and games. However, as the market matures, there will be a natural transition towards greater adoption of the paid versions.

Companies need to focus on identifying the best influence pathways for companies while also triggering new personalized experiences for consumers. Appropriate use of digital information technologies will be the key to these endeavours. The following two key digital technologies that are taking the world by storm are:

- The Internet
- The mobile

While a lot has already been said about the Internet, let us now focus on the mobile. Mobile penetration in India is very high, and the mobile has turned to be the first device for a significant number of Indian audiences to access the Internet. Mobile games and applications are very popular in India and this is going to develop into a ₹2700-crore market by 2016, driven by strong smartphone growth and expanding 3G user base.

Marketers are investing their faith and resources on Apps, in the hope of monetizing them successfully, and are constantly on the lookout for engaging more and more consumers by luring them through an increased use of gamification and image-based Apps.

This puts gamification as a serious investment by marketers. While global hospitality major, Marriott, developed a gaming concept similar to the popular Farmville, cosmetics brand L'Oreal developed 'L'Oreal Reveal' for business management aspirants. Games are demonstrating an increased share of revenue, which means that progress has clearly been made towards monetization of games.

EXHIBIT 16.2 Nestle replaces Captcha words with KitKat game

Captcha represent the security feature that requires website visitors to rewrite distorted words to prove that they are human and not a computer bot. Captchas are used to prevent bots from using various types of computing services or collecting certain types of sensitive information. Applications include preventing bots from taking part in online polls, registering for free *e*-mail accounts (which may then be used to send spam), and collecting *e*-mail addresses.

Confectionary brand, KitKat embraced an online interactive advertisement format that gave users a break from frustrating Captcha forms. However, 'PlayCaptcha' adopted by Nestle-owned chocolate bar asks users to open a virtual KitKat by swiping along the foil by using their finger on a touch screen or a mouse on a PC.

Innovative brands are trying to develop new ways to allow their consumers to enjoy their products. KitKat had developed a 'Have a Break' brand equity for its brand. Campaigns developed were significantly inventive and positioned the brand as a youthful, fun-loving, spirited brand which resonated with the consumers.

THE RISE OF TECHNOLOGY

Every digital interaction represents an opportunity to provide something extraordinary to the consumer, through vigorous software development, programming, increased data access and retrieval, and interface possibilities.

Banks and Apps

- The Commonwealth Bank of Australia launched a new smartphone App, which impacts the house-hunting experience. When a prospective buyer likes a house, he/she clicks a picture. Image-recognition software and location-based technologies are used. Subsequently, the App identifies the property and provides transactional details and pricing. After this, the App connects with the buyer's personal financial data, to study the individual's financial status. In case the buyer may want to apply for a mortgage, the App investigates the possibility and calculates the amount.
- The HDFC India App allows consumers to enjoy mobile banking features and functionalities by allowing them to verify their account balance, transfer funds, and pay their bills.
- ICICI India launched a mobile banking App titled iMobile. The App allows consumers to check out credit cards and loan accounts. Consumers are allowed to check balances and also make payments and transfer funds to another account.

Some online marketers already use features in devices such as cameras and touch screens to help consumers see what apparel and accessories may actually look like when worn.

Evolving technologies and consumer behaviour should make it easier for organizations to redesign many complex experiences. For example, companies offering inherently complicated products or services could overlay a game interface on certain Web pages to let consumers play at trading-off different options and prices. Visual-recognition technology could allow consumers to scan health-care bills, receipts, statements, and appointments into one integrated calendar and cash-management system. Already, start-ups in travel, expense, and sales force management are experimenting with approaches that streamline processes and make interactions more inviting—using touch and swipe to make changes, gestures to activate large displays, and data in phones to recognize consumers and automatically customize interfaces.

EXHIBIT 16.3 Cadbury celebrations

Cadbury created a Facebook App on the occasion of Raksha Bandhan in India, for its product brand Cadbury's Celebrations. The company had launched a collection of Cadbury's chocolates to be gifted on the special occasion. The campaign launched for the promotion of this collection was called—Songs for Sisters. Brothers could share messages for their sisters on the brand's social media platforms. These messages were subsequently converted into songs by India's leading bands. The freshly created video songs were shared across social media platform to generate memorable experiences for fans.

GAMIFICATION AND GAME-BASED MARKETING

Gamification is emerging as a marketing trend and it is vital for marketing to address the analysis of games used in gamification, in terms of their structure and mechanism, and their subsequent transference to the area of marketing activities.

What is Gamification?

Gamification is the application of structure and mechanics of games (points, rewards, levels, challenges, and trophies) to the real world, in order to boost the engagement of users, change their behaviour, and solve problems of various kinds.[2]

> **EXHIBIT 16.4 Accenture and gamification**
>
> Accenture introduced a four-level gamification tool to increase the workplace productivity of its young, savvy individuals, in a bid to keep them motivated and engrossed with the work environment.
>
> The game lets employees roll the dice and attempt questions on a wide range of topics relating to ethics and compliance. Successful employees who clear all levels of the game are designated bosses of virtual organizations. The fun and engaging experience is further enriched when companies allow individuals to view scores of their competitors. People have always been obsessed with winning and games give them the pleasurable experience of winning while being a user.

Shifts in the Marketplace

- As vast volumes of information start flooding the lives of consumers today, they have started choosing what to consume and what to ignore. Today's consumers decide what to listen to and watch, by making full use of mute buttons, social networks, and pre-taping systems.
- Spending time on social media is the latest trend. Asking friends what they like, dislike, or recommend is a lifestyle component. The power of recommendations given by friends is more important than the power of traditional advertising.
- Consumers have limited time and methods that can bring in convenience to their life are much appreciated. It is significantly more about good experiences, and the Internet is now creating ways by which consumers can get both convenience and positive experiences.
- Consumers have become focused on the consumer brand experience, and have started paying not for the unique selling proposition (USP), but for the time spent with a brand. It is more about creation of brand associations and product-oriented memories.
- The traditional advertising model, where the consumer was a passive recipient, is fading away.
- Marketers lay a lot of emphasis on achieving high levels of consumer engagement because that is what subsequently generates profitability.

In this context, *gamification can be used by a marketer to drive consumer engagement and subsequently garner consumer loyalty*, as games are being perceived as tools that can cut through the clutter of a crowded brand marketplace, and socially networked environments to attract, retain, and monetize customers.

How can Gamification Benefit Marketing?

Companies need to understand how to add games and game mechanics to their marketing mix, how to use games to influence behaviour and reach business goals, and use 'game-based marketing' to boost revenues.

The use of games can benefit marketing (Fig. 16.1) in the following ways:

- To play a game, users (potential consumers) have to login first. This helps companies build a database of potential clients by collecting the email ids of players.
- Games allow companies to attract fans in social media by also constituting an important element of competition.
- Games allow education and integration of members of a group or branch.
- Games can benefit marketing through the mechanism of recommendation of a game, publication of results, and the possibility of comparing results.
- Games can provide consumers with a positive, fun-filled, and entertaining experience.
- Games can serve as branding tools by creating a positive image for the product or brand. They can allow the recipients to get in touch with the brand over a long period through the Internet and other platforms such as mobile phones, CD, and DVD discs.
- Games permit companies to simulate real-life situations that customers identify with, easily, in such a way that the target group gets more engaged.

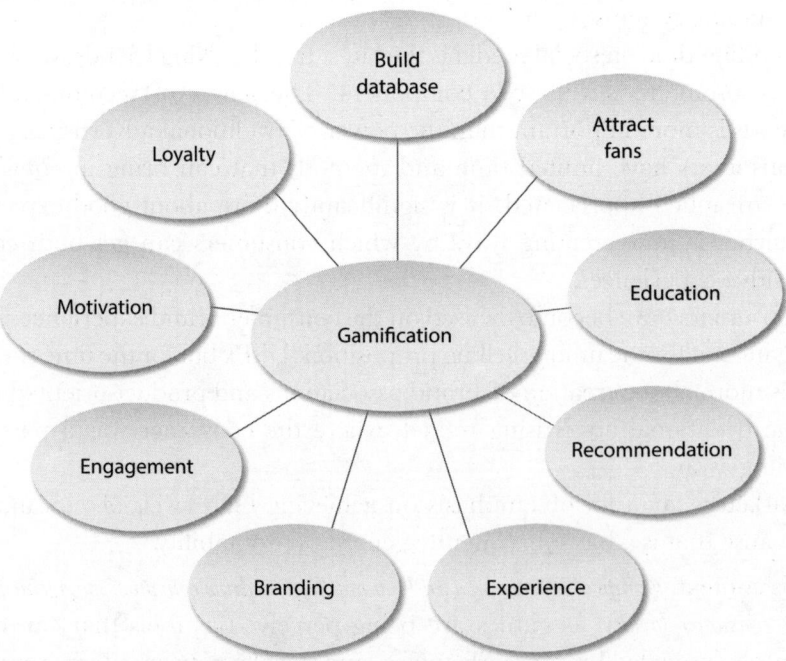

Fig. 16.1 Gamification and marketing

- Games motivate consumers to take particular actions, which in effect will result in loyalty, and attachment to a brand represented by a particular institution.
- In the social media space, players can express their loyalty by sharing information, inviting friends, and informing them about the received awards. Thanks to this, people start talking about the brand associated with a particular game. This gives a brand the opportunity to stand out from the crowd and become the market leader.

Companies will benefit by selecting the appropriate situation, which can be transformed into a game and which will entice their target market. The situation should correspond to the essence of a particular brand and the lifestyle of clients. A good starting point for designing a gamification system is using particular rituals and daily habits, which the clients may associate with a particular brand.

EXHIBIT 16.5 L'Oréal—Reveal—Recruitment through gamification

Reveal by L'Oréal is an inventive, individual online game that combines a scintillating exposure to several intuitive experiences with evaluation and learning modules, specifically built by experts from academic, business, and psychometric worlds, for online engagement of individuals.

Reveal by L'Oréal allows the player to discover his/her own abilities and preferences by stimulating his/her knowledge. Candidates play the game via an avatar which interacts with other virtual employees and carries out various tasks and challenges in diverse organizational roles such as business development, finance, marketing, research and development, and the supply chain. At the end of the game, they receive personalized feedback on how different jobs at L'Oréal would suit them.

CONSUMER MOTIVATION FOR PLAYING ONLINE GAMES

For gamification to become a successful marketing strategy, companies need to develop long synergistic relationships with consumers, based on fun and entertainment. In this context, players' intention to play online games is of considerable interest. Knowledge of the same, subsequently, allows creators, sponsors, and operators of online games to benefit greatly from improved understandings of the driving factors behind players' intention.

Research has shown that consumers have the following three primary motivations for playing online games (Fig. 16.2):
- Enjoyment and a fun-filled experience
- Trust
- Ability to believe information on an online gaming site they perceive as trustworthy

Companies motivate consumers to play so that consumer brand affinity increases.

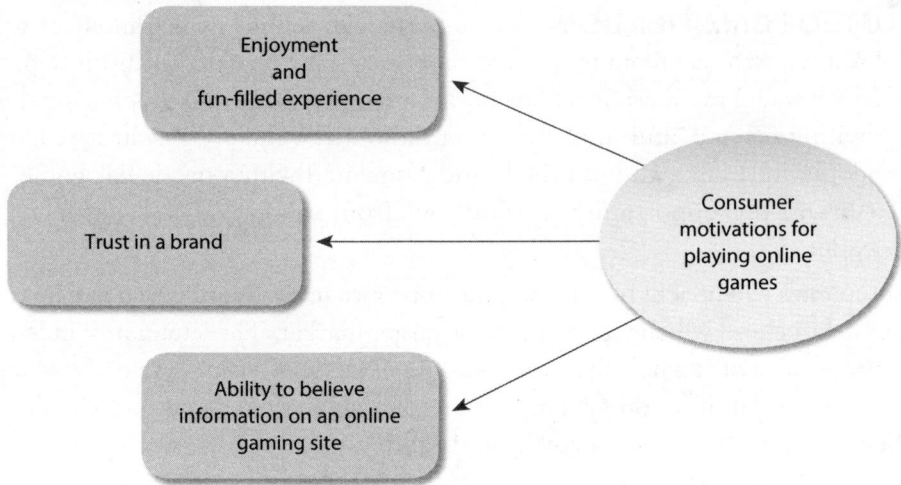

Fig. 16.2 Consumer motivations for playing online games

GAMIFICATION AND THE CONSUMER BRAND AFFINITY SPECTRUM

Most players (consumers) depict exploratory browsing behaviour. They venture online to pass time or engage in a fun-filled experience. If they end up playing a game created by a product brand, which defines an enjoyable experience for them (Fig. 16.3) it will also help the companies in the following ways:

- Engagement between brand and consumer is achieved
- As player uncertainty towards the online experience diminishes, their trust in the associated brand increases
- Players who trust the brand, because of the 'appropriateness' of their experience, tend to believe the brand more
- Believability breeds involvement. The consumer subsequently returns to the game website
- Involvement develops a positive attitude of the players to the brand website as they perceive that the brand will not engage in opportunistic behaviour

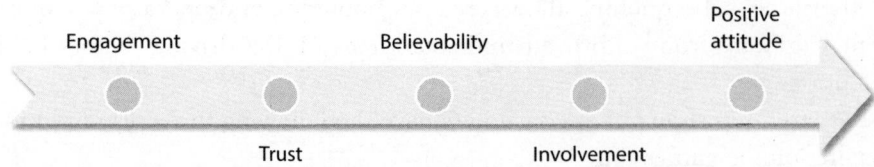

Fig. 16.3 The consumer brand affinity spectrum

Games are typically known to cause feel-good chemical reactions and alter human responses to stimuli.

THE ANATOMY OF GAMIFICATION

Games—Elements, Structure, and Narrative

According to Jim Banister, the owner and creative director of consulting agency Spectrum DNA, games consist of five basic *elements*[3] (Fig. 16.4). They are as follows:

- *Context* Rules, regulations giving a structure to the narration, which at the same time impose limitations
- *Content* The things we can perceive with our senses
- *Community* Interaction between players
- *Trade* Exchange of value
- *Tools and Code* Limitations associated with the used technology, engine of the game

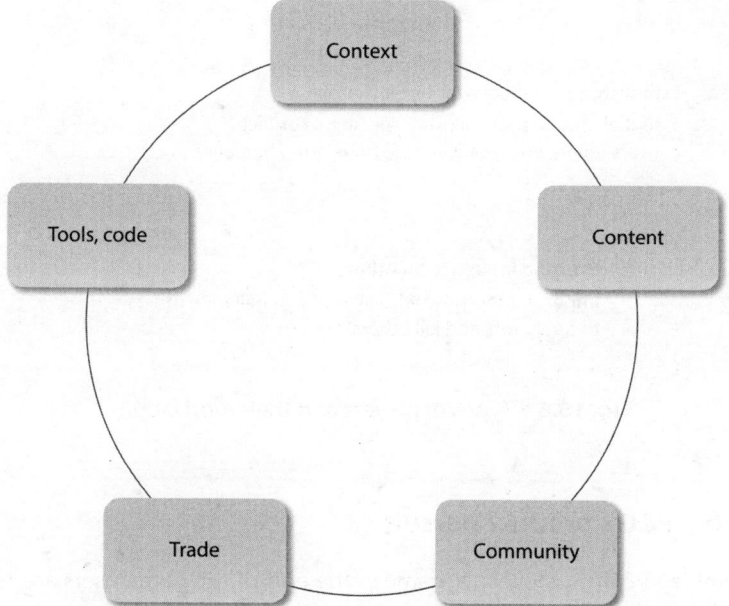

Fig. 16.4 The anatomy of gamification: Elements of games

The *structure* of every game consists of the following elements (Fig. 16.5):

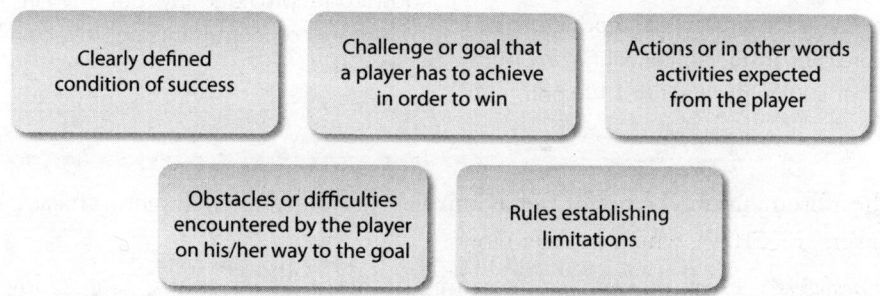

Fig. 16.5 The structure of a game

Types of Players and their Motivation

According to Richard Bartle, the author of, 'Games People Play', Professor of the University of Essex, players are motivated by four main factors (Fig. 16.6):

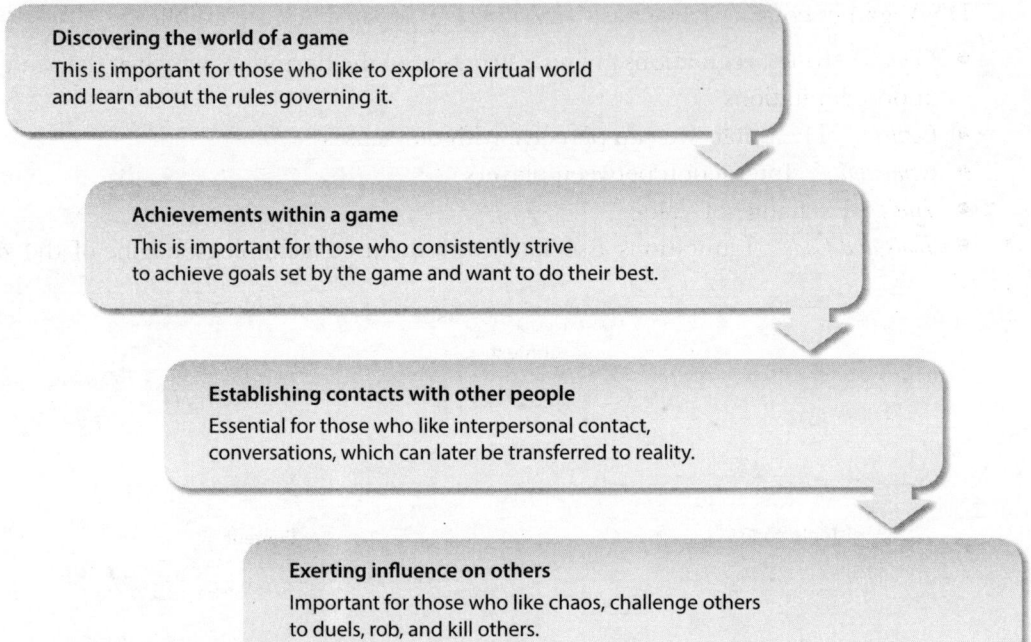

Discovering the world of a game
This is important for those who like to explore a virtual world and learn about the rules governing it.

Achievements within a game
This is important for those who consistently strive to achieve goals set by the game and want to do their best.

Establishing contacts with other people
Essential for those who like interpersonal contact, conversations, which can later be transferred to reality.

Exerting influence on others
Important for those who like chaos, challenge others to duels, rob, and kill others.

Fig. 16.6 Types of players and their motivations

EXHIBIT 16.6 P&G's product pursuit

Procter and Gamble (P&G) launched a game called Product Pursuit. In a virtual supermarket type setting, players tend to catch an avalanche of products. This gives consumers an exposure to the world of P&G's products. With *unruly children* and *stock boys* trying to disrupt a player's game, players are invited to collect P&G products to win a high score. For instance, collecting a *Gillette* gives a player 300 points and *Crest* 150 points. At the end of the game users are 'rewarded' with a fact about P&G.

For instance, at 2150 points, a player is rewarded with a fact like 'As a marketing professional with P&G, you will be responsible for leveraging the knowledge provided by our market research in order to communicate effectively with customers.'

The aforementioned types of behaviour have led Bartle to define four basic categories of players (Fig. 16.7), which are as follows:

- *Achievers* These players like to acquire points and earn status. They enjoy the process of playing and want to play well. They like working with others and sharing the joys and defeats of the game.

THE FUTURE OF MARKETING—GAMIFICATION AND APPS 419

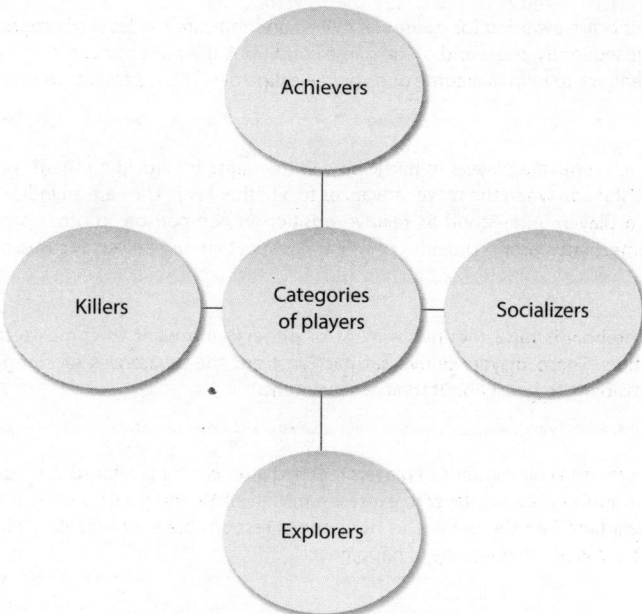

Fig. 16.7 Categories of players

- *Socializers* These players enjoy the social component of playing games, such as interacting, forming alliances, and collaborating.
- *Explorers* These players take pleasure in game playing activities and elements, such as accumulating points or badges, uncovering shortcuts, or figuring out puzzles.
- *Killers* These players thrive on competition and have a win-at-all-costs mentality.

In addition to Bartle's four player types, the gaming field also includes the 'naïve' players, players who participate unintentionally. They earn frequent flyers points but do not use them, or accumulate bank rewards that they never redeem. Such a player slows down the game play unless marketers can capture their attention and convert them into active participants. Whether a game is funny depends not on the motive, but on the mechanics. This is something that can capture a player's attention for a long time.

Game Mechanisms and Dynamics

Mechanics is about the functional elements of a game (Fig. 16.8). Dynamics is about the interaction of the player with mechanics—building it properly leads to a situation in which the game becomes attractive for players following various motivations. Sometimes these terms can be used in the same meaning. The following are further combinations of dynamics together with appropriate mechanics:[4]

Flow

As already discussed in Chapter 3, flow is a mental state which can be described as concentrated motivation. It is achieved by means of full emotional immersion in the experience of the carried-out task, which is characterized by an appropriately high level

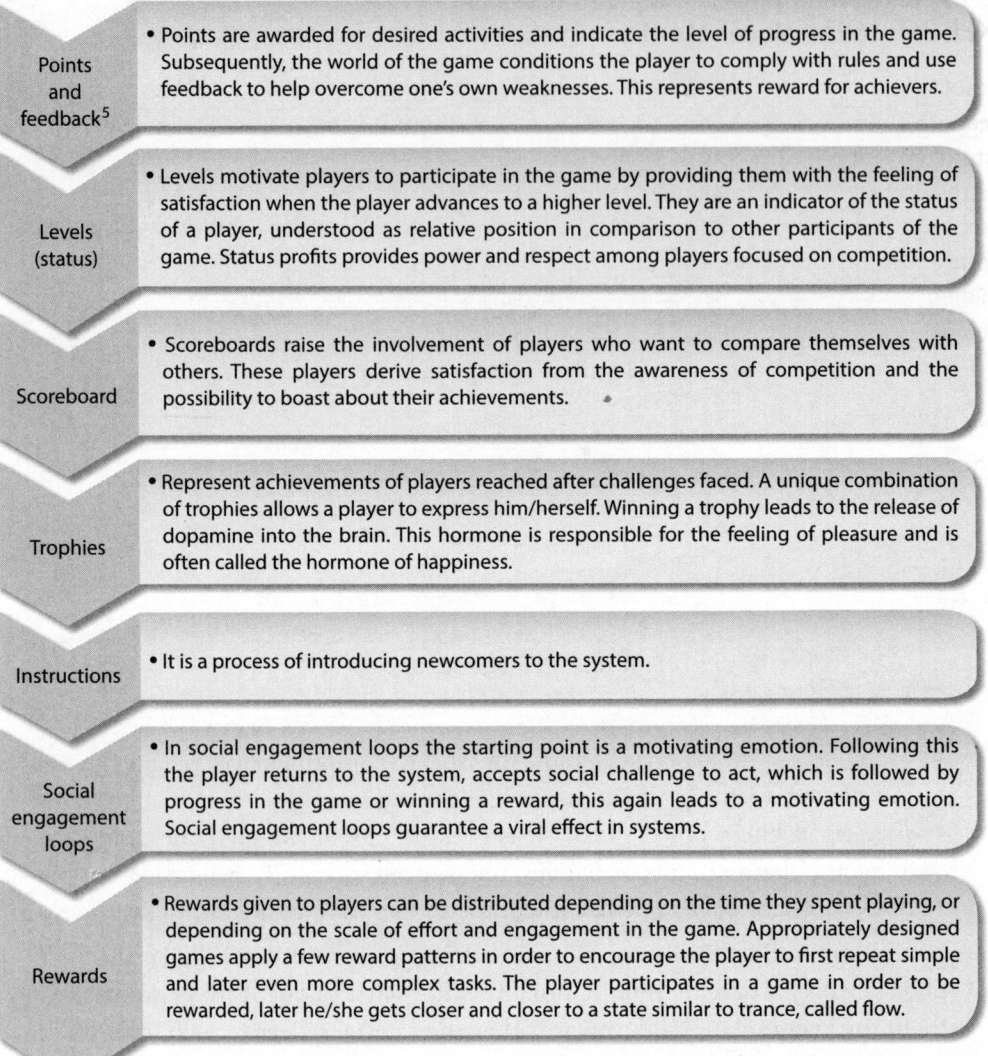

Fig. 16.8 Game mechanics and dynamics

of difficulty (it is assumed that the skill level of the person participating in the challenge is just as high).

Leading into the state of flow can be achieved slowly, by ordering players to repeat certain tasks until they fully master them and later raising the level of game's difficulty. Players who have entered the state of flow experience the feeling of exaltation, the feeling that they are using their potential to the greatest possible extent, the feeling of maximum engagement and satisfaction. This is the state sometimes experienced by sportsmen, creators, managers, employees who achieve a breakthrough in their projects. Every success starts in the state of flow.

> **EXHIBIT 16.7 VocabMonk**
>
> VocabMonk is a gamified and personalized vocabulary-building tool, with a social touch to foster competitive learning driven by powerful and researched Artificial Intelligence algorithms. The company is trying to project *VocabMonk* as a one-stop shop for personalized vocabulary building. The emphasis is on following a personalized approach and assisting candidates in competitive exams such as GRE, GMAT, CAT, and SAT. The company uses eclectic vocabulary-building tools to create an easy-to-use virtual assistant that constantly gauges and analyses individual performance, using concepts such as gamification, embedding small casual games within activities, creating challenges between users, and virtual currency.

USE OF GAMES AS MARKETING TOOLS

- *Well-designed games can produce significant psychological rewards*[6]

Gamification takes advantage of the players' internal motivators; at the same time regular contests, represented by loyalty programmes, which involve winning prizes and trophies, are based on external motivators—people participate in them to win the prizes and not to have fun. In gamification systems, prizes are an additional element intensifying engagement. Needless to say, the facade of a higher status plays a significant role in maintaining consumer engagement.

- *Well-designed games help formulate the right consumer attitudes*

Gamification can be adapted to the individual needs of a consumer, and can also help in formulating social attitudes, promote healthy lifestyle, and popularize education, because it can influence the behaviour of players in their daily life.

- *Games create a conducive online environment for marketing*

Games are competing with advertising for consumer attention, and simply placing advertisements inside popular titles does not help marketing regain the lost affections of the customers. Whole communities can be built around brands. A good example of this is the fan-pages on Facebook. Communities built on the basis of gamification create an environment in which clients contact each other and the brand is discussed in a congenial setting. Under such circumstances, subtle messages and suggestions directed to recipients are received and absorbed better. Such a gamification system gets players involved for a long time, gives them the satisfaction from progress in the game, and the struggle for status.

THE WORLD OF APPS

Apps are adding a completely new dimension to marketing today. An 'App' can be defined as a software application typically developed by a product brand to allow a consumer to gain information about a product or service, thereby forming an opinion or completing a transaction.

Applications or Apps, as they are termed, are optimized for the devices on which they are to be downloaded on and accessed from. Marketers are using them for the following reasons:

- Enhancing their reach
- Positioning brands
- Stimulating impulsive buying by increasing visual appeal
- Stimulating consumer engagement
- Leveraging consumer interactivity and participation

Benefits to consumers include *convenience* and *user-friendliness*. The App industry is tapping multi-devices where Apps can be accessible across all the platforms (iOS, Android, smart TVs, and every other gadget) to make it convenient for the consumer. Apps have the ability to sync the data offline and provide new and innovative content.

Marketers and Apps

- *Enhancing reach*

Apps can be used by companies to target a multitude of consumers, specially, by integrating them with social media tools.

EXHIBIT 16.8 Apps and Indian movies

When *Bhaag Milkha Bhaag*, the inspiring biographical sports film on Milkha Singh was launched in India, the movie started its promotions on social media, well in advance, by sharing teasers and facts about the athlete. A series of Facebook Apps were used for promoting the movie. These Apps enabled the fans to get sneak peeks about the movie and helped them bond further. While a *First Look Club* enabled fans to get exclusive content, *Chase Your Dream* enabled fans to share a realistic dream where the App would create customized cover photos for the fans, and the fans could create their own posters in the Milkha Fan Art App. The *Bhaag Milkha Bhaag* gaming application further allowed fans to experience the adventure of the movie, by running as Milkha, playing adventure-packed racing games, grabbing medals, and seeing themselves on top of the game centre leader board.

A typical consumer is attuned to the world of downloading an online App or a mobile application to fulfil his/her routine activities—be it reserving a train ticket, a movie ticket, ordering a meal, searching for information, or conducting a banking transaction.

- *Positioning brands*

Campaigns with distinct message strategies are used to position brands specifically. When an App depicts a specific brand campaign, a complete new way of interacting with consumers can evolve. This method increases consumer engagement and strengthens brand loyalty through interactivity.

EXHIBIT 16.9 Cadbury's Bournvita

Cadbury, India launched a new campaign for its chocolate-flavoured health drink, Bournvita. The campaign was called 'Taiyari Jeet ki', and stressed on the importance of inculcating good habits in children, by bringing in a winning attitude.

Cadbury had always positioned itself as a health drink. This specific campaign focussed on ingraining good value systems in children, thereby widening the spectrum of the brand's positioning. A Facebook application enabled fans to kick off good habits with the help of their friends. On Twitter, the brand hosted contests around the hashtag #BVTGoodHabits, where users had to share positive practices. The brand found support in its endeavour, from mothers across twitter and other social media platforms.

- *Stimulating impulsive buying*

Having a product App on an iPhone, iPad, or an Xbox, brings the product into the consumers' hand, thereby giving it more visibility. A higher visual appeal triggers a consumer buy, specifically, if it is supported by convenience.

EXHIBIT 16.10 Pizza Hut—Chomp-a-Thon

Pizza Hut allows consumers to place an order using an App. The App claims that it is very easy to order a pizza, anytime, from anywhere, even while consumers are playing on an Xbox. Consumers can enjoy the menu, explore daily specials, and order favourite items. The App enables users to find the closest Pizza Hut store. A high visual appeal stimulates more daily buys.

Pizza Hut launched an exciting social media campaign emphasizing the message that 'size matters'. This happened when the brand launched a 23% bigger pan pizza. An exciting social media campaign gave away 23% discount vouchers for the same.

A pizza eating marathon, termed as the chomp-a-thon was hosted on a Facebook App. Participants were asked to chomp away a virtual pizza in the quickest time possible. Twitter influencers were also roped in to create the buzz on Twitter while users were encouraged to share why size matters in different areas of life.

- *Stimulating consumer engagement*

Companies are benefitting by peer-to-peer interactions between consumers. When consumers share experiences or pictures, they are in a way endorsing a brand they are engaged with.

> **EXHIBIT 16.11 Woodland shoes**
>
> Woodland, the footwear brand, conducted a Facebook hunt for the 'Woodland Extreme Explorer'. With this the company created a brand personality reflecting its adventurous spirit. Applicants needed to share their pictures/videos depicting their adventurous side on a cool Facebook App, where these were put up for voting. The contest rewarded the winner by giving him/her an all-expenses paid trip to explore the planet.

- *Leveraging consumer interactivity and participation*

Several Apps are letting brands capitalize on user contributions, interactions, conversations, and uploads.

> **EXHIBIT 16.12 Instagram and Digital Marketing**
>
> Instagram is an online photo sharing, video sharing, and social networking service. The App enables its users to take pictures and videos, apply digital filters to them, and share them on a variety of social networking services, such as Facebook, Twitter, Tumblr, and Flickr. Users are also able to record and share short videos lasting for up to 15 seconds.
>
> Brands have been successfully able to leverage Instagram for their own promotion, with the human being's innate desire to capture important life-defining moments and celebrate them by sharing pictures with their friends. Needless to say, these defining moments have some brand or the other associated with them, for example, the acquisition of a VW car, a new Nakshatra diamond necklace, or a trip to a foreign land, through say, Cox and Kings.
>
> Instagram is distributed through the Apple App Store, Google Play, and Windows Phone Store and is fast emerging as the most popular photo and video sharing App in terms of downloads ahead of YouTube.
>
> Image-driven data and photo-sharing applications are being used by marketers for a wide range of activities such as product demos, highlighting special offers and events, product differentiation, and enhanced engagements. Brands are very active on Instagram because of the instant connect offered by the visual medium. These brands include Levis, Redbull, Nike amongst several others.

APPS AND THE INDIAN DIASPORA

Apps can be used for a multitude of tasks. The following section traverses through a series of popular Apps being used by the Indian diaspora (Fig. 16.9).

Apps for Social Media Management

These Apps allow users to hang out on their preferred social networking platforms, keep tabs on most of their social efforts in one place, and even manage multiple profiles.

Fig. 16.9 Apps and the Indian diaspora

They also allow users to personalize their pictures with quotes and thoughts to share on social networks by integrating text messages and quotes with Instagram pictures for an interesting effect and user appeal. The Pinterest App also allows users to upload pictures from a camera and editing photos (Fig. 16.10).

Fig. 16.10 Apps for social media management

Apps for Financial Transactions

These Apps allow consumers to complete their following financial transactions (Fig. 16.11):
- Paying invoices
- Request and receive payment for products and services
- Deposit cheques
- Track cash sales
- Plug in mobile card readers to swipe cards

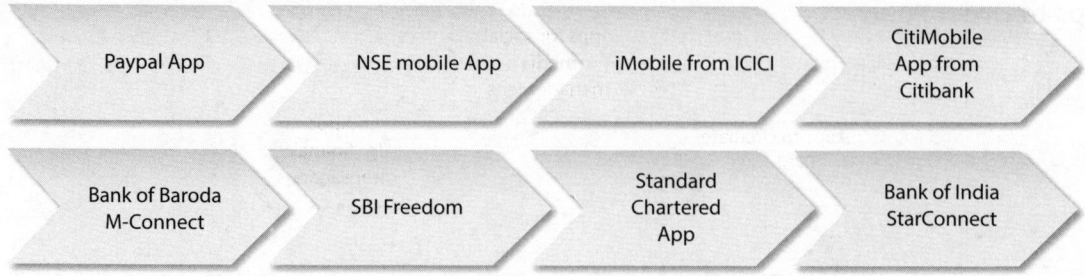

Fig. 16.11 Apps for financial transactions

- Facilitate online shopping
- Convenient method for mobile trading through comprehensive trading and market monitoring platforms
- Live stream of stock quotes

Apps to Facilitate Circulation of News

Apps have been floated by newspapers and news channels to bring the breaking news to the consumers. Apps also provide unrivalled coverage of national, international, city, sports, entertainment, lifestyle, business, health, science and technology topics from India's most-read newspapers and most-watched news channels (Fig. 16.12).

Fig. 16.12 Apps to facilitate circulation of news

Apps to Facilitate Social Networking

These Apps allows users to click pictures, share important moments on social networking sites, and also retouch, capture, and collage pictures (Fig. 16.13). Apps like Meetup allow users to find events by location, interest, and date. These Meetups exemplify social networking by helping marketers create, promote, and participate in gatherings in local consumer communities.

Fig. 16.13 Apps to facilitate social networking

Apps to Order Food

Apps are being used by consumers to order food from restaurants and food outlets at the nearest locations (Fig. 16.14).

Fig. 16.14 Apps to order food

Apps to Improve Workplace Productivity

Apps like Google Analytics help companies to access analytics to keep up the pace with data-driven projects in real time. The Google Analytics App allows users to access significant key performance indicators (KPIs), analyse traffic-related data, visitor paths, etc. Apps like Trello allow individuals to track the performance of a complete project, using a project collaboration tool. Group project Apps help keep communication open, address problems (with solutions) as they arise, keep workflow on schedule, and manage deadlines (Fig. 16.15).

Fig. 16.15 Apps to improve workplace productivity

Apps to Download Books

Apps represent an amazing way to download and read books (Fig. 16.16). Users can download the latest best-selling books or their favourite classics—day or night, can browse libraries, tap a book to open it, flip through pages with a swipe or a tap, and bookmark or add notes to their favourite passages.

Fig. 16.16 Apps to download books

Apps to Create Content

There are a number of Apps that enable users to create content and post it online (Fig. 16.17). For instance, Apps enable blogging; even from relatively smaller mobile platforms. Several consumer review websites like MouthShut have developed Apps, to

Fig. 16.17 Apps to create content

reach out to millions of consumers. The MouthShut mobile App provides reviews and allows individuals to post content, that is, reviews on a variety of products and services across the top six most-used categories: automotive, mobile, movies, health and beauty, travel and restaurants, and online shopping. Reviews are sorted in four divisions, which are popular, most-reviewed products, rating, and recommendations. The App also looks up restaurants as per the preference: proximity, type of cuisine, ratings by consumers, and recommendations. The App can be used to spot the exact location of a restaurant, hospital, pubs, hotels, and much more.

Apps to Watch TV Shows

These Apps let consumers watch disparate Indian TV shows across different languages, absolutely free. The Apps not only notify consumers when new episodes of their favourite TV programmes are available for viewing online, but also give them access to archives of hundreds of past episodes (Fig. 16.18).

Fig. 16.18 Apps to watch TV shows

CASE STUDY: The 16th Indian Lok Sabha Elections—The Era of Online Apps, Facebook, Google, and Twitter

In the 16th Indian Lok Sabha elections, political parties focused significantly on two primary issues: development and progressive governance. The objective was to appeal to the youth. However, the challenge this time was different. The parties were aware of changes in society, education, and Internet literacy. They were sensitive to the fact that they were dealing with an increasingly Internet-savvy population and new tools would have to be used, to lure these voters.

Segment Profile

Year 2014 saw the inclusion of over 2.3 crore young Indian voters in the 18- to 19-year-old category who were freshly enrolled and would vote for the first time. Society was witnessing a major change, the mainstream media was a mass medium, and the young population was Internet friendly. Political parties could not overlook these changes in the environment and hence grew the affinity for social networks and Apps.

Significant political parties in the fray included the following:
- The Bhartiya Janata Party
- The Indian National Congress
- The Aam Admi Party

While the Bharatiya Janata Party (BJP) was an early adopter of social media, the Congress had an on and off tryst with the virtual medium, but gained credit eventually. However, it was the Aam Aadmi Party which saw an organic growth on social media, specifically around the time it formed the government in New Delhi, at the end of 2013, prior to the elections. The surprising growth of the party had captured the attention of the mainstream media, which gave it a lot of visibility and the young party was quick to capitalize on this visibility using social media.

On one hand were the Indian political parties, who were making an effort to reach out to the voters on the social networking platforms. On the other hand were the companies behind these social networking platforms, which were hoping to use the elections to increase usage of their platform. Innovative changes made by Facebook, Twitter, and Google facilitated and encouraged conversations along with election coverage and relevant information.

Apps in Use

Several Apps proliferated during the elections. Some of them were as follows:
- Election India
- India Elections 2014
- The Elect for India App

While some of these Apps allowed voters to perform a quick search for a candidate, party or constituency, take the daily elections opinion poll, and view recent polls analysis, the others allowed voters to track the social sentiment around the elections, along with the option of viewing the interactive visualizations to monitor the results of the elections.

The following figure depicts the functions performed by the *Elect for India* App (Fig. 16.19).

The Indian Elections and Google

The Indian elections saw the popularity of another medium for interaction between the voter and the hopeful political aspirants—*Google Hangout*. Search giant, Google, allowed group video chatting amongst 10 people, using Hangout. This was first successfully used in the third quarter of 2012 by Gujarat Chief Minister, Narendra Modi. Google Hangout was being used by politicians like Barack Obama in the past for interacting with larger audiences. Success of the usage of the medium soon saw a complete group of political aspirants using it, in order to appeal to the digitally savvy audiences.

Google included a *Pledge to Vote* visual section which Google also included an interesting trends section that showed the 'Google Score' (Fig. 16.20).

- Users could check the 2009 election results. Users could cast their opinion vote and see the opinion results.
- Users could check the voting schedule for 2014 elections.
- Users could check the latest news and videos related to current elections.
- Users could share candidate details to their Facebook friends.
- Users could share reviews about this application on their Facebook and Twitter accounts.

Fig. 16.19 The Elect for India App

- **Google pledge to vote:** Asked users to show their support by taking a pledge to vote, the page also showed an interactive map which quickly filled up with pledges. One could zoom in and hover on the pledges to see what people were saying.
- **Google score:** Based on the amount of search activity performed by prospective voters in the last 24 hours using Google Search and YouTube for a political leader. Google Score also took into consideration the amount of engagement the political leader was drawing on Google+.

Fig. 16.20 The Indian elections and Google

Facebook—Register to Vote

Facebook, India's most popular social network, added the following special features for the Indian Election, 2014 (Fig. 16.21):

- A 'Register To Vote' feature in its *Life Event* section
- Creation of the *Indian Political Interest Lists*
- Launched the Election Tracker—A performance dashboard of the leading political parties and politicians
- Launch of the 'Candidates 2014 on Facebook Talks Live'.

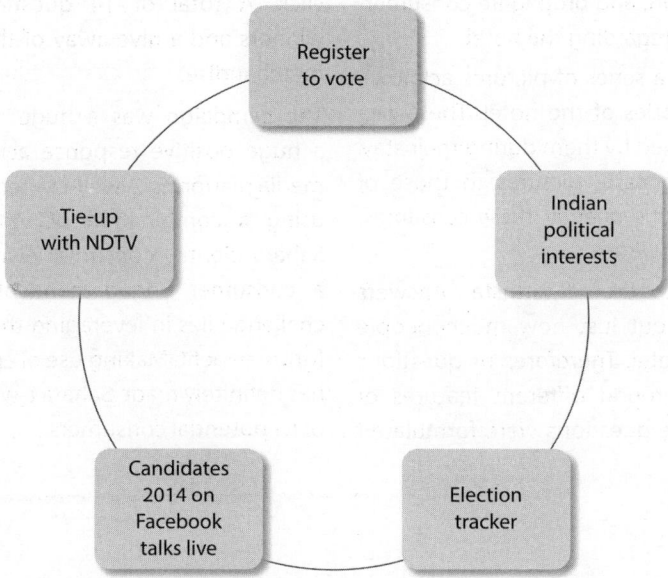

Fig. 16.21 The Indian elections and Facebook

Facebook tied up with NDTV and gave Indian voters a chance to interact with political leaders live. Audiences interacted with top politicians including West Bengal CM, Mamata Banerjee, and AAP leader, Arvind Kejriwal. The interviews were also aired on the NDTV news channel and were streamed live online.

Twitter and Lok Sabha Elections 2014

Twitter is characterized by micro-blogging—content, that is, short and on target, courtesy the 140 character requirement. The medium found immense appeal amongst the politicians and also became an online battle ground between rival parties.

The ease of usage and the rapid proliferation of content made it a hangout of veterans such as Narendra Modi, Arvind Kejriwal, Shashi Tharoor, Sushma Swaraj, amongst others. The content hosted on Twitter soon became the basis for political debates on television. Twitter, India set up a dedicated vertical whose mandate was to get political parties, politicians, and influencers to engage with their audience on Twitter.

Acceptance of the virtual world and the convenience provided by the medium to reach the masses was the flavour of the year.

EXHIBIT 16.13   Sahara Star, India—A visually appealing online campaign

Consumers of the hotel, Sahara Star, India, used Pinterest to pin pictures of the hotel online. This Pinterest board was created for them, by the organization, as part of a campaign to use the online media to share and propagate consumer-generated content regarding the hotel.

Consumers posted a series of pictures acknowledging fond memories of the hotel. These pictures had been clicked by them during their stay. These ranged from party pictures to those of lavish bathrooms. Subsequently, these consumers were contacted via Twitter.

Sahara formulated the #StarInsta Answers campaign to find out just how much people know about the hotel. Therefore, 14 questions were formulated around different features of the Sahara Star. The questions were formulated in such a way that only those who had actually been present at the hotel would have been able to answer them correctly. The twist was—the answer had to be in the form of an Instagram click. A total of 14 questions, 14 days, 14 winners and a give away of the hotel's choicest merchandise.

The campaign was a huge success and drew a huge positive response across diverse social media platforms. A well-crafted online campaign, using a combination of virtual tools helped Sahara identify consumer evangelists and build a consumer engagement platform. The true challenge lies in leveraging these consumers for future benefit. Making use of contemporary tools has definitely made Sahara a winner, in the minds of its potential consumers.

Questions:

1. How did Facebook, Twitter, and Google use innovative techniques to facilitate conversations and election coverage?
2. How did political parties pro-actively react to the changes in society, education, and Internet literacy and make use of the Internet to target the youth? Discuss.

PRACTITIONER PERSPECTIVE

Mobile Apps have become the official channel to drive content and services to consumers. As users continue to adopt and interact with Apps, it is their data—what they say, what they do, where they go—that is transforming the App interaction paradigm.

Brian Blau, Research Director, Gartner

The Lok Sabha elections would be a key partnership platform for Twitter in India this year.

Rishi Jaitly, India Head of Twitter

SUMMARY

Digital marketing is about to enter a more challenging territory. Building on the vast increase in consumer power brought on by the digital age, marketing is headed towards being on demand—not just always 'on', but also always relevant, responsive to the consumer's desire for marketing that cuts through the noise with pinpoint delivery. What is fuelling on-demand marketing is the continued, symbiotic evolution of technology and consumer expectations. Already, search technologies have made product information ubiquitous; social media encourages consumers to share, compare, and rate experiences; and mobile devices add a 'wherever' dimension to the digital environment. Playing games, both online and using the mobile and the use of Apps, both online and using the mobile, are becoming rampant—in fact, it is the new lifestyle trend today. Subsequently, it is the monetization of these games and Apps, that is, the next logical step marketers can take in this direction. India is one of the biggest mobile markets in the world in terms of the sheer mobile penetration and the fact that mobile has turned to be the first device for a significant number of Indian audiences to access the Internet. Mobile gaming too is a phenomenon catching up in India. Mobile games and applications in India are expected to be ₹2700-crore market by 2016, driven by strong smartphone growth and expanding 3G-userbase. As per recorded data, more than 50% of mobile Internet traffic and paid content revenues come from smartphones, dominated by Google and Apple App stores.

Concept Review Questions

1. How are Apps changing the face of marketing?
2. What shifts in the marketplace have paved a way for gamification as a marketing tool?
3. How can companies make use of games for marketing?
4. Write short notes on the following:
   (a) Elements and structure of games
   (b) Types of players
   (c) Mechanics and dynamics of games
5. Detail how marketers can make use of the following Apps to their advantage:
   (a) Google Analytics
   (b) Hootsuite
   (c) Tweegram
6. 'Facebook will eventually be able to mine the world's largest database of photographs, linking individual people to their activities'. Comment.
7. How are companies making use of Instagram for digital marketing?
8. Companies are fast moving towards cracking the code for monetization of games. How have Marriott and L'Oréal used gamification to their advantage?

Critical Thinking Questions

1. Identify a set of five Apps (not discussed in the chapter) being used by consumers for various purposes. Detail their functions and value to consumers.
2. Identify a set of online games being used by organizations to promote their products.
3. How did the world of the Internet change the face of Indian Elections? Conduct research online to identify the politician who was able to use the digital world to his/her advantage most effectively. Profile the activities in detail.

Practising Digital Marketing

1. Create a conceptual model for developing an *App* for a product or brand of your choice.
   (a) Develop the objective for which the App needs to be created
   (b) The profile of the target consumers who will benefit from the App
   (c) Create a power-point slide to depict the interface of the App in the context of input and output screens that will be visible to the consumers

   The exercise can be done in groups of three to four participants.

2. Create a *gaming idea* for a product or brand of your choice.
   (a) Create a storyboard to depict what the game will do.
   (b) Develop an analysis of how the game will be beneficial to enhance the brand–consumer relationship.

References

1. Dahlstrom, P. and Edelman, D., *The Coming Era of On-demand Marketing*, McKinsey Quarterly, 2013.
2. Deterding, Sebastian, et al., (2011). 'Gamification using game-design elements in non-gaming contexts'. *Proceedings of the 2011 Annual Conference Extended Abstracts on Human Factors in Computing Systems*. ACM.
3. Exhibits 16.4 to 16.7 have been sourced from 31 Interesting Indian Social Media Campaigns of Quarter 3, 2013 http://lighthouseinsights.in/31-interesting-indian-social-media-campaigns-of-quarter-3-2013.html/.
4. Wrona, K., *Gamification and Games, Their Potential for Application in Marketing Strategies*, 2012.
5. Zichermann, G. and Linder, J., *Game-based Marketing: Inspire Customer Loyalty Through Rewards, Challenges, and Contests* 2010, 19.
6. Zichermann, G. and Linder, J., *Game-based Marketing*, John Wiley and Sons, 2010.

Index

A
A Broad Look at the B2C and B2B Scenarios 154
A Consumer Co-creation Model using INV Based on Metcalf Law (C-INV) 372
Apps and the Indian Diaspora 424

B
Behavioural Internet 17
Behavioural Segmentation 326
Behavioural Targeting 18, 331
Behavioural Targeting vs Contextual Targeting 76
Benefit Segmentation 328
Benefits of Electronic Customer Relationship Management Technology in Online Banking 102
Bonding for Customer Relationship 105
Brand Customer Centricity 186
Brand Experience 176
Brand Positioning Online 332
Brand Post Popularity 398
Brands and Emotions 187
Building Collaborative Customer Relationships 276
Building Consumer Engagement through Content Management 285
Business Models 233
Business-to-consumer 2.0 114

C
Campaign Management 298, 308
Campaign Management using Corporate Blogs 305
Campaign Management using Facebook 302
Campaign Management using Twitter 303
Changing Marketing Landscape 4
Co-creation Communities for Brands 362
Co-creation Communities—Some Exhibits 368
Collaborative Web and E-enterprise 122
and the Enterprise 118
Consumer Brand Emotion 188
Consumer Engagement 276
Consumer Motivation for Playing Online Games 415
Consumer Price Sensitivity 377
Consumer Price Sensitivity Model using K-means Cluster Analysis 376
Consumer Psychographic Profiles and Consumer Segmentation 328
Consumer Segmentation 50
Based on Consumer Sentiment Score 312
in Virtual Space 326
Different Methods for 322
Consumer Targeting 328
Consumer Traits 52
Consumer Trustworthiness Regression Model using Netnography (CTR) 371
Consumer Visit Schedules and Click-through Rates 403
Consumer-generated Media and Consumer Behaviour 345
and Opinion Leaders 346
Consumers
and Online Shopping Issues 53
and Online Space 353
New Influential Constituency 170
Correlation between Consumer-generated Media and Sales 347
Cultural Implications of Key Web Characteristics 71
Customer Liking, Satisfaction, and Involvement 311
Customer Relationship Management (CRM) 94, 307
and the Customer Lifecycle 104
Business-to-consumer Dimensions 110
Goals of 97
Processes 102
Role of 103
Customer Value Analysis and the Internet 229
Customer-centric Business Management 226
Customer-centric Web Business Models 224
Cyberbranding 170

D
Database Marketing 84
Demographic Segmentation 326
Deterministic Targeting 329
Diamond–Water Paradox 198
Digital Brand Ecosystem 173
Digital Change Implications of 33
Digital Ecosystem 67, 341
Digital Marketing Optimization 28

E

E-commerce Applications 262
Electronic Customer Relationship Management 107
E-marketing and Consumer Segmentation 22
E-marketing and CRM 19
E-marketing and Online Advertising 21
E-marketing and Sales and Trade Promotion 24
E-marketing Communication Modes 16
E-marketing—Strengths and Applications 14
Emerging Consumer Segments in India 335
Empirical Models to Leverage Product/Brand Online Communities 368
Engagement Marketing 277
E-price 55
E-procurement 261
E-products—Creating Customer Value in an Online World 46
E-promotion 56
Evaluating Consumer Sentiment using Sentiwordnet 1.0 312

F

Facebook—The Origin 387
Financial Services and the Internet 240
Finding Top Loyalty Drivers 291
Fundamental Advantages Offered by the Internet 257

G

Gamification and Game-based Marketing 412
Gamification and the Consumer Brand Affinity Spectrum 416
Gearing up for New Online Consumers 86

Generation Y—Expectations and Influence 31
Geographical Segmentation 326

H

How Companies can use Blogs for Effective Campaign Management 315

I

Identifying Influencers in Conversations 351
Impact of a Facebook Fan 397
Implications for Organizations 34
Inbound Marketing and Co-creation 159
Indian Web Market 243
Integrated Marketing Communication and the Internet 21
Integration and Alignment 292
Internet and Business 13
Internet Cookies and Traffic Building 202
Internet Marketing Metrics 208
Internet Traffic Plan 200

K

Key Customer Relationship Management Applications 111
Keyword Advertising 205
Keyword Portfolio Evaluation 205
Keyword Value 205
Knowledge as a Value Proposition 343
Knowledge Discovery and Data Mining 322

M

Marketing Segmentation 49
Marketing with Networks 139
Measuring Campaign Effectiveness I 314

Measuring Campaign Effectiveness II—Quantitative Tag Analysis 314
Measuring E-commerce Success 264
Mining Consumer-generated Media 348
Models of Website Visits 73
Monitoring E-commerce Brands and Social Media in the Indian Market 267

N

Need for Digital Engagement 29
Need for Greater Organizational Adaptability 290
Netiquette—The Facebook Etiquette for Brands 392
Next-generation CRM—A Mobile App and a Community 116
Non-deterministic Targeting 330
New Age E-enterprise 116

O

Online Consumer Behaviour 70
Online Distribution and Procurement 253
Online Marketing Domains 16
Online Marketplaces 260
Online Shopping in the Era of Social Networking 284
Online Targeting 329
Online Value 55

P

Peer Reviews, Word of Mouth, and the Dissatisfied Customer 346
Popularity of Brand Pages 327
Positioning 55, 337
Predictive Targeting 330
Price Effects in Online Domain 245

Psychographic
  Segmentation   326
Purchase Importance   248

R

Research Illustration   80
Revenue Benefits   237
Rise of Technology   411
Role of Internet in Impacting
  Consumer Price Sensitivity   244

S

SAP Web Channel Experience
  Management   114
Search Engine Marketing   203
Search Marketing Methods
  for Traffic Building   200
Segmentation   337
Sentiment Mining   309
Site Optimization   205
Social Curation
  and Brands   155
Social Media   136
  Analytics   142
  Model by McKinsey   137
  Tools   150

The Road Ahead   160
Social Plugins and their
  Contribution to Marketing   283
Social Web   153
Social World   142
Spiral of Prosperity Model   258

T

Tagging and Folksonomies   307
Targeting   54, 337
  and the Enterprise   118
The Value of the Power of
  Influence   347
The Virtual World   4
Top 10 Brands in India
  and their Facebook
  Presence   403
Traditional Distribution
  Management Issues   256
Traffic Volume and Quality   202
Traffic-building Goals   203
Twitter Marketing   304

U

Using Corporate Blog as a CRM
  2.0 Tool   309

Using Consumer Brand
  Knowledge and Consumer
  Brand Emotion to Develop
  Consumer Engagement   184

V

Value Uncertainty   248
Value of a Customer
  Contact   224
Viral Marketing   155

W

Web 2.0   135
Web 2.0 and Marketing   78
Web and Consumer
  Decision-making Process   76
Web and the New
  Corporation   8
Web Benefits to Firms   231
Web Chain Analysis   228
Web Chain of Events   227
Website Characteristics Affecting
  Online Purchase Decision   57
Websites and Internet
  Marketing   208
World of Apps   421

About the Author

Vandana Ahuja is working as Professor of Marketing at Amity Business School, Noida. Prior to this, she was the Dean—Research and Professor of Marketing at IILM Graduate School of Management, Greater Noida. Dr Ahuja has also worked as Area Chair, Marketing, and faculty at the Jaypee Business School, NOIDA, the business arm of the Jaypee Institute of Information Technology, India. She holds a PhD degree in Management in the area of Corporate Blogging as a Tool for Interactive Marketing and CRM. She has over 22 years of experience in the academia and corporate sector and teaches e-marketing, sales and distribution management, and B2B marketing. Prof. Ahuja previously worked with the IT arm of the Jaypee Group, where she was involved in business development and marketing communication activities for teaching solution Bhartiyavidya. Prior to this, she had worked as a Business Manager with NIIT in India, where she was responsible for corporate training, business development, and marketing.

Dr Ahuja is the proud recipient of the AMP-ILDC women achievers award for excellence in Management Teaching and has conducted several MDPs and training sessions for the corporate world. She is an avid researcher and has published several manuscripts in international and national journals and also serves on the Editorial Board of several international journals. She has organized and chaired several national and international conferences and has guided several PhD students in the domain of management.

Prof. Ahuja was the Convenor of the International Conference on Advances in Management and Technology 2015 jointly organized by Jaypee Business School (JBS) in association with University of Nebraska, Omaha, USA. She was the Conference Co-chair for the National Conference on Social Media and EMarketing organized by JBS in 2014.

Related Titles

Marketing Research: Concepts, Practices, and Cases, 1e
[9780195676969]

Sunanda Easwaran, *Prin. L. N. Welingkar Institute of Management Development and Research, Bengaluru* and **Sharmila J. Singh**, *National Qualitative Head, GfK Mode India, Mumbai*

It is a comprehensive textbook specially designed to meet the needs of management students. The book combines the quantitative and qualitative aspects of marketing research, and addresses its utility for both the researcher and the end-user. The text provides in-depth coverage of the key elements of the subject: its theoretical foundations, techniques of planning and design, research methodology for the implementation of quantitative and qualitative techniques, presentation and interpretation of findings through reports, and the use of marketing research techniques for developing and evaluating marketing strategies.

Key Features
- Addresses both the quantitative and qualitative research aspects of marketing management
- Provides practical guidelines on the relationship between the researcher and the manager, the scope of research, and what the user may expect from research
- Includes step-wise SPSS commands for conducting discriminant analysis, factor analysis, cluster analysis, and multi-dimensional scaling

E-Business, 1e
[9780198069843]

Parag Kulkarni, *CEO and Chief Scientist at EKLaT Research, Pune*, **Sunita Jahirabadkar**, *Assistant Professor, Dept of Computer Engineering, Cummins College of Engineering, Pune*, and **Pradip Chande**, *Group Director, TRUBA Group of Institutes, Indore*

It is a comprehensive textbook designed for students of business management. It integrates *e*-commerce with the strategic aspects of *e*-business, with the help of numerous examples, exhibits, figures, and case studies. The book covers different aspects of *e*-business including models, strategies, security and reliability, and evaluation and audit. It provides in-depth coverage of important issues related to *e*-business, such as creation of *e*-business plans and website development, *e*-market, back-end systems, online payment systems, business intelligence (BI), and knowledge management (KM). It also delves into the management and techno-managerial aspects of running an *e*-business.

Key Features
- Includes chapters on KM and BI in *e*-business, Internet security, Internet payment, and website development
- Discusses contemporary issues and current trends, such as mobile computing, *m*-commerce, Internet banking, and the IT Act, 2000

Brand Management: Principles and Practices, 1e
[9780198069867]

Kirti Dutta, *Assistant Professor, BULMIM, New Delhi*

It is a comprehensive textbook designed for students of postgraduate management programmes specializing in marketing. It explores the core concepts of branding and illustrates them through numerous examples, exhibits, figures, images, case studies, and videos.

Key Features
- Provides rich learning from brand practices of Indian brands like Kingfisher, Maggi, Airtel, Aircel, Micromax, ITC, and LIC
- Discusses practices of global and Indian companies such as Singapore Airlines, Lux, Amul, and Tata Group, and includes exhibits with marketing insights from industry
- Includes exclusive chapters on creating a brand, understanding organizational culture, consumer behaviour, *e*-branding, and managing brand architecture

Advertising Management, 2e
[9780198074120]

Jaishri Jethwaney, *Professor, Indian Institute of Maas Communication, New Delhi*, and **Shruti Jain**, *CCO and Global Head-CSR, EXL Service*

The second edition of this book is a comprehensive textbook tailored to meet the syllabi requirements of management students, mass media, and stand-alone courses on advertising. Interspersed with examples, exhibits, and real-life cases, the book provides an in-depth coverage of the key components, namely advertising and promotions, media strategy and planning, and agency relationships.

Key Features
- Examines the advertising strategies followed by business organizations
- Explores the emerging issues in advertising management from an Indian perspective
- New topics such as measurement of brand equity, positioning platforms, media scheduling, and sales force sales promotion

Other Related Titles

9780195689082	Jauhari & Dutta: *Services*	9780198062929	Krishna: *Consumer Behaviour*
9780195667585	Apte: *Services Marketing*	9780198077091	Kumar: *Marketing Channels*